OPTICAL
CODING THEORY
with PRIME

OPTICAL
CODING THEORY
with PRIME

Wing C. Kwong • Guu-Chang Yang

CRC Press
Taylor & Francis Group
Boca Raton   London   New York

CRC Press is an imprint of the
Taylor & Francis Group, an **informa** business

CRC Press
Taylor & Francis Group
6000 Broken Sound Parkway NW, Suite 300
Boca Raton, FL 33487-2742

© 2013 by Taylor & Francis Group, LLC
CRC Press is an imprint of Taylor & Francis Group, an Informa business

No claim to original U.S. Government works

Printed and bound in Great Britain by TJ International, Padstow, Cornwall
Version Date: 20130318

International Standard Book Number-13: 978-1-4665-6780-1 (Hardback)

Library of Congress Cataloging-in-Publication Data

Kwong, Wing C.
  Optical coding theory with prime / authors, Wing C. Kwong, Guu-Chang Yang.
  pages cm
  Summary: "The new field of optical coding theory helps in designing new classes of optical codes for various coding-based optical applications, such as the well-known optical code division multiple access (CDMA). While there are books on coding theory for wireless communications, there is no book specifically dedicated to optical coding theory. In a clear, concise manner, this book presents the mathematical concepts essential to optical coding theory. It covers Galois fields, vector space, matrix theory, Markov chain, and algebraic tools for performance analysis. After providing readers with the mathematical tools, the authors describe applications of optical codes in various coding schemes along with supporting hardware technologies. They also focus on 1-D, 2-D, and 3-D prime codes"-- Provided by publisher.
  Includes bibliographical references and index.
  ISBN 978-1-4665-6780-1 (hardback)
  1. Optical communications. 2. Coding theory. 3. Numbers, Prime. I. Yang, Guu-Chang. II. Title.

TK5103.59.K84 2013
003'.54--dc23
                                                                          2013003959

Visit the Taylor & Francis Web site at
http://www.taylorandfrancis.com

and the CRC Press Web site at
http://www.crcpress.com

Dedication

With love and affection for our families
Joey, Michelle, Rebecca, Sofina, and Tracy

Contents

List of Figures

List of Tables

Preface

Ten years have passed since our first-of-its-kind book on optical code-division multiple access (CDMA), *Prime Codes with Applications to CDMA Optical and Wireless Networks*, published by Artech House in 2002. The book covered optical coding theory, performance analytical techniques, and proof-of-principle experiments for the specialized field of optical CDMA, from the mid-1980s to early 2002. It not only provided the first comprehensive text, but also facilitated research and education in this emerging field. Since the early 1990s, numerous developments in optical CDMA have been contributed by worldwide researchers. Some of the major works were collected in the book, *Optical Code Division Multiple Access: Fundamentals and Applications*, edited by P. R. Prucnal and published by Taylor & Francis in 2006. The book covered the whole spectrum of the field of optical CDMA, including its history and developments, physical hardware technologies, modern experimental testbeds, and potential applications. Being considered renowned experts in optical coding theory, we contributed one chapter, "Optical CDMA Codes," in the book.

Similar to its wireless counterpart, optical CDMA can be classified into two main research categories: hardware technology and coding technique. Nevertheless, optical CDMA is unable to receive benefits from existing wireless-CDMA technologies or coding techniques because optical fiber is generally not good at preserving phase information. Optical CDMA also encounters different operating environments and issues, thus requiring unconventional coding as well as transmission techniques and technologies. A new field, optical coding theory, has emerged and been developed for the design and analysis of families of optical codes for a variety of optical-CDMA applications. Furthermore, optical CDMA currently follows a similar historical path of wireless CDMA in the sense that the advances in hardware technologies must be supported in tandem with contemporary coding techniques. Although there are books on the coding theory of wireless communications, there is no book specifically dedicated to the subject matter of optical coding theory.

Since the mid-1980s, optical codes have been primarily designed for providing multiple and simultaneous access in CDMA-based optical communication systems and networks, such as local area networks. In addition, optical coding is now receiving attention in environments requiring address or user identification by means of optical codes, such as optical wireless, optical switched networks, passive optical networks, fiber-sensor systems, data-obscurity transmission, IP routing, and fault tolerance, monitoring, and identification in optical systems and networks. Nowadays, optical coding theory, which is not limited to optical-CDMA applications anymore, includes construction of optical codes for various optical applications, improvements in performance analytical techniques of optical codes, and development of novel optical coding techniques supported by the latest hardware technologies.

Optical coding theory and its applications to coding-based optical systems and networks have been studied for the past three decades. Until the mid-1990s, optical codes were based on one-dimensional (1-D) coding in time or wavelength. To provide sufficient performance, very long 1-D optical codes were needed, thus requiring ultrashort optical pulses and rendering such systems impractical. We were among the leaders in directing research momentum to two-dimensional (2-D) coding in time and wavelength simultaneously. Since then, research in the area of 2-D coding techniques has flourished. Our series of work on the theoretical and application aspects of various families of prime codes played a major role in such developments. Our contributions established the foundation of algebraic 1-D and 2-D optical coding, which made high-rate, high-capacity, coding-based optical systems and networks feasible. In the late 1990s, research on quality-of-service (QoS) control and services prioritization in multirate, multimedia coding-based optical systems by means of specially designed optical codes began attracting attention. The impact is prominent as future systems are expected to support services with different rates, QoSs, and priorities.

Our work on optical coding theory has been scattered over numerous archival journals. To collect these important works in one place coherently, we write this first-of-its-kind monograph to cover the fundamentals and development of optical coding theory with a focus on various families of prime codes and their potential applications to coding-based optical systems and networks. Prerequisites include a basic knowledge of linear algebra and coding theory, as well as a foundation in probability and communications theory. A theorem–proof approach is used so that theories are broken down into digestible form and readers will be able to understand main messages without searching through tedious proofs. Examples are used to illustrate the fundamental concepts and to show how prime codes are constructed and analyzed. The performances of prime codes in a variety of applications are also detailed. In addition to targeting researchers in the field, this book also covers working knowledge of optical coding theory and prime codes for the design of coding-based optical systems and networks for engineers. We hope that systems engineers, research and development professionals, professors, graduate students, and mathematicians who are interested in optical coding theory and its applications find this book useful and informative.

The first part of this book sorts out the mathematical concepts and formulations that are important in the second part. Chapter 1 covers the preliminary materials that are necessary to the understanding and application of the essential algebraic techniques of optical coding theory, such as Galois fields, vectors, matrices, Markov chains, and Gaussian and combinatorial analytical tools. In addition to providing readers with the necessary mathematical tools, the applications of optical codes in various coding schemes and the study of supporting hardware technologies are given in Chapter 2. The second part of this book starts out with the constructions and properties of various families of 1-D asynchronous prime codes with illustrative examples and performance analyses in Chapter 3. Chapter 4 investigates 1-D synchronous prime codes and follows with examples of applications. Chapter 5 studies 2-D asynchronous prime codes with various coding flexibilities, expanded cardinalities, and variable performances. The concepts of shifted-code keying and multicode keying for high-rate transmission of multiple bits per symbol are also introduced. Chapter 6

discusses 2-D synchronous prime codes, which possess true code orthogonality at
the expense of synchronization. Chapter 7 investigates the use of multilength prime
codes for supporting multiple-rate, multimedia services in optical systems and networks. The uses of code weight and code power to control the QoS of multimedia services are also analyzed. Finally, this book concludes with the construction of
three-dimensional prime codes in Chapter 8.

We would like to thank Professors Paul R. Prucnal and Thomas E. Fuja, our Ph.D.
advisors and long-time friends, for their professional guidance, inspiration, and assis-
tance all these years. We are also grateful to Dr. Cheng-Yuan Chang of the National
United University, Taiwan, for proofreading this book, and his past, present, and future involvement and contributions to our endeavor in the advancement of optical
coding theory and optical CDMA. We are thankful to the U.S. Defense Advanced
Research Projects Agency, the National Science Council of Republic of China, Hofstra University, and National Chung Hsing University for their generous support. We
thank the IEEE for publishing our findings in its journals and Artech House for grant-
ing us permission to use materials from our previous book. Finally, we would like
to pay tribute to numerous pioneers and contributors in the field of optical CDMA.
Without their dedication and collective contributions, the field would not have flourished and reached today's status. To our best knowledge, their published, archival
articles and books are cited accordingly in the bibliographies of this book, wherever
suitable. To name a few, C. A. Brackett, F. R. K. Chung, P. A. Davies, G. J. Foschini,
J. P. Heritage, J. Y. N. Hui, P. V. Kumar, P. R. Prucnal, J. A. Salehi, M. A. Santoro,
A. A. Shaar, V. K. Wei, G. Vannucci, and, last but not least, A. M. Weiner are some
of the early pioneers in the field of optical CDMA with archival journal articles being
published before 1990. We tried our best to be inclusive in the citations. If any rel-
evant literature or personnel is found omitted, please contact us and we will amend
this accordingly in a future edition.

Wing C. Kwong
Princeton Junction, New Jersey

Guu-Chang Yang
Taichung, Taiwan

About the Authors

Wing C. Kwong received his B.S. degree from the University of California, San Diego, California, in 1987, and his Ph.D. degree from Princeton University, Princeton, New Jersey, in 1992, both in electrical engineering.

In 1992, Dr. Kwong joined the faculty of Hofstra University, Hempstead, New York, where he is currently a professor with the Department of Engineering and the newly established School of Engineering and Applied Science. He co-authored the first-of-its-kind technical book on optical code-division multiple access (CDMA), *Prime Codes with Applications to CDMA Optical and Wireless Networks*, G.-C. Yang and W. C. Kwong, Norwood, MA: Artech House, 2002, and contributed one chapter to another optical-CDMA book, *Optical Code Division Multiple Access: Fundamentals and Applications*, (ed.) P. R. Prucnal, Boca Raton, FL: Taylor & Francis, 2006. He has published numerous professional articles, and chaired technical sessions and served on technical program committees at international conferences. He has given seminars and tutorials in optical coding theory and optical CDMA in various cities and countries, such as Canada, Hong Kong (China), South Korea, Singapore, Taiwan, and the United States. His research interests include optical and wireless communication systems and multiple-access networks, optical interconnection networks, and ultrafast all-optical signal processing techniques.

Dr. Kwong is a senior member of the IEEE and currently an associate editor of the *IEEE Transactions on Communications*. He was the recipient of the NEC Graduate Fellowship awarded by the NEC Research Institute, Princeton, New Jersey, in 1991. He received the Young Engineer Award from the IEEE (Long Island chapter) in 1998.

Guu-Chang Yang received his B.S. degree from the National Taiwan University, Taipei, Taiwan, in 1985, and his M.S. and Ph.D. degrees from the University of Maryland, College Park, Maryland, in 1989 and 1992, respectively, all in electrical engineering.

From 1988 to 1992, Dr. Yang was a research assistant in the System Research Center, University of Maryland. In 1992, he joined the faculty of the National Chung Hsing University, Taichung, Taiwan, where he is currently a professor with the Department of Electrical Engineering and the Graduate Institute of Communication Engineering. He was the chairman of the Department of Electrical Engineering from 2001 to 2004. He co-authored the first-of-its-kind technical book on optical code-division multiple access (CDMA), *Prime Codes with Applications to CDMA Optical and Wireless Networks*, G.-C. Yang and W. C. Kwong, Norwood, MA: Artech House, 2002, and contributed one chapter to another optical-CDMA book, *Optical Code Division Multiple Access: Fundamentals and Applications*, (ed.) P. R. Prucnal,

Boca Raton, FL: Taylor & Francis, 2006. His research interests include wireless and optical communication systems, modulation and signal processing techniques, and applications of CDMA.

Dr. Yang serves as the area coordinator of the National Science Council's Telecommunications Program from 2012 to 2014, the co-coordinator of the National Science Council's National Networked Communication Program from 2010 to 2013, and the chairman of the IEEE Communications Society (Taipei Chapter) from 2013 to 2014. He also served as the vice chairman of the IEEE Communications Society (Taipei Chapter) from 2011 to 2012, the chairman of the IEEE Information Theory Society (Taipei Chapter) from 2003 to 2005, and the vice chairman of the IEEE Information Theory Society (Taipei Chapter) from 1999 to 2000. He became an IEEE Fellow in 2012 for contributions to optical CDMA. He received the Distinguished Research Award from the National Science Council in 2004, and the Outstanding Young Electrical Engineer Award in 2003 and the Distinguished Electrical Engineering Professor Award in 2012, both from the Chinese Institute of Electrical Engineering. He also received the Best Teaching Award from the Department of Electrical Engineering, National Chung Hsing University from 2001 to 2004 and in 2008.

1 Fundamental Materials and Tools

Modern algebra [1–5] provides mathematical concepts and tools fundamental to the study of *Optical Coding Theory*. The theory finds applications in coding-based optical systems and networks, for example, involving optical code-division multiple access (O-CDMA) and multiplexing [6–22]. Various families of the prime codes studied in this book are based on the arithmetic of finite or Galois fields of some prime numbers [1, 2, 21–23].

This chapter covers the essential concepts and algebraic tools that are useful for understanding the subject matter in this book. It begins with a review of Galois fields, followed by vector and matrix theories. Important code parameters, such as Hamming weight and distance, correlation functions, and cardinality upper bound, that characterize optical codes are defined. Afterward, the concept of Markov chains is studied [24,25]. Algebraic tools to analyze the performances of optical codes are also developed. In particular, Gaussian approximation is a quick, utilitarian tool for performance analysis, especially in the absence of structural information of the optical codes under study [21, 22, 24–26]. More accurate combinatorial tools for analyzing code performances with soft-limiting and hard-limiting receivers, and with and without the classical chip-synchronous assumption, are also formulated [27–37]. Finally, the definition of spectral efficiency, another figure of merit for comparing optical codes, is introduced [38–43].

1.1 GALOIS FIELDS

Optical coding theory relies on modern algebra, which uses a different arithmetic system, rather than the familiar real and complex number systems. A field in modern algebra consists of elements defined with four mathematical operations: addition, subtraction, multiplication, and division. If the number of elements in a field is finite, this field is called a finite field or *Galois field*, in the memory of Évariste Galois (1811–1832) [1–3]. Because optical coding theory, especially with prime codes, is usually based on the principles of Galois fields of prime numbers, the fundamentals of fields in modern algebra are first reviewed before proceeding with the rest of the book.

Definition 1.1

A field F contains a set of elements and four operators—addition $(+)$, subtraction $(-)$, multiplication $(\times)$, and division $(\div)$—defined with the following properties:

1. *Closure.* If a and b are elements in F, the sum $a+b$ and the product $a \times b$ are also elements in F.
2. *Additive Identity and Inverse.* If a is an element in F and

$$a+0=0+a=a$$

$$a+(-a)=(-a)+a=0$$

then "0" is the unique additive identity element, called *zero*, in F, and $-a$ is its unique additive inverse in F.
3. *Multiplicative Identity and Inverse.* If a is a nonzero element in F and

$$a \times 1 = 1 \times a = a$$

$$a \times a^{-1} = a^{-1} \times a = 1$$

then "1" is the unique multiplicative identity element, called *unity*, in F, and a^{-1} is its unique multiplicative inverse in F.
4. *Commutativity.* If a and b are elements in F, the commutative law implies that

$$a+b=b+a$$

$$a \times b = b \times a$$

5. *Associativity.* If a, b, and c are elements in F, the associative law implies that
$$a+(b+c)=(a+b)+c$$
$$a \times (b \times c) = (a \times b) \times c$$

6. *Distributivity.* If a, b, and c are elements in F, the distributive law implies that
$$(a+b) \times c = (a \times c) + (b \times c)$$

7. *Subtractibility.* If a and b are elements in F, then the subtraction $a-b$ implies that
$$a-b=a+(-b)$$

due to the existence of the additive inverse $-b$.
8. *Divisibility.* If a is an element in F and b is a nonzero element in F, then the division $a \div b$ implies that

$$a \div b = a \times b^{-1}$$

due to the existence of the multiplicative inverse b^{-1}.

■

Theorem 1.1

The additive and multiplicative identity elements in a field F are both unique. The additive inverse of any element in F is unique and the inverse of the additive inverse gives back the element itself. The multiplicative inverse of any nonzero element in F is unique and the inverse of the multiplicative inverse gives back the element itself.

Proof Assume that 0 and $0'$ are additive identity elements in F. Also assume that 1 and $1'$ are multiplicative identity element in F. Their uniqueness is proved by

$$0 = 0 + 0' = 0' + 0 = 0'$$
$$1 = 1 \times 1' = 1' \times 1 = 1'$$

Assume that $-a$ and $-a'$ are additive inverses for an element a in F. Also assume that b^{-1} and b'^{-1} are multiplicative inverses for a nonzero element b in F. Their uniqueness is proved by

$$-a = (-a) + [a + (-a')] = [(-a) + a] + (-a') = -a'$$
$$b^{-1} = b^{-1} \times (b \times b'^{-1}) = (b^{-1} \times b) \times b'^{-1} = b'^{-1}$$

Due to the properties of additive inverse: $(-a) + a = a + (-a) = 0$, multiplicative inverse: $b^{-1} \times b = b \times b^{-1} = 1$, and the uniqueness of inverses, it can be shown that $-(-a) = a$ and $(b^{-1})^{-1} = b$. So, a is an additive inverse of $-a$ and b is a multiplicative inverse of b^{-1}. ∎

Definition 1.2

The *order* of a field is the number of elements in the field. A field with a finite order p is called a finite field or Galois field $GF(p)$ for a positive integer p. If p is a prime number, such a finite field is also called a *prime field*. ∎

The order of a field can be finite or infinite. The set of all real numbers under traditional arithmetic is a classical example of a field with an infinite order. The set of all positive real numbers under traditional arithmetic is a counterexample because additive identity element "0" and additive inverses cannot be found in the set. Another counterexample is the set of all integers under ordinary arithmetic because multiplicative inverses, except "1," do not exist in the set.

In optical coding theory, finite (or Galois) fields with nonnegative integers under modulo arithmetic are of primary interest. In particular, various families of the prime codes in this book have optimal code properties when the codes are constructed over $GF(p)$ of a prime p. Such a prime field can be categorized by the set of all modulo-p

integers with modulo-p additions and multiplications, whereas modulo-p subtractions and divisions are defined implicitly.

For example, the smallest finite field is GF(2) $= \{0,1\}$, which is also a prime field. This field contains only the zero and unity elements, and the modulo-2 additions and multiplications are summarized as

+	0	1		×	0	1
0	0	1		0	0	0
1	1	0		1	0	1

The next finite field is GF(3) $= \{0,1,2\}$, which is also a prime field, with the modulo-3 additions and multiplications summarized as

+	0	1	2		×	0	1	2
0	0	1	2		0	0	0	0
1	1	2	0		1	0	1	2
2	2	0	1		2	0	2	1

The finite field GF(4) $= \{0,1,2,3\}$ is not a prime field because its additions and multiplications are not exactly modulo-4, as summarized below:

+	0	1	2	3		×	0	1	2	3
0	0	1	2	3		0	0	0	0	0
1	1	0	3	2		1	0	1	2	3
2	2	3	0	1		2	0	2	3	1
3	3	2	1	0		3	0	3	1	2

GF(4), also denoted as GF(2^2), is called an *extension field* of GF(2) because elements "0" and "1" in GF(4) operate the same way as those in GF(2). In fact, the two tables of GF(4) are generated by applying the primitive polynomial $x^2 + x + 1$ over GF(2) [1–5].

Definition 1.3

The *order* of a nonzero element a in a finite field GF(p) of a positive integer p is the smallest positive integer i satisfying $a^i = 1 \pmod{p}$. ∎

The order of an element is not the same as the order of a finite field. The latter is the number of elements in a finite field and always equal to p in GF(p). Because there are $p-1$ nonzero elements in GF(p), the order of an element cannot be greater than $p-1$. For example, the maximum order of a nonzero element in the prime field GF(3) $= \{0,1,2\}$ is 2. By inspection, only the element "2" in GF(3) can reach the maximum order because $2^1 = 2$ and $2^2 = 1 \pmod{3}$.

Definition 1.4

A field F' is called a *subfield* of another field F if F contains all elements of F' and these elements in F carry all of the properties of F'. F is then called an *extension field* of F'. ∎

Exemplified by GF(2) and GF(4), a prime field GF(p) is a subfield of GF(p^m) for a prime p and an integer $m > 1$. This is because GF(p^m) contains all elements of GF(p), and these elements operate the same way as those in GF(p).

For example, GF(2) is also a subfield of GF(2^3) = GF(8) = $\{0, 1, 2, 3, 4, 5, 6, 7\}$. One example of the addition and multiplication tables of GF(8) is given by

+	0	1	2	3	4	5	6	7
0	0	1	2	3	4	5	6	7
1	1	0	3	2	5	4	7	6
2	2	3	0	1	6	7	4	5
3	3	2	1	0	7	6	5	4
4	4	5	6	7	0	1	2	3
5	5	4	7	6	1	0	3	2
6	6	7	4	5	2	3	0	1
7	7	6	5	4	3	2	1	0

×	0	1	2	3	4	5	6	7
0	0	0	0	0	0	0	0	0
1	0	1	2	3	4	5	6	7
2	0	2	4	6	3	1	7	5
3	0	3	6	5	7	4	1	2
4	0	4	3	7	6	2	5	1
5	0	5	1	4	2	7	3	6
6	0	6	7	1	5	3	2	4
7	0	7	5	2	1	6	4	3

For reference, the tables are generated by applying the primitive polynomial $x^3 + x + 1$ over GF(2) [1–5]. Although it is beyond the scope of this book, a slightly different multiplication table of GF(8) can also be generated with another primitive polynomial $x^3 + x^2 + 1$ over GF(2).

Definition 1.5

The *characteristic* of a field F is the smallest number of times for the multiplicative identity element to add up to generate the additive identity element. ∎

By the definition, the characteristics of GF(p) and GF(p^m) of a prime p are both equal to p. For example, the characteristics of GF(2) and GF(4) are equal to 2 because their additive identity element "1" can be obtained by adding up the multiplicative identity element two times such that $1 + 1 = 0$ (mod 2) and $1 + 1 = 0$ (mod 4). The characteristic of GF(7) is 7 because $1 + 1 + 1 + 1 + 1 + 1 + 1 = 0$ (mod 7).

1.1.1 Primitive Elements

An important category of elements in a finite field are *primitive* elements. These elements are useful for constructing other elements in the finite field or extending the finite field. Every finite field contains at least one primitive element.

Definition 1.6

A primitive element α is an element in a finite field that can generate every element, except zero, in the finite field by successive powers of α.   ■

Theorem 1.2

The first $p - 1$ successive powers of a primitive element of GF(p) generate all the $p - 1$ nonzero elements of GF(p) for a positive integer p. Each primitive element is an element of maximum order, which is equal to $p - 1$ in GF(p).

Proof Assume that α is a primitive element of GF(p) and has an order of $p - 1$. Let $\alpha^i = \alpha^j$ and $0 < j < i < p$. Dividing α^j on both sides results in $\alpha^{i-j} = 1 \pmod{p}$, which violates the assumption of α having the order of $p - 1$ because $i - j$ is always less than $p - 1$. So, α^i must all be distinct for all $i \in [1, p - 1]$. To maintain the order of $p - 1$, $\alpha^i \neq 0 \pmod{p}$ is needed for all $i \in [1, p - 1]$. Otherwise, the successive powers $\{\alpha^{i+1}, \alpha^{i+2}, \ldots, \alpha^{p-1}\}$ will be all 0s. So, the smallest nonzero power of α that gives $\alpha^i = 1$ must be $i = p - 1$. Because $p - 1$ is also the number of nonzero elements in GF(p), α has the maximum order.   ■

By observation, the possible orders of nonzero elements in GF(p) are the divisors of $p - 1$. For example, as $p - 1 = 6$ in GF(7), the possible orders of the elements in GF(7) are 1, 2, 3, and 6. Of course, the element "1" always has order 1. The successive powers of the element "2" are $2^1 = 2$, $2^2 = 4$, and $2^3 = 2 \times 4 = 1 \pmod 7$. So, "2" has the order of 3 and is not a primitive element of GF(7). The element "3" is a primitive element of GF(7) because it has the order of 6 as $3^1 = 3$, $3^2 = 2$, $3^3 = 3 \times 2 = 6$, $3^4 = 3 \times 6 = 4$, $3^5 = 3 \times 4 = 5$, and $3^6 = 3 \times 5 = 1 \pmod 7$. Applying a similar successive-power test to the elements "4," "5," and "6," the orders of 3, 6, and 2 are obtained, respectively. So, "3" and "5" are the primitive elements of GF(7).

Theorem 1.3

For a given positive integer i, the $p - 1$ products of $\alpha^i \alpha^j$ are all distinct in GF(p) for all $j \in [1, p - 1]$, where p is a positive integer.

Proof According to Theorem 1.2, every α^p can be factorized out of the product

$\alpha^i \alpha^j$ because $\alpha^p = \alpha^0 = 1$. This factorization is equivalent to the application of a modulo-p addition onto the exponent of α^{i+j} and leaves the same set of exponents of α as that in Theorem 1.2.   ∎

TABLE 1.1
Multiplication Table of GF(p), Written in the Form of a Primitive Element α

$\times$	0	α^0	α^1	α^2	$\cdots$	α^{p-1}
0	0	0	0	0	$\cdots$	0
α^0	0	α^0	α^1	α^2	$\cdots$	α^{p-1}
α^1	0	α^1	α^2	α^3	$\cdots$	α^0
α^2	0	α^2	α^3	α^4	$\cdots$	α^1
$\vdots$	$\vdots$	$\vdots$	$\vdots$	$\vdots$	$\ddots$	$\vdots$
α^{p-1}	0	α^{p-1}	α^0	α^1	$\cdots$	α^{p-2}

According to Theorems 1.2 and 1.3, a primitive element α of GF(p) can be used to construct a multiplication table of GF(p), as shown in Table 1.1. For example, by substituting α in the table with a primitive element "2" of GF(5), a multiplication table of GF(5) is constructed as

$\times$	0	1	2	3	4
0	0	0	0	0	0
1	0	1	2	3	4
2	0	2	4	1	3
3	0	3	1	4	2
4	0	4	3	2	1

after some row- and column-rearrangement.

1.2   VECTOR SPACE

A *vector space*, an important concept closely related to linear algebra and matrix theory, is a collection of vectors that carry the same but certain properties [4, 5]. Two classical examples of vector space are the two-dimensional and three-dimensional Euclidean spaces in geometry, in which a vector $\mathbf{v}$ is interpreted as a directed line and written as an ordered set of Cartesian coordinates (v_x, v_y) and (v_x, v_y, v_z), respectively. The coordinates are obtained from the projections of $\mathbf{v}$ onto the x, y, and z axes.

The concept of vector space over a finite field under modulo addition and multiplication is of particular interest in optical coding theory because one-dimensional optical codes can be represented as vectors over a finite field.

Definition 1.7

A vector space V over a field F contains a set of elements, called *vectors*, in which each vector consists of an ordered set of elements in F, called *scalars*, and two operators—*vector addition* and *scalar multiplication*—defined with the following properties:

1. *Closure.* If $\mathbf{v}_1$ and $\mathbf{v}_2$ are vectors in V and c is a scalar in F, the sum $\mathbf{v}_1 + \mathbf{v}_2$ and the product $c\mathbf{v}_1$ are also vectors in V.

2. *Additive Identity and Inverse.* If $\mathbf{v}$ is a vector in V and

$$\mathbf{v} + \mathbf{0} = \mathbf{0} + \mathbf{v} = \mathbf{v}$$

$$\mathbf{v} + (-\mathbf{v}) = (-\mathbf{v}) + \mathbf{v} = \mathbf{0}$$

   then "$\mathbf{0}$" is the unique additive identity vector, called zero vector, in V, and $-\mathbf{v}$ is its unique additive inverse vector in V.

3. *Commutativity.* If $\mathbf{v}_1$ and $\mathbf{v}_2$ are vectors in V, the commutative law implies that

$$\mathbf{v}_1 + \mathbf{v}_2 = \mathbf{v}_2 + \mathbf{v}_1$$

4. *Associativity.* If $\mathbf{v}$ is a vector in V, and c_1 and c_2 are scalars in F, the associative law implies that

$$(c_1 c_2)\mathbf{v} = c_1(c_2\mathbf{v})$$

5. *Distributivity.* If $\mathbf{v}_1$ and $\mathbf{v}_2$ are vectors in V, and c_1 and c_2 are scalars in F, the distributive law implies that

$$c_1(\mathbf{v}_1 + \mathbf{v}_2) = c_1\mathbf{v}_1 + c_1\mathbf{v}_2$$

$$(c_1 + c_2)\mathbf{v}_1 = c_1\mathbf{v}_1 + c_2\mathbf{v}_1$$

6. *Multiplicativity.* If $\mathbf{v}$ is a vector in V, c is a scalar in F, and "0" and "1" are the additive and multiplicative identity elements in F, respectively, then $c\mathbf{0} = \mathbf{0}$, $0\mathbf{v} = \mathbf{0}$, and $1\mathbf{v} = \mathbf{v}$.

∎

Definition 1.8

An n-tuple over a field F is an ordered set of n elements, denoted by $(v_1, v_2, \ldots, v_i, \ldots, v_n)$, where v_i is an element in F. The collection of these n-tuples forms a vector space F^n.

∎

If $(u_1, u_2, \ldots, u_i, \ldots, u_n)$ and $(v_1, v_2, \ldots, v_i, \ldots, v_n)$ are n-tuples over a field F and c is a scalar of F, their vector addition produces

$$(u_1, u_2, \ldots, u_i, \ldots, u_n) + (v_1, v_2, \ldots, v_i, \ldots, v_n)$$
$$= (u_1 + v_1, u_2 + v_2, \ldots, u_i + v_i, \ldots, u_n + v_n)$$

and their scalar multiplication produces

$$c(u_1, u_2, \ldots, u_i, \ldots, u_n) = (c u_1, c u_2, \ldots, c u_i, \ldots, c u_n)$$

whereas $u_i + v_i$ and $c u_i$ are also elements in F.

Definition 1.9

The *inner product* of n-tuples $\mathbf{u} = (u_1, u_2, \ldots, u_i, \ldots, u_n)$ and $\mathbf{v} = (v_1, v_2, \ldots, v_i, \ldots, v_n)$ over a field F is defined as

$$
\begin{aligned}
\mathbf{u} \cdot \mathbf{v} &= (u_1, u_2, \ldots, u_i, \ldots, u_n) \cdot (v_1, v_2, \ldots, v_i, \ldots, v_n) \\
&= u_1 v_1 + u_2 v_2 + \cdots + u_i v_i + \cdots + u_n v_n
\end{aligned}
$$

which results in a scalar in F, where u_i, v_i, and $u_i v_i$ are elements in F. ∎

In addition, the inner products of n-tuples $\mathbf{u}$, $\mathbf{v}$, and $\mathbf{w}$ over F produce

$$
\begin{aligned}
\mathbf{u} \cdot \mathbf{v} &= \mathbf{v} \cdot \mathbf{u} \\
(c\mathbf{u}) \cdot \mathbf{v} &= c(\mathbf{u} \cdot \mathbf{v}) \\
\mathbf{w} \cdot (\mathbf{u} + \mathbf{v}) &= (\mathbf{w} \cdot \mathbf{u}) + (\mathbf{w} \cdot \mathbf{v})
\end{aligned}
$$

for a scalar c in F, due to the properties of vector space in Definition 1.7.

Two n-tuples over F are said to be *orthogonal* if their inner product is 0. A nonzero n-tuple over F can be orthogonal to itself.

1.2.1 Linear Operations in Vector Space over a Field

To construct and study the properties of one-dimensional optical codes, linear operations in vector space over a finite field are needed. Such linear operations resemble the usual operations in solving simultaneous linear equations, but are now performed in a finite field.

Definition 1.10

If $\{\mathbf{v}_1, \mathbf{v}_2, \ldots, \mathbf{v}_i, \ldots, \mathbf{v}_m\}$ are vectors in a vector space V over a field F and $\{a_1, a_2, \ldots, a_i, \ldots, a_m\}$ are scalars in F, the form

$$a_1 \mathbf{v}_1 + a_2 \mathbf{v}_2 + \cdots + a_i \mathbf{v}_i + \cdots + a_m \mathbf{v}_m$$

is called a *linear combination* of these vectors.

These vectors are said to be *linearly dependent* if

$$a_1 \mathbf{v}_1 + a_2 \mathbf{v}_2 + \cdots + a_i \mathbf{v}_i + \cdots + a_m \mathbf{v}_m = \mathbf{0}$$

for $\{a_1, a_2, \ldots, a_i, \ldots, a_m\}$ not all equal to 0s; otherwise, they are said to be *linearly independent*.

If there exists a set of linearly independent vectors that can generate every vector in V by means of linear combinations, these linearly independent vectors are said to *span V* and form a *basis* of V. If the number of these linearly independent vectors is finite, V is called a finite-dimensional vector space and its *dimension* is also equal to this number.   ∎

By definition, any set of linearly independent vectors that span V cannot contain the zero vector $\mathbf{0}$; otherwise, they are linearly dependent. Also, linearly independent vectors cannot be obtained by any linear combination of other vectors in V.

There exists at least one set of linearly independent vectors that can form a basis of a vector space. For example, a set of linearly independent vectors, in which each vector contains a single 1 as one element and 0s as the remaining elements, is a natural choice for a basis. These vectors are called *unit vectors* and there are n of them for an n-dimensional vector space.

For example, the two unit vectors $(0,1)$ and $(1,0)$, which resemble the two Cartesian coordinate axes in two-dimensional Euclidean space, form a basis of a two-dimensional vector space V_2 over GF(2) with four distinct vectors:

$$(0,0) = 0(0,1) + 0(1,0)$$
$$(0,1) = 1(0,1) + 0(1,0)$$
$$(1,0) = 0(0,1) + 1(1,0)$$
$$(1,1) = 1(0,1) + 1(1,0)$$

Unit vectors are not the only basis vectors for a vector space. For example, $(0,1)$ and $(1,1)$ can also form a basis of V_2. Nevertheless, a basis consisting of unit vectors only is called a *normal orthogonal* or *orthonormal* basis.

Definition 1.11

A vector space V' is called a *subspace* of another vector space V if V contains all vectors of V' and these vectors follow the vector-addition and scalar-multiplication properties of V.   ∎

By definition, it is only necessary to show closure under vector addition and scalar multiplication in order to verify the existence of a subspace, whereas other properties of a vector space are implied. Closure under scalar multiplication guarantees that the zero vector is always in the subspace. So, a subspace exists even if it has only one vector—the zero vector.

Theorem 1.4

If all vectors in a set V' are formed by the linear combinations of a subset of linearly independent vectors in a vector space V over a field F, V' is called a subspace of V and this subset of linearly independent vectors forms a basis of V'. Additive identity elements and inverses exist and the commutative, associative, and distributive laws also hold in V'.

Proof Let the subset of linearly independent vectors in V be $\{v_1, v_2, \ldots, v_i, \ldots, v_m\}$. By definition, V also contains vectors created by the linear combinations of these vectors. So, all vectors in V' are found in V. Also, let $v_a = a_1 v_1 + a_2 v_2 + \cdots + a_i v_i + \cdots + a_m v_m$ and $v_b = b_1 v_1 + b_2 v_2 + \cdots + b_i v_i + \cdots + b_m v_m$ be vectors in V' for some scalars $\{a_1, a_2, \ldots, a_i, \ldots, a_m\}$ and $\{b_1, b_2, \ldots, b_i, \ldots, b_m\}$ in F, and c be a scalar in F. Their sum and product

$$v_a + v_b = (a_1 + b_1)v_1 + (a_2 + b_2)v_2 + \cdots + (a_i + b_i)v_i + \cdots + (a_m + b_m)v_m$$

$$c v_a = c a_1 v_1 + c a_2 v_2 + \cdots + c a_i v_i + \cdots + c a_m v_m$$

belong to V' because $a_i + b_i$ and $c a_i$ are also in F for all $i \in [1, m]$ due to closure of F under addition and multiplication. So, V' is a subspace of V.

By definition, a vector subspace is also a vector space. So, this subset of linearly independent vectors spans and forms a basis of V', and the properties and laws of V are inherited. The existence of additive identity elements and inverses can be shown by applying $c = 0$ and $c = -1$ such that

$$0 v_a = 0 v_1 + 0 v_2 + \cdots + 0 v_i + \cdots + 0 v_m = 0$$

$$-v_a = (-a_1)v_1 + (-a_2)v_2 + \cdots + (-a_i)v_i + \cdots + (-a_m)v_m$$

result, where "0" is the (scalar) zero in F and $-a_i$ is the additive inverse of a_i in F for all $i \in [1, m]$. ∎

Using the unit vector $v_1 = (0, 1)$ of V_2 over GF(2) as an example, linear combinations of the form $a_1 v_1$ with a scalar a_1 in GF(2) result in two vectors $(0, 0)$ and $(0, 1)$, which constitute a subspace V_2'. So, the unit vector v_1 forms a basis of V_2'.

1.3 MATRIX THEORY

Matrix theory is another important concept and famous for systematically and efficiently solving a system of simultaneous linear equations in compact form [4, 5].

Matrix theory over a finite field under modulo addition and multiplication is of particular interest in optical coding theory because two-dimensional optical codes can be represented as matrices over a finite field.

1.3.1 Basic Definitions

An $m \times n$ matrix **A** over a field F is an array of mn elements, arranged in m rows and n columns as

$$
\mathbf{A} = \begin{bmatrix}
a_{11} & a_{12} & \cdots & a_{1j} & \cdots & a_{1n} \\
a_{21} & a_{22} & \cdots & a_{2j} & \cdots & a_{2n} \\
\vdots & \vdots & \ddots & \vdots & \ddots & \vdots \\
a_{i1} & a_{i2} & \cdots & a_{ij} & \cdots & a_{in} \\
\vdots & \vdots & \ddots & \vdots & \ddots & \vdots \\
a_{m1} & a_{m2} & \cdots & a_{mj} & \cdots & a_{mn}
\end{bmatrix} = [a_{ij}]
$$

where a_{ij} is an element in F and located in the ith row and jth column of **A**. If m equals n, such a matrix is called a *square matrix*.

A $1 \times n$ matrix has only one row and is also called a *row vector*.

An $m \times 1$ matrix has only one column and is also called a *column vector*.

A *zero matrix* **0** has all its mn elements equal to the zero element in F.

The *main diagonal* of a matrix contains the elements, a_{ii}, extending diagonally from the top-left corner to the bottom-right corner, with equal column and row numbers.

A *triangular matrix* is an $n \times n$ square matrix with all its elements, either below or above the main diagonal, equal to the zero element in F. The upper and lower triangular matrices are denoted as

$$
\mathbf{U} = \begin{bmatrix}
a_{11} & a_{12} & a_{13} & \cdots & a_{1n} \\
0 & a_{22} & a_{23} & \cdots & a_{2n} \\
0 & 0 & a_{33} & \cdots & a_{3n} \\
\vdots & \vdots & \vdots & \ddots & \vdots \\
0 & 0 & 0 & \cdots & a_{nn}
\end{bmatrix}
\qquad
\mathbf{L} = \begin{bmatrix}
a_{11} & 0 & 0 & \cdots & 0 \\
a_{21} & a_{22} & 0 & \cdots & 0 \\
a_{31} & a_{32} & a_{33} & \cdots & 0 \\
\vdots & \vdots & \vdots & \ddots & \vdots \\
a_{n1} & a_{n2} & a_{n3} & \cdots & a_{nn}
\end{bmatrix}
$$

respectively.

A *diagonal matrix* is an $n \times n$ square matrix with all its elements, except those in the main diagonal, equal to the zero element in F such that $a_{ij} = 0$ for all $i \neq j$.

An *identity matrix* **I** is an $n \times n$ diagonal matrix with all its elements in the main diagonal equal to the unity element in F. For example,

$$
\begin{bmatrix}
1 & 0 \\
0 & 1
\end{bmatrix}
\qquad\qquad
\begin{bmatrix}
1 & 0 & 0 \\
0 & 1 & 0 \\
0 & 0 & 1
\end{bmatrix}
$$

The *transpose* of an $m \times n$ matrix $\mathbf{A} = [a_{ij}]$ exchanges the rows and columns of $\mathbf{A}$ to generate an $n \times m$ matrix $\mathbf{A}^t = [a_{ij}]^t = [a_{ji}]$. For example,

$$\mathbf{A} = \begin{bmatrix} 1 & 4 & 7 \\ 2 & 5 & 8 \\ 3 & 6 & 9 \end{bmatrix} \qquad \mathbf{A}^t = \begin{bmatrix} 1 & 2 & 3 \\ 4 & 5 & 6 \\ 7 & 8 & 9 \end{bmatrix}$$

The transpose of an upper triangular matrix is a lower triangular matrix.
The transpose of a lower triangular matrix is an upper triangular matrix.

A matrix can be partitioned into an array of smaller disjoint matrices, called *submatrices*. The total numbers of rows and columns of all submatrices must add up to those of the whole matrix. For example, matrix $\mathbf{A}$ can be partitioned into

$$\mathbf{A} = \begin{bmatrix} 1 & 5 & 9 \\ 2 & 6 & 10 \\ 3 & 7 & 11 \\ 4 & 8 & 12 \end{bmatrix} = \begin{bmatrix} \mathbf{A}_1 \\ \mathbf{A}_2 \end{bmatrix} = \begin{bmatrix} \mathbf{A}_{11} & \mathbf{A}_{12} \\ \mathbf{A}_{21} & \mathbf{A}_{22} \end{bmatrix}$$

and the submatrices can be expressed in different forms, such as

$$\mathbf{A}_1 = \begin{bmatrix} 1 & 5 & 9 \\ 2 & 6 & 10 \end{bmatrix} \qquad \mathbf{A}_2 = \begin{bmatrix} 3 & 7 & 11 \\ 4 & 8 & 12 \end{bmatrix}$$

$$\mathbf{A}_{11} = \begin{bmatrix} 1 \end{bmatrix} \qquad \mathbf{A}_{12} = \begin{bmatrix} 5 & 9 \end{bmatrix}$$

$$\mathbf{A}_{21} = \begin{bmatrix} 2 \\ 3 \\ 4 \end{bmatrix} \qquad \mathbf{A}_{22} = \begin{bmatrix} 6 & 10 \\ 7 & 11 \\ 8 & 12 \end{bmatrix}$$

Two same-dimension matrices are said to be equal only if their respective elements are all identical.

1.3.2 Basic Operations and Properties

Let $\mathbf{A}$ and $\mathbf{B}$ be $m \times n$ matrices over a field F and c be an element in F, their sum and product

$$\mathbf{A} + \mathbf{B} = \begin{bmatrix} a_{11}+b_{11} & a_{12}+b_{12} & \cdots & a_{1n}+b_{1n} \\ a_{21}+b_{21} & a_{22}+b_{22} & \cdots & a_{2n}+b_{2n} \\ \vdots & \vdots & \ddots & \vdots \\ a_{m1}+b_{m1} & a_{m2}+b_{m2} & \cdots & a_{mn}+b_{mn} \end{bmatrix} = [a_{ij}+b_{ij}]$$

$$c\mathbf{A} = \begin{bmatrix} ca_{11} & ca_{12} & \cdots & ca_{1n} \\ ca_{21} & ca_{22} & \cdots & ca_{2n} \\ \vdots & \vdots & \ddots & \vdots \\ ca_{m1} & ca_{m2} & \cdots & ca_{mn} \end{bmatrix} = [ca_{ij}]$$

are $m \times n$ matrices over F, where a_{ij}, b_{ij}, $a_{ij} + b_{ij}$, and $c\,a_{ij}$ are elements in F. Addition of matrices with different dimensions is not defined.

Addition and scalar multiplication of matrices are both associative and commutative due to the same properties in F.

Matrix multiplication, say $\mathbf{D} = \mathbf{AB}$, is defined only if the number of columns in $\mathbf{A}$ is equal to the number of rows in $\mathbf{B}$. The product is an $m \times n$ matrix $\mathbf{D} = [d_{ij}]$ over a field F if $\mathbf{A} = [a_{il}]$ is an $m \times k$ matrix and $\mathbf{B} = [b_{lj}]$ is a $k \times n$ matrix, both over F. The (i,j) th element in $\mathbf{D}$ is the sum of the products of the elements in the ith row in $\mathbf{A}$ and the respective elements in the jth column in $\mathbf{B}$ such that

$$d_{ij} = \sum_{l=1}^{k} a_{il} b_{lj}$$

where d_{ij}, a_{il}, and b_{lj} are elements in F for $i \in [1,m]$, $l \in [1,k]$, and $j \in [1,n]$. For example,

$$\mathbf{A} = \begin{bmatrix} 1 & 2 & 3 \\ 4 & 5 & 6 \end{bmatrix} \qquad \mathbf{B} = \begin{bmatrix} 1 & 2 \\ 3 & 4 \\ 5 & 6 \end{bmatrix} \qquad \mathbf{AB} = \begin{bmatrix} 22 & 28 \\ 49 & 64 \end{bmatrix}$$

It is easy to verify that matrix multiplication is distributive and associative. For example,

$$
\begin{aligned}
\mathbf{A}(\mathbf{B} + \mathbf{C}) &= \mathbf{AB} + \mathbf{AC} \\
(\mathbf{B} + \mathbf{C})\mathbf{A} &= \mathbf{BA} + \mathbf{CA} \\
(\mathbf{AB})\mathbf{C} &= \mathbf{A}(\mathbf{BC})
\end{aligned}
$$

for matrices $\mathbf{A}$, $\mathbf{B}$, and $\mathbf{C}$ over a field F. However, matrix multiplication is generally not commutative. For example, it is usually found that $\mathbf{AB} \neq \mathbf{BA}$.

The product of two upper triangular matrices produces an upper triangular matrix.

The product of two lower triangular matrices produces a lower triangular matrix.

The *inverse* $\mathbf{A}^{-1}$ of an $n \times n$ square matrix $\mathbf{A}$ over a field F is an $n \times n$ square matrix over F, satisfying

$$\mathbf{A}^{-1}\mathbf{A} = \mathbf{A}\mathbf{A}^{-1} = \mathbf{I}$$

where $\mathbf{I}$ is the $n \times n$ identity matrix over F.

If its inverse exists, a matrix is called *nonsingular*. Otherwise, it is called *singular*. The inverse of a triangular matrix is also a triangular matrix.

Theorem 1.5

If $\mathbf{D} = \mathbf{AB}$ and the inverses of $\mathbf{A}$ and $\mathbf{B}$ both exist over a field F, then

$$\mathbf{D}^{-1} = \mathbf{B}^{-1}\mathbf{A}^{-1}$$

Proof Because $\mathbf{A}^{-1}$ and $\mathbf{B}^{-1}$ both exist, it is easy to show that

$$(\mathbf{B}^{-1}\mathbf{A}^{-1})\mathbf{D} = \mathbf{B}^{-1}\mathbf{A}^{-1}\mathbf{A}\mathbf{B} = \mathbf{B}^{-1}\mathbf{I}\mathbf{B} = \mathbf{B}^{-1}\mathbf{B} = \mathbf{I}$$
$$\mathbf{D}(\mathbf{B}^{-1}\mathbf{A}^{-1}) = \mathbf{A}\mathbf{B}\mathbf{B}^{-1}\mathbf{A}^{-1} = \mathbf{A}\mathbf{I}\mathbf{A}^{-1} = \mathbf{A}\mathbf{A}^{-1} = \mathbf{I}$$

So, the inverse of $\mathbf{D}$ is $\mathbf{B}^{-1}\mathbf{A}^{-1}$, by definition.   ∎

1.3.3   Determinant

The *determinant* of an $n \times n$ square matrix $\mathbf{A} = [a_{ij}]$ is defined as a sum of signed n-fold product terms and denoted as

$$|\mathbf{A}| = \sum (-1)^q a_{1p_1} a_{2p_2} \cdots a_{ip_i} \cdots a_{np_n}$$

Each product term contains one permutation of one element from each row and column of $\mathbf{A}$. Because each permutation is determined by a distinct set of n subscripts $\{p_1, p_2, \ldots, p_i, \ldots, p_n\}$ and $p_i \in [1, n]$, there are in total $n!$ such permutations and, in turn, $n!$ product terms. The summation is performed over all these $n!$ product terms with the sign $(-1)^q$ determined by whether the number of elements q that need to be reordered in order to obtain one distinct permutation is even or odd.

As a recursive method of calculating the determinant of $\mathbf{A} = [a_{ij}]$ in terms of the sum of the n determinants of $(n-1) \times (n-1)$ submatrices, the Laplace expansion formula is given by [4, 5]

$$|\mathbf{A}| = \sum_{j=1}^{n} (-1)^{i+j} a_{ij} |\mathbf{M}_{ij}|$$

for a fixed $i \in [1, n]$. $\mathbf{M}_{ij}$ denotes the $(n-1) \times (n-1)$ submatrix after the row and column containing a_{ij} in $\mathbf{A}$ have been removed. While $|\mathbf{M}_{ij}|$ is called the *minor* of a_{ij}, $(-1)^{i+j}|\mathbf{M}_{ij}|$ is called the *cofactor* of a_{ij}.

For example, for $n = 3$ and $i = 2$, the determinant of $\mathbf{A}$ can be calculated by

$$
\begin{aligned}
|\mathbf{A}| &= \begin{vmatrix} a_{11} & a_{12} & a_{13} \\ a_{21} & a_{22} & a_{23} \\ a_{31} & a_{32} & a_{33} \end{vmatrix} \\
&= (-1)^{2+1} a_{21} \begin{vmatrix} a_{12} & a_{13} \\ a_{32} & a_{33} \end{vmatrix} + (-1)^{2+2} a_{22} \begin{vmatrix} a_{11} & a_{13} \\ a_{31} & a_{33} \end{vmatrix} \\
&\quad + (-1)^{2+3} a_{23} \begin{vmatrix} a_{11} & a_{12} \\ a_{31} & a_{32} \end{vmatrix} \\
&= -a_{21} \left[(-1)^{1+1} a_{12} a_{33} + (-1)^{1+2} a_{13} a_{32} \right] \\
&\quad + a_{22} \left[(-1)^{1+1} a_{11} a_{33} + (-1)^{1+2} a_{13} a_{31} \right] \\
&\quad - a_{23} \left[(-1)^{1+1} a_{11} a_{32} + (-1)^{1+2} a_{12} a_{31} \right] \\
&= -a_{21}(a_{12} a_{33} - a_{13} a_{32}) + a_{22}(a_{11} a_{33} - a_{13} a_{31}) - a_{23}(a_{11} a_{32} - a_{12} a_{31})
\end{aligned}
$$

It is found that the determinant of a triangular matrix is the product of all elements on the main diagonal. So, the determinant of a square matrix can be readily obtained by first transforming it into a triangular matrix.

An $n \times n$ square matrix has a nonzero determinant if and only if its n rows (or columns) are linearly independent. It is because linear independency implies that no matrix row-wise (or column-wise) transformation, such as the sum of scalar products of rows (or columns), can produce a row (or column) with all zero elements, except when the scalars in the scalar products are all 0s.

This property supports the computation of a matrix inverse by means of a determinant. For an $n \times n$ square matrix $\mathbf{A}$, the substitution of a_{ij} with a_{kj} in the Laplace expansion formula results in

$$\sum_{j=1}^{n} (-1)^{i+j} a_{kj} |\mathbf{M}_{ij}| = \begin{cases} |\mathbf{A}| & \text{for } i = k \\ 0 & \text{otherwise} \end{cases}$$

If $\mathbf{B} = [b_{ij}]$ is the inverse of $\mathbf{A}$, then the element in the ith row and jth column of $\mathbf{B}$ can be readily computed by the cofactor of a_{ji} as

$$b_{ij} = \frac{(-1)^{i+j} |\mathbf{M}_{ji}|}{|\mathbf{A}|}$$

where $|\mathbf{A}| \neq 0$.

1.3.4   Eigenvalues and Eigenvectors

An *eigenvector* of a square matrix is a nonzero vector that maintains in the same direction but is scaled by a fixed value, called an *eigenvalue*, after being multiplied by the matrix. Eigenvalues and eigenvectors find applications in linear algebra, such as matrix factorization into canonical form [4, 5].

Definition 1.12

A nonzero vector $\mathbf{v}$ is an *eigenvector* of a square matrix $\mathbf{A}$ if there exists a scalar c, called an *eigenvalue* of $\mathbf{A}$, such that $\mathbf{A}\mathbf{v} = c\mathbf{v}$ or $(\mathbf{A} - c\mathbf{I})\mathbf{v} = 0$.   ∎

By definition, the eigenvalues of $\mathbf{A}$ are found by calculating the roots of $|\mathbf{A} - c\mathbf{I}| = 0$. The eigenvector $\mathbf{v}$ associated with an eigenvalue is computed by substituting the eigenvalue back into $(\mathbf{A} - c\mathbf{I})\mathbf{v} = 0$ and then solving for the elements of $\mathbf{v}$.

For example, the eigenvalues of matrix

$$\mathbf{A} = \begin{bmatrix} 3 & 4 \\ 2 & 1 \end{bmatrix}$$

are found by evaluating the determinant

$$|\mathbf{A} - c\mathbf{I}| = \begin{vmatrix} 3 - c & 4 \\ 2 & 1 - c \end{vmatrix} = 0$$

and then solving $(3-c)(1-c) - 2 \times 4 = c^2 - 4c - 5 = 0$. The eigenvalues of $\mathbf{A}$ are found to be "-1" and "5." The eigenvectors associated with the eigenvalue "-1" is computed by further solving

$$[\mathbf{A} - (-1)\mathbf{I}]\mathbf{v} = \begin{bmatrix} 4 & 4 \\ 2 & 2 \end{bmatrix} \begin{bmatrix} v_1 \\ v_2 \end{bmatrix} = \begin{bmatrix} 0 \\ 0 \end{bmatrix}$$

and, in turn, $4v_1 + 4v_2 = 0$ and $2v_1 + 2v_2 = 0$. A nontrivial solution to these two equations is $v_2 = -v_1$. The eigenvectors of the eigenvalue "-1" are then given by $v_1(1, -1)^t$ with v_1 being arbitrary. For instance, by setting $v_1 = 1$, $(1, -1)^t$ becomes an eigenvector associated with the eigenvalue "-1." Similarly, $(2, 1)^t$ is an eigenvector associated with the eigenvalue "5" if $v_1 = 1$ is also assumed.

If c is an eigenvalue of $\mathbf{A}$, αc is the eigenvalue of $\alpha\mathbf{A}$ for a scalar α.

If c is an eigenvalue of a nonsingular matrix $\mathbf{A}$, $1/c$ is the eigenvalue of $\mathbf{A}^{-1}$.

The eigenvalues of an upper or lower triangular matrix are the elements on the main diagonal.

If the eigenvalues of a nonsingular matrix $\mathbf{A}$ are all distinct, the associated eigenvectors are all linearly independent, as implied in the following theorem.

Theorem 1.6

If $\mathbf{A}$ is an $n \times n$ nonsingular matrix with n distinct eigenvalues, there exists an $n \times n$ nonsingular matrix $\mathbf{B}$ such that $\mathbf{B}^{-1}\mathbf{A}\mathbf{B}$ is a diagonal matrix. $\mathbf{A}$ is said to be *diagonalizable*.

Proof Let $\mathbf{A}$ be an $n \times n$ matrix with eigenvectors $\{\mathbf{b}_1, \mathbf{b}_2, \ldots, \mathbf{b}_n\}$ associated with n distinct eigenvalues $\{c_1, c_2, \ldots, c_n\}$, respectively. Assume that these eigenvectors are linearly dependent. Hence, there exists an integer $k \in [1, n-1]$ such that $\{\mathbf{b}_1, \mathbf{b}_2, \ldots, \mathbf{b}_k\}$ are linearly independent but $\{\mathbf{b}_1, \mathbf{b}_2, \ldots, \mathbf{b}_{k+1}\}$ are linearly dependent. This gives $\alpha_1\mathbf{b}_1 + \alpha_2\mathbf{b}_2 + \cdots + \alpha_{k+1}\mathbf{b}_{k+1} = 0$ for some scalars $\{\alpha_1, \alpha_2, \ldots, \alpha_{k+1}\}$ not all equal to 0. Multiplying by $\mathbf{A}$ on both sides results in $\alpha_1\mathbf{A}\mathbf{b}_1 + \alpha_2\mathbf{A}\mathbf{b}_2 + \cdots + \alpha_{k+1}\mathbf{A}\mathbf{b}_{k+1} = 0$. By definition, $\mathbf{A}\mathbf{b}_i = c_i\mathbf{b}_i$ for all $i \in [1, n]$. So, the equation can be further written as $\alpha_1 c_1 \mathbf{b}_1 + \alpha_2 c_2 \mathbf{b}_2 + \cdots + \alpha_{k+1} c_{k+1} \mathbf{b}_{k+1} = 0$. Subtracting it from the original equation and then multiplying c_{k+1} on both sides of the difference results in $\alpha_1(c_1 - c_{k+1})\mathbf{b}_1 + \alpha_2(c_2 - c_{k+1})\mathbf{b}_2 + \cdots + \alpha_k(c_k - c_{k+1})\mathbf{b}_k = 0$. Because $\{\mathbf{b}_1, \mathbf{b}_2, \ldots, \mathbf{b}_k\}$ are assumed linearly independent, it can be concluded that $\alpha_i(c_i - c_{k+1})\mathbf{b}_i = 0$ for all $i \in [1, k]$. As these eigenvalues are all distinct, this gives $c_i - c_{k+1} \neq 0$ and α_i must be zero for all $i \in [1, k+1]$, which contradicts the not-all-zero-scalar and linear-dependent assumptions. So, the n eigenvectors associated with the n distinct eigenvalues must be linearly independent.

Assume that these n linear-independent eigenvectors form the columns of an $n \times n$ matrix $\mathbf{B}$. By definition, there exists $\mathbf{B}^{-1}$. If $\mathbf{A}\mathbf{b}_i = c_i\mathbf{b}_i$ for $i \in [1, n]$ are expressed in matrix form as $\mathbf{AB} = \mathbf{BC}$, then

$$\mathbf{C} = \begin{bmatrix} c_1 & 0 & \cdots & 0 \\ 0 & c_2 & \cdots & 0 \\ \vdots & \vdots & \ddots & \vdots \\ 0 & 0 & \cdots & c_n \end{bmatrix}$$

is an $n \times n$ diagonal matrix containing all n distinct eigenvalues of $\mathbf{A}$. The multiplication of $\mathbf{B}^{-1}$ on both sides results in $\mathbf{B}^{-1}\mathbf{AB} = \mathbf{C}$, a diagonal matrix. ∎

While direct multiplication is a straightforward method of calculating small powers of a square matrix, the task becomes difficult for large powers. If the square matrix has all distinct eigenvalues, Theorem 1.6 makes large-power calculations easier by computing the powers of a diagonal matrix as

$$\begin{aligned} \mathbf{A}^k &= \left(\mathbf{BCB}^{-1}\right)^k \\ &= (\mathbf{BCB}^{-1})(\mathbf{BCB}^{-1})\cdots(\mathbf{BCB}^{-1}) \\ &= \mathbf{BCIC}\cdots\mathbf{ICB}^{-1} \\ &= \mathbf{BC}^k\mathbf{B}^{-1} \end{aligned}$$

in which $\mathbf{C}^k$ is simply given by

$$\mathbf{C}^k = \begin{bmatrix} c_1^k & 0 & \cdots & 0 \\ 0 & c_2^k & \cdots & 0 \\ \vdots & \vdots & \ddots & \vdots \\ 0 & 0 & \cdots & c_n^k \end{bmatrix}$$

1.4 HAMMING DISTANCE AND WEIGHT

Hamming weight and distance are two important parameters in characterizing an optical code that consists of a collection of codewords.

The *Hamming weight*, commonly called code weight, of a code is the number of nonzero elements in each of its codewords.

The *Hamming distance* between two codewords that have the same number of code elements is the number of positions in which the respective elements of the two codewords differ.

Their Hamming distance is also the Hamming weight on the difference of two codewords. So, the Hamming weight of a codeword is the Hamming distance between the codeword and the all-zero codeword.

For example, the Hamming weights of the codewords 1010010010 and 0100011001 are both 4 and their Hamming distance is 6.

The *minimum distance* of a code is the smallest Hamming distance that can be found between any pair of codewords in the code set.

1.5   CORRELATION FUNCTIONS

Autocorrelation and cross-correlation functions are important parameters in characterizing optical codes [17, 18, 21, 22, 27]. Because some optical codes are constructed in vector form and some are in matrix form, these correlation functions are here defined as one-dimensional (1-D) and two-dimensional (2-D). The autocorrelation function consists of two parts—the peak and sidelobes—and is useful for initial code acquisition and synchronization between the transmitter-receiver pair. The autocorrelation peak is usually equal to the Hamming (or code) weight and determines how well an optical codeword is detected at its receiver in the presence of *mutual interference* caused by interfering codewords. It is desirable to design optical codes with the autocorrelation sidelobes as low as possible for minimizing *self-interference*. The cross-correlation function represents the degree of mutual interference caused by interfering codewords and can be defined as *aperiodic*, *periodic*, or *in-phase*, depending on the coding schemes in use (e.g., see Chapter 2). The aperiodic cross-correlation function measures the strength of mutual interference as a function of the amount of (code-element) shifts applied to one of the two correlating codewords. The periodic cross-correlation function is defined similar to the aperiodic one, except that the shifts are performed cyclically—as if the shifted codeword is concatenated once—so that the correlation process does not involve any null caused by the "shift-out" of the shifted codeword. The in-phase cross-correlation function assumes that the two correlating codewords are aligned accordingly during the correlation process. So, in-phase cross-correlation results in just a value, not a function of any shift. Optical codes are traditionally designed with these cross-correlation functions as close to zero as possible for minimizing mutual interference.

1.5.1   1-D Auto- and Cross-Correlation Functions

The 1-D correlation functions are defined for optical codes that use one coding feature (e.g., time or wavelength) to convey information. For example, 1-D unipolar temporal-amplitude codes convey nonzero code elements with optical pulses in time.

Definition 1.13

For two distinct 1-D codewords (or N-tuples) $C = (c_0, c_1, \ldots, c_i, \ldots, c_{N-1})$ and $C' = (c'_0, c'_1, \ldots, c'_i, \ldots, c'_{N-1})$ and an integer $\tau \in [0, N-1]$, the 1-D periodic discrete cross-correlation function between C and C' at a given τ-shift is defined as

$$\Theta_{C,C'}(\tau) = \sum_{i=0}^{N-1} c_i c'_{i \oplus \tau}$$

where c_i and c'_i represent the code elements in the ith positions of C and C', respectively, and "$\oplus$" denotes a modulo-N addition.

For the 1-D in-phase cross-correlation function, τ is set to a fixed value, such as $\tau = 0$.

For the 1-D aperiodic cross-correlation function, the modulo-N addition is replaced by an ordinary addition so that the shifts are noncyclic.

Setting $C = C'$, $\Theta_{C,C}(\tau)$ defines the 1-D discrete autocorrelation function of C. When $\tau = 0$, this function gives the autocorrelation peak, which is equal to the Hamming (or code) weight. Otherwise, it gives the autocorrelation sidelobe at a τ-shift.

The *maximum cross-correlation function* is the largest cross-correlation value that can be obtained between any two correlating N-tuples, say C and C', in the code set and defined as

$$\Theta_{\max} = \max\{\Theta_{C,C'}(\tau), \text{for all } \tau \in [0, N-1]\}$$

The *average cross-correlation function* between two N-tuples is taken by averaging the sum of their cross-correlation values from all N τ-shifts and given by

$$\overline{\Theta}_{C,C'} = \frac{1}{N} \sum_{\tau=0}^{N-1} \Theta_{C,C'}(\tau)$$

∎

The 1-D periodic cross-correlation function between any two N-tuples (i.e., codewords) counts the number of positions where both N-tuples have the same nonzero code elements at any τ cyclic-shift. For example, if the code set contains binary $(0, 1)$ N-tuples, the nonzero code elements are simply binary 1s. The aperiodic definition implies that the τ-shift is noncyclic. In these 1-D definitions, τ is referred to as only one kind of shift in either time or wavelength, depending on which coding feature is used. The in-phase cross-correlation function is just one value because it is just one case, usually $\tau = 0$, in the periodic cross-correlation function.

1.5.2   2-D Auto- and Cross-Correlation Functions

The 2-D correlation functions are defined for optical codes that use two coding features (e.g., time and wavelength) to convey information. For example, 2-D unipolar spectral-temporal-amplitude codes convey nonzero code elements by multiwavelength optical pulses in time.

Definition 1.14

For any two distinct 2-D codewords (or $L \times N$ matrices) $\mathbf{C} = [c_{i,j}]$ and $\mathbf{C}' = [c_{i,j}]$ and two integers $\tau_1 \in [0, L-1]$ and $\tau_2 \in [0, N-1]$, the 2-D periodic discrete cross-correlation function between $\mathbf{C}$ and $\mathbf{C}'$ at given τ_1- and τ_2-shifts is defined as

$$\Theta_{\mathbf{C},\mathbf{C}'}(\tau_1, \tau_2) = \sum_{i=0}^{L-1} \sum_{j=0}^{N-1} c_{i,j} c'_{i \hat{\oplus} \tau_1, j \oplus \tau_2}$$

where $c_{i,j}$ and $c'_{i,j}$ represent the code elements in the ith rows and jth columns of $\mathbf{C}$ and $\mathbf{C}'$, respectively, "$\hat{\oplus}$" denotes a modulo-L addition, and "$\oplus$" denotes a modulo-N addition.

For the 2-D in-phase cross-correlation function, τ_1 and τ_2 are set to their own fixed values, such as $\tau_1 = 0$ and $\tau_2 = 0$.

For the 2-D aperiodic cross-correlation function, the modulo-L and modulo-N additions are replaced by ordinary additions so that the shifts are noncyclic.

Setting $\mathbf{C} = \mathbf{C}'$, $\Theta_{\mathbf{C},\mathbf{C}}(\tau_1, \tau_2)$ defines the 2-D discrete autocorrelation function of $\mathbf{C}$. When $\tau_1 = \tau_2 = 0$, this function gives the autocorrelation peak, which is equal to the Hamming (or code) weight. Otherwise, it gives the autocorrelation sidelobe at τ_1- and τ_2-shifts.

The maximum cross-correlation function is the largest cross-correlation value that can be obtained between any two correlating $L \times N$ matrices, say $\mathbf{C}$ and $\mathbf{C}'$, in the code set and defined as

$$\Theta_{\max} = \max\{\Theta_{\mathbf{C},\mathbf{C}'}(\tau_1, \tau_2), \text{ for all } \tau_1 \in [0, L-1] \text{ and } \tau_2 \in [0, N-1]\}$$

The average cross-correlation function between two $L \times N$ matrices is taken by averaging the sum of their cross-correlation values obtained from all L τ_1-shifts and N τ_2-shifts and given by

$$\overline{\Theta}_{\mathbf{C},\mathbf{C}'} = \frac{1}{LN} \sum_{\tau_1=0}^{L-1} \sum_{\tau_2=0}^{N-1} \Theta_{\mathbf{C},\mathbf{C}'}(\tau_1, \tau_2)$$

∎

The 2-D periodic cross-correlation function between any two $L \times N$ matrices (i.e., codewords) counts the number of positions where both $L \times N$ matrices have the same nonzero code elements at any τ_1 and τ_2 cyclic-shifts. For example, if the code set contains binary $(0, 1)$ $L \times N$ matrices, the nonzero code elements are simply binary 1s. The aperiodic definition implies that the τ_1- and τ_2-shifts are noncyclic. In these 2-D definitions, τ_1 and τ_2 are referred to as two different kinds of shifts. For example, if τ_1 is for wavelength shift, then τ_2 is for time shift, or vice versa. The in-phase cross-correlation function is just one value because it is just one case, usually $\tau_1 = 0$ and $\tau_2 = 0$, in the periodic cross-correlation function.

1.6 CARDINALITY UPPER BOUND

The upper bound of the cardinality (or code size) of a family of 1-D or 2-D optical codes depends on the code length N, code weight w, the number of wavelengths L, the maximum autocorrelation sidelobe λ_a, and the maximum periodic cross-correlation function λ_c in use [17, 18, 21, 22, 44].

Theorem 1.7

The cardinality upper bound of any family of 2-D (binary unipolar) optical codes is formulated as

$$\Phi(L \times N, w, \lambda_a, \lambda_c) \leq \frac{L(LN-1)(LN-2)\cdots(LN-\lambda_c)\lambda_a}{w(w-1)(w-2)\cdots(w-\lambda_c)}$$

where $\lambda_c > 0$ and $\lambda_a > 0$. For 1-D (binary unipolar) optical codes, $L = 1$ is set.

Proof The derivation is based on Johnson's cardinality bound of 1-D optical orthogonal codes [17, 18, 44]. By computing the cyclic separations of adjacent pulses in every codeword (of weight w) in the code set, w cyclic adjacent-pulse separations per codeword can be obtained. To have λ_c as the maximum periodic cross-correlation function, the cross-correlation set for each codeword in the code set is obtained by grouping every λ_c of the consecutive cyclic adjacent-pulse separations of the codeword in accordance with the method in [45]. As a result, there exist a total of $w\binom{w-1}{\lambda_c}/(\lambda_a L)$ disjoint elements in the cross-correlation set of each codeword [46], and the cross-correlation sets of all codewords must be distinct. The factor L accounts for the fact that the cross-correlation process is performed cyclically in the horizontal (i.e., time) direction only. Because there are $\binom{LN-1}{\lambda_c}$ possible ways to select λ_c elements in the cross-correlation sets, the cardinality upper bound is given by

$$\Phi(L \times N, w, \lambda_a, \lambda_c) \leq \frac{\binom{LN-1}{\lambda_c}}{w\binom{w-1}{\lambda_c}/(\lambda_a L)}$$

where $\binom{x}{y} = x!/[y!(x-y)!]$ for integers $x \geq y \geq 0$. After some manipulations, the final form of the theorem is derived. ∎

For example, the cardinality of the carrier-hopping prime codes in Section 5.1, which have $L = w \leq p_1$, $N = p_1 p_2 \cdots p_k$, $\lambda_a = 0$, and $\lambda_c = 1$, is upper-bounded by

$$
\begin{aligned}
\Phi(w \times p_1 p_2 \cdots p_k, w, 0, 1) &\leq \Phi(w \times p_1 p_2 \cdots p_k, w, 1, 1) \\
&\leq \frac{w(w p_1 p_2 \cdots p_k - 1)}{w(w-1)} \\
&= p_1 p_2 \cdots p_k + \frac{p_1 p_2 \cdots p_k - 1}{w-1}
\end{aligned}
$$

according to Theorem 1.7, where $p_1 \leq p_2 \leq \cdots \leq p_k$ are prime numbers. For comparison, the actual cardinality of the carrier-hopping prime codes is given in Section 5.1 as $p_1 p_2 \cdots p_k$, which approaches the upper bound for a large w. So, the codes are said to have asymptotic optimal cardinality.

1.7 MARKOV CHAIN

To analyze the performance of optical codes, the cross-correlation function plays an important role because it counts the number of pulse overlaps (or so-called hits) between any two correlating codewords. For code weight w, there are up to w pulse positions for the hits to occur, and these positions can be modeled as the *states* of a *Markov chain* [24, 25]. The probability of changing the number of hits from one value to another value can be computed from the probability of transferring from one state to another state in such a Markov chain.

Containing a finite number of states, a Markov chain is a discrete random process with a (memoryless) Markov property. The Markov property states that the conditional probability distributions of states are all independent and the conditional probability of next state depends only on the present state. Let random variables $\{X_0, X_1, X_2, \ldots, X_i\}$ represent the independent probability distributions of $i+1$ states, labeled with distinct integers ranging from 0 to i. The Markov property implies that $\Pr(X_i = x_i \mid X_{i-1} = x_{i-1}, X_{i-2} = x_{i-2}, \ldots, X_0 = x_0) = \Pr(X_i = x_i \mid X_{i-1} = x_{i-1})$.

The changes of state in a Markov chain are called *transitions*. The probabilities associated with state changes are called transition probabilities. Due to the Markov property, $p_{i,j} = \Pr(X_j = j \mid X_i = i)$ represents the transition probability of transferring from state i to state j. A directed graph with paths, labeled by the transition probabilities, going from one state to other states is commonly used to characterize a Markov chain, such as the one in Figure 1.1.

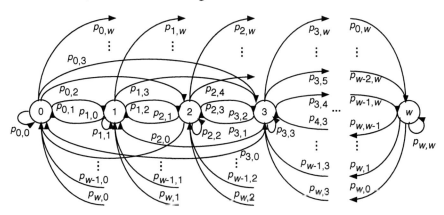

FIGURE 1.1 State transition diagram of a Markov chain with transition probabilities, $p_{i,j}$, where i and $j \in [0, w]$.

Let $\mathbf{P}$ denote the transition matrix containing a complete set of the transition probabilities of the Markov chain in Figure 1.1 such that

$$\mathbf{P} = \begin{bmatrix} p_{0,0} & p_{0,1} & \cdots & p_{0,w} \\ p_{1,0} & p_{1,1} & \cdots & p_{1,w} \\ \vdots & \vdots & \ddots & \vdots \\ p_{w,0} & p_{w,1} & \cdots & p_{w,w} \end{bmatrix}$$

This square matrix has nonnegative elements. Because the total probability of transferring out from any state must be equal to 1, each row sums to one and $\sum_{j=0}^{w} p_{i,j} = 1$.

To analyze a Markov chain, higher-order transition probabilities are sometimes computed. The kth-order transition probabilities can be calculated by multiplying the first-order transition matrix $\mathbf{P}$ by itself k times, denoted by [24]

$$\mathbf{P}^k = \begin{bmatrix} p_{0,0}^{(k)} & p_{0,1}^{(k)} & \cdots & p_{0,w}^{(k)} \\ p_{1,0}^{(k)} & p_{1,1}^{(k)} & \cdots & p_{1,w}^{(k)} \\ \vdots & \vdots & \ddots & \vdots \\ p_{w,0}^{(k)} & p_{w,1}^{(k)} & \cdots & p_{w,w}^{(k)} \end{bmatrix}$$

where $p_{i,j}^{(k)}$ is the probability of starting from state i and arriving at state j after k transitions. The probability that any k consecutive transitions taking on particular values is computed by

$$\begin{aligned} \Pr&(X_k = x_k, X_{k-1} = x_{k-1}, X_{k-2} = x_{k-2}, \ldots, X_0 = x_0) \\ &= \Pr(X_k = x_k \mid X_{k-1} = x_{k-1}) \Pr(X_{k-1} = x_{k-1} \mid X_{k-2} = x_{k-2}) \cdots \\ &\quad \times \Pr(X_1 = x_1 \mid X_0 = x_0) \Pr(X_0 = x_0) \\ &= \mathbf{PP} \cdots \mathbf{P} \Pr(X_0 = x_0) \\ &= \mathbf{P}^k \Pr(X_0 = x_0) \end{aligned}$$

where $\Pr(X_0 = x_0)$ is the initial state probability.

1.8 ALGEBRAIC TOOLS FOR PERFORMANCE ANALYSIS

Gaussian approximation is a quick estimation method to analyze code performance by applying the Central Limit Theorem [24–26]. Such an approximation is useful especially when the structural information of optical codes is not available. Otherwise, combinatorial methods usually produce more accurate code performance [21, 22, 27–37].

In general, the choice of signaling waveform of optical codes affects the designs of transmitter and receiver and, most importantly, the detection process, as studied in Chapter 2. There are two basic detection techniques—namely *coherent* (for optical field) and *incoherent* (for optical intensity). While coherent detection refers to how a receiver detects optical signals with knowledge of phase information, incoherent detection refers to the case without such knowledge. Operating on optical intensity, incoherent detection generally does not require phase tracking or system-wise synchronization and hardware complexity of the receiver is reduced, but usually at the expense of code performance.

Because binary unipolar codes, which contain $(0, 1)$ code elements, are usually transmitted in the form of optical intensity, they require incoherent detection and are also called incoherent codes. As bipolar codes, which contain $(-1, +1)$ code elements, are usually transmitted in form of optical phase, they require coherent detection and are also called coherent codes. Because this book studies optical coding theory with emphasis on prime codes, which are mainly incoherent codes, the term *optical codes* generally refers to this kind of code, which does not require phase tracking or system-wise synchronization, unless stated otherwise.

According to the definition of periodic cross-correlation function, the amount of interference seen at a receiver involves the correlation of its address codeword with two consecutive codewords from one interferer in order to obtain one complete cross-correlation process. This corresponds to the reception of two data bits in series from the same interferer. So, the error probability seen at the receiver can be written as

$$
\begin{aligned}
P_e &= \Pr(\text{error} \mid K \text{ simultaneous users}) \\
&= \sum_{x=0}^{1} \sum_{y=0}^{1} \Pr(\text{error} \mid K \text{ simultaneous users, interferer sends bits xy}) p_{xy}
\end{aligned}
$$

where p_{xy} is the probability of sending a data bit $x = \{0, 1\}$ followed by a data bit $y = \{0, 1\}$. There are, in total, four data-bit patterns and, in turn, four error-probability terms. Two terms in P_e, which correspond to $(x, y) = (0, 1)$ and $(1, 0)$, are contributed by partial cross-correlations and usually difficult to compute, especially when the cross-correlation function is greater than 1.

For unipolar codes, these two partial-correlation terms are usually bounded by the term of "bits 11" if on-off-keying modulation is assumed [21, 30]. So, the error probability can be simplified as

$$
P_e \approx \sum_{x=0}^{1} \Pr(\text{error} \mid K \text{ simultaneous users, interferer sends bit x}) p_x
$$

where p_x is the probability of sending a data bit $x = \{0, 1\}$.

For bipolar codes, the two partial-correlation terms are usually not bounded. For example, Gold sequences of various lengths have different partial-correlation values [6, 22, 47, 48]. So, other means, such as code length and weight, are used to first compute the signal-to-interference power ratio (SIR) and then the code performance is formulated in the form of a Gaussian approximation.

In the following sections, some general analytical techniques, based on Gaussian approximation and combinatorial methods, are formulated. Special analytical techniques that only apply to specific optical codes are given in their respective chapters.

1.8.1 Gaussian Approximation for Unipolar Codes

Using incoherent *on-off keying* (OOK) modulation, every user sends out a unipolar codeword corresponding to the address (signature) codeword of its intended receiver for a data bit 1, but nothing is transmitted for a data bit 0. At a receiver, unipolar codewords from all simultaneous users are correlated with the receiver's address codeword. If a correct codeword arrives, an autocorrelation function with a high peak results. The autocorrelation peak is usually equal to the code weight. For incorrect codewords, cross-correlation functions are generated and they create mutual interference. The aggregated cross-correlation functions and the autocorrelation function (if it exists) are then sampled and threshold-detected. If the sum of all functions in the sampling time, which is usually set at the expected (time) position of the auto-correlation peak, is as high as a predetermined decision-threshold level, a data bit 1 is recovered. Otherwise, a bit 0 is decided.

Assume that every simultaneous user sends data bit 0s and 1s with equal but independent probabilities: $p_0 = p_1 = 1/2$. Let q_i denote the probability that the cross-correlation value between an interfering codeword and the address codeword of a receiver in the sampling time is i and is defined as

$$q_i = \sum_{x=0}^{1} \Pr(\text{cross-correlation value} = i, \text{receiver receives bit x}) p_x$$

$$= 0.5\Pr(\text{cross-correlation value} = i, \text{receiver receives bit 1})$$

This kind of probability is commonly referred to as *hit* probability. The probability term with bit $x = 0$ is equal to 0 in OOK because no codeword is transmitted and, thus, no interference is generated for a data bit 0. The hit probability generally depends on the code parameters, such as weight and length, of the unipolar codewords in use and will be given in their respective chapters.

For unipolar codes with the maximum cross-correlation function of λ_c, each interfering codeword may contribute up to λ_c pulses (or hits) toward the cross-correlation function. So, the total number of hits seen by a receiver in the sampling time is given by $\sum_{k=0}^{\lambda_c} k l_k$, where l_k represents the number of interfering codewords contributing $k \in [0, \lambda_c]$ hits toward the cross-correlation function. The conditional probability of having the correlation value $Z = \sum_{k=0}^{\lambda_c} k l_k$ is given by a multinomial distribution as

$$\Pr(Z \text{ hits} \mid K \text{ users, receiver receives bit 0}) = \frac{(K-1)!}{l_0! l_1! \cdots l_{\lambda_c}!} q_0^{l_0} q_1^{l_1} \cdots q_{\lambda_c}^{l_{\lambda_c}}$$

As there are $K - 1 = \sum_{k=0}^{\lambda_c} l_k$ interferers (or interfering codewords), the conditional error probability of the receiver, which is actually receiving a bit 0, can be written as

$$\Pr(\text{error} \mid K \text{ simultaneous users, receiver receives bit 0})$$
$$= \Pr(Z \geq Z_{\text{th}} \mid K \text{ simultaneous users, receiver receives bit 0})$$
$$= 1 - \sum_{\sum_{k=0}^{\lambda_c} k l_k = 0}^{Z_{\text{th}}} \frac{(K-1)!}{l_0! l_1! \cdots l_{\lambda_c}!} q_0^{l_0} q_1^{l_1} \cdots q_{\lambda_c}^{l_{\lambda_c}}$$
$$\approx 1 - \int_0^{Z_{\text{th}}} \frac{1}{\sqrt{2\pi\sigma_0^2}} e^{\frac{-(x-m_0)^2}{2\sigma_0^2}} dx$$
$$\approx 1 - \int_{-\infty}^{Z_{\text{th}}} \frac{1}{\sqrt{2\pi\sigma_0^2}} e^{\frac{-(x-m_0)^2}{2\sigma_0^2}} dx$$

where Z_{th} is the threshold level used to decide whether the receiver is receiving a data bit 0 or 1. In the derivation, the multinomial distribution is approximated as Gaussian with mean

$$m_0 = (K-1) \sum_{i=0}^{\lambda_c} iq_i$$

and variance

$$\sigma_0^2 = (K-1) \left[\sum_{i=1}^{\lambda_c} \sum_{j=0}^{i-1} (i-j)^2 q_i q_j \right]$$

for a sufficiently large K, due to the Central Limit Theorem. It is assumed that the cross-correlation functions of these $K-1$ interferers are independent and identically distributed random variables. As each cross-correlation function takes on a value ranging from 0 to λ_c, the individual mean and variance are then given by $m = \sum_{i=0}^{\lambda_c} iq_i$ and $\sigma^2 = \sum_{i=0}^{\lambda_c} (i-j)^2 q_i = \sum_{i=1}^{\lambda_c} \sum_{j=0}^{i-1} (i-j)^2 q_i q_j$, respectively. The Central Limit Theorem states that the probability distribution of the sum of these $K-1$ random variables approaches a Gaussian distribution when K is sufficiently large [24, 25].

If a codeword, which represents the transmission of a data bit 1, arrives at a receiver with matching address codeword, an autocorrelation function with a high peak results. The total number of pulses seen by the receiver in the sampling time includes the autocorrelation peak and hits (generated by interfering codewords), and can be as large as $w + \sum_{k=0}^{\lambda_c} k l_k$. The autocorrelation peak is usually equal to the code weight w of the unipolar codewords in use. So, the conditional probability of having the correlation value $Z = w + \sum_{k=0}^{\lambda_c} k l_k$ is also given by a multinomial distribution and the conditional error probability of the receiver, which is actually receiving a bit 1, can be written as

$$\Pr(\text{error} \mid K \text{ simultaneous users, receiver receives bit 1})$$
$$= \Pr(Z < Z_{th} \mid K \text{ simultaneous users, receiver receives bit 1})$$
$$= 1 - \sum_{w + \sum_{k=0}^{\lambda_c} k l_k = Z_{th}}^{w+(K-1)\lambda_c} \frac{(K-1)!}{l_0! l_1! \cdots l_{\lambda_c}!} q_0^{l_0} q_1^{l_1} \cdots q_{\lambda_c}^{l_{\lambda_c}}$$
$$\approx 1 - \int_{Z_{th}}^{w+(K-1)\lambda_c} \frac{1}{\sqrt{2\pi\sigma_1^2}} e^{\frac{-(x-m_1)^2}{2\sigma_1^2}} \, dx$$
$$\approx 1 - \int_{Z_{th}}^{\infty} \frac{1}{\sqrt{2\pi\sigma_1^2}} e^{\frac{-(x-m_1)^2}{2\sigma_1^2}} \, dx$$

with mean

$$m_1 = w + (K-1) \sum_{i=0}^{\lambda_c} iq_i$$

and variance

$$\sigma_1^2 = \sigma_0^2 = (K-1)\left[\sum_{i=1}^{\lambda_c}\sum_{j=0}^{i-1}(i-j)^2 q_i q_j\right]$$

for a sufficiently large K, due to the Central Limit Theorem.

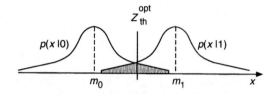

FIGURE 1.2 Typical relationship of two symmetric Gaussian conditional probability density functions, $p(x|0)$ and $p(x|1)$, where Z_{th}^{opt} is the optimal decision threshold [21, 26].

To minimize decision error, the optimal decision threshold Z_{th}^{opt} must be determined. First, consider the conditional probability density functions in the two conditional error probabilities:

$$p(x|0) = \frac{1}{\sqrt{2\pi\sigma_0^2}} e^{\frac{-(x-m_0)^2}{2\sigma_0^2}}$$

$$p(x|1) = \frac{1}{\sqrt{2\pi\sigma_1^2}} e^{\frac{-(x-m_1)^2}{2\sigma_1^2}}$$

The general relationship of these two (symmetric) Gaussian-distributed conditional probability density functions is illustrated in Figure 1.2. The optimal decision threshold Z_{th}^{opt} is usually located at the point of intersection of these functions. As shown in the figure, the shaded areas to the left and right of Z_{th}^{opt} indicate the regions of errors caused by the conditional error probabilities Pr(error | K simultaneous users, receiver receives bit 1) and Pr(error | K simultaneous users, receiver receives bit 0), respectively.

The optimization of Z_{th} involves the so-called likelihood ratio test [26] with the conditional probability density functions $p(x|0)$ and $p(x|1)$ following the rules:

1. If $p(x|0)p(0) > p(x|1)p(1)$, choose data bit 0.
2. If $p(x|1)p(1) > p(x|0)p(0)$, choose data bit 1.

If $p(0) = p(1)$, the optimal threshold occurs at the location of x where $p(x|0) = p(x|1)$. The optimal threshold level for minimizing the error probability is found to be

$$x = Z_{th}^{opt} = \frac{m_0 + m_1}{2}$$

Substituting Z_{th}^{opt} into the two conditional error probabilities, they eventually become

$$\text{Pr(error} \mid K \text{ simultaneous users, receiver receives bit 1)}$$

$$= \text{Pr(error} \mid K \text{ simultaneous users, receiver receives bit 0)}$$

$$\approx 1 - \int_{-\infty}^{Z_{th}^{opt}} \frac{1}{\sqrt{2\pi\sigma_0^2}} e^{\frac{-(x-m_0)^2}{2\sigma_0^2}} \, dx$$

$$= Q \left(\frac{Z_{th}^{opt} - m_0}{\sqrt{\sigma_0^2}} \right)$$

$$= Q \left(\frac{w}{2\sqrt{\sigma_0^2}} \right)$$

where $Q(x) = (1/\sqrt{2\pi}) \int_x^{\infty} \exp\left(-y^2/2\right) dy$ is the complementary error function.

The Gaussian-approximated error probability of unipolar codes with the maximum cross-correlation function of λ_c in OOK is finally derived as

$$
\begin{aligned}
P_{e|G \text{ unipolar}} &= \sum_{x=0}^{1} \text{Pr(error} \mid K \text{ simultaneous users, receiver receives bit } x)p_x \\
&= Q \left(\frac{1}{2} \sqrt{\frac{w^2}{(K-1)\sum_{i=1}^{\lambda_c}\sum_{j=0}^{i-1}(i-j)^2 q_i q_j}} \right) \\
&= Q \left(\frac{\sqrt{\text{SIR}}}{2} \right)
\end{aligned}
\qquad (1.1)
$$

where the factor $1/2$ is due to OOK with equal probability of transmitting data bit 1s and 0s, and the terms inside the square root are collectively identified as the signal-to-interference power ratio (SIR).

1.8.2   Gaussian Approximation for Bipolar Codes

Using coherent bipolar modulation, every user sends out a bipolar codeword corresponding to the address (signature) codeword of its intended receiver for a data bit 1, but transmits the phase-conjugate form of the same codeword for a data bit 0. The advantage of bipolar codes, such as Walsh codes and maximal-length sequences [22, 47, 48], is the capability of having zero in-phase cross-correlation functions for preventing mutual interference. However, these kinds of bipolar codes require perfect code synchronization to operate, meaning that all simultaneous users need to transmit in the same orientation—should it be time or wavelength. As a result, a coherent system is usually a synchronous system if zero mutual interference is desired. On other hand, if perfect code synchronization is not possible, Gold sequences, a family of asynchronous bipolar codes with multiple periodic cross-correlation functions, can be used at the expense of stronger mutual interference.

The Gaussian-approximated error probability of bipolar codes is generally given by [47]

$$P_{e|G \text{ bipolar}} = Q\left(\sqrt{\text{SIR}}\right)$$

Comparing to Equation (1.1), the factor $1/2$ disappears because data bit 0s are now conveyed by the phase-conjugate form of bipolar codewords. The actual form of the SIR depends on the bipolar codes in use. For example, the asynchronous Gold sequences of length N are found to have SIR $= 2N/(K-1)$ [22,47].

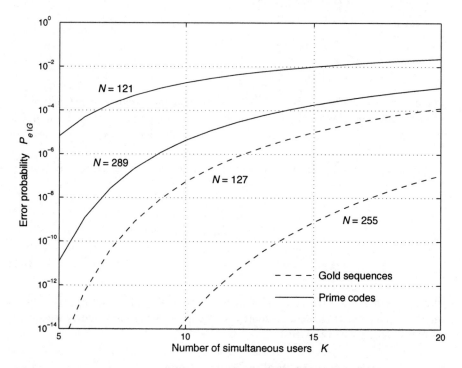

FIGURE 1.3 Gaussian error probability of (unipolar) 1-D prime codes and (bipolar) Gold sequences for various code length N.

Figure 1.3 plots the Gaussian-approximated error probabilities of the (unipolar) 1-D prime codes in Section 3.1 and (bipolar) Gold sequences against the number of simultaneous users K. In this example, the prime codes have $\lambda_c = 2$, length $N = p^2 = \{121, 289\}$, and weight $w = p = \{11, 17\}$, while Gold sequences have $N = w = \{127, 255\}$, where p is a prime number. Their code lengths are selected to be similar for a fair comparison. From Section 3.1, the hit probabilities of the prime codes are given by $q_0 = (7p^2 - p - 2)/(12p^2)$, $q_1 = (2p^2 + p + 2)/(6p^2)$, and $q_2 = (p-2)(p+1)/(12p^2)$. The variance in Equation (1.1) becomes $\sum_{i=1}^{2}\sum_{j=0}^{i-1}(i-j)^2 q_i q_j = (5p^2 - 2p - 4)/(12p^2)$. As shown in the figure, the error probabilities of both code families improve as w or N increases because of higher autocorrelation peaks (determined by w) or lower hit probabilities. However, their error probabilities get worse as K increases, due to stronger mutual interference. In general, Gold sequences perform better than the prime codes because the former have code weight equal to code length and data bit 0s are transmitted with phase-conjugate codes, resulting in a higher SIR.

1.8.3 Combinatorial Analysis for Unipolar Codes

In addition to Gaussian approximation, a more accurate combinatorial method can be applied to analyze the performance of unipolar codes in OOK modulation.

As mentioned in Section 1.8.1, for unipolar codes with the maximum cross-correlation value of λ_c, each interfering codeword (or interferer) may contribute up to λ_c hits toward the cross-correlation function. For a given K simultaneous users, the total number of interferers is given by $K - 1 = \sum_{k=0}^{\lambda_c} l_k$, and the total number of hits seen by the receiver in the sampling time is given by $\sum_{k=0}^{\lambda_c} k l_k$, where l_k represents the number of interfering codewords contributing k hits toward the cross-correlation function. The conditional probability of having $Z = \sum_{k=0}^{\lambda_c} k l_k$ hits contributed by these interfering codewords follows a multinomial distribution. Furthermore, in OOK, a decision error occurs whenever the received data bit is 0, but the total number of hits seen by the receiver in the sampling time is as high as the decision threshold Z_{th}. So, the error probability of unipolar codes with the maximum cross-correlation function of λ_c in OOK is formulated as [21, 27, 30]

$$
\begin{aligned}
P_e &= \frac{1}{2} \Pr(Z \geq Z_{\text{th}} \mid K \text{ simultaneous users, receiver receives bit 0}) \\
&= \frac{1}{2} \sum_{\sum_{k=0}^{\lambda_c} k l_k \geq Z_{\text{th}}} \frac{(K-1)!}{l_0! l_1! \cdots l_{\lambda_c}!} q_0^{l_0} q_1^{l_1} \cdots q_{\lambda_c}^{l_{\lambda_c}} \\
&= \frac{1}{2} - \frac{1}{2} \sum_{l_1=0}^{Z_{\text{th}}-1} \sum_{l_2=0}^{\lfloor (Z_{\text{th}}-1-l_1)/2 \rfloor} \cdots \sum_{l_{\lambda_c}=0}^{\lfloor (Z_{\text{th}}-1-\sum_{k=1}^{\lambda_c-1} k l_k)/\lambda_c \rfloor} \frac{(K-1)!}{l_0! l_1! \cdots l_{\lambda_c}!} q_0^{l_0} q_1^{l_1} \cdots q_{\lambda_c}^{l_{\lambda_c}}
\end{aligned}
$$

where the factor $1/2$ is due to OOK with equal probability of transmitting data bit 1s and 0s, q_i denotes the probability of having $i \in [0, \lambda_c]$ hits (contributed by each interfering codeword) toward the cross-correlation function in the sampling time, $\sum_{k=0}^{\lambda_c} l_k = K - 1$, and $\lfloor \cdot \rfloor$ is the floor function. Because q_i is a probability term, it is always true that $\sum_{i=0}^{\lambda_c} q_i = 1$.

For example, the error probability of unipolar codes with $\lambda_c = 2$ in OOK is given by

$$
P_e = \frac{1}{2} - \frac{1}{2} \sum_{l_1=0}^{Z_{\text{th}}-1} \sum_{l_2=0}^{\lfloor (Z_{\text{th}}-1-l_1)/2 \rfloor} \frac{(K-1)!}{l_0! l_1! l_2!} q_0^{l_0} q_1^{l_1} q_2^{l_2} \tag{1.2}
$$

where $l_0 + l_1 + l_2 = K - 1$, $q_0 + q_1 + q_2 = 1$, and Z_{th} is usually set to w for optimal decision.

1.8.4   Hard-Limiting Analysis for Unipolar Codes

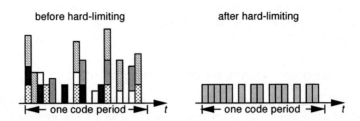

FIGURE 1.4   Hard-limiting of 5 unipolar codewords of weight 5 with unequal pulse height.

It is known that a hard-limiter can be placed at the front end of a receiver in order to lessen the near-far problem and the localization of strong interference in the received signal [21, 30, 33, 34, 37]. As illustrated in Figure 1.4, multiplexed codewords can have strong interference at some pulse positions, and pulses from various geographical locations can have different heights (or intensities) due to different amounts of propagation loss. The hard-limiter equalizes the pulse intensity and interference strength and, in turn, improves code performance. While a receiver with a hard-limiter is called a hard-limiting receiver, a regular receiver, such as those studied in Sections 1.8.1 through 1.8.3, is usually referred to as a soft-limiting receiver.

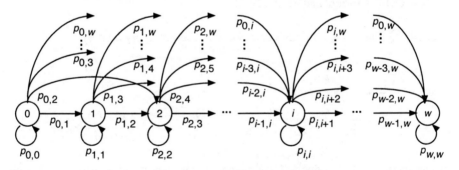

FIGURE 1.5   State transition diagram of a Markov chain with transition probabilities, $p_{i,j}$, where state i represents that i pulse positions in the address codeword (of weight w) of a hard-limiting receiver are being hit [34].

In a hard-limiting receiver, the mutual interference seen at all nonempty pulse positions of the received signal are equalized and then each equalized pulse will contribute equally toward the cross-correlation function. Assume that unipolar codes with weight w and the maximum cross-correlation function of λ_c are in use. Let $i = \{0, 1, \ldots, w\}$ represent the states in the Markov chain of Figure 1.5 such that i of the w pulse positions of the address codeword of the hard-limiting receiver are hit by interfering codewords. So, the transition probability $p_{i,j}$ of transferring from state i

to state j in the Markov chain is given by [34, 37]

$$
p_{i,j} = \begin{cases} \sum_{l=k}^{\lambda_c} \frac{\binom{i}{l-k}\binom{w-i}{k}}{\binom{w}{l}} q_l & \text{if } j = i+k \\ 0 & \text{otherwise} \end{cases}
$$

where $k \in [0, \lambda_c]$, q_l denotes the hit probability of having $l \in [0, \lambda_c]$ hits (contributed by each interfering codeword) toward the cross-correlation function in the sampling time, and the binomial coefficient is defined as

$$
\binom{x}{y} = \frac{x!}{y!(x-y)!}
$$

for integers $x \geq y \geq 0$, and $\binom{x}{y} = 0$ if $x < y$. Because $p_{i,j} = 0$ for all $i > j$, the transition probabilities can be collected into an upper triangular matrix as

$$
\mathbf{P} = \begin{bmatrix} p_{0,0} & p_{0,1} & \cdots & p_{0,w} \\ 0 & p_{1,1} & \cdots & p_{1,w} \\ \vdots & \vdots & \ddots & \vdots \\ 0 & 0 & \cdots & p_{w,w} \end{bmatrix}
$$

and the main-diagonal elements, $p_{i,i}$ for $i \in [0, w]$, are the eigenvalues of $\mathbf{P}$. With these $w+1$ eigenvalues, $\mathbf{P}$ is diagonalizable and $\mathbf{P} = \mathbf{ABA}^{-1}$ for some $(w+1) \times (w+1)$ matrices $\mathbf{B}$, $\mathbf{A}$, and $\mathbf{A}^{-1}$, according to Theorem 1.6, where $\mathbf{A}^{-1}$ is the inverse of $\mathbf{A}$. So, $\mathbf{B}$ is a diagonal matrix with its main-diagonal elements equal to the eigenvalues of $\mathbf{P}$. The columns of $\mathbf{A}$ contain the associated eigenvectors of $\mathbf{P}$. Further, from Section 1.3.4, the $(K-1)$th power of $\mathbf{P}$ can be written as

$$
\mathbf{P}^{K-1} = \mathbf{AB}^{K-1}\mathbf{A}^{-1}
$$

where $K-1$ represents the number of interferers (or interfering codewords) and

$$
\mathbf{B}^{K-1} = \begin{bmatrix} p_{0,0}^{K-1} & 0 & \cdots & 0 \\ 0 & p_{1,1}^{K-1} & \cdots & 0 \\ \vdots & \vdots & \ddots & \vdots \\ 0 & 0 & \cdots & p_{w,w}^{K-1} \end{bmatrix}
$$

Because $\mathbf{A}$ is made up of eigenvectors associated with the $w+1$ eigenvalues of $\mathbf{P}$, $\mathbf{A}$ and $\mathbf{A}^{-1}$ are found to be [5, 34, 37]

$$
\mathbf{A} = \begin{bmatrix} 1 & \binom{w}{1} & \binom{w}{2} & \cdots & \binom{w}{w} \\ 0 & 1 & \binom{w-1}{1} & \cdots & \binom{w-1}{w-1} \\ 0 & 0 & 1 & \cdots & \binom{w-2}{w-2} \\ \vdots & \vdots & \vdots & \ddots & \vdots \\ 0 & 0 & 0 & \cdots & 1 \end{bmatrix}
$$

$$\mathbf{A}^{-1} = \begin{bmatrix} 1 & -\binom{w}{1} & \binom{w}{2} & \cdots & (-1)^{w}\binom{w}{w} \\ 0 & 1 & -\binom{w-1}{1} & \cdots & (-1)^{w-1}\binom{w-1}{w-1} \\ 0 & 0 & 1 & \cdots & (-1)^{w-2}\binom{w-2}{w-2} \\ \vdots & \vdots & \vdots & \ddots & \vdots \\ 0 & 0 & 0 & \cdots & 1 \end{bmatrix}$$

Let $\mathbf{h}^{(l)} = (h_0^{(l)}, h_1^{(l)}, \ldots, h_i^{(l)}, \ldots, h_w^{(l)})$ be a vector collecting all possible interference patterns created by l interferers, in which $h_i^{(l)}$ represents the probability of having i of the w pulse positions in the address codeword of the hard-limiting receiver being hit by these l interferers. For $K-1$ interferers, $\mathbf{h}^{(K-1)}$ can be recursively written as [24]

$$\mathbf{h}^{(K-1)} = \mathbf{h}^{(K-2)}\mathbf{P} = \cdots = \mathbf{h}^{(0)}\mathbf{P}^{K-1} = (1,0,\ldots,0)\mathbf{A}\mathbf{B}^{K-1}\mathbf{A}^{-1}$$

where "1" represents the initial condition of having one interferer and "0" represents the initial condition of having none. After some manipulations, it is found that

$$h_i^{(K-1)} = \frac{w!}{i!(w-i)!} \sum_{j=0}^{i}(-1)^{i-j}\frac{i!}{j!(i-j)!}p_{j,j}^{K-1}$$

For a hard-limiting receiver, an error occurs when the received data bit is 0 but the address codeword has the number of pulse positions that are hit by interfering codewords being as high as the decision threshold Z_{th}. So, the error probability of unipolar codes with a maximum cross-correlation function of λ_c in a hard-limiting receiver in OOK is formulated as

$$\begin{aligned} P_{e,\text{hard}} &= \frac{1}{2}\sum_{i=Z_{th}}^{w} h_i^{(K-1)} \\ &= \frac{1}{2}\sum_{i=Z_{th}}^{w}\frac{w!}{i!(w-i)!}\sum_{j=0}^{i}(-1)^{i-j}\frac{i!}{j!(i-j)!}\left[\sum_{k=0}^{\lambda_c}\frac{j!(w-k)!}{w!(j-k)!}q_k\right]^{K-1} \end{aligned}$$

where the factor $1/2$ is due to OOK with equal probability of transmitting data bit 1s and 0s.

For example, the hard-limiting error probability of unipolar codes with $\lambda_c = 2$ in OOK is given by

$$P_{e,\text{hard}} = \frac{1}{2}\sum_{i=0}^{w}(-1)^{w-i}\frac{w!}{i!(w-i)!}\left[q_0 + \frac{iq_1}{w} + \frac{i(i-1)q_2}{w(w-1)}\right]^{K-1} \tag{1.3}$$

where Z_{th} is usually set to w for optimal decision.

Figure 1.6 plots the Gaussian-approximated, soft-limiting, and hard-limiting error probabilities [from Equations (1.1), (1.2), and (1.3), respectively] of the 1-D prime codes in Section 3.1 against the number of simultaneous users K. In this example, the prime codes have $\lambda_c = 2$, length $N = p^2 = \{169, 289\}$, and weight $w = p = \{13, 17\}$.

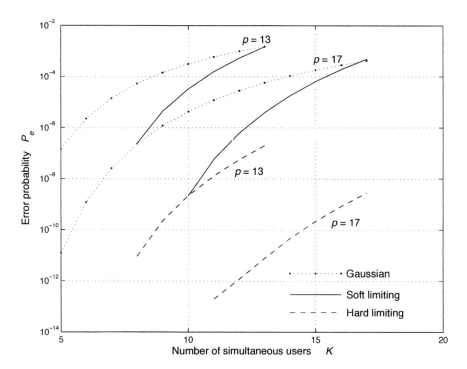

FIGURE 1.6 Gaussian, soft-limiting, and hard-limiting error probabilities of the 1-D prime codes for $p = \{13, 17\}$.

From Section 3.1, the hit probabilities are given by $q_0 = (7p^2 - p - 2)/(12p^2)$, $q_1 = (2p^2 + p + 2)/(6p^2)$, and $q_2 = (p - 2)(p + 1)/(12p^2)$. The variance in Equation (1.1) becomes $\sum_{i=1}^{2} \sum_{j=0}^{i-1} (i - j)^2 q_i q_j = (5p^2 - 2p - 4)/(12p^2)$. In general, the error probabilities improve as p increases due to heavier code weight $w = p$ and longer code length $N = p^2$. However, the error probabilities get worse as K increases because of stronger mutual interference. The Gaussian curve is worse than the soft-limiting curve for the same p, but both curves converge as K increases. This agrees with the understanding that Gaussian approximation generally gives pessimistic performance, and its accuracy improves with K in accordance with the Central Limit Theorem. The hard-limiting receiver always results in better performance than the soft-limiting one because the former lowers the amount of interference. The difference in error probability enlarges as p increases.

1.8.5   Soft-Limiting Analysis without Chip Synchronization

The combinatorial analyses in Sections 1.8.3 and 1.8.4 assume that simultaneously transmitting unipolar codewords are bit asynchronous but chip synchronous, for ease of mathematical treatment. With the chip-synchronous assumption, the timings of all transmitting codewords are perfectly aligned in time slots (or so-called chips), even though their bit frames need not be so. It is known that the chip-synchronous assumption provides a performance upper bound, while the more realistic chip-asynchronous assumption, in which unipolar codewords can be transmitted and detected at any time instant, results in more accurate performance [27, 30, 34–37].

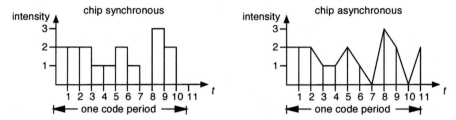

FIGURE 1.7 Cross-correlation functions between two 1-D codewords, 10110010000 and 10011000100, under the chip-synchronous and chip-asynchronous assumptions [21, 35, 37].

Figure 1.7 illustrates an example of the periodic cross-correlation functions between two 1-D codewords, 10110010000 and 10011000100, for both assumptions. The chip-synchronous cross-correlation function is discrete, and its values within one chip interval are found to be $\{2, 2, 2, 1, 1, 2, 1, 0, 3, 2, 0\}$, consecutively. However, the chip-asynchronous cross-correlation function is not discrete but is a (linear) function of time because its values now depend on the amount of pulse overlap due to the relative shifts of these two codewords, as illustrated in Figure 1.7. As a result, the chip-asynchronous cross-correlation function involves partial overlap of pulses (or nothing) from two consecutive chips intervals. On average, the cross-correlation values within one chip interval are found to be $\{2, 2, 3/2, 1, 3/2, 3/2, 1/2, 3/2, 5/2, 1, 1\}$, consecutively, in this example.

As defined earlier, q_i is the (hit) probability of having a periodic cross-correlation value of $i \in [0, \lambda_c]$ in a chip interval under the chip-synchronous assumption, where λ_c is the maximum cross-correlation function of the unipolar codes in use. However, under the chip-asynchronous assumption, two consecutive chip intervals must be considered, and $q_{i,j}$ here defined as the (hit) probability of having the (chip-synchronous) cross-correlation value in the preceding chip interval equal to $i \in [0, \lambda_c]$ and the (chip-synchronous) cross-correlation value in the present chip interval equal to $j \in [0, \lambda_c]$. The hit probabilities are related by [21, 35, 37]

$$q_i = \frac{1}{2} \sum_{j=0}^{\lambda_c} (q_{i,j} + q_{j,i})$$

$$\sum_{i=0}^{\lambda_c} \sum_{j=0}^{\lambda_c} q_{i,j} = 1$$

$$\sum_{i=0}^{\lambda_c} q_i = 1$$

In general, $q_{i,j}$ and $q_{j,i}$ are different when $\lambda_c > 1$, but equal for the case of $\lambda_c = 1$, for $i \neq j$.

Each interferer (or interfering codeword) may contribute up to λ_c hits toward the cross-correlation function at any time instance. For a given K simultaneous users, the total number of interferers is given by $K - 1 = \sum_{i=0}^{\lambda_c} \sum_{j=0}^{\lambda_c} l_{i,j}$ and the total number of hits seen by the receiver in the sampling time is given by $\sum_{i=0}^{\lambda_c} \sum_{j=0}^{\lambda_c} (i+j)l_{i,j}$, where $l_{i,j}$ is the number of interfering codewords contributing i hits in the preceding chip interval and j hits in the present chip interval. The conditional probability of having $Z = \sum_{i=0}^{\lambda_c} \sum_{j=0}^{\lambda_c} (i+j)l_{i,j}$ hits contributed by these interferers follows a multinomial distribution and is given by

$$\Pr(Z \text{ hits} \mid K \text{ users, receiver receives bit } 0) = \frac{(K-1)!}{\prod_{i=0}^{\lambda_c} \prod_{j=0}^{\lambda_c} l_{i,j}!} \prod_{i=0}^{\lambda_c} \prod_{j=0}^{\lambda_c} q_{i,j}^{l_{i,j}}$$

As illustrated in Figure 1.7, the cross-correlation value in a chip interval is a linear function of time. Let $X_{i,j,k}$ be a continuous random variable representing the cross-correlation value in a chip interval caused by codeword k, which belongs to one of the $l_{i,j}$ interfering codewords. So, $X_{i,j,k}$ is uniformly distributed over the interval $[i, j)$ when $0 \leq i \leq j \leq \lambda_c$, or the interval $[j, i)$ when $0 \leq j \leq i \leq \lambda_c$. The expected value (or mean) and variance of $X_{i,j,k}$ are then given by $E[X_{i,j,k}] = \int_i^j [x/(j-i)]dx = (i+j)/2$ and $Var[X_{i,j,k}] = E[X_{i,j,k}^2] - E[X_{i,j,k}]^2 = \int_i^j [x^2/(j-i)]dx - (i+j)^2/4 = (i-j)^2/12$, respectively. Considering all $k \in [1, l_{i,j}]$ cases, the overall mean and variance are then given, respectively, by

$$m = E\left[\sum_{i=0}^{\lambda_c} \sum_{j=0}^{\lambda_c} \sum_{k=1}^{l_{i,j}} X_{i,j,k}\right] = \sum_{i=0}^{\lambda_c} \sum_{j=0}^{\lambda_c} \frac{i+j}{2} l_{i,j}$$

$$\sigma^2 = Var\left[\sum_{i=0}^{\lambda_c} \sum_{j=0}^{\lambda_c} \sum_{k=1}^{l_{i,j}} X_{i,j,k}\right] = \sum_{i=0}^{\lambda_c} \sum_{j=0}^{\lambda_c} \frac{(i-j)^2}{12} l_{i,j}$$

An error occurs when the total number of hits seen by the receiver in the sampling time is as high as the decision threshold Z_{th}. According to the Central Limit Theorem, the conditional error probability is then given by

$$\Pr(Z \geq Z_{th} \mid Z \text{ hits}) = \Pr\left(\sum_{i=0}^{\lambda_c} \sum_{j=0}^{\lambda_c} \sum_{k=1}^{l_{i,j}} X_{i,j,k} \geq Z_{th}\right)$$

$$= Q\left(\frac{Z_{th} - m}{\sqrt{\sigma^2}}\right)$$

where $Q(x) = (1/\sqrt{2\pi}) \int_x^\infty \exp\left(-y^2/2\right) dy$ is the complementary error function.

Finally, the error probability of unipolar codes with the maximum cross-correlation function of λ_c in a soft-limiting receiver in OOK under the chip-asynchronous assumption is formulated as [35, 37]

$$
\begin{aligned}
P_{e,\text{asyn}} &= \frac{1}{2}\Pr(Z \geq Z_{\text{th}} \mid K \text{ simultaneous users, receiver receives bit } 0) \\[2mm]
&= \frac{1}{2} - \frac{1}{2}\sum_{\substack{\sum_{i=0}^{\lambda_c}\sum_{j=0}^{\lambda_c}(i+j)l_{i,j}=0}}^{Z_{\text{th}}-1} \frac{(K-1)!}{\prod_{i=0}^{\lambda_c}\prod_{j=0}^{\lambda_c} l_{i,j}!}\prod_{i=0}^{\lambda_c}\prod_{j=0}^{\lambda_c} q_{i,j}^{l_{i,j}}\left[1 - Q\left(\frac{Z_{\text{th}}-m}{\sqrt{\sigma^2}}\right)\right] \\[2mm]
&= \frac{1}{2} - \frac{1}{2}\sum_{l_{0,1}=0}^{Z_{\text{th}}-1}\sum_{l_{1,0}=0}^{Z_{\text{th}}-1-l_{0,1}}\sum_{l_{1,1}=0}^{\lfloor(Z_{\text{th}}-1-l_{0,1}-l_{1,0})/2\rfloor} \cdots \\[2mm]
&\quad \sum_{l_{\lambda_c,\lambda_c}=0}^{\lfloor(Z_{\text{th}}-1-\sum_{i=0}^{\lambda_c}\sum_{j=0}^{\lambda_c}(i+j)l_{i,j})/\lambda_c\rfloor}\frac{(K-1)!}{\prod_{i=0}^{\lambda_c}\prod_{j=0}^{\lambda_c} l_{i,j}!}\prod_{i=0}^{\lambda_c}\prod_{j=0}^{\lambda_c} q_{i,j}^{l_{i,j}} \\[2mm]
&\quad \times \left[1 - Q\left(\frac{Z_{\text{th}} - \frac{1}{2}\sum_{i=0}^{\lambda_c}\sum_{j=0}^{\lambda_c}(i+j)l_{i,j}}{\sqrt{\frac{1}{12}\sum_{i=0}^{\lambda_c}\sum_{j=0}^{\lambda_c}(i-j)^2 l_{i,j}}}\right)\right]
\end{aligned}
\tag{1.4}
$$

where the factor $1/2$ is due to OOK with equal probability of transmitting data bit 1s and 0s, $K-1 = \sum_{i=0}^{\lambda_c}\sum_{j=0}^{\lambda_c} l_{i,j}$, and $\lfloor \cdot \rfloor$ is the floor function.

For examples, the chip-asynchronous, soft-limiting error probability of unipolar codes with $\lambda_c = 1$ in OOK is given by

$$
\begin{aligned}
P_{e,\text{asyn}} &= \frac{1}{2} - \frac{1}{2}\sum_{l_{0,1}=0}^{Z_{\text{th}}-1}\sum_{l_{1,0}=0}^{Z_{\text{th}}-1-l_{0,1}}\sum_{l_{1,1}=0}^{Z_{\text{th}}-1-l_{0,1}-l_{1,0}}\frac{(K-1)!}{l_{0,0}!l_{0,1}!l_{1,0}!l_{1,1}!}q_{0,0}^{l_{0,0}}q_{0,1}^{l_{0,1}}q_{1,0}^{l_{1,0}}q_{1,1}^{l_{1,1}} \\[2mm]
&\quad \times \left[1 - Q\left(\frac{Z_{\text{th}} - (l_{0,1}+l_{1,0}+2l_{1,1})/2}{\sqrt{(l_{0,1}+l_{1,0})/12}}\right)\right]
\end{aligned}
\tag{1.5}
$$

where $l_{0,0} + l_{0,1} + l_{1,0} + l_{1,1} = K - 1$, $q_{0,0} + q_{0,1} + q_{1,0} + q_{1,1} = 1$, and Z_{th} is usually set to w for optimal decision.

Figure 1.8 plots the soft-limiting error probabilities [from P_e in Equation (1.2) and $P_{e,\text{asyn}}$ in Equation (1.5)] of the 2-D carrier-hopping prime codes in Section 5.1 against the number of simultaneous users K under the chip-synchronous and chip-asynchronous assumptions, respectively. In this example, the carrier-hopping prime codes have $\lambda_c = 1$, $L = \{7, 11\}$ wavelengths, length $N = w^2 = \{49, 121\}$, and weight $w = \{7, 11\}$. From Section 5.1, the hit probabilities are given by $q_1 = w^2/(2LN)$, $q_{1,1} = w(w-1)/[2N(N-1)]$, $q_{1,0} = q_{0,1} = q_1 - q_{1,1}$, and $q_{0,0} = 1 - q_1 - q_{0,1}$. In general, the error probabilities of both assumptions improve as w or N increases because of higher autocorrelation peaks or lower hit probabilities. However, their error probabilities get worse as K increases because of stronger mutual interference. As expected, the performance of the chip-asynchronous case is always better than the chip-synchronous case because the latter gives the performance upper bound. The difference in their error probabilities increases with w or N and is found to be about two to three orders of magnitude in this example. To validate the accuracy of the

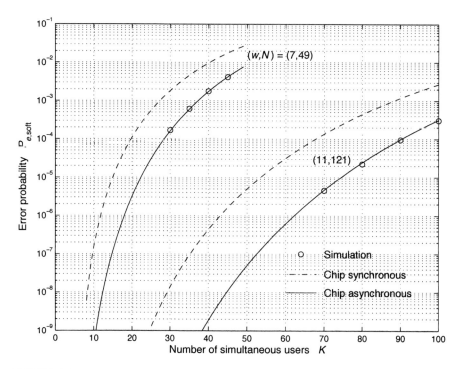

FIGURE 1.8 Soft-limiting error probabilities of the 2-D carrier-hopping prime codes under the chip-synchronous and chip-asynchronous assumptions for code length $N = \{49, 121\}$ and weight $w = \{7, 11\}$.

chip-asynchronous analysis, the results of computer simulation are also plotted in the figure and found closely matching the chip-asynchronous curves. The computer simulation is performed by cross-correlating codewords randomly selected from the code set. The number of correlating codewords is determined by the number of simultaneous users selected for the simulation. The transmission starting time of each codeword is chosen from a random decimal number in the range of $[0, 1)$, corresponding to a fraction of one chip interval, for emulating chip asynchronism. The total number of data bits involved in each simulation should be at least one hundred times the reciprocal of the targeting error probability in order to obtain sufficient iterations.

Theorem 1.8

The chip-asynchronous mean and variance in $P_{e,\text{asyn}}$ of Equation (1.4) can also be formulated in terms of hit probabilities as [21, 35, 37]:

$$m_{\text{asyn}} = \sum_{i=0}^{\lambda_c} i q_{i,i} + \sum_{i=0}^{\lambda_c} \sum_{j=0}^{i-1} \left(\frac{i+j}{2} \right) (q_{i,j} + q_{j,i}) = \frac{w^2}{2N}$$

$$\sigma_{\text{asyn}}^2 = \sum_{i=0}^{\lambda_c} i^2 q_{i,i} + \sum_{i=0}^{\lambda_c} \sum_{j=0}^{i-1} \left[(i-j)j + \frac{(i-j)^2}{3} + j^2 \right] (q_{i,j} + q_{j,i}) - \left(\frac{w^2}{2N} \right)^2$$

The chip-synchronous mean and variance in Section 1.8.1 can be formulated as

$$m_{\text{syn}} = \sum_{i=0}^{\lambda_c} i q_i = \frac{w^2}{2N}$$

$$\sigma_{\text{syn}}^2 = \sum_{i=0}^{\lambda_c} i^2 q_i - \left(\frac{w^2}{2N} \right)^2$$

The difference between these two variances is derived as

$$\sigma_{\text{syn}}^2 - \sigma_{\text{asyn}}^2 = \sum_{i=0}^{\lambda_c} \sum_{j=0}^{i-1} \frac{(i-j)^2}{6} (q_{i,j} + q_{j,i})$$

which indicates that the chip-asynchronous cross-correlation function always generates less interference than the chip-synchronous one. This characteristic can be translated into better code performance in the chip-asynchronous case and verifiable by applying the variances to the Gaussian-approximated error probability of Equation (1.1).

For the special case of $\lambda_c = 1$ and $q_1 \approx q_{1,1}$, these two variances can be further related by

$$\sigma_{\text{asyn}}^2 \approx \frac{2}{3} \sigma_{\text{syn}}^2$$

Proof As illustrated in Figure 1.7, the chip-asynchronous periodic cross-correlation value is a function of the relative shift τ between two correlation codewords. The shift consists of integral and fractional parts as $\tau = \tau_c + \tau_f$. While τ_c is an integer multiple of a whole chip interval, τ_f is a fraction of a whole chip interval and a random variable with the probability density function uniformly distributed in the open interval $(0, 1)$. So, the chip-asynchronous periodic cross-correlation function $I_{r,\text{asyn}}$ in the rth chip can be written as [21]

$$I_{r,\text{asyn}} = I_r + \tau_f (I_{r \oplus 1} - I_r)$$

where I_r is the chip-synchronous periodic cross-correlation value at the rth chip for $r \in [0, N-1]$ and "$\oplus$" denotes a modulo-N addition. When $I_{r,\text{asyn}}$ is plotted against the amount of time shift τ, the shape of the chip-asynchronous periodic cross-correlation function within the chip interval $[r, r \oplus 1)$ can be a triangle, rectangle, or trapezoid, with an average value equal to $(I_r + I_{r \oplus 1})/2$ (e.g., see Figure 1.7). Denote $q_{i,j}$ as the (hit) probability of having $I_r = i$ and $I_{r \oplus 1} = j$. The average chip-asynchronous periodic cross-correlation value can be written as the mean (or expected value) such that

$$
\begin{aligned}
m_{\text{asyn}} &= \sum_{i=0}^{\lambda_c} \sum_{j=0}^{\lambda_c} \left\{ \int_0^1 \left[I_r + \tau_f (I_{r \oplus 1} - I_r) \right] d\tau_f \right\} q_{i,j} \\
&= \sum_{i=0}^{\lambda_c} i q_{i,i} + \sum_{i=0}^{\lambda_c} \sum_{j=0}^{i-1} \left\{ \int_0^1 \left[j + \tau_f (i - j) \right] q_{i,j} d\tau_f \right\} \\
&\quad + \sum_{j=0}^{\lambda_c} \sum_{i=0}^{j-1} \left\{ \int_0^1 \left[i + \tau_f (j - i) \right] q_{i,j} d\tau_f \right\}
\end{aligned}
$$

The final form in the theorem is derived after some manipulations. The mean is also equal to $w^2/2N$ because there always are at most w^2 hits between two correlating codewords (of weight w and length N) over N chips in OOK.

The chip-asynchronous variance is derived by taking the expected value of the second moment of having $I_r = i$ and $I_{r \oplus 1} = j$ minus the squared mean such that

$$
\begin{aligned}
\sigma_{\text{asyn}}^2 &= \sum_{i=0}^{\lambda_c} \sum_{j=0}^{\lambda_c} \left\{ \int_0^1 \left[I_r + (I_{r \oplus 1} - I_r) \tau_f \right]^2 d\tau_f \right\} q_{i,j} - \left(\frac{w^2}{2N} \right)^2 \\
&= \sum_{i=0}^{\lambda_c} i^2 q_{i,i} + \sum_{i=0}^{\lambda_c} \sum_{j=0}^{i-1} \left\{ \int_0^1 \left[j + \tau_f (i - j) \right]^2 q_{i,j} d\tau_f \right\} \\
&\quad + \sum_{j=0}^{\lambda_c} \sum_{i=0}^{j-1} \left\{ \int_0^1 \left[i + \tau_f (j - i) \right]^2 q_{i,j} d\tau_f \right\} - \left(\frac{w^2}{2N} \right)^2 \\
&= \sum_{i=0}^{\lambda_c} i^2 q_{i,i} + \sum_{i=0}^{\lambda_c} \sum_{j=0}^{i-1} \left\{ \int_0^1 \left[j^2 + 2j(i - j)\tau_f + (i - j)^2 \tau_f^2 \right] q_{i,j} d\tau_f \right\} \\
&\quad + \sum_{j=0}^{\lambda_c} \sum_{i=0}^{j-1} \left\{ \int_0^1 \left[i^2 + 2i(j - i)\tau_f + (j - i)^2 \tau_f^2 \right] q_{i,j} d\tau_f \right\} - \left(\frac{w^2}{2N} \right)^2
\end{aligned}
$$

The final form in the theorem is derived after some manipulations.

For the chip-synchronous mean and variance in Section 1.8.1, $m_{\text{syn}} = w^2/(2N)$ because there are at most w^2 hits between two correlating codewords (of weight w and length N) over N chips in OOK. The chip-synchronous variance is derived as

$$
\sigma_{\text{syn}}^2 = \sum_{i=0}^{\lambda_c} \sum_{j=0}^{i-1} (i - j)^2 (q_i + q_j) = \sum_{i=0}^{\lambda_c} i^2 q_i - \left(\frac{w^2}{2N} \right)^2
$$

by applying $\sum_{i=0}^{\lambda_c} q_i = 1$ and $\sum_{i=0}^{\lambda_c} i q_i = w^2/(2N)$.

So, the difference between these two variances becomes

$$
\begin{aligned}
\sigma_{\text{syn}}^2 - \sigma_{\text{asyn}}^2 &= \sum_{i=0}^{\lambda_c} i^2 q_i - \sum_{i=0}^{\lambda_c} i^2 q_{i,i} - \sum_{i=0}^{\lambda_c} \sum_{j=0}^{i-1} \left[(i-j)j + \frac{(i-j)^2}{3} + j^2 \right] (q_{i,j} + q_{j,i}) \\
&= \sum_{i=0}^{\lambda_c} \sum_{j=0}^{i-1} \left\{ \frac{i^2}{2} + \frac{j^2}{2} - \left[(i-j)j + \frac{(i-j)^2}{3} + j^2 \right] \right\} (q_{i,j} + q_{j,i})
\end{aligned}
$$

by applying $q_i = 0.5 \sum_{j=0}^{\lambda_c} (q_{i,j} + q_{j,i})$. The final form of the theorem is derived after some manipulations.

For the special case of $\lambda_c = 1$, the chip-asynchronous interference variance can be rearranged as [21]

$$
\begin{aligned}
\sigma_{\text{asyn}}^2 &= \frac{q_{1,0} + q_{0,1}}{3} + q_{1,1} - q_1^2 \\
&= \frac{2}{3}(q_1 - q_{1,1}) + q_{1,1} - q_1^2 \\
&= \frac{2}{3}(q_{1,1} - q_1^2) \\
&\approx \frac{2}{3} \sigma_{\text{syn}}^2
\end{aligned}
$$

when $q_1 \approx q_{1,1}$. The properties $q_i = 0.5 \sum_{j=0}^{1} (q_{i,j} + q_{j,i})$, $\sum_{k=0}^{1} \sum_{j=0}^{1} q_{j,k} = 1$, $q_0 + q_1 = 1$, and $q_{1,0} = q_{0,1} = q_1 - q_{1,1}$ are applied in the derivation. ■

1.8.6 Hard-Limiting Analysis without Chip Synchronization

The more realistic chip-asynchronous assumption can also be applied to the hard-limiting receiver for more accurate performance analysis.

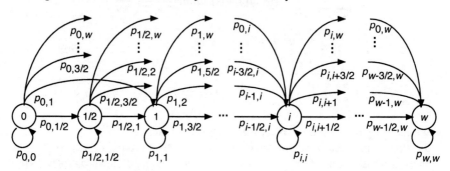

FIGURE 1.9 State transition diagram of the Markov chain with transition probabilities $p_{i,j}$, where state i represents i pulse sub-positions in the address codeword (of weight w) of a hard-limiting receiver are being hit [37].

As illustrated in Figure 1.7, the chip-asynchronous cross-correlation value in a chip interval is a linear function of time. By taking the average cross-correlation value within a chip interval, the contribution of an interfering pulse can be assumed to have a strength of one half of a hit on average. For unipolar codes with a maximum cross-correlation function of λ_c and weight w, the w pulse positions are here divided into $2w$ sub-positions and such a one-half-hit may now occur in one of these $2w$ sub-positions after hard-limiting. Let $i = \{0, 1/2, 1, 3/2, \ldots, w - 1/2, w\}$ represent the states in the Markov chain of Figure 1.9 such that i of the w pulse positions of the address codeword of the hard-limiting receiver are hit by interfering codewords. Then, the transition probability $p_{i,j}$ of transferring from state i to state j in the Markov chain is given by [37]

$$p_{i,j} = \begin{cases} \sum_{s=k}^{\lambda_c} \sum_{t=k}^{\lambda_c} \dfrac{\binom{2i}{s+t-2k}\binom{2w-2i}{2k}}{\binom{2w}{s+t}} q_{s,t} & \text{if } j = i+k \\ 0 & \text{otherwise} \end{cases}$$

where $k = \{0, 1/2, 1, 3/2, \ldots, \lambda_c - 1/2, \lambda_c\}$, and $q_{s,t}$ denotes the (chip-asynchronous) hit probability defined in Section 1.8.5. Because $p_{i,j} = 0$ for all $i > j$, the transition probabilities can be collected into an upper triangular matrix as

$$\mathbf{P} = \begin{bmatrix} p_{0,0} & p_{0,1/2} & p_{0,1} & \cdots & p_{0,w} \\ 0 & p_{1/2,1/2} & p_{1/2,1} & \cdots & p_{1/2,w} \\ 0 & 0 & p_{1,1} & \cdots & p_{1,w} \\ \vdots & \vdots & \vdots & \ddots & \vdots \\ 0 & 0 & 0 & \cdots & p_{w,w} \end{bmatrix}$$

and the main-diagonal elements, $p_{i,i}$ for $i = \{0, 1/2, 1, 3/2, \ldots, w - 1/2, w\}$, are the eigenvalues of $\mathbf{P}$. With these $2w + 1$ eigenvalues, $\mathbf{P}$ is diagonalizable and $\mathbf{P} = \mathbf{A}\mathbf{B}\mathbf{A}^{-1}$ for some $(2w + 1) \times (2w + 1)$ matrices $\mathbf{B}$, $\mathbf{A}$, and $\mathbf{A}^{-1}$, according to Theorem 1.6, where $\mathbf{A}^{-1}$ is the inverse of $\mathbf{A}$. $\mathbf{B}$ is a diagonal matrix with its main-diagonal elements equal to the eigenvalues of $\mathbf{P}$. The columns of $\mathbf{A}$ contain the associated eigenvectors of $\mathbf{P}$.

Following the derivation in Section 1.8.4, and given $K - 1$ interferers,

$$\mathbf{B}^{K-1} = \begin{bmatrix} p_{0,0}^{K-1} & 0 & 0 & \cdots & 0 \\ 0 & p_{1/2,1/2}^{K-1} & 0 & \cdots & 0 \\ 0 & 0 & p_{1,1}^{K-1} & \cdots & 0 \\ \vdots & \vdots & \vdots & \ddots & \vdots \\ 0 & 0 & 0 & \cdots & p_{w,w}^{K-1} \end{bmatrix}$$

$$\mathbf{A} = \begin{bmatrix} 1 & \binom{2w}{1} & \binom{2w}{2} & \cdots & \binom{2w}{2w} \\ 0 & 1 & \binom{2w-1}{1} & \cdots & \binom{2w-1}{2w-1} \\ 0 & 0 & 1 & \cdots & \binom{2w-2}{2w-2} \\ \vdots & \vdots & \vdots & \ddots & \vdots \\ 0 & 0 & 0 & \cdots & 1 \end{bmatrix}$$

$$
\mathbf{A}^{-1} = \begin{bmatrix}
1 & -\binom{2w}{1} & \binom{2w}{2} & \cdots & (-1)^{2w}\binom{2w}{2w} \\
0 & 1 & -\binom{2w-1}{1} & \cdots & (-1)^{2w-1}\binom{2w-1}{2w-1} \\
0 & 0 & 1 & \cdots & (-1)^{2w-2}\binom{2w-2}{2w-2} \\
\vdots & \vdots & \vdots & \ddots & \vdots \\
0 & 0 & 0 & \cdots & 1
\end{bmatrix}
$$

can be obtained and eventually the probability of having i of the w pulse positions in the address codeword of the hard-limiting receiver being hit by $K-1$ interferers is given by

$$
h_i^{(K-1)} = \frac{(2w)!}{(2i)!(2w-2i)!}\sum_{j=0}^{2i}(-1)^{2i-j}\frac{(2i)!}{j!(2i-j)!}p_{j/2,j/2}^{K-1}
$$

for $i = \{0, 1/2, 1, 3/2, \ldots, w-1/2, w\}$.

For a hard-limiting receiver, an error occurs when the received data bit is 0 but the address codeword has the number of pulse positions that are hit by interfering codewords being as high as the decision threshold Z_{th}. So, an error occurs only when there are as many as Z_{th} pulse positions in the address codeword seeing a sum of one hit after hard-limiting. This sum of one hit comes from the case when both sub-positions of a pulse position are hit with one-half-hit at the same time. If there exist n such pulse positions, the remaining $w-n$ pulse positions of the address codeword see either one-half-hit or no hit. Let r be the number of pulse positions in which only one sub-position is hit. The total number of combinations that there are n pulse positions seeing one-hit and r of them seeing one-half-hit is then given by $\binom{w}{n}\sum_{r=0}^{w-n}\binom{w-n}{r}2^r$. Furthermore, the probability of a total of $2n+r$ sub-positions being hit by $K-1$ interferers is given by $h_{(2n+r)/2}^{(K-1)}/\binom{2w}{2n+r}$.

So, the error probability of unipolar codes with the maximum cross-correlation function of λ_c in a hard-limiting receiver in OOK under the chip-asynchronous assumption is finally formulated as [37]

$$
\begin{aligned}
P_{e,\text{asyn,hard}} &= \frac{1}{2}\sum_{n=Z_{th}}^{w}\left[\binom{w}{n}\sum_{r=0}^{w-n}\binom{w-n}{r}2^r\right]\frac{h_{(2n+r)/2}^{(K-1)}}{\binom{2w}{2n+r}} \\
&= \frac{1}{2}\sum_{n=Z_{th}}^{w}\frac{w!}{n!(w-n)!}\sum_{r=0}^{w-n}\frac{(w-n)!}{r!(w-n-r)!}2^r\sum_{j=0}^{2n+r}(-1)^{2n+r-j} \\
&\quad\times\frac{(2n+r)!}{j!(2n+r-j)!}\left[\sum_{s=0}^{\lambda_c}\sum_{t=0}^{\lambda_c}\frac{j!(2w-s-t)!}{(2w)!(j-s-t)!}q_{s,t}\right]^{K-1}
\end{aligned}
$$

where the factor $1/2$ is due to OOK with equal probability of transmitting data bit 1s and 0s.

For example, the chip-asynchronous, hard-limiting error probability of unipolar codes with $\lambda_c = 1$ in OOK is given by

$$P_{e,\text{asyn,hard}} = \frac{1}{2} \sum_{i=0}^{2w} (-1)^{2w-i} \frac{2w!}{i!(2w-i)!} \left[q_{0,0} \right.$$
$$\left. + \frac{i(q_{0,1}+q_{1,0})}{2w} + \frac{i(i-1)q_{1,1}}{2w(2w-1)} \right]^{K-1} \quad (1.6)$$

where Z_{th} is usually set to w for optimal decision.

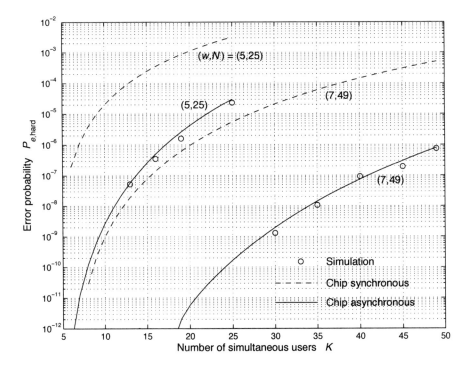

FIGURE 1.10 Hard-limiting error probabilities of the 2-D carrier-hopping prime codes under the chip-synchronous and chip-asynchronous assumptions for length $N = \{25,49\}$ and weight $w = \{5,7\}$.

Figure 1.10 plots the hard-limiting error probabilities [from $P_{e,\text{hard}}$ in Equation (1.3) and $P_{e,\text{asyn,hard}}$ in Equation (1.6)] of the 2-D carrier-hopping prime codes in Section 5.1 against the number of simulations users K under the chip-synchronous and chip-asynchronous assumptions, respectively. In this example, the carrier-hopping prime codes have $\lambda_c = 1$, $L = \{5,7\}$ wavelengths, length $N = w^2 = \{25,49\}$, and weight $w = \{5,7\}$. While Equation (1.3) was originally derived for $\lambda_c = 2$ codes, it can be applied to the $\lambda_c = 1$ carrier-hopping prime codes by simply setting $q_2 = 0$. From Section 5.1, the hit probabilities are given by $q_1 = w^2/(2LN)$, $q_{1,1} = w(w-1)/[2N(N-1)]$, $q_{1,0} = q_{0,1} = q_1 - q_{1,1}$, and $q_{0,0} = 1 - q_1 - q_{0,1}$. In general, the error probabilities of both assumptions improve as w or N increases due to higher autocorrelation peaks or lower hit probabilities. However, their error probabilities get worse as K increases because of stronger mutual interference. As expected, the performance of the chip-asynchronous case is always better than the chip-synchronous case because the latter gives the performance upper bound. The difference in their error probabilities increases with w or N and is found to be about two to three orders of magnitude in this example. To validate the accuracy of the hard-limiting, chip-asynchronous analysis, the results of computer simulation are also plotted in the figure and found to closely match the chip-asynchronous curves. The computer simulation is performed similar to that of Figure 1.8, but nonzero amplitude levels of the multiplexed signal at any time instant is clipped to the same level in order to emulate the hard-limiting operation.

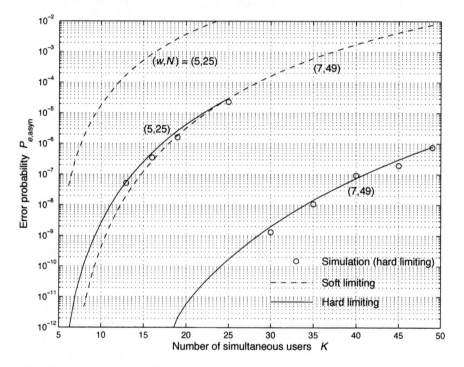

FIGURE 1.11 Chip-asynchronous error probabilities of the 2-D carrier-hopping prime codes with and without hard-limiting for length $N = \{25, 49\}$ and weight $w = \{5, 7\}$.

Figure 1.11 plots the soft- and hard-limiting error probabilities [from $P_{e,\mathrm{asyn}}$ in Equation (1.5) and $P_{e,\mathrm{asyn,hard}}$ in Equation (1.6), respectively] of the 2-D carrier-hopping prime codes in Section 5.1 against the number of simultaneous users K under the chip-asynchronous assumption. The same code parameters as in Figure 1.10 are used. As expected, the hard-limiting case always results in better performance than the soft-limiting case, and the difference in their error probabilities is about three to four orders of magnitude in this example.

1.8.7 Spectral Efficiency

In addition to error probability, spectral efficiency (SE) is another figure of merit for comparing optical codes. SE considers data transfer rate R_{bit} (in bits/s), number of simultaneous users K (for a given error probability), number of wavelength channels L (in Hz), and number of time slots (or code length) N as a whole, and is generally defined as [38–43]

$$SE \ (bits/s/Hz) = \frac{Aggregated \ data \ transfer \ rate}{Total \ transmission \ bandwidth} = \frac{KR_{bit}}{L\Lambda} = \frac{KR_{chip}}{LN\Lambda}$$

where Λ is the wavelength spacing per wavelength channel, including guard bands, and $R_{chip} = NR_{bit}$ is the chip rate. The target is to obtain the SE as large as possible for high efficiency or good bandwidth utilization. The definition assumes the use of 2-D codes, but also applies to 1-D codes by setting $L = 1$.

1.9 SUMMARY

In this chapter, various linear algebraic tools that are essential to the construction and analyses of bipolar and unipolar (also known as coherent and incoherent) optical codes were reviewed and developed. The definitions of Hamming distance and weight, correlation functions, and cardinality upper bound, which are useful for code classifications, were established. The concept and application of the Markov chain in optical coding theory were introduced. The use of Gaussian approximation to simplify performance analysis of unipolar and bipolar codes was studied. The performances of optical codes in a soft- and hard-limiting receiver were analyzed using combinatorial methods. The hard-limiting receiver was shown to perform better than the soft-limiting receiver. Finally, the performances of optical codes in both types of receivers without the classical pessimistic chip-synchronization assumption were investigated. Reflecting the actual effect of mutual interference, the more realistic chip-asynchronous assumption was shown to give more accurate code performance. The theoretical analytical models were validated by computer simulations.

REFERENCES

1. Blake, I. F., Mullin, R. C. (1976). *An Introduction to Algebraic and Combinatorial Coding Theory*. New York: Academic Press.
2. Berlekamp, E. R. (1984). *Algebraic Coding Theory*. (Revised 1984 edition). Walnut Creek, CA: Aegean Park Press.
3. Lin, S., Costello, Jr., D. J. (2004). *Error Control Coding*. (second edition). Englewood Cliffs, NJ: Prentice Hall.
4. Strang, G. (2006). *Linear Algebra and Its Applications*. (fourth edition). Belmont, CA: Thomson, Brooks/Cole.
5. Lay, D. C. (2011). *Linear Algebra and Its Applications*. (fourth edition). Reading, MA: Addison-Wesley.
6. Tamura, S., Nakano, S., Okazaki, K. (1985). Optical code-multiplex transmission by Gold sequences. *J. Lightwave Technol.* 3(1):121–127.

7. Hui, J. (1985). Pattern code modulation and optical decoding—A novel code-division multiplexing technique for multifiber networks. *IEEE J. Selected Areas Commun.* 3(6):916–927.

8. Prucnal, P. R., Santoro, M., Fan, T. (1986). Spread spectrum fiber-optic local area network using optical processing. *J. Lightwave Technol.* 4(5):547–554.

9. Prucnal, P. R., Santoro, M., Sehgal, S. (1986). Ultrafast all-optical synchronous multiple access fiber networks. *IEEE J. Selected Areas Commun.* 4(9):1484–1493.

10. Foschini, G. J., Vannucci, G. (1987). Spread Spectrum Code-Division-Multiple-Access (SS-CDMA) Lightwave Communication System. US Patent 4,703,474. Issue date: October 27, 1987.

11. Foschini, G. J. (1988). Using spread-spectrum in a high-capacity fiber-optic local network. *J. Lightwave Technol.* 6(3):370–379.

12. Vannucci, G. (1989). Combining frequency-division and code-division multiplexing in a high-capacity optical network. *IEEE Network* 3(2):21–30.

13. Brackett, C. A., Heritage, J. P., Salehi, J. A., Weiner, A. M. (1989). Optical Telecommunications System Using Code Division Multiple Access. US Patent 4,866,699. Issue date: September 12, 1989.

14. Salehi, J. A. (1989). Emerging optical code-division multiple access communication systems. *IEEE Network* 3(2):31–39.

15. Salehi, J. A., Weiner, A. M., Heritage, J. P. (1990). Coherent Ultrashort Light Pulse Code-Division Multiple Access Communication Systems. *J. Lightwave Technol.* 8(3):478–491.

16. Salehi, J. A. (1989). Code division multiple-access techniques in optical fiber networks. I. Fundamental principles. *IEEE Trans. Commun.* 37(8):824–833.

17. Chung, F. R. K., Salehi, J. A., Wei, V. K. (1989). Optical orthogonal codes: Design, analysis, and applications. *IEEE Trans. Info. Theory* 35(3):595–604.

18. Chung, H., Kumar, P. V. (1990). Optical orthogonal codes—New bounds and an optimal construction. *IEEE Trans. Info. Theory* 36(4):866–873.

19. Varanasi, M. K., Aazhang, B. (1991). Near-optimum detection in synchronous code-division multiple-access systems. *IEEE Trans. Commun.* 39(5):725–736.

20. Kwong, W. C., Perrier, P. A., Prucnal, P. R. (1991). Performance comparison of asynchronous and synchronous code-division multiple-access techniques for fiber-optic local area networks. *IEEE Trans. Commun.* 39(11):1625–1634.

21. Yang, G.-C., Kwong, W. C. (2002). *Prime Codes with Applications to CDMA Optical and Wireless Networks.* Norwood, MA: Artech House.

22. Prucnal, P. R. (ed.) (2006). *Optical Code Division Multiple Access: Fundamentals and Applications.* Boca Raton, FL: Taylor & Francis Group.

23. Shaar, A. A., Davies, P. A. (1983). Prime sequences: Quasi-optimal sequences for OR channel code division multiplexing. *Electron. Lett.* 19(21):888–890.

24. Leon-Garcia, A. (1994). *Probability and Random Processes for Electrical Engineering.* (second edition). Reading, MA: Addison-Wesley.

25. Papoulis, A., Pillai, S. U. (2002). *Probability, Random Variables, and Stochastic Processes.* (fourth edition). New York: McGraw-Hill.

26. Poor, H. V. (1988). *An Introduction to Signal Detection and Estimation.* New York: Springer-Verlag.

27. Salehi, J. A., Brackett, C. A. (1989). Code division multiple-access techniques in optical fiber networks. II. System performance analysis. *IEEE Trans. Commun.* 37(8):834–842.

28. Brady, D., Verdu, S. (1991). A semiclassical analysis of optical code division multiple

access. *IEEE Trans. Commun.* 39(1):85–93.

29. Lam, A. W., Hussain, A. M. (1992). Performance analysis of direct-detection optical CDMA communication systems with avalanche photodiodes. *IEEE Trans. Commun.* 40(4):810–820.

30. Azizoğlu, M. Y., Salehi, J. A., Li, Y. (1992). Optical CDMA via temporal codes. *IEEE Trans. Commun.* 40(7):1162–1170.

31. Walker, E. L. (1994). A theoretical analysis of the performance of code division multiple access communications over multimode optical fiber channels. Part I. Transmission and detection. *IEEE J. Selected Areas Commun* 12(4):751–761.

32. Shalaby, H. M. H. (1995). Performance analysis of optical synchronous CDMA communication systems with PPM signaling. *IEEE Trans. Commun.* 43(234):624–634.

33. Ohtsuki, T., Sato, K., Sasase, I., Mori, S. (1996). Direct-detection optical synchronous CDMA systems with double optical hard-limiters using modified prime sequence codes. *IEEE J. Selected Areas Commun.* 14(9):1879–1887.

34. Chen, J.-J., Yang, G.-C. (2001). CDMA fiber-optic systems with optical hard limiters. *J. Lightwave Technol.* 18(7):950–958.

35. Hsu, C.-C., Yang, G.-C., Kwong, W. C. (2007). Performance analysis of 2-D optical codes with arbitrary cross-correlation values under the chip-asynchronous assumption. *IEEE Commun. Lett.* 11(2):170–172.

36. Hsu, C.-C., Chang, Y.-C., Yang, G.-C., Chang, C.-L., Kwong, W. C. (2007). Performance analysis of 2-D O-CDMA codes without the chip-synchronous assumption. *IEEE Trans. Selected Areas Commun.* 25(6):135–143.

37. Hsu, C.-C., Yang, G.-C., Kwong, W. C. (2008). Hard-limiting performance analysis of 2-D optical codes under the chip-asynchronous assumption. *IEEE Trans. Commun.* 56(5):762–768.

38. Chang, T.-W. F., Sargent, E. H. (2003). Optimizing spectral efficiency in multiwavelength optical CDMA system. *IEEE Trans. Commun.* 51(9):1442–1445.

39. Mendez, A. J., Gagliardi, R. M., Hernandez, V. J., Bennett, C. V., Lennon, W. J. (2004). High-performance optical CDMA system based on 2-D optical orthogonal codes. *J. Lightwave Technol.* 22(11):2409–2419.

40. Rochette, M., Ayotte, S., Rusch, L. A. (2005). Analysis of the spectral efficiency of frequency-encoded OCDMA systems with incoherent sources. *J. Lightwave Technol.* 23(4):1610–1619.

41. Chang, C.-Y., Chen, H.-T., Yang, G.-C., Kwong, W. C. (2007). Spectral efficiency study of quadratic-congruence carrier-hopping prime codes in multirate optical CDMA systems. *IEEE J. Selected Areas Commun.* 25(9):118–128.

42. Galli, S., Menendez, R., Narimanov, E., Prucnal, P. R. (2008). A novel method for increasing the spectral efficiency of optical CDMA. *IEEE Trans. Commun.* 56(12):2133–2144.

43. Chen, H.-W., Yang, G.-C., Chang, C.-Y., Lin, T.-C., Kwong, W. C. (2009). Spectral efficiency study of two multirate schemes for optical CDMA with/without symbol synchronization. *J. Lightwave Technol.* 27(14):2771–2778.

44. Yang, G.-C., Fuja, T. (1995). Optical orthogonal codes with unequal auto- and cross-correlation constraints. *IEEE Trans. Info. Theory* 41(1):96–106.

45. Yang, G.-C., Kwong, W. C. (1995). On the construction of 2^n codes for optical code-division multiple-access. *IEEE Trans. Commun.* 43(2/3/4):495–502.

46. Yang, G.-C., Kwong, W. C. (1996). Two-dimensional spatial signature patterns. *IEEE Trans. Commun.* 44(2):184–191.

47. Lam, A. W., Tantaratana, S. (1994). *Theory and Application of Spread-Spectrum Systems—A Self Study Course*, Piscataway, NJ: IEEE Press.
48. Dinan, E. H., Jabbari, B. (1998). Spreading codes for direct sequence CDMA and wideband CDMA cellular networks. *IEEE Commun. Mag.* 36(9):48–54.

2 Optical Coding Schemes

Since the mid-1980s, there have been steady developments in coding techniques and enabling technologies in the field of coding-based optical systems and networks, exemplified by Optical Code-Division Multiple Access (O-CDMA) and multiplexing [1–34]. With the advances in optical hardware tewachnology, the large bandwidth expansion required by optical codes can now be accommodated and multiple-user O-CDMA experimental testbeds operating at 10 Gbits/s have been demonstrated [34–37]. For instance, there are two main categories of optical coding schemes— synchronous and asynchronous—depending on whether synchronization (usually in time or wavelength) is needed among optical codewords. While both kinds of coding schemes have their pros and cons, asynchronous coding, in general, allows simultaneous users to access the same optical transmission medium independently with no wait time, scheduling, or coordination. Compared to conventional asynchronous schemes, such as Carrier-Sense Multiple Access with Collision Detection (CSMA/CD) [38], asynchronous coding makes more efficient use of the transmission medium because a user does not need to wait for the medium to become idle before gaining access. The number of collisions among the signals of simultaneous users increases and access delay gets worse when conventional asynchronous schemes are used in a high-speed or heavy traffic-load environment. Asynchronous coding is, however, more suitable for this kind of system environment. Furthermore, because the traffic in a local area network is typically bursty, asynchronous multiple-access schemes, such as incoherent O-CDMA, are more efficient than synchronous multiple-access schemes, exemplified by Optical Time-Division Multiple Access (O-TDMA), in which a fixed portion (i.e., time) of the medium is dedicated to a particular user.

In addition to O-CDMA and O-TDMA, Wavelength-Division Multiple Access (WDMA) is another optical multiple-access scheme that has been attracting attention. As listed in Table 2.1, these three schemes have their pros and cons; which scheme to use depends on the system environment [10, 33, 39].

As shown in Table 2.2, based on the choices of signaling format, detection method, synchronization requirement, coding domain, and code format, optical coding schemes can be generally classified into seven main categories:

1. Temporal amplitude coding (1-D)
2. Temporal phase coding (1-D)
3. Spectral amplitude coding (1-D)
4. Spectral phase coding (1-D)
5. Spatial-temporal amplitude coding (2-D)
6. Spectral-temporal amplitude coding (2-D)
7. Spatial/polarization-spectral-temporal coding (3-D)

TABLE 2.1

Comparisons of Common Optical Multiple-Access Schemes

	Advantages	Disadvantages
O-TDMA	• Dedicated channels • Suitable for continuous traffic • High throughput • Deterministic access	• Inefficient in bursty traffic • System-wise synchronization • Hard limit on the number of active and possible users
WDMA	• Dedicated channels • Suitable for continuous traffic • High throughput • Deterministic access • (Time) asynchronous access	• Inefficient in bursty traffic • Need wavelength management and stabilization • Hard limit on the number of active and possible users
O-CDMA	• Efficient in bursty traffic • (Time) asynchronous access • Soft limit on the number of active and possible users • Flexible user allocation	• Collisions • Random, statistical access • Performance degrades with number of active users

Source: Reproduced with permission from Guu-Chang Yang and Wing C. Kwong, *Prime Codes with Applications to CDMA Optical and Wireless Networks*, Norwood, MA: Artech House, Inc., 2002. © 2002 by Artech House, Inc.

The first two categories involve one-dimensional (1-D) coding in the time domain. The schemes in category 1 are based on incoherent signal processing and detection that operate on the intensity of optical pulses; the optical pulses are spread out in time [1–8, 33, 34, 40–42]. While the schemes in this category are the easiest of all categories to implement and (time) asynchronous in general, they require the use of 1-D pseudo-orthogonal binary $(0, 1)$ codes, such as optical orthogonal codes and the asynchronous prime codes in Chapter 3 [33, 43–47], with low cross-correlation functions. On the other hand, by applying code synchronism, a variation in temporal amplitude coding allows the use of shifted 1-D pseudo-orthogonal codes, such as the synchronous prime codes in Chapter 4, in order to improve code cardinality and performance at the expense of system-wise synchronization [2, 33, 40]. Borrowing a concept from wireless communications, the schemes in category 2 utilize optical fields by applying 0 or π phase shifts to time-spreading optical pulses [10–13]. Using coherent signal processing and detection, the schemes in this category allow the use of orthogonal bipolar $(-1, +1)$ codes, such as maximal-length sequences and Walsh codes [48, 49], with zero (in-phase) cross-correlation functions for minimizing mutual interference. However, perfect code synchronization is required to maintain the orthogonality of bipolar codes. In addition, phase coding requires special fibers to preserve phase information during transmission. Nevertheless, these two 1-D tempo-

TABLE 2.2

Classifications of Optical Coding Schemes

Signaling format	Optical intensity	Optical field		
Detection method	Incoherent	Coherent		
Synchronization	Asynchronous	Synchronous		
Coding domain	Temporal	Spectral	Spatial	Polarization
Code format	Unipolar $(0, 1)$	Bipolar $(-1, +1)$		

ral coding techniques require a very long code length in order to support a sufficient number of simultaneous users and possible subscribers. As a result, ultrashort optical pulses and high-speed electronics are required. The schemes in both categories are susceptible to fiber dispersion and nonlinearities.

In categories 3 and 4, 1-D amplitude and phase coding are performed in the wavelength domain, respectively [15–21, 35, 50–52]. The spectral nature of optical codes is decoupled from the temporal nature of data; code length is now independent of data rate, and system-wise (time) synchronization is not needed. A broadband optical pulse is first dispersed into multiple wavelengths (or so-called wavelength spreading), spectral coding is then performed by passing these wavelengths through intensity or phase modulators, and the coded wavelengths are finally recombined to form a spectral codeword. Code length is determined by the resolution of the wavelength-spreading and coding devices, which, in turn, limit the number of possible subscribers because the cardinalities of the optical codes in use are usually related to code length. With a special decoder design, orthogonal bipolar codes, such as maximal-length sequences and Walsh codes, can be used in both categories for minimizing mutual interference. Furthermore, binary $(0, 1)$ codes, which have a low, fixed, in-phase cross-correlation function, such as the synchronous prime codes in Chapter 4, can also been used in spectral amplitude coding with a special decoder.

To support many users in temporal amplitude coding, 1-D binary $(0, 1)$ codes, such as the optical orthogonal codes and prime codes (in Chapters 3 and 4), have been designed with good correlation properties—thumbtack-shape autocorrelation and low cross-correlation functions—in order to optimize the discrimination between the correct-address codeword and interfering codewords. So, good 1-D binary $(0, 1)$ codes need to have long code length in order to spread out the effect of mutual interference. In other words, very large bandwidth expansion and high-speed coding hardware are required to support sufficient numbers of simultaneous users and possible subscribers. One possible way to lessen this problem is to utilize 2-D coding, such as adding space or wavelength as the second coding dimension to the 1-D temporal-amplitude (or so-called time-spreading) codes. The spatial-temporal amplitude coding schemes in category 5 allow the use of free space, multiple fibers, or multicore fibers with 2-D binary $(0, 1)$ codes being transmitted in the time and space domains simultaneously [22–27, 53]. The spectral-temporal amplitude (so-called wavelength-hopping time-spreading or, in short, wavelength-time) coding schemes in category 6 require coding in the time and wavelength domains, in which fast wavelength hopping is involved in the pulses of 2-D binary $(0,1)$ codes [14,28–30,33,34,36,37,54–61]. In general, 2-D codes, such as the 2-D prime codes in Chapters 5 and 6, provide lower probability of interception and offer coding scalability and flexibility due to the use of two coding dimensions. These features in the physical layer can be beneficial in supporting time-sensitive obscure transmissions in strategic or military systems, where real-time encryption delay is critical and software encryption at high speed is rather difficult [62].

To further reduce code length or improve code performance, the combination of three coding dimensions has been proposed in category 7. For example, the three-dimensional (3-D) spatial-spectral-temporal coding schemes in [32, 63] transport wavelength-time pulses via multiple fibers with the use of 3-D unipolar codes, such as the 3-D prime codes in Chapter 8. The 3-D polarization-spectral-temporal coding scheme in [31] carries wavelength-time pulses along with the two polarizations of light via an optical fiber.

Future coding-based optical systems and networks are expected to support multimedia services with different bit rates, quality-of-services (QoSs), and priority. For instance, the use of specially designed 1-D and 2-D binary $(0,1)$ codes with multiple lengths and variable weights but fixed low cross-correlation functions has been proposed for supporting these types of multimedia services [33,34,64–68]. By using the multilength prime codes in Chapter 7, one system clock and lasers with the same pulse-width (or so-called chip-width) can be used for all services, simplifying system hardware and timing requirements. Also, studies have shown that shorter codewords, which are assigned to higher bit-rate services, have better code performance and, in turn, higher service priorities—an inherent characteristic in multilength coding.

To achieve high bit rate or spectral efficiency in coding-based optical systems and networks, the concept of multiple-bit-per-symbol transmission has been introduced by means of pulse-position modulation, multicode keying, and shifted-code keying [69–76]. The advantages of symbol transmission are threefold: the effective bit rate is increased by the number of bits per symbol, in essence, trading hardware complexity for reducing bandwidth expansion and electronic speed; spectral efficiency is improved; and user code obscurity is enhanced because bit 0s are also transmitted in codewords and eavesdroppers cannot determine the transmission of bit 0s or 1s by simply detecting the absence or presence of optical intensity in the downlink fiber [62]. The prime codes that are suitable for multicode keying and shifted-code keying are also studied in this book.

The rest of this chapter is organized as follows. The coding techniques and enabling hardware technologies of the seven categories of optical coding schemes are reviewed in Sections 2.1 through 2.7. The special technique of supporting multirate, multimedia services in coding-based optical systems and networks by means of multiple-length codes is studied in Section 2.8. Afterward, Section 2.9 introduces multicode keying and shifted-code keying for increasing bit rate. Additional designs of coding devices, based on arrayed waveguide gratings [57–60,77] and fiber Bragg gratings [78–82], are investigated in Section 2.10. Finally, various potential applications of optical coding, in addition to O-CDMA, are discussed in Section 2.11.

2.1 1-D TEMPORAL AMPLITUDE CODING

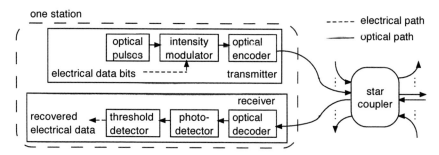

FIGURE 2.1   A typical coding-based optical system model. (Source: Reproduced with permission from Guu-Chang Yang and Wing C. Kwong, *Prime Codes with Applications to CDMA Optical and Wireless Networks*, Norwood, MA: Artech House, Inc., 2002. © 2002 by Artech House, Inc.)

Figure 2.1 outlines the basic configuration of a typical coding-based optical system and network. It consists of multiple stations (or users) linked to a shared optical medium via optical fibers or free space [1, 33]. The shared medium usually consists of an optical multiplexing/demultiplexing device, such as a star coupler. The device is used to combine optical codewords from and then distribute to all stations. Each station consists of a pair of optical transmitter and receiver, whose structures depend on the coding scheme in use.

In incoherent on-off keying (OOK) modulation, a user sends out an optical codeword corresponding to the address (signature) codeword of its intended receiver for a data bit 1, but nothing for a data bit 0. Figure 2.2(a) shows the timing diagrams of a continuous stream of optical clock pulses of width T_c and repetition rate $1/T$. Figure 2.2(b) shows an example of low-bandwidth nonreturn-to-zero electrical data bits of period T at one station in Figure 2.1. Electro-optic OOK conversion is performed using the voltages of data bits to control the opening and closing of the intensity modulator in the transmitter [1, 33]. Every data bit 1, which carries a high voltage, will close the switch and let pass one clock pulse, resulting in a high-bandwidth data-modulated optical signal, as shown in Figure 2.2(c). Assume that 1-D time-spreading binary $(0, 1)$ codewords are used as the address codewords of the stations. To accommodate the 1s and 0s of the codewords, each bit period T is subdivided into a number of time slots (or so-called chips) of width T_c, giving code length $N = T/T_c$. Following the data-bit pattern in this illustration, Figure 2.2(d) shows the corresponding time-spreading binary $(0, 1)$ codewords generated by an optical encoder. Finally, these codewords are multiplexed with the codewords from all stations at the star coupler, as exemplified in Figure 2.2(e).

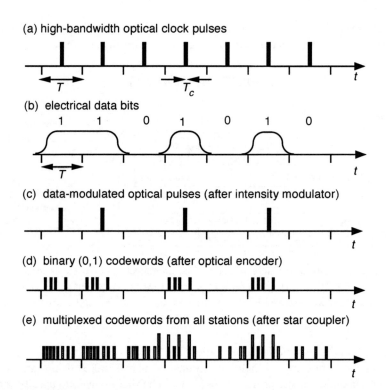

FIGURE 2.2 Signal formats at various stages of an optical transmitter. (Source: Reproduced with permission from Guu-Chang Yang and Wing C. Kwong, *Prime Codes with Applications to CDMA Optical and Wireless Networks*, Norwood, MA: Artech House, Inc., 2002. © 2002 by Artech House, Inc.)

At each receiver, an optical decoder, which operates as an inverse filter of its corresponding optical encoder, correlates its own address (signature) codeword with any received codeword. Assuming chip synchronism, the decoder output is written as a discrete periodic correlation function, according to Section 1.5. If a codeword arrives at the correct destination, an autocorrelation function with a high peak is generated. Otherwise, the codeword is treated as interference and a cross-correlation function results. So, it is necessary to maximize the autocorrelation peaks but to minimize the cross-correlation functions in order to optimize the discrimination between the correct codewords and interfering codewords. An electrical pulse is generated whenever an autocorrelation peak is detected at the threshold detector. Such a pulse indicates the reception of a data bit 1; otherwise, a data bit 0 is recovered.

Prucnal et al. [2] proposed the first-of-its-kind tunable incoherent optical encoder, in which a parallel configuration of fixed fiber-optic delay-lines and intensity modulators was used, for temporal amplitude coding. Figure 2.3 shows the block diagram of a revised version of such a parallel design. The encoder consists of a $1 \times w$ optical power splitter, a set of w electronically tunable (fiber-optic or waveguide) delay-lines,

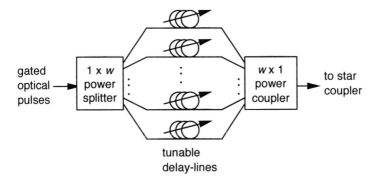

FIGURE 2.3   Tunable optical encoder in a parallel coding configuration [2, 33].

and a $w \times 1$ optical power coupler, where w is the code weight (or number of pulses) of the 1-D time-spreading binary $(0, 1)$ codes in use. At the encoder input, the power splitter divides an incoming gated optical pulse, which represents the transmission of a data bit 1, into w pulses. These w pulses are delayed individually by their own tunable delay-lines, according to the locations of the mark chips (or binary 1s) in the address codeword of the intended receiver. Finally, these pulses are combined by the coupler to form the desired codeword for transmission.

As fixed delay-lines were assumed in Prucnal's original design [2], tunability was achieved by first generating pulses in all possible time-delays and then selecting only w of them in according to the address codeword of the intended receiver. So, the original setup required the use of a $1 \times N$ power splitter, a set of N fixed (fiber-optic or waveguide) delay-lines, N intensity modulators (one per line), and an $N \times 1$ power coupler, where N is the code length. Each of these N delay-lines takes a distinct value from the set of $\{0, T_c, 2T_c, \ldots, (N-1)T_c\}$, where T_c is the chip-width. The w properly delayed pulses are selected by closing w intensity modulators.

The setup of the decoder is identical to that of the encoder, except that only w fixed-delay paths are needed if a fixed-address-receiver configuration is assumed. The decoder correlates incoming codewords by accumulating the reversely delayed pulses to give a high autocorrelation peak if there exists a codeword matching the decoder's address codeword. Otherwise, a low cross-correlation function results and is considered as interference.

The advantage of this parallel coding configuration is the capability of performing incoherent optical processing without the need for fast-response photodetectors or high-speed electronics. Also, it can universally generate any 1-D time-spreading binary $(0, 1)$ code, such as all of the prime codes in Chapters 3 and 4. However, this kind of parallel structure creates a very stringent power requirement because each optical pulse is split into many pulses in the encoders and decoders. In addition, the number of delay-lines adds up to a huge number, and this kind of parallel coding devices is usually bulky and lossy.

Figure 2.4 shows the block diagram of a tunable incoherent optical encoder in

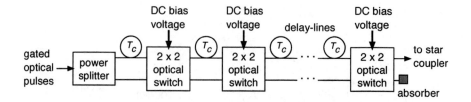

FIGURE 2.4 Tunable optical encoder in a serial coding configuration [33,41,42].

a serial coding configuration [33, 41, 42]. This setup improves the power, size, and delay-length requirements of the parallel configuration. The encoder consists of a series of 2×2 optical switches, which are connected with two separate (fiber-optic or waveguide) delay-lines between two adjacent switches. Each pair of delay-lines generates a differential time-delay of one chip-width T_c. The DC-bias voltages of the 2×2 optical switches are individually controlled so that each switch is configured to operate in either 3-dB or bar state independently. At an encoder input, the power splitter divides an incoming gated optical pulse (of width T_c), which represents the transmission of a data bit 1, into two pulses. The amount of differential time-delays is accumulated as these two pulses pass through a series of bar-state switches. The bar state allows optical pulses at the two inputs of a switch to directly exit the corresponding outputs without any change. After the proper amount of differential time-delays has been created, both pulses are combined at a 3-dB-state switch and then split into four pulses—two pulses at each output. Functioning like a 2×2 passive coupler, a 3-dB state switch duplicates optical pulses arriving at its two inputs and makes them available at the two outputs. The process repeats until the desired number of pulses, which are properly arranged according to the address codeword of the intended receiver, is generated. If there are n switches in the 3-dB state, a time-spreading binary $(0, 1)$ codeword with 2^n pulses can be generated. For example, if the second, sixth, and thirteenth switches are set to the 3-dB state, 2, 6, and 13 chips of differential time-delays are accumulated to generate the codeword 1010001010000101000101.

The setup of the optical decoder is similar to that of the encoder, except that the 3-dB-state 2×2 optical switches are now replaced by 2×2 passive couplers if a fixed-address-receiver configuration is assumed. Only $n + 1$ 2×2 passive couplers are needed, and the delay-lines between two couplers are used to generate the differential time-delays of two groups of pulses directly. For example, to have an address (signature) codeword of 1010001010000101000101 in the decoder, four 2×2 passive couplers are needed, and the delay-lines between two couplers are arranged to generate the differential time-delays of 2, 6, and 13 chips, correspondingly.

While this serial configuration improves the power, size, and delay-length requirements of the parallel configuration, it can only generate certain families of 1-D time-spreading binary $(0, 1)$ codes that have replicative pulse separations, such as 1-D even-spaced codes, 2^n codes, and 2^n prime codes in Section 3.5 [33, 41, 42].

Making use of the block structure of some optical codes, such as the 1-D prime codes in Chapter 3, the power splitting/combining loss and number of optical

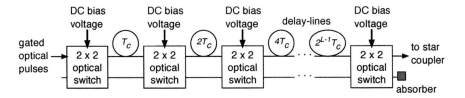

FIGURE 2.5 Tunable incoherent optical encoder in an improved serial coding configuration [33,41,42].

switches in the serial coding configuration can be reduced substantially. For instance, each of the prime codewords (in Section 3.1) of length p^2 and weight p can be divided into p blocks, and each block has a single one (or a pulse) and $p-1$ 0s, where p is a prime number. If all p pulses in a prime code can be generated by a laser with a repetition rate p/T, the power loss created by pulse splitting and combining at the optical splitter and switches can be avoided, where T is the bit period, as explained in the following.

Shown in Figure 2.5 is an improved serial tunable encoder. It consists of a series of $L+1$ 2×2 optical switches, which are connected with two separate (fiber-optic or waveguide) delay-lines between two adjacent switches, where $L = \lceil \log_2 p \rceil$ and $\lceil \cdot \rceil$ is the ceiling function [33,41,42]. The DC-bias voltages of the 2×2 optical switches are individually controlled so that each switch is configured to operate in either cross or bar state independently. While the bar state allows an optical pulse at an input of a switch to directly exit the corresponding output, the cross state allows the pulse to cross over to the opposite output. The differential time-delays are all distinct and assigned with values equal to the product of the chip-width T_c and consecutive powers of 2. This design is based on the tunable O-TDMA coder proposed by Prucnal et al. in [83,84], in which any discrete time delay of $\{0, T_c, 2T_c, \ldots, (p-1)T_c\}$ chips can be generated by setting the 2×2 optical switches in either cross or bar states, accordingly. The last 2×2 optical switch is used to route the properly delayed pulse to the output of the encoder. With this last switch in place, the use of intensity modulators for performing electro-optic conversion of data bits (see Figures 2.1 and 2.2) can be eliminated. This is because all p pulses within a bit period can be simply routed to the unused output of the last switch for every data bit 0. Similarly, as in the 2^n prime codewords in Section 3.5, a block may have no pulse but all p 0s, any optical pulse within such a block can also be routed to this unused output.

Because optical pulses are now entering this improved serial encoder at a rate of p/T, p-fold increases in the speed of electronics and the repetition rate of lasers are required, as compared to the serial design in Figure 2.4. Nevertheless, there is no power loss due to splitting and combining of optical pulses, and only $\lceil \log_2 p \rceil + 1$ optical switches are required in the improved serial design, resulting in substantial cost savings and size reduction, and making the design more suitable for waveguide implementation.

2.2 1-D TEMPORAL PHASE CODING

Temporal amplitude coding can only accommodate 1-D binary $(0,1)$ codes and is restricted to the use of incoherent processing and detection because optical intensity is used for transmission. This kind of incoherent system is usually asynchronous in nature because these optical codes, such as the prime codes in Chapter 3, are designed to operate without system-wise time synchronization. Due to nonscheduled transmission and nonzero mutual interference, temporal amplitude coding supports only a limited number of subscribers and even fewer simultaneous users before a rapid deterioration of code performance occurs. By introducing 0 or π phase shifts to optical pulses, temporal phase coding supports orthogonal bipolar $(-1, +1)$ codes, such as maximal-length sequences and Walsh codes [48, 49], with zero (in-phase) cross-correlation functions. Rather than using OOK, temporal phase coding transmits a conjugated form of the bipolar codewords in use for data bit 0s, resulting in better code performance than temporal amplitude coding [10–13, 15, 16]. However, this kind of coherent system is usually synchronous in nature because bipolar codes require system-wise synchronization in order to maintain code orthogonality. Also, the need for phase preservation in optical fibers often hinders the development of temporal phase coding.

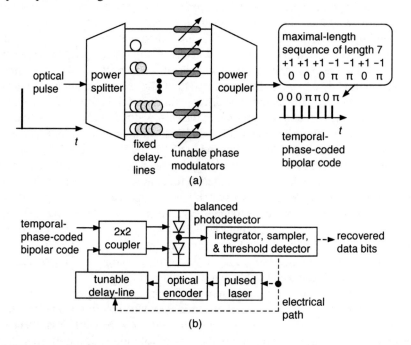

FIGURE 2.6 Temporal phase coding: (a) tunable encoder; (b) tunable decoder [10–13, 15, 16].

Figure 2.6 shows a typical tunable coherent encoder and decoder for temporal phase coding [10–13, 15, 16]. Assume that bipolar codes of length and weight of both equal to N are used. A narrow optical pulse is first split into N pulses. These pulses are then delayed by fixed (fiber-optic or waveguide) delay-lines, and 0 or π phase shifts are introduced by tunable phase modulators. These phase-coded pulses are finally recombined to form a temporal-phase codeword. In this scheme, a station (or user) transmits the address (bipolar) codeword of its intended receiver for a data bit 1, but a data bit 0 is conveyed by the same codeword with conjugated phase shifts. In a receiver, phase tracking and correlation of arriving bipolar codewords (from all stations) with the receiver's address codeword are usually done by optical heterodyne detection in a phase-locked loop, as shown in Figure 2.6(b) [10, 12, 13]. The recovery of data bits is performed by a balanced photodetector and an electronic, integrating, sampling, and thresholding circuit.

Another type of temporal-phase-coding device consists of superstructured fiber Bragg gratings [79, 80]. Phase modulation is performed by segments of (0 or π) phase-shifted fiber Bragg gratings placed inside a piece of optical fiber. The locations of the segments determine the spacings of the pulses and, in general, are not easily tunable.

2.3   1-D SPECTRAL PHASE CODING

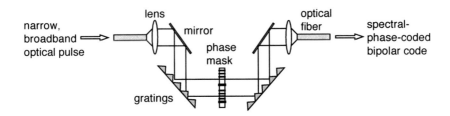

FIGURE 2.7   Spectral phase coding in free space [19–21, 35].

Because spectral phase coding transmits phase-modulated codes in the wavelength domain, the code length is independent of data rate, and codes are inherently synchronous as long as the coded spectra all align to a common wavelength reference plane. In this kind of scheme, each station (or user) is assigned an orthogonal bipolar codeword, such as maximal-length sequences and Walsh codewords, as its address signature. A user transmits the (bipolar) address codeword of its intended receiver for a data bit 1, but a data bit 0 is conveyed by the same codeword with conjugated phase shifts. As shown in Figure 2.7, a narrow, broadband optical pulse is first dispersed in wavelengths by gratings [19–21, 35]. Phase coding is then performed by passing spectral components through a phase mask, in which the pixels can be made electronically programmable with the use of liquid-crystal-based phase modulators. The phase-coded spectral components are finally recombined by (inverse) gratings to form a spectral-phase codeword. The length of the bipolar codes in use is determined by the wavelength resolutions of the gratings and phase mask. The decoder has the same setup as the encoder but with a conjugated phase mask.

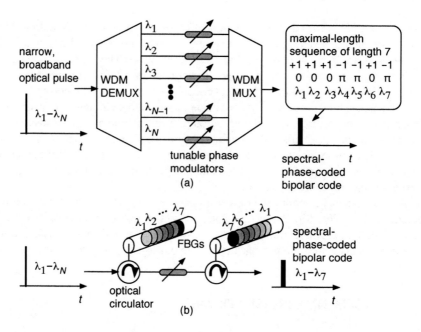

FIGURE 2.8   Spectral phase coding in (a) waveguide and (b) fiber [21, 30, 34–36, 86].

In addition to free-space, spectral phase coding can also be performed in waveguide and fiber. In Figure 2.8(a), spectral spreading is done by a wavelength-division-multiplexing (WDM) demultiplexer (DEMUX), such as thin-film filters, arrayed-waveguide-grating devices, holographic Bragg reflectors, and micro-disk resonators [30,34,36,37,77,85,86]. Phase coding is then performed by passing the spectral components through tunable phase modulators. The phase-coded spectral components are finally recombined by a wavelength multiplexer (MUX) to form a spectral-phase codeword.

Similarly, based on the time-domain spectral-phase encoder by Gao et al. in [21], spectral spreading can be done by placing segments of fiber Bragg gratings (FBGs) with different center wavelengths inside a piece of optical fiber, as shown in Figure 2.8(b). Those spectral components matching the center wavelengths get reflected back to the fiber input and routed through an optical circulator to a rapidly tunable phase modulator. Because different FBGs are placed at different locations of the fiber, time delays (or time spreading) are introduced to the reflected wavelengths. The phase modulator then performs 0 or π phase shifts to the time-spreading wavelengths one-by-one, according to the (bipolar) address codeword of the intended receiver. A second piece of optical fiber with reversed placement of FBGs as those of the first piece of optical fiber is used to (time) realign the phase-coded spectral components, finally forming the desired spectral-phase codeword.

2.4   1-D SPECTRAL AMPLITUDE CODING

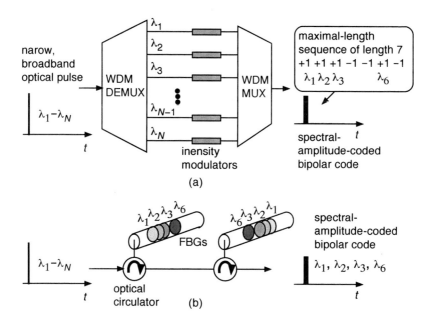

FIGURE 2.9   Spectral amplitude coding in (a) waveguide and (b) fiber.

In spectral amplitude coding, OOK is assumed as each data bit 1 is conveyed by a bipolar $(-1, +1)$ codeword, but data 0s are not transmitted [15–18, 50–52]. In addition, amplitude coding means that optical intensity is used for transmission. So, only the "+1" elements of bipolar codewords are transmitted in wavelengths but the "−1" code elements are not. The three kinds of spectral-phase encoders in Section 2.3 can be modified for spectral amplitude coding. For the free-space encoder, amplitude masks with transparent and opaque pixels are used in lieu of phase masks. For the waveguide-type encoder, intensity modulators replace phase modulators, as shown in Figure 2.9(a). For the fiber-based encoder [17, 51, 52], only fiber Bragg gratings (FBGs) with center wavelengths matching those of the "+1" elements of the bipolar codeword in use exist inside the two pieces of optical fiber, as shown in Figure 2.9(b). The wavelengths matching those of the "+1" code elements are reflected back to the input of the first piece of optical fiber and then routed to the second piece of optical fiber for (time) realignment.

Because spectral amplitude coding only transmits the "+1" elements of the bipolar codewords, an optical differential receiver, which consists of a "true" decoder, a "conjugated" decoder, and a pair of balanced photodetectors, is designed to emulate the "−1" code elements [16–18, 51, 52]. The decoders, which function as inverse filters, are made of the same structure as the encoders. The true decoder is used to collect incoming wavelengths that match those wavelengths of the "+1" elements of its (bipolar) address codeword, and the conjugated decoder collects the rest of the

incoming wavelengths. The "-1" code-elements are emulated at the balanced photodetectors, which allow the electrical current obtained from the true decoder being
subtracted by the electrical current obtained from the conjugated decoder.

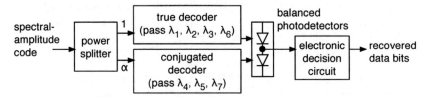

FIGURE 2.10 Spectral-amplitude differential receiver for the maximal-length sequence
$(+1, +1, +1, -1, -1, +1, -1)$, where α is the output ratio of the power splitter, which is equal
to 1 when orthogonal bipolar codes are in use [16–18, 51, 52].

station	address code	bit	transmitted signal
1	$\lambda_1 \lambda_2 \lambda_3\, 0\, 0\, \lambda_6\, 0$	1	$\lambda_1 \lambda_2 \lambda_3\, 0\, 0\, \lambda_6\, 0$
2	$0\, \lambda_2 \lambda_3 \lambda_4\, 0\, 0\, \lambda_7$	0	$0\ \ 0\ \ 0\ \ 0\ \ 0\ \ 0\ \ 0$
3	$\lambda_1\, 0\, \lambda_3 \lambda_4 \lambda_5\, 0\, 0$	1	$\lambda_1\, 0\, \lambda_3 \lambda_4 \lambda_5\, 0\, 0$
4	$0\, \lambda_2\, 0\, \lambda_4 \lambda_5 \lambda_6\, 0$	1	$0\, \lambda_2\, 0\, \lambda_4 \lambda_5 \lambda_6\, 0$
5	$0\, 0\, \lambda_3\, 0\, \lambda_5 \lambda_6 \lambda_7$	1	$0\, 0\, \lambda_3\, 0\, \lambda_5 \lambda_6 \lambda_7$
6	$\lambda_1\, 0\, 0\, \lambda_4\, 0\, \lambda_6 \lambda_7$	0	$0\ \ 0\ \ 0\ \ 0\ \ 0\ \ \ 0\ \ 0$
7	$\lambda_1 \lambda_2\, 0\, 0\, \lambda_5\, 0\, \lambda_7$	1	$\lambda_1 \lambda_2\, 0\, 0\, \lambda_5\, 0\, \lambda_7$

multiplexed signal $= 3\lambda_1\, 3\lambda_2\, 3\lambda_3\, 2\lambda_4\, 4\lambda_5\, 3\lambda_6\, 2\lambda_7$

	receiver 1		receiver 2	
	autocorrelation	intensity	cross-correlation	intensity
true decoder output	$3\lambda_1\, 3\lambda_2\, 3\lambda_3\, 0$ $0\, 3\lambda_6\, 0$	12	$0\, 3\lambda_2\, 3\lambda_3\, 2\lambda_4$ $0\, 0\, 2\lambda_7$	10
conjugated decoder output	$0\, 0\, 0\, 2\lambda_4$ $4\lambda_5\, 0\, 2\lambda_7$	8	$3\lambda_1\, 0\, 0\, 0$ $4\lambda_5\, 3\lambda_6\, 0$	10
balanced photo-detector output		4		0

FIGURE 2.11 Example of the spectral-amplitude decoding process with zero mutual interference, where the maximal-length sequences of length 7 are used.

For example, the spectral-amplitude differential receiver for the maximal-length
sequence $(+1, +1, +1, -1, -1, +1, -1)$ of length 7 is shown in Figure 2.10. The
true decoder detects wavelengths λ_1, λ_2, λ_3, and λ_6, where λ_i is the ith wavelength
used to carry the ith sequence element that is equal to "$+1$." The conjugated decoder
then detects wavelengths λ_4, λ_5, and λ_7. Assume that the cyclic-shifted versions of
this maximal-length sequence are used as the other bipolar codewords; they sup-
port at most 7 possible subscribers (or stations). Figure 2.11 illustrates an example
of the autocorrelation and cross-correlation processes in the receivers of stations 1

and 2, respectively. In this example, representing the transmission of data bit 1s, the spectral-amplitude (address) codewords of stations 1, 3, 4, 5, and 7 are being transmitted simultaneously, multiplexed, and distributed to the receivers of all stations. While the receivers of stations 1, 3, 4, 5, and 7 expect to see autocorrelation functions, the receivers of stations 2 and 6 will see cross-correlation functions because no matching (address) codeword is transmitted to these two receivers for data bit 0s in OOK. So, the wavelengths arriving at receivers 1 and 2 at one time instant are $3\lambda_1$, $3\lambda_2$, $3\lambda_3$, $2\lambda_4$, $4\lambda_5$, $3\lambda_6$, and $2\lambda_7$. For receiver 1, the total number of wavelengths detected at the upper photodetector is 12 (from $3\lambda_1 + 3\lambda_2 + 3\lambda_3 + 3\lambda_6$) and that at the lower photodetector is 8 (from $2\lambda_4 + 4\lambda_5 + 2\lambda_7$). The balanced photodetectors give an autocorrelation peak of $12 - 8 = 4$ units of electrical current. For receiver 2, the upper photodetector sees ten wavelengths (from $3\lambda_2 + 3\lambda_3 + 2\lambda_4 + 2\lambda_7$) and the lower photodetector also sees 10 wavelengths (from $3\lambda_1 + 4\lambda_5 + 3\lambda_6$), resulting in $10 - 10 = 0$ unit of electrical current—zero cross-correlation value—at the output of the balanced photodetectors.

In addition to bipolar $(-1, +1)$ codes, spectral amplitude coding also supports the use of binary $(0, 1)$ codes, but these codes need to have a low, fixed in-phase cross-correlation function λ_c [51, 52]. Because spectral coding does not involve time spreading, the correlation process is not a function of time anymore. So, the cross-correlation function is called in-phase and has one value only. If the amount of mutual interference caused by each interfering codeword at the output of the true decoder is λ_c, the conjugated decoder will output $w - \lambda_c$ [51]. By adjusting the splitting ratio of the power splitter in Figure 2.10 to $\alpha = \lambda_c/(w - \lambda_c)$, the net interference at the output of the conjugated decoder will then become $\alpha(w - \lambda_c) = \lambda_c$. As a result, the mutual interference seen at both decoders can completely be cancelled out at the balanced photodetectors, even through pseudo-orthogonal binary $(0, 1)$ codes, such as the synchronous prime codes in Chapter 4, are used, as long as their in-phase cross-correlation functions are equal to a constant number.

Instead of OOK, a variation of spectral amplitude coding conveys data bit 0 by transmitting the conjugate wavelengths of bipolar codewords [82]. In this scheme, the "-1" elements of bipolar codewords are transmitted in wavelengths but the "$+1$" elements are not whenever data bit 0s are conveyed. By transmitting both data bit 1s and 0s, this scheme results in code-performance improvement, similar to that of spectral phase coding. However, only restricted families of bipolar codes, such as Walsh codes and "balanced" maximal-length sequences [34, 57–60], which have code lengths equal to some even numbers and code weights equal to half of the code lengths, are used in order to maintain zero mutual interference.

2.5   2-D SPATIAL-TEMPORAL AMPLITUDE CODING

To lessen the long-code-length and large-bandwidth-expansion problems in 1-D temporal amplitude coding, spatial-temporal amplitude coding uses 2-D binary $(0, 1)$ codewords to carry data bit 1s in space and time simultaneously [22–27, 53]. The spatial domain is provided by multiple transmission channels, such as free space, multiple fibers, or a multiple-core fiber.

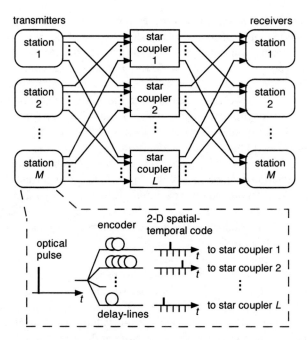

FIGURE 2.12 Spatial-temporal amplitude coding in multiple fibers and star couplers. (Source: Reproduced with permission from Guu-Chang Yang and Wing C. Kwong, *Prime Codes with Applications to CDMA Optical and Wireless Networks*, Norwood, MA: Artech House, Inc., 2002. © 2002 by Artech House, Inc.)

Figure 2.12 shows an example of spatial-temporal-amplitude-coding systems with multiple optical fibers and star couplers [22, 23]. Assume that there are M stations and each of them is assigned a 2-D binary $(0, 1)$ codeword of size $L \times N$ as its address signature, where L is the number of spatial channels (provided by optical fibers and star couplers, in this example) and N is the number of time slots [33, 53]. A narrow optical pulse, which represents the transmission of a data bit 1, is first split into L pulses; each pulse is time-delayed to one of the N time slots, according to the address codeword of the intended receiver. These L pulses are then conveyed separately via their own optical fibers and multiplexed with the corresponding pulses from other stations at the star couplers. The decoders in the receivers reverse the process to give correlation functions.

Figure 2.13 illustrates an example of encoding and decoding processes of 2-D binary pixels in spatial-temporal amplitude coding [24, 26]. With the support of 2-D binary $(0, 1)$ codes [33, 53], the technique is suitable for parallel transmission and simultaneous access of multiple digitized 2-D images. There is no need to perform the bottleneck-prone parallel-to-serial or serial-to-parallel conversion because the pixels of every digitized image are transmitted in parallel. The concept also applies to free-space optics, in lieu of the multicore fiber or fiber bundle [25]. In this

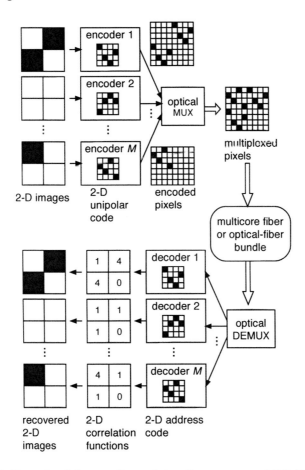

FIGURE 2.13 Example of the encoding and decoding processes of 2-D binary pixels in spatial-temporal amplitude coding, where black squares represent dark pixels and the number in each square of the 2-D correlation functions represents the darkness level after correlation.

example, 2-D images of 2×2 binary pixels are transmitted, and each black pixel is encoded at an optical encoder with a 4×4 2-D unipolar codeword, forming an array of 8×8 coded pixels. These encoded pixels are then multiplexed with the corresponding encoded pixels from other stations at an optical MUX. Afterward, the multiplexed arrays of 8×8 encoded pixels are transmitted in parallel via multicore fiber, optical-fiber bundle, or free space, and later distributed to all stations by an optical DEMUX. If an array of coded pixels arrives at the correct decoder, an auto-correlation function, which is represented by a high (darkness-level) number, results. Otherwise, a cross-correlation function, which is represented by a low number, results and is treated as interference. By threshold-detecting the darkness levels, the binary pixels of the transmitted 2-D image are recovered.

2.6   2-D SPECTRAL-TEMPORAL AMPLITUDE CODING

If deployment of multicore fiber or optical-fiber bundle is not possible or too compli-
cated, one alternative is to use a hybrid WDM-coding scheme [33, 54, 55], in which
1-D time-spreading codewords are used in conjunction with multiple wavelengths.
Every codeword is reusable and can be sent out simultaneously at different wavelengths, if needed. The selection of codewords of a specific wavelength at a receiver
is done by an optical WDM filter placed in front of the optical decoder. The code
length and, in turn, the speed of hardware are reduced due to the lessening in the
number of simultaneous users in each wavelength. However, unless there is a central controller coordinating the wavelength usage among simultaneous users, wavelengths cannot usually be utilized evenly, and the scheme fails to achieve the optimal
performance, as discussed in Section 5.1 [33, 55].

Another approach, spectral-temporal amplitude (or wavelength-time) coding,
imbeds multiple wavelengths within 1-D time-spreading codewords as the second coding dimension [14, 28–30, 33, 34, 36, 37, 55–61]. The scheme involves fast
wavelength hopping, and the wavelength-hop takes place at every pulse of a time-
spreading codeword, instead of having the same wavelength for all pulses within
each codeword as in the aforementioned hybrid WDM-coding scheme. Using the
same number of wavelengths and code length, 2-D wavelength-time codes, such as
the prime codes in Chapter 5, have a larger cardinality than and can perform as well
as the 1-D time-spreading codes used in the hybrid WDM-coding scheme.

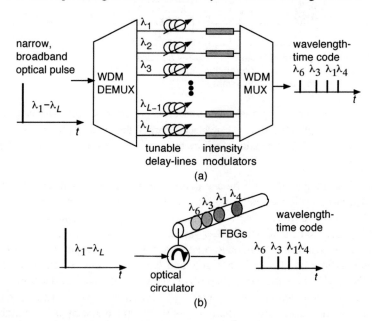

FIGURE 2.14   Spectral-temporal-amplitude encoders in (a) waveguide and (b) fiber [34, 36,
78, 81, 82].

Figure 2.14(a) shows a waveguide-based, spectral-temporal-amplitude encoder, which consists of WDM MUX/DEMUX devices, such as thin-film filters, arrayed-waveguide-grating (AWG) devices, holographic Bragg reflectors, and micro-disk resonators [30, 34, 36, 37, 77, 85, 86], combined with tunable time-delay elements. A narrow, broadband laser pulse, which represents the transmission of a data bit 1, is split into L pulses of distinct wavelengths, where L is the number of wavelengths used in the wavelength-time codes. These multiwavelength pulses are time-delayed by tunable delay-lines, according to the address codeword of the intended receiver. If a wavelength is not used in the codeword, it will be blocked by an intensity modulator along that wavelength path. This encoder is integrable by fabricating the components all in the waveguide. The all-fiber approach in Figure 2.14(b) places segments of fiber Bragg gratings (FBGs) with different center wavelengths inside a piece of optical fiber. The locations of these wavelength segments, which are usually not tunable, determine the spacings of the corresponding wavelength pulses [78–82]. More examples on AWG- and FBG-based encoder/decoder designs that are tunable are given in Section 2.10.

2.7 THREE-DIMENSIONAL CODING

To further improve the number of simultaneous users and subscribers, higher coding dimension can be achieved by combining temporal, spatial, and spectral coding [32, 63]. Furthermore, the use of the two polarizations of optical field to replace the use of multiple fibers in the spatial domain has been proposed [31]. 3-D unipolar codes are needed to support this kind of coding schemes. The prime codes that support 3-D coding are studied in Chapter 8 [33].

2.8 MULTIRATE AND MULTIPLE-QoS CODING

So far in this chapter, only one type of service with identical bit rate is assumed to exist in coding-based optical systems and networks. However, future systems are expected to support a variety of services, such as data, voice, and video, with different bit rates, QoSs, and even priorities. It is known that coherent (phase) coding schemes have better performance than incoherent (amplitude) coding schemes because the former allow the use of orthogonal bipolar codes [34]. Nevertheless, coherent coding requires strict phase control with the use of special optical fibers in order to maintain code orthogonality. The code choices in coherent coding are mostly limited to bipolar codes, such as maximal-length sequences and Walsh codes. This kind of code has restrictive code cardinality, which is about the same as the code length, giving a hard limit on the number of possible subscribers. Also, bipolar codes are very sensitive to any change in the code structure, and code orthogonality can be easily destroyed due to induced phase fluctuations during transmission in optical fiber. On the other hand, the unipolar codes used in incoherent coding schemes have totally opposite characteristics. First of all, they are less sensitive to phase changes, and regular optical fiber can be used because optical intensity is transmitted. Second, with pseudo-orthogonality (or nonzero cross-correlations), the unipolar code structure is more flexible and less restrictive in the relationships among code cardinality, weight, and length. Unipolar codes allow trading among performance, number of simultaneous users, and number of subscribers. Third, there exist unipolar codes for 1-D, 2-D, and even 3-D coding, while bipolar codes are all 1-D. Fourth, special unipolar codes can be designed with multiple lengths and variable weights without sacrificing the cross-correlation function. These features support multirate, multimedia services in incoherent coding systems and networks with different bit rates, QoSs, and priorities [33, 34, 64–68]. The prime codes that support this kind of coding schemes are studied in Chapter 7.

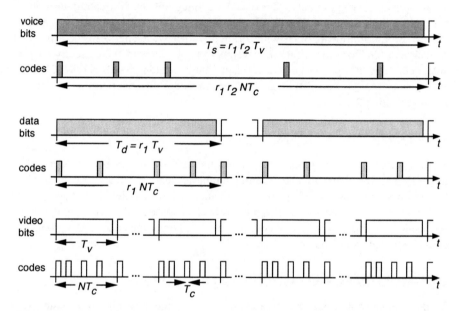

FIGURE 2.15 Timing diagrams of three types of multirate, multimedia services supported by multilength coding. (Source: Reproduced with permission from Guu-Chang Yang and Wing C. Kwong, *Prime Codes with Applications to CDMA Optical and Wireless Networks*, Norwood, MA: Artech House, Inc., 2002. © 2002 by Artech House, Inc.)

To illustrate an application of multilength coding, three types of multirate, multimedia services (i.e., digitized voice, data, and video) are assumed in Figure 2.15 [33, 34]. Real-time video transmission, which has a continuous traffic pattern, is usually assigned the highest priority and requires the highest bit rate, whereas the bursty voice service requires the lowest priority and bit rate. Assume that video-service bit rate $1/T_v$ is an integer multiple of the data-service bit rate $1/T_d$ (i.e., $1/T_v = r_1/T_d$), which, in turn, is a multiple of the voice-service bit rate $1/T_s$ (i.e., $1/T_d = r_2/T_s$), where r_1 and r_2 are the expansion factors. For the service (i.e., video) with the highest bit rate, code length N is assumed, where $T_v = NT_c$ and T_c is the pulse-width (or chip-width). Because the same chip-width T_c is used for all services, the medium-rate service (i.e., data) requires optical codewords of r_1 times longer than that of the highest-rate service in order to support the rate $1/T_d = 1/(r_1 T_v) = 1/(r_1 N T_c)$. Similarly, the lowest-rate service (i.e., voice) requires codewords of $r_1 r_2$ times longer than that of the video service in order to support the rate $1/T_s = 1/(r_1 r_2 T_v) = 1/(r_1 r_2 N T_c)$. To support these three types of services, 1-D or 2-D unipolar codewords of lengths N, $r_1 N$, and $r_1 r_2 N$ are constructed with the same maximum cross-correlation function that is independent of code length [33, 34, 64–68]. The shortest codewords are then assigned to the real-time services (i.e., video) with the highest bit-rate and priority, whereas the longest codewords are for the voice services. Because the analyses in Chapter 7 show that the shortest codewords have the best performance, the QoS of critical real-time video transmission is guaranteed. This unique priority feature, however, cannot be found in conventional single-length coding schemes. In addition, one system clock and lasers with the same pulse-width can be used for all types of services in this multilength approach, simplifying system hardware and timing requirements.

Furthermore, two multirate asynchronous O-CDMA schemes were proposed by Maric and Lau in [87]. For example, in the parallel-mapping multiple-code scheme [69, 87], each user is assigned multiple 1-D codewords. If a user needs to transmit at a rate of M times the basic bit rate, every M serial bits are first converted into M parallel bits. Then, each parallel bit 1 is conveyed by one of the assigned M codewords, but nothing is transmitted for a bit 0. As a result, the number of codewords that are transmitted at the same time ranges from 0 to M, depending on the user's bit rate and the number of parallel bit 1s after the serial-to-parallel conversion. Because of the need of transmitting many codewords simultaneously, optical codes with huge cardinality are required in this scheme. Nevertheless, the scheme is still asynchronous in nature because user-to-user synchronization is not needed, even though multiple codewords are simultaneously transmitted by every user.

2.9   MULTICODE KEYING AND SHIFTED-CODE KEYING

To support higher bit-rate transmission without increasing the speed of optics and electronics, three methods of multiple-bit-per-symbol transmission have been proposed [70–75]. In pulse-position modulation (PPM) coding, each bit period is divided into 2^m nonoverlapping PPM frames [70,73]. Each user is assigned one distinct (address) codeword and all m serial data bits are converted into one of 2^m possible symbols. A symbol is transmitted by placing the codeword entirely inside one of the 2^m PPM frames designated for that symbol. As illustrated in Figure 2.16, every two serial data bits are grouped to form one of the four possible symbols and, in turn, the symbol is conveyed by transmitting the codeword entirely within one of the four PPM frames. As a result, the total number of time slots is increased by a factor of 2^m in this nonoverlapping PPM scheme and so is the transmission bandwidth.

Another method of transmitting symbols is by means of multicode keying [69, 75, 76], in which each user is assigned 2^m distinct codewords to represent m serial data bits per symbol. One of these codewords is conveyed each time in order to represent the transmission of one of the 2^m symbols. Figure 2.17 shows an example of four-code keying, in which every two serial data bits are grouped to form

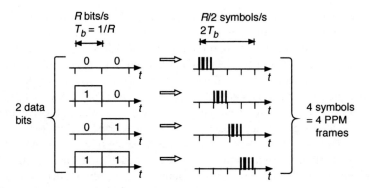

FIGURE 2.16　Example of PPM coding with 4 symbols, represented by 4 PPM frames, where T_b is the bit period and R is the bit rate [70, 71, 73].

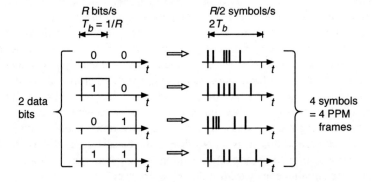

FIGURE 2.17　Example of multicode keying with 4 symbols, represented by 4 distinct codewords, where T_b is the bit period and R is the bit rate [69, 75, 76].

one of the four possible symbols and, in turn, the symbol is conveyed by one of the four distinct codewords. This multicode-keying approach does not need system-wise synchronization but only needs the communicating transmitter-receiver pair be synchronized, the same requirement as any asynchronous OOK coding scheme anyway. However, multicode keying requires an 2^m-fold increase in the number of codewords, all with the same low cross-correlation function. Details about the cross-correlation requirements and the prime codes that are suitable for multicode keying can be found in Section 5.6.

Without the need for huge code cardinality, shifted-code keying assigns each user with one codeword and its $2^m - 1$ (time or wavelength) shifted copies to represent the 2^m symbols of m serial data bits per symbol [69, 74]. Figure 2.18 shows an example of shifted-code keying with 4 symbols, in which 4 time positions (within a bit period) are used as the transmission start-time of a codeword. This scheme is different from the nonoverlapping PPM scheme [70, 73] in such a way that no increase in the

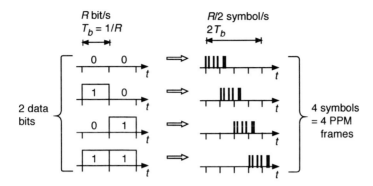

FIGURE 2.18 Example of shifted-code keying with 4 symbols, represented by shifting a codeword to one of the four time positions, where T_b is the bit period and R is the bit rate [69, 74].

number of time slots or the bandwidth expansion is needed. The overlapping PPM scheme in [71,72] belongs to a case of the shifted-code-keying scheme. Shifted-code keying does not require system-wise synchronization or a 2^m-fold increase in code cardinality. Depending on time or wavelength shifts, two tunable transmitter-receiver designs are given in Figures 2.19 and 2.20 [74]. The prime codes that are suitable for shifted-code keying can be found in Section 5.3.

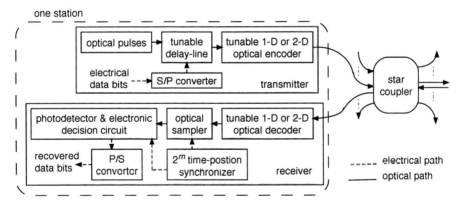

FIGURE 2.19 Tunable transmitter and receiver for shifted-code keying with time-shifted codewords.

Shown in Figure 2.19 is a tunable transmitter and receiver for shifted-code keying with 1-D or 2-D time-spreading codewords and their time-shifted copies [74]. The transmitter consists of a serial-to-parallel (S/P) data-to-symbol converter, a tunable delay-line, and a tunable 1-D or 2-D optical encoder. The S/P data-to-symbol converter groups every m serial data bits to form one of the 2^m symbols. A narrow laser pulse is then delayed to one of the 2^m time positions by the tunable delay-line; the amount of time-delay depends on which symbol is transmitted. The delay-line only needs to be tuned as fast as the symbol rate and consists of the improved serial encoder in Section 2.1 [83, 84]. This optical pulse is then passed through the tunable optical encoder to form the address codeword of its intended receiver with the proper amount of time shift. The receiver consists of a tunable 1-D or 2-D optical decoder, an optical sampler, a 2^m time-position synchronizer, a photodetector, an electronic decision circuit, and a P/S symbol-to-data converter. Because only one time-shifted codeword is transmitted during one symbol period, the intended receiver will see at most one autocorrelation peak per symbol period, but the peak's time position depends on which symbol is received. Time-gated by the 2^m time-position synchronizer, the optical sampler inspects the existence of such a peak at these 2^m positions. The optical sampler consists of optical interferometric devices, such as terahertz optical asymmetric demultiplexers and nonlinear optical loop mirrors [88, 89]. These devices can periodically generate an optical sampling window of size as narrow as several picoseconds by means of ultrafast optical nonlinear effects. So, they can be used to gate very narrow optical features, such as autocorrelation peaks, which appear at most once in each symbol period. Optical signals, such as noise and cross-correlation functions, falling outside the sampling windows are dropped. The received symbol is then determined by the electronic decision circuitry after photodetection. Finally, the data bits are recovered at the P/S symbol-to-data converter.

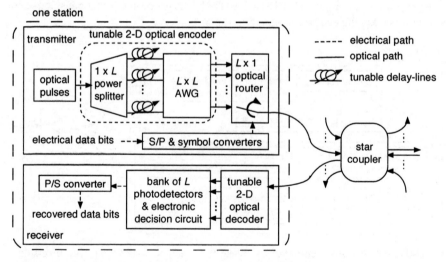

FIGURE 2.20 Tunable transmitter and receiver for shifted-code keying with wavelength-shifted codewords.

Shown in Figure 2.20 is a tunable transmitter and receiver for shifted-code keying with 2-D wavelength-time codewords and their wavelength-shifted copies [74]. These 2-D wavelength-time codewords are assumed to have L distinct wavelengths, and each wavelength is used at most once per codeword, such as the wavelength-shifted carrier-hopping prime codes in Section 5.3. Because L wavelengths can gen-

erate at most L wavelength-shifted copies of a codeword, 2^m-ary shifted-code keying requires $2^m \leq L$. The transmitter consists of an S/P data-to-symbol converter,
an $L \times 1$ optical router, and a tunable 2-D optical encoder. The encoder, which generates wavelength-shifted codewords, consists of a $1 \times L$ power splitter, a set of L
tunable delay-lines, and an $L \times L$ arrayed-waveguide-gratings (AWG) device with
periodic-wavelength assignment [57–60,77]. Wavelength periodicity means that exit
wavelengths at the AWG output ports are rotatable, depending on which input port is
injected with a laser pulse. Assume that the wavelengths of the pulses at output ports
1, 2, 3, and 4 are λ_1, λ_2, λ_3, and λ_4, respectively, when input port 1 of a 4×4 AWG
device is injected with a broadband optical pulse. The wavelengths of the pulses are
then rotated up once and become λ_2, λ_3, λ_4, and λ_1, at output ports 1, 2, 3, and
4, respectively, when input port 2 is injected with the pulse. In this encoder, a nar-
row, broadband laser pulse is first split into L pulses at the power splitter, and these
pulses are delayed by the tunable delay-lines, according to the address codeword of
its intended receiver. All possible wavelength shifts of the codeword are performed
at the $L \times L$ AWG device. Depending on which symbol is transmitted, only one of
the AWG output ports, which has the proper wavelength-shifted codeword, is picked
by the $L \times 1$ optical router.

The receiver consists of one tunable 2-D optical decoder, a bank of L photodetectors, an electronic decision circuit, and a P/S symbol-to-data converter. The decoder,
which has an identical setup as the encoder, is used to reverse the amounts of time
delay and wavelength shift introduced by its corresponding encoder. Because only
one wavelength-shifted codeword is transmitted during one symbol period, the intended receiver will see at most one autocorrelation peak per symbol period at one
of the L output ports of the optical decoder. By identifying which output port has
the autocorrelation peak, the received symbol is finally determined by the electronic
decision circuitry after photodetection. Finally, the data bits are recovered at the P/S
symbol-to-data converter.

2.10   ENABLING HARDWARE TECHNOLOGIES

2.10.1   Wavelength-Aware Hard-Limiting Detector

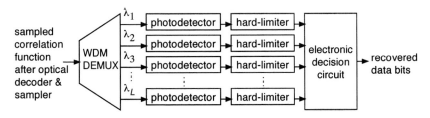

FIGURE 2.21   Wavelength-aware hard-limiting detector for 2-D wavelength-time codes
[91].

As studied in Chapter 1, a hard-limiter can be placed at the front end of an optical decoder to prevent interference from becoming heavily localized in small sections of a cross-correlation function [56, 67, 90]. In concept, the hard-limiter can also equalize the interference strength at nonempty chip positions and eliminate the near-far problem due to unequalized powers of received codewords caused by different transmission distances. However, a fast-response, all-optical hard-limiter that can work with ultrashort optical pulses is still under research. To alleviate this deficiency, Baby et al. [91] proposed a wavelength-aware hard-limiting detector for 2-D wavelength-time codes, as shown in Figure 2.21. This detector is placed at the output of an optical sampler, which is, in turn, connected to the output of a 2-D optical decoder in a receiver. The role of the optical sampler is to periodically generate an optical sampling window of size as narrow as several picoseconds in order to gate autocorrelation peaks, but to remove noise and cross-correlation functions that fall outside the sampling window [88, 89]. The opening of the sampling window is synchronized to the expected time locations of the autocorrelation peaks, which appear at most once in the same time location per bit period, after the correlation process at the optical decoder. With the use of an optical sampler, slower-response photodetectors and electronics can now be used in the wavelength-aware hard-limiting detector. This is because the detector only needs to discriminate the energy strength of the gated signal exiting the optical sampler, but a precise opto-electronic conversion—the actual shape—of the narrow gated signal is not necessary. If strong energy is detected, an autocorrelation peak is decided and a data bit 1 is recovered.

To provide 2-D hard-limiting functionality, the wavelength-aware hard-limiting detector consists of a wavelength DEMUX, a bank of photodetectors and electronic hard-limiters, and an electronic decision circuit. In this setup, the L wavelengths of the gated signal are individually photodetected and hard-limited. Because each wavelength is only counted once after hard-limiting, the probability of getting a decision error is reduced if the strong energy seen at the gated signal is caused by one or more wavelengths being repeated many times in the cross-correlation function. The setup is particularly useful for 2-D wavelength-time codes that use every wavelength exactly once in each codeword, such as the carrier-hopping prime codes in Section 5.1. This is because the gated signal always contains all L wavelengths after hard-limiting if it contains an autocorrelation peak. Finally, by recombining and threshold-detecting the hard-limited signals at the electronic decision circuit, a data bit 1 will be recovered if there still exists an autocorrelation peak.

2.10.2 Fiber Bragg Gratings

Fiber Bragg gratings (FBGs), which periodically vary the refractive index in an optical fiber core, can be used to build in-fiber distributed Bragg (wavelength) reflectors [34, 78–81]. This type of reflector can be used as a WDM device, such as in-fiber wavelength filters and sensors. Shown in Figure 2.22 is a FBG-based, 2-D tunable wavelength-time encoder introduced by Chen [81]. Tunability is achieved using an optical router with an array of multiple FBG fibers. While M different rows are designed with different FBG arrangements for generating M different wavelength-time codewords, a $1 \times M$ optical router is used to route an incoming narrow, broadband

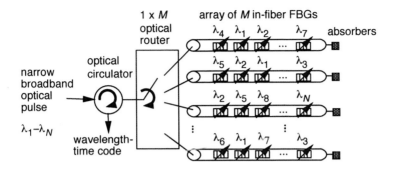

FIGURE 2.22 2-D tunable wavelength-time encoder with in-fiber FBGs [81].

optical pulse to one of these rows. The optical circulator routes the generated codeword to the encoder output.

When a narrow, broadband optical pulse is injected into a section of FBGs, the
input wavelength, which matches the Bragg wavelength $\lambda_B = 2n_{\text{eff}}\Lambda$ of the FBGs,
will be reflected, but the rest of the wavelengths will pass through the FBGs, where
Λ is the resonance grating period and n_{eff} is the effective index of the unmodified
mode [34, 78, 81]. Because there are multiple sections of distinct-Bragg-wavelength
FBGs within a piece of optical fiber, the location of each section determines the
time position of a certain wavelength pulse in a wavelength-time codeword. In addition to the setup in Figure 2.22, a limited degree of tunability can also be achieved
by introducing equal strain to the FBGs in a piece of optical fiber such that these
FBGs see the same amount of Bragg-wavelength shift. The amount of wavelength
shift in a FBG is determined by $\Delta\lambda_{\text{shift}} = 0.8\lambda_B(\Delta L/L)$, where L is the FBG length
and ΔL is the amount of fiber stretch. For example, a typical section of FBGs is of
length $L = 10$ mm, and the maximum amount of strain that can be created is about
$\Delta L = 0.1$ mm, giving $\Delta L/L = 0.01$. At $\lambda_B \approx 1550$ nm, the corresponding wavelength
shift is about $\Delta\lambda_{shift} \approx 12.4$ nm. Assume that the spacing between adjacent wavelengths is 0.8 nm (or 100 GHz in frequency), the number of available wavelengths
obtained by straining the FBGs can be as high as $12.4/0.8 = 15$. By mounting in-
fiber FBGs onto a piezoelectric transducer for strain induction, different wavelength-
shifted codewords, such as those in the shifted carrier-hopping prime codes in Section 5.3, are generated.

2.10.3 Arrayed Waveguide Gratings

Shown in Figure 2.23 is a tunable AWG-based coding device that can be used to
generate 1-D spectral-phase codes, 1-D spectral-amplitude codes, and 2-D spectral-
temporal-amplitude codes. This device features four kinds of tunability. The first
kind of tunability is on the spreading and rotation of the spectral components of
broadband optical pulses. It is achieved by the use of an optical router in conjunction
with the wavelength periodicity of the AWG [57–60, 77]. For an $M \times M$ AWG device

with periodic-wavelength assignment, exit wavelengths at the output ports are rotatable, depending on which input port is injected with a broadband optical pulse. The $1 \times M$ optical router is used to route an incoming pulse to one of the M input ports of the AWG device. The second kind of tunability is supported by tunable delay-lines along each wavelength path for temporal coding. The third kind of tunability is provided by phase modulators for phase coding. The fourth kind of tunability is due to the use of intensity modulators for preserving or dropping optical pulses in some wavelength paths. The properly wavelength-shifted, time-delayed, phase-modulated, and/or intensity-modulated pulses are finally combined at the WDM MUX to generate the desired 1-D spectral-phase codeword, 1-D spectral-amplitude codeword, or 2-D spectral-temporal-amplitude codeword.

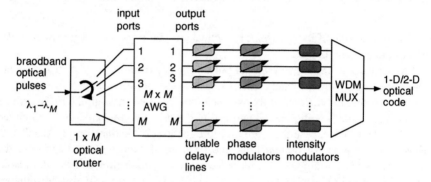

FIGURE 2.23 Tunable AWG-based encoder for 1-D spectral (phase and amplitude) coding and 2-D spectral-temporal coding.

TABLE 2.3

Periodic-Wavelength Assignment of an 8×8 AWG

	Output Port							
	1	2	3	4	5	6	7	8
input port 1	λ_1	λ_2	λ_3	λ_4	λ_5	λ_6	λ_7	λ_8
input port 2	λ_2	λ_3	λ_4	λ_5	λ_6	λ_7	λ_8	λ_1
input port 3	λ_3	λ_4	λ_5	λ_6	λ_7	λ_8	λ_1	λ_2
input port 4	λ_4	λ_5	λ_6	λ_7	λ_8	λ_1	λ_2	λ_3
input port 5	λ_5	λ_6	λ_7	λ_8	λ_1	λ_2	λ_3	λ_4
input port 6	λ_6	λ_7	λ_8	λ_1	λ_2	λ_3	λ_4	λ_5
input port 7	λ_7	λ_8	λ_1	λ_2	λ_3	λ_4	λ_5	λ_6
input port 8	λ_8	λ_1	λ_2	λ_3	λ_4	λ_5	λ_6	λ_7

For an $M \times M$ AWG device with wavelength periodicity, the exit wavelengths, denoted $\lambda_{(i+j) \bmod M}$, at output port j can be represented as a modulo-M addition determined by which input port i is injected with a broadband optical pulse, where i and $j \in [1, M]$. For example, consider an 8×8 AWG device. Assume that the exit wavelengths at the output ports $j = \{1,2,3,4,5,6,7,8\}$ are $\{\lambda_1, \lambda_2, \lambda_3, \lambda_4, \lambda_5, \lambda_6, \lambda_7, \lambda_8\}$, respectively, when input port $i = 1$ is injected with an optical pulse. Then, the exit wavelengths at the output ports $j = \{1,2,3,4,5,6,7,8\}$ are rotated once and become $\{\lambda_2, \lambda_3, \lambda_4, \lambda_5, \lambda_6, \lambda_7, \lambda_8, \lambda_1\}$, respectively, when input port $i = 2$ receives the optical pulse. Table 2.3 tabulates the wavelength at each output port of this 8×8 AWG device as a function of which input port (or row) is applied with a broadband optical pulse. By turning the optical router to the desired input port and tapping into the appropriate output ports, the spectral components of an optical pulse can be separated and rotated rapidly.

TABLE 2.4

Transmission Wavelengths of Spectral-Amplitude Code Based on the Maximal-Length Sequences of Length 7 and Walsh Code of Length 8

	Maximal-Length Sequences	**Wavelength Usage**
C_1	$(+1,+1,+1,-1,-1,+1,-1)$	$\lambda_1 \, \lambda_2 \, \lambda_3 \, \lambda_6$
C_2	$(-1,+1,+1,+1,-1,-1,+1)$	$\lambda_2 \, \lambda_3 \, \lambda_4 \, \lambda_7$
C_3	$(+1,-1,+1,+1,+1,-1,-1)$	$\lambda_1 \, \lambda_3 \, \lambda_4 \, \lambda_5$
C_4	$(-1+1,-1,+1,+1,+1,-1)$	$\lambda_2 \, \lambda_4 \, \lambda_5 \, \lambda_6$
C_5	$(-1,-1,+1,-1,+1,+1,+1)$	$\lambda_3 \, \lambda_5 \, \lambda_6 \, \lambda_7$
C_6	$(+1,-1,-1,+1,-1,+1,+1)$	$\lambda_1 \, \lambda_4 \, \lambda_6 \, \lambda_7$
C_7	$(+1,+1,-1,-1,+1,-1,+1)$	$\lambda_1 \, \lambda_2 \, \lambda_5 \, \lambda_7$

	Walsh Codes	**Wavelengths Usage**
C_1	$(+1,-1,+1,-1,+1,-1,+1,-1)$	$\lambda_1 \, \lambda_3 \, \lambda_5 \, \lambda_7$
C_2	$(+1,+1,-1,-1,+1,+1,-1,-1)$	$\lambda_1 \, \lambda_2 \, \lambda_5 \, \lambda_6$
C_3	$(+1,-1,-1,+1,+1,-1,-1,+1)$	$\lambda_1 \, \lambda_4 \, \lambda_5 \, \lambda_8$
C_4	$(+1,+1,+1,+1,-1,-1,-1,-1)$	$\lambda_1 \, \lambda_2 \, \lambda_3 \, \lambda_4$
C_5	$(+1,-1,+1,-1,-1,+1,-1,+1)$	$\lambda_1 \, \lambda_3 \, \lambda_6 \, \lambda_8$
C_6	$(+1,+1,-1,-1,-1,-1,+1,+1)$	$\lambda_1 \, \lambda_2 \, \lambda_7 \, \lambda_8$
C_7	$(+1,-1,-1,+1,-1,+1,+1,-1)$	$\lambda_1 \, \lambda_4 \, \lambda_6 \, \lambda_7$

To generate 1-D spectral-amplitude codes based on the maximal-length sequence $(+1,+1,+1,-1,-1,+1,-1)$ of length 7, the encoder is configured with $M = 7$, all delay-lines being set to give zero time-delay, and the phase modulators giving zero phase shift. In this configuration, every "+1" element in the maximal-length sequence is transmitted with a wavelength that is determined by the "+1" element's position. The "−1" elements are not transmitted, which is done by turning off the intensity modulators along the corresponding wavelength path. So, the resulting spectral-amplitude codeword C_1 contains $\lambda_1 \lambda_2 \lambda_3 \lambda_6$. There exist totally 7 orthogonal spectral-amplitude codewords $\{C_1, C_2, C_3, \ldots, C_7\}$ by cyclic-shifting this maximal-length sequence, as given in Table 2.4 [10]. Codeword C_i is generated when the 1×7 optical router is turned to input port $i \in [1,7]$ of the 7×7 AWG device.

To generate spectral-amplitude codes based on the "+1" elements of other bipolar codes, such as Walsh codes and "modified" maximal-length sequences of length M [49, 59, 60], wavelength periodicity of the AWG is not useful. (The modified maximal-length sequences of length N are constructed by padding a "−1" to the ends of every maximal-length sequences of length $N - 1$ in order to have the same number of "+1" and "−1" in each sequence.) By setting the $1 \times M$ optical router to one input port and all delay-lines to zero time shift, code generation is tunable through the use of the intensity modulators to select which wavelengths to preserve or drop [16]. Also given in Table 2.4 are Walsh code of length 8, whereas 8 wavelengths are used to represent the "+1" elements in the codewords in accordance to the "+1" element's positions.

Similarly, for 1-D spectral phase coding of bipolar codes, the phase modulators come into play in order to add π phase shifts to the "−1" elements of the codes. For 2-D spectral-temporal amplitude coding, time spreading is achieved by tunable delay-lines in addition to the wavelength selection by the intensity modulators. Variations of this tunable spectral encoder have been proposed for various optical coding schemes in [57–60].

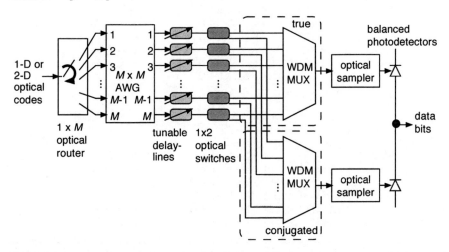

FIGURE 2.24 Tunable AWG-based optical balanced receivers for 1-D spectral (phase and amplitude) coding and 2-D spectral-temporal coding.

Figure 2.24 shows a tunable optical balanced receiver that can be used to correlate 1-D spectral-phase codes, 1-D spectral-amplitude codes, and 2-D spectral-temporal-amplitude codes. The receiver consists of a $1 \times M$ optical router, an $M \times M$ AWG device, a set of M tunable delay-lines and 1×2 optical switches, two WDM MUXs, two optical samplers, and a pair of balanced photodetectors. Because each receiver is assigned with one 1-D or 2-D spectral codeword as its address signature, the top

WDM MUX is used to collect incoming wavelengths that match those wavelengths in its assigned (address) spectral codeword, and the bottom WDM MUX collects the rest of the wavelengths arriving at the receiver. For the case of 1-D spectral ampli- tude coding, the "+1" elements of a bipolar codeword, such as the maximal-length sequences, are conveyed by wavelengths, the "−1" elements are emulated through subtraction at the balanced photodetectors. This is done by routing the wavelengths corresponding to the "−1" elements of the address codeword to the bottom WDM MUX by properly setting the 1×2 optical switches. The tunable delay lines are all set to give zero time-delay. Wavelength tunability is achieved by the $1 \times M$ optical router, which routes incoming 1-D spectral-amplitude codewords to one of the in- put ports of the $M \times M$ AWG device for the proper amount of wavelength rotations. Optical samplers are used to improve the signal-to-interference ratio and reduce the bandwidth requirement of the balanced photodetectors. If one of the arriving code- words matches the address codeword of the receiver, an autocorrelation peak results and is then passed to an electronic hard-limiter/regenerator for data-bit-1 recovery.

For other bipolar codes, such as Walsh codes and modified maximal-length se- quences, tunability is achieved via the use of 1×2 optical switches to route the wavelengths corresponding to the "+1" and "−1" elements of the address codeword to the true and conjugated decoders, respectively. Also, the tunable delay-lines are all set to give zero time-delay. For 2-D spectral-temporal amplitude coding, time despreading is performed by the tunable delay-lines. The unused wavelengths are routed to the bottom WDM MUX and then ignored by disabling the lower optical sampler.

2.11   POTENTIAL APPLICATIONS

As hardware technologies mature, optical coding has been gathering attention and proposed for various applications [33, 34, 36, 37, 39, 60, 92–104]. Experimental O- CDMA testbeds at 10 Gbit/s have been successfully demonstrated. For example, Brés et al. [36] demonstrated an incoherent, tunable, wavelength-time-coding testbed sup- porting 8 simultaneous users by means of four-code keying with the carrier-hopping prime codes in Section 5.1. Hernandez et al. [35] demonstrated a coherent, spectral- phase-coding testbed, supporting 32 simultaneous users by transmitting 8 Walsh codewords in two time slots and two polarizations with forward error correction. Both coherent and incoherent (or synchronous versus asynchronous) coding have their pros and cons. Which one to use depends on the application and operation en- vironment. In fact, they can be used together to complement their deficiencies. For example, coding-based passive optical networks have been recently proposed with the downlink traffic transported by coherent (or synchronous) codes and the uplink traffic carried by incoherent (or asynchronous) codes [60, 92].

Desirable features of optical coding, in particular 2-D spectral-temporal ampli- tude coding, include dynamic bandwidth assignment, efficient in bursty traffic, asyn- chronous and uncoordinated statistical multiple-user access, high scalability for sup- porting more users by simply adding codewords, flexible code-cardinality enlarge- ment by means of increasing the number of wavelengths and/or time slots independently, performance degradation gracefully under heavy traffic, potential data obscurity, and the support of multiple bit rates, variable QoS, multimedia services. It is predictable that optical coding, in particular O-CDMA, is slowly replacing O-TDMA and WDMA as means of contention resolution in optical systems, and gradual upgrade strategies from O-TDMA or WDMA to O-CDMA are being sought. For example, O-CDMA has been proposed to incorporate into various network applications, such as local and metropolitan area networks, burst-mode switching, ring networks, passive optical networks, optical interconnects, optical wireless, optical interconnects, optical microarea networks, and O-CDMA-to-WDM gateways for long-haul WDM backbone [33, 34, 36, 39, 92, 93, 95–97, 99, 101]. In addition, optical coding finds other applications, such as IP-routing, in-service monitoring, and fiber fault surveillance in optical networks and sensor identification in fiber-sensor systems, which use optical codes for the purpose of address or user identification [94, 98, 100, 104].

Last but not least, optical coding theory has unexpectedly found application in the area of preventing four-wave-mixing crosstalk in high-capacity, long-haul, repeaterless, WDM lightwave systems due to fiber nonlinearities. While Forghieri et al. [105, 106] proposed the use of unequal channel spacings in order to prevent four-wave-mixing crosstalk from falling in wavelength channels and solved for the channel spacings by means of integer linear programming with computer exhaustive search, Kwong et al. [107, 108] formulated optimal solutions algebraically by recognizing that the problem was identical to the construction 1-D temporal-amplitude codes with ideal autocorrelation sidelobes.

2.12 SUMMARY

In this chapter, various coding techniques and enabling hardware technologies of the seven major categories of optical coding schemes were investigated. Supporting the transmission of multirate, multimedia services by means of multiple-length codes, and increasing bit rate by means of multicode and shifted-code keying were also reviewed. AWG- and FBG-based programmable encoder/decoder designs were investigated. Finally, the potential applications of optical coding were discussed.

Among these major optical coding schemes, 2-D spectral-temporal amplitude (or wavelength-time) coding is found to be the most advantageous because of 1) simplicity: asynchronous access (no need of global clock), little scheduling, supporting bursty traffic, gradual performance degradation under heavy load, and less sensitive to fiber nonlinearities; 2) ease of implementation: tunable and supporting dynamic services, such as variable QoS and multiple data rates; 3) larger code size and flexible coding in wavelength and time independently; 4) more functionalities: supporting multiple bit rates and QoS by varying code length and weight, better obscurity by means of hopping in wavelength and time, and supporting multicode and shifted-code keying for better spectral efficiency and code obscurity; and 5) better scalability and compatibility: trading bandwidth for scalability, compatible with WDM technology, and supporting overlay and gradual upgrade strategies.

REFERENCES

1. Prucnal, P. R. , Santoro, M. A., Fan, T. R. (1986). Spread spectrum fiber-optic local area network using optical processing. *J. Lightwave Technol.* 4(5):547–554.

2. Prucnal, P. R., Santoro, M. A., Sehgal, S. K. (1986). Ultra-fast all-optical synchronous multiple access fiber networks. *IEEE J. Selected Areas Commun.* 4(9):1484–1493.

3. Foschini, G. J., Vannucci, G. (1987). Spread Spectrum Code-Division-Multiple-Access (SS-CDMA) Lightwave Communication System. US Patent 4,703,474. Issue date: October 27, 1987.

4. Foschini, G. J. (1988). Using spread-spectrum in a high-capacity fiber-optic local network. *J. Lightwave Technol.* 6(3):370–379.

5. Vannucci, G. (1989). Combining frequency-division and code-division multiplexing in a high-capacity optical network. *IEEE Network* 3(2):21–30.

6. Salehi, J. A. (1989). Code division multiple-access techniques in optical fiber networks. I: Fundamental principles. *IEEE Trans. Commun.* 37(8):824–833.

7. Brackett, C. A., Heritage, J. P., Salehi, J. A., Weiner, A. M. (1989). Optical Telecommunications System Using Code Division Multiple Access. US Patent 4,866,699. Issue date: September 12, 1989.

8. Salehi, J. A. (1989). Emerging optical code-division multiple access communications systems. *IEEE Network Mag.* 1(2):31–39.

9. Salehi, J. A., Weiner, A. M., Heritage, J. P. (1990). Coherent ultrashort light pulse code-division multiple access communication systems. *J. Lightwave Technol.* 8(3):478–491.

10. Huang, W., Nizam, M. H. M., Andonovic, I., Tur, M. (2000). Coherent optical CDMA (OCDMA) systems used for high-capacity optical fiber networks—System description, OTDMA comparison, and OCDMA/WDMA networking. *J. Lightwave Technol.* 18(6):765–778.

11. Marhic, M. E. (1993). Coherent optical CDMA networks. *J. Lightwave Technol.* 11(5/6):895–864.

12. Huang, W., Andonovic, I., Tur, M. (1998). Decision-directed PLL for coherent optical pulse CDMA systems in the presence of multiuser interference, laser phase noise, and shot noise. *J. Lightwave Technol.* 16(10):1786–1794.

13. Andonovic, I., Tur, M., Huang, W. (1999). Coherent optical pulse CDMA systems based on coherent correlation detection. *IEEE Trans. Commun.* 47(2):261–271.

14. Mendez, A. J., Gagliardi, R. M., Hernandez, V. J., Bennett, C. V., Lennon, W. J. (2004). High-performance optical CDMA system based on 2-D optical orthogonal codes. *J. Lightwave Technol.* 22(11):2409–2419.

15. Nguyen, L., Dennis, T., Aazhang, B., Young, J. F. (1997). Experimental demonstration of bipolar codes for optical spectral amplitude CDMA communication. *J. Lightwave Technol.* 15(9):1647–1653.

16. Lam, C. F., Tong, D. T. K., Wu, M. C., Yablonovitch, E. (1998). Experimental demonstration of bipolar optical CDMA system using a balanced transmitter and complementary spectral encoding. *IEEE Photon. Technol. Lett.* 10(10):1504–1506.

17. Huang, J.-F., Hsu, D.-Z. (2000). Fiber-grating-based optical CDMA spectral coding with nearly orthogonal *M*-sequence codes. *IEEE Photon. Technol. Lett.* 12(9):1252–1254.

18. Lin, C.-H., Wu, J., Tsao, H.-W., Yang, C.-L., (2005). Spectral amplitude-coding optical CDMA system using Mach-Zehnder interferometers. *J. Lightwave Technol.* 23(4):1543–1555.

19. Sardesai, H. P., Chang, C.-C., Weiner, A. M. (1998). A femtosecond code-division multiple-access communication system test bed. *J. Lightwave Technol.* 16(11):1953–

1964.

20. Cong, W., Yang, C., Scott, R. P., Hernandez, V. J., Fontaine, N. K., Kolner, B. H., Heritage, J. P., Yoo, S. J. B. (2006). Demonstration of 160- and 320-Gb/s SPECTS O-CDMA network testbeds. *IEEE Photon. Technol. Lett.* 18(15):1567–1569.

21. Gao, Z., Wang, X., Kataoka, N., Wada, N. (2011). Rapid reconfigurable OCDMA system using single-phase modulator for time-domain spectral phase encoding/decoding and DPSK data modulation. *J. Lightwave Technol.* 29(3):348–354.

22. Hui, J. Y. N. (1985). Pattern code modulation and optical decoding: A novel code division multiplexing technique for multifiber network. *IEEE J. Selected Areas Commun.* 3(3):916–927.

23. Park, E., Mendez, A. J., Garmire, E. M. (1992). Temporal/spatial optical CDMA networks—Design, demonstration, and comparison with temporal networks. *IEEE Photon. Technol. Lett.* 4(10):1160–1162.

24. Kitayama, K. (1994). Novel spatial spread spectrum based fiber optic CDMA networks for image transmission. *IEEE J Selected Areas Commun.* 12(5):762–772.

25. Hassan, A. A., Hershey, J. E., Riza, N. A. (1995). Spatial optical CDMA. *IEEE J. Selected Areas Commun.* 13(3):609–613.

26. Kwong, W. C., Yang, G.-C. (1998). Image transmission in multicore-fiber code-division multiple-access networks. *IEEE Commun. Lett.* 2(10):285–287.

27. Yeh, B.-C., Lin, C.-H., Yang, C.-L., Wu, J. (2009). Noncoherent spectral/spatial optical CDMA system using 2-D diluted perfect difference codes. *J. Lightwave Technol.* 27(13):2420–2432.

28. Tančevski, L., Andonovic, I. (1996). Hybrid wavelength hopping/time spreading schemes for use in massive optical networks with increased security. *J. Lightwave Technol.* 14(12):2636–2647.

29. Fathallah, H., Rusch, L. A., LaRochelle, S., (1999). Passive optical fast frequency-hop CDMA communications system. *J. Lightwave Technol.* 17(3):397–405.

30. Yu, K., Shin, J., Park, N. (2000). Wavelength-time spreading optical CDMA system using wavelength multiplexers and mirrored fiber delay lines. *IEEE Photon. Technol. Lett.* 12(9):1278–1280.

31. McGeehan, J. E., Nezam, S. M. R. M., Saghari, P., Willner, A. E., Omrani, R., Kumar, P. V. (2005). Experimental demonstration of OCDMA transmission using a three-dimensional (time-wavelength-polarization) codeset. *J. Lightwave Technol.* 23(10):3282–3289.

32. Yeh, B.-C., Lin, C.-H., Wu, J. (2009). Noncoherent spectral/time/spatial optical CDMA system using 3-D perfect difference codes. *J. Lightwave Technol.* 27(6):744–759.

33. Yang, G.-C., Kwong, W. C. (2002). *Prime Codes with Applications to CDMA Optical and Wireless Networks*, Norwood, MA: Artech House.

34. Prucnal, P. R. (ed.) (2006). *Optical Code Division Multiple Access: Fundamentals and Applications*. Boca Raton, FL: Taylor & Francis Group.

35. Hernandez, V. J., Cong, W. , Hu, J., Yang, C., Fontaine, N. K., Scott, R. P., Ding, Z., Kolner, B. H., Heritage, J. P., Yoo, S. J. B. (2007). A 320-Gb/s capacity (32-user × 10 Gb/s) SPECTS O-CDMA network testbed with enhanced spectral efficiency through forward error correction. *J. Lightwave Technol.* 25(1):79–86.

36. Brés, C.-S., Glesk, I., Prucnal, P. R. (2006). Demonstration of an eight-user 115-Gchip/s incoherent OCDMA system using supercontinuum generation and optical time gating. *IEEE Photon. Technol. Lett.* 18(7):889–891.

37. Brés, C.-S., Prucnal, P. R. (2007) Code-empowered lightwave networks. *J. Lightwave*

Technol. 25(10):2911–2921.

38. Kleinrock, L., Tobagi, F. A. (1995). Packet switching in radio channels: Part I. Carrier sense multiple-access modes and their throughput delay characteristics. *IEEE Trans. Commun.* 23(12):1400–1416.

39. Stok, A., Sargent, E. H. (2002). System performance comparison of optical CDMA and WDMA in a broadcast local area network. *IEEE Commun. Lett.* 6(9):409–411.

40. Kwong, W. C., Perrier, P. A., Prucnal, P. R. (1991). Performance comparison of asynchronous and synchronous code-division multiple-access techniques for fiber-optic local area networks. *IEEE Trans. Commun.* 39(11):1625–1634.

41. Kwong, W. C., Yang, G.-C., Zhang, J.-G. (1996). 2^n prime-sequence codes and coding architecture for optical code-division multiple-access. *IEEE Trans. Commun.* 44(9):1152–1162.

42. Yang, G.-C., Kwong, W. C. (1995). On the construction of 2^n codes for optical code-division multiples-access. *IEEE Trans. Commun.* 43(2–4):495–502.

43. Shaar, A. A., Davies, P. A. (1983). Prime sequences: Quasi-optimal sequences for OR channel code division multiplexing. *Electron. Lett.* 19(21):888–890.

44. Chung, F. R. K., Salehi, J. A., Wei, V. K. (1989). Optical orthogonal codes: Design, analysis, and applications. *IEEE Trans. Info. Theory* 35(5):595–604.

45. Chung, H., Kumar, P. V. (1990). Optical orthogonal codes—New bounds and an optimal construction. *IEEE Trans. Info. Theory* 36(4):866–873.

46. Yang, G.-C., Fuja, T. (1995). Optical orthogonal codes with unequal auto- and cross-correlation constraints. *IEEE Trans. Info. Theory* 41(1): 96–106.

47. Yang, G.-C. (1996). Variable-weight optical orthogonal codes for CDMA networks with multiple performance requirements. *IEEE Trans. Commun.* 44(1):47–55.

48. Lam, A. W., Tantaratana, S. (1994). *Theory and Application of Spread-Spectrum Systems—A Self Study Course,* Piscataway, NJ: IEEE Press.

49. Dinan, E. H., Jabbari, B. (1998). Spreading codes for direct sequence CDMA and wideband CDMA cellular networks. *IEEE Commun. Mag.* 36(9):48–54.

50. Zaccarin, D., Kavehrad, M. (1994). Performance evaluation of optical CDMA systems using non-coherent detection bipolar codes. *J. Lightwave Technol.* 12(1):96–105.

51. Wei, Z., Shalaby, H. M. H., Ghafouri-Shiraz, H. (2001). Modified quadratic congruence codes for fiber Bragg-grating-based spectral-amplitude-coding optical CDMA systems. *J. Lightwave Technol.* 19(9):1274–1281.

52. Wei, Z., Ghafouri-Shiraz, H. (2002). Unipolar codes with ideal in-phase cross-correlation for spectral amplitude-coding optical CDMA systems. *IEEE Trans. Commun.* 50(8):1209–1212.

53. Yang, G.-C., Kwong, W. C. (1996). Two dimensional spatial signature patterns. *IEEE Trans. Commun.* 44(2):184–191.

54. Perrier, P. A., Prucnal, P. R. (1988). Wavelength-division integration of services in fiber-optic networks. *Inter. J. Digital Analog Cabled Systems* 1(3):149–157.

55. Yang, G.-C., Kwong, W. C. (1997). Performance comparison of multiwavelength CDMA and WDMA+CDMA for fiber-optic networks. *IEEE Trans. Commun.* 45(11):1426–1434.

56. Kwong, W. C., Yang, G.-C., Baby, V., Brès, C.-S., Prucnal, P. R. (2005). Multiple-wavelength optical orthogonal codes under prime-sequence permutations for optical CDMA. *IEEE Trans. Commun.* 53(1):117–123.

57. Kwong, W. C., Yang, G.-C., Liu, Y.-C. (2005). A new family of wavelength-time optical CDMA codes utilizing programmable arrayed waveguide gratings. *IEEE J. Selected*

Areas Commun. 23(8):1564–1571.

58. Kwong, W. C., Yang, G.-C., Chang, C.-Y. (2005). Wavelength-hopping time-spreading optical CDMA with bipolar codes. *J. Lightwave Technol.* 23(1):260–267.

59. Hsieh, C.-P., Chang, C.-Y., Yang, G.-C., Kwong, W. C. (2006). A bipolar-bipolar code for asynchronous wavelength-time optical CDMA. *IEEE Trans. Commun.* 54(7):1190–1194.

60. Hu, H.-W., Chen, H.-T., Yang, G.-C., Kwong, W. C. (2007). Synchronous Walsh-based bipolar-bipolar code for CDMA passive optical networks. *J. Lightwave Technol.* 25(8):1910–1917.

61. Baby, V., Glesk, I., Runser, R. J., Fischer, R., Huang, Y.-K., Brés, C.-S., Kwong,W. C., Curtis, T. H., Prucnal, P. R. (2005). Experimental demonstration and scalability analysis of a four-node 102-Gchip/s fast frequency-hopping time-spreading optical CDMA network. *IEEE Photon. Technol. Lett.* 17(1):253–255.

62. Shake, T. H. (2005). Security performance of optical CDMA against eavesdropping. *J. Lightwave Technol.* 23(2):655–670.

63. Kim, S., Yu, K., Park, N. (2000). A new family of space/wavelength/time spread three-dimensional optical code for OCDMA networks. *J. Lightwave Technol.* 18(4):502–511.

64. Kwong, W. C., Yang, G.-C. (2001). Double-weight signature pattern codes for multicore-fiber code-division multiple-access networks. *IEEE Commun. Lett.* 5(5):203–205.

65. Kwong, W. C., Yang, G.-C. (2002). Design of multilength optical orthogonal codes for optical CDMA multimedia networks. *IEEE Trans. Commun.* 50(8):1258–1265.

66. Kwong, W. C., Yang, G.-C. (2004). Multiple-length, multiple-wavelength optical orthogonal codes for optical CDMA systems supporting multirate, multimedia services. *IEEE J. Selected Areas Commun.* 22(9):1640–1647.

67. Kwong, W. C., Yang, G.-C. (2005). Multiple-length extended carrier-hopping prime codes for optical CDMA systems supporting multirate, multimedia services. *J. Lightwave Technol.* 23(11):3653–3662.

68. Baby, V., Kwong, W. C., Chang, C.-Y., Yang, G.-C., Prucnal, P. R. (2007). Performance analysis of variable-weight, multilength optical codes for wavelength-time O-CDMA multimedia systems. *IEEE Trans. Commun.* 55(7):1325–1333.

69. Chen, H.-W., Yang, G.-C., Chang, C.-Y., Lin, T.-C., Kwong, W. C. (2009). Spectral efficiency study of two multirate schemes for optical CDMA with/without symbol synchronization. *J. Lightwave Technol.* 27(14):2771–2778.

70. Shalaby, H. M. H. (1995). Performance analysis of optical synchronous CDMA communication systems with PPM signaling. *IEEE Trans. Commun.* 43(2):624–634.

71. Shalaby, H. M. H. (1999). A performance analysis of optical overlapping PPM-CDMA communication systems. *J. Lightwave Technol.* 17(3):426–433.

72. Kim, J. Y., Poor, H. V. (2001). Turbo-coded optical direct-detection CDMA system with PPM modulation. *J. Lightwave Technol.* 19(3):312–323.

73. Kamakura, K., Yashiro, K. (2003). An embedded transmission scheme using PPM signaling with symmetric error-correcting codes for optical CDMA. *J. Lightwave Technol.* 21(7):1601–1611.

74. Narimanov, E., Kwong, W. C., Yang, G.-C., Prucnal, P. R. (2005). Shifted carrier-hopping prime codes for multicode keying in wavelength-time O-CDMA. *IEEE Trans. Commun.* 53(12):2150–2156.

75. Chang, C.-Y., Yang, G.-C., Kwong, W. C. (2006). Wavelength-time codes with maximum cross-correlation functions of two for multicode keying optical CDMA. *J. Light-*

wave Technol. 24(3):1093–1100.

76. Chang, C.-Y., Chen, H.-T., Yang, G.-C., Kwong, W. C. (2007). Spectral efficiency study of quadratic-congruence carrier-hopping prime codes in multirate optical CDMA system. *IEEE J. Selected Areas Commun.* 25(9):118–128.

77. Takahashi, H., Oda, K., Toba, H., Inoue, Y. (1995). Transmission characteristics of arrayed waveguide $N \times N$ wavelength multiplexer. *J. Lightwave Technol.* 13(3):447–455.

78. Chen, L. R., Benjamin, S. D., Smith, P. W. E., Sipe, J. E. (1998). Applications of ultrashort pulse propagation in Bragg gratings for wavelength-division multiplexing and code-division multiple access *IEEE J. Quantum Electron.* 34(11):2117–2129.

79. Teh, P. C., Petropoulos, P., Ibsen, M., Richardson, D. J. (2000). A comparative study of the performance of seven- and 63-chip optical code-division multiple-access encoders and decoders based on superstructured fiber Bragg gratings. *J. Lightwave Technol.* 19(9):1352–1365.

80. Teh, P. C., Petropoulos, P., Ibsen, M., Richardson, D. J. (2001). Phase encoding and decoding of short pulses at 10 Gb/s using superstructured fiber Bragg gratings. *IEEE Photon. Technol. Lett.* 13(2):154–156.

81. Chen, L. R. (2001). Flexible fiber Bragg grating encoder/decoder for hybrid wavelength-time optical CDMA. *IEEE Photon. Technol. Lett.*, 13(11):1233–1235.

82. Zeng, F., Wang, Q., Yao, J. (2007). Sequence-inversion-keyed optical CDMA coding/decoding scheme using an electrooptic phase modulator and fiber Bragg grating arrays. *IEEE J. Selected Topics Quantum Electron.* 13(5):1508–1515.

83. Prucnal, P. R., Krol, M., Stacy, J. (1991). Demonstration of a rapidly tunable optical time-division multiple-access coder. *IEEE Photon. Technol. Lett.* 3(2):170–172.

84. Deng, K.-L., Runser, R. J., Toliver, P., Glesk, I., Prucnal, P. R. (2000). A highly-scalable, rapidly-reconfigurable, multicasting-capable, 100 Gb/s photonic switched interconnect based upon OTDM technology. *J. Lightwave Technol.* 18(12):1892–1904.

85. Djordjev, K., Choi, S.-J., Dapkus, R. D. (2002). Microdisk tunable resonant filters and switches. *IEEE Photon. Technol. Lett.* 14(6):828–830.

86. Huang, Y.-K., Baby, V., Prucnal, P. R., Greiner, C. M., Iazikov, D., Mossberg, T. W. (2005). Integrated holographic encoder for wavelength-hopping/time-spreading optical CDMA. *IEEE Photon. Technol. Lett.* 17(4):825–827.

87. Maric, S. V., Lau, V. K. N. (1998). Multirate fiber-optic CDMA: System design and performance analysis. *J. Lightwave Technol.*, 16(1):9–17.

88. Lee, J.-H., Teh, P. C., Petropoulos, P., Ibsen, M., Richardson, D. J. (2002). A grating-based OCDMA coding-decoding system incorporating a nonlinear optical loop mirror for improved code recognition and noise reduction. *J. Lightwave Technol.* 20(1):36–46.

89. Sokoloff, J. P., Prucnal, P. R., Glesk, I., Kane, M. (1993). A terahertz optical asymmetric demultiplexer (TOAD). *IEEE Photon. Technol. Lett.* 5(7):787–790.

90. Hsu, C.-C., Yang, G.-C., Kwong, W. C. (2008). Hard-limiting performance analysis of 2-D optical codes under the chip-asynchronous assumption, *IEEE Trans. Commun.* 56(5):762–768.

91. Baby, V., Brés, C.-S., Glesk, I., Xu, L., Prucnal, P. R. (2004). wavelength aware receiver for enhanced 2D OCDMA system performance. *Electron. Lett.* 40(6):385–387.

92. Lundqvist, H., Karlsson, G. (2005). On error-correction coding for CDMA PON. *J. Lightwave Technol.* 23(8):2342–2351.

93. Menendez, R. C., Toliver, P., Galli, S., Agarwal, A., Banwell, T., Jackel, J., Young, J., Etemad, S. (2005). Network applications of cascaded passive code translation for WDM-compatible spectrally phase-encoded optical CDMA. *J. Lightwave Technol.*

23(10):3219–3231.

94. Yeh, C., Chi, S. (2005). Optical fiber-fault surveillance for passive optical networks in S-band operation window. *Optics Express* 13(14):5494–5498.

95. Meenakshi, M., Andonovic, I. (2006). Code-based all optical routing using two-level coding. *J. Lightwave Technol.* 24(4):1627–1637.

96. Khattab, T., Alnuweiri, H. (2007). Optical CDMA for all-optical sub-wavelength switching in core GMPLS networks. *J. Selected Areas Commun.* 25(5):905–921.

97. Farnoud, F., Ibrahimi, M., Salehi, J. A. (2007). A packet-based photonic label switching router for a multirate all-optical CDMA-based GMPLS switch. *IEEE J. Selected Topics Quantum Electron.* 13(5):1522–1530.

98. Fathallah, H. A., Rusch, L. A. (2007). Code division multiplexing for in-service out-of-band monitoring of live FTTH-PONs. *J. Optical Networking* 6(7):819–829.

99. Ghaffari, B. M., Matinfar, M. D., Salehi, J. A. (2008). Wireless optical CDMA LAN: Digital design concepts. *IEEE Trans. Commun.* 56(12):2145–2155.

100. Rad, M. M., Fathallah, H. A., Rusch, L. A. (2008). Fiber fault monitoring for passive optical networks using hybrid 1-D/2-D coding. *IEEE Photon. Technol. Lett.* 20(24):2054–2056.

101. Sowailem, M. Y. S., Morsy, M. H. S., Shalaby, H. M. H. (2009). Employing code domain for contention resolution in optical burst switched networks with detailed performance analysis. *J. Lightwave Technol.* 27(23):5284–5294.

102. Beyranvand, H., Salehi, J. A. (2009). All-optical multiservice path switching in optical code switched GMPLS core network. *J. Lightwave Technol.* 27(12):2001–2012.

103. Deng, Y., Wang, Z., Kravtsov, K., Chang, J., Hartzell, C., Fok, M. P., Prucnal, P. R. (2010). Demonstration and analysis of asynchronous and survivable optical CDMA ring networks. *J. Optical Commun. Networking* 2(4):159–165.

104. Rad, M. M., Fathallah, H. A., Rusch, L. A. (2010). Fiber fault PON monitoring using optical coding: Effects of customer geographic distribution. *IEEE Trans. Commun.* 58(4):1172–1181.

105. Forghieri, F., Tkach, R. W., Chraplyvy, A. R., Marcuse, D. (1994). Reduction of four-wave mixing crosstalk in WDM systems using unequally spaced channels. *IEEE Photon. Technol. Lett.*, 6(6):754–756.

106. Forghieri, F., Gnauck, A. H., Tkach, R. W., Chraplyvy, A. R., Derosier, R. M. (1994). Repeaterless transmission of eight channels at 10 Gb/s over 137 km (11 Tb/s-km) of dispersion-shifted fiber using unequal channel spacing. *IEEE Photon. Technol. Lett.* 6(11):1374–1376.

107. Kwong, W. C., Yang, G.-C. (1997). An algebraic approach to the unequal-spaced channel-allocation problem in WDM lightwave systems. *IEEE Trans. Commun.* 45(3):352–359

108. Chang, K.-D., Yang, G.-C., Kwong, W. C. (2000). Determination of FWM products in unequal-spaced-channel WDM lightwave systems. *J. Lightwave Technol.* 18(12):2113–2122.

3 1-D Asynchronous Prime Codes

Based on the concept of linear congruence [1,2], prime codes were traditionally designed to have low cross-correlation functions and support asynchronous transmissions. In 1978, Cooper and Nettleton [3] introduced the first version of prime codes for cellular mobile frequency-hopping spread-spectrum communication systems, supporting asynchronous transmissions from mobile units to a base station [4–7]. In 1981, Titlebaum [8] introduced a family of frequency-time prime codes for coherent multiuser radar and asynchronous frequency-hopping spread-spectrum communication systems. Belonging to a family of extended cyclic Reed–Solomon codes, these prime codes are maximum distance separable cyclic codes [1,2]. In 1983, Shaar and Davis [9] introduced a family of prime sequences and binary unipolar codewords, collectively called the original prime codes in this book, for asynchronous temporal-amplitude O-CDMA. In 1986, Prucnal et al. [10,11] demonstrated the first all-optical encoder and decoder, which employed fiber-optic delay-lines, for the generation and correlation of these prime codes.

In this chapter, the constructions, properties, and performances of several families of 1-D asynchronous prime codes—in particular, the original prime codes, extended prime codes, generalized prime codes, and 2^n prime codes—are studied [12–17]. The constructions of several families of optical orthogonal codes (OOCs) [18–32], another category of 1-D binary unipolar codes designed for incoherent temporal amplitude coding, are illustrated. These OOCs can be used to generate some families of 2-D prime codes in Chapters 5 and 6 [20–22].

3.1 ORIGINAL PRIME CODES

The original prime codes, initially designed for temporal amplitude coding, were introduced by Shaar and Davis [9]. Based on Galois field GF(p) of a prime number p, a prime sequence $S_i = (s_{i,0}, s_{i,1}, \ldots, s_{i,j}, \ldots, s_{i,p-1})$ is constructed by the element

$$s_{i,j} = ij \pmod{p} \tag{3.1}$$

where $s_{i,j}$, i, and j are all in GF(p). There are a total of p prime sequences, S_i, indexed by $i = \{0, 1, \ldots, p-1\}$.

Each of these p prime sequences is mapped into a binary $(0,1)$ codeword $C_i = (c_{i,0}, c_{i,1}, \ldots, c_{i,l}, \ldots, c_{i,p^2-1})$, indexed by $i = \{0, 1, \ldots, p-1\}$, of length p^2 with the code element [9, 12, 17]

$$c_{i,l} = \begin{cases} 1 & \text{if } l = s_{i,j} + jp \text{ for } j = \{0, 1, \ldots, p-1\} \\ 0 & \text{otherwise} \end{cases} \tag{3.2}$$

Each code element $c_{i,l}$ is traditionally called a *chip*. The binary 1s (or pulses) in the codewords are called *mark* chips.

Because there are p pulses in each codeword, the weight and cardinality of the original prime codes of length p^2 over GF(p) are both equal to p. It is the characteristic of asynchronous codes, and these original prime codes, that the code weight w can be less than p by simply dropping $p - w$ pulses from every codeword, without affecting the cross-correlation properties.

TABLE 3.1

Prime Sequences and Codewords over GF(5)

i	S_i	C_i
0	0 0 0 0 0	10000 10000 10000 10000 10000
1	0 1 2 3 4	10000 01000 00100 00010 00001
2	0 2 4 1 3	10000 00100 00001 01000 00010
3	0 3 1 4 2	10000 00010 01000 00001 00100
4	0 4 3 2 1	10000 00001 00010 00100 01000

TABLE 3.2

Prime Sequences and Codewords over GF(7)

i	S_i	C_i
0	0 0 0 0 0 0 0	1000000 1000000 1000000 1000000 1000000 1000000 1000000
1	0 1 2 3 4 5 6	1000000 0100000 0010000 0001000 0000100 0000010 0000001
2	0 2 4 6 1 3 5	1000000 0010000 0000100 0000001 0100000 0001000 0000010
3	0 3 6 2 5 1 4	1000000 0001000 0000001 0010000 0000010 0100000 0000100
4	0 4 1 5 2 6 3	1000000 0000100 0100000 0000010 0010000 0000001 0001000
5	0 5 3 1 6 4 2	1000000 0000010 0001000 0100000 0000001 0000100 0010000
6	0 6 5 4 3 2 1	1000000 0000001 0000010 0000100 0001000 0010000 0100000

For illustration, Tables 3.1 and 3.2 show the prime sequences and binary $(0, 1)$ codewords over GF(5) and GF(7), respectively.

Assuming chip synchronism for mathematical convenience, the amount of mutual interference generated by these prime codes is characterized by the discrete 1-D periodic cross-correlation function defined in Section 1.5. This periodic cross-correlation function counts the number of coincidences of pulses (or so-called *hits*) between any two correlating codewords. This is a function of the amount of relative discrete shift (in terms of the number of time slots or chips) between the two codewords. For each codeword, its own correlation represents an autocorrelation function with a higher peak, which is usually equal to the code weight. Because the coding algorithm is based on the concept of linear congruence in the number theory [8], the correlation properties of the prime codes can be proved algebraically.

Theorem 3.1

The autocorrelation peaks of the original prime codes over GF(p) of a prime p and weight w are equal to w, where $w \le p$. The periodic cross-correlation functions of the codes are at most 2, but at most 1 if the codeword C_0 is one of the correlating codewords [9, 17].

Proof Let C_i and $C_{i'}$ be two distinct prime codewords for i and $i' = \{1, 2, \ldots, p-1\}$, where $i \neq i'$. Because each element in a prime sequence determines the chip position of a pulse in a group of p chips in Equation (3.2), every binary codeword can be divided into p blocks and each block has p chips. So, there is exactly one pulse in the jth block of C_i, located in chip position ij (mod p), where $j = \{0, 1, \ldots, p-1\}$. Let $C_i^{(\tau)}$ represent the shifted version of C_i after C_i has been (right) cyclic-shifted by τ chips. Assume that $x \in [0, p-1]$, $y \in [0, p-1]$, and $\tau = xp + y$. So, $y = \tau$ (mod p) enumerates the p chip positions in each block. Due to the τ-shifts, there may exist up to two pulses in the jth block of $C_i^{(\tau)}$ and two possible cases to consider:

1. If $[i(j-x) \pmod{p}] + y < p$, then one pulse is in chip position $[i(j-x) \pmod{p}] + y$. This pulse comes from the $(j-x)$th block of C_i, being shifted into the jth block of $C_i^{(\tau)}$.
2. If $[i(j-x-1) \pmod{p}] + y \ge p$, then one pulse is in chip position $[i(j-x-1) \pmod{p}] + y - p$. This pulse comes from the $(j-x-1)$th block of C_i, being shifted into the jth block of $C_i^{(\tau)}$.

If there is a hit (or pulse overlap) in the jth blocks of $C_i^{(\tau)}$ and $C_{i'}$, then either one or both of the following equations must hold:

$$[i(j-x) \pmod{p}] + y = i'j \pmod{p} \tag{3.3}$$

$$[i(j-x-1) \pmod{p}] + y - p = i'j \pmod{p} \tag{3.4}$$

Because they are linear functions of j over GF(p), at most one solution of j can be found in each equation. As the number of blocks containing a hit cannot exceed the number of solutions of j, there may exist two hits in at most two blocks. So, the maximum periodic cross-correlation function is 2.

For $i = 0$, there is always at most one pulse in any block for any τ-shift in $C_0^{(\tau)}$. So, the periodic cross-correlation function is at most 1 as the aforementioned two-pulse-per-block cases do not exist.

Finally, the autocorrelation peaks of w are due to the code weight $w \le p$. ∎

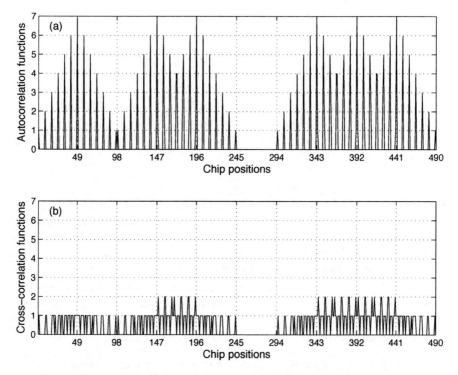

FIGURE 3.1 Examples of (a) autocorrelation functions of the original prime codeword C_1 and (b) cross-correlation functions of C_1 and C_2, both over GF(7) and of length 49 and weight 7, for the transmission of data-bit stream 1011001110 in OOK.

Figure 3.1 shows the autocorrelation functions of the original prime codeword C_1 and cross-correlation functions of C_1 and C_2, both over GF(7) and of length 49 and weight 7, for the transmission of data-bit stream 1011001110 in on-off-keying (OOK) modulation. In OOK, each data bit 1 is conveyed by a codeword, but nothing is transmitted for a data bit 0. As shown in Figure 3.1, the autocorrelation peaks are equal to 7 and the periodic cross-correlation functions are at most 2, agreeing with Theorem 3.1.

3.1.1 Performance Analysis

In this section, the performance of the original prime codes, which have the maximum periodic cross-correlation function of 2, is analyzed. The negative effect of physical noises is ignored in order to concentrate on the effect of mutual interference created by interfering codewords. The analyses in this book assume interference-limited scenarios with infinite signal-to-interference power ratio (SIR) so that the true performance of optical codes can be studied.

According to Section 1.8.1, the Gaussian error probability of the original prime codes over GF(p) of a prime p and weight $w \leq p$ in OOK is given by

$$P_{e|G} = Q\left(\frac{\sqrt{\text{SIR}}}{2}\right) = Q\left(\frac{1}{2}\sqrt{\frac{w^2}{(K-1)\sigma^2}}\right) \tag{3.5}$$

where $Q(x) = (1/\sqrt{2\pi})\int_x^\infty \exp\left(-y^2/2\right)dy$ is the complementary error function, SIR is defined as the ratio of the autocorrelation peak, which is usually equal to w, squared to the total interference variance $(K-1)\sigma^2$, and $K-1$ is the number of interfering codewords. By the Central Limit Theorem, this approximation is valid for a large number of simultaneous users (or simultaneously transmitting codewords) K.

Theorem 3.2

For the original prime codes over GF(p) of a prime p with cardinality $\Phi = p$, length $N = p^2$, and weight $w \leq p$, the hit probabilities, q_i, of having the periodic cross-correlation values $i = \{0,1,2\}$ (in the sampling time) are formulated as [17]

$$q_2 \leq \frac{w(w^2-1)(p-2)}{12(p-1)p^3}$$

$$q_1 = \frac{w^2}{2p^2} - 2q_2$$

$$q_0 = 1 - \frac{w^2}{2p^2} + q_2$$

respectively, whereas equality occurs when $w = p$.

The variance of the interference caused by each interfering codeword is found to be

$$\sigma^2 = \sum_{i=1}^{2}\sum_{j=0}^{i-1}(i-j)^2 q_i q_j = q_0 q_1 + 4q_0 q_2 + q_1 q_2$$

Proof Assuming OOK and that data bit 0s and 1s are equiprobable, the hit probabilities of a prime codeword, say C_i, correlating with another codeword in the code set are related by [17,33]

$$0 \times q_0^i + 1 \times q_1^i + 2 \times q_2^i = \frac{w^2}{2N} = \frac{w^2}{2p^2}$$

and $q_0^i + q_1^i + q_2^i = 1$, according to Section 1.8.1, where $i = \{0,1,\ldots,\Phi-1\}$. Let Z denote the cross-correlation value seen by the intended receiver (in the sampling time), V denote the interferer's codeword, and U denote the receiver's address codeword. From [17], the probability of getting two hits is given by

$$
\begin{aligned}
q_2^i &= \Pr(Z = 2, V = C_{i'} \mid U = C_i, i' \neq i) \\
&= \sum_{i'=0, i' \neq i}^{w-1} \Pr(Z = 2, V = C_{i'}, U = C_i) \Pr(V = C_{i'} \mid U = C_i) \\
&= \frac{1}{\Phi - 1} \sum_{i'=0, i' \neq i}^{w-1} \Pr(Z = 2, V = C_{i'}, U = C_i) \\
&= \frac{1}{2(\Phi - 1)} \sum_{i'=0, i' \neq i}^{w-1} \Pr(Z = 2, V = C_{i'}, U = C_i \mid \text{interferer } i' \text{ sent bit 1}) \\
&\leq \frac{1}{2(\Phi - 1)} \times \frac{\sum_{y=1}^{w-1} y(w-y) - i(w-i)}{p^2} \\
&\leq \frac{(w-1)w(w+1) - 6i(w-i)}{12(\Phi - 1)p^2}
\end{aligned}
$$

The derivation is based on the facts that there is no interference for a data bit 0 in OOK, interferer i' sends data bit 1s and 0s with equal probability, $\Pr(V = C_{i'} \mid U = C_i) = 1/(\Phi - 1)$ due to the existence of $\Phi - 1$ possible interferers, and there are p^2 possible cyclic shifts due to code length $N = p^2$. Follow the proof of Theorem 3.1, for code weight $w \leq p$, it is found that the number of solutions of j in Equation (3.4) is $w - y$ if the number of solutions of j in Equation (3.3) is y. The term $i(w-i)$ represents the number of hits being overcounted due to $i' = 0$, in which Equation (3.3) does not hold. In this case, if the number of solutions of j in Equation (3.3) is i, the number of solutions of j in Equation (3.4) is $w - i$.

Finally, averaging q_2^i for all codewords with $i = \{0, 1, \dots, \Phi - 1\}$ results in

$$
q_2 \leq \frac{1}{p} \sum_{i=1}^{\Phi-1} \frac{(w-1)w(w+1) - 6i(w-i)}{12(\Phi - 1)p^2} = \frac{w(w^2 - 1)(\Phi - 2)}{12\Phi(\Phi - 1)p^2}
$$

where $6i(w-i) = 0$ if $i > w$. Similarly, q_1 and q_0 are derived by averaging $q_1^i = w^2/(2p^2) - 2q_2^i$ and $q_0^i = 1 - w^2/(2p^2) + q_2^i$ for all $i = \{0, 1, \dots, \Phi - 1\}$.

According to Section 1.8.1, the variance of each interfering codeword is given by $\sigma^2 = \sum_{i=1}^{\lambda_c} \sum_{j=0}^{i-1}(i - j)^2 q_i q_j$ with $\lambda_c = 2$ for the original prime codes. After some manipulations, the final form in the theorem is derived. ∎

Following the combinatorial methods in Sections 1.8.3 and 1.8.4, the chip-synchronous, soft- and hard-limiting error probabilities of the original prime codes over $GF(p)$ of a prime p with length $N = p^2$, weight $w \leq p$, and the maximum periodic cross-correlation function of 2 in OOK are given by [17,33–35]

$$
P_{e,\text{soft}} = \frac{1}{2} - \frac{1}{2} \sum_{l_1=0}^{Z_{\text{th}}-1} \sum_{l_2=0}^{\lfloor (Z_{\text{th}}-1-l_1)/2 \rfloor} \frac{(K-1)!}{l_1! l_2! (K-1-l_1-l_2)!} q_1^{l_1} q_2^{l_2} q_0^{K-1-l_1-l_2} \qquad (3.6)
$$

and

$$P_{e,\text{hard}} = \frac{1}{2} \sum_{h=Z_{\text{th}}}^{w} \frac{w!}{h!(w-h)!} \sum_{i=0}^{h} (-1)^{h-i} \frac{h!}{i!(h-i)!} \left[q_0 + \frac{i q_1}{w} + \frac{i(i-1)q_2}{w(w-1)} \right]^{K-1} \quad (3.7)$$

respectively, where the decision threshold $Z_{\text{th}} = w$ is usually applied for optimal decision and $\lfloor \cdot \rfloor$ is the floor function.

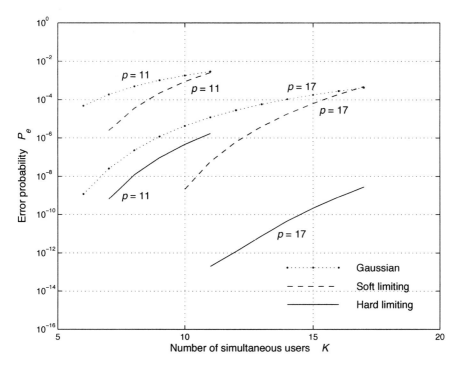

FIGURE 3.2 Error probabilities of the original prime codes over GF(p) for $N = p^2$ and $w = p = \{11, 17\}$.

Figure 3.2 plots the Gaussian [from Equation (3.5)], and chip-synchronous, soft-limiting [from Equation (3.6)] and hard-limiting [from Equation (3.7)] error probabilities of the original prime codes over GF(p) against the number of simultaneous users K for $p = \{11, 17\}$. In general, the error probabilities improve as p increases because of heavier code weight ($w = p$) and longer length ($N = p^2$), resulting in higher autocorrelation peaks and lower hit probabilities, respectively. The error probabilities get worse as K increases due to stronger mutual interference. The hard-limiting error probabilities are always better than the soft-limiting counterparts for the same p. While the Gaussian method provides a fast tool to approximate code performance, it tends to overestimate the error probability, especially when K is small. As K increases, the Gaussian curves approach the soft-limiting curves because the accuracy of the approximation improves in accordance with the Central Limit Theorem.

3.2   EXTENDED PRIME CODES

For binary $(0,1)$ codes, the periodic cross-correlation functions are always nonzero and need to be as low as possible in order to minimize the amount of mutual interference. With this goal in mind, the extended prime codes are here designed to have the maximum periodic cross-correlation function of 1. This is achieved by padding every "block" in the original prime codewords with $p-1$ trailing 0s. (See the proof of Theorem 3.1 for the definition of "block.")

Based on $\mathrm{GF}(p)$ of a prime number p, each of the p prime sequences, S_i, given in Equation (3.1) is now mapped into a binary $(0,1)$ codeword $E_i = (e_{i,0}, e_{i,1}, \ldots, e_{i,l}, \ldots, e_{i,p(2p-1)-1})$, indexed by $i = \{0, 1, \ldots, p-1\}$, with the code element [13, 17]

$$e_{i,l} = \begin{cases} 1 & \text{if } l = s_{i,j} + j(2p-1) \text{ for } j = \{0,1,\ldots,p-1\} \\ 0 & \text{otherwise} \end{cases}$$

This construction results in the extended prime codes of cardinality p, length $p(2p-1)$, and weight p.

Similar to the original prime codes, the code weight w can be less than p by simply dropping $p-w$ pulses from every extended prime codeword without affecting the cross-correlation properties.

For illustration, Table 3.3 shows the prime sequences and extended prime codewords over $\mathrm{GF}(5)$.

TABLE 3.3

Extended Prime Codewords over GF(5)

i	S_i	E_i
0	0 0 0 0 0	100000000 100000000 100000000 100000000 100000000
1	0 1 2 3 4	100000000 010000000 001000000 000100000 000010000
2	0 2 4 1 3	100000000 001000000 000010000 010000000 000100000
3	0 3 1 4 2	100000000 000100000 010000000 000010000 001000000
4	0 4 3 2 1	100000000 000010000 000100000 001000000 010000000

Theorem 3.3

The autocorrelation peaks of the extended prime codes over $\mathrm{GF}(p)$ of a prime p and weight w are equal to w, where $w \leq p$. The periodic cross-correlation functions of the codes are at most 1 [13, 17].

Proof The proof is similar to that of Theorem 3.1. Let E_i and $E_{i'}$ be two distinct extended prime codewords for i and $i' = \{1, 2, \ldots, p-1\}$, where $i \neq i'$. Based on the construction, every extended prime codeword can be divided into p blocks, each block has $2p - 1$ chips, and there is only one pulse per block. So, there is exactly one pulse in the jth block of E_i, located in chip position ij (mod p), where $j = \{0, 1, \ldots, p-1\}$. Let $E_i^{(\tau)}$ represent the shifted version of E_i after E_i has been (right) cyclic-shifted by τ chips. Assume that $x \in [0, p-1]$, $y \in [0, 2p-2]$, and $\tau = x(2p - 1) + y$. So, $y = \tau$ (mod $2p - 1$) enumerates the $2p - 1$ chip positions in each block. Due to the τ-shift, there may exist up to two pulses in the jth block of $E_i^{(\tau)}$ and two possible cases to consider:

1. If $[i(j-x)$ (mod $p)] + y < 2p - 1$, then one pulse is in chip position $[i(j-x)$ (mod $p)] + y$. This pulse comes from the $(j-x)$th block of E_i, being shifted into the jth block of $E_i^{(\tau)}$.
2. If $[i(j-x-1)$ (mod $p)] + y \geq 2p - 1$, then one pulse is in chip position $[i(j-x-1)$ (mod $p)] + y - p$. This pulse comes from the $(j-x-1)$th block of E_i, being shifted into the jth block of $E_i^{(\tau)}$.

If there is a hit in the jth blocks of $E_i^{(\tau)}$ and $E_{i'}$, then one of the following equations must hold:

$$[i(j-x) \quad (\text{mod } p)] + y = i'j \quad (\text{mod } p)$$

$$[i(j-x-1) \quad (\text{mod } p)] + y - 2p + 1 = i'j \quad (\text{mod } p)$$

Because they are linear functions of j over GF(p), at most one solution of j can be found in each equation. While the first equation requires $y < p$, the second one requires $y \geq p$, if both τ and y are fixed. It is impossible to find two j-values that satisfy both equations at the same time. So, there only exists one hit in at most one block and the periodic cross-correlation function is at most 1.

For $i = 0$, there is always at most one pulse in any block for any τ-shift in $E_0^{(\tau)}$. So, the periodic cross-correlation function is at most 1.

Finally, the autocorrelation peaks of w are due to the code weight $w \leq p$. ∎

Figure 3.3 shows the autocorrelation functions of the extended prime codeword E_2 and cross-correlation functions of E_2 and E_3, both over GF(5) and of length 45 and weight 5, for the transmission of data-bit stream 1011001110 in OOK. The autocorrelation peaks are equal to 5 and the periodic cross-correlation functions are at most 1, agreeing with Theorem 3.3.

3.2.1 Performance Analysis

Because the extended prime codes over GF(p) of a prime p with length $N = p(2p - 1)$ and weight $w \leq p$ have the maximum periodic cross-correlation function of 1,

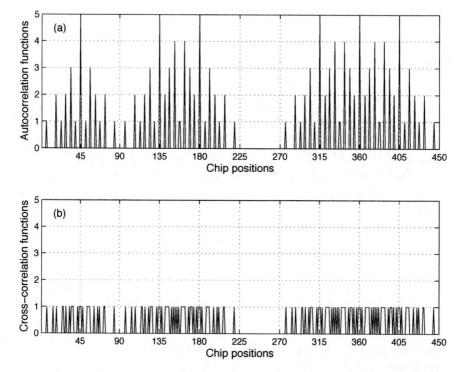

FIGURE 3.3 Examples of (a) autocorrelation functions of the extended prime codeword E_2 and (b) cross-correlation functions of E_2 and E_3, both over GF(5) and of length 45 and weight 5, for the transmission of data-bit stream 1011001110 in OOK.

their Gaussian error probability $P_{e|G}$ in OOK is also given by Equation (3.5), but with a different interference variance σ^2, which is formulated in Theorem 3.4.

According to Sections 1.8.3 and 1.8.4, the chip-synchronous, soft- and hard-limiting error probabilities of the extended prime codes over GF(p) of a prime p with length $N = p(2p - 1)$, weight $w \leq p$, and the maximum periodic cross-correlation function of 1 in OOK are given by

$$P_{e,\text{soft}} = \frac{1}{2} - \frac{1}{2} \sum_{l_1=0}^{Z_{\text{th}}-1} \frac{(K-1)!}{l_1!(K-1-l_1)!} q_1^{l_1} q_0^{K-1-l_1} \tag{3.8}$$

and

$$P_{e,\text{hard}} = \frac{1}{2} \sum_{h=Z_{\text{th}}}^{w} \frac{w!}{h!(w-h)!} \sum_{i=0}^{h} (-1)^{h-i} \frac{h!}{i!(h-i)!} \left(q_0 + \frac{i q_1}{w} \right)^{K-1} \tag{3.9}$$

respectively, where q_i is the probability of getting $i = \{0, 1\}$ hits in the sampling time of the cross-correlation function, and the decision threshold $Z_{\text{th}} = w$ is usually applied for optimal decision.

Theorem 3.4

For the extended prime codes over GF(p) of a prime p with length $N = p(2p - 1)$ and weight $w \leq p$, the hit probabilities, q_i, of having the periodic cross-correlation values of $i = \{0, 1\}$ (in the sampling time) are formulated as [13, 17]

$$q_1 = \frac{w^2}{2p(2p - 1)}$$

$$q_0 = 1 - q_1$$

The variance of the interference caused by each interfering codeword is found to be

$$\sigma^2 = \sum_{i=1}^{1} \sum_{j=0}^{i-1} (i - j)^2 q_i q_j = q_0 q_1$$

Proof The proof is similar to that of Theorem 3.2, but now the maximum periodic cross-correlation function is 1. So, $q_0 + q_1 = 1$ and $\sum_{i=0}^{1} i q_i = w^2/(2N) = w^2/[2p(2p - 1)]$, in which w^2 represents the number of possible hits in the cross-correlation function, $1/N$ represents the number of possible shifts in a codeword of length N, and $1/2$ comes from the assumption of equiprobable data bit-1 and bit-0 transmissions in OOK. According to Section 1.8.1, the variance of each interfering codeword is given by $\sigma^2 = \sum_{i=1}^{\lambda_c} \sum_{j=0}^{i-1} (i - j)^2 q_i q_j$ with $\lambda_c = 1$ for the extended prime codes. After some manipulations, the final form in the theorem is derived. ∎

Figure 3.4 plots the Gaussian [from Equation (3.5)], and chip-synchronous, soft-limiting [from Equation (3.8)] and hard-limiting [from Equation (3.9)] error probabilities of the extended prime codes over GF(p) against the number of simultaneous users K for $p = \{7, 11\}$. The hit probabilities and variance come from Theorem 3.4. In general, the error probabilities improve as p increases because of heavier code weight ($w = p$) and longer length [$N = p(2p - 1)$], resulting in higher autocorrelation peaks and lower hit probabilities, respectively. There is no decision error when $K < w$ because the extended prime codes have the maximum periodic cross-correlation function of 1. However, the error probabilities get worse as K increases due to stronger mutual interference. The hard-limiting error probabilities are always better than the soft-limiting counterparts for the same p, as expected. While the Gaussian method provides a fast tool to approximate code performance, it tends to overestimate the error probability, especially when K is small. As K increases, the Gaussian curves approach the soft-limiting curves because the accuracy of the approximation improves in accordance with the Central Limit Theorem.

Figure 3.5 plots the chip-synchronous, hard-limiting error probabilities [from Equations (3.7) and (3.9)] of the original and extended prime codes against the number of simultaneous users K for $p = \{7, 11\}$. Their code lengths are given by

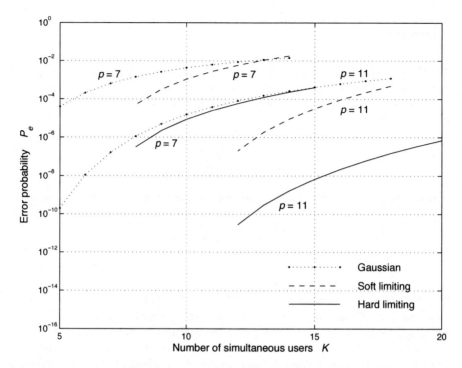

FIGURE 3.4 Error probabilities of the extended prime codes over GF(p) for $N = p(2p-1)$ and $w = p = \{7, 11\}$.

$N = p^2$ and $N = p(2p-1)$, respectively. As expected, the extended prime codes always perform better for the same p because they have a smaller maximum periodic cross-correlation function and longer code length.

3.3   GENERALIZED PRIME CODES

The original and extended prime codes have a strict relationship between code length and cardinality. For example, the original prime codes over GF(p) of a prime p have length and cardinality equal to p^2 and p, respectively. So, a quadruple increase in the code length is needed in order to double the code cardinality. In this section, the generalized prime codes are constructed to provide a more flexible relationship between code length and cardinality without affecting the correlation properties.

Based on GF(p) of a prime number p and a positive integer k, a generalized prime sequence $S_{i_k, i_{k-1}, \ldots, i_1} = (s_{i_k, i_{k-1}, \ldots, i_1, 0}, s_{i_k, i_{k-1}, \ldots, i_1, 1}, \ldots, s_{i_k, i_{k-1}, \ldots, i_1, j}, \ldots, s_{i_k, i_{k-1}, \ldots, i_1, p-1})$ is constructed by the element [17]

$$s_{i_k, i_{k-1}, \ldots, i_1, j} = (i_k \odot_p j) + (i_{k-1} \odot_p j)p + (i_{k-2} \odot_p j)p^2 + \cdots + (i_1 \odot_p j)p^{k-1}$$

where $i_1, i_2, \ldots, i_k$, and j are all in GF(p) and "$\odot_p$" denotes a modulo-p multiplication. There are a total of p^k generalized prime sequences, $S_{i_k, i_{k-1}, \ldots, i_1}$, indexed by i_1,

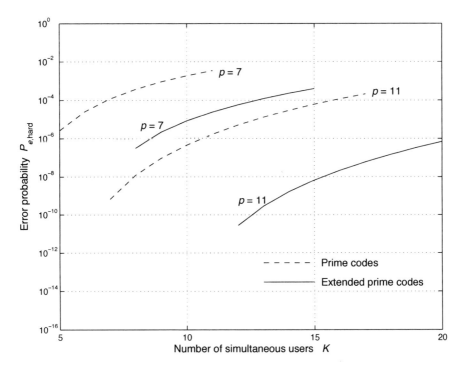

FIGURE 3.5 Chip-synchronous, hard-limiting error probabilities of the original and extended prime codes over $GF(p)$ for $N = p^2$ and $N = p(2p - 1)$, respectively, and $w = p = \{7, 11\}$.

$i_2, \ldots,$ and $i_k = \{0, 1, \ldots, p - 1\}$.

Each of these p^k generalized prime sequences is mapped into a binary $(0, 1)$ codeword $G_{i_k, i_{k-1}, \ldots, i_1} = (g_{i_k, i_{k-1}, \ldots, i_1, 0}, \ g_{i_k, i_{k-1}, \ldots, i_1, 1}, \ \ldots, \ g_{i_k, i_{k-1}, \ldots, i_1, l}, \ldots, \ g_{i_k, i_{k-1}, \ldots, i_1, p^{k+1}-1})$, indexed by $i_1, i_2, \ldots,$ and $i_k = \{0, 1, \ldots, p - 1\}$, with the code element [17]

$$g_{i_k, i_{k-1}, \ldots, i_1, l} = \begin{cases} 1 & \text{if } l = s_{i_k, i_{k-1}, \ldots, i_1, j} + jp^k \text{ for } j = \{0, 1, \ldots, p - 1\} \\ 0 & \text{otherwise} \end{cases}$$

This construction results in generalized prime codes of cardinality p^k, length p^{k+1}, and weight p.

Similar to the original and extended prime codes, the code weight w can be less than p by simply dropping $p - w$ pulses from every generalized prime codeword, without affecting the cross-correlation properties.

To have a cardinality of p^2, the code length is now equal to p^3 by setting $k = 2$ in the generalized prime codes, instead of p^4 in the original prime codes in Section 3.1. The latter belong to the special case of $k = 1$ in the generalized prime codes.

For illustration, Table 3.4 shows the generalized prime sequences and binary $(0, 1)$ codewords over $GF(3)$ with $k = 2$.

TABLE 3.4

Generalized Prime Sequences and Codewords over GF(3) with $k = 2$

(i_2, i_1)	S_{i_2,i_1}	G_{i_2,i_1}
(0,0)	0 0 0	100000000 100000000 100000000
(0,1)	0 1 2	100000000 010000000 001000000
(0,2)	0 2 1	100000000 001000000 010000000
(1,0)	0 3 6	100000000 000100000 000000100
(1,1)	0 4 8	100000000 000010000 000000001
(1,2)	0 5 7	100000000 000001000 000000010
(2,0)	0 6 3	100000000 000000100 000100000
(2,1)	0 7 5	100000000 000000010 000001000
(2,2)	0 8 4	100000000 000000001 000010000

Source: Reproduced with permission from Guu-Chang Yang and Wing C. Kwong, *Prime Codes with Applications to CDMA Optical and Wireless Networks*, Norwood, MA: Artech House, Inc., 2002. © 2002 by Artech House, Inc.

Theorem 3.5

The autocorrelation peaks of the generalized prime codes over GF(p) of a prime p and weight w are equal to w, where $w \leq p$. The periodic cross-correlation function of the codes are at most 2, but at most 1 if the codeword $G_{0,0,\ldots,0}$ is one of the correlating codewords [17].

Proof The proof is similar to that of Theorem 3.1. Let $G_{i_k,i_{k-1},\ldots,i_1}$ and $G_{i'_k,i'_{k-1},\ldots,i'_1}$ be two distinct generalized prime codewords for $i_1, i_2, \ldots$, and $i_k = \{0, 1, \ldots, p-1\}$, where $(i_k, i_{k-1}, \ldots, i_1) \neq (i'_k, i'_{k-1}, \ldots, i'_1) \neq (0, 0, \ldots, 0)$. Based on the construction, every generalized prime codeword can be divided into p blocks, each block has p^k chips, and there is only one pulse per block. So, there is exactly one pulse in the jth block of $G_{i_k,i_{k-1},\ldots,i_1}$, located in chip position $(i_k \odot_p j) + (i_{k-1} \odot_p j)p + \cdots + (i_1 \odot_p j)p^{k-1}$, where $j = \{0, 1, \ldots, p-1\}$. Let $G_{i_k,i_{k-1},\ldots,i_1}^{(\tau)}$ represent the shifted version of $G_{i_k,i_{k-1},\ldots,i_1}$ after $G_{i_k,i_{k-1},\ldots,i_1}$ has been (right) cyclic-shifted by τ chips. Assume that $x \in [0, p-1]$, $y \in [0, p^k - 1]$, and $\tau = xp^k + y$. So, $y = \tau \pmod{p^k}$ enumerates the p^k chip positions in each block. Due to the τ-shift, there may exist up to two pulses in the jth block of $G_{i_k,i_{k-1},\ldots,i_1}^{(\tau)}$ and two possible cases to consider:

1. If $\{[i_k \odot_p (j-x)] + [i_{k-1} \odot_p (j-x)]p + \cdots + [i_1 \odot_p (j-x)]p^{k-1}\} + y < p^k$,

then one pulse is in chip position $\{[i_k \odot_p (j-x)] + [i_{k-1} \odot_p (j-x)]p +$
$\cdots + [i_1 \odot_p (j-x)]p^{k-1}\} + y$. This pulse comes from the $(j-x)$th block of
$G_{i_k,i_{k-1},\ldots,i_1}$, being shifted into the jth block of $G_{i_k,i_{k-1},\ldots,i_1}^{(\tau)}$.

2. If $\{[i_k \odot_p (j-x-1)] + [i_{k-1} \odot_p (j-x-1)]p + \cdots + [i_1 \odot_p (j-x-$
$1)]p^{k-1}\} + y \geq p^k \pmod{p^k}$, then one pulse is in chip position $\{[i_k \odot_p (j-$
$x-1)] + [i_{k-1} \odot_p (j-x-1)]p + \cdots + [i_1 \odot_p (j-x-1)]p^{k-1}\} + y - p^k$. This
pulse comes from the $(j-x-1)$th block of $G_{i_k,i_{k-1},\ldots,i_1}$, being shifted into
the jth block of $G_{i_k,i_{k-1},\ldots,i_1}^{(\tau)}$.

If there is a hit in the jth blocks of $G_{i_k,i_{k-1},\ldots,i_1}^{(\tau)}$ and $G_{i_k',i_{k-1}',\ldots,i_1'}$, then either one or
both of the following equations must hold:

$$\{[i_k \odot_p (j-x)] + [i_{k-1} \odot_p (j-x)]p + \cdots + [i_1 \odot_p (j-x)]p^{k-1}\} + y$$
$$= \{[i_k' \odot_p (j-x)] + [i_{k-1}' \odot_p (j-x)]p + \cdots + [i_1' \odot_p (j-x)]p^{k-1}\}$$

$$\{[i_k \odot_p (j-x-1)] + [i_{k-1} \odot_p (j-x-1)]p + \cdots$$
$$+[i_1 \odot_p (j-x-1)]p^{k-1}\} + y - p^k = \{[i_k' \odot_p (j-x-1)]$$
$$+[i_{k-1}' \odot_p (j-x-1)]p + \cdots + [i_1' \odot_p (j-x-1)]p^{k-1}\}$$

Because they are linear functions of j over $GF(p)$, at most one solution of j can be
found in each equation. As the number of blocks containing a hit cannot exceed the
number of solutions of j, there may exist two hits in at most two blocks. So, the
maximum periodic cross-correlation function is 2.

For $(i_k, i_{k-1}, \ldots, i_1) = (0, 0, \ldots, 0)$, there is always at most one pulse in any block
for any τ-shift in $G_{0,0,\ldots,0}^{(\tau)}$. So, the periodic cross-correlation function is at most 1 as
the aforementioned two-pulse-per-block cases do not exist.

Finally, the autocorrelation peaks of w are due to the code weight $w \leq p$. ∎

3.3.1 Performance Analysis

Because the generalized prime codes represent the general case of the original prime
codes in Section 3.1 and also have the maximum periodic cross-correlation function
of 2, their Gaussian, and chip-synchronous, soft- and hard-limiting error probabilities
in OOK follow Equations (3.5), (3.6), and (3.7), respectively. However, an accurate
model of the hit probabilities of the generalized prime codes are difficult to obtain
because of the irregular hit patterns. With some generalizations, the worst-case two-
hit probability q_2 are derived in the following theorem.

Theorem 3.6

For the generalized prime codes over $GF(p)$ of a prime p with cardinality $\Phi = p^k$,
length $N = p^{k+1}$, and weight $w \leq p$, the hit probabilities, q_i, of having the periodic

cross-correlation values of $i = \{0,1,2\}$ (in the sampling time) are formulated as

$$q_2 \leq \frac{w(w^2-1)(p-2)(2p-1)^{k-1}}{12p^{2k+1}(p^k-1)}$$

$$q_1 = \frac{w^2}{2p^{k+1}} - 2q_2$$

$$q_0 = 1 - \frac{w^2}{2p^{k+1}} + q_2$$

The variance of the interference caused by each interfering codeword is found to be

$$\sigma^2 = \sum_{i=1}^{2}\sum_{j=0}^{i-1}(i-j)^2 q_i q_j = q_0 q_1 + 4q_0 q_2 + q_1 q_2$$

Proof Assume the worst-case scenario in the occurrence of two-hits. Define T_k as the total number of two-hits seen in the cross-correlation functions among the p^k generalized prime codewords of length $N = p^{k+1}$ and weight $w \leq p$ for a given $k \geq 1$.

For $k = 1$, the total number of two-hits among the p codewords is found to be

$$T_1 \leq \frac{w(w^2-1)(p-2)}{6}$$

according to Theorem 3.2. This is because the original prime codes belong to the case of $k = 1$ in the generalized prime codes.

For $k = 2$, the total number of two-hits due to one of the p codewords, G_{i_2,i_1} with $i_2 = 0$ and $i_1 = \{0,1,\ldots,p-1\}$, correlating with the other $p^2 - 1$ codewords in the code set is equal to T_1, which represents the total number of two-hits obtained when $k = 1$. This is because the codewords, G_{0,i_1}, are generated from the generalized prime sequences that have the same elements as those of $k = 1$. For other codewords, G_{i_2,i_1} with $i_2 = \{1,2,\ldots,p-1\}$ and $i_1 = \{0,1,\ldots,p-1\}$, the total number of two-hits due to the p codewords for a fixed i_2 is found to be less than or equal to $2T_1$, by inspection. So, the total number of two-hits among all p^2 codewords is found to be

$$T_2 \leq T_1 + 2(p-1)T_1$$
$$= \frac{w(w^2-1)(p-2)(2p-1)}{6}$$

Similary, for $k = 3$, the total number of two-hits due to one of the p^2 codewords, G_{i_3,i_2,i_1} with $i_3 = 0$, $i_2 = \{0,1,\ldots,p-1\}$, and $i_1 = \{0,1,\ldots,p-1\}$, correlating with the other $p^3 - 1$ codewords in the code set is equal to T_2. For the other codewords, G_{i_3,i_2,i_1} with $i_3 = \{1,2,\ldots,p-1\}$, $i_2 = \{0,1,\ldots,p-1\}$, and $i_1 = \{0,1,\ldots,p-1\}$, the total number of two-hits due to the p^2 codewords for a fixed i_3 is found to be less than or equal to $2T_2$, by inspection. So, the total number of two-hits among all p^3 codewords is found to be

$$
\begin{aligned}
T_3 &\leq T_2 + 2(p-1)T_2 \\
&\leq (2p-1)^2 T_1 \\
&= \frac{w(w^2-1)(p-2)(2p-1)^2}{6}
\end{aligned}
$$

By applying this recursive relationship, T_k is generally found to be

$$
\begin{aligned}
T_k &\leq (2p-1)^{k-1} T_1 \\
&= \frac{w(w^2-1)(p-2)(2p-1)^{k-1}}{6}
\end{aligned}
$$

So, the worst-case two-hit probability can be derived as

$$
q_2 \approx \frac{T_k}{2\Phi(\Phi-1)p^{k+1}}
$$

The derivation is based on the fact that no interference is generated for a data bit 0 in OOK, interferers send data bit-1 and bit-0 with equal probability, the total number of hits is averaged out by the code cardinality $\Phi = p^k$, there are $\Phi - 1$ possible interfering codewords contributing two-hits, and there are $N = p^{k+1}$ chip positions for the two-hits to occur. After some manipulations, the final form of q_2 is derived.

For $k = 1$, the generalized prime codes become the original prime codes in Section 3.1. In this case, the form of q_2 is exact because it is identical to the q_2 in Theorem 3.2. For the cases of $k > 1$, the accuracy of q_2 suffers as k increases.

Following Theorem 3.1, the hit probabilities are related by

$$
\sum_{i=0}^{2} i q_i = \frac{w^2}{2N} = \frac{w^2}{2p^{k+1}}
$$

and $q_0 + q_1 + q_2 = 1$.

According to Section 1.8.1, the variance of each interfering codeword is given by $\sigma^2 = \sum_{i=1}^{\lambda_c} \sum_{j=0}^{i-1} (i-j)^2 q_i q_j$ with $\lambda_c = 2$ for the generalized prime codes. After some manipulations, the final form in the theorem is derived. ∎

Figure 3.6 plots the Gaussian [from Equation (3.5)], and chip-synchronous, soft-limiting [from Equation (3.6)] and hard-limiting [from Equation (3.7)] error probabilities of the generalized prime codes over $GF(p)$ against the number of simultaneous users K for $p = 11$ and $k = \{1, 2\}$. The hit probabilities and variance come from Theorem 3.6. In general, the error probabilities improve as p or k increases because of heavier code weight ($w = p$) or longer length ($N = p^{k+1}$), resulting in higher autocorrelation peaks and lower hit probabilities, respectively. However, the error probabilities get worse as K increases due to stronger mutual interference. The hard-limiting error probabilities are always better than the soft-limiting counterparts for

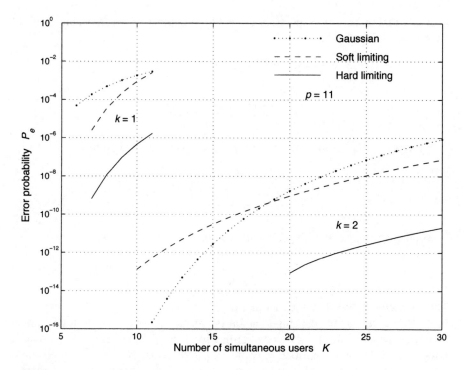

FIGURE 3.6 Error probabilities of the generalized prime codes over $GF(p)$ for $N = p^{k+1}$ and $w = p = 11$ and $k = \{1, 2\}$.

the same p, as expected. The three curves for the case of $k = 1$ exactly follow those curves (labeled with $p = 11$) in Figure 3.2 because Theorems 3.2 and 3.6 are identical when $k = 1$. Nevertheless, the two-hit probability q_2 in Theorem 3.6 presents an upper bound when $k > 1$. The general relationship between the Gaussian and soft-limiting error probabilities, as shown in the $k = 1$ curves (e.g., see Figure 3.2), does not apply anymore. This can be reflected in the $k = 2$ Gaussian and soft-limiting curves in Figure 3.6, in which the Gaussian curve continues to higher error probability, instead of converging with the latter, as K increases beyond 18.

3.4 2^n PRIME CODES

In addition to cardinality and performance, code structure is another important design parameter because it affects the power budget, size, cost, and, in turn, feasibility of the coding scheme in use [16, 17]. For example, 2^n codes [14–16, 36] have a repetitive, symmetric structure that is suitable for the power-, cost-, and size-conscious serial coding configuration in Section 2.1. In this section, 2^n prime codes, which retain the algebraic properties of prime codes as well as the symmetric structure of 2^n codes, are constructed [15, 16]. The properties and construction steps in this section can also be applied to convert some OOCs to valid 2^n codes by following [14].

First introduced by Chang and Marhic [36], 2^n codes contains binary $(0,1)$ codewords of weight 2^n for a positive integer n. The pulse separations in each codeword are highly repetitive because the pattern of the current 2^m pulses depends on that of the previous 2^{m-1} pulses, where $m \in [2,n]$. Due to this repetitiveness, it is more convenient to represent the pulse pattern in terms of cyclic adjacent-pulse separations (in number of chips or time slots) [14–22].

Definition 3.1

For a given positive integer n, a valid 2^n codeword has the (chip) separation of any two adjacent pulses, denoted $(t_0, t_1, \ldots, t_i, \ldots, t_{2^n-1})$, satisfying the *cyclic-adjacent-pulse-separation constraint* [14, 17]

$$t_{x+(2^{z-1}-1)+m \pmod{2^n}} = t_{y+(2^{z-1}-1)+m \pmod{2^n}}$$

in which $x \in [0, 2^n - 2]$ and $y \in [0, 2^n - 2]$ are both distinct and divisible by 2^z, for some $m \in [0, 2^n - 1]$ and $z \in [1, n-1]$. The term t_i denotes the (chip) separation between the ith and $(i+1)$th consecutive pulses of the codeword. To obtain the cyclic adjacent-pulse separation t_{2^n-1} between the last and first pulses, the codeword is assumed to wrap around. ∎

For example, if $n = 2$, each 2^2 codeword has the cyclic adjacent-pulse separations (t_0, t_1, t_2, t_3). As $x \in [0,2]$, $y \in [0,2]$, $z = 1$, and $m \in [0,3]$, a valid 2^2 codeword will satisfy either one of the cyclic-adjacent-pulse-separation constraints: $t_0 = t_2$ for $m = \{0,2\}$, or $t_1 = t_3$ for $m = \{1,3\}$. For illustration, codewords 101000010100000, 100100100000100, and 110000100000100 have their cyclic adjacent-pulse separations given by $(2,5,2,6)$, $(3,3,6,3)$, and $(1,5,6,3)$, respectively. Based on the cyclic-adjacent-pulse-separation constraints in this example, the first two codewords are valid 2^2 codewords, but the last one is not.

As in the original prime codes over $\mathrm{GF}(p)$ of a prime p in Section 3.1, each prime sequence $S_i = (s_{i,0}, s_{i,1}, \ldots, s_{i,j}, \ldots, s_{i,p-1})$ is mapped into a binary $(0,1)$ codeword C_i with every element $s_{i,j}$ in Equation (3.1) representing the position of a pulse in the jth block of the codeword. So, the cyclic adjacent-pulse separations of C_i can be found by the respective elements in S_i as

$$t_j = \begin{cases} s_{i,(j+z_j \pmod{p})} - s_{i,j} + z_j p & \text{for } j = \{0, 1, \ldots, p-2\} \\ s_{i,z_j-1} - s_{i,j} + z_j p & \text{for } j = p-1 \end{cases} \qquad (3.10)$$

A valid 2^n prime sequence over $\mathrm{GF}(p)$ of a prime p is then generated by keeping the 2^n elements that satisfy the cyclic-adjacent-pulse-separation constraint in Definition 3.1, but removing the remaining $p - 2^n$ elements for some $m \in [0, p-1]$ and $z_j \in [1, p-2^n+1]$, where $p \geq 2^n$. For given n and p, the prime sequences that can be converted to valid 2^n prime sequences are governed by Theorem 3.7.

Theorem 3.7

Over GF(p) of a prime p, the prime sequences, S_0, S_i, and S_{p-i}, that can be converted to valid 2^n prime sequences are those with indices $i = \{1, 2, \ldots, (p-1)/2\}$ satisfying [15–17]

$$\frac{2(p-u)(2^v - 1)}{2^n - 2^{n-v} + 1} \le i \le \frac{(p-u)(2^{v+1} - 1)}{2^n - 2^{n-v-1} - 1}$$

for all $u = \{0, 1, \ldots, p - 2^n\}$ and $v = \{0, 1, \ldots, n - 2\}$.

Proof Each element $s_{i,j} = ij \pmod{p}$ in a prime sequence $S_i = (s_{i,0}, s_{i,1}, \ldots, s_{i,j}, \ldots, s_{i,p-1})$ consists of one distinct integer in the set of $\{0, 1, \ldots, p-1\}$, where i and $j \in [0, p-1]$. Define group $G_k = (s_{i,k}, s_{i,k+1}, \ldots, s_{i,k+l})$ as an ordered set of $l + 1$ of these p distinct elements with $s_{i,k} < s_{i,k+1} < \cdots < s_{i,k+l}$ for $k \in [0, p-1]$ and these $l + 1$ elements are not contained in other groups, for an integer $l \ge 0$. Let k_r represent the starting index of group $G_{k_r} = (s_{i,k_r}, s_{i,k_r+1}, \ldots, s_{i,k_{r+1}-1})$. So, $k_r = \lceil rp/i \rceil < p$ for any $r = \{0, 1, \ldots, i-1\}$, where $\lceil \cdot \rceil$ is the ceiling function. There are always i groups, G_{k_0}, G_{k_1}, ..., G_{k_r}, ..., and $G_{k_{i-1}}$, for a given prime sequence S_i.

Let $|G_{k_r}| = k_{r+1} - k_r$ for $r = \{0, 1, \ldots, i-2\}$ or $|G_{k_r}| = p - k_{i-1}$ for $r = i - 1$ denote the number of elements (or cardinality) in group G_{k_r}. Because $k_{r+1} = \lceil (r+1)p/i \rceil$ and $k_r = \lceil rp/i \rceil$, it is found that $\lfloor p/i \rfloor \le k_{r+1} - k_r \le \lceil p/i \rceil$ for $r = \{0, 1, \ldots, i-1\}$, where $\lfloor \cdot \rfloor$ is the floor function. So, $|G_{k_r}|$ is always equal to $\lfloor p/i \rfloor$ or $\lceil p/i \rceil$.

In summary, the set of these i groups of S_i contains all the p elements of S_i with $s_{i,k_r} = ik_r \pmod{p}$ as the first element of G_{k_r} for $r = \{0, 1, \ldots, i-1\}$. It can be shown that the cardinalities of these groups always come in one of the two following patterns [15–17]:

Pattern 1: If $s_{i,k_1} < \lceil i/2 \rceil$, the cardinality pattern is given by

> $W \lceil p/i \rceil$-element groups $+ 1 \lfloor p/i \rfloor$-element group
> $+ [X_1 \lceil p/i \rceil$-element groups $+ 1 \lfloor p/i \rfloor$-element group]
> $+ [\cdots]$
> $+ [X_l \lceil p/i \rceil$-element groups $+ 1 \lfloor p/i \rfloor$-element group]
> $+ [\cdots]$
> $+ [X_g \lceil p/i \rceil$-element groups $+ 1 \lfloor p/i \rfloor$-element group]

Pattern 2: If $s_{i,k_1} \ge \lceil i/2 \rceil$, the cardinality pattern is given by

> $[1 \lceil p/i \rceil$-element group $+ Y_1 \lfloor p/i \rfloor$-element groups]
> $+ [\cdots]$
> $+ [1 \lceil p/i \rceil$-element group $+ Y_l \lfloor p/i \rfloor$-element groups]
> $+ [\cdots]$
> $+ [1 \lceil p/i \rceil$-element group $+ Y_g \lfloor p/i \rfloor$-element groups]
> $+ 1 \lceil p/i \rceil$-element group $+ Z \lfloor p/i \rfloor$-element groups

where "+" represents "followed by," "[$\cdots$]" indicates optional entities, and W and Z are positive integers. In addition, X_l is equal to $W - 1$ or W, and Y_l is equal to $Z - 1$ or Z. The total numbers of entities in Patterns 1 and 2 are determined by $W + 1 + \sum_{l=1}^{g}(X_l + 1) = i$ and $Z + 1 + \sum_{l=1}^{g}(Y_l + 1) = i$, respectively.

To establish these two cardinality patterns, two new definitions—*chain* and *turn*—are introduced here. A chain with a positive or negative slope is a set of consecutive groups, say G_{k_r}, $G_{k_{r+1}}$, ..., and $G_{k_{r+l}}$, with their first elements $s_{i,k_r} > s_{i,k_{r+1}} > \cdots > s_{i,k_{r+l}}$ or $s_{i,k_r} < s_{i,k_{r+1}} < \cdots < s_{i,k_{r+l}}$, respectively, for a nonnegative integer $l < i - r$. A turn is a group located at the pivot where a positive-slope chain turns into a negative-slope chain or vice versa.

The first group G_{k_0} always has $\lceil p/i \rceil$ elements because $|G_{k_0}| = k_1 - k_0 = \lceil p/i \rceil$. The last group $G_{k_{i-1}}$ always has $\lfloor p/i \rfloor$ elements because $|G_{k_{i-1}}| = p - k_{i-1} = \cdots = \lceil p/i \rceil - 1$. For those groups in between, it can be shown in the following that groups of positive-slope chains have $\lceil p/i \rceil$ elements, but groups of negative-slope chains have $\lfloor p/i \rfloor$ elements. Assume G_{k_r} as the group at the turn, $G_{k_{r-1}}$ as the last group in a positive-slope chain, and $G_{k_{r+1}}$ as the first group in a negative-slope chain. So, the first elements in these three groups are related by $s_{i,k_{r-1}} < s_{i,k_r}$ and $s_{i,k_r} > s_{i,k_{r+1}}$. Because $s_{i,k_{r+1}} = ik_{r+1} \pmod{p}$, $s_{i,k_r} = ik_r \pmod{p}$, $k_{r+1} = \lceil (r+1)p/i \rceil$, and $k_r = \lceil rp/i \rceil$, it can be shown that $ik_r > ik_{r+1} - p$ for $r = \{1, 2, \ldots, i-2\}$. Similarly, the last element $s_{i,k_r-1} = ik_r - i \pmod{p}$ of $G_{k_{r-1}}$ is found greater than the last element $s_{i,k_{r+1}-1} = ik_{r+1} - i \pmod{p}$ of G_{k_r}, resulting in $|G_{k_{r-1}}| = \lceil p/i \rceil$, $|G_{k_r}| = \lfloor p/i \rfloor$, and $|G_{k_{r+1}}| = \lfloor p/i \rfloor$. In summary, every group in the first chain before the first turn has $\lceil p/i \rceil$ elements, and the chain has a positive slope. Between the first and second turns is the second chain, in which every group has $\lfloor p/i \rfloor$ elements and the chain has a negative slope. Similarly, between the second and third turns is the third chain, in which every group has $\lceil p/i \rceil$ elements and the chain has a positive slope. This alternating cardinality pattern is repeated until a negative-slope chain with the last group $G_{k_{i-1}}$ is reached.

When $s_{i,k_1} < \lceil i/2 \rceil$, let G_{k_r}, $G_{k_{r+1}}$, and $G_{k_{r+2}}$ be three consecutive groups in a negative-slope chain. The first elements of these groups are related by $s_{i,k_{r+1}} = s_{i,k_r} + i\lfloor p/i \rfloor$ and $s_{i,k_{r+2}} = s_{i,k_{r+1}} + i\lfloor p/i \rfloor = s_{i,k_r} + 2i\lfloor p/i \rfloor$ due to $|G_{k_r}| = |G_{k_{r+1}}| = \lfloor p/i \rfloor$. As $s_{i,k_1} = i\lceil p/i \rceil \pmod{p} < \lceil i/2 \rceil$, this gives $i\lfloor p/i \rfloor < \lceil i/2 \rceil - i$ and $s_{i,k_{r+2}} < s_{i,k_r} + 2\lceil i/2 \rceil - 2i < s_{i,k_r} - (i-1) \le (i-1) - (i-1) = 0$ for any $r = \{0, 1, \ldots, i-1\}$. This violates the fact that $s_{i,k_r} \ge 0$ for all $r = \{0, 1, \ldots, i-1\}$. So, $G_{k_{r+2}}$ cannot belong to the negative-slope chain, and $G_{k_{r+1}}$ is the turn. In this case, S_i appears as Pattern 1 because there are always W or X_l $\lceil p/i \rceil$-element groups followed by one $\lfloor p/i \rfloor$-element group.

When $s_{i,k_1} \ge \lceil i/2 \rceil$, let G_{k_r}, $G_{k_{r+1}}$, and $G_{k_{r+2}}$ be three consecutive groups in the positive-slope chain. The first elements of these groups are related by $s_{i,k_{r+1}} = s_{i,k_r} + i\lceil p/i \rceil$ and $s_{i,k_{r+2}} = s_{i,k_{r+1}} + i\lceil p/i \rceil = s_{i,k_r} + 2i\lceil p/i \rceil$ due to $|G_{k_r}| = |G_{k_{r+1}}| = \lceil p/i \rceil$. As $s_{i,k_0} = 0$ and $s_{i,k_r} \in [1, p-1]$ for all $r \ne 0$, this gives $s_{i,k_1} = s_{i,k_0} + i\lceil p/i \rceil = i\lceil p/i \rceil \pmod{p} \ge \lceil i/2 \rceil$ and $s_{i,k_{r+2}} \ge s_{i,k_r} + 2\lceil i/2 \rceil \ge i$. These violate the fact that $s_{i,k_r} = i\lceil rp/i \rceil \pmod{p} < rp + i = i$ for all $r = \{0, 1, \ldots, i-1\}$. So, $G_{k_{r+2}}$ cannot belong to the positive-slope chain, and $G_{k_{r+1}}$ is the turn. In this case, S_i appears as Pattern 2 because there is always one $\lceil p/i \rceil$-element group followed by Z or Y_l $\lfloor p/i \rfloor$-element groups.

For example, if $p = 17$ and $i = 4$, the prime sequence is given by $S_4 = (0,7,14,4,11,1,8,15,5,12,2,9,16,6,13,3,10)$. By definition, S_4 can be partitioned into 7 groups: $G_{k_0} = G_0 = (0,7,14)$, $G_{k_1} = G_4 = (4,11)$, $G_{k_2} = G_1 = (1,8,15)$, $G_{k_3} = G_5 = (5,12)$, $G_{k_4} = G_2 = (2,9,16)$, $G_{k_5} = G_6 = (6,13)$, and $G_{k_6} = G_3 = (3,10)$, with $\lfloor p/i \rfloor = 2$ or $\lceil p/i \rceil = 3$ elements. By inspection, G_4 is a turn between the positive-slope chain of $\{G_0, G_4\}$ and the negative-slope chain of $\{G_4, G_1\}$. Also, G_1 is a turn between the negative-slope chain of $\{G_4, G_1\}$ and the positive-slope chain of $\{G_1, G_5\}$. Similarly, G_5 is a turn between the positive-slope chain of $\{G_1, G_5\}$ and the negative-slope chain of $\{G_5, G_2\}$. Finally, G_2 is a turn between the negative-slope chain of $\{G_5, G_2\}$ and the positive-slope chain of $\{G_2, G_6, G_3\}$. This arrangement results in Pattern 2 as $s_{4,k_1} = 16 \geq \lceil 4/2 \rceil$.

Based on Equation (3.10), the cyclic separation between two adjacent pulses in any group of S_i is given by $t_j = s_{i,j+1} - s_{i,j} + p = \cdots = i$ (mod p) if $z_j = 1$. Similarly, the cyclic separation between two adjacent pulses in any two consecutive groups, say G_{k_r} and $G_{k_{r+1}}$, of S_i is given by $t_j = s_{i,k_r+1} - s_{i,k_r} + p = \cdots = i$ (mod p). Together with Patterns 1 and 2, the number of possible cases to determine whether the cyclic-adjacent-pulse-separation constraint in Definition 3.1 is satisfied can be substantially reduced. In particular, a prime sequence that can be converted into a valid 2^n prime sequence should contain one of the following group arrangements [15–17]:

1.   A (2^n or more)-element group.
2.   A (2^{n-1} or more)-element group + a (2^{n-1} or more)-element group.
3.   A ($2^{n-1} - 1$ or 2^{n-1})-element group + a 2^{n-1}-element group + a ($2^{n-1} - 1$ or 2^{n-1})-element group.
4*.   At least 2^2 consecutive (2^{n-2} or more)-element groups.
4.   A (2^{n-2} or $2^{n-2} + 1$)-element group + 2 consecutive 2^{n-2}-element group + a (2^{n-2} or $2^{n-2} + 1$)-element group.
5.   A ($2^{n-2} - 1$ or 2^{n-2})-element group + 3 consecutive 2^{n-2}-element groups + a ($2^{n-2} - 1$ or 2^{n-2})-element group.
6*.   At least 2^3 consecutive (2^{n-3} or more)-element groups.
6.   A (2^{n-3} or $2^{n-3} + 1$)-element group + 6 consecutive 2^{n-3}-element group + a (2^{n-3} or $2^{n-3} + 1$)-element group.

     $\vdots$ $\vdots$

$2(n-1)$*.   At least 2^{n-1} consecutive (2 or more)-element groups.
$2(n-1)$.   A (2 or 3)-element group + ($2^{n-1} - 2$) consecutive 2-element groups + a (2 or 3)-element group.
$2(n-1)+1$.   A (1 or 2)-element group + ($2^{n-1} - 1$) consecutive 2-element groups + a (1 or 2)-element group.

where "+" represents "followed by."

Case 1 assumes that all 2^n pulses in a 2^n codeword come from a single group, which has at least 2^n elements. Because the cyclic adjacent-pulse separations in any group are all identical, Definition 3.1 is satisfied due to $t_j = t_{j+1 \text{ (mod } p)} = \cdots =$

$t_{j+2^n-2 \pmod p}$ for some $j \in [0, p-1]$. If there exists a prime sequence S_i with i such that the equality $\lfloor p/i \rfloor = 2^n - 1$ is satisfied, at least one group with $\lceil p/i \rceil = 2^n$ elements can be found because the groups of S_i must follow Pattern 1 or 2. So, this case is satisfied and this S_i can be converted to a valid 2^n prime sequence.

Case 2 assumes that all 2^n pulses in a 2^n codeword come from two groups, which have at least 2^{n-1} elements per group, and each group accounts for half of these pulses. Because the cyclic adjacent-pulse separations in any group are all identical, Definition 3.1 is also satisfied due to $t_j = t_{j+1 \pmod p} = \cdots = t_{j+2^{n-1}-2 \pmod p}$ and $t_{j+2^{n-1} \pmod p} = t_{j+2^{n-1}+1 \pmod p} = \cdots = t_{j+2^n-2 \pmod p}$ for some $j \in [0, p-1]$. If there exists a prime sequence S_i with i such that the inequality $2^n - 1 \geq p/i \geq [2^{n-1} + (2^{n-1} + (2^{n-1} - 1))l]/(2l+1) \geq 2^{n-1} - 1/2$ is satisfied for an integer $l \geq 0$, this S_i can be converted to a valid 2^n prime sequence. The lower and upper limits of this inequality come from the extreme group-cardinality arrangements constrained by Pattern 1 or 2.

Case 3 assumes that all 2^n pulses in a 2^n codeword come from three groups, in which 2^{n-2}, 2^{n-1}, and 2^{n-2} pulses are from the front ($2^{n-1} - 1$ or 2^{n-1})-element, middle 2^{n-1}-element, and back ($2^{n-1} - 1$ or 2^{n-1})-element groups, respectively. So, Definition 3.1 is also satisfied due to $t_j = t_{j+1 \pmod p} = \cdots = t_{j+2^{n-2}-2 \pmod p} = t_{j+2^{n-2} \pmod p} = t_{j+2^{n-2}+1 \pmod p} = \cdots = t_{j+3\times 2^{n-2}-2 \pmod p} = t_{j+3\times 2^{n-2} \pmod p} = t_{j+3\times 2^{n-2}+1 \pmod p} = \cdots = t_{j+2^n-2 \pmod p}$ and $t_{j+2^{n-2}-1 \pmod p} = t_{j+3\times 2^{n-2}-1 \pmod p}$ for some $j \in [0, p-1]$. If there exists a prime sequence S_i with i such that the inequality $[2^{n-1} + 2^{n-1} + (2^{n-1} - 1)]/3 \geq p/i \geq [(2^{n-1} + (2^{n-1} - 1))l + 2^{n-1}]/(2l+1)$ and, in turn, $2^{n-1} - 1/3 \geq p/i \geq 2^{n-1} - 1/2$ is satisfied for an integer $l \geq 0$, this S_i can be converted to a valid 2^n prime sequence. The lower and upper limits of this inequality come from the extreme group-cardinality arrangements constrained by Pattern 1 or 2.

Case 4 assumes that all 2^n pulses in a 2^n codeword come from four (2^{n-2} or $2^{n-2} + 1$)-element groups. Case 5 assumes five ($2^{n-2} - 1$ or 2^{n-2})-element groups. Both cases can be considered together because they deal with groups with 2^{n-2} elements. Following the aforementioned cases, if there exists a prime sequence S_i with i such that the inequality $[((2^{n-2} + 1) + 2^{n-2})l + 2^{n-2}]/(2l+1) \geq p/i \geq [(2^{n-2} + 2^{n-2} + (2^{n-2} - 1))l + 2^{n-2}]/(3l+1)$ and, in turn, $2^{n-2} + 1/2 \geq p/i \geq 2^{n-2} - 1/3 = [2^n(1 - 1/4) - 1]/(2+1)$ is satisfied for an integer $l > 0$, this S_i can be converted to a valid 2^n prime sequence.

Case 4* assumes that all 2^n pulses in a 2^n codeword come from at least four groups, which have at least 2^{n-2}-elements per group. While the first and last sets of 2^{n-2} pulses are from the front and back groups, the remaining two sets of the 2^{n-2} pulses are from two of the groups in between. Definition 3.1 is satisfied if the cyclic adjacent-pulse separations between any two adjacent sets of the 2^{n-2} pulses are chosen such that $t_j = t_{j+1 \pmod p} = \cdots = t_{j+2^{n-2}-2 \pmod p} = t_{j+2^{n-2} \pmod p} = t_{j+2^{n-2}+1 \pmod p} = \cdots = t_{j+2^{n-1}-2 \pmod p} = t_{j+2^{n-1} \pmod p} = t_{j+2^{n-1}+1 \pmod p} = \cdots = t_{j+3\times 2^{n-2}-2 \pmod p} = t_{j+3\times 2^{n-2} \pmod p} = t_{j+3\times 2^{n-2}+1 \pmod p} = \cdots = t_{j+2^n-2 \pmod p}$ and $t_{j+2^{n-2}-1 \pmod p} = t_{j+3\times 2^{n-2}-1 \pmod p}$ for some $j \in [0, p-1]$. In this case, the elements in the unused groups are removed in order to maintain 2^n pulses. So, the total number of remaining elements in S_i is now equal to $p - u$ if u denotes the number of removed elements. Because $2^{n-2} + 1/2 \geq (p-u)/i \geq [2^n(1 - 1/4) - 1]/(2 + 1)$, an inequality similar to that in Case 4 results. If $u \leq p - 2^n$, the term $(p - u)/i$ in the inequality is replaced by $(p - u - u')/i$, where u' denotes the number of removed elements satisfying $u' \leq p - 2^n - u$.

In general, for $k = \{2, 3, \ldots, n - 1\}$, Case $2k$ assumes that all 2^n pulses of a 2^n codeword come from 2^k $(2^{n-k} + 1$ or $2^{n-k})$-element groups, while Case $2k + 1$ assumes $2^k + 1$ $(2^{n-k}$ or $2^{n-k} - 1)$-element groups. Both cases can be considered together because they deal with groups with 2^{n-k} elements. If there exists a prime sequence S_i with i such that the inequality $[((2^{n-k} + 1) + (2^k - 3)2^{n-k})l + 2^{n-k}]/[(2^k - 2)l + 1] \geq p/i \geq [((2^k - 2)2^{n-k} + (2^{n-k} - 1))l + 2^{n-k}]/[(2^k - 1)l + 1]$ and, in turn, $2^{n-k} + 1/[2(2^{k-1} - 1)] \geq p/i \geq [2^n - 2^{n-k} - 1]/(2^k - 1) = [2^n(1 - 1/2^k) - 1]/[2(2^{k-1} - 1) + 1]$ is satisfied for an integer $l \geq 0$, this S_i can be converted to a valid 2^n prime sequence. The lower and upper limits of this inequality come from the extreme group-cardinality arrangements constrained by Pattern 1 or 2.

Similarly, for $k = \{2, 3, \ldots, n - 1\}$, Case $2k^*$ assumes that all 2^n pulses in a 2^n codeword come from at least 2^k groups, which have at least 2^{n-k} elements per group. While the first and last sets of 2^{n-k} pulses are from the front and back groups, the remaining $2^{n-k} - 2$ sets of the 2^{n-k} pulses are from $2^{n-k} - 2$ of the groups in between. Definition 3.1 is satisfied if the cyclic adjacent-pulse separations between any two adjacent sets of the 2^{n-k} pulses are chosen accordingly. In this case, the elements in the unused groups are removed in order to maintain 2^n pulses. So, the total number of remaining elements in S_i is now equal to $p - u$ if u denotes the number of removed elements. Because $2^{n-k} + 1/[2(2^{k-1} - 1)] \geq (p - u)/i \geq [2^n(1 - 1/2^k) - 1]/[2(2^{k-1} - 1) + 1]$, an inequality similar to that in Case $2k$ results. If $u \leq p - 2^n$, $(p - u)/i$ in the inequality is replaced by $(p - u - u')/i$, where u' denotes the number of removed elements satisfying $u' \leq p - 2^n - u$.

Finally, by combining all cases, the inequality

$$\frac{2^n(1 - \frac{1}{2^{v+1}}) - 1}{2(2^v - 1) + 1} \leq \frac{p - u}{i} \leq 2^{n-v-1} + \frac{1}{2(2^v - 1)}$$

is derived, where $u = \{0, 1, \ldots, p - 2^n\}$, $v = \{0, 1, \ldots, n - 2\}$, and $i = \{1, 2, \ldots, (p - 1)/2\}$. After some manipulations, the final form in the theorem is derived. ∎

Using $n = 3$ and $p = 11$ as an example, the prime sequences that can be converted to valid 2^n prime sequences are S_0, S_i, and S_{11-i} with i satisfying the inequalities $0 \leq i \leq (11 - u)/3$ and $2(11 - u)/5 \leq i \leq 3(11 - u)/5$, where $u = \{0, 1, \ldots, 11 - 2^3\}$ and $i = \{1, 2, \ldots, (11 - 1)/2\}$. These inequalities become $0 \leq i \leq 3.7$ and $4.4 \leq i \leq 6.6$ for $u = 0$, $0 \leq i \leq 3.3$ and $4.0 \leq i \leq 6.0$ for $u = 1$, $0 \leq i \leq 3.0$ and $3.6 \leq i \leq 4.4$ for $u = 2$, and $0 \leq i \leq 2.7$ and $3.2 \leq i \leq 4.8$ for $u = 3$. By combining them, $i = \{0, 1, 2, 3, 4, 5, 6\}$ is obtained, meaning that all 11 prime sequences over GF(11) can be converted into valid 2^3 prime sequences.

Under a certain relationship between p and n, the validity rule of 2^n prime sequences in Theorem 3.7 can be simplified in the following theorem. As p gets larger, there are more freedom—pulses to choose from—in the pulse-removal process. Theorem 3.8 finds the minimum p value so that the whole set of prime sequences over $GF(p)$ is qualified for conversion to valid 2^n codewords for a given n.

Theorem 3.8

All p prime sequences over $GF(p)$ of a prime p can be converted to valid 2^n prime sequences if

$$p \geq 2^{n+1} - 6$$

is satisfied [15–17].

Proof The prime sequences removed in Theorem 3.7 are those with the index i failing Cases $2k^*$ for some $k = \{2, 3, \ldots, n-1\}$. For Case 4^*, the groups between the front and back groups must have $2^{n-1} - 1, 2^{n-1} - 1, \ldots, 2^{n-1} - 1$, and $2^{n-1} - 2$ elements, consecutively, due to Pattern 1. The number of removed elements in the $2^2 - 2$ groups, which provide the $2^2 - 2$ sets of the 2^{n-2} pulses, is then equal to $2(2^{n-1} - 1 - 2^{n-2})$. To obtain 2^n pulses, $p - 2^n$ elements are removed from a prime sequence and then $p - 2^n$ needs to be as large as $2^n - 2 - 2^{n-1}$ and finally $p \geq 2^{n+1} - 2^{n-1} - 2$ so that a failed prime sequence (in Theorem 3.7) can now be converted to a valid 2^n prime sequence by means of unused-element removal.

For Case 6^*, the groups between the front and back groups must have $2^{n-2}, 2^{n-2}, 2^{n-2} - 1, 2^{n-2}, 2^{n-2}, 2^{n-2} - 1, \ldots, 2^{n-2}, 2^{n-2}$, and $2^{n-2} - 1$ elements, consecutively, due to Pattern 1. The number of removed elements in the $2^3 - 2$ groups, which provide the $2^3 - 2$ sets of the 2^{n-3} pulses, is equal to $4(2^{n-2} - 2^{n-3}) + 2(2^{n-2} - 1 - 2^{n-3})$. So, $p - 2^n$ needs to be as large as $2^n - 2 - 2^{n-2}$ and finally $p \geq 2^{n+1} - 2^{n-2} - 2$ so that a failed prime sequence (in Theorem 3.7) can now be converted to a valid 2^n prime sequence by means of unused-element removal.

In general, for $k = \{3, 4, 5, \ldots, n-1\}$, Case $2k^*$, the groups between the front and back groups must have $2^{n-k+1}, 2^{n-k+1}, \ldots, 2^{n-k+1}, 2^{n-k+1} - 1, 2^{n-k+1}, 2^{n-k+1}, \ldots, 2^{n-k+1}, 2^{n-k+1} - 1, \ldots, 2^{n-k+1}, 2^{n-k+1}, \ldots, 2^{n-k+1}, 2^{n-k+1} - 1$ elements, consecutively, due to Pattern 1. The number of removed elements in the $2^k - 2$ groups, which provide the $2^k - 2$ sets of the 2^{n-k} pulses, is equal to $(2^k - 4)(2^{n-k+1} - 2^{n-k}) + 2(2^{n-k+1} - 1 - 2^{n-k})$. So, $p - 2^n$ needs to be as large as $2^n - 2 - 2^{n-k+1}$ and finally $p \geq 2^{n+1} - 2^{n+1-k} - 2$ so that a failed prime sequence (in Theorem 3.7) can now be converted to a valid 2^n prime sequence by means of unused-element removal.

The maximum of $2^{n+1} - 2^{n+1-k} - 2$ is reached when $k = n - 1$ and the final form of the theorem is derived. ∎

For example, if $n = 3$, the smallest prime number satisfying Theorem 3.8 is

$p = 11$. So, all 11 prime sequences over GF(11) can be converted to valid 2^3 prime sequences, which agree with the results in Theorem 3.7.

Finally, the generation algorithm of the 2^n prime codes can be summarized as follows [15–17]:

1. For a given prime number $p \geq 2^n$, apply Theorems 3.7 and 3.8 to determine which prime sequence S_i can be converted to a valid 2^n prime sequence.

2. For every S_i with i satisfying the inequality in Theorem 3.7 with $u = 0$, apply Equation (3.10) with $z_j = 1$ to determine its cyclic adjacent-pulse separations. Those consecutive elements, say $s_{i,j}$ and $s_{i,j+1}$, with cyclic adjacent-pulse separations satisfying the constraint in Definition 3.1 with some $m \in [0, p-1]$ are kept unchanged. The remaining elements are replaced by Xs. This step converts S_i to a valid 2^n prime sequence S_i'.

3. For every S_i with i satisfying the inequality in Theorem 3.7 with $u = \{1, 2, \ldots, p - 2^n\}$, apply Equation (3.10) with $z_j = \{1, 2, \ldots, p - 2^n + 1\}$ to determine its cyclic adjacent-pulse separations. Those elements, say $s_{i,j}$ and $s_{i,(j+z_j \pmod p)}$, with cyclic adjacent-pulse separations satisfying the constraint in Definition 3.1 with some $m \in [0, p-1]$ are kept unchanged. The remaining elements are replaced by Xs. This step modifies S_i, which is excluded from Step 2, into a valid 2^n prime sequence S_i'.

4. Every valid 2^n prime sequence S_i' is mapped into a binary $(0, 1)$ codeword $C_i' = (c_{i,0}', c_{i,1}', \ldots, c_{i,k}', \ldots, c_{i,p^2-1}')$ of length p^2 and weight 2^n, according to the rule

$$c_{i,k}' = \begin{cases} 1 & \text{for } k = s_{i,j} + jp \text{ and } s_{i,j} \neq X \\ 0 & \text{otherwise} \end{cases}$$

where i and $j \in [0, p-1]$. The role of X is to generate p 0s. If needed, the codeword is rotated until it starts with a 1, followed by the 1s and 0s generated from unchanged elements, $s_{i,j}$'s, and ends with the consecutive 0s generated from Xs.

5. (*Optional*) Compute the separations between the first and last 1s of all 2^n prime codewords generated in the above steps and denote T as the maximum separation. The 2^n prime codes generated in Step 4 are still pseudo-orthogonal as long as there exists at least $T + 1$ 0s at the end of each codeword. So, if $p^2 > 2T + 1$, the code length can be lower-bounded by $2T + 1$, with the last $p^2 - 2T - 1$ consecutive 0s in each codeword being removed. Otherwise, the code length remains as p^2.

For illustration, Table 3.5 shows the prime sequences over GF(11) and Table 3.6 shows their cyclic adjacent-pulse separations with $z_j = 1$ and $n = 3$, where separations satisfying the cyclic-adjacent-pulse-separation constraint are bold-faced. Table 3.7 tabulates the valid 2^3 prime sequences over GF(11), based on the aforementioned generation algorithm, which, in turn, generates the 11 2^3 prime codewords over GF(11). The elements not satisfying the cyclic-adjacent-pulse-separation constraint are replaced by Xs.

TABLE 3.5
Prime Sequences over GF(11)

$S_0 =$	0	0	0	0	0	0	0	0	0	0	0
$S_1 =$	0	1	2	3	4	5	6	7	8	9	10
$S_2 =$	0	2	4	6	8	10	1	3	5	7	9
$S_3 =$	0	3	6	9	1	4	7	10	2	5	8
$S_4 =$	0	4	8	1	5	9	2	6	10	3	7
$S_5 =$	0	5	10	4	9	3	8	2	7	1	6
$S_6 =$	0	6	1	7	2	8	3	9	4	10	5
$S_7 =$	0	7	3	10	6	2	9	5	1	8	4
$S_8 =$	0	8	5	2	10	7	4	1	9	6	3
$S_9 =$	0	9	7	5	3	1	10	8	6	4	2
$S_{10} =$	0	10	9	8	7	6	5	4	3	2	1

TABLE 3.6
Cyclic Adjacent-Pulse Separations for Prime Sequences over GF(11) with $z_j = 1$ and $n = 3$

$S_0 =$	11	11	11	11	11	11	11	11	11	11	11
$S_1 =$	12	12	12	12	12	12	12	12	12	12	1
$S_2 =$	13	13	13	13	13	2	13	13	13	13	2
$S_3 =$	14	14	14	3	14	14	14	3	14	14	3
$S_4 =$	15	15	4	15	15	4	15	15	4	15	4
$S_5 =$	16	16	5	16	5	16	5	16	5	16	5
$S_6 =$	17	6	17	6	17	6	17	6	17	6	6
$S_7 =$	18	7	18	7	7	18	7	7	18	7	7
$S_8 =$	19	8	8	19	8	8	8	19	8	8	8
$S_9 =$	20	9	9	9	9	20	9	9	9	9	9
$S_{10} =$	21	10	10	10	10	10	10	10	10	10	10

TABLE 3.7
Valid 2^3 Prime Sequences over GF(11)

$S_0 =$	X	X	0	0	0	0	0	0	0	0	X
$S_1 =$	X	X	2	3	4	5	6	7	8	9	X
$S_2 =$	X	X	4	6	8	10	1	3	5	7	X
$S_3 =$	X	X	6	9	1	4	7	10	2	5	X
$S_4 =$	X	4	8	1	5	X	X	6	10	3	7
$S_5 =$	X	X	10	4	9	3	8	2	7	1	X
$S_6 =$	X	X	1	7	2	8	3	9	4	10	X
$S_7 =$	X	7	3	10	6	X	X	5	1	8	4
$S_8 =$	X	X	5	2	10	7	4	1	9	6	X
$S_9 =$	X	X	7	5	3	1	10	8	6	4	X
$S_{10} =$	X	X	9	8	7	6	5	4	3	2	X

Because the 2^n prime codewords are formed by properly removing $p - 2^n$ 1s in some original prime codewords over $GF(p)$ of a prime p, the correlation properties are preserved and the cross-correlation functions are still at most 2.

3.4.1 Performance Analysis

As the maximum periodic cross-correlation function of the 2^n prime codes over $GF(p)$ of a prime p with cardinality $\Phi = p$, length $N = p^2$, and weight $w = 2^n$ is equal to 2, their Gaussian and chip-synchronous, soft-, and hard-limiting error probabilities follow Equations (3.5), (3.6), and (3.7), respectively. Similarly, the hit probabilities and variance of interference follow those in Theorem 3.2.

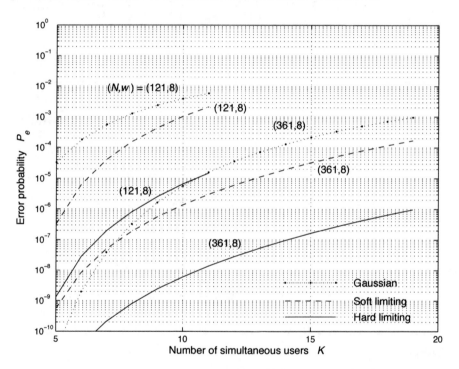

FIGURE 3.7 Error probabilities of the 2^n prime codes over $GF(p)$ for $N = p^2$, $w = 2^n$, $p = \{11, 19\}$, and $n = 3$.

Figure 3.7 plots the Gaussian [from Equation (3.5)], and chip-synchronous, soft-limiting [from Equation (3.6)] and hard-limiting [from Equation (3.7)] error probabilities of the 2^n prime codes over $GF(p)$ against the number of simultaneous users K for $N = p^2$, $w = 2^n$, $p = \{11, 19\}$, and $n = 3$. The hit probabilities and variance come from Theorem 3.2. In general, the error probabilities improve as n or p increases because of heavier code weight or longer code length, resulting in higher autocorrelation peaks or lower hit probabilities, respectively. However, the error probabilities get worse as K increases due to stronger mutual interference. The hard-limiting error probabilities are always better than the soft-limiting counterparts for the same p or n, as expected. Because the two-hit probability q_2 in Theorem 3.2 presents an upper bound, the general relationship between the Gaussian and soft-limiting error probabilities (e.g., see Figures 3.2 and 3.4) does not apply anymore. This can be reflected in the Gaussian and soft-limiting curves in Figure 3.7, in which the Gaussian curves are always higher than the latter in this example.

3.5 OPTICAL ORTHOGONAL CODES

Optical orthogonal codes (OOCs), first proposed by Chung et al. [18], belong to another category of 1-D binary $(0, 1)$ codes designed for incoherent, temporal ampli-tude coding. OOCs are sparse in the code element "1" (or mark chips) and specially designed in order to have autocorrelation sidelobes and periodic cross-correlation functions as low as possible [18–32]. Various algebraic techniques related to error control codes, such as projective geometry, block designs, and difference sets, have been applied to the OOC constructions [24, 37–41].

Definition 3.2

A family of $(N, w, \lambda_a, \lambda_c)$ OOCs is defined as a collection of 1-D binary $(0, 1)$ code-words with length N, weight w, the maximum autocorrelation sidelobe λ_a, and the maximum periodic cross-correlation function λ_c such that the 1-D auto- and cross-correlation constraints in Definition 1.13 (in Section 1.5) are satisfied. ∎

A balanced incomplete block design (BIBD), denoted $B[v, b, r, k, \lambda]$, is an arrange-ment of v distinct objects into b blocks. Each block contains exactly k objects, each object occurs in exactly r different blocks, and every pair of distinct objects occurs together in exactly λ blocks, where $v > k$ and $\lambda \geq 1$ [37–39]. These five parameters are related by $bk = vr$ and $r(k-1) = \lambda(v-1)$. For example, Chung et al. [18] con-structed $(N, w, 1, 1)$ OOCs using the BIBD with $\lambda = 1$, while Chung and Kumar [19] reported $(N, w, 2, 2)$ OOCs.

In this section, several constructions of $(N, w, 1, 1)$ OOCs, which are based on the BIBD, with optimal cardinality are illustrated [19, 20, 40]. Afterward, $(N, w, 1, 2)$ and $(N, w, 2, 1)$ OOCs are constructed by relaxing the autocorrelation or cross-correlation constraint in order to achieve larger code cardinality [20, 21]. Finally, the perfor-mances of these OOCs are discussed.

3.5.1 Constructions of (N, w, 1, 1) OOC

In [37], the BIBD was used to construct $(N, w, 1, 1)$ OOCs of weight $w = \{3, 4, 5\}$. Wilson [40] generalized the construction to arbitrary w, as summarized in the fol-lowing [19]:

1. Let $w = 2m$ and set $N = w(w-1)t + 1$ to be a prime number, where m and t are positive integers. Also let α be a primitive element of GF(N) and the values calculated from $\log_\alpha(\alpha^{2mkt} - 1)$ be all distinct and nonzero modulo-m for $k \in [1, m]$. So, binary $(0, 1)$ codewords with pulses located in chip positions

$$\{(0, \alpha^{mi}, \alpha^{mi+2mt}, \alpha^{mi+4mt}, \ldots, \alpha^{mi+4m(m-1)t}) : i = \{0, 1, \ldots, t-1\}\}$$

form a family of $(N, w, 1, 1)$ OOCs of "even" weight $w = 2m$ and cardinality $t = (N-1)/(w^2 - w)$.

2. Let $w = 2m + 1$ and set $N = w(w-1)t + 1$ to be a prime number, where m and t are positive integers. Also let α be a primitive element of GF(N) and the values calculated from $\log_\alpha(\alpha^{2mkt} - 1)$ be all distinct modulo-m for $k \in [1, m]$. So, binary $(0, 1)$ codewords with pulses located in chip positions

$$\{(\alpha^{mi}, \alpha^{mi+2mt}, \alpha^{mi+4mt}, \ldots, \alpha^{mi+4m^2t}) : i = \{0, 1, \ldots, t-1\}\}$$

form a family of $(N, w, 1, 1)$ OOCs of "odd" weight $w = 2m + 1$ and cardinality $t = (N-1)/(w^2 - w)$.

These two Wilson constructions resulted in optimal code cardinality as the cardinality upper bound in Section 1.6 was met with equality [19].

Hanani [38] constructed a family of $(N, 6, 1, 1)$ OOCs using the BIBD with different parameters. Yang [20] generalized Hanani construction for even $w = 4m + 2$ and odd $w = 4m + 3$, as summarized in the following:

1. Let $w = 4m + 2$ and set $N = w(w-1)t + 1$ to be a prime number, where m and t are positive integers. Also let α be a primitive element of GF(N) and the conditions $\alpha^{k(8m+2)t+y} - 1 = \alpha^{i_k}$ for $k \in [0, m]$, $\alpha^{k(8m+2)t} - \alpha^y = \alpha^{j_k}$, $\alpha^{k(8m+2)t} - 1 = \alpha^{r_k}$, and $\alpha^{k(8m+2)t+y} - \alpha^y = \alpha^{s_k}$ for $k \in [1, m]$ be all satisfied for some integer $y \in [1, (8m+2)t - 1]$. The integers i_k, j_k, r_k, and s_k are all distinct modulo-$(4m+1)$. So, binary $(0, 1)$ codewords with pulses located in chip positions

$$\{(\alpha^{(4m+1)i}, \alpha^{y+(4m+1)i}, \alpha^{(8m+2)t+(4m+1)i}, \alpha^{(8m+2)t+y+(4m+1)i}, \ldots,$$
$$\alpha^{(8m+2)2mt+(4m+1)i}, \alpha^{(8m+2)2mt+y+(4m+1)i}) : i = \{0, 1, \ldots, t-1\}\}$$

form a family of $(N, w, 1, 1)$ OOCs of even weight $w = 4m + 2$ and cardinality $t = (N-1)/(w^2 - w)$.

2. Let $w = 4m + 3$ and set $N = w(w-1)t + 1$ to be a prime number, where m and t are positive integers. Also let α be a primitive element of GF(N) and the conditions $\alpha^{k(8m+6)t+y} - 1 = \alpha^{i_k}$ for $k \in [0, m]$, $\alpha^{k(8m+6)t} - \alpha^y = \alpha^{j_k}$, $\alpha^{k(8m+6)t} - 1 = \alpha^{r_k}$, and $\alpha^{k(8m+6)t+y} - \alpha^y = \alpha^{s_k}$ for $k \in [1, m]$ be all satisfied for some integer $y \in [1, (8m+6)t - 1]$. The integers i_k, j_k, r_k, and s_k are all distinct modulo-$(4m+3)$. So, binary $(0, 1)$ codewords with pulses located in chip positions

$$\{(0, \alpha^{(4m+3)i}, \alpha^{y+(4m+3)i}, \alpha^{(8m+6)t+(4m+3)i}, \alpha^{(8m+6)t+y+(4m+3)i}, \ldots,$$
$$\alpha^{(8m+6)2mt+(4m+3)i}, \alpha^{(8m+6)2mt+y+(4m+3)i}) : i = \{0, 1, \ldots, t-1\}\}$$

form a family of $(N, w, 1, 1)$ OOCs of odd weight $w = 4m + 3$ and cardinality $t = (N-1)/(w^2 - w)$.

These two Yang constructions also resulted in optimal code cardinality as the cardinality upper bound in Section 1.6 was met with equality [20].

Let $N = 151$, $w = 6$, $m = 1$, $t = 5$, $y = 17$, and $\alpha = 6$. Based on Yang construction with $w = 4m + 2$, the conditions are found to be $6^y - 1 = 70 = 6^{99}$, $6^{50+y} - 1 = 6 = 6^1$, $6^{50} - 6^y = 112 = 6^{47}$, $6^{50} - 1 = 31 = 6^{28}$, and $6^{50+y} - 6^y = 87 = 6^{45}$ due to $i_0 = 99$, $i_1 = 1$, $j_1 = 47$, $r_1 = 28$, and $s_1 = 45$ and they are all distinct module-5. This example results in five $(151, 6, 1, 1)$ OOC codewords over GF(151) with pulses located in chip positions $(1, 7, 32, 71, 73, 118)$, $(39, 40, 72, 75, 92, 135)$, $(8, 38, 56, 105, 115, 131)$, $(10, 18, 23, 123, 132, 147)$, and $(2, 14, 64, 85, 142, 146)$.

3.5.2 Constructions of $(N, w, 1, 2)$ OOC

According to the cardinality upper bound in Section 1.6, code cardinality can be improved by relaxing the maximum periodic cross-correlation function λ_c. In [20], Yang demonstrated how the BIBDs in Section 3.5.1 could be modified for the constructions of $(N, w, 1, 2)$ OOCs with expanded cardinality, as summarized in this section.

The Wilson and Yang constructions in Section 3.5.1 can be extended to generate $(N, w, 1, 2)$ OOCs with twice as many codewords as their optimal $(N, w, 1, 1)$ counterparts by replacing the index $i \in [0, t - 1]$ with $i \in [0, 2t - 1]$ and applying the concept of "coordinate-reversed" imaging [20]. For example, by modifying Wilson construction for odd-weight, pulses are now located in chip positions

$$\{(\alpha^{mi}, \alpha^{mi+2mt}, \alpha^{mi+4mt}, \ldots, \alpha^{mi+4m^2t}) : i = \{0, 1, \ldots, 2t - 1\}\}$$

where $w = 2m + 1$, $N = w(w-1)t + 1$, and α is a primitive element of GF(N) such that the values calculated from $\log_\alpha(\alpha^{2mkt} - 1)$ are all distinct modulo-m for $k \in [1, m]$. Because $\alpha^{w(w-1)t} = 1$ and $\alpha^{w(w-1)t/2} = -1$, it is found that the chip positions computed from $i \in [t, 2t - 1]$ are coordinate-reversed images of those computed from $i \in [0, t - 1]$. So, codewords with pulses located in the union of these two types of chip positions

$$\{(\alpha^{mi}, \alpha^{mi+2mt}, \alpha^{mi+4mt}, \ldots, \alpha^{mi+4m^2t}) \cup (-\alpha^{mi}, -\alpha^{mi+2mt},$$
$$-\alpha^{mi+4mt}, \ldots, -\alpha^{mi+4m^2t}) : i = \{0, 1, \ldots, t - 1\}\}$$

form a family of $(N, w, 1, 2)$ OOCs of odd weight $w = 2m + 1$ and cardinality $2t$, where $t = (N-1)/(w^2 - w)$.

Let $N = 41$, $w = 5$, $m = 2$, and $t = 2$. Wilson constructions generate two $(41, 5, 1, 1)$ OOC codewords with pulses located in chip positions $(1, 10, 16, 18, 37)$ and $(5, 8, 9, 21, 39)$. By taking the coordinate-reversed images, two new codewords with pulses located in chip positions $(4, 23, 25, 31, 40)$ and $(2, 20, 32, 33, 36)$ are obtained, resulting in four $(41, 5, 1, 2)$ OOC codewords.

In [20], Yang further extended these $(N, w, 1, 2)$-OOC constructions in order to obtain w (for even weight) and $w - 1$ (for odd weight) times as many codewords as the optimal $(N, w, 1, 1)$ OOCs in Section 3.5.1. The main difference is the inclusion of index j.

1. Let $w = 2m$ and set $N = w(w - 1)t + 1$ to be a prime number, where m and t are positive integers. Also let α be a primitive element of GF(N) and the values calculated from $\log_\alpha(\alpha^{2mkt} - 1)$ be all distinct and nonzero modulo-m for $k \in [1, m]$. So, binary $(0, 1)$ codewords with pulses located in chip positions

$$\{(0, \alpha^{j+mi}, \alpha^{j+mi+2mt}, \alpha^{j+mi+4mt}, \ldots, \alpha^{j+mi+4m(m-1)t}) :$$
$$i = \{0, 1, \ldots, 2t - 1\}, j = \{0, 1, \ldots, m - 1\}\}$$

form a family of $(N, w, 1, 2)$ OOCs of even weight $w = 2m$ and cardinality wt, where $t = (N - 1)/(w - 1)$.

2. Let $w = 2m + 1$ and set $N = w(w - 1)t + 1$ to be a prime number, where m and t are positive integers. Also let α be a primitive element of GF(N) and the values calculated from $\log_\alpha(\alpha^{2mkt} - 1)$ be all distinct modulo-m for $k \in [1, m]$. So, binary $(0, 1)$ codewords with pulses located in chip positions

$$\{(\alpha^{j+mi}, \alpha^{j+mi+2mt}, \alpha^{j+mi+4mt}, \ldots, \alpha^{j+mi+4m^2t}) :$$
$$i = \{0, 1, \ldots, 2t - 1\}, j = \{0, 1, \ldots, m - 1\}\}$$

form a family of $(N, w, 1, 2)$ OOCs of odd weight $w = 2m + 1$ and cardinality $(w - 1)t$, where $t = (N - 1)/w$.

Let $N = 41$, $w = 5$, $m = 2$, and $t = 2$. The first example in this section, which has four $(41, 5, 1, 2)$ OOC codewords, corresponds to the case of $j = 0$. For the case of $j = 1$, four new codewords with pulses located in chip positions $(6, 14, 17, 19, 26)$, $(11, 12, 28, 34, 38)$, $(15, 22, 24, 27, 35)$, and $(3, 7, 13, 29, 30)$ are obtained, resulting in eight $(41, 5, 1, 2)$ OOC codewords.

3.5.3 Constructions of $(N, w, 2, 1)$ OOC

The autocorrelation constraint λ_a is useful in the code-synchronization process between the communicating transmitter-receiver pair. Once the time frame of the arrival (correct address) codeword or, more precisely, the expected position of the autocorrelation peak is located, the role of the autocorrelation constraint becomes less important than that of the cross-correlation constraint. It is because the latter determines the severity of mutual interference. Also, from the cardinality upper bound in Section 1.6, code cardinality is directly proportional to λ_a, meaning that doubling λ_a will double code cardinality without scarifying code performance. So, Yang and Fuja [21] constructed two families of $(N, w, 2, 1)$ OOCs, as summarized in the following:

The first construction is for $(N, w, 2, 1)$ OOCs with $w = 2m$ and $w = 2m + 1$, which results in optimal code cardinality as cardinality upper bound in Section 1.6 is met with equality [21].

1. Let $w = 2m$ and set $N = (w^2t/2) + 1$ to be a prime number, where m and t are positive integers. Also let α be a primitive element of GF(N) and the values calculated from $\log_\alpha(\alpha^{mkt} - 1)$ be all distinct modulo-m for $k \in [1, m]$. So, binary $(0, 1)$ codewords with pulses located in chip positions

$$\{(\alpha^{mi}, \alpha^{m(i+t)}, \alpha^{m(i+2t)}, \ldots, \alpha^{m[i+2(m-1)t]}) : i = \{0, 1, \ldots, t-1\}\}$$

form a family of $(N, w, 2, 1)$ OOCs of even weight $w = 2m$ and cardinality $t = 2(N-1)/w^2$.

2. Let $w = 2m + 1$ and set $N = [(w^2 - 1)t/2] + 1$ to be a prime number, where m and t are positive integers. Also, let α be a primitive element of GF(N) and the values calculated from $\log_\alpha(\alpha^{(m+1)kt} - 1)$ be all distinct and nonzero modulo-$(m+1)$ for $k \in [1, m]$. So, binary $(0, 1)$ codewords with pulses located in chip positions

$$\{(0, \alpha^{(m+1)i}, \alpha^{(m+1)(i+t)}, \alpha^{(m+1)(i+2t)}, \ldots,$$
$$\alpha^{(m+1)[i+2(m-1)t]}) : i = \{0, 1, \ldots, t-1\}\}$$

form a family of $(N, w, 2, 1)$ OOCs of odd weight $w = 2m + 1$ and cardinality $t = 2(N-1)/(w^2 - 1)$.

Let $N = 37$, $w = 5$, $m = 2$, $t = 3$, and $\alpha = 2$. Based on the construction with $w = 2m + 1$, the conditions are found to be $2^{3t} - 1 = 30 = 2^{14}$ and $2 = 2^1$. This example results in three $(37, 5, 2, 1)$ OOC codewords over GF(37) with pulses located in chip positions $(0, 1, 6, 31, 36)$, $(0, 8, 11, 26, 29)$, and $(0, 10, 14, 23, 27)$.

The second construction is for $(N, w, 2, 1)$ OOCs with $w = 4m$ and $w = 4m + 1$ [21].

1. Let $w = 4m$ and set $N = (w^2t/2) + 1$ to be a prime number, where m and t are positive integers. Also let α be a primitive element of GF(N) and the conditions $\alpha^{k4mt+y} - 1 = \alpha^{ik}$ for $k \in [0, m-1]$, $\alpha^{k4mt} - \alpha^y = \alpha^{jk}$, $\alpha^{k4mt} - 1 = \alpha^{rk}$, and $\alpha^{k4mt+y} - \alpha^y = \alpha^{sk}$ for $k \in [1, m]$ be all satisfied for some integer $y \in [1, 4mt - 1]$. The integers i_k, j_k, r_k, and s_k are all distinct modulo-$4m$. So, binary $(0, 1)$ codewords with pulses located in chip positions

$$\{(\alpha^{4mi}, \alpha^{y+4mi}, \alpha^{4mt+4mi}, \alpha^{4mt+y+4mi}, \ldots,$$
$$\alpha^{(2m-1)4mt+4mi}, \alpha^{(2m-1)4mt+y+4mi}) : i = \{0, 1, \ldots, t-1\}\}$$

form a family of $(N, w, 2, 1)$ OOCs of even weight $w = 4m$ and cardinality $t = 2(N-1)/w^2$.

2. Let $w = 4m + 1$ and set $N = [(w^2 - 1)t/2] + 1$ to be a prime number, where m and t are positive integers. Also, let α be a primitive element of GF(N) and the conditions $\alpha^{k(4m+2)t+y} - 1 = \alpha^{ik}$ for $k \in [0, m-1]$, $\alpha^{k(4m+2)t} - \alpha^y = \alpha^{jk}$, $\alpha^{k(4m+2)t} - 1 = \alpha^{rk}$, and $\alpha^{k(4m+2)t+y} - \alpha^y = \alpha^{sk}$ for $k \in [1, m]$ be all satisfied for some integer $y \in [1, (4m+2)t - 1]$. The integers y, i_k, j_k,

r_k, and s_k are all distinct and nonzero modulo-$(4m+2)$. So, binary $(0,1)$ codewords with pulses located in chip positions

$$\{(0, \alpha^{(4m+2)i}, \alpha^{y+(4m+2)i}, \alpha^{(4m+2)t+(4m+2)i}, \alpha^{(4m+2)t+y+(4m+2)i}, \ldots,$$
$$\alpha^{(4m+2)(2m-1)t+(4m+2)i}, \alpha^{(4m+2)(2m-1)t+y+(4m+2)i}) :$$
$$i = \{0, 1, \ldots, t-1\}\}$$

form a family of $(N, w, 2, 1)$ OOCs of odd weight $w = 4m+1$ and cardinality $t = 2(N-1)/(w^2-1)$.

Let $N = 41$, $w = 4$, $m = 1$, $t = 5$, $y = 3$, and $\alpha = 6$. Based on the construction with $w = 4m$, the conditions are found to be $6^y - 1 = 10 = 6^8$, $6^{20} - 6^y = 29 = 6^7$, $6^{20} - 1 = 39 = 6^6$, and $6^{20+y} - 6^y = 19 = 6^9$ due to $i_0 = 8$, $j_1 = 7$, $r_1 = 6$, and $s_1 = 9$, and they are all distinct module-4. This example results in four $(41, 4, 2, 1)$ OOC codewords over GF(41) with pulses located in chip positions $(1, 11, 30, 40)$, $(12, 16, 25, 29)$, $(10, 13, 28, 31)$, $(3, 4, 37, 38)$, and $(7, 18, 23, 34)$.

3.5.4 Performance Analysis

To study the performances of these OOCs, the maximum periodic cross-correlation function λ_c is an important factor because it determines the severity of mutual interference. Because the $(N, w, 1, 1)$ and $(N, w, 2, 1)$ OOCs have $\lambda_c = 1$ and the $(N, w, 1, 2)$ OOCs have $\lambda_c = 2$, their performance analyses follow those of the extended prime codes (of $\lambda_c = 1$) in Section 3.2 and the original prime codes (of $\lambda_c = 2$) in Section 3.1, respectively.

The Gaussian-approximated error probability $P_{e|G}$ of these OOCs can be calculated from Equation (3.5). This approximation is a function of code weight w, the number of interferes (or interfering codewords) $K-1$, and the interference variance $\sigma^2 = \sum_{i=1}^{\lambda_c} \sum_{j=0}^{i-1} (i-j)^2 q_i q_j$, where q_i denotes the hit probability of having the periodic cross-correlation value (in the sampling time) of $i = \{0, 1, \ldots, \lambda_c\}$.

For the $(N, w, 1, 2)$ OOCs, the interference variance is given by $\sigma^2 = q_0 q_1 + 4q_0 q_2 + q_1 q_2$, where $q_0 = 1 - q_1 - q_2$, $q_1 = [w^2/(2N)] - 2q_2$, and $q_2 = w^2/(2N)/(\Phi - 1)$. The derivation of q_2 comes from the fact that the only chance of getting two hits in the $(N, w, 1, 2)$ OOCs is between a codeword and its coordinate-reversed image. There are at most $\Phi - 1$ possible interfering codewords and a total of w^2 hits over N chip positions, where Φ is the cardinality of the $(N, w, 1, 2)$ OOCs in use.

For the $(N, w, 1, 1)$ and $(N, w, 2, 1)$ OOCs, the interference variance is given by $\sigma^2 = q_0 q_1$, where $q_0 = 1 - q_1$ and $q_1 = w^2/(2N)$.

In addition, combinatorial methods can be applied for more accurate performance analysis of these OOCs. For the $(N, w, 1, 1)$ and $(N, w, 2, 1)$ OOCs, the chip-synchronous, soft- and hard-limiting error probabilities follow Equations (3.8) and (3.9), respectively. For the $(N, w, 1, 2)$ OOCs, the chip-synchronous, soft- and hard-limiting error probabilities follow Equations (3.6) and (3.7), respectively.

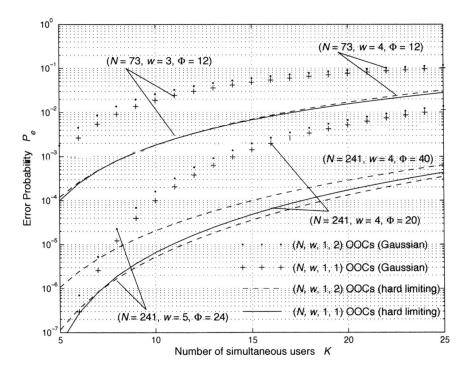

FIGURE 3.8 Error probabilities of the $(N, w, 1, 1)$ and $(N, w, 1, 2)$ OOCs for $N = \{73, 241\}$ and $w = \{3, 4, 5\}$.

Figure 3.8 plots the Gaussian [from Equation (3.5)] and chip-synchronous, hard-limiting [from Equation (3.7)] error probabilities of the $(N, w, 1, 1)$ and $(N, w, 1, 2)$ OOCs against the number of simultaneous users K for code length $N = \{73, 241\}$ and code weight $w = \{3, 4, 5\}$. From Section 3.5.1, the cardinality of the $(N, w, 1, 1)$ OOCs is given by $\Phi = (N - 1)/(w^2 - w)$. This gives $\Phi = 12$ in the $(73, 3, 1, 1)$ OOCs and $\Phi = 20$ in the $(241, 4, 1, 1)$ OOCs. Similarly, the cardinality of the $(N, w, 1, 2)$ OOCs created by the coordinate-reversed method in Section 3.5.2 is given by $\Phi = 2(N - 1)/(w^2 - w)$, which is two times the cardinality of the $(N, w, 1, 1)$ OOCs. In general, the error probabilities improve as N or w increases because of lower hit probabilities or higher autocorrelation peaks. However, the error probabilities get worse as K increases due to stronger mutual interference. While the Gaussian method provides a fast tool to approximate code performance, it tends to overestimate the error probability and gives the performance upper bound, especially when K is small. The hard-limiting error probabilities (the solid and dashed curves) are better than their Gaussian counterparts (the plus and dot curves) because the former give more accurate performance. Although not shown in the figure, the soft-limiting error-probability curve will be situated in between the Gaussian and hard-limiting curves for a given set of w and N.

The $(N,w,1,1)$ OOCs have the periodic cross-correlation functions of at most 1 at the expense of limited code cardinality. The $(N,w,1,2)$ OOCs have larger cardinality but generally result in poor performance due to higher cross-correlation values. This can be illustrated from the dashed curve of the $(241,4,1,2)$ OOCs with $\Phi = 40$, which is always worse than the solid curve of the $(241,4,1,1)$ OOCs, in Figure 3.8. On the other hand, the $(241,4,1,2)$ OOCs created by the coordinate-reversed method in Section 3.5.2 double the cardinality of the $(241,4,1,1)$ OOCs.

Code length and cardinality are two important figures of merit in system implementation. This is because the former determines the amount of bandwidth expansion and the latter controls the number of possible subscribers. So, the code weight of the $(N,w,1,2)$ OOCs in Figure 3.8 are chosen such that the code length and cardinality are similar to those of the $(N,w,1,1)$ OOCs for a fair comparison. For the same length and similar cardinality as the corresponding $(N,w,1,1)$ OOCs, the $(73,w,1,2)$ OOCs are chosen with $w = 4$ in order to have $\Phi = 12$, and the $(241,5,1,2)$ OOCs are used to give $\Phi = 24$, according to the coordinate-reversed method in Section 3.5.2. With this code-weight adjustment, Figure 3.8 shows that the $(N,w,1,1)$ and $(N,w,1,2)$ OOCs perform closely to each other (plus versus dotted curves; solid versus dashed curves). This efficient exchange of large code cardinality for heavier code weight demonstrates the flexibility of the $(N,w,1,2)$ OOCs, compensating for the performance loss due to higher cross-correlation function.

3.6   SUMMARY

In this chapter, the algebraic constructions and properties of various 1-D asynchronous prime codes were studied. Numerical examples on comparing their Gaussian, soft-limiting, and hard-limiting code performances under the chip-synchronous assumption were also given. Over $GF(p)$ of a prime p, the original prime codes, which form the basis of other prime codes in this book, have length p^2, weight $w \leq p$, and cardinality p. To reduce the periodic cross-correlation functions from 2 to 1, the extended prime codes over $GF(p)$ were constructed, which have the same weight and cardinality as the original prime codes, but different length of $p(2p-1)$. To provide flexibility in the relationship of code length and cardinality without sacrificing the correlation properties, the generalized prime codes of length p^{k+1}, weight $w \leq p$, and cardinality p^k were constructed for a positive integer k. The 2^n prime codes of length p^2, weight 2^n, and cardinality $\Phi \leq p$ were studied. The codes preserve the algebraic properties of 2^n codes and prime codes, supporting the power-, size-, and cost-conscious serial coding configuration in Section 2.1. Finally, the constructions of several families of 1-D OOCs, which are useful for the constructions of some families of 2-D prime codes in Chapters 5 and 6, were illustrated.

REFERENCES

1. Roth, R. M., Seroussi, G. (1986). On cyclic MDS codes of length q over $GF(q)$. *IEEE Trans. Info. Theory* 32(2):284–285.

2. Sarwate, D. V. (1994). Reed–Solomon codes and the design of sequences for spread-spectrum multiple-access communications. *Reed–Solomon Codes and Their Applications*. Wicker, S. B., Bhargava, V. K. (Eds.). Piscataway, NJ: IEEE Press.

3. Cooper, G., Nettleton, R. (1978). A spread-spectrum technique for high-capacity mobile communications. *IEEE Trans. Vehicular Technol.* 27(4):264–275.

4. Pickholtz, R. L., Schilling, D. L., Milstein, L. B. (1982). Theory of spread-spectrum communications—A tutorial. *IEEE Trans. Commun.* 30(5):855–884.

5. Dixon, R. C. (1984). *Spread Spectrum Systems.* (second edition). New York: John Wiley & Sons.

6. Kohno, R., Meidan, R., Milstein, L. B. (1995). Spread spectrum access methods for wireless communications. *IEEE Commun. Mag.* 33(1):58–67.

7. Glisic, S., Vucetic, B. (1997). *Spread-Spectrum CDMA Systems for Wireless Communications.* Norwood, MA: Artech House.

8. Titlebaum, E. L. (1981). Time-frequency hop signals. Part I. Coding based upon the theory of linear congruences. *IEEE Trans. Aerospace Electron. Systems* 17(4):490–494.

9. Shaar, A., Davies, P. (1983). Prime sequences: Quasi-optimal sequences for OR channel code division multiplexing. *Electron. Lett.* 19(21):888–890.

10. Prucnal, P. R., Santoro, M. A., Fan, T. R. (1986). Spread spectrum fiber optic local area network using optical processing. *J. Lightwave Technol.* 4(5):547–554.

11. Prucnal, P. R., Santoro, M. A., Sehgal, S. K. (1986). Ultra-fast all-optical synchronous multiple access fiber networks. *IEEE J. Selected Areas Commun.* 4(9):1484–1493.

12. Kwong, W. C., Perrier, P. A., Prucnal, P. R. (1991). Performance comparison of asynchronous and synchronous code division multiple access techniques for fiber-optic local area network. *IEEE Trans. Commun.* 39(11):1625–1634.

13. Yang, G.-C., Kwong, W. C. (1995). Performance analysis of optical CDMA with prime code. *Electron. Lett.* 31(7):569–570.

14. Yang, G.-C., Kwong, W. C. (1995). On the construction of 2^n codes for optical code-division multiple-access. *IEEE Trans. Commun.* 43(2–4):495–502.

15. Kwong, W. C., Yang, G.-C. (1995). Construction of 2^n prime codes for optical code-division multiple-access. *IEE Proc. Commun.* 142(3):141–150.

16. Kwong, W. C., Yang, G.-C., Zhang, J.-G. (1996). 2^n prime codes and coding architecture for optical code-division multiple-access. *IEEE Trans. Commun.* 44(9):1152–1162.

17. Yang, G.-C., Kwong, W. C. (2002). *Prime Codes with Applications to CDMA Optical and Wireless Networks.* Norwood, MA: Artech House.

18. Chung, F. R. K., Salehi, J. A., Wei, V. K. (1989). Optical orthogonal codes: Design, analysis, and applications. *IEEE Trans. Info. Theory* 35(5):595–604.

19. Chung, H., Kumar, P. V. (1990). Optical orthogonal codes—New bounds and an optimal construction. *IEEE Trans. Info. Theory* 36(4):866–873.

20. Yang, G.-C. (1995). Some new families of optical orthogonal codes for code-division multiple-access fibre-optic networks. *IEE Proc. Commun.* 142(6):363–368.

21. Yang, G.-C., Fuja, T. (1995). Optical orthogonal codes with unequal auto- and cross-correlation constraints. *IEEE Trans. Info. Theory* 41(1):96–106.

22. Yang, G.-C., (1996). Variable-weight optical orthogonal codes for CDMA networks with multiple performance requirements. *IEEE Trans. Commun.* 44(1):47–55.

23. Buratti, M. (1995). A powerful method for constructing difference families and optimal optical orthogonal codes. *Designs, Codes Cryptography* 5(1):13–25.

24. Fuji-Hara, R., Miao, Y. (2000). Optical orthogonal codes: Their bounds and new optimal constructions. *IEEE Trans. Info. Theory* 46(7):2396–2406.

25. Ge, G., Yin, J. (2001). Constructions for optimal $(v, 4, 1)$ optical orthogonal codes. *IEEE Trans. Info. Theory* 47(7):2998–3004.

26. Fuji-Hara, R., Miao, Y., Yin, J. (2001). Optimal $(9v, 4, 1)$ optical orthogonal codes *SIAM J. Discrete Mathematics* 14(2):256–266.

27. Buratti, M. (2002). Cyclic designs with block size 4 and related optimal optical orthogonal codes. *Designs, Codes and Cryptography* 26(1-3):111–125.

28. Chu, W., Golomb, S. W. (2003). A new recursive construction for optical orthogonal codes. *IEEE Trans. Info. Theory* 49(11):3072–3076.

29. Chang, Y., Fuji-Hara, R., Miao, Y. (2003). Combinatorial constructions of optimal optical orthogonal codes with weight 4. *IEEE Trans. Info. Theory* 49(5):1283–1292.

30. Chang, Y., Ji, L. (2004). Optimal $(4up, 5, 1)$ optical orthogonal codes. *J. Combinatorial Designs* 12(5):346–361.

31. Abel, R. J. R., Buratti, M. (2004). Some progress on $(v, 4, 1)$ difference families and optical orthogonal codes. *J. Combinatorial Theory Series A* 106(1):59–75.

32. Chu W., Colbourn, C. J. (2004). Recursive constructions for optimal $(n, 4, 2)$-OOCs. *J. Combinatorial Designs* 12(5)333–345.

33. Azizoğlu, M. Y., Salehi, J. A., Li, Y. (1992). Optical CDMA via temporal codes. *IEEE Trans. Commun.* 40(7):1162–1170.

34. Chen, J.-J., Yang, G.-C. (2001). CDMA fiber-optic systems with optical hard limiters. *IEEE J. Lightwave Technol.* 18(7):950–958.

35. Hsu, C.-C., Yang, G.-C., Kwong, W. C. (2008). Hard-limiting performance analysis of 2-D optical codes under the chip-asynchronous assumption. *IEEE Trans. Commun.* 56(5):762–768.

36. Chang, Y. L., Marhic, M. E. (1990). 2^n codes for optical CDMA and associated networks. In *Proceedings: IEEE/LEOS Summer Topical Meetings*, Monterey, California, July 23–24.

37. Bose, R. C. (1939). On the construction of balanced incomplete block design. *Annals Human Genetics* 9(4):353–399.

38. Hanani, H. (1961). The existence and construction of balanced incomplete block designs. *The Annals Mathematical Statistics* 32(2):361–386.

39. Colbourn, M. J., Colbourn, C. J. (1984). Recursive constructions for cyclic block designs. *J. Statistical Planning Inference* 10(1):97–103.

40. Wilson, R. M., (1972). Cyclotomy and difference families in elementary Abelian groups. *J. Number Theory* 4(1):17–47.

41. Zhi, C., Pingzhi, F., Fan, J. (1992). Disjoint difference sets, difference triangle sets, and related codes. *IEEE Trans. Info. Theory* 38(2):518–522.

4 1-D Synchronous Prime Codes

As studied in Chapter 2, whenever optical intensity is used for transmission, incoherent coding and detection can be employed. Incoherent coding is also (time) asynchronous in nature. So, pseudo-orthogonal binary $(0,1)$ codes that have close-to-zero periodic cross-correlation functions, such as the 1-D prime codes in Chapter 3, have been designed for asynchronous applications. Multiple access of simultaneous users is supported without the need for waiting, scheduling, or coordination [1–10]. Because nonscheduled transmissions create randomness and may accumulate strong mutual interference, asynchronous coding can only support a limited number of subscribers and even fewer simultaneous users.

In general, due to rigorous transmission scheduling and coordination, synchronous coding produces higher throughput (or successful transmissions) and accommodates more subscribers and simultaneous users than asynchronous coding [10–14]. The term *synchronous* usually refers to the requirement that transmissions of all simultaneous users originate at a certain reference frame, namely in time or wavelength, at all time. The trade-off is that perfect synchronization, especially in the time domain, is difficult to achieve. In applications with real-time or high-throughput requirements, such as digitized video transmission, synchronous coding is more efficient. On the other hand, in applications where traffic tends to be bursty or real-time transmission is not critical, such as digitized voice and data transmissions, asynchronous coding is more suitable due to its simplicity and flexibility in resource utilization.

Synchronous coding can support more possible subscribers because cyclic-shifted versions of incoherent codewords can be treated as distinct codewords, substantially increasing code cardinality. In addition, *in-phase* cross-correlation functions are now considered, instead of periodic ones in Chapter 3. So, synchronous (incoherent) coding requires new optical codes with fixed, low, in-phase cross-correlation functions [5, 11, 12, 15]. As studied in this chapter, some of these synchronous codes even have zero in-phase cross-correlation functions and create zero mutual interference.

In this chapter, 1-D synchronous prime codes are constructed for accommodating synchronous simultaneous accesses [5, 10]. The properties and performance of these synchronous prime codes are also analyzed. Afterward, the construction, properties, and performance of 1-D synchronous multilevel prime codes are studied [16]. The codes have multiple levels of in-phase cross-correlation function and code cardinality. This property supports a flexible exchange between the numbers of subscribers and simultaneous users. Finally, potential applications, in which synchronous coding is particularly suitable, are discussed [5, 12, 17]. By combining both Optical Time-

Division Multiple Access (O-TDMA) and synchronous O-CDMA in the same synchronous network, multimedia services with different traffic requirements and bit rates can be integrated. The timing problem that results from the difference in bit rates of different service types can be eliminated using just a single clock rate.

4.1 SYNCHRONOUS PRIME CODES

Based on the Galois field $GF(p)$ of a prime number p, a synchronous prime sequence $S_{i_2,i_1} = (s_{i_2,i_1,0}, s_{i_2,i_1,1}, \ldots, s_{i_2,i_1,j}, \ldots, s_{i_2,i_1,w-1})$ is constructed by the element

$$s_{i_2,i_1,j} = i_2 j + i_1 \pmod{p}$$

where $s_{i_2,i_1,j}$, i_1, i_2, and j are all in $GF(p)$, and $w \le p$. There are a total of p^2 synchronous prime sequences, S_{i_2,i_1}, indexed by i_1 and $i_2 = \{0, 1, \ldots, p-1\}$.

Each of these p^2 synchronous prime sequences is mapped into a binary $(0,1)$ codeword $C_{i_2,i_1} = (c_{i_2,i_1,0}, c_{i_2,i_1,1}, \ldots, c_{i_2,i_1,l}, \ldots, c_{i_2,i_1,wp-1})$, indexed by i_1 and $i_2 = \{0, 1, \ldots, p-1\}$, with the code element [5, 10, 12]

$$c_{i_2,i_1,l} = \begin{cases} 1 & \text{if } l = s_{i_2,i_1,j} + jp \text{ for } j = \{0, 1, \ldots, p-1\} \\ 0 & \text{otherwise} \end{cases}$$

This construction results in the synchronous prime codes with cardinality p^2, length wp, and weight $w \le p$.

For illustration, Table 4.1 shows the first 35 (out of a total of 49) synchronous prime sequences and binary $(0,1)$ codewords of length $wp = 49$ and weight $w = 7$ over $GF(7)$.

These p^2 synchronous prime codewords can be partitioned into p subsets (indexed by $i_2 \in [0, p-1]$), and each subset has p codewords (indexed by $i_1 \in [0, p-1]$). The first synchronous codeword, $C_{i_2,0}$, in every subset originates from a codeword of the asynchronous prime codes in Section 3.1, and acts as a seed for generating other synchronous codewords in the subset. So, the synchronous prime codes are p times larger in cardinality than the asynchronous counterparts over the same $GF(p)$.

In the synchronous prime codes, the peak of the cross-correlation function between any two codewords can be as high as the autocorrelation peak, but is never found at the expected autocorrelation-peak position of the codewords. (This autocorrelation-peak position is called the *in-phase* position, and this notation is used in this book whenever synchronous codes are concerned.) By synchronizing to the in-phase position, a receiver can distinguish the true autocorrelation peak from adjacent cross-correlation peaks.

Theorem 4.1

The autocorrelation peaks of the synchronous prime codes over $GF(p)$ of a prime p and weight w are equal to w, where $w \le p$. The in-phase cross-correlation functions

TABLE 4.1
First 35 Synchronous Prime Sequences and Codewords over GF(7)

(i_2,i_1)	S_{i_2,i_1}	C_{i_2,i_1}
(0,0)	0 0 0 0 0 0 0	1000000 1000000 1000000 1000000 1000000 1000000 1000000
(0,1)	1 1 1 1 1 1 1	0100000 0100000 0100000 0100000 0100000 0100000 0100000
(0,2)	2 2 2 2 2 2 2	0010000 0010000 0010000 0010000 0010000 0010000 0010000
(0,3)	3 3 3 3 3 3 3	0001000 0001000 0001000 0001000 0001000 0001000 0001000
(0,4)	4 4 4 4 4 4 4	0000100 0000100 0000100 0000100 0000100 0000100 0000100
(0,5)	5 5 5 5 5 5 5	0000010 0000010 0000010 0000010 0000010 0000010 0000010
(0,6)	6 6 6 6 6 6 6	0000001 0000001 0000001 0000001 0000001 0000001 0000001
(1,0)	0 1 2 3 4 5 6	1000000 0100000 0010000 0001000 0000100 0000010 0000001
(1,1)	1 2 3 4 5 6 0	0100000 0010000 0001000 0000100 0000010 0000001 1000000
(1,2)	2 3 4 5 6 0 1	0010000 0001000 0000100 0000010 0000001 1000000 0100000
(1,3)	3 4 5 6 0 1 2	0001000 0000100 0000010 0000001 1000000 0100000 0010000
(1,4)	4 5 6 0 1 2 3	0000100 0000010 0000001 1000000 0100000 0010000 0001000
(1,5)	5 6 0 1 2 3 4	0000010 0000001 1000000 0100000 0010000 0001000 0000100
(1,6)	6 0 1 2 3 4 5	0000001 1000000 0100000 0010000 0001000 0000100 0000010
(2,0)	0 2 4 6 1 3 5	1000000 0010000 0000100 0000001 0100000 0001000 0000010
(2,1)	1 3 5 0 2 4 6	0100000 0001000 0000010 1000000 0010000 0000100 0000001
(2,2)	2 4 6 1 3 5 0	0010000 0000100 0000001 0100000 0001000 0000010 1000000
(2,3)	3 5 0 2 4 6 1	0001000 0000010 1000000 0010000 0000100 0000001 0100000
(2,4)	4 6 1 3 5 0 2	0000100 0000001 0100000 0001000 0000010 1000000 0010000
(2,5)	5 0 2 4 6 1 3	0000010 1000000 0010000 0000100 0000001 0100000 0001000
(2,6)	6 1 3 5 0 2 4	0000001 0100000 0001000 0000010 1000000 0010000 0000100
(3,0)	0 3 6 2 5 1 4	1000000 0001000 0000001 0010000 0000010 0100000 0000100
(3,1)	1 4 0 3 6 2 5	0100000 0000100 1000000 0001000 0000001 0010000 0000010
(3,2)	2 5 1 4 0 3 6	0010000 0000010 0100000 0000100 1000000 0001000 0000001
(3,3)	3 6 2 5 1 4 0	0001000 0000001 0010000 0000010 0100000 0000100 1000000
(3,4)	4 0 3 6 2 5 1	0000100 1000000 0001000 0000001 0010000 0000010 0100000
(3,5)	5 1 4 0 3 6 2	0000010 0100000 0000100 1000000 0001000 0000001 0010000
(3,6)	6 2 5 1 4 0 3	0000001 0010000 0000010 0100000 0000100 1000000 0001000
(4,0)	0 4 1 5 2 6 3	1000000 0000100 0100000 0000010 0010000 0000001 0001000
(4,1)	1 5 2 6 3 0 4	0100000 0000010 0010000 0000001 0001000 1000000 0000100
(4,2)	2 6 3 0 4 1 5	0010000 0000001 0001000 1000000 0000100 0100000 0000010
(4,3)	3 0 4 1 5 2 6	0001000 1000000 0000100 0100000 0000010 0010000 0000001
(4,4)	4 1 5 2 6 3 0	0000100 0100000 0000010 0010000 0000001 0001000 1000000
(4,5)	5 2 6 3 0 4 1	0000010 0010000 0000001 0001000 1000000 0000100 0100000
(4,6)	6 3 0 4 1 5 2	0000001 0001000 1000000 0000100 0100000 0000010 0010000

of the codes are at most 1, but equal to 0 if the correlating codewords come from the same subset or index $i_2 = \{0, 1, \ldots, p - 1\}$ [5, 10, 12].

Proof Let C_{i_2,i_1} and $C_{i_2',i_1'}$ be two distinct synchronous prime codewords from two different subsets for i_1, i_2, i_1', and $i_2' = \{0, 1, \ldots, p - 1\}$, where $i_2 \neq i_2'$. Based on the construction, every synchronous codeword can be divided into w blocks, each block has p chips, and there is exactly one pulse per block, where $w \leq p$. Label the p chip positions in each of these w blocks with consecutive numbers from 0 to $p - 1$. So, the pulse in the jth block of C_{i_2,i_1} is located in chip position $i_2 j + i_1 \pmod{p}$, where $j = \{0, 1, \ldots, w - 1\}$. Also, the pulse in the jth block of $C_{i_2',i_1'}$ is located in chip position $i_2' j + i_1' \pmod{p}$. If there is a hit in the jth blocks of C_{i_2,i_1} and $C_{i_2',i_1'}$, then

$$i_2 j + i_1 = i_2' j + i_1' \pmod{p}$$

must hold. Because this equation is a linear function of j over $GF(p)$, at most one solution of j can be found. As the number of blocks containing a hit cannot exceed the number of solutions of j, there only exists one hit in at most one block. So, the maximum in-phase cross-correlation function is 1.

For any two distinct codewords C_{i_2,i_1} and $C_{i_2',i_1'}$ from the same subset (or $i_2 = i_2'$ but $i_1 \neq i_1'$), if there is a hit in their jth blocks, then

$$i_2 j + i_1 = i_2 j + i_1' \pmod{p}$$

which is not a function of j over $GF(p)$. The equation implies $i_1 = i_1'$, which violates the assumption of distinct C_{i_2,i_1} and $C_{i_2',i_1'}$. So, the maximum in-phase cross-correlation function is 0.

Finally, the autocorrelation peaks of w are due to the code weight $w \leq p$.   ■

Figure 4.1 shows the autocorrelation functions of the synchronous prime codeword $C_{1,2}$, cross-correlation functions of $C_{1,2}$ and $C_{1,4}$ (from the same subset $i_2 = 1$), and cross-correlation functions of $C_{1,2}$ and $C_{2,1}$ (from two different subsets), all over $GF(7)$ and of length 49 and weight 7, for the transmission of data-bit stream 1011001110 in on-off-keying (OOK) modulation. In OOK, each data bit 1 is conveyed by a codeword, but nothing is transmitted for a data bit 0. The vertical grid lines indicate the expected positions of the autocorrelation peaks—the in-phase positions. The autocorrelation peaks at the in-phase positions are equal to the code weight, which is equal to 7 in this example. The cross-correlation values at the in-phase positions are at most 0 and 1 in Figures 4.1(b) and (c), respectively, agreeing with Theorem 4.1. However, the cross-correlation values can be as high as the autocorrelation peaks at other chip positions.

4.1.1   Performance Analysis

According to Section 1.8, the synchronous prime codes, which have the in-phase cross-correlation functions of at most 1, can accommodate up to $K = w - 1$ simul-

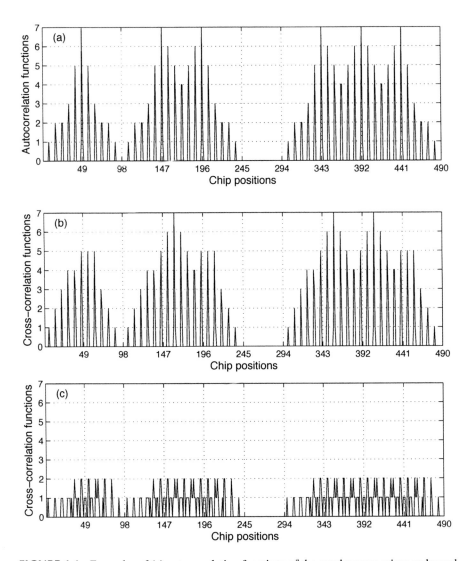

FIGURE 4.1   Examples of (a) autocorrelation functions of the synchronous prime codeword $C_{1,2}$; (b) cross-correlation functions of $C_{1,2}$ and $C_{1,4}$ (from the same subset); and (c) cross-correlation functions of $C_{1,2}$ and $C_{2,1}$ (from two different subsets), all over GF(7) and of length 49 and weight 7, for the transmission of data-bit stream 1011001110 in OOK. The vertical grid lines indicate the in-phase positions.

taneous users without any decision error if the decision threshold is set to the code weight w. However, when $K \geq w$, decision errors may occur in a receiver due to its inability to distinguish an autocorrelation peak from the aggregated in-phase cross-correlation function.

Theorem 4.2

The chip-synchronous, soft-limiting error probability of the synchronous prime codes over GF(p) of a prime p with cardinality p^2, length wp, weight w, and the maximum in-phase cross-correlation function of 1 in OOK is formulated as [5, 10]

$$P_e = \frac{1}{2^K} \left\{ \frac{K!}{w!(K-w)!} \left[1 - \frac{p^w w!(p^2 - w)!}{p^2!} \right] + \sum_{i=w+1}^{K} \frac{K!}{i!(K-i)!} \right\} \quad (4.1)$$

if $K \geq w$; otherwise, $P_e = 0$.

Proof Because the synchronous prime codes have the in-phase cross-correlation functions of at most 1, the total amount of mutual interference seen by the desired receiver at the in-phase positions can be as high as the autocorrelation peaks and reach the decision threshold when $K \geq w$. According to Section 1.8, the probability of error can be written as

$$P_e = \sum_{i=0}^{K} \text{Pr}(\text{error} \mid K \text{ simultaneous users}, i \text{ users sent 1})$$
$$\times \text{Pr}(i \text{ users sent 1} \mid K \text{ simultaneous users})$$
$$= \frac{\binom{K}{i}}{2^K} \sum_{i=0}^{K} \text{Pr}(\text{error} \mid K \text{ simultaneous users}, i \text{ users sent 1})$$

for $K \in [w, p^2 - 1]$. The derivation is based on the assumptions that each simultaneous user generates data bit 1s and 0s with equal probability in OOK. There are $\binom{K}{i}$ ways to pick i simultaneous users that transmit data bit-1s, out of 2^K possible cases.

Due to the subset property in Theorem 4.1, there are three cases to consider. If the number of simultaneous users that transmit data bit-1s is less than w (or $i < w$), there will be no error and then $\text{Pr}(i \text{ users sent 1} \mid K \text{ simultaneous users}) = 0$. However, if the number of simultaneous users that transmit data bit-1s is greater than w (or $i > w$), at least one receiver will make wrong decisions and then $\text{Pr}(i \text{ users sent 1} \mid K \text{ simultaneous users}) = 1$. Finally, when $i = w$, errors may occur if the two correlating codewords originate from two different subsets. There are p^w ways to pick the codewords, out of $\binom{p^2}{w}$ possible ways, from two different subsets. So, $\text{Pr}(\text{error} \mid K \text{ simultaneous users}, i \text{ sent 1}) = 1 - p^w / \binom{p^2}{w}$ if $i = w$. By combining these three cases and after some manipulations, the final form of Equation (4.1) is derived. ∎

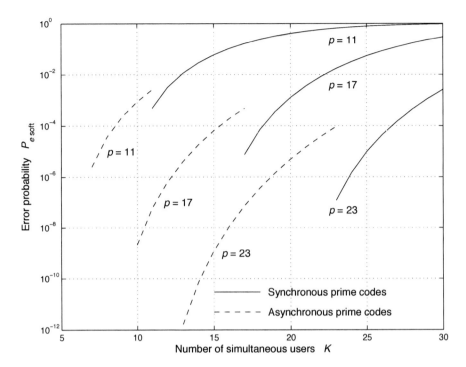

FIGURE 4.2 Chip-synchronous, soft-limiting error probabilities of the asynchronous and synchronous prime codes over GF(p) for $w = p = \{11, 17, 23\}$.

Figure 4.2 plots the chip-synchronous, soft-limiting error probabilities of the asynchronous prime codes [from Equation (3.6)] and synchronous prime codes [from Equation (4.1)] over GF(p) against the number of simultaneous users K for $w = p = \{11, 17, 23\}$. In general, the error probabilities improve as p increases because of heavier code weight ($w = p$) and longer code length ($N = p^2$), resulting in higher autocorrelation peaks and lower hit probabilities, respectively. However, the error probabilities get worse as K increases due to stronger mutual interference. The synchronous prime codes always outperform the asynchronous ones because the former have the maximum (in-phase) cross-correlation value of 1, but the latter have the maximum (periodic) cross-correlation value of 2. Their performance difference gets wider as p increases. In addition, the synchronous prime codes support up to p^2 possible subscribers and have no decision error when $K < w$. The asynchronous prime codes can only support up to p possible subscribers and have decision errors even for a small K. These explain why the solid curves start but the dashed curves stop at $K = p$ in this example.

Because Gaussian approximation has been derived for studying the performance of the asynchronous prime codes in Section 3.1, the Gaussian error probability of the synchronous prime codes is here derived for the sake of comparison.

Theorem 4.3

The Gaussian error probability of the synchronous prime codes over GF(p) of a prime p with length wp and weight w in OOK is formulated as [5, 10]

$$P_{e|G} = Q\left(\frac{wp}{\sqrt{(K-1)w(2p-w)}}\right) \tag{4.2}$$

where $Q(x) = (1/\sqrt{2\pi})\int_x^\infty \exp\left(-y^2/2\right) dy$ is the complementary error function.

Proof According to Section 1.8.1, the Gaussian error probability is given by

$$
\begin{aligned}
P_{e|G} &= Q\left(\frac{1}{2}\sqrt{\frac{w^2}{(K-1)\sum_{i=1}^{\lambda_c'}\sum_{j=0}^{i-1}(i-j)^2 q_i q_j}}\right) \\
&= Q\left(\frac{w}{2\sqrt{(K-1)q_0 q_1}}\right)
\end{aligned}
$$

where the factor $1/2$ comes from the assumption of equiprobable data bit-1 and bit-0 transmissions in OOK, and the maximum in-phase cross-correlation function λ_c' is set to 1 for the synchronous prime codes. The hit probabilities, q_i, of having the in-phase cross-correlation values of $i = \{0,1\}$ are given by

$$q_1 = \frac{w^2}{2N} = \frac{w^2}{2wp} = \frac{w}{2p}$$

and $q_0 = 1 - q_1$. The numerator in q_1 counts the number of possible pulse-overlaps (or hits) in each cross-correlation function. In the denominator, N represents the number of possible chip positions for the hits to occur, and $1/2$ accounts for OOK. After some manipulations, the final form of $P_{e|G}$ in the theorem is derived. ∎

Figure 4.3 plots the Gaussian error probabilities of the asynchronous prime codes [from Equation (3.5)] and synchronous prime codes [from Equation (4.2)] against the number of simultaneous users K for $w = p = \{11, 17, 23\}$. In general, the trend of the curves follows that of Figure 4.2 with similar explanations. By comparing the dashed curves in Figures 4.2 and 4.3, it is found that Gaussian approximation tends to overestimate the error probabilities when K is small. However, it underestimates the error probabilities when K is large, as seen from the solid curves of both figures.

4.2 SYNCHRONOUS MULTILEVEL PRIME CODES

The synchronous prime codes in Section 4.1 are constructed with small cardinality due to the maximum in-phase cross-correlation function of 1. One way to improve

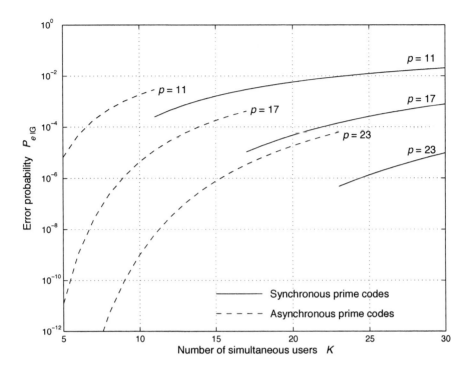

FIGURE 4.3 Gaussian error probabilities of the asynchronous and synchronous prime codes over GF(p) for $w = p = \{11, 17, 23\}$.

code cardinality is by relaxing the maximum cross-correlation function at the expense of code performance [5, 16]. In this section, synchronous multilevel prime codes, which have multiple levels of in-phase cross-correlation functions and code cardinalities, are constructed [16]. By partitioning the codes into a tree structure of subsets of codewords, the in-phase cross-correlation values is varied to attain different code performances and cardinalities. Some subsets of codewords can even achieve orthogonality (or zero cross-correlation value). In addition, the synchronous multilevel prime codes can be used in spectral amplitude coding [15] due to their fixed in-phase cross-correlation functions, as discussed in Section 2.4. The codes reduce phase-induced-intensity noise, a major deleterious effect in spectral-amplitude-coding systems, because they are sparse in the number of mark chips (or pulses).

Based on GF(p) of a prime p and a positive integer n, a synchronous multilevel prime sequence $S_{i_{n+1}, i_n, \ldots, i_1} = (s_{i_{n+1}, i_n, \ldots, i_1, 0}, \; s_{i_{n+1}, i_n, \ldots, i_1, 1}, \; \ldots, s_{i_{n+1}, i_n, \ldots, i_1, j}, \ldots, s_{i_{n+1}, i_n, \ldots, i_1, w-1})$ is constructed by the element

$$s_{i_{n+1}, \ldots, i_2, i_1, j} = i_{n+1} j^n + i_n j^{n-1} + \cdots + i_1 j^0 \pmod{p}$$

where $s_{i_{n+1}, \ldots, i_2, i_1, j}$, $i_1, i_2, \ldots, i_{n+1}$, and j are all in GF(p), and $w \le p$. There are a total of p^{n+1} synchronous multilevel prime sequences, $S_{i_{n+1}, i_n, \ldots, i_1}$, indexed by $i_1, i_2,$

..., and $i_{n+1} = \{0, 1, \ldots, p-1\}$.

Each of these p^{n+1} synchronous multilevel prime sequences is mapped into a binary $(0, 1)$ codeword $C_{i_{n+1}, i_n, \ldots, i_1} = (c_{i_{n+1}, i_n, \ldots, i_1, 0}, c_{i_{n+1}, i_n, \ldots, i_1, 1}, \ldots, c_{i_{n+1}, i_n, \ldots, i_1, l}, \ldots, c_{i_{n+1}, i_n, \ldots, i_1, wp-1})$, indexed by i_1, i_2, ..., and $i_{n+1} = \{0, 1, \ldots, p-1\}$, with the code element [16]

$$c_{i_{n+1}, \ldots, i_2, i_1, l} = \begin{cases} 1 & \text{if } l = s_{i_{n+1}, i_n, \ldots, i_1, j} + jp \text{ for } j = \{0, 1, \ldots, p-1\} \\ 0 & \text{otherwise} \end{cases}$$

This construction results in the synchronous multilevel prime codes with cardinality p^{n+1}, length wp, and weight $w \le p$.

The synchronous multilevel prime codes increase code cardinality and then support more possible subscribers by having the maximum in-phase cross-correlation function λ_c' as high as n. The codes can be partitioned as a tree structure of $n+1$ levels, as illustrated in Figure 4.4. Starting from the root on the left-hand side, level $n+1$ has one set of $\Phi = p^{n+1}$ codewords of $\lambda_c' = n$. In level n, these p^{n+1} codewords are partitioned into p subsets, and each subset has $\Phi = p^n$ codewords of $\lambda_c' = n-1$. In level $n-1$, every subset of p^n codewords in level n are further partitioned into p subsets, giving a total of p^2 subsets, and each subset has $\Phi = p^{n-1}$ codewords of $\lambda_c' = n-2$. This partition process continues to level 1, in which there are in total p^n subsets and $\Phi = p$ codewords in each subset with $\lambda_c' = 0$. Code orthogonality (or zero mutual interference) is achieved within every subset in level 1, an important characteristic of the synchronous multilevel prime codes. The synchronous prime codes in Section 4.1 belong to one subset in level 2.

Theorem 4.4

The autocorrelation peaks of the synchronous multilevel prime codes over $GF(p)$ of a prime p and weight w are equal to w, where $w \le p$ [16]. The in-phase cross-correlation functions of the codes are at most n, but at most $k-1$ if the correlating codewords come from the same subset of level $k \in [1, n+1]$.

Proof The proof is similar to that of Theorem 4.1 Let $C_{i_{n+1}, i_n, \ldots, i_1}$ and $C_{i'_{n+1}, i'_n, \ldots, i'_1}$ be two distinct synchronous multilevel prime codewords for i_1, i_2, ..., i_{n+1}, i'_1, i'_2, ..., and $i'_{n+1} = \{0, 1, \ldots, p-1\}$, where $(i_{n+1}, i_n, \ldots, i_1) \ne (i'_{n+1}, i'_n, \ldots, i'_1)$. Based on the construction, every synchronous codeword can be divided into w blocks, each block has p chips, and there is exactly one pulse per block, where $w \le p$. Label the p chip positions in each of these w blocks with the consecutive numbers from 0 to $p-1$. So, the pulse in the jth block of $C_{i_{n+1}, i_n, \ldots, i_1}$ is located in chip position $i_{n+1}j^n + i_n j^{n-1} + \cdots + i_1 j^0 \pmod{p}$, where $j = \{0, 1, \ldots, w-1\}$. Also, the pulse in the jth block of $C_{i'_{n+1}, i'_n, \ldots, i'_1}$ is located in chip position $i'_{n+1}j^n + i'_n j^{n-1} + \cdots + i'_1 j^0$

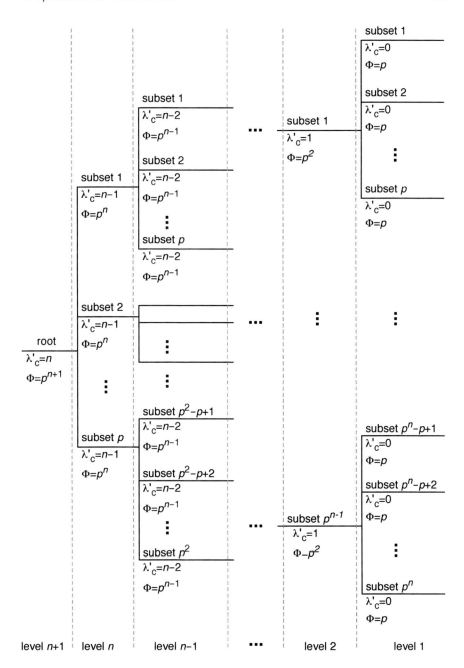

FIGURE 4.4 Tree structure of the synchronous multilevel prime codes over $GF(p)$ of a prime p and a positive integer n, where Φ is the code cardinality in each subset.

(mod p). If there is a hit in the jth blocks of $C_{i_{n+1},i_n,\ldots,i_1}$ and $C_{i'_{n+1},i'_n,\ldots,i'_1}$, then

$$i_{n+1}j^n + i_n j^{n-1} + \cdots + i_1 j^0 = i'_{n+1}j^n + i'_n j^{n-1} + \cdots + i'_1 j^0 \quad (\text{mod } p)$$

must hold. Because this equation is an nth-power function of j over $GF(p)$, at most n solutions of j can be found. So, the maximum in-phase cross-correlation function is at most n.

For any two distinct codewords $C_{i_{n+1},i_n,\ldots,i_1}$ and $C_{i'_{n+1},i'_n,\ldots,i'_1}$ from the same subset $(i_{n+1} = i'_{n+1}, i_n = i'_n, \cdots,$ and $i_{k+1} = i'_{k+1}$, but $i_k \neq i'_k$, $i_{k-1} \neq i'_{k-1}$, $\cdots$, and $i_1 \neq i'_1$) of level $k \in [1, n+1]$, if there is a hit in the jth blocks of $C_{i_{n+1},i_n,\ldots,i_1}$ and $C_{i'_{n+1},i'_n,\ldots,i'_1}$, then

$$i_{n+1}j^n + i_n j^{n-1} + \cdots + i_{k+1}j^k + i_k j^{k-1} + i_{k-1}j^{k-2} + \cdots + i_1 j^0$$
$$= i_{n+1}j^n + i_n j^{n-1} + \cdots + i_{k+1}j^k + i'_k j^{k-1} + i'_{k-1}j^{k-2} + \cdots + i'_1 j^0 \quad (\text{mod } p)$$

must hold. Because it is a $(k-1)$th-power function of j over $GF(p)$, at most $k-1$ solutions of j can be found. So, the maximum in-phase cross-correlation function is $k-1$.

Finally, the autocorrelation peaks of w are due to the code weight $w \leq p$.   ∎

Using $n = 2$ and $p = w = 5$ as an example, there exist 125 synchronous trilevel prime codewords over $GF(5)$ of length $wp = 25$ and weight $w = 5$, indexed by i_1, i_2, and $i_3 \in [0,4]$. The 25 synchronous trilevel prime sequences and binary $(0,1)$ codewords with the index $i_3 = 1$ are tabulated in Table 4.2. The subset partition is done by fixing the indices i_2 and i_3. While all 125 codewords in the code set have $\lambda'_c = 2$, the 25 codewords with a fixed i_3 (e.g., Table 4.2 with $i_3 = 1$) have $\lambda'_c = 1$, and every 5 codewords with fixed i_2 and i_3 have $\lambda'_c = 0$. The 25 synchronous prime codewords over $GF(5)$ in Table 4.1 correspond to the special case of $i_3 = 0$ in level 2 of these synchronous trilevel prime codes.

4.2.1 Performance Analysis

According to Section 1.8.3, the chip-synchronous, soft-limiting error probability of the synchronous multilevel prime codes over $GF(p)$ of a prime p with weight $w \leq p$ and the maximum in-phase cross-correlation function $\lambda'_c = n$ in OOK is given by

$$P_{e,\text{soft}} = \frac{1}{2} - \frac{1}{2} \sum_{l_1=0}^{Z_{\text{th}}-1} \sum_{l_2=0}^{\lfloor (Z_{\text{th}}-1-l_1)/2 \rfloor} \cdots \sum_{l_n=0}^{\lfloor (Z_{\text{th}}-1-\sum_{k=1}^{n-1} k l_k)/n \rfloor}$$
$$\frac{(K-1)!}{l_0! l_1! \cdots l_n!} q_0^{l_0} q_1^{l_1} \cdots q_n^{l_n} \tag{4.3}$$

where $K = \sum_{k=0}^n l_k + 1$ is the number of simultaneous users and the decision threshold $Z_{\text{th}} = w$ is usually applied for optimal decision.

TABLE 4.2

Twenty-Five Synchronous Trilevel Prime Sequences and Codewords over GF(5) with $i_3 = 1$ and $n = 2$

(i_3, i_2, i_1)	S_{i_3, i_2, i_1}	C_{i_3, i_2, i_1}
(1,0,0)	0 1 4 4 1	10000 01000 00001 00001 01000
(1,0,1)	1 2 0 0 2	01000 00100 10000 10000 00100
(1,0,2)	2 3 1 1 3	00100 00010 01000 01000 00010
(1,0,3)	3 4 2 2 4	00010 00001 00100 00100 00001
(1,0,4)	4 0 3 3 0	00001 10000 00010 00010 10000
(1,1,0)	0 2 1 2 0	10000 00100 01000 00100 10000
(1,1,1)	1 3 2 3 1	01000 00010 00100 00010 01000
(1,1,2)	2 4 3 4 2	00100 00001 00010 00001 00100
(1,1,3)	3 0 4 0 3	00010 10000 00001 10000 00010
(1,1,4)	4 1 0 1 4	00001 01000 10000 01000 00001
(1,2,0)	0 3 3 0 4	10000 00010 00010 10000 00001
(1,2,1)	1 4 4 1 0	01000 00001 00001 01000 10000
(1,2,2)	2 0 0 2 1	00100 10000 10000 00100 01000
(1,2,3)	3 1 1 3 2	00010 01000 01000 00010 00100
(1,2,4)	4 2 2 4 3	00001 00100 00100 00001 00010
(1,3,0)	0 4 0 3 3	10000 00001 10000 00010 00010
(1,3,1)	1 0 1 4 4	01000 10000 01000 00001 00001
(1,3,2)	2 1 2 0 0	00100 01000 00100 10000 10000
(1,3,3)	3 2 3 1 1	00010 00100 00010 01000 01000
(1,3,4)	4 3 4 2 2	00001 00010 00001 00100 00100
(1,4,0)	0 0 2 1 2	10000 10000 00100 01000 00100
(1,4,1)	1 1 3 2 3	01000 01000 00010 00100 00010
(1,4,2)	2 2 4 3 4	00100 00100 00001 00010 00001
(1,4,3)	3 3 0 4 0	00010 00010 10000 00001 10000
(1,4,4)	4 4 1 0 1	00001 00001 01000 10000 01000

Theorem 4.5

For the synchronous multilevel prime codes over $GF(p)$ of a prime p with cardinality p^{n+1}, length $N = wp$, weight $w \leq p$, and $\lambda'_c = n$, the hit probabilities, q_i, of having the in-phase cross-correlation values of $i = \{0, 1, \ldots, n\}$ are formulated as [16]

$$q_i = \frac{h_{n,i}}{2(p^{n+1} - 1)}$$

$$\sum_{i=0}^{n} i q_i = \frac{w(p^n - 1)}{2(p^{n+1} - 1)}$$

and $\sum_{i=0}^{n} q_i = 1$, where $h_{n,i}$ is the total number of times of getting i hits in the in-phase cross-correlation functions, given by

$$h_{n,0} = 2(p^{n+1} - 1) - h_{n,n} - h_{n,n-1} - \cdots - h_{n,1}$$

$$h_{n,1} = w(p^n - 1) - nh_{n,n} - (n-1)h_{n,n-1} - \cdots - 2h_{n,2}$$

$$h_{n,i} = \frac{(h_{n-1,i-1} + h_{n-2,i-1} + \cdots + h_{i-1,i-1})h_{i,i}}{h_{i-1,i-1}}$$

$$h_{n,n} = \frac{w!(p-1)}{n!(w-n)!}$$

Proof While the factor $1/2$ comes from the assumption of equiprobable data bit-1 and bit-0 transmissions in OOK and the denominator $p^{n+1} - 1$ represents the possible number of interfering codewords, the hit probability q_i is computed by evaluating $h_{n,i}$ recursively. To account for zero interference in the p orthogonal codewords in each subset of level 1, it is found that

$$\sum_{i=0}^{n} i q_i = \frac{w^2}{2N} \times \frac{p^{n+1} - p}{p^{n+1} - 1} = \frac{w}{2p} \times \frac{p(p^n - 1)}{p^{n+1} - 1}$$

where $p^{n+1} - p$ represents the total number of interfering codewords, excluding those orthogonal to the address codeword of the receiver in study.

The equations of $h_{n,0}$ and $h_{n,1}$ come from the rearrangements of $q_i = h_{n,i}/[2(p^{n+1} - 1)]$ in $\sum_{i=0}^{n} q_i = 1$ and $\sum_{i=0}^{n} i q_i = w(p^n - 1)/[2(p^{n+1} - 1)]$, respectively.

Starting from the root of the tree structure, codewords in level $n + 1$ can be partitioned into p subsets and only one subset has the same i_{n+1} value as the address codeword. So, there are $p - 1$ subsets of interfering codewords contributing at most n hits in the in-phase cross-correlation function, out of a total of w possible hits. This accounts for the equation of $h_{n,n}$. Furthermore, $h_{n-1,i}$ counts the number of times of getting i hits contributed by the interfering codewords in level n with the same i_{n+1} subset as the address codeword. Because the cross-correlation property of the codewords is uniform, the term $(h_{n,i} - h_{n-1,i})/h_{n-1,i-1}$ is always a constant, whereas $h_{n,i} - h_{n-1,i}$ counts the number of times of getting i hits contributed by the interfering codewords in level $n+1$ with different i_{n+1} subsets from the address codeword. Continuing down the tree level-by-level, the relationship found in the term $(h_{n,i} - h_{n-1,i})/h_{n-1,i-1}$ holds as a recursive function of n and results in

$$\frac{h_{n,i} - h_{n-1,i}}{h_{n-1,i-1}} = \frac{h_{n-1,i} - h_{n-2,i}}{h_{n-2,i-1}} = \cdots = \frac{h_{i,i} - h_{i-1,i}}{h_{i-1,i-1}}$$

in which $h_{i-1,i} = 0$ is assumed because $h_{i-1,i}$ does not exist, by definition. After some manipulations, the final form of $h_{n,i}$ in the theorem is derived. ∎

To complete the evaluation of the hit probabilities in Theorem 4.5, $h_{n,n}$, $h_{n,n-1}$, ..., and $h_{n,0}$ are found from the following steps:

Step 1: Set $n = 1$.

    a. For $i = 1$, the equation of $h_{n,n}$ gives $h_{1,1} = w(p-1)$.

Step 2: Increase n by one to $n = 2$.

    a. For $i = 2$, the equation of $h_{n,n}$ gives $h_{2,2} = w(w-1)(p-1)/2$.
    b. For $i = 1$, the equation of $h_{n,1}$ gives $h_{2,1} = w(p^2-1) - 2h_{2,2} = w(p-1)(p-w+2)$.

Step 3: Increase $n = j - 1$ by one to $n = j$, for all $j = \{3,4,5,\ldots,\lambda_c'\}$.

    a. For $i = j$, the equation of $h_{n,n}$ gives $h_{j,j} = w!(p-1)/[j!(w-j)!]$.
    b. For $i = \{j-1, j-2, \ldots, 2\}$, the equation of $h_{n,i}$ gives $h_{j,j-1}$, $h_{j,j-2}$, ..., and $h_{j,2}$, respectively.
    c. For $i = 1$, the equation of $h_{n,1}$ gives $h_{j,1} = w(p^j-1) - jh_{j,j} - (j-1)h_{j,j-1} - \cdots - 2h_{j,2}$.

Step 4: Repeat Step 3 if $n \leq \lambda_c'$; otherwise, go to Step 5.

Step 5: Finally, $h_{n,0} = 2(p^{n+1} - 1) - h_{n,n} - h_{n,n-1} - \cdots - h_{n,1}$ is obtained.

Because the synchronous multilevel prime codes have zero in-phase cross-correlation values among the p codewords within every subset in level 1, orthogonal codewords can be chosen from the same subset when $K \leq p$, resulting in zero mutual interference and error probability. Otherwise, codewords should be chosen from more than one subset in level 1, sacrificing code performance. If there exist $K \in [p+1, p^2]$ simultaneous users, codewords are selected from multiple subsets of level 1 but all these subsets of level 1 should come from one subset of level 2 in order to limit λ_c' to 1. Similarly, if $K \in [p^2+1, p^3]$, codewords from one subset of level 3 are chosen in order to contain λ_c' to 2. In general, if $K \in [p^l+1, p^{l+1}]$, codewords are selected from one subset of level $l+1$ in order to limit λ_c' to l, where $l \in [0,n]$.

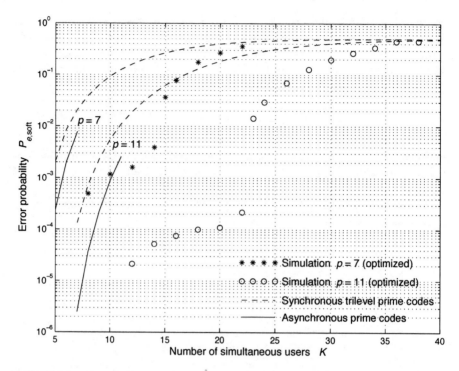

FIGURE 4.5 Chip-synchronous, soft-limiting error probabilities of the synchronous trilevel prime codes and the asynchronous prime codes, both over $GF(p)$, for $w = p = \{7, 11\}$.

Figure 4.5 plots the chip-synchronous, soft-limiting error probabilities of the synchronous multilevel prime codes with $n = 2$ [from Equation (4.3)] and the asynchronous prime codes [from Equation (3.7)], both over $GF(p)$, against the number of simultaneous users K for $w = p = \{7, 11\}$. Both codes have the maximum cross-correlation function of 2, but the first one is in-phase and the second one is periodic. For the dashed and solid curves, simultaneous users randomly select codewords from the sets of p^3 and p codewords, respectively—the maximum cardinality of both code families. In general, the error probabilities improve as p increases because of heavier code weight ($w = p$) and longer code length ($N = p^2$), resulting in higher autocorrelation peaks and lower hit probabilities. However, the error probabilities get worse as K increases due to stronger mutual interference. The synchronous trilevel prime codes (dashed curves) perform worse than the asynchronous prime codes (solid curves) for the same p. This is because the dominating hit probability q_2 of the former (from Theorem 4.5) is always larger than that of the latter (from Theorem 3.2). On the other hand, the synchronous trilevel prime codes have a factor of p^2 larger cardinality and support more possible subscribers. The solid curves of the asynchronous prime codes stop at $K = p = \{7, 11\}$, correspondingly, because of the limited cardinality of p, but the dashed curves of the synchronous trilevel prime codes can potentially continue to $K = p^3$.

Figure 4.5 also shows an example of how the performance of the synchronous trilevel prime codes can be optimized as functions of K and the number of orthogonal codewords in each subset of level 1. The asterisks and circles in the figure represent the computer-simulation performance of the synchronous trilevel prime codes with the orthogonal codewords being choosing "subset-by-subset." Both asterisks and circles start from $K > p$ because codewords coming from the same subset are orthogonal and then $P_{e,\text{soft}} = 0$ when $K \leq p$. For the example of $p = 11$, the error probability of the asynchronous prime codes begins to worsen even when K is as small as 7. When $K \in [p+1, 2p]$, the error probability (e.g., circles with $K \in [12, 22]$) of the synchronous trilevel prime codes gets worse gradually. This is because synchronous codewords are now being selected from two subsets and code orthogonality is broken slowly as K increases beyond p. There is a big jump when K changes from $2p$ to $2p + 1$ (e.g., circles at $K = 22$ and $K = 23$) because a codeword is now selected from a third subset and it interferes with all $2p$ codewords in the two subsets. In summary, the synchronous trilevel prime codes always perform much better than the asynchronous prime codes when $K \leq p$, and the former provide an option of supporting more subscribers at the expense of worsened performance and requiring code synchronization.

4.3 SYNCHRONOUS CODING APPLICATIONS

Because time synchronization is difficult to achieve in large-scale systems or networks, the environments that are suitable for the applications of asynchronous and synchronous coding are different. In environments such as small-scale networks, where synchronization is relatively easy to achieve, synchronous coding is more attractive than asynchronous coding. This is because the former supports a larger number of subscribers for the same bandwidth expansion, and allows error-free transmission when the number of simultaneous users is less than the code weight (or autocorrelation peak). However, in interexchange or long-haul networks, in which network synchronization is rather difficult to achieve, asynchronous coding becomes more attractive. Due to the traffic nature, coding-based passive optical networks (PONs) have been recently proposed with the downlink traffic—from the central station to subscribers—transported by synchronous coding and the uplink traffic—from subscribers to the central station—carried by asynchronous coding [13].

Furthermore, the idea of integrating multimedia services with different traffic or bit-rate requirements by means of O-TDMA and synchronous O-CDMA in the same system or network has been proposed by Santoro [17]. O-TDMA, a synchronous multiple-access scheme, divides a bit period into N time slots. Each user is assigned a time slot as its own address. Assuming OOK, a user transmits an optical pulse in the time slot corresponding to the address of its destination for every data bit 1, but data bit 0s are not conveyed. So, N users can transmit simultaneously without collisions as long as their transmissions are all synchronized and no multiple users are accessing the same destination. Although O-TDMA only supports N (orthogonal) addresses and so is the number of subscribers, it supports the largest number of simultaneous users of all multiple-access schemes and is more suited for services with high traffic density or real-time, critical transmissions, such as digitized video or high-priority services. On the other hand, synchronous O-CDMA, like its asynchronous counterpart, supports more possible subscribers due to the use of optical codes and is then more suitable for services with low traffic density, bursty traffic pattern, and less-time-sensitive transmission, such as digitized voice or data.

In multimedia systems, one challenge is posed by the requirement of multiple clock signals in order to support different bit rates and traffic patterns of various service types. Figure 4.6 illustrates an example of how three types of services (i.e., digitized data, voice, and video) can be supported in such an integrated O-TDMA and synchronous O-CDMA system by means of one clock signal only. To illustrate how the system works, it is here assumed that the clock rate is equal to the video bit rate $1/T_v$, which is, in turn, an integer multiple of the data bit rate $1/T_d$, and also $1/T_d$ is an integer multiple of the voice bit rate $1/T_u$. Signals of different service types are time-multiplexed into transmission frames of duration T_v and $N = T_v/T_c$ time slots. As illustrated in the time-slot assignment at the bottom of Figure 4.6, some time slots in each frame are reserved for continuous-traffic, high-bit-rate video services. One video service occupies one of these time slots and is transmitted in O-TDMA. The remaining time slots in each frame are reserved for bursty-traffic, low-bit-rate data and voice services, which are transmitted in synchronous O-CDMA. Each one of these (remaining) time slots in a frame can accommodate the transmission of multiple simultaneous users of one low-rate service type by multiplexing one chip of the codeword from each simultaneous user. Due to the use of distinct synchronous codewords of the same length for simultaneous users in one service type, the autocorrelation peaks of different users will occur in different frames, even though these users are transmitting at the same time slots in every frame. Also, simultaneous users of different service types can easily be distinguished at a receiver because the autocorrelation peaks of different users will occur at different time slots, even though they may exist in the same frame. This is also because the data and voice services have different bit periods and then the codewords of these two service types have different lengths, which are equal to T_d/T_v and T_u/T_v, respectively.

By integrating O-TDMA and synchronous O-CDMA in the same system or network, the timing problem caused by the difference in bit rates of different service types can be eliminated using just a single clock. This can also simplify the coordination issue of using O-TDMA for bursty-traffic, low-bit-rate data and voice services. This is because users of each service type will need to take turns to transmit in the same time slot of consecutive frames if O-TDMA is used, requiring time-slot interleavers of some sort. Another way to integrate multiple-rate, multimedia services is by dedicating a wavelength to each service type [18]. This method allows the choice of a suitable multiple-access scheme within each service type, but the requirement of multiple clock signals still exists and poses an issue.

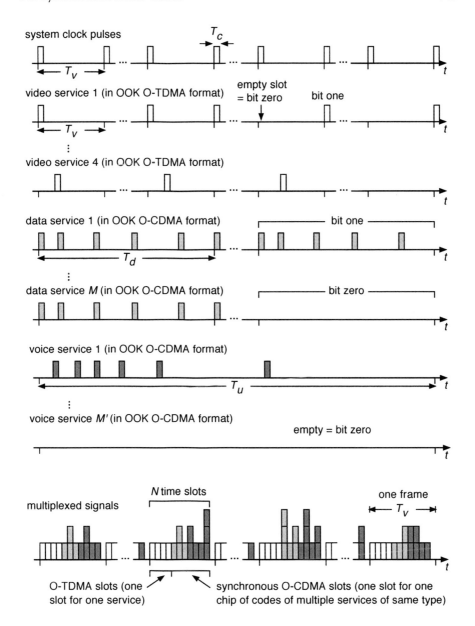

FIGURE 4.6 Example of three types of services supported by O-TDMA and synchronous O-CDMA in OOK. Bit ones of each service are conveyed in the service's preselected transmission format, but bit 0s are not transmitted [5, 10, 17].

4.4 SUMMARY

In this chapter, the construction, properties, and performance of 1-D synchronous prime codes were studied. Designed with in-phase cross-correlation functions of at most 1, the 1-D synchronous prime codes over $GF(p)$ have a cardinality of p^2, a factor of p larger than that of the 1-D asynchronous prime codes in Section 3.1. The 1-D synchronous multilevel prime codes over $GF(p)$ with arbitrary maximum in-phase cross-correlation functions were also studied. By partitioning the codewords into subsets of different levels, the cross-correlation values can be varied in order to attain different code performances and cardinalities. Because there are p orthogonality codewords in every subset of the lowest level, zero error probability can be achieved by choosing codewords from the same subset when the number of simultaneous users is no larger than p.

The use of synchronous O-CDMA in conjunction with O-TDMA in multimedia synchronous systems or networks was illustrated, in which multiple services with different traffic or bit-rate requirements were integrated using just a single clock signal. Taken together with the improvements in the number of subscribers, synchronous coding is more attractive than asynchronous coding in local-area environments with real-time or high-throughput requirements in which a large number of subscribers are to be interconnected and synchronization is relatively easy to achieve.

REFERENCES

1. Prucnal, P. R., Santoro, M. A., Fan, T. R. (1986). Spread spectrum fiber optic local area network using optical processing. *J. Lightwave Technol.* 4(5):547–554.
2. Santoro, M. A., Prucnal, P. R. (1987). Asynchronous fiber optic local area network using CDMA and optical correlation. *Proc. IEEE* 75(9):1336–1338.
3. Salehi, J. A., (1989). Code division multiple-access techniques in optical fiber networks. I. Fundamental principles. *IEEE Trans. Commun.* 37(8):824–833.
4. Salehi, J. A., (1989). Emerging optical code division multiple access communications systems. *IEEE Network Mag.* 1(2):31–39.
5. Yang, G.-C, Kwong, W. C. (2002). *Prime Codes with Applications to CDMA Optical and Wireless Networks.* Norwood, MA: Artech House.
6. Prucnal, P. R. (ed.) (2006). *Optical Code Division Multiple Access: Fundamentals and Applications.* Boca Raton, FL: Taylor & Francis Group.
7. Shaar, A. A., Davies, P. A. (1983). Prime sequences: Quasi-optimal sequences for OR channel code division multiplexing. *Electron. Lett.* 19(21):888–890.
8. Chung, F. R. K., Salehi, J. A., Wei, V. K. (1989). Optical orthogonal codes: Design, analysis, and applications. *IEEE Trans. Info. Theory* 35(3):595–604.
9. Chung, H., Kumar, P. V. (1990). Optical orthogonal codes—New bounds and an optimal construction. *IEEE Trans. Info. Theory* 36(4):866–873.
10. Kwong, W. C., Perrier, P. A., Prucnal, P. R. (1991). Performance comparison of asynchronous and synchronous code division multiple access techniques for fiber-optic local area network. *IEEE Trans. Commun.* 39(11):1625–1634.
11. Prucnal, P. R., Santoro, M. A., Sehgal, S. K. (1986). Ultra-fast all-optical synchronous multiple access fiber networks. *IEEE J. Selected Areas Commun.* 4(9):1484–1493.

12. Kwong, W. C., Prucnal, P. R. (1990). Synchronous CDMA demonstration for fiber-optic networks with optical processing. *Electron. Lett.* 26(22):1990–1992.

13. Hu, H.-W., Chen, H.-T., Yang, G.-C., Kwong, W. C., (2007). Synchronous Walsh-based bipolar-bipolar code for CDMA passive optical networks. *J. Lightwave Technol.* 25(8):1910–1917.

14. Lalmahomed, A., Karbassian, M. M., Ghafouri-Shiraz, H. (2010). Performance analysis of enhanced-MPC in incoherent synchronous O-CDMA. *J. Lightwave Technol.* 28(1):39–46.

15. Wei, Z., Ghafouri-Shiraz, H. (2002). Unipolar codes with ideal in-phase cross-correlation for spectral-amplitude-coding O-CDMA systems. *IEEE Trans. Commun.* 50(8):1209–1212.

16. Hsieh, C.-H., Yang, G.-C., Chang, C.-Y., Kwong, W. C. (2009). Multilevel prime codes for O-CDMA systems. *J. Optical Commun. Networking* 1(7):600–607.

17. Santoro, M. A., (1989). An integrated-services digital-access fiber-optic broadband local area network with optical processing. In *Proceedings: 4th Tirrenia International Workshop on Digital Communications, Meeting on Coherent Optical Communications and Photonics Switching*, Tirrenia, Pisa, Italy, September 19–23, G. Prati (ed.) New York: Elsevier, pp. 285–296.

18. Perrier, P. A., Prucnal, P. R. (1988). Wavelength division integration of services in fiber-optic networks. *Inter. J. Digital Analog Cabled Systems* 1(3):149–157.

5 2-D Asynchronous Prime Codes

To support many subscribers and simultaneous users, long 1-D optical codes, such as the prime codes in Chapters 3 and 4, are needed in order to achieve sufficient code cardinality and performance. As a result, large bandwidth expansion and high processing speed in coding and decision hardware are required [1, 2]. One possible way to lessen these penalties is to use 1-D optical codes in conjunction with wavelength-division multiplexing (WDM) in the hybrid WDM-coding scheme [3,4]. In the scheme, every codeword is reusable and can be sent out simultaneously at different wavelengths by different users. Because the number of transmitting codewords is reduced by spreading them out in different wavelengths, the desired code performance becomes achievable with shorter code length. However, unless there is a central controller to evenly distribute all wavelengths to simultaneous users, the WDM-coding scheme has been shown to suffer from the problem of uneven user-wavelength distribution and the theoretical performance may not be achievable [4].

A better approach is to use 2-D optical codes, in which the optical pulses within each codeword carry different wavelengths [1, 2, 5–13]. Although the use of 2-D optical codes increases system complexity, this approach adds coding flexibility and, more importantly, improves code cardinality and performance [1, 2, 14, 15]. For example, Tančevski et al. [16] introduced the so-called prime-hop codes, which have every pulse in each 1-D optical codeword conveyed in a distinct wavelength, resulting in a class of 2-D optical codes with zero autocorrelation sidelobes and periodic cross-correlation functions of at most 1. For a given prime number p, the prime-hop codes use p wavelengths and have length, weight, and cardinality of p^2, p, and $p(p - 1)$, respectively, providing a factor of $p - 1$ larger cardinality than the 1-D prime codes in Section 3.1.

In this chapter, six families of 2-D asynchronous prime codes [5–13, 17–22], which provide flexible choices of optical codes with various relationships among code length, code weight, code cardinality, number of wavelengths, and correlation properties, are constructed and analyzed. (While the second coding dimension is referred to as "wavelengths" in this chapter, spatial or fiber-optic channels can also be used to substitute for wavelengths in the 2-D optical codes, as discussed in Section 2.5.) The applications of some of these 2-D prime codes in multicode keying and shifted-code keying are investigated [9, 10]. These two keying schemes increase the bit rate by means of transmitting multiple bits per symbol. Afterward, several 2-D construction methods, in which the wavelengths of the pulses in 1-D time-spreading codes are permuted by following the orders of the elements of shifted prime and quadratic-congruence sequences, are studied [13, 17–23]. Finally, the constructions of two families of 2-D optical orthogonal codes are illustrated [4, 14].

5.1 CARRIER-HOPPING PRIME CODES

In addition to code length, 2-D optical codes are also defined by an additional coding dimension, which is conveyed by multiple transmission channels, such as free space, optical fibers, or wavelengths, depending on the coding schemes studied in Sections 2.5 and 2.6. So, the correlation functions of 2-D optical codes also depend on the number of transmission channels, in addition to code weight and length, as discussed in Section 1.5.

Definition 5.1

A family of 2-D optical codes is a collection of binary $(0,1)$ $L \times N$ matrices (i.e., codewords), each of weight w and length N, with L (e.g., free-space, fiber-optic, or wavelength) channels, satisfying the following autocorrelation and cross-correlation constraints [1]:

- *Autocorrelation.* For an integer $\tau \in [1, N-1]$, the discrete 2-D autocorrelation sidelobe of a code matrix $\mathbf{x}$ is no greater than a nonnegative integer λ_a such that

$$\sum_{i=0}^{L-1} \sum_{j=0}^{N-1} x_{i,j} x_{i,j\oplus\tau} \leq \lambda_a$$

  where $x_{i,j} = \{0,1\}$ is an element of $\mathbf{x}$ at the ith row and jth column, and "$\oplus$" denotes a modulo-N addition. For $\tau = 0$, the function gives the autocorrelation peak, which is usually equal to code weight w.

- *Cross-correlation.* For an integer $\tau \in [0, N-1]$, the discrete 2-D periodic cross-correlation function of two distinct code matrices $\mathbf{x}$ and $\mathbf{y}$ is no greater than a positive integer λ_c such that

$$\sum_{i=0}^{L-1} \sum_{j=0}^{N-1} x_{i,j} y_{i,j\oplus\tau} \leq \lambda_c$$

  where $y_{i,j} = \{0,1\}$ is an element of $\mathbf{y}$ at the ith row and jth column.

∎

In general, the number of transmission channels, L, represents the number of rows and the number of time slots (or code length), N, denotes the number of columns in the code matrices. For ease of representation, a pulse (or binary 1) in each code matrix (i.e., codeword) can equivalently be written as an ordered pair. (Because time slots are also referred as *chips* in optical codes, these pulses are called *mark* chips.) There are w ordered pairs in a codeword of weight w. An ordered pair (λ_v, t_h) records the vertical (v) and horizontal (h) displacements of a pulse from the bottom-leftmost

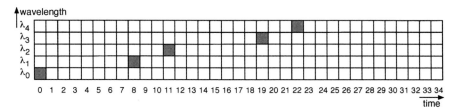

FIGURE 5.1 A carrier-hopping prime codeword of weight 5 with 5 wavelengths and 35 time slots. Each dark square indicates the chip (time) location and transmitting wavelength of an optical pulse in the codeword.

corner of a code matrix. So, λ_v represents the transmitting channel (e.g., free space, fiber, or wavelength) and t_h shows the chip (time) location of a pulse in the code matrix. For example, Figure 5.1 shows a 5×35 matrix of a carrier-hopping prime codeword of weight 5 with 5 wavelengths and 35 time slots.

Given a set of k prime numbers $p_k \geq p_{k-1} \geq \cdots \geq p_1$, binary $(0,1)$ matrices, $\mathbf{x}_{i_k,i_{k-1},\ldots,i_1}$, with the ordered pairs [1,2]

$$\{[(0,0),(1,i_1+i_2p_1+\cdots+i_kp_1p_2\cdots p_{k-1}),$$
$$(2,2\odot_{p_1}i_1+(2\odot_{p_2}i_2)p_1+\cdots+(2\odot_{p_k}i_k)p_1p_2\cdots p_{k-1}),\ldots,$$
$$(w-1,(w-1)\odot_{p_1}i_1+((w-1)\odot_{p_2}i_2)p_1+\cdots$$
$$+((w-1)\odot_{p_k}i_k)p_1p_2\cdots p_{k-1})]:i_1=\{0,1,\ldots,p_1-1\},$$
$$i_2=\{0,1,\ldots,p_2-1\},\ldots,i_k=\{0,1,\ldots,p_k-1\}\}$$

form the carrier-hopping prime codes with cardinality $p_1p_2\cdots p_k$, $L=w$ wavelengths, length $N=p_1p_2\cdots p_k$, and weight $w\leq p_1$, where "$\odot_{p_j}$" denotes a modulo-p_j multiplication for $j=\{1,2,\ldots,k\}$.

Using $k=1$ and $p_1=w=7$ as an example, there exist 7 carrier-hopping prime codewords of $L=7$ wavelengths, length $N=7$, and weight $w=7$, denoted by $\mathbf{x}_0=[(0,0),(1,0),(2,0),(3,0),(4,0),(5,0),(6,0)]$, $\mathbf{x}_1=[(0,0),(1,1),(2,2),(3,3),(4,4),(5,5),(6,6)]$, $\mathbf{x}_2=[(0,0),(1,2),(2,4),(3,6),(4,1),(5,3),(6,5)]$, $\mathbf{x}_3=[(0,0),(1,3),(2,6),(3,2),(4,5),(5,1),(6,4)]$, $\mathbf{x}_4=[(0,0),(1,4),(2,1),(3,5),(4,2),(5,6),(6,3)]$, $\mathbf{x}_5=[(0,0),(1,5),(2,3),(3,1),(4,6),(5,4),(6,2)]$, and $\mathbf{x}_6=[(0,0),(1,6),(2,5),(3,4),(4,3),(5,2),(6,1)]$. The codewords can also be represented in terms of wavelength-time sequences, such as $\mathbf{x}_2=\lambda_0\lambda_4\lambda_1\lambda_5\lambda_2\lambda_6\lambda_3$.

Using $k=2$, $p_1=w=5$, and $p_2=7$ as an example, there exist 35 carrier-hopping prime codewords of $L=5$ wavelengths, length $N=35$, and weight $w=5$, denoted by $\mathbf{x}_{i_2,i_1}=[(0,0),(1,i_1+5i_2),(2,2\odot_5 i_1+(2\odot_7 i_2)5),(3,3\odot_5 i_1+(3\odot_7 i_2)5),(4,4\odot_5 i_1+(4\odot_7 i_2)5)]$ for $i_1\in[0,4]$ and $i_2\in[0,6]$. Shown in Figure 5.1 is $\mathbf{x}_{3,1}=[(0,0),(1,8),(2,11),(3,19),(4,22)]$, which can also be represented as the wavelength-time sequence $\lambda_0 0000\ 000\lambda_1 0\ 0\lambda_2 000\ 0000\lambda_3\ 00\lambda_4 00\ 00000\ 00000$.

The prime-hop codes in [16], which have a cardinality of $p_1(p_1-1)$, belong to a subset of the carrier-hopping prime codes with $k=2$ and $w=p_1=p_2$, and support p_1 less codewords than the carrier-hopping prime codes.

Because each code matrix consists of one pulse per row and per column, the carrier-hopping prime codes have zero autocorrelation sidelobes—an important feature that minimizes self-interference and facilitates code tracking in receivers—and the following correlation properties.

Theorem 5.1

The autocorrelation peaks and sidelobes of the carrier-hopping prime codes of weight w are equal to w and 0, respectively, where $w \leq p_1$. The periodic cross-correlation functions of the codes are at most 1 [1].

Proof Let $\mathbf{x}_{i_k, i_{k-1}, \ldots, i_1}$ and $\mathbf{x}_{i'_k, i'_{k-1}, \ldots, i'_1}$ be two distinct carrier-hopping prime codewords with $(i_k, i_{k-1}, \ldots, i_1) \neq (i'_k, i'_{k-1}, \ldots, i'_1)$. If there exist two hits of pulses in any relative horizontal cyclic shift τ between these two codewords, then

$$
\begin{aligned}
&j_1 \odot_{p_1} i_1 + (j_1 \odot_{p_2} i_2)p_1 + \cdots + (j_1 \odot_{p_k} i_k)p_1 p_2 \cdots p_{k-1} + \tau \\
&= j_1 \odot_{p_1} i'_1 + (j_1 \odot_{p_2} i'_2)p_1 + \cdots + (j_1 \odot_{p_k} i'_k)p_1 p_2 \cdots p_{k-1}
\end{aligned}
$$

$$
\begin{aligned}
&j_2 \odot_{p_1} i_1 + (j_2 \odot_{p_2} i_2)p_1 + \cdots + (j_2 \odot_{p_k} i_k)p_1 p_2 \cdots p_{k-1} + \tau \\
&= j_2 \odot_{p_1} i'_1 + (j_2 \odot_{p_2} i'_2)p_1 + \cdots + (j_2 \odot_{p_k} i'_k)p_1 p_2 \cdots p_{k-1}
\end{aligned}
$$

must hold simultaneously for a $j_1 = \{0, 1, \ldots, w-1\}$ and a $j_2 = \{0, 1, \ldots, w-1\}$, where $j_1 \neq j_2$. The subtraction of these two equations results in

$$
\begin{aligned}
&[(j_1 \odot_{p_1} i_1 - j_2 \odot_{p_1} i_1) - (j_1 \odot_{p_1} i'_1 - j_2 \odot_{p_1} i'_1)] \\
&+ [(j_1 \odot_{p_2} i_2 - j_2 \odot_{p_2} i_2) - (j_1 \odot_{p_2} i'_2 - j_2 \odot_{p_2} i'_2)]p_1 + \cdots \\
&+ [(j_1 \odot_{p_k} i_k - j_2 \odot_{p_k} i_k) - (j_1 \odot_{p_k} i'_k - j_2 \odot_{p_k} i'_k)]p_1 p_2 \cdots p_{k-1} = 0
\end{aligned}
$$

which is valid only when $i_m = i'_m$ for all $m = \{1, 2, \ldots, k\}$. This violates the assumption of distinct $\mathbf{x}_{i_k, i_{k-1}, \ldots, i_1}$ and $\mathbf{x}_{i'_k, i'_{k-1}, \ldots, i'_1}$. So, the periodic cross-correlation function is at most 1.

Because all pulses in a codeword are in different wavelengths, the autocorrelation sidelobes are always 0. Finally, the autocorrelation peaks of w are due to the code weight $w \leq p_1$. ∎

According to Section 1.6, the cardinality upper bound of the carrier-hopping prime codes with cardinality $p_1 p_2 \cdots p_k$, $L = w$ wavelengths, length $N = p_1 p_2 \cdots p_k$, weight $w \leq p_1$, and the maximum periodic cross-correlation function of 1 is given by [1]

$$\Phi_{upper} \leq \frac{w(wp_1p_2\cdots p_k - 1)}{w(w-1)}$$

$$= p_1p_2\cdots p_k + \frac{p_1p_2\cdots p_k - 1}{w-1}$$

The upper bound is equal to $1 + 1/(w-1) - 1/[(w-1)p_1p_2\cdots p_k]$ times the actual cardinality. The factor approaches 1 for a large w. So, the carrier-hopping prime codes are asymptotically optimal in cardinality.

5.1.1 Performance Analysis

According to Section 1.8.3, the chip-synchronous, soft-limiting error probability of the carrier-hopping prime codes with $L = w$ wavelengths, length $N = p_1p_2\cdots p_k$, weight $w \leq p_1$, and the maximum periodic cross-correlation function of 1 in OOK is given by

$$P_e = \frac{1}{2} - \frac{1}{2} \sum_{i=0}^{Z_{th}-1} \frac{(K-1)!}{i!(K-1-i)!} q_1^i q_0^{K-1-i} \tag{5.1}$$

where K is the number of simultaneous users and the decision threshold $Z_{th} = w$ is usually applied for optimal decision.

As the carrier-hopping prime codes have one pulse per row and per column in each codeword, the one-hit probability of the pulses in an interfering codeword overlapping with the pulses in the address codeword (of a receiver) in the sampling time of their periodic cross-correlation function is formulated as [1]

$$q_1 = \frac{w^2}{2LN} = \frac{w^2}{2 \times w \times p_1p_2\cdots p_k} = \frac{w}{2p_1p_2\cdots p_k}$$

and $q_0 + q_1 = 1$, where the factor $1/2$ comes from the assumption of equiprobable data bit-1 and bit-0 transmissions in OOK, and q_i is the probability of having $i = \{0, 1\}$ hits in the sampling time of the periodic cross-correlation functions.

Figure 5.2 plots the chip synchronous, soft-limiting error probabilities of the carrier-hopping prime codes with $k = 2$, $L = w$ wavelengths, and length $N = p_1p_2$ against the number of simultaneous users K for $p = p_1 = p_2 = \{11, 13, 17\}$ and weight $w = \{p - 2, p\}$. The solid and dashed curves show the effect of code weight to code performance. In general, the error probabilities improve as p increases because of heavier code weight, more wavelengths, and longer code length in use, resulting in higher autocorrelation peaks and lower hit probabilities. However, the error probabilities get worse as K increases due to stronger mutual interference.

To contrast 2-D coding with hybrid WDM-coding, the 1-D prime codes in Section 3.1 are here applied to the latter and compared with the 2-D carrier-hopping prime codes. By using $k = 2$, $L = w = p_1 = p_2 = p$, and $N = p_1p_2 = p^2$, both code families have the same cardinality, number of wavelengths, length, and weight

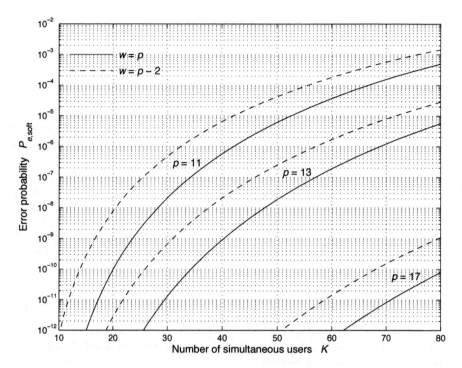

FIGURE 5.2 Chip-synchronous, soft-limiting error probabilities of the carrier-hopping prime codes with $k = 2$, $L = w$, and $N = p_1 p_2$ for $p = p_1 = p_2 = \{11, 13, 17\}$ and $w = \{p-2, p\}$.

for a fair comparison in terms of bandwidth expansion LN and number of possible subscribers. The main differences are that the 1-D prime codes have the maximum periodic cross-correlation function of 2, the same wavelength is used by all pulses within each 1-D prime codeword, and the same codeword can be conveyed by different wavelengths simultaneously in the hybrid WDM-coding scheme. So, the chip-synchronous, soft-limiting error probability of these 1-D prime codewords with p wavelengths in hybrid WDM-coding and OOK is formulated as [1,4]

$$P_{e,\text{hybrid}} = \frac{1}{2} - \frac{1}{2} \sum_{l_1=0}^{\lceil K/p \rceil - 1} \sum_{l_2=0}^{\lfloor (\lceil K/p \rceil - 1 - l_1)/2 \rfloor} \frac{(\lceil K/p \rceil - 1)!}{l_1! l_2! (\lceil K/p \rceil - 1 - l_1 - l_2)!}$$
$$\times q_1^{l_1} q_2^{l_2} q_0^{\lceil K/p \rceil - 1 - l_1 - l_2}$$

where $l_1 + l_2 < \lceil K/p \rceil$, q_i is the probability of having $i = \{0,1,2\}$ hits in the sampling time of the periodic cross-correlation functions, and $\lceil \cdot \rceil$ is the ceiling function. From Section 3.1, $q_2 = w(w^2 - 1)(p-2)/[12(p-1)p^3]$, $q_1 = w^2/(2p^2) - 2q_2$, and $q_0 = 1 - w^2/(2p^2) + q_2$. Assume that a central controller is used to evenly distribute these p wavelengths to all K simultaneous users. There exist at most $\lceil K/p \rceil$ users transmitting simultaneously in each wavelength. This corresponds to the best scenario, and $P_{e,\text{hybrid}}$ represents the performance lower bound. Error-free transmission can theoretically be achieved when the number of simultaneous users in each wavelength is less than $w/2$ (or $\lceil K/p \rceil < w/2$). This is because the 1-D prime codes have the maximum periodic cross-correlation function of 2 and the decision threshold is usually set to w for optimal decision.

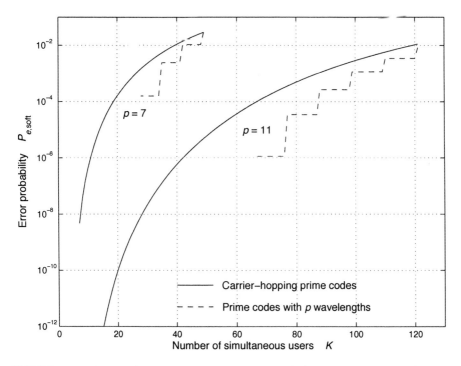

FIGURE 5.3 Chip-synchronous, soft-limiting error probabilities of the carrier-hopping prime codes and the 1-D prime codes (in hybrid WDM-coding), both with $L = w = p$ and $N = p^2$ for $p = \{7, 11\}$. (A central controller is assumed in the hybrid scheme.)

Figure 5.3 plots the chip-synchronous, soft-limiting error probabilities of the ($k = 2$) carrier-hopping prime codes and the 1-D prime codes in hybrid WDM-coding, both with $L = p$ wavelengths, length $N = p_1 p_2 = p^2$, and weight $w = p$, against the number of simultaneous users K for $p = p_1 = p_2 = \{7, 11\}$. In general, the error probabilities improve as p increases because of more wavelengths, longer code length, and heavier code weight in use. These, in turn, lower the hit probabilities and heighten the autocorrelation peaks. However, the error probabilities get worse as K increases due to stronger mutual interference. The step-like dashed curves represent the performance lower bound of hybrid WDM-coding. This lower bound can only be achieved theoretically with the use of a central controller to evenly distribute all simultaneously transmitting 1-D prime codewords over $L = p$ wavelengths. The curves start at the points where the number of simultaneous users in each wavelength is less than $w/2$ (or $\lceil K/p \rceil \leq w/2$). The performances (solid curves) of the carrier-hopping prime codes, which are shown worse than those of the 1-D prime codes in hybrid WDM-coding, are here compared to the performance lower bound of the latter. The dashed curves are increasingly better than the solid curves at small K as p increases. This is because hybrid WDM-coding allows simultaneously transmitting codewords to be spread out into more wavelengths. On the other hand, the solid curves converges with the dashed curves when the traffic load is heavy (or large K), showing comparable performance to the lower bound. However, without the central controller, the performance of the 1-D prime codes in hybrid WDM-coding will become worse than that of the carrier-hopping prime codes, even under light traffic load.

5.2 MULTILEVEL CARRIER-HOPPING PRIME CODES

Optical codes are usually constructed with cross-correlation functions of at most 1 in order to minimize the amount of mutual interference. As a result, code cardinality is significantly restricted due to the cardinality upper bounds in Section 1.6. One way of improving code cardinality is to increase code length, as done in the carrier-hopping prime codes in Section 5.1. It is also known that larger code cardinality can be accomplished by relaxing the maximum cross-correlation function at the expense of code performance [1, 2, 10–12, 14–16]. In this section, *multilevel* carrier-hopping prime codes, which provide flexible relationships among code length, cardinality, and cross-correlation functions, with asymptotically optimal cardinality are constructed.

Based on $GF(p)$ of a prime p and two positive integers k and n, binary $(0,1)$ matrices, $x_{i_{k,n},i_{k,n-1},\dots,i_{k,1},i_{k-1,n},i_{k-1,n-1},\dots,i_{1,1}}$, with the ordered pairs [11, 12]

$$
\begin{aligned}
\{&[(0,0),(1,x_{i_{k,n},i_{k,n-1},\dots,i_{k,1},i_{k-1,n},i_{k-1,n-1},\dots,i_{1,1},1}),\\
&(2,x_{i_{k,n},i_{k,n-1},\dots,i_{k,1},i_{k-1,n},i_{k-1,n-1},\dots,i_{1,1},2}),\dots,\\
&(j,x_{i_{k,n},i_{k,n-1},\dots,i_{k,1},i_{k-1,n},i_{k-1,n-1},\dots,i_{1,1},j}),\dots,\\
&(w-1,x_{i_{k,n},i_{k,n-1},\dots,i_{k,1},i_{k-1,n},i_{k-1,n-1},\dots,i_{1,1},w-1})]:\\
&i_{s,t}=\{0,1,\dots,p-1\}\text{ for }s=\{1,2,\dots,k\}\text{ and }t=\{1,2,\dots,n\}\}
\end{aligned}
$$

and the jth code element, which determines the chip (time) location of the jth wavelength, given by

$$
\begin{aligned}
&x_{i_{k,n},i_{k,n-1},\dots,i_{k,1},i_{k-1,n},i_{k-1,n-1},\dots,i_{1,1},j}\\
&=\sum_{m=1}^{k}p^{m-1}[i_{m,n}j^{n}+i_{m,n-1}j^{n-1}+\dots+i_{m,1}j\ (\text{mod }p)]
\end{aligned}
$$

form the multilevel carrier-hopping prime codes with cardinality p^{nk}, $L=w$ wavelengths, length $N=p^{k}$, weight $w\leq p$, and the maximum periodic cross-correlation function $\lambda_{c}=n\leq w$.

Theorem 5.2

The autocorrelation peaks and sidelobes of the multilevel carrier-hopping prime codes over $GF(p)$ of a prime p and weight w are equal to w and 0, respectively, where $w \leq p$. The periodic cross-correlation functions of the codes are at most n, where $n \leq w$.

Proof The proof is similar to that of Theorem 5.1. Let $\mathbf{x}_{i_{k,n},i_{k,n-1},\ldots,i_{k,1},i_{k-1,n},i_{k-1,n-1},\ldots,i_{1,1}}$ and $\mathbf{x}_{i'_{k,n},i'_{k,n-1},\ldots,i'_{k,1},i'_{k-1,n},i'_{k-1,n-1},\ldots,i'_{1,1}}$ be two distinct multilevel carrier-hopping prime codewords with $(i_{k,n}, i_{k,n-1}, \ldots, i_{k,1}, \ldots, i_{k-1,n}, i_{k-1,n-1}, \ldots, i_{1,1}) \neq (i'_{k,n}, i'_{k,n-1}, \ldots, i'_{k,1}, i'_{k-1,n}, i'_{k-1,n-1}, \ldots, i'_{1,1})$. If there exists at least one hit in any relative horizontal cyclic shift τ between the two codewords, the difference in the ordered pairs of all their corresponding code elements, say at the jth chip location, becomes

$$\sum_{m=1}^{k} p^{m-1} \left[i_{m,n} j^n + i_{m,n-1} j^{n-1} + \cdots + i_{m,1} j \pmod{p} \right] + \tau$$

$$- \sum_{m=1}^{k} p^{m-1} \left[i'_{m,n} j^n + i'_{m,n-1} j^{n-1} + \cdots + i'_{m,1} j \pmod{p} \right] = 0$$

for a $j = \{0, 1, \ldots, w-1\}$. Because this equation is an nth-power function of j over $GF(p)$, it is impossible to have more than n solutions of j. So, the periodic cross-correlation functions are at most n.

Because all pulses in a codeword are in different wavelengths, the autocorrelation sidelobes are always 0. Finally, the autocorrelation peaks of w are due to the code weight $w \leq p$.   ∎

Illustrated in Figure 5.4, the p^{nk} multilevel carrier-hopping prime codewords can be partitioned into a tree structure of n levels. Starting from the root on the left-hand side, level n has one set of $\Phi = p^{nk}$ codeword of (the maximum periodic cross-correlation function) $\lambda_c = n$. In level $n-1$, these p^{nk} codewords are partitioned into p^k subsets, and each subset has $\Phi = p^{(n-1)k}$ codewords of $\lambda_c = n-1$. In level $n-2$, every subset of $p^{(n-1)k}$ codewords in level $n-1$ are further partitioned into p^k subsets, giving a total of p^{2k} subsets, and each subset has $\Phi = p^{(n-2)k}$ codewords of $\lambda_c = n-2$. This partition process continues to level 1, in which there are in total $p^{(n-1)k}$ subsets and $\Phi = p^k$ codewords in each subset with $\lambda_c = 1$. This partition property allows the selection of codewords of certain cardinality and performance because the maximum cross-correlation function is a major factor determining code performance. If code performance is more important than cardinality, codewords from lower levels of the tree structure are selected. If cardinality is more important, codewords from higher levels can be used at the expense of code performance.

One subset in level 1 is actually the same set of the carrier-hopping prime codes in Section 5.1, and a portion of one subset in level 2 is the quadratic-congruence

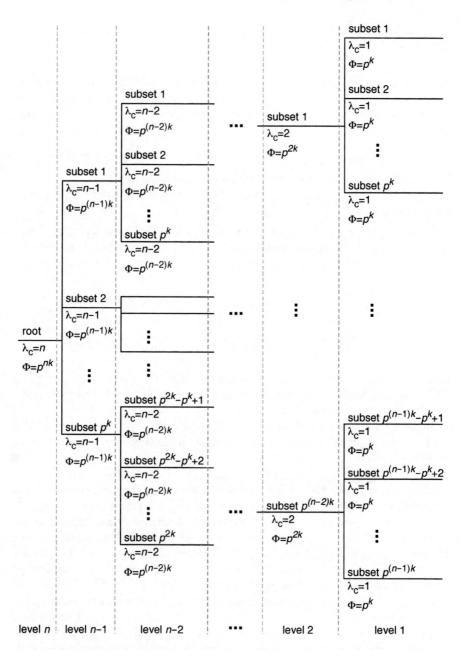

FIGURE 5.4   Tree structure of the multilevel carrier-hopping prime codes over $GF(p)$ of a prime p and positive integers n and k, where λ_c is the maximum periodic cross-correlation function and Φ is the code cardinality in each subset.

carrier-hopping prime codes in Section 5.6 [10]. Unlike the quadratic-congruence carrier-hopping prime codes, the multilevel carrier-hopping prime codes always give asymptotically optimal cardinality for any k and n. The quadratic-congruence codes [23] and cubic-congruence codes [24] are two special cases of the multilevel carrier-hopping prime codes with $n = 2$ and 3, respectively, and both $k = 1$.

Theorem 5.3

The multilevel carrier-hopping prime codes can be partitioned into n levels of subsets of codewords, in which the periodic cross-correlation function between any two codewords from the same subset in level l is at most l, where $l \in [1,n]$ and $n \leq w$.

Proof The proof follows that of Theorem 5.2. Let $\mathbf{x}_{i_{k,n}, i_{k,n-1}, \dots, i_{k,1}, i_{k-1,n}, i_{k-1,n-1}, \dots, i_{1,1}}$ and $\mathbf{x}_{i'_{k,n}, i'_{k,n-1}, \dots, i'_{k,1}, i'_{k-1,n}, i'_{k-1,n-1}, \dots, i'_{1,1}}$ be two distinct multilevel carrier-hopping prime codewords from the same subset in level $l \in [1,n]$, where $(i_{k,n}, i_{k,n-1}, \dots, i_{k,l+1}, i_{k-1,n}, i_{k-1,n-1}, \dots, i_{1,l+2}, i_{1,l+1}) = (i'_{k,n}, i'_{k,n-1}, \dots, i'_{k,l+1}, i'_{k-1,n}, i'_{k-1,n-1}, \dots, i'_{1,l+2}, i'_{1,l+1})$ but $(i_{k,l}, i_{k,l-1}, \dots, i_{k,1}, i_{k-1,l}, i_{k-1,l-1}, \dots, i_{1,1}) \neq (i'_{k,l}, i'_{k,l-1}, \dots, i'_{k,1}, i'_{k-1,l}, i'_{k-1,l-1}, \dots, i'_{1,1})$. If there exists one hit in any relative horizontal cyclic shift τ between the two codewords, the difference in the ordered pairs of all their corresponding code elements, say at the jth chip location, becomes

$$\sum_{m=1}^{k} p^{m-1}[i_{m,l} j^l + i_{m,l-1} j^{l-1} + \cdots + i_{m,1} j \pmod{p}] + \tau$$

$$-\sum_{m=1}^{k} p^{m-1}[i'_{m,l} j^l + i'_{m,l-1} j^{l-1} + \cdots + i'_{m,1} j \pmod{p}] = 0$$

for a $j = \{0, 1, \dots, w - 1\}$. Because this equation is a lth-power function of j over $GF(p)$, it is impossible to have more than l solutions of j. The periodic cross-correlation property in the theorem is then proved. ∎

Using $k = 1$, $n = 2$, $p = 5$, and $L = w = 4$ as an example, this bilevel carrier-hopping prime code of length $N = 5$ has 25 codewords, denoted by $\mathbf{x}_{i_{1,2}, i_{1,1}} = [(0,0), (1, i_{1,2} + i_{1,1}), (2, 4i_{1,2} + 2i_{1,1}), (3, 9i_{1,2} + 3i_{1,1})]$ for $i_{1,1} \in [0,4]$ and $i_{1,2} \in [0,4]$. In level 2, all 25 codewords have $\lambda_c = 2$. In level 1, the 5 codewords with the same $i_{1,2}$ index (or subset) have $\lambda_c = 1$, but those with different $i_{1,2}$ indices have $\lambda_c = 2$. For example, $\mathbf{x}_{0,1} = [(0,0), (1,1), (2,2), (3,3)]$ has at most one hit (in the sampling time of the periodic cross-correlation function) when it correlates with the other 4 codewords from the same $i_{1,2} = 0$ subset of level 1. The 5 codewords, $\mathbf{x}_{1,0} = [(0,0), (1,1), (2,4), (3,4)]$, $\mathbf{x}_{1,1} = [(0,0), (1,2), (2,1), (3,2)]$, $\mathbf{x}_{1,2} = [(0,0), (1,3), (2,3), (3,0)]$, $\mathbf{x}_{1,3} = [(0,0), (1,4), (2,0), (3,3)]$, and $\mathbf{x}_{1,4} = [(0,0), (1,0), (2,2), (3,1)]$, from the $i_{1,2} = 1$ subset of level 1 have at most two hits with $x_{0,1}$.

Using $k = 2$, $n = 3$, $p = 5$, and $L = w = 5$ as an example, this trilevel carrier-hopping prime code of length $N = 25$ has 15625 codewords, denoted by $x_{i_{2,3},i_{2,2},i_{2,1},i_{1,3},i_{1,2},i_{1,1}} = [(0,0),(1,5(i_{2,3} + i_{2,2} + i_{2,1}) + i_{1,3} + i_{1,2} + i_{1,1}),(2,5(8i_{2,3} + 4i_{2,2} + 2i_{2,1}) + 8i_{1,3} + 4i_{1,2} + 2i_{1,1}),(3,5(27i_{2,3} + 9i_{2,2} + 3i_{2,1}) + 27i_{1,3} + 9i_{1,2} + 3i_{1,1}),(4,5(64i_{2,3} + 16i_{2,2} + 4i_{2,1}) + 64i_{1,3} + 16i_{1,2} + 4i_{1,1})]$ for $i_{2,3}$, $i_{2,2}$, $i_{2,1}$, $i_{1,3}$, $i_{1,2}$, and $i_{1,1} \in [0,4]$. In level 3, all 15625 codewords have $\lambda_c = 3$. In level 2, codewords with the same $i_{1,3}$ and $i_{2,3}$ indices (or subset) have $\lambda_c = 2$, but those with different $i_{1,3}$ or $i_{2,3}$ indices have $\lambda_c = 3$. In level 1, codewords with the same $i_{1,2}$, $i_{1,3}$, $i_{2,2}$, and $i_{2,3}$ indices have $\lambda_c = 1$. For example, $x_{0,0,1,0,0,0} = [(0,0),(1,5),(2,10),(3,15),(4,20)]$ has at most three hits (in the sampling time of the periodic cross-correlation function) when it correlates with codewords, such as $x_{0,0,1,1,1,3} = [(0,0),(1,5),(2,13),(3,15),(4,22)]$ and $x_{4,0,0,0,0,0} = [(0,0),(1,20),(2,10),(3,15),(4,5)]$, from different $i_{1,3}$ or $i_{2,3}$ subsets in level 3. However, $x_{0,0,1,0,0,0}$ has at most two hits when it correlates with codewords, such as $x_{0,4,2,0,4,1} = [(0,0),(1,5),(2,3),(3,14),(4,13)]$, from the same $i_{1,3}$ and $i_{2,3}$ subset in level 2. Finally, $x_{0,0,1,0,0,0}$ has at most one hit when it correlates with the other 24 codewords, such as $x_{0,0,2,0,0,1} = [(0,0),(1,11),(2,22),(3,8),(4,19)]$, from the same $i_{1,2}$, $i_{1,3}$, $i_{2,2}$, and $i_{2,3}$ subset in level 1.

According to Section 1.6, the cardinality upper bound of the multilevel carrier-hopping prime codes with cardinality p^{nk}, $L = w$ wavelengths, length $N = p^k$, weight $w \le p$, and the maximum periodic cross-correlation function of n is given by

$$\Phi_{upper} \le \frac{w(wp^k - 1)(wp^k - 2)\cdots(wp^k - n)}{w(w-1)(w-2)\cdots(w-n)}$$

This upper bound approaches the actual cardinality when w is large. So, the multilevel carrier-hopping prime codes are asymptotically optimal in cardinality.

5.2.1 Performance Analysis

According to Section 1.8.4, the chip-synchronous, hard-limiting error probability of the multilevel carrier-hopping prime codes over $GF(p)$ of a prime p with weight $w \le p$ and the maximum periodic cross-correlation function of n in OOK is given by

$$P_{e,hard} = \frac{1}{2} \sum_{h=Z_{th}}^{w} \frac{w!}{h!(w-h)!} \sum_{i=0}^{h} (-1)^{h-i} \frac{h!}{i!(h-i)!} \left[\sum_{j=0}^{n} \frac{i!(w-j)!}{w!(i-j)!} q_j \right]^{K-1}$$

where K is the number of simultaneous users, and the decision threshold $Z_{th} = w$ is usually applied for optimal decision.

Theorem 5.4

For the multilevel carrier-hopping prime codes over $GF(p)$ of a prime p with cardinality p^{nk}, $L = w$ wavelengths, length $N = p^k$, weight $w \le p$, and $\lambda_c = n$, the hit probabilities, q_i, of having the periodic cross-correlation values of $i = \{0, 1, \ldots, n\}$ (in the sampling time) are formulated as [11, 12]

$$q_i = \frac{h_{n,i}}{2p^k(p^{nk} - 1)}$$

$$\sum_{i=0}^{n} iq_i = \frac{w}{2p^k}$$

and $\sum_{i=0}^{n} q_i = 1$, where $h_{n,i}$ is the total number of times of getting i hits in the sampling time of the periodic cross-correlation functions, given by

$$h_{n,0} = 2p^k(p^{nk} - 1) - h_{n,n} - h_{n,n-1} - \cdots - h_{n,1}$$

$$h_{n,1} = w(p^{nk} - 1) - nh_{n,n} - (n-1)h_{n,n-1} - \cdots - 2h_{n,2}$$

$$h_{n,i} = \frac{(h_{n-1,i-1} + h_{n-2,i-1} + \cdots + h_{i-1,i-1})h_{i,i}}{h_{i-1,i-1}}$$

$$h_{n,n} = \frac{w!(p^k - 1)}{n!(w - n)!}$$

Proof The hit probability q_i is computed by evaluating $h_{n,i}$ recursively, where $1/2$ comes from the assumption of equiprobable data bit-1 and bit-0 transmissions in OOK, p^k represents the number of possible time shifts in codewords of length p^k, and $p^{nk} - 1$ denotes the possible number of interfering codewords. The equations of $h_{n,0}$ and $h_{n,1}$ come from the rearrangements of $q_i = h_{n,i}/[2p^k(p^{nk} - 1)]$ in $\sum_{i=0}^{n} q_i = 1$ and $\sum_{i=0}^{n} iq_i = w^2/(2LN) = w/(2p^k)$, respectively.

Starting from the root of the tree structure, codewords in level n can be partitioned into p^k subsets, and only one subset has the same $(i_{1,n}, i_{2,n}, \ldots, i_{k,n})$ values as the address codeword (of a receiver). So, there are $p^k - 1$ subsets of interfering codewords contributing at most n hits in the periodic cross-correlation functions, out of a total of w possible hits. This accounts for the equation of $h_{n,n}$. Furthermore, $h_{n-1,i}$ counts the number of times of getting i hits contributed by the interfering codewords in level n with the same $(i_{1,n}, i_{2,n}, \ldots, i_{k,n})$ subset as the address codeword. Because the cross-correlation property of the codewords is uniform, the term $(h_{n,i} - h_{n-1,i})/h_{n-1,i-1}$ is always a constant, in which $h_{n,i} - h_{n-1,i}$ counts the number of times of getting i hits contributed by the interfering codewords in level n with different $(i_{1,n}, i_{2,n}, \ldots, i_{k,n})$ subsets from the address codeword. Continuing down the tree level-by-level, the relationship found in the term $(h_{n,i} - h_{n-1,i})/h_{n-1,i-1}$ holds as a recursive function of n and results in

$$\frac{h_{n,i} - h_{n-1,i}}{h_{n-1,i-1}} = \frac{h_{n-1,i} - h_{n-2,i}}{h_{n-2,i-1}} = \cdots = \frac{h_{i,i} - h_{i-1,i}}{h_{i-1,i-1}}$$

in which $h_{i-1,i} = 0$ is assumed because $h_{i-1,i}$ does not exist, by definition. After some manipulations, the final form of $h_{n,i}$ in the theorem is derived. ∎

To complete the evaluation of the hit probabilities in Theorem 5.4, $h_{n,n}$, $h_{n,n-1}$, ..., and $h_{n,0}$ are found from the following steps:

Step 1: Set $n = 1$.

    a. For $i = 1$, the equation of $h_{n,n}$ gives $h_{1,1} = w(p^k - 1)$.

Step 2: Increase n by one to $n = 2$.

    a. For $i = 2$, the equation of $h_{n,n}$ gives $h_{2,2} = w(w-1)(p^k - 1)/2$.
    b. For $i = 1$, the equation of $h_{n,1}$ gives $h_{2,1} = w(p^{2k} - 1) - 2h_{2,2} = w(p^k + 2 - w)(p^k - 1)$.

Step 3: Increase $n = j - 1$ by one to $n = j$, for all $j = \{3, 4, 5, \ldots, \lambda_c\}$.

    a. For $i = j$, the equation of $h_{n,n}$ gives $h_{j,j} = w!(p^k - 1)/[j!(w-j)!]$.
    b. For $i = \{j-1, j-2, \ldots, 2\}$, the equation of $h_{n,i}$ gives $h_{j,j-1}, h_{j,j-2}, \ldots$, and $h_{j,2}$, respectively.
    c. For $i = 1$, the equation of $h_{n,1}$ gives $h_{j,1} = w(p^{jk} - 1) - jh_{j,j} - (j - 1)h_{j,j-1} - \cdots - 2h_{j,2}$.

Step 4: Repeat Step 3 if $n \leq \lambda_c$; otherwise, go to Step 5.

Step 5: Finally, $h_{n,0} = 2p^k(p^{nk} - 1) - h_{n,n} - h_{n,n-1} - \cdots - h_{n,1}$ is obtained.

Because the multilevel carrier-hopping prime codes have the periodic cross-correlation function of at most 1 among the p^k codewords within every subset in level 1, codewords can be chosen from the same subset to minimize the mutual interference when $K \leq p^k$. Otherwise, codewords should be chosen from more than one subset in level 1, further sacrificing code performance. If there exist $K \in [p^k + 1, p^{2k}]$ simultaneous users, codewords are selected from multiple subsets of level 1 but all these subsets of level 1 should come from one subset of level 2 in order to limit λ_c to 2. Similarly, if $K \in [p^{2k} + 1, p^{3k}]$, codewords from one subset of level 3 are chosen in order to limit λ_c to three. In general, if $K \in [p^{lk} + 1, p^{(l+1)k}]$, codewords are selected from one subset of level l in order to limit λ_c to l, where $l \in [1, n]$.

Figure 5.5 plots the chip-synchronous, hard-limiting error probabilities of the multilevel carrier-hopping prime codes with $k = 1$, $L = w$ wavelengths, length $N = p = 89$, and weight w against the number of simultaneous users K for $n = \{1, 2, 3\}$ and $w = \{11, 14, 17\}$. In general, the error probabilities improve as L or w increases because of lower hit probabilities or higher autocorrelation peaks. However, the error probabilities get worse as K or n increases due to stronger mutual interference. Because the code cardinality is given by p^{nk}, there is a trade-off between code performance and cardinality. Furthermore, as seen in the curves of $L = w = 14$ and $N = 89$, the biggest difference in the code performance occurs between the codewords with $n = 1$ and $n = 2$, and the worsening in error probability slows down when $n \geq 3$. This is because the hit probabilities get worse and cannot depreciate much further as n increases beyond 3.

Figure 5.6 plots the chip-synchronous, hard-limiting error probabilities of the multilevel carrier-hopping prime codes with $n = 3$, $L = 7$ wavelengths, length

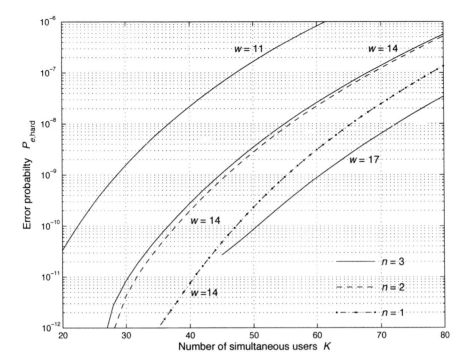

FIGURE 5.5 Chip-synchronous, hard-limiting error probabilities of the multilevel carrier-hopping prime codes with $k = 1$ and $N = 89$ for $n = \{1, 2, 3\}$ and $L = w = \{11, 14, 17\}$.

$N = p^k$, and weight $w = 7$ against the number of simultaneous user K for $p = \{7, 11, 13, 17\}$ and $k = \{1, 2, 3\}$. In general, the error probabilities improve as p or k increases because of longer length $N = p^k$ and then lower hit probabilities. However, the error probabilities get worse as K increases due to stronger mutual interference. Both Figures 5.5 and 5.6 illustrate how bandwidth expansion LN can be sacrificed for the sake of better code performance.

Figure 5.7 shows an example of how the performance of the multilevel carrier-hopping prime codes with $k = 1$, $n = 2$, $L = 8$ wavelengths, length $N = p = 23$, and weight $w = 8$ can be optimized as a function of the number of simultaneous users K. In this code set, there are $p^{nk} = 529$ codewords with the maximum periodic cross-correlation function $\lambda_c = n = 2$ in the top level (or level $n = 2$). These 529 codewords can be partitioned into twenty-three subsets of codewords in level 1, in which each subset consists of 23 codewords with $\lambda_c = 1$. The dashed curve shows the performance of all 529 codewords (of $\lambda_c = 2$) in level 2, in which codewords are selected randomly. To optimize the code performance as a function of K, transmitting codewords are first chosen from the same subset of level 1 when $K \leq 23$, and then from level 2 in order to select the remaining $K - 23$ codewords when $23 < K \leq 23^2$. The solid-cross curve, which stops at $K = 23$, shows an optimized performance, whereas the first twenty-three transmitting codewords are selected from one subset

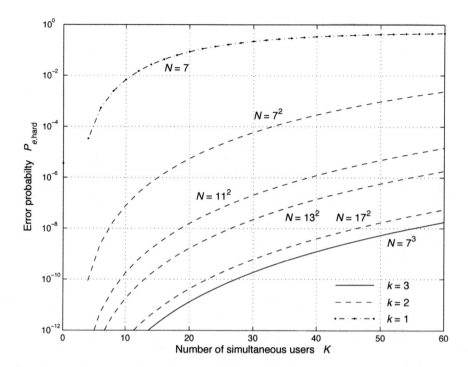

FIGURE 5.6 Chip-synchronous, hard-limiting error probabilities of the trilevel carrier-hopping prime codes with $L = w = 7$ and $N = p^k$ for $p = \{7, 11, 13, 17\}$ and $k = \{1, 2, 3\}$.

(with $\lambda_c = 1$) of level 1. The solid-circle curve, which starts at $K > 23$, shows an optimized performance when more $\lambda_c = 2$ codewords from another subset of level 1 are added. The curve slowly approaches the dashed curve when K increases beyond 23. By partitioning the codewords into multiple levels, code cardinality and cross-correlation function can be selected to suit different code-performance requirements.

5.3   SHIFTED CARRIER-HOPPING PRIME CODES

In incoherent coding, OOK is usually assumed, in which a user transmits data bit 1s with the address codeword of its intended receiver, but bit 0s are not conveyed. As discussed in Section 2.9, shifted-code keying increases the bit rate by transmitting multiple bits per symbol [9]. In this section, shifted carrier-hopping prime codes are studied. Each user employs one carrier-hopping prime codeword (in Section 5.1) and its 2^m (time or wavelength)-shifted copies to carry 2^m possible symbols in each symbol period, corresponding to m data bits per symbol. In this approach, the shifted carrier-hopping prime codes have ideal correlation properties—zero autocorrelation sidelobes for perfect symbol identification, zero *intrasymbol* cross-correlation values among the shifted codewords of the same user, and *intersymbol* cross-correlation values of at most 1 among the codewords of different users.

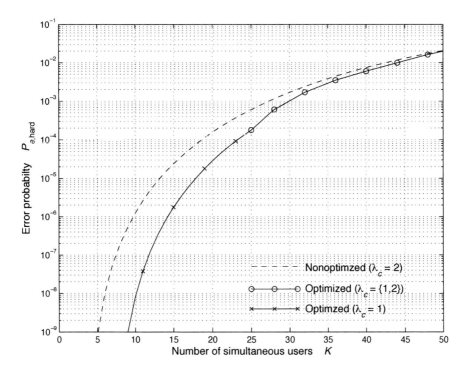

FIGURE 5.7 Chip-synchronous, hard-limiting error probabilities of the bilevel carrier-hopping prime codes with $k = 1$, $L = w = 8$, and $N = 23$, optimized as a function of K.

Definition 5.2

A family of 2-D shifted optical codes is a collection of binary $(0,1)$ $L \times N$ matrices (i.e., codewords), each of weight w and length N, with L (e.g., spatial, fiber-optic, or wavelength) channels, satisfying the following correlation constraints [9]:

- *Autocorrelation* (λ_a). Identical to the autocorrelation constraint in Definition 5.1.
- *Intersymbol cross-correlation* (λ_c). Identical to the periodic cross-correlation constraint in Definition 5.1.
- *Intrasymbol cross-correlation* (λ_c'). The discrete 2-D (in-phase) cross-correlation function of a code matrix $\mathbf{x}$ and its cyclic-shifted copy $\mathbf{x}'$ is no greater than a non-negative integer λ_c' such that

$$\sum_{i=0}^{L-1}\sum_{j=0}^{N-1} x_{i,j}x_{i,j}' \leq \lambda_c'$$

where $x_{i,j} = \{0,1\}$ is an element of $\mathbf{x}$ and $x_{i,j}' = \{0,1\}$ is an element of $\mathbf{x}'$

at the ith row and jth column. (Note: The cross-correlation value at the expected location of the autocorrelation peak of $\mathbf{x}$ is here considered and is not a function of any τ-shift.)

■

5.3.1   Construction 1: Time Shifts

Given a set of k prime numbers $p_k \geq p_{k-1} \geq \cdots \geq p_1$, binary $(0,1)$ matrices, $\mathbf{x}_{i_k,i_{k-1},\ldots,i_1,l}$, with the ordered pairs [9]

$$\{[(0,l),(1,(i_1+i_2p_1+\cdots+i_kp_1p_2\cdots p_{k-1})\oplus l),$$
$$(2,(2\odot_{p_1}i_1+(2\odot_{p_2}i_2)p_1+\cdots+(2\odot_{p_k}i_k)p_1p_2\cdots p_{k-1})\oplus l),\ldots,$$
$$(w-1,((w-1)\odot_{p_1}i_1+((w-1)\odot_{p_2}i_2)p_1+\cdots$$
$$+((w-1)\odot_{p_k}i_k)p_1p_2\cdots p_{k-1})\oplus l)]:i_1=\{0,1,\ldots,p_1-1\}$$
$$i_2=\{0,1,\ldots,p_2-1\},\ldots,i_k=\{0,1,\ldots,p_k-1\},$$
$$l=\{0,1,\ldots,p_1p_2\cdots p_k-1\}\}$$

form the time-shifted carrier-hopping prime codes with cardinality $(p_1p_2\cdots p_k)^2$, $L=w$ wavelengths, length $N=p_1p_2\cdots p_k$, and weight $w\leq p_1$, where "$\odot_{p_j}$" denotes a modulo-p_j multiplication for $j=\{1,2,\ldots,k\}$ and "$\oplus$" denotes a modulo-$p_1p_2\cdots p_k$ addition.

These $(p_1p_2\cdots p_k)^2$ time-shifted carrier-hopping prime codewords can be partitioned into $p_1p_2\cdots p_k$ groups (indexed by i_1, i_2, ..., and i_k) and there are $p_1p_2\cdots p_k$ shifted codewords (indexed by l) in each group. The first codeword $\mathbf{x}_{i_k,i_{k-1},\ldots,i_1,0}$ in every group comes from a codeword of the carrier-hopping prime codes in Section 5.1, which acts as a seed to generate the other shifted codewords in the group.

Using $k=2$, $L=w=4$, $p_1=5$, and $p_2=7$ as an example, this time-shifted carrier-hopping prime code of length $N=p_1p_2=35$ has 35 groups and 35 shifted codewords in each group, denoted by $\mathbf{x}_{i_2,i_1,l}=[(0,l),(1,(i_1+5i_2)\oplus l.),(2,(2\odot_5 i_1+(2\odot_7 i_2)5)\oplus l),(3,(3\odot_5 i_1+(3\odot_7 i_2)5)\oplus l),(4,(4\odot_5 i_1+(4\odot_7 i_2)5)\oplus l)]$ for $i_1\in[0,4]$, $i_2\in[0,6]$, and $l\in[0,34]$, where "$\oplus$" denotes a modulo-35 addition. For example, $\mathbf{x}_{2,2,0}=[(0,0),(1,12),(2,24),(3,1),(4,13)]$ is the first codeword in the $(i_2=2,i_1=2)$-group and $\mathbf{x}_{2,2,2}=[(0,2),(1,14),(2,26),(3,3),(4,15)]$ is a copy of $\mathbf{x}_{2,2,0}$ after two cyclic time-shifts.

5.3.2   Construction 2: Wavelength Shifts

Wavelength shifts can also be applied to the carrier-hopping prime codes in Section 5.1 with $k=1$ only. This restriction exists because time shifts and wavelength shifts are generally not compatible, and wavelength shifts with $k>1$ result in codes with the intersymbol cross-correlation functions of greater than 1.

Given a prime number p_1, binary $(0,1)$ matrices, $\mathbf{x}_{i_1,l}$, with the ordered pairs [9]

$$\{[(0\oplus_{p_1}l,0),(1\oplus_{p_1}l,i_1),(2\oplus_{p_1}l,2\odot_{p_1}i_1),\ldots,((p_1-1)\oplus_{p_1}l,$$
$$(p_1-1)\odot_{p_1}i_1)]:i_1=\{1,2,\ldots,p_1-1\},l=\{0,1,\ldots,p_1-1\}\}$$

form the wavelength-shifted carrier-hopping prime codes with cardinality $(p_1 - 1)p_1$, $L = w$ wavelengths, length $N = p_1$, and weight $w = p_1$.

To obtain the wavelength-shifted carrier-hopping prime codewords of weight $w < p_1$, those ordered pairs with the first components whose values (or wavelength numbers) are greater than $w - 1$ are removed.

These $(p_1 - 1)p_1$ wavelength-shifted carrier-hopping prime codewords can be partitioned into $p_1 - 1$ groups (indexed by i_1), and there are p_1 shifted codewords (indexed by l) in each group. The first codeword $\mathbf{x}_{i_1,0}$ in every group is coming from one of the $k = 1$ carrier-hopping prime codewords in Section 5.1, which acts as a seed to generate the other shifted codewords in the group.

Using $L = w = N = p_1 = 7$ as an example, this wavelength-shifted carrier-hopping prime code has 6 groups and 7 shifted codewords in each group, denoted by $\mathbf{x}_{i_1,l} = [(l,0),(1 \oplus_7 l, i_1),(2 \oplus_7 l, 2 \odot_7 i_1),\ldots,(6 \oplus_7 l, 6 \odot_7 i_1)]$ for $i_1 \in [1,6]$ and $l \in [0,6]$. For example, $\mathbf{x}_{1,0} = [(0,0),(1,1),(2,2),(3,3),(4,4),(5,5),(6,6)]$ is the first codeword in the $(i_1 = 1)$-group and $\mathbf{x}_{1,2} = [(0,5),(1,6),(2,0),(3,1),(4,2),(5,3),(6,4)]$ is a copy of $\mathbf{x}_{1,0}$ after two cyclic wavelength-shifts. If $w = 5$, these two codewords become $\mathbf{x}_{1,0} = [(0,0),(1,1),(2,2),(3,3),(4,4)]$ and $\mathbf{x}_{1,2} = [(0,5),(1,6),(2,0),(3,1),(4,2)]$ after the removal of those ordered pairs with the first components whose values are greater than $w - 1 = 4$.

Theorem 5.5

The autocorrelation peaks and sidelobes of the shifted carrier-hopping prime codes of weight w are equal to w and 0, respectively, where $w \leq p_1$. The intersymbol (periodic) cross-correlation functions of the codewords from different groups are at most 1. The intrasymbol (in-phase) cross-correlation functions of the codewords from the same group are equal to 0 [9].

Proof Let $\mathbf{x}_{i_k,i_{k-1},\ldots,i_1,l}$ and $\mathbf{x}_{i'_k,i'_{k-1},\ldots,i'_1,l'}$ be two distinct time-shifted carrier-hopping prime codewords with $(i_k,i_{k-1},\ldots,i_1,l) \neq (i'_k,i'_{k-1},\ldots,i'_1,l')$. If there exist two hits of pulses in any relative horizontal cyclic shift τ between the two codewords, then

$$[j_1 \odot_{p_1} i_1 + (j_1 \odot_{p_2} i_2)p_1 + \cdots + (j_1 \odot_{p_k} i_k)p_1 p_2 \cdots p_{k-1}] \oplus l + \tau$$
$$= [j_1 \odot_{p_1} i'_1 + (j_1 \odot_{p_2} i'_2)p_1 + \cdots + (j_1 \odot_{p_k} i'_k)p_1 p_2 \cdots p_{k-1}] \oplus l'$$

$$[j_2 \odot_{p_1} i_1 + (j_2 \odot_{p_2} i_2)p_1 + \cdots + (j_2 \odot_{p_k} i_k)p_1 p_2 \cdots p_{k-1}] \oplus l + \tau$$
$$= [j_2 \odot_{p_1} i'_1 + (j_2 \odot_{p_2} i'_2)p_1 + \cdots + (j_2 \odot_{p_k} i'_k)p_1 p_2 \cdots p_{k-1}] \oplus l'$$

must hold simultaneously for a $j_1 = \{0,1,\ldots,p_1 p_2 \cdots p_k - 1\}$ and a $j_2 = \{0,1,\ldots,p_1 p_2 \cdots p_k - 1\}$, where $j_1 \neq j_2$. The subtraction of these two equations results in

$$[(j_1 - j_2) \odot_{p_1} i_1 - (j_1 - j_2) \odot_{p_1} i_1'] + [(j_1 - j_2) \odot_{p_2} i_2 - ((j_1 - j_2) \odot_{p_2} i_2']p_1$$
$$+ \cdots + [(j_1 - j_2) \odot_{p_k} i_k - (j_1 - j_2) \odot_{p_k} i_k']p_1 p_2 \cdots p_{k-1} = 0$$

which is valid only when $i_m = i_m'$ for all $m = \{1, 2, \ldots, k\}$. This violates the assumption of distinct $\mathbf{x}_{i_k, i_{k-1}, \ldots, i_1, l}$ and $\mathbf{x}_{i_k', i_{k-1}', \ldots, i_1', l'}$. So, the intersymbol (periodic) cross-correlation function is at most 1.

Because all pulses in a codeword are in different wavelengths, the autocorrelation sidelobes are always 0. The autocorrelation peaks of w are due to the code weight $w \leq p_1$.

Because the intrasymbol (in-phase) cross-correlation function is defined between a codeword with its shifted copies, the function follows the maximum autocorrelation-sidelobe value, which is equal to 0 no matter how many horizontal shifts are applied to a codeword.

The proof for the wavelength-shifted carrier-hopping prime codes follows the above procedure with the corresponding ordered pairs of the wavelength-shifted codes and $k = 1$. ∎

5.3.3 Performance Analysis

In this section, the performances of the time- and wavelength-shifted carrier-hopping prime codes in shifted-code keying are analyzed. The analysis also applies to multi-code keying, which transmits symbols by means of different optical codes. In general, the performance of optical codes in OOK is determined only by the intersymbol (periodic) cross-correlation constraint λ_c. The intrasymbol (in-phase) cross-correlation constraint λ_c' comes into play when shifted-code or multicode keying is in use, as discussed in Section 2.9.

Theorem 5.6

For the shifted carrier-hopping prime codes with L wavelengths, length N, weight $w \leq p_1$, $\lambda_c = 1$, and $\lambda_c' = 0$ in shifted-code keying, the hit probabilities, q_i, of having intersymbol (periodic) cross-correlation values of $i = \{0, 1\}$ (in the sampling time) are given by

$$q_1 = \frac{w^2}{LN}$$

and $q_0 = 1 - q_1$.

The chip-synchronous, hard-limiting bit error probability of these shifted carrier-hopping prime codes in 2^m-ary shifted-code keying is formulated as [9]

$$
\begin{aligned}
P_{e,\text{hard,shifted}} \;=\; & \frac{2^m}{2(2^m-1)} \left\{ 1 - \sum_{t=0}^{2^m-1} \left(\frac{1}{t+1} \right) \frac{(2^m-1)!}{t!(2^m-1-t)!} \right. \\
& \left. \times [\Pr(w)]^t \left[\sum_{v=0}^{w-1} \Pr(v) \right]^{2^m-1-t} \right\}
\end{aligned}
\tag{5.2}
$$

where m is the number of data bits per symbol,

$$
\Pr(v) = \frac{w!}{v!(w-v)!} \sum_{i=0}^{v} (-1)^{v-i} \frac{v!}{i!(v-i)!} \left(q_0 + \frac{iq_1}{w} \right)^{K-1}
$$

and K is the number of simultaneous users.

Proof The derivation of q_1 follows that of $\lambda_c = 1$ optical codes in OOK (e.g., see Section 5.1), except that the factor $1/2$ is not needed because of continuous symbol transmission in shifted-code or multicode keying.

With the shifted carrier-hopping prime codes in use, each user conveys m data bits (per symbol) by transmitting one of the 2^m shifted copies (or symbols) of the address codeword of its intended receiver. As these 2^m shifted codewords have zero intrasymbol cross-correlation functions ($\lambda_c' = 0$) among themselves, the hard-limiting probability of having a peak of v appearing at any one of 2^m-1 wrong decoders in a receiver is given by $\Pr(v)$ in the theorem, which is derived by following Section 1.8.4 [9,10,25]. The derivation of $\Pr(v)$ and the use of $w!/[v!(w-v)!]$ are based on the assumption that the peak v, out of w possible pulses, is caused by the accumulation of interference generated by $K-1$ interferers.

The probability that t decoders have a correlation value of at least s and 2^m-1-t decoders have a correlation value of less than s is given by

$$
\Pr(s,t) = \frac{(2^m-1)!}{t!(2^m-1-t)!} [\Pr(s)]^t \left[\sum_{v=0}^{s-1} \Pr(v) \right]^{2^m-1-t}
$$

Because the probability of choosing the correct decoder is $1/(t+1)$ and there are 2^m symbols, the general chip-synchronous, hard-limiting bit error probability of optical codes with $\lambda_c' = 0$ in 2^m-ary shifted-code or multicode keying is derived as [9,10,25]

$$
P_{e,\text{hard,keying}} = \frac{2^m}{2(2^m-1)} \left[1 - \sum_{s=Z_{\text{th}}}^{w} \frac{w!}{s!(w-s)!} \sum_{t=0}^{2^m-1} \frac{1}{t+1} \Pr(s,t) \right]
$$

where the decision threshold $Z_{\text{th}} = w$ is usually applied for optimal decision. After some manipulations, the final form of $P_{e,\text{hard,keying}}$ in the theorem is derived. ∎

For comparison, the chip-synchronous, hard-limiting bit error probability of the carrier-hopping prime codes (in Section 5.1) with the maximum periodic cross-correlation function of one in OOK is given by

$$P_{e,\text{hard,OOK}} = \frac{1}{2} \sum_{h=Z_{\text{th}}}^{w} \frac{w!}{h!(w-h)!} \sum_{i=0}^{h} (-1)^{h-i} \frac{h!}{i!(h-i)!} \left(q_0' + \frac{iq_1'}{w} \right)^{K-1} \qquad (5.3)$$

according to Section 1.8.4, where $q_1' = w^2/(2LN)$ and $\sum_{i=0}^{1} q_i' = 1$.

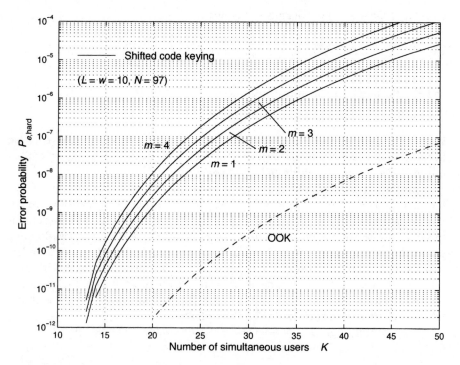

FIGURE 5.8 Chip-synchronous, hard-limiting bit error probabilities of the carrier-hopping prime codes of $L = w = 10$ and $N = 97$ in OOK and 2^m-ary shifted-code keying for $m = \{1,2,3,4\}$.

Figure 5.8 plots the chip-synchronous, hard-limiting bit error probabilities of the carrier-hopping prime codes in OOK [from Equation (5.3)] and the shifted carrier-hopping prime codes in 2^m-ary shifted-code keying [from Equation (5.2)], both of $k = 1, L = w$ wavelengths, length $N = p_1 = 97$, and weight $w = 10$ against the number of simultaneous users K for $m = \{1,2,3,4\}$. In general, the error probabilities get worse as K increases because of stronger mutual interference. The worsening in the error probabilities (solid curves) of shifted-code keying is relatively large when being compared to those (dashed curves) of OOK because the hit probabilities in OOK are reduced by half as data bit 0s are not conveyed. Furthermore, the error probabilities get worse as m increases because more data bits will be decided incorrectly if a symbol decision error occurs. The results show that there is a trade-off between code performance and the choice of m. For the benefit of higher bit rate or enhancing user code obscurity, error probability suffers. If bit rate or code obscurity is not important, one should use OOK. Otherwise, the choice of $m = 2$ or 3 provides a good compromise among code performance, hardware complexity, and bit rate.

With the time-shifted carrier-hopping prime codes in use, each user conveys symbols with time-shifted copies of the address codeword of its intended receiver. A time-shifted copy will be followed by another time-shifted copy in order to represent the transmission of two consecutive but different symbols of the same user. Depending on their time-shift directions, these two copies may arrive at the receivers of other users with shorter (time) separation than those with no time shift. As a result, the maximum intersymbol (periodic) cross-correlation function may get worse from 1 to 2 (or $\lambda_c = 2$), but the occurrence of two hits is at most once over one symbol period for the extreme case of $w = N$. The chances of this happening are even smaller as the ratio w/N decreases; most of the time, λ_c is still equal to 1.

For comparison, the two-hit is here assumed to occur at most x times over one symbol period. The hit probability q_i of getting $i = \{0, 1, 2\}$ hits in the sampling time of the intersymbol (periodic) cross-correlation function can then be modified as [9]

$$q_2 = \frac{w^2}{LN} \times \frac{x}{N} \tag{5.4}$$

$$q_1 = \frac{w^2}{LN} - 2q_2 = \frac{w(N - 2x)}{N^2} \tag{5.5}$$

and $\sum_{i=0}^{2} q_i = 1$. For $\lambda_c = 2$ and $\lambda_c' = 0$, the probability of having a peak of v appearing at any one of $2^m - 1$ wrong decoders becomes

$$\Pr(v) = \frac{w!}{v!(w-v)!} \sum_{i=0}^{v} (-1)^{v-i} \frac{v!}{i!(v-i)!} \left[q_0 + \frac{iq_1}{w} + \frac{i(i-1)q_2}{w(w-1)} \right]^{K-1} \tag{5.6}$$

Substituting Equations (5.4) through (5.6) into Equation (5.2), the chip-synchronous, hard-limiting bit error probability of these time-shifted carrier-hopping prime codes for the two-hit happening x times per symbol period is derived.

Figure 5.9 plots the chip-synchronous, hard-limiting bit error probabilities of the time-shifted carrier-hopping prime codes of $k = 1$, $L = w$ wavelengths, length $N = p_1 = 101$, and weight $w = 10$ in 2^3-ary shifted-code keying [from Equations (5.2) and (5.4) through (5.6)] against the number of simultaneous users K for $x = \{0, 1, 2, 3\}$. In general, the error probabilities get worse as x increases, but the worsening is relatively small. The inclusion of $x = \{2, 3\}$ is just for comparison as they should not occur. So, the error probabilities are always bounded by the $(x = 0)$- and $(x = 1)$-curves, and the $(x = 1)$-curve is valid only for the extreme case of $w = N$.

5.3.4 Spectral Efficiency Study

Following Equations (5.2) and (5.4) through (5.6), the chip-synchronous, hard-limiting bit error probability of the shifted carrier-hopping prime codes in shifted-code keying is dominated by the case of $t = 1$. As $\sum_{v=0}^{w} \Pr(v) = 1$, it is found

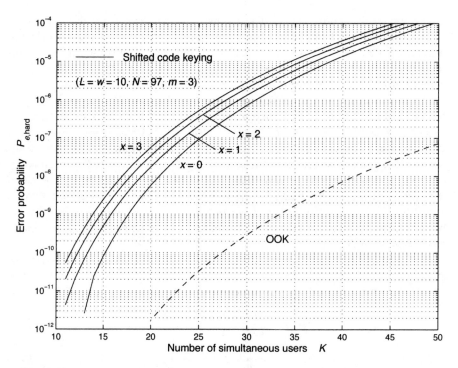

FIGURE 5.9 Chip-synchronous, hard-limiting bit error probabilities of the time-shifted carrier-hopping prime codes of $L = w = 10$ and $N = 97$ in 2^3-ary shifted-code keying for $x = \{0, 1, 2, 3\}$.

that $\sum_{v=0}^{w-1} \Pr(v) = 1 - \Pr(w)$ and $[\sum_{v=0}^{w-1} \Pr(v)]^{2^m-2} \approx 1$ when $w > 5$. So, the chip-synchronous, hard-limiting bit error probability with $Z_{\text{th}} = w$ can be approximated as [9, 25]

$$P_{e,\text{hard,shifted}} \approx \frac{2^m}{4} \sum_{i=0}^{w} (-1)^{w-i} \frac{w!}{i!(w-i)!} \left[q_0 + \frac{i q_1}{w} + \frac{i(i-1)q_2}{w(w-1)} \right]^{K-1} \qquad (5.7)$$

Although the maximum intersymbol cross-correlation function of the time-shifted carrier-hopping prime codes can get worse from 1 to 2, the probability of getting two-hits is limited by the probability of getting one-hits because $q_1 + 2q_2 = w^2/(LN)$. The occurrence of any two-hit in the cross-correlation function will reduce the chance of getting 2 one-hits. If there exists no two-hit, the one-hit probability is then given by $q_1'' = w^2/(LN) = w/N$ for $L = w$. Assume that the occurrence of a two-hit is caused by two interfering codewords and each of them contributes one hit at the same time. Define $\alpha = q_1/q_1'' = q_1/(w/N)$ as the ratio of the probability of getting a one-hit with some two-hits presence to the probability of getting a one-hit without any two-hit presence. So, α is a real number in the closed interval of $[0, 1]$, and $1 - \alpha$ represents the ratio of getting a two-hit due to the reduction in the presence of 2 one-hits. When $\alpha = 1$, no two-hit exists due to $q_2 = 0$. When $\alpha = 0$, no one-hit exists due to $q_1 = 0$. The amount of interference generated by each interfering codeword can be written as

$$I = \alpha \times 1 + (1 - \alpha) \times 2 = 2 - \frac{q_1}{w/N}$$

and $I \in [1, 2]$ due to $\alpha \in [0, 1]$.

Now, consider the case of using the wavelength-shifted carrier-hopping prime codes with cardinality $(p-1)p$, $L = w$ wavelengths, length $N = p$, and weight $w \leq p$ in shifted-code keying. The two-hit probability can be derived as

$$
\begin{aligned}
q_2 &= \frac{\sum_{i=1}^{p-1} \frac{iw}{p} \times \frac{(p-i)w}{p} \times \frac{2^m - 1}{2^m}}{p \times p \times (p-1)} \\
&= \frac{(N+1)}{6N} \times \left(\frac{w}{N}\right)^2 \times \frac{2^m - 1}{2^m}
\end{aligned}
$$

Because the number of available wavelengths is $L = w$, the intersymbol (periodic) cross-correlation function can be caused by a preceding symbol of the interfering codeword overlapping the correct user's address codeword at iw/p chip locations and a present symbol overlapping at $(p-i)w/p$ chip locations, where $i \in [1, p-1]$. The probability of having different preceding and present symbols is given by $(2^m - 1)/2^m$. In the denominator, the first p accounts for the number of possible wavelength shifts in each of the wavelength-shifted carrier-hopping prime codewords. The second p represents the number of possible time shifts in a code of length $N = p$. The term $p - 1$ represents the number of valid wavelength shifts as identical preceding and present symbols do not generate any two-hits. Furthermore, $\sum_{i=0}^{2} i q_i = w^2/(LN)$ gives

$$q_1 = \frac{w^2}{LN} - 2q_2 = \frac{w}{N} - \frac{w^2(N+1)(2^m - 1)}{3N^3 2^m}$$

Because $I = 2 - q_1/(w/N)$, the wavelength-shifted carrier-hopping prime codes have

$$I = 1 + \frac{w(N+1)(2^m - 1)}{3N^2 2^m} \leq 1 + \frac{N^2 2^m}{3N^2 2^m} \approx \frac{4}{3}$$

by assuming $w < N$. So, for the wavelength-shifted carrier-hopping prime codes, I is bound by $[1, 4/3]$, instead of $[1, 2]$ in the time-shifted carrier-hopping prime codes.

Based on the aforementioned derivation, the chip synchronous, hard-limiting bit error probability, approximated in Equation (5.7) with $Z_{th} = w$, of the time- and wavelength-shifted carrier-hopping prime codes in shifted-code keying can be modified as

$$P_{e,\text{hard,shifted}} \approx \frac{2^m}{4} \sum_{i=0}^{w} (-1)^{w-i} \frac{w!}{i!(w-i)!} \left(q_0'' + \frac{iq_1''}{w}\right)^{IK_{\text{SCK}} - 1}$$

with $I \in [1, 2]$ and $I \in [1, 4/3]$, respectively, where K_{SCK} is the number of simultaneous users in shifted-code keying (SCK). As $q_1'' = w^2/(LN)$ is twice that of

$q_1' = w^2/(2LN)$ in OOK in Equation (5.3), the amount of interference seen in shifted-code keying is about twice that in OOK. To have the same form as Equation (5.3), $P_{e,\text{hard,shifted}}$ can be rewritten by setting $m = 1$ and doubling $IK_{\text{SCK}} - 1$ as [25]

$$P_{e,\text{hard},m=1 \text{ shifted}} \approx \frac{1}{2} \sum_{i=0}^{w} (-1)^{w-i} \frac{w!}{i!(w-i)!} \left(q_0' + \frac{iq_1'}{w} \right)^{2(IK_{\text{SCK}}-1)} \tag{5.8}$$

By comparing Equations (5.3) and (5.8) term-by-term, the relationship of

$$K_{\text{SCK}} \approx \frac{K_{\text{OOK}} + 1}{2I}$$

is established.

According to Section 1.8.7, spectral efficiency (SE) in shifted-code and multicode keying can be generally defined as

$$\text{SE} = \frac{KmR_{\text{bit}}}{L\Lambda} = \frac{Km}{L\Lambda} \times \frac{R_{\text{chip}}}{N} \propto \frac{Km}{LN}$$

where K is the number of simultaneous users for a given error probability, mR_{bit} is the aggregated bit rate for 2^m-ary modulation and bit rate R_{bit}, $R_{\text{chip}} = NR_{\text{bit}}$ is the chip rate, and Λ is the (wavelength) channel spacing. For OOK, $m = 1$ is used. Usually, R_{chip}/Λ is fixed when families of optical codes or coding schemes are compared. So, the SE comparison in this section can be simplified by computing $Km/(LN)$.

The SE of the time- and wavelength-shifted carrier-hopping prime codes in shifted-code keying with $m = 1$ is then approximated as

$$\text{SE}_{m=1 \text{ shifted}} \quad \propto \quad \frac{K_{\text{SCK}} \times 1}{LN}$$

$$\approx \quad \frac{K_{\text{OOK}}}{2ILN} + \frac{1}{2ILN}$$

where $I \in [1,2]$ and $[1,4/3]$, respectively. Because $\text{SE}_{\text{OOK}} = K_{\text{OOK}}/(LN)$, shifted-code keying with $m = 1$ always results in a smaller SE than OOK, giving no benefit to using the former, besides the reason of user code obscurity.

For a general case of $m > 1$, it is found that the factor 2^m has less influence than the exponential term (to the K_{SCK}th power) in Equation (5.8). So, the SE of the time- and wavelength-shifted carrier-hopping prime codes in 2^m-ary shifted-code keying is generally approximated as

$$\text{SE}_{\text{shifted}} \underset{\sim}{\propto} \frac{(K_{\text{OOK}} + 1)m}{2ILN}$$

For example, the SE of shifted-code keying with $m = 2$ is given by

$$\text{SE}_{m=2 \text{ shifted}} \underset{\sim}{\propto} \frac{K_{\text{OOK}}}{ILN} + \frac{1}{ILN}$$

To have the SE of shifted-code keying with $m = 2$ better than that of OOK, the condition $\text{SE}_{m=2 \text{ shifted}} > \text{SE}_{\text{OOK}}$ should be satisfied. After some manipulations, the condition requires $I < 1 + 1/K_{OOK} \approx 1$. Because I must be at least equal to 1 in the time- and wavelength-shifted carrier-hopping prime codes, there is no benefit to using 2^2-ary shifted-code keying over OOK, besides the reason of user code obscurity.

Similarly, the condition of having $SE_{m=3 \text{ shifted}} > SE_{OOK}$ is given by

$$\frac{3K_{OOK}}{2ILN} + \frac{3}{2ILN} > \frac{K_{OOK}}{LN}$$

After some simplifications, the condition becomes

$$I < \frac{3K_{OOK}+3}{2K_{OOK}} \approx \frac{3}{2}$$

for a large K_{OOK}. Compared to $I \in [1,4/3]$ in the wavelength-shifted carrier-hopping prime codes, the SE of 2^3-ary shifted-code keying is better than that of OOK (with the carrier-hopping prime codes in Section 5.1). However, it is uncertain in the time-shifted carrier-hopping prime codes with $m = 3$ because they require $I \in [1,2]$.

In general, whether the SE of 2^m-ary shifted-code keying is better than that of OOK depends on the values of m and I. While the kind of shifted codes determines the I value, the SE of shifted-code keying is directly proportional to m, which is also related to the hardware complexity. In other words, shifted-code keying allows trading off system complexity for spectral efficiency.

For the SE study of 2-D coding schemes, system parameters, such as bandwidth expansion LN, chip rate R_{chip}, and (wavelength) channel spacing Λ, are usually assumed as fixed resources. So, the SE comparison can be simplified by considering the product of Km. To determine which scheme has a larger SE, it is equivalent to find out which term, $K_{SCK}m$ versus K_{OOK}, has a larger quantity for a given error probability.

Figure 5.10 plots the SEs of the wavelength-shifted carrier-hopping prime codes in 2^m-ary shifted-code keying and the carrier-hopping prime codes (in Section 5.1) in OOK against the bandwidth expansion LN, where $L = w = 10$, $m = \{1,2,3\}$, $R_{chip}/\Lambda = 1$, and $P_{e,\text{hard}} \approx 10^{-9}$. The numbers of simultaneous users K_{SCK} that achieve $P_{e,\text{hard}} \approx 10^{-9}$ for the shifted-code-keying (solid) curves are calculated from Equation (5.7) with the corresponding m values. Similarly, Equation (5.3) is used to compute K_{OOK} that achieves $P_{e,\text{hard}} \approx 10^{-9}$ for the OOK (dashed) curve. Figure 5.10 shows that shifted-code keying has a smaller SE than OOK when $m = 1$, but starts having a larger SE when $m \geq 3$. In addition, the rate of increase in the SE of shifted-code keying grows with m almost linearly. In the SE aspect, it is beneficial to use shifted-code keying with a large m.

Figure 5.11 plots the numbers of simultaneous users K supported by the wavelength-shifted carrier-hopping prime codes in 2^m-ary shifted-code keying and by the carrier-hopping prime codes (in Section 5.1) in OOK against the bandwidth-expansion factor LN, where $L = w = 10$, $m = \{1,2,3,4\}$, $R_{chip}/\Lambda = 1$, and $P_{e,\text{hard}} \approx 10^{-9}$. The numbers of simultaneous users K_{SCK} that achieve $P_{e,\text{hard}} \approx 10^{-9}$ for the shifted-code-keying curves are calculated from Equation (5.7) with the corresponding m values. Similarly, Equation (5.3) is used to compute K_{OOK} that achieves

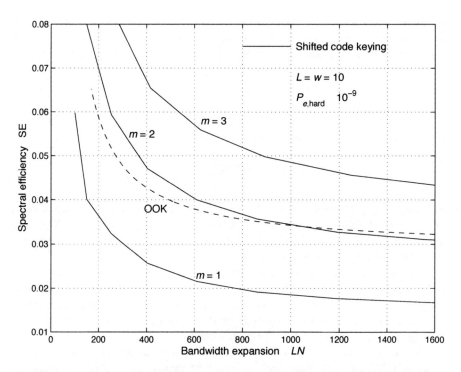

FIGURE 5.10 SE versus bandwidth-expansion factor LN of the 2^m-ary wavelength-shifted and OOK carrier-hopping prime codes, where $L = w = 10$, $m = \{1, 2, 3\}$, and $P_e \approx 10^{-9}$.

$P_{e,\text{hard}} \approx 10^{-9}$ for the OOK curve. In general, the number of simultaneous users improves as the bandwidth expansion LN increases because of lower hit probabilities. The OOK curve is always better than the shifted-code-keying curves because hit probabilities are reduced by half in the former. As shown in the dashed-circle curve, the approximation method, which is based on $K_{\text{SCK}} \approx (K_{\text{OOK}} + 1)/(2I)$, provides a fast but quite accurate way to compute the SE of shifted-code keying when $m \leq 3$. Figure 5.11 also shows that K decreases as m increases for a fixed LN. Although the chance of getting decision errors increases with the number of data bits represented by a symbol, the SE of shifted-code keying is directly proportional to mK_{SCK}, which compensates for the loss in K_{SCK} and provides a net gain in the SE as m increases. This agrees with the results in Figure 5.8.

5.4 EXTENDED CARRIER-HOPPING PRIME CODES

The carrier-hopping prime codes studied so far are based on an assumption that the number of time slots is always more than the number of available wavelengths. However, this assumption may not be valid in high bit-rate systems, in which the number of time slots is limited. For example, 10+ Gbits/s systems can support about 30 time slots in current technology [2, 26]. Such a small number of time slots can only ac-

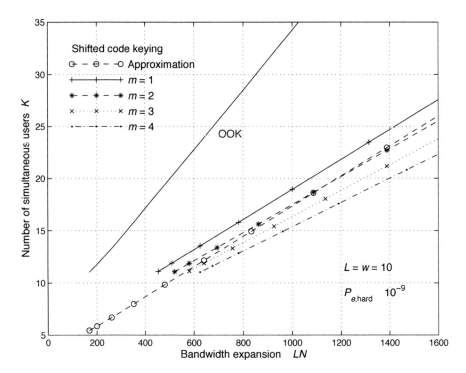

FIGURE 5.11 Number of simultaneous users K versus bandwidth-expansion factor LN of the 2^m-ary wavelength-shifted and OOK carrier-hopping prime codes, where $L = w = 10$, $m = \{1,2,3,4\}$, and $P_e \approx 10^{-9}$.

commodate limited numbers of simultaneous users and possible subscribers, even in 2-D optical codes. Nevertheless, this limitation can be improved in wavelength-time codes by increasing the number of available wavelengths, say through the use of lasers with broadened supercontinuum spectrum [27]. Families of 2-D optical codes that require the use of more wavelengths than time slots will be useful for these kinds of applications.

By interchanging the two components in every ordered pair of the carrier-hopping prime codes (in Section 5.1) of cardinality $p_1 p_2 \cdots p_k$, $L = p_1$ wavelengths, length $N = p_1 p_2 \cdots p_k$, and weight $w \le p_1$, extended carrier-hopping prime codes of $L = p_1 p_2 \cdots p_k$, $N = p_1$, and weight $w \le p_1$ are constructed through a series of modulo additions and multiplications. The extended carrier-hopping prime codes have huge cardinality, zero autocorrelation sidelobes, and periodic cross-correlation functions of still at most 1. Furthermore, they can be divided into many groups, in which the codewords in each group are wavelength-shifted copies of each other. An application of this wavelength-group property is to support the flexible, programmable AWG- and FBG-based coding hardware in Section 2.10 and, in turn, to save coding hardware cost.

Given a set of k prime numbers $p_k \geq p_{k-1} \geq \cdots \geq p_1$, binary $(0,1)$ matrices, $\mathbf{x}_{i_k,i_{k-1},\ldots,i_1,l_k,l_{k-1},\ldots,l_1}$, with the ordered pairs [6]

$$
\begin{aligned}
&[(l_1 + l_2 p_1 + l_3 p_1 p_2 + \cdots + l_k p_1 p_2 \cdots p_{k-1}, 0), ((i_1 \oplus_{p_1} l_1) + (i_2 \oplus_{p_1} l_2)p_1 \\
&+ (i_3 \oplus_{p_1} l_3)p_1 p_2 + \cdots + (i_k \oplus_{p_1} l_k)p_1 p_2 \cdots p_{k-1}, 1), (((2 \odot_{p_1} i_1) \oplus_{p_1} l_1) \\
&+ ((2 \odot_{p_2} i_2) \oplus_{p_1} l_2)p_1 + ((2 \odot_{p_3} i_3) \oplus_{p_1} l_3)p_1 p_2 + \cdots \\
&+ ((2 \odot_{p_k} i_k) \oplus_{p_1} l_k)p_1 p_2 \cdots p_{k-1}, 2), \ldots, ((((w-1) \odot_{p_1} i_1) \oplus_{p_1} l_1) \\
&+ (((w-1) \odot_{p_2} i_2) \oplus_{p_1} l_2)p_1 + (((w-1) \odot_{p_3} i_3) \oplus_{p_1} l_3)p_1 p_2 + \cdots \\
&+ (((w-1) \odot_{p_k} i_k) \oplus_{p_1} l_k)p_1 p_2 \cdots p_{k-1}, w-1)]
\end{aligned} \tag{5.9}
$$

in which the indices are separated into k groups as

group 1: $i_1 = \{0,1,\ldots,p_1-1\}, i_2 = \{0,1,\ldots,p_2-1\},\ldots,$
$i_k = \{1,2,\ldots,p_k-1\}, l_1 = \{0,1,\ldots,p_1-1\}, l_2 = \{0,1,\ldots,p_2-1\},\ldots,$
$l_{k-1} = \{0,1,\ldots,p_{k-1}-1\}, l_k = 0;$
group 2: $i_1 = \{0,1,\ldots,p_1-1\}, i_2 = \{0,1,\ldots,p_2-1\},\ldots,$
$i_{k-1} = \{1,2,\ldots,p_{k-1}-1\}, i_k = 0, l_1 = \{0,1,\ldots,p_1-1\},$
$l_2 = \{0,1,\ldots,p_2-1\},\ldots,l_{k-2} = \{0,1,\ldots,p_{k-2}-1\}, l_{k-1} = 0,$
$l_k = \{0,1,\ldots,p_k-1\};$

$\vdots$

group $k-1$: $i_1 = \{0,1,\ldots,p_1-1\}, i_2 = \{1,2,\ldots,p_2-1\},$
$i_3 = i_4 = \cdots = i_k = 0, l_1 = \{0,1,\ldots,p_1-1\}, l_2 = 0, l_3 = \{0,1,\ldots,p_3-1\},$
$l_4 = \{0,1,\ldots,p_4-1\}],\ldots,l_k = \{0,1,\ldots,p_k-1\};$
group k: $i_1 = \{1,2,\ldots,p_1-1\}, i_2 = i_3 = \cdots = i_k = 0, l_1 = 0,$
$l_2 = \{0,1,\ldots,p_2-1\}, l_3 = \{0,1,\ldots,p_3-1\},\ldots,l_k = \{0,1,\ldots,p_k-1\}$

and the ordered pairs

$$
\begin{aligned}
&[(l_1 + l_2 p_1 + l_3 p_1 p_2 + \cdots + l_k p_1 p_2 \cdots p_{k-1}, 0), ((i_1 \oplus_{p_1} l_1) \\
&+ (i_2 \oplus_{p_1} l_2)p_1 + (i_3 \oplus_{p_1} l_3)p_1 p_2 + \cdots + (i_k \oplus_{p_1} l_k)p_1 p_2 \cdots p_{k-1}, 0), \\
&(((2 \odot_{p_1} i_1) \oplus_{p_1} l_1) + ((2 \odot_{p_2} i_2) \oplus_{p_1} l_2)p_1 + ((2 \odot_{p_3} i_3) \oplus_{p_1} l_3)p_1 p_2 \\
&+ \cdots + ((2 \odot_{p_k} i_k) \oplus_{p_1} l_k)p_1 p_2 \cdots p_{k-1}, 0),\ldots, \\
&((((w-1) \odot_{p_1} i_1) \oplus_{p_1} l_1) + (((w-1) \odot_{p_2} i_2) \oplus_{p_1} l_2)p_1 \\
&+ (((w-1) \odot_{p_3} i_3) \oplus_{p_1} l_3)p_1 p_2 + \cdots \\
&+ (((w-1) \odot_{p_k} i_k) \oplus_{p_1} l_k)p_1 p_2 \cdots p_{k-1}, 0)]
\end{aligned} \tag{5.10}
$$

in which the indices are separated into k groups as

group 1: $i_1 = \{0,1,\ldots,p_1-1\}, i_2 = \{0,1,\ldots,p_2-1\},\ldots,$
$i_{k-1} = \{0,1,\ldots,p_{k-1}-1\}, i_k = 1, l_1 = \{0,1,\ldots,p_1-1\},$
$l_2 = \{0,1,\ldots,p_2-1\},\ldots,l_{k-1} = \{0,1,\ldots,p_{k-1}-1\}, l_k = 0;$

group 2: $i_1 = \{0, 1, \ldots, p_1 - 1\}, i_2 = \{0, 1, \ldots, p_2 - 1\}, \ldots,$

$i_{k-2} = \{0, 1, \ldots, p_{k-2} - 1\}, i_{k-1} = 1, i_k = 0, l_1 = \{0, 1, \ldots, p_1 - 1\},$

$l_2 = \{0, 1, \ldots, p_2 - 1\}, \ldots, l_{k-2} = \{0, 1, \ldots, p_{k-2} - 1\}, l_{k-1} = 0,$

$l_k = \{0, 1, \ldots, p_k - 1\};$

$$\vdots$$

group $k - 1$: $i_1 = \{0, 1, \ldots, p_1 - 1\}, i_2 = 1, i_3 = i_4 = \cdots = i_k = 0,$

$l_1 = \{0, 1, \ldots, p_1 - 1\}, l_2 = 0, l_3 = \{0, 1, \ldots, p_3 - 1\},$

$l_4 = \{0, 1, \ldots, p_4 - 1\}, \ldots, l_k = \{0, 1, \ldots, p_k - 1\};$

group k: $i_1 = 1, i_2 = i_3 = \cdots = i_k = 0, l_1 = 0, l_2 = \{0, 1, \ldots, p_2 - 1\},$

$l_3 = \{0, 1, \ldots, p_3 - 1\}, \ldots, l_k = \{0, 1, \ldots, p_k - 1\}$

form the extended carrier-hopping prime codes with cardinality $(p_1 p_2 \cdots p_{k-1})^2 p_k + (p_1 p_2 \cdots p_{k-2})^2 p_{k-1} p_k + \cdots + p_1^2 p_2 p_3 \cdots p_k + p_1 p_2 \cdots p_k$, $L = p_1 p_2 \cdots p_k$ wavelengths, length $N = p_1$, and weight $w \leq p_1$, where "$\odot_{p_i}$" denotes a modulo-p_j multiplication for $j = \{1, 2, \ldots, k\}$ and "$\oplus_{p_1}$" denotes a modulo-p_1 addition.

Using $k = 2$, $w = p_1 = 3$, and $p_2 = 5$ as an example, this extended carrier-hopping prime code of $L = p_1 p_2 = 15$ wavelengths and length $N = p_1 = 3$ has 45 codewords from group 1 and 15 codewords from group 2. The codewords in group 1 are denoted by $\mathbf{x}_{i_2, i_1, l_2, l_1} = [(l_1, 0), ((i_1 \oplus_3 l_1) + 3i_2, 1), (((2 \odot_3 i_1) \oplus_3 l_1) + (2 \odot_5 i_2)3, 2)]$ for $i_1 \in [0, 2]$, $i_2 \in [1, 4]$, $l_1 \in [0, 2]$, and $l_2 = 0$, and $\mathbf{x}_{i_2, i_1, l_2, l_1} = [(l_1, 0), ((i_1 \oplus_3 l_1) + 3i_2, 0), (((2 \odot_3 i_1) \oplus_3 l_1) + (2 \odot_5 i_2)3, 0)]$ for $i_1 \in [0, 2]$, $i_2 = 1$, $l_1 \in [0, 2]$, and $l_2 = 0$. The codewords in group 2 are denoted by $\mathbf{x}_{i_2, i_1, l_2, l_1} = [(3l_2, 0), (i_1 + 3l_2, 1), (2 \odot_3 i_1 + 3l_2, 2)]$ for $i_1 \in [1, 2]$, $i_2 = 0$, $l_1 = 0$, and $l_2 \in [0, 4]$, and $\mathbf{x}_{i_2, i_1, l_2, l_1} = [(3l_2, 0), (i_1 + 3l_2, 0), (2 \odot_3 i_1 + 3l_2, 0)]$ for $i_1 = 1$, $i_2 = 0$, $l_1 = 0$, and $l_2 \in [0, 4]$. For example, $\mathbf{x}_{1,1,0,1} = [(1, 0), (5, 1), (6, 2)]$ and $[(1, 0), (5, 0), (6, 0)]$, $\mathbf{x}_{2,0,0,0} = [(0, 0), (6, 1), (12, 2)]$, $\mathbf{x}_{3,2,0,2} = [(2, 0), (10, 1), (2, 2)]$, and $\mathbf{x}_{4,2,0,1} = [(1, 0), (12, 1), (11, 2)]$ are some codewords in group 1. Also, $\mathbf{x}_{0,1,1,0} = [(3, 0), (4, 1), (5, 2)]$ and $[(3, 0), (4, 0), (5, 0)]$, and $\mathbf{x}_{0,2,1,0} = [(3, 0), (5, 1), (4, 2)]$ are some codewords in group 2. These ordered pairs can also be represented in terms of wavelength-time sequences, such as $\mathbf{x}_{1,1,0,1} = \lambda_1 \lambda_5 \lambda_6$.

Theorem 5.7

The autocorrelation peaks and sidelobes of the extended carrier-hopping prime codes of weight w are equal to w and 0, respectively, where $w \leq p_1$. The periodic cross-correlation functions of the codes are at most 1 [6].

Proof The proof is similar to that of Theorem 5.1. Let $\mathbf{x}_{i_k, i_{k-1}, \ldots, i_1, l_k, l_{k-1}, \ldots, l_1}$ and $\mathbf{x}_{i'_k, i'_{k-1}, \ldots, i'_1, l'_k, l'_{k-1}, \ldots, l'_1}$ be two distinct extended carrier-hopping prime codewords from

Equation (5.9) with $(i_k, i_{k-1}, \ldots, i_1) \neq (i'_k, i'_{k-1}, \ldots, i'_1)$. If there exist two hits of pulses in any relative horizontal cyclic shift τ between the two codewords, then

$$
\begin{aligned}
&(j_1 \odot_{p_1} i_1) \oplus_{p_1} l_1 + ((j_1 \odot_{p_2} i_2) \oplus_{p_1} l_2)p_1 + ((j_1 \odot_{p_3} i_3) \oplus_{p_1} l_3)p_1 p_2 + \cdots \\
&+ ((j_1 \odot_{p_k} i_k) \oplus_{p_1} l_k)p_1 p_2 \cdots p_{k-1} = ((j_1 \oplus_{p_1} \tau) \odot_{p_1} i'_1) \oplus_{p_1} l'_1 \\
&+ (((j_1 \oplus_{p_1} \tau) \odot_{p_2} i'_2) \oplus_{p_1} l'_2)p_1 + (((j_1 \oplus_{p_1} \tau) \odot_{p_3} i'_3) \oplus_{p_1} l'_3)p_1 p_2 + \cdots \\
&+ (((j_1 \oplus_{p_1} \tau) \odot_{p_k} i'_k) \oplus_{p_1} l'_k)p_1 p_2 \cdots p_{k-1}
\end{aligned}
$$

$$
\begin{aligned}
&(j_2 \odot_{p_1} i_1) \oplus_{p_1} l_1 + ((j_2 \odot_{p_2} i_2) \oplus_{p_1} l_2)p_1 + ((j_2 \odot_{p_3} i_3) \oplus_{p_1} l_3)p_1 p_2 + \cdots \\
&+ ((j_2 \odot_{p_k} i_k) \oplus_{p_1} l_k)p_1 p_2 \cdots p_{k-1} = ((j_2 \oplus_{p_1} \tau) \odot_{p_1} i'_1) \oplus_{p_1} l'_1 \\
&+ (((j_2 \oplus_{p_1} \tau) \odot_{p_2} i'_2) \oplus_{p_1} l'_2)p_1 + (((j_2 \oplus_{p_1} \tau) \odot_{p_3} i'_3) \oplus_{p_1} l'_3)p_1 p_2 + \cdots \\
&+ (((j_2 \oplus_{p_1} \tau) \odot_{p_k} i'_k) \oplus_{p_1} l'_k)p_1 p_2 \cdots p_{k-1}
\end{aligned}
$$

must hold simultaneously for a $j_1 = \{0, 1, \ldots, p_1 p_2 \cdots p_k - 1\}$ and a $j_2 = \{0, 1, \ldots, p_1 p_2 \cdots p_k - 1\}$, where $j_1 \neq j_2$. The subtraction of these two equations results in

$$
\begin{aligned}
&[(j_1 \odot_{p_1} i_1 - j_2 \odot_{p_1} i_1) - (j_1 \odot_{p_1} i'_1 - j_2 \odot_{p_1} i'_1)] \\
&+ [(j_1 \odot_{p_2} i_2 - j_2 \odot_{p_2} i_2) - (j_1 \odot_{p_2} i'_2 - j_2 \odot_{p_2} i'_2)]p_1 + \cdots \\
&+ [(j_1 \odot_{p_k} i_k - j_2 \odot_{p_k} i_k) - (j_1 \odot_{p_k} i'_k - j_2 \odot_{p_k} i'_k)]p_1 p_2 \cdots p_{k-1} = 0
\end{aligned}
$$

which is valid only when $i_m = i'_m$ for all $m = \{1, 2, \ldots, k\}$. This violates the assumption of distinct $\mathbf{x}_{i_k, i_{k-1}, \ldots, i_1, l_k, l_{k-1}, \ldots, l_1}$ and $\mathbf{x}_{i'_k, i'_{k-1}, \ldots, i'_1, l'_k, l'_{k-1}, \ldots, l'_1}$. So, the periodic cross-correlation function is at most 1.

Because all pulses in a codeword are in different wavelengths, the autocorrelation sidelobes are always 0. The autocorrelation peaks of w are due to the code weight $w \leq p_1$.

Because the construction in Equation (5.10) uses the same first components in the ordered pairs as those in Equation (5.9), the correlation properties of the codes from Equation (5.10) follow those from Equation (5.9). ∎

According to Equations (5.9) and (5.10), the extended carrier-hopping prime codes can be divided into k groups, depending on the code indices. Each of these k groups of the codewords can be further divided into a number of subgroups with a special wavelength-shift property. Within a subgroup, the codewords are wavelength-shifted copies of each other. To preserve the maximum periodic cross-correlation function of 1, the codewords that belong to the same subgroup of $\mathbf{x}_{i_k, i_{k-1}, \ldots, i_1, 0, 0, \ldots, 0}$ are those of $\mathbf{x}_{i_k, i_{k-1}, \ldots, i_1, l_k, l_{k-1}, \ldots, l_1}$ with $l_1 \in [0, p_1 - 1]$, $l_2 \in [0, p_2 - 1]$, …, and $l_k \in [0, p_k - 1]$. However, any two codewords $\mathbf{x}_{i_k, i_{k-1}, \ldots, i_1, 0, 0, \ldots, 0}$ and $\mathbf{x}_{i'_k, i'_{k-1}, \ldots, i'_1, 0, 0, \ldots, 0}$ with $(i_1, i_2, \ldots, i_k) \neq (i'_1, i'_2, \ldots, i'_k)$ do not belong to the same subgroup because they are coming from two distinct codewords and not wavelength-shifted copies of each other.

Theorem 5.8

To preserve the periodic cross-correlation functions of at most 1, an extended carrier-hopping prime codeword $x_{i_k,i_{k-1},...,i_1,0,0,...,0}$ can generate $(p_1 - t_1)(p_2 - t_2) \cdots (p_k - t_k)$ wavelength-shifted codewords in a subgroup for $t_m = \max\{j_m \odot_{p_m} i_m : j_m \in [0, w - 1]\}$, where "$\odot_{p_m}$" denotes a modulo-$p_m$ multiplication and $m = \{1, 2, \ldots, k\}$ [6].

Proof Let $x_{i_k,i_{k-1},...,i_1,l_k,l_{k-1},...,l_1}$ and $x_{i'_k,i'_{k-1},...,i'_1,l'_k,l'_{k-1},...,l'_1}$ be two distinct extended carrier-hopping prime codewords from Equation (5.9) with $(i_k, i_{k-1}, \ldots, i_1) \neq (i'_k, i'_{k-1}, \ldots, i'_1)$. If codeword $x_{i'_k,i'_{k-1},...,i'_1,l'_k,l'_{k-1},...,l'_1}$ is a wavelength-shifted copy of $x_{i_k,i_{k-1},...,i_1,l_k,l_{k-1},...,l_1}$, all w wavelengths of both codewords match correspondingly at a relative vertical shift $\tau = \tau_1 + \tau_2 p_1 + \cdots + \tau_k p_1 p_2 \cdots p_{k-1}$ such that

$$
\begin{aligned}
(j_1 \odot_{p_1} i_1) \oplus_{p_1} l_1 + ((j_2 \odot_{p_2} i_2) \oplus_{p_1} l_2) p_1 + \cdots \\
+ ((j_k \odot_{p_k} i_k) \oplus_{p_1} l_k) p_1 p_2 \cdots p_{k-1} + \tau = (j_1 \odot_{p_1} i'_1) \oplus_{p_1} l'_1 \\
+ ((j_2 \odot_{p_2} i'_2) \oplus_{p_1} l'_2) p_1 + \cdots + ((j_k \odot_{p_k} i'_k) \oplus_{p_1} l'_k) p_1 p_2 \cdots p_{k-1}
\end{aligned}
$$

must hold for a $\tau_1 \in [0, p_1 - 1]$, $\tau_2 \in [0, p_2 - 1]$, $\ldots$, and $\tau_k \in [0, p_k - 1]$. This gives w individual equations, $((j_m \odot_{p_m} i_m) \oplus_{p_1} l_m) + \tau_m = ((j_m \odot_{p_m} i'_m) \oplus_{p_1} l'_m)$, which must be satisfied simultaneously for all $j_m \in [0, w - 1]$ with $m = \{1, 2, \ldots, k\}$. To satisfy these equations, $i_m = i'_m$ is first required for all $m = \{1, 2, \ldots, k\}$. This implies that all wavelength-shifted codewords in a subgroup must have the same indices i_1, i_2, $\ldots$, and i_k.

Furthermore, l_m, l'_m, and τ_m determine the amount of relative wavelength-shifts for $m = \{1, 2, \ldots, k\}$. For a fixed l_m, l'_m is controlled by τ_m and belongs to the set of $\{0, 1, \ldots, p_m - 1\}$. So, l'_m can be used to determine the amount of distinct wavelength-shifts that can be applied to the codeword for a given τ_m. The maximum value of $j_m \odot_{p_m} i_m$ in the aforementioned w equations determines the maximum number of distinct wavelength-shifts. As $l'_m \in [0, p_m - 1]$, the maximum number of wavelength-shifted codewords is given by $(p_1 - t_1)(p_2 - t_2) \cdots (p_k - t_k)$ for some $t_m = \max\{j_m \odot_{p_m} i_m : j_m \in [0, w - 1]\}$, where $m = \{1, 2, \ldots, k\}$. ∎

Based on Theorem 5.8, the construction of the wavelength-shifted codewords in a subgroup begins with $x_{i_k,i_{k-1},...,i_1,0,0,...,0}$ with some $i_m = 0$ for $m = \{1, 2, \ldots, k\}$. For each $i_m = 0$, the corresponding t_m becomes 0 and the factor $p_m - t_m$ becomes p_m, maximizing the number of wavelength-shifted codewords. For each $i_m \neq 0$, the corresponding t_m becomes $p_m - 1$ and the factor $p_m - t_m$ becomes 1. For example, if $i_2 = i_3 = \cdots = i_k = 0$ and $i_1 \in [1, p_1 - 1]$, then $t_2 = t_3 = \cdots = t_k = 0$ and $p_1 - 1$ subgroups with $p_2 p_3 \cdots p_k$ codewords per subgroup can be obtained.

Again, using $k = 2$, $p_1 = w = 3$, and $p_2 = 5$ as an example, there exist $p_2 = 5$ subgroups with $p_1 = 3$ wavelength-shifted codewords per subgroup in group 1, and $p_1 = 3$ subgroups with $p_2 = 5$ wavelength-shifted codewords per subgroup in group 2. For instance, the subgroup with $i_1 = 0$ and $i_2 = 3$ contains 3 wavelength-shifted codewords, $x_{3,0,0,0} = [(0,0),(9,1),(3,2)]$, $x_{3,0,0,1} = [(1,0),(10,1),(4,2)]$, and $x_{3,0,0,2} = [(2,0),(11,1),(5,2)]$, in group 1. The subgroup with $i_1 = 1$ and $i_2 = 0$ contains 5 wavelength-shifted codewords, $x_{0,1,0,0} = [(0,0),(1,1),(2,2)]$, $x_{0,1,1,0} = [(3,0),(4,1),(5,2)]$, $x_{0,1,2,0} = [(6,0),(7,1),(8,2)]$, $x_{0,1,3,0} = [(9,0),(10,1),(11,2)]$, and $x_{0,1,4,0} = [(12,0),(13,1),(14,2)]$, in group 2.

According to Section 1.6, the cardinality upper bound of the extended carrier-hopping prime codes with cardinality $(p_1 p_2 \cdots p_{k-1})^2 p_k + (p_1 p_2 \cdots p_{k-2})^2 p_{k-1} p_k + \cdots + p_1 p_2 \cdots p_k$, $L = p_1 p_2 \cdots p_k$ wavelengths, length $N = p_1$, weight $w \leq p_1$, and the maximum periodic cross-correlation function of 1 is given by [25]

$$
\begin{aligned}
\Phi_{\text{upper}} \quad &\leq \quad \frac{p_1 p_2 \cdots p_k (p_1 p_2 \cdots p_k p_1 - 1)}{w(w-1)} \\[2mm]
&= \quad \frac{p_1^3 (p_2 p_3 \cdots p_k)^2}{w(w-1)} - \frac{p_1 p_2 \cdots p_k}{w(w-1)}
\end{aligned}
$$

The upper bound is larger than the actual cardinality by a factor of approximately $1 - w(w-1)p_1^{-1}[p_k^{-1} + (p_{k-1}p_k)^{-1} + \cdots + (p_1 p_2 \cdots p_k)^{-1}]$. The factor approaches 1 for a large p_k. So, the extended carrier-hopping prime codes are asymptotically optimal in cardinality.

5.4.1   Performance Analysis

Because the maximum periodic cross-correlation function is 1, the chip-synchronous, soft-limiting error probability of the extended carrier-hopping prime codes with $L = p_1 p_2 \cdots p_k$ wavelengths, length $N = p_1$, and weight $w \leq p_1$ in OOK follows Equation (5.1).

The wavelength-group property of the extended carrier-hopping prime codes lowers the hit probabilities because codewords coming from the same subgroup contain no common wavelengths and are orthogonal. To account for this, the one-hit probability can be formulated as [25]

$$
q_1 = \frac{w^2}{2LN} \times F_k = \frac{w^2}{2 p_1^2 p_2 p_3 \cdots p_k} \times F_k
$$

where the factor $1/2$ comes from the assumption of equiprobable data bit-1 and bit-0 transmissions in OOK. The term $F_k = \sum_{\text{all subgroups}} \Pr(\text{one hit in two correlating codewords}|\text{both codewords from same subgroup}) \times \Pr(\text{the subgroup chosen from the code set})$ represents the ratio of the number of interfering codewords contributing one hit (in the sampling time of the periodic cross-correlation functions) to the total number of interfering codewords. The number of terms in F_k increases with the number of subgroups, which is determined by k. For example, for $k = 2$, group 1 contains p_2 subgroups with p_1 codewords per subgroup, and group 2 consists of p_1 subgroups with p_2 codewords per subgroup. So,

$$
F_2 = \frac{\Phi_2 - p_1}{\Phi_2 - 1} \times \frac{p_1}{\Phi_2} \times p_2 + \frac{\Phi_2 - p_2}{\Phi_2 - 1} \times \frac{p_2}{\Phi_2} \times p_1 + \frac{\Phi_2 - 1}{\Phi_2 - 1} \times \frac{\Phi_2 - 2 p_1 p_2}{\Phi_2} \times 1
$$

where $\Phi_2 = p_1^2 p_2 + p_1 p_2$ is the cardinality of the $k = 2$ extended carrier-hopping prime codes with $L = p_1 p_2$ wavelengths, length $N = p_1$, and weight $w \leq p_1$, and $\Phi_2 - 1$ represents the number of possible interfering codewords. For $k = 3$, group 1 contains p_3 subgroups with $p_1 p_2$ codewords per subgroup and $(p_2 - 1)p_2 p_3$ subgroups with p_1 codewords per subgroup, group 2 gives p_2 subgroups with $p_1 p_3$ codewords per subgroup, and group 3 gives p_1 subgroups with $p_2 p_3$ codewords per subgroup. So,

$$
\begin{aligned}
F_3 &= \frac{\Phi_3 - p_1 p_2}{\Phi_3 - 1} \times \frac{p_1 p_2}{\Phi_3} \times p_3 + \frac{\Phi_3 - p_1}{\Phi_3 - 1} \times \frac{p_1}{\Phi_3} \times (p_2 - 1)p_2 p_3 \\
&+ \frac{\Phi_3 - p_1 p_3}{\Phi_3 - 1} \times \frac{p_1 p_3}{\Phi_3} \times p_2 + \frac{\Phi_3 - p_2 p_3}{\Phi_3 - 1} \times \frac{p_2 p_3}{\Phi_3} \times p_1 \\
&+ \frac{\Phi_3 - 1}{\Phi_3 - 1} \times \frac{\Phi_3 - p_1 p_2^2 p_3 - 2 p_1 p_2 p_3}{\Phi_3} \times 1
\end{aligned}
$$

where $\Phi_3 = (p_1 p_2)^2 p_3 + p_1^2 p_2 p_3 + p_1 p_2 p_3$ is the cardinality of the $k = 3$ extended carrier-hopping prime codes with $L = p_1 p_2 p_3$ wavelengths, length $N = p_1$, and weight $w \leq p_1$.

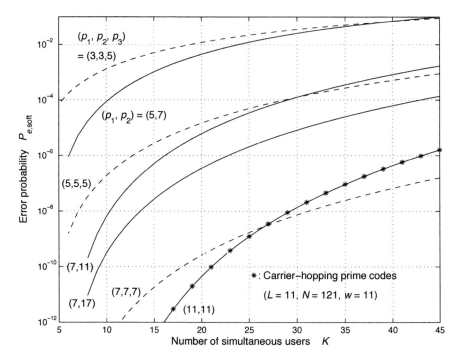

FIGURE 5.12 Chip-synchronous, soft-limiting error probabilities of the extended carrier-hopping prime codes for various prime numbers and $k = \{2, 3\}$.

Figure 5.12 plots the chip-synchronous, soft-limiting error probabilities of the extended carrier-hopping prime codes of $L = p_1 p_2 \cdots p_k$ wavelengths, length $N = p_1$, and weight $w = p_1$ against the number of simultaneous users K for various prime numbers and $k = \{2,3\}$. In general, the error probabilities improve as L or N increases because of lower hit probabilities. However, the error probabilities get worse as K increases due to stronger mutual interference. The $(5,7)$- and $(3,3,5)$-curves converge as K increases, demonstrating the flexibility of the codes in selecting L and N. If N is restricted, a larger L can be used in order to achieve a targeted error probability. Represented by "$*$," the error probability of the carrier-hopping prime codes of $L = 11$, $N = 121$, and $w = 11$ (in Section 5.1) is included in the figure for comparing with the extended carrier-hopping prime codes of $L = 121$, $N = 11$, and $w = 11$. Both cases overlap exactly because they utilize the same bandwidth expansion LN and hit probabilities. However, the former only supports 121 codewords, while the extended carrier-hopping prime codes support 1452 codewords. If code performance is more important than cardinality, one can simply use subgroups of wavelength-shifted codewords such that F_k and, in turn, q_1 are reduced accordingly.

5.5 EXPANDED CARRIER-HOPPING PRIME CODES

The carrier-hopping prime codes in Section 5.1 have cardinality $p_1 p_2 \cdots p_k$, length $p_1 p_2 \cdots p_k$, and weight $w \leq p_1$, with w wavelengths. With the availability of mode-locked lasers with flattened broadband supercontinuum optical spectrum as wide as 100 nm [27], there exist scenarios, especially in high bit-rate coding systems, that more wavelengths are present than are actually needed in the codes. If there are wp' wavelengths, a simple way to utilize the extra wavelengths is to separate them into p' groups (of w wavelengths in each group). Then, the same $p_1 p_2 \cdots p_k$ carrier-hopping prime codewords are reusable in each group of wavelengths, supporting $p' p_1 p_2 \cdots p_k$ codewords (or subscribers) in such a hybrid WDM-coding scheme. Nevertheless, to achieve even larger cardinality, each of the $p_1 p_2 \cdots p_k$ carrier-hopping prime codewords can be taken as a seed so that $w^2 + p'$ groups of the expanded carrier-hopping prime codewords are constructed, as shown in this section [5,7,8].

Given a set of prime numbers $p_k \geq p_{k-1} \geq \cdots \geq p_1$ and p' with $p' \geq w$ and $wp' \leq p_1$, binary $(0,1)$ matrices, $\mathbf{x}_{i_k,i_{k-1},\ldots,i_1,l_2,l_1}$ and $\mathbf{x}_{i_k,i_{k-1},\ldots,i_1,l_3}$, with the ordered pairs [5,7,8]

$$
\begin{aligned}
&\{[(l_1, l_1 \odot_{p_1} i_1 + (l_1 \odot_{p_2} i_2)p_1 + \cdots + (l_1 \odot_{p_k} i_k)p_1 p_2 \cdots p_{k-1}), \\
&((l_1 \oplus_w l_2) + w, [(l_1 \oplus_w l_2) + w] \odot_{p_1} i_1 + ([(l_1 \oplus_w l_2) + w] \odot_{p_2} i_2)p_1 \\
&+ \cdots + ([(l_1 \oplus_w l_2) + w] \odot_{p_k} i_k)p_1 p_2 \cdots p_{k-1}), ((l_1 \oplus_w (2 \odot_{p'} l_2)) + 2w, \\
&([l_1 \oplus_w (2 \odot_{p'} l_2)] + 2w] \odot_{p_1} i_1 + ([l_1 \oplus_w (2 \odot_{p'} l_2)) + 2w] \odot_{p_2} i_2)p_1 \\
&+ \cdots + ([l_1 \oplus_w (2 \odot_{p'} l_2)) + 2w] \odot_{p_k} i_k)p_1 p_2 \cdots p_{k-1}), \ldots, \\
&(l_1 \oplus_w ((w-1) \odot_{p'} l_2)) + (w-1)w, [l_1 \oplus_w ((w-1) \odot_{p'} l_2)) \\
&+ (w-1)w] \odot_{p_1} i_1 + ([l_1 \oplus_w ((w-1) \odot_{p'} l_2)) + (w-1)w] \odot_{p_2} i_2)p_1 \\
&+ \cdots + ([l_1 \oplus_w ((w-1) \odot_{p'} l_2)) + (w-1)w] \odot_{p_k} i_k)p_1 p_2 \cdots p_{k-1}),] : \\
&i_1 = \{0,1,\ldots,p_1-1\}, i_2 = \{0,1,\ldots,p_2-1\}, \ldots, i_k = \{0,1,\ldots,p_k-1\}, \\
&l_1 = \{0,1,\ldots,w-1\}, l_2 = \{0,1,\ldots,w-1\}\}
\end{aligned}
\tag{5.11}
$$

and

$$\{[(l_2w, l_2w \odot_{p_1} i_1 + (l_2w \odot_{p_2} i_2)p_1 + \cdots + (l_2w \odot_{p_k} i_k)p_1p_2 \cdots p_{k-1}),$$
$$(l_2w+1, (l_2w+1) \odot_{p_1} i_1 + ((l_2w+1) \odot_{p_2} i_2)p_1 + \cdots$$
$$+ ((l_2w+1) \odot_{p_k} i_k)p_1p_2 \cdots p_{k-1}), \ldots, (l_2w+w-1,$$
$$(l_2w+w-1) \odot_{p_1} i_1 + ((l_2w+w-1) \odot_{p_2} i_2)p_1 + \cdots$$
$$+ ((l_2w+w-1) \odot_{p_k} i_k)p_1p_2 \cdots p_{k-1})] : i_1 = \{0,1,\ldots,p_1-1\},$$
$$i_2 = \{0,1,\ldots,p_2-1\}, \ldots, i_k = \{0,1,\ldots,p_k-1\},$$
$$l_3 = \{0,1,\ldots,p'-1\}\} \tag{5.12}$$

form the expanded carrier-hopping prime codes with cardinality $(w^2+p')p_1p_2 \cdots p_k$, $L = wp'$ wavelengths, length $N = p_1p_2 \cdots p_k$, and weight $w \le p'$, where "$\odot_{p'}$" denotes a modulo-p' multiplication and "$\oplus_w$" denotes a modulo-w addition.

For comparison, the cardinality of these expanded carrier-hopping prime codes is $(w^2+p')/p'$ times that of the carrier-hopping prime codes (in Section 5.1) with $L = w$, $N = p_1p_2 \cdots p_k$, and $w \le p_1$ if the latter are used with p' groups of w wavelengths per group in the hybrid WDM-coding scheme.

Using $k = 2$, $w = p' = 3$, $p_1 = 11$, and $p_2 = 13$ as an example, the carrier-hopping prime code (in Section 5.1) of length $N = p_1p_2 = 143$ and weight 3 has 143 codewords, denoted by $\mathbf{x}_{i_2,i_1} = [(0,0),(1,i_1+11i_2),(2,2 \odot_{11} i_1 + (2 \odot_{13} i_2)11)]$ for $i_1 \in [0,10]$ and $i_2 \in [0,12]$. Simply separating the $wp' = 9$ available wavelengths into 3 groups with 3 wavelengths in each group, these 143 carrier-hopping prime codewords are reusable in each group in the hybrid WDM-coding scheme, supporting 429 possible subscribers. Nevertheless, from Equations (5.11) and (5.12), each of these carrier-hopping prime codewords can generate $w^2 + p' = 12$ groups of the expanded carrier-hopping prime codewords of length $N = 143$ and weight $w = 3$ with a total cardinality of 1,716, denoted by $\mathbf{x}_{i_2,i_1,l_2,l_1} = [(l_1, l_1 \odot_{11} i_1 + (l_1 \odot_{13} i_2)11), ((l_1 \oplus_3 l_2)+3, [(l_1 \oplus_3 l_2)+3] \odot_{11} i_1 + ([(l_1 \oplus_3 l_2)+3] \odot_{13} i_2)11), ((l_1 \oplus_3 (2 \odot_3 l_2))+6, [(l_1 \oplus_3 (2 \odot_3 l_2))+6] \odot_{11} i_1 + ([(l_1 \oplus_3 (2 \odot_3 l_2))+6] \odot_{13} i_2)11)]$ and $\mathbf{x}_{i_2,i_1,l_3} = [(3l_3, (3l_3) \odot_{11} i_1 + ((3l_3) \odot_{13} i_2)11), (3l_3+1, (3l_3+1) \odot_{11} i_1 + ((3l_3+1) \odot_{13} i_2)11), (3l_3+2, (3l_3+2) \odot_{11} i_1 + (3l_3+2) \odot_{13} i_2)11)]$, respectively, for $i_1 \in [0,10]$, $i_2 \in [0,12]$, $l_1 \in [0,2]$, $l_2 \in [0,2]$, and $l_3 \in [0,2]$. For example, $\mathbf{x}_{5,2,2,1} = [(1,57),(3,68),(8,56)]$, $\mathbf{x}_{5,2,2,2} = [(2,114),(4,85),(6,45)]$, and $\mathbf{x}_{5,2,1} = [(3,28),(4,85),(5,142)]$.

Theorem 5.9

The autocorrelation peaks and sidelobes of the expanded carrier-hopping prime codes of weight w are equal to w and 0, respectively, where $w \le p'$. The periodic cross-correlation functions of the codes are at most 1. The periodic cross-correlation functions of the w codewords within each one of the $wp_1p_2 \cdots p_k$ groups, from Equation (5.11), and the p' codewords within each one of the $p_1p_2 \cdots p_k$ groups, from Equation (5.12), are equal to 0 [5,7].

Proof Let $\mathbf{x}_{i_k,i_{k-1},\ldots,i_1,l_2,l_1}$ and $\mathbf{x}_{i'_k,i'_{k-1},\ldots,i'_1,l'_2,l'_1}$ be two distinct expanded carrier-hopping prime codewords, originating from two carrier-hopping prime codewords $\mathbf{x}_{i_k,i_{k-1},\ldots,i_1}$ and $\mathbf{x}_{i'_k,i'_{k-1},\ldots,i'_1}$, respectively, with $(i_k,i_{k-1},\ldots,i_1,l_2,l_1) \neq (i'_k,i'_{k-1},\ldots,i'_1,l'_2,l'_1)$. The periodic cross-correlation functions are at most 1 because the ordered pairs of $\mathbf{x}_{i_k,i_{k-1},\ldots,i_1,l_2,l_1}$ and $\mathbf{x}_{i'_k,i'_{k-1},\ldots,i'_1,l'_2,l'_1}$ belong to those of $\mathbf{x}_{i_k,i_{k-1},\ldots,i_1}$ and $\mathbf{x}_{i'_k,i'_{k-1},\ldots,i'_1}$, which have the periodic cross-correlation functions of at most 1. Similarly, the same property holds for any two codewords $\mathbf{x}_{i_k,i_{k-1},\ldots,i_1,l_3}$ and $\mathbf{x}_{i'_k,i'_{k-1},\ldots,i'_1,l'_3}$.

Let $\mathbf{x}_{i_k,i_{k-1},\ldots,i_1,l_2,l_1}$ and $\mathbf{x}_{i_k,i_{k-1},\ldots,i_1,l'_2,l'_1}$ be two distinct expanded carrier-hopping prime codewords, originating from the same carrier-hopping prime codeword $\mathbf{x}_{i_k,i_{k-1},\ldots,i_1}$, with $(l_2,l_1) \neq (l'_2,l'_1)$. If there exist two hits of pulses in any relative horizontal cyclic shift between the two codewords, then

$$l_1 \oplus_w (j_1 \odot_{p'} l_2) + j_1 w = l'_1 \oplus_w (j'_1 \odot_{p'} l'_2) + j'_1 w$$

$$l_1 \oplus_w (j_2 \odot_{p'} l_2) + j_2 w = l'_1 \oplus_w (j'_2 \odot_{p'} l'_2) + j'_2 w$$

must hold simultaneously for a set of j_1, j'_1, j_2, and $j'_2 = \{0,1,\ldots,w-1\}$, where $j_1 \neq j_2$ and $j'_1 \neq j'_2$. Because $l_1 \oplus_w (j_1 \odot_{p'} l_2)$ and $l'_1 \oplus_w (j'_1 \odot_{p'} l'_2)$ are both less than w, it requires $j_1 = j'_1$ for the first equation to hold. Similarly, $j_2 = j'_2$ is needed for the second equation to hold. The subtraction of both equations results in

$$(j_1 - j_2) \odot_{p'} l_2 = (j_1 - j_2) \odot_{p'} l'_2$$

which is valid only when $l_2 = l'_2$. Substituting $l_2 = l'_2$ back into the first equation results in $l_1 = l'_1$. These two conditions violate the assumption of distinct $\mathbf{x}_{i_k,i_{k-1},\ldots,i_1,l_2,l_1}$ and $\mathbf{x}_{i_k,i_{k-1},\ldots,i_1,l'_2,l'_1}$. So, the periodic cross-correlation functions are at most 1.

When $l_2 = l'_2$, both equations are valid only if $l_1 = l'_1$. So, the periodic cross-correlation functions are equal to 0 for a fixed l_2. This gives w groups of w orthogonal codewords in each group, from Equation (5.11), for each of the $p_1 p_2 \cdots p_k$ carrier-hopping prime codewords.

The periodic cross-correlation functions are equal to 0 for any two distinct codewords $\mathbf{x}_{i_k,i_{k-1},\ldots,i_1,l_3}$ and $\mathbf{x}_{i_k,i_{k-1},\ldots,i_1,l'_3}$ because all pulses in both codewords are in different wavelengths. This gives one group of p' orthogonal codewords, from Equation (5.12), for each of the $p_1 p_2 \cdots p_k$ carrier-hopping prime codewords.

Because all pulses in a codeword are in different wavelengths, the autocorrelation sidelobes are always 0. Finally, the autocorrelation peaks of w are due to the code weight $w \leq p'$. ∎

According to Section 1.6, the cardinality upper bound of the expanded carrier-hopping prime codes with cardinality $(w^2 + p')p_1 p_2 \cdots p_k$, $L = wp'$ wavelengths, length $N = p_1 p_2 \cdots p_k$, weight $w \leq p'$, and the maximum cross-correlation function of 1 is given by [5, 7]

$$\Phi_{\text{upper}} \leq \frac{wp'(wp' p_1 p_2 \cdots p_k - 1)}{w(w-1)}$$

The upper bound is approximately $p'^2/(w^2+p')$ times of the actual cardinality. The factor approaches 1 for a large w. So, the expanded carrier-hopping prime codes are asymptotically optimal in cardinality.

5.5.1 Performance Analysis

Because the maximum periodic cross-correlation function is 1, the chip-synchronous, soft-limiting error probability of the expanded carrier-hopping prime codes with $L = wp'$ wavelengths, length $N = p_1 p_2 \cdots p_k$, and weight $w \leq p'$ in OOK follows Equation (5.1).

The group property of the expanded carrier-hopping prime codes lowers the hit probabilities because codewords coming from the same group contain no common wavelengths and are orthogonal. The one-hit probability can be formulated as [5,7]

$$q_1 = \frac{w^2}{2LN} \times F = \frac{w}{2p'p_1p_2\cdots p_k} \times F \qquad (5.13)$$

where the factor $1/2$ comes from the assumption of equiprobable data bit-1 and bit-0 transmissions in OOK. The term $F = \sum_{\text{all groups}} \text{Pr}(\text{one hit in two correlating codewords}|\text{both from same group}) \times \text{Pr}(\text{the group chosen from the code set})$ represents the ratio of the number of interfering codewords contributing one hit (in the sampling time of the periodic cross-correlation functions) to the total number of interfering codewords. So, F is used to discount the codewords with zero mutual interference and derived as

$$
\begin{aligned}
F &= \frac{\Phi - 1 - (w-1)p_1p_2\cdots p_k}{\Phi - 1} \times \frac{w^2}{w^2 + p'} \\
&\quad + \frac{\Phi - 1 - (p'-1)p_1p_2\cdots p_k}{\Phi - 1} \times \frac{p'}{w^2 + p'} \\
&= 1 - \frac{(w^3 - w^2 + p'^2 - p')p_1p_2\cdots p_k}{(\Phi - 1)(w^2 + p')}
\end{aligned}
$$

where $\Phi = (w^2 + p')p_1p_2\cdots p_k$ is the code cardinality. The first product term in F accounts for the $wp_1p_2\cdots p_k$ groups of w orthogonal codewords in each group from Equation (5.11). There are $(w-1)p_1p_2\cdots p_k$ codewords not using the same set of wavelengths as the address codeword (of a receiver), out of $\Phi - 1$ possible interfering codewords. There exist w^2 such groups, out of $w^2 + p'$ groups. The second product term in F accounts for the $p_1p_2\cdots p_k$ groups of p' orthogonal codewords in each group from Equation (5.12). There are $(p' - 1)p_1p_2\cdots p_k$ codewords not using the same set of wavelengths as the address codeword. There exist p' such groups, out of $w^2 + p'$ groups.

The hybrid WDM-coding scheme utilizes the wp' wavelengths by separating them into p' groups of w wavelengths per group. So, codewords from different groups will not interfere with each other because they contain different wavelengths, even though each group uses the same carrier-hopping prime codewords (in Section 5.1) with $L = w$ wavelengths, length $N = p_1 p_2 \cdots p_k$, and weight $w \leq p_1$. If codewords are uniformly selected from these p' groups of codewords by a central controller, there will be at most $\lceil K/p' \rceil$ codewords transmitting simultaneously from each group, where $\lceil \cdot \rceil$ is the ceiling function. The chip-synchronous, soft-limiting error probability of the carrier-hopping prime codes with p' groups of w wavelengths per group in hybrid WDM-coding can be formulated as [5,7]

$$P_{e,\text{hybrid}} = \frac{1}{2} \sum_{i=w}^{\lceil K/p' \rceil - 1} \frac{(\lceil K/p' \rceil - 1)!}{i!(\lceil K/p' \rceil - 1 - i)!} (q_1')^i (1 - q_1')^{\lceil K/p' \rceil - 1 - i}$$

where $q_1' = w^2/(2LN) = w/(2p_1 p_2 \cdots p_k)$ is the one-hit probability. This $P_{e,\text{hybrid}}$ equation corresponds to the best scenario and gives the theoretical lower bound of error probability due to the use of the central controller to distribute codewords of different wavelength groups to the simultaneous users evenly. Error-free transmission can theoretically be achieved when the number of simultaneous users in each wavelength group is less than w (or $\lceil K/p' \rceil < w$). This is because the carrier-hopping prime codes have the maximum periodic cross-correlation function of 1 and the decision threshold is usually set to w for optimal decision. Without the central controller, the performance lower bound will not be achievable.

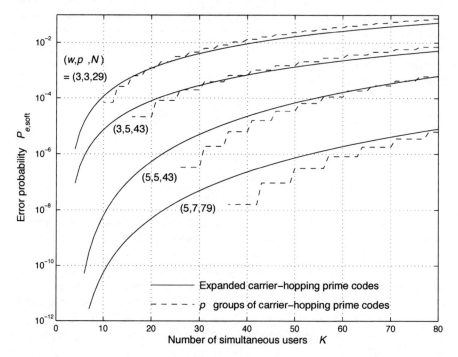

FIGURE 5.13 Chip-synchronous, soft-limiting error probabilities of the expanded carrier-hopping prime codes and the carrier-hopping prime codes in hybrid WDM-coding with p' groups of wavelengths. (A central controller is assumed in the hybrid scheme.)

Figure 5.13 plots the chip-synchronous, soft-limiting error probabilities of the expanded carrier-hopping prime codes of $L = wp'$ wavelengths, length $N = p_1$, and weight w, and the carrier-hopping prime codes (in Section 5.1) of $L = w$ and $N = p_1$ in hybrid WDM-coding with p' groups of w wavelengths per group against the number of simultaneous users K for $p_1 = \{29, 43, 79\}$, $w = \{3, 5\}$, and $p' = \{3, 5, 7\}$, where $k = 1$. In general, the error probabilities improve as L, N, or w increases because of lower hit probabilities or higher autocorrelation peaks. However, the error probabilities get worse as K increases due to stronger mutual interference. The step-like dashed curves represent the performance lower bound of the hybrid scheme, which can only be achieved theoretically with the help of the central controller. The dashed curves start having decision errors when the number of interfering codewords in each group is greater than the code weight (or $\lceil K/p' \rceil - 1 > w$). The performance of the expanded carrier-hopping prime codes (solid curves) is here compared to the performance lower bound of the carrier-hopping prime codes in the hybrid scheme with the central controller. So, the expanded carrier-hopping prime codes generally have better performance than the latter when the central controller is not used. The dashed curves are increasingly better than the solid curves at small K when p' increases because the hybrid scheme spreads the interfering codewords out into more wavelength groups. Also, the dashed curves converge with the solid curves when the traffic load is heavy (or $\lceil K/p' \rceil - 1 >> w$). In this scenario, both curves show comparable performance, even compared to the lower bound of the hybrid scheme.

In the aforementioned analysis, chip synchronism has been assumed for mathematical convenience but results in pessimistic performance. In reality, codewords can arrive at a receiver at any time, and chip-asynchronous analysis can reflect more accurate performance. According to Section 1.8.5, the chip-asynchronous, soft-limiting error probability of the expanded carrier-hopping prime codes with $L = wp'$ wavelengths, length $N = p_1 p_2 \cdots p_k$, weight $w \le p'$, and the maximum periodic cross-correlation function of 1 in OOK is given by

$$
\begin{aligned}
P_{e,\text{asyn}} = {} & \frac{1}{2} - \frac{1}{2} \sum_{i_{0,1}=0}^{Z_{\text{th}}-1} \sum_{i_{1,0}=0}^{Z_{\text{th}}-1-i_{0,1}} \frac{(K-1)!}{i_{0,1}! i_{1,0}! (K-1-i_{0,1}-i_{1,0})!} q_{0,1}^{i_{0,1}} q_{1,0}^{i_{1,0}} \\
& \times q_{0,0}^{K-1-i_{0,1}-i_{1,0}} \left[1 - Q \left(\frac{w - (i_{0,1} + i_{1,0} + 2i_{1,1})/2}{\sqrt{(i_{0,1}+i_{1,0})/12}} \right) \right]
\end{aligned}
$$

where the decision threshold $Z_{\text{th}} = w$ is usually applied for optimal decision and $Q(x) = (1/\sqrt{2\pi}) \int_x^\infty \exp\left(-y^2/2\right) dy$ is the complementary error function.

With the chip-asynchronous assumption, the periodic cross-correlation functions in every two consecutive chips (or time slots) is now considered because the two correlating codewords may not exactly align in every chip interval anymore.

Theorem 5.10

For the expanded carrier-hopping prime codes of $L = wp'$ wavelengths, length

$N = p_1 p_2 \cdots p_k$, and weight $w \leq p'$, the chip-asynchronous, hit probabilities, $q_{i,j}$, of having the periodic cross-correlation value in the preceding chip equal to $i = \{0, 1\}$ and the periodic cross-correlation value in the present chip equal to $j = \{0, 1\}$ are formulated as [5, 7]

$$q_{1,1} = \frac{q_1(p_1 - 1)}{p_1 p_2 \cdots p_k - 1}$$

$$q_{1,0} = \frac{q_1 p_1(p_2 p_3 \cdots p_k - 1)}{p_1 p_2 \cdots p_k - 1}$$

$$q_{0,0} = 1 - \frac{q_1(2 p_1 p_2 \cdots p_k - p_1 - 1)}{p_1 p_2 \cdots p_k - 1}$$

where q_1 is the chip-synchronous one-hit probability given in Equation (5.13).

Proof Let $\mathbf{x}_{i_k,i_{k-1},\ldots,i_1,l_2,l_1}$ and $\mathbf{x}_{i'_k,i'_{k-1},\ldots,i'_1,l'_2,l'_1}$ be two distinct expanded carrier-hopping prime codewords with $(i_k, i_{k-1}, \ldots, i_1, l_2, l_1) \neq (i'_k, i'_{k-1}, \ldots, i'_1, l'_2, l'_1)$. Two consecutive chips in the periodic cross-correlation function between the two codewords can be hit at the same time only when the (chip) separation of two adjacent pulses in one codeword differs from that in the other codeword by 1, or there are two consecutive pulses in either codeword. According to Equation (5.11), the cyclic adjacent-pulse separations in these two codewords are determined by $[(i_s - i'_s) \pmod{p_s}] p_1 p_2 \cdots p_{s-1}$ for $s = \{2, 3, \ldots, k\}$. So, it is possible to have two consecutive hits only when $i_s = i'_s$ for all $s = \{2, 3, \ldots, k\}$. It is then found that

$$q_{1,1} = q_1 \times \frac{p_1 - 1}{p_1 p_2 \cdots p_k - 1}$$

where $(p_1 - 1)/(p_1 p_2 \cdots p_k - 1)$ is the probability of choosing these two codewords from the same group, indexed by $i_1 \neq i'_1$, $i_2 = i'_2$, ..., and $i_k = i'_k$, out of $p_1 p_2 \cdots p_k - 1$ possible interfering codewords. Because the codewords have the chip-synchronous periodic cross-correlation functions of at most 1, $q_i = (1/2) \sum_{j=0}^{1}(q_{i,j} + q_{j,i})$, $\sum_{k=0}^{1} \sum_{j=0}^{1} q_{j,k} = 1$, and $q_0 + q_1 = 1$, according to Section 1.8.5. After some manipulations, $q_{1,0} = q_{0,1} = q_1 - q_{1,1}$ and $q_{0,0} = 1 - 2 q_{1,0} - q_{1,1}$, and eventually the final form of the hit probabilities in the theorem are derived.

The proof for the codewords, $\mathbf{x}_{i_k,i_{k-1},\ldots,i_1,l_3}$, in Equation (5.12) follows the same rationale with l_1 and l_2 being replaced by l_3. ∎

Figure 5.14 plots the chip-synchronous and chip-asynchronous, soft-limiting error probabilities of the expanded carrier-hopping prime codes of $L = wp'$ wavelengths, length $N = p_1 = \{23, 47, 83\}$, and weight $w = \{3, 5\}$ against the number of simultaneous users K for $p' = \{3, 5, 7\}$ and $k = 1$. As expected, the error probabilities of the chip-asynchronous case (solid curves) are superior to those of the chip-synchronous case (dashed curves). In this example, the chip-synchronous assumption results in overestimating the code performance by one to three orders of magnitude, depending on the values of w, p', and N.

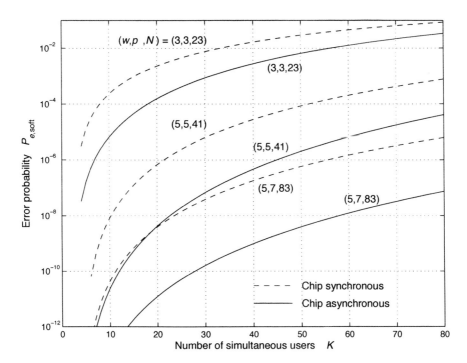

FIGURE 5.14 Soft-limiting error probabilities of the expanded carrier-hopping prime codes with and without the chip-synchronous assumption for $w = \{3,5\}$, $p' = \{3,5,7\}$, and $N = \{23, 41, 83\}$.

5.6 QUADRATIC-CONGRUENCE CARRIER-HOPPING PRIME CODES

Except for the multilevel carrier-hopping prime codes, the 2-D optical codes studied in this chapter are constructed with the periodic cross-correlation functions of at most 1 in order to minimize the effect of mutual interference. It is known that larger code cardinality can be achieved by relaxing the cross-correlation function at the expense of code performance. In addition to supporting many possible subscribers, large code cardinality can also accommodate multicode keying.

In this section, the quadratic-congruence carrier-hopping prime codes are constructed by adding a quadratic-congruence (QC) operator, such as $i^2 l$ (mod p_1) or $i(i+1)l/2$ (mod p_1), to the ordered pairs of the carrier-hopping prime codes (in Section 5.1) of $L = w$ wavelengths, length $N = p_1 p_2 \cdots p_k$, and weight $w \leq p_1$, where $l = \{0, 1, \ldots, p_1 - 1\}$ is the group number of the codes, and $i = \{0, 1, \ldots, p_1 - 1\}$ [10, 28]. The $l = 0$ group of the quadratic-congruence carrier-hopping prime codes corresponds to the carrier-hopping prime codes without any QC operation.

Given a set of k prime numbers $p_k \geq p_{k-1} \geq \cdots \geq p_1$, binary $(0, 1)$ matrices,

$\mathbf{x}_{i_k,i_{k-1},\ldots,i_1,l}$, with the ordered pairs [10, 28]

$$\{[(0,0),(1,i_1+i_2p_1+\cdots+i_kp_1p_2\cdots p_{k-1}),$$
$$(2,2\odot_{p_1}i_1+(2\odot_{p_2}i_2)p_1+\cdots+(2\odot_{p_k}i_k)p_1p_2\cdots p_{k-1}),\ldots,$$
$$(p_1-1,(p_1-1)\odot_{p_1}i_1+((p_1-1)\odot_{p_2}i_2)p_1+\cdots$$
$$+((p_1-1)\odot_{p_k}i_k)p_1p_2\cdots p_{k-1})]:i_1=\{0,1,\ldots,p_1-1\},$$
$$i_2=\{0,1,\ldots,p_2-1\},\ldots,i_k=\{0,1,\ldots,p_k-1\},l=0\}$$

and

$$\{[(i_1,0),(1\oplus_{p_1}i_1,[(1\cdot2)/2]\odot_{p_1}l+i_2p_1+\cdots+i_kp_1p_2\cdots p_{k-1}),$$
$$(2\oplus_{p_1}i_1,[(2\cdot3)/2]\odot_{p_1}l+(2\odot_{p_2}i_2)p_1+\cdots+(2\odot_{p_k}i_k)p_1p_2\cdots p_{k-1}),\ldots,$$
$$((p_1-1)\oplus_{p_1}i_1,[(p_1-1)p_1/2]\odot_{p_1}l+((p_1-1)\odot_{p_2}i_2)p_1+\cdots$$
$$+((p_1-1)\odot_{p_k}i_k)p_1p_2\cdots p_{k-1})]:i_1=\{0,1,\ldots,p_1-1\},$$
$$i_2=\{0,1,\ldots,p_2-1\},i_3=\{0,1,\ldots,p_3-1\},\ldots,$$
$$i_k=\{0,1,\ldots,p_k-1\},l=\{1,2,\ldots,p_1-1\}\}$$

form the quadratic-congruence carrier-hopping prime codes with cardinality $p_1^2p_2\cdots p_k$, $L=w$ wavelengths, length $N=p_1p_2\cdots p_k$, and weight $w=p_1$, where "$\odot_{p_j}$" denotes a modulo-p_j multiplication for $j=\{1,2,3,\ldots,k\}$.

To have weight $w<p_1$, those ordered pairs with the first components (or wavelength numbers) whose values are greater than $w-1$ can be removed without affecting the cross-correlation properties.

These $p_1^2p_2\cdots p_k$ quadratic-congruence carrier-hopping prime codewords can be partitioned into p_1 groups (indexed by l), and there are $p_1p_2\cdots p_k$ codewords (indexed by i_1, i_2, ..., and i_k) in each group.

Theorem 5.11

The autocorrelation peaks and sidelobes of the quadratic-congruence carrier-hopping prime codes of weight w are equal to w and 0, respectively, where $w\leq p_1$. The periodic cross-correlation functions of the codes are at most 2, but at most 1 if the correlating codewords are from the same group $l=\{0,1,\ldots,p_1-1\}$ [10,28].

Proof The proof is similar to that of Theorem 5.1, except that the linear-congruence operators in the ordered pairs are now replaced by quadratic ones. So, the maximum periodic cross-correlation function for any two distinct codewords, $\mathbf{x}_{i_k,i_{k-1},\ldots,i_1,l}$ and $\mathbf{x}_{i'_k,i'_{k-1},\ldots,i'_1,l'}$, in the quadratic-congruence carrier-hopping prime codes is at most 2 when $l\neq l'$.

For any two codewords in the same group l with the same indices $(i_2,i_3,\ldots,i_k)$, the periodic cross-correlation functions are at most 1 because the autocorrelation sidelobes of the quadratic-congruence codes are at most 1 [1, Section 6.5]. For any two codewords in the same group l with indices $(i_2, i_3, \ldots, i_k) \neq (i'_2, i'_3, \ldots, i'_k)$, the periodic cross-correlation functions are also at most 1 due to the same cross-correlation property of the carrier-hopping prime codes in Section 5.1.

Because all pulses in a codeword are in different wavelengths, the autocorrelation sidelobes are always 0. Finally, the autocorrelation peaks of w are due to the code weight $w \leq p_1$. ∎

Using $k = 1$ and $L = w = p_1 = 5$ as an example, this quadratic-congruence carrier-hopping prime code of length 5 has 5 groups of 5 codewords in each group, denoted by $\mathbf{x}_{i_1,0} = [(0,0), (1,i_1), (2, 2 \odot_5 i_1), (3, 3 \odot_5 i_1), (4, 4 \odot_5 i_1)]$ and $\mathbf{x}_{i_1,l} = [(i_1, 0), (1 \oplus i_1, l), (2 \oplus i_1, 3 \odot_5 l), (3 \oplus i_1, 6 \odot_5 l), (4 \oplus i_1, 10 \odot_5 l)]$ for $i_1 \in [0,4]$ and $l \in [1,4]$. For example, the 5 codewords, $\mathbf{x}_{0,2} = [(0,0), (1,2), (2,1), (3,2), (4,0)]$, $\mathbf{x}_{1,2} = [(0,0), (1,0), (2,2), (3,1), (4,2)]$, $\mathbf{x}_{2,2} = [(0,2), (1,0), (2,0), (3,2), (4,1)]$, $\mathbf{x}_{3,2} = [(0,1), (1,2), (2,0), (3,0), (4,2)]$, and $\mathbf{x}_{4,2} = [(0,2), (1,1), (2,2), (3,0), (4,0)]$, in group $l = 2$ have the periodic cross-correlation functions of at most 1. The 5 codewords, $\mathbf{x}_{0,1} = [(0,0), (1,1), (2,3), (3,1), (4,0)]$, $\mathbf{x}_{1,1} = [(0,0), (1,0), (2,1), (3,3), (4,1)]$, $\mathbf{x}_{2,1} = [(0,1), (1,0), (2,0), (3,1), (4,3)]$, $\mathbf{x}_{3,1} = [(0,3), (1,1), (2,0), (3,0), (4,1)]$, and $\mathbf{x}_{4,1} = [(0,1), (1,3), (2,1), (3,0), (4,0)]$, in group $l = 1$ have the periodic cross-correlation functions of at most 2 when they correlate with the codewords in group $l = 2$.

Using $k = 2$, $L = w = 4$, and $p_1 = p_2 = 5$ as an example, this quadratic-congruence carrier-hopping prime code of length 25 has 5 groups of 25 codewords in each group, denoted by $\mathbf{x}_{i_2,i_1,0} = [(0,0), (1, i_1 + 5i_2), (2, 2 \odot_5 i_1 + (2 \odot_5 i_2)5), (3, 3 \odot_5 i_1 + (3 \odot_5 i_2)5), (4, 4 \odot_5 i_1 + (4 \odot_5 i_2)5)]$ and $\mathbf{x}_{i_2,i_1,l} = [(i_1, 0), (1 \oplus i_1, 1 \odot_5 l + (1 \odot_5 i_2)5), (2 \oplus i_1, 3 \odot_5 l + (2 \odot_5 i_2)5), (3 \oplus i_1, 6 \odot_5 l + (3 \odot_5 i_2)5), (4 \oplus i_1, 10 \odot_5 l + (4 \odot_5 i_2)5)]$ for $i_1 \in [0,4]$, $i_2 \in [0,4]$, and $l \in [1,4]$. To have weight $w = 4$, the ordered pairs that have their first components with values greater than 4 are dropped. The codewords $\mathbf{x}_{1,0,1} = [(0,0), (1,6), (2,13), (3,16)]$, $\mathbf{x}_{2,3,1} = [(0,23), (1,6), (2,15), (3,0)]$, and $\mathbf{x}_{1,1,4} = [(0,20), (1,0), (2,9), (3,12)]$ are three examples. The codeword $\mathbf{x}_{1,0,1}$ has the maximum periodic cross-correlation function of 1 when it correlates with $\mathbf{x}_{2,3,1}$ in the same group $l = 1$, but 2 when it correlates with $\mathbf{x}_{1,1,4}$ in a different group.

5.6.1 Performance Analysis

According to Section 1.8.4, the chip-synchronous, hard-limiting error probability of the quadratic-congruence carrier-hopping prime codes with $L = w$ wavelengths, length $N = p_1 p_2 \cdots p_k$, weight $w \leq p_1$, and the maximum periodic cross-correlation function of 2 in OOK is given by

$$P_{e,\text{hard}} = \frac{1}{2} \sum_{h=Z_{\text{th}}}^{w} \frac{w!}{h!(w-h)!} \sum_{i=0}^{h} (-1)^{h-i} \frac{h!}{i!(h-i)!} \left[q_0 + \frac{iq_1}{w} + \frac{i(i-1)q_2}{w(w-1)} \right]^{K-1} \quad (5.14)$$

where K is the number of simultaneous users and the decision threshold $Z_{\text{th}} = w$ is usually applied for optimal decision.

Theorem 5.12

For the quadratic-congruence carrier-hopping prime codes of $L = w$ wavelengths, length $N = p_1 p_2 \cdots p_k$, and weight $w \leq p_1$, the hit probabilities, q_i, of having the periodic cross-correlation values of $i = \{0,1,2\}$ (in the sampling time) are formulated as [10, 28]

$$q_2 = \frac{(p_1 - 1)(w - 1)w}{4 p_1 p_2 \cdots p_k (p_1^2 p_2 \cdots p_k - 1)}$$

$$q_1 = \frac{w}{2 p_1 p_2 \cdots p_k} - 2 q_2$$

$$q_0 = 1 - q_1 - q_2$$

Proof The two-hit probability is generally derived as

$$q_2 = \frac{1}{2} \times \frac{\binom{p_1}{2} - (p_1 - w)w - \binom{p_1 - w}{2}}{p_1 p_2 \cdots p_k} \times \frac{(p_1 - 1) p_1 p_2 \cdots p_k}{p_1^2 p_2 \cdots p_k - 1} \times \frac{1}{N}$$

where the factor $1/2$ comes from the assumption of equiprobable data bit-1 and bit-0 transmissions in OOK. The term $\binom{p_1}{2}$ represents the number of possible cyclic adjacent-pulse separations among the p_1 pulses in a codeword, $(p_1 - w)w$ represents the number of possible separations among w pulses after $p_1 - w$ pulses have been removed, and $\binom{p_1 - w}{2}$ represents the number of possible separations among the $p_1 - w$ removed pulses. The denominator $p_1 p_2 \cdots p_k$ represents the number of codewords in the same group. The term $(p_1 - 1) p_1 p_2 \cdots p_k / (p_1^2 p_2 \cdots p_k - 1)$ represents the probability of choosing an interfering codeword coming from a different group of the address codeword, out of a total of $p_1^2 p_2 \cdots p_k$ codewords. The last term $1/N$ represents the number of possible time shifts in a codeword of length $N = p_1 p_2 \cdots p_k$. By applying $\sum_{i=0}^{2} i q_i = w^2 / (2LN) = w / (2 p_1 p_2 \cdots p_k)$ and $\sum_{i=0}^{2} q_i = 1$ and after some manipulations, the final forms of the hit probabilities in the theorem are derived. ∎

Figure 5.15 plots the chip-synchronous, hard-limiting error probabilities of the quadratic-congruence carrier-hopping prime codes [from Equation (5.14)] and the carrier-hopping prime codes [from Equation (5.3)] of both $k = 1, L = 9$ wavelengths, length $N = p_1 = \{19, 47, 103\}$, and weight $w = 9$ against the number of simultaneous users K. The error probabilities of the quadratic-congruence carrier-hopping prime codes are always worse than those of the carrier-hopping prime codes due to a larger maximum periodic cross-correlation function. The trade-off is that the latter have only p_1 codewords, while the former have p_1^2 codewords. As the solid curves assume all quadratic-congruence carrier-hopping prime codes having the same maximum periodic cross-correlation function of 2, the actual code performance is bounded by

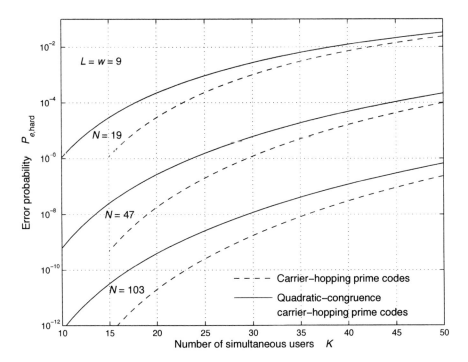

FIGURE 5.15 Chip-synchronous, hard-limiting error probabilities of the quadratic-congruence carrier-hopping prime codes and the carrier-hopping prime codes of both $L = w = 9$ and $N = \{19, 47, 103\}$.

the solid and dashed curves. This is because the group property has the codewords mixed with periodic cross-correlation functions of at most 1 and 2.

5.6.2 Multicode and Shifted-Code Keying

The enlarged cardinality of the quadratic-congruence carrier-hopping prime codes supports multicode keying. In multicode keying, each user is assigned multiple codewords, which represent the transmission of different symbols (of multiple data bits per symbol). As discussed in Definition 5.2, the total amount of interference seen by a receiver in multicode keying consists of the intersymbol (periodic) cross-correlation functions generated by the codewords of interfering users and the intrasymbol (in-phase) cross-correlation functions caused by different symbols (or codewords) of the correct user.

In this section, the quadratic-congruence carrier-hopping prime codes are partitioned into $p_1 p_2 \cdots p_k$ groups (indexed by i_2, i_3, ..., i_k and l) and there are p_1 codewords (indexed by i_1) in each group. In this way, $p_1 p_2 \cdots p_k$ subscribers can be accommodated, and each of them is assigned 2^m codewords for 2^m-code keying, supporting 2^m symbols with m bits per symbol, where $2^m \leq p_1$. This partition method allows the largest number of possible subscribers with the intrasymbol (in-phase) cross-correlation functions no greater than 1, while the intersymbol (periodic) cross-correlation functions are at most 2.

Theorem 5.13

With $p_1 p_2 \cdots p_k$ groups of p_1 codewords per group, the chip-synchronous, hard-limiting error probability of the quadratic-congruence carrier-hopping prime codes with $L = w$ wavelengths, length $N = p_1 p_2 \cdots p_k$, and weight $w \leq p_1$ in 2^m-code keying is formulated as [10, 28]

$$P_{e,\text{hard,multicode}} = \frac{2^m}{2(2^m - 1)} \left[1 - \left(\frac{p_1 - 1}{p_1} \right) \sum_{t=0}^{2^m - 1} \left(\frac{1}{t+1} \right) \text{Pr}'(w,t) \right.$$

$$\left. - \left(\frac{1}{p_1} \right) \sum_{t=0}^{2^m - 1} \left(\frac{1}{t+1} \right) \text{Pr}(w-1,t) \right]$$

where $2^m \leq p_1$,

$$\text{Pr}'(w,t) = \frac{(2^m - 1)!}{t!(2^m - 1 - t)!} \left[\text{Pr}'(w) \right]^t \left[\sum_{v=0}^{w-1} \text{Pr}'(v) \right]^{2^m - 1 - t}$$

$$\text{Pr}(w,t) = \frac{(2^m - 1)!}{t!(2^m - 1 - t)!} \left[\text{Pr}(w) \right]^t \left[\sum_{v=0}^{w-1} \text{Pr}(v) \right]^{2^m - 1 - t}$$

$$\text{Pr}'(v) = \begin{cases} \frac{p_1}{N} \left(1 - \frac{v+1}{p_1} \right) \text{Pr}(v) + \frac{N - p_1}{N} \text{Pr}(v) & \text{for } v = 0 \\ \frac{p_1}{N} \left[\frac{v}{p_1} \text{Pr}(v-1) + \left(1 - \frac{v+1}{p} \right) \text{Pr}(v) \right] + \frac{N - p_1}{N} \text{Pr}(v) & \text{for } v \in [1, w-1] \\ \frac{p_1}{N} \left[\frac{v}{p_1} \text{Pr}(v-1) + \text{Pr}(v) \right] + \frac{N - p_1}{N} \text{Pr}(v) & \text{for } v = w \end{cases}$$

$$\text{Pr}(v) = \frac{w!}{v!(w-v)!} \sum_{i=0}^{v} (-1)^{v-i} \frac{v!}{i!(v-i)!} \left[q_0' + \frac{i q_1'}{w} + \frac{i(i-1) q_2'}{w(w-1)} \right]^{K-1}$$

and the hit probabilities are given by

$$q_2' = \frac{(p_1 - 1)(w - 1)w}{2 p_1 p_2 \cdots p_k (p_1^2 p_2 \cdots p_k - 1)}$$

$$q_1' = \frac{w}{p_1 p_2 \cdots p_k} - 2 q_2'$$

$$q_0' = 1 - q_1' - q_2'$$

Proof The hit probabilities follow those in Theorem 5.12, except that the factor $1/2$ is removed in multicode keying due to continuous symbol transmission.

The proof of the error probabilities follows that of Theorem 5.6. A decision error in a decoder occurs when interfering codewords cause the aggregated cross-correlation function (in the sampling time) greater than or equal to w. Given that there are $K - 1$ interfering codewords and each generates at most two hits in a time slot over one symbol period, the hard-limiting probability of having a peak of v appearing at any one of $2^m - 1$ wrong decoders in a receiver is given by $\mathrm{Pr}(v)$ in the theorem, which is derived by following Section 1.8.4. So, a symbol decision error occurs when more than one decoder has a correlation value of at least w. The derivation of the probability $\mathrm{Pr}(w,t)$ that t decoders have a correlation value of at least w and $2^m - 1 - t$ decoders have a correlation value of less than w can be broken into two cases, depending on the code structure and cross-correlation properties of the codewords in group $l = 0$ and groups $l = \{1,2,\ldots,p_1 - 1\}$ separately. The intrasymbol cross-correlation functions of the 2^m codewords with the same indices $(i_2,i_3,\ldots,i_k)$ in group $l = 0$ are always equal to 0 when the first pulses of these codewords are excluded, resulting in $\mathrm{Pr}(w,t) = \binom{2^m-1}{t}[\mathrm{Pr}(w)]^t[\sum_{v=0}^{w-1}\mathrm{Pr}(v)]^{2^m-1-t}$. However, the intrasymbol cross-correlation functions of the codewords in groups $l = \{1,2,\ldots,p_1 - 1\}$ can be 0 or 1, depending on the indices of the codewords.

In general, with nonzero intrasymbol cross-correlation functions λ_c', each user's own codewords will create self-interference. To account for this, let A_j^v denote the conditional probability of the number of hits (seen by any one of the $2^m - 1$ wrong decoders) being increased from v to $v+j$ for $j = \{1,2,\ldots,\lambda_c'\}$. The probability of having a peak of v at any one of $2^m - 1$ wrong decoders in a receiver then becomes

$$\mathrm{Pr}'(v) = \sum_{j=1}^{\lambda_c'} A_j^v \mathrm{Pr}(v-j) + \left(1 - \sum_{j=1}^{\lambda_c'} A_j^{v+j}\right)\mathrm{Pr}(v)$$

where $A_j^{v+j} = 0$ when $v + j > w$. The computation of A_j^v depends on the optical codes in use.

If $v = 0$, it is found that $\mathrm{Pr}'(v) = (p_1/N)[1 - (v + 1)/p_1]\mathrm{Pr}(v) + [(N - p_1)/N]\mathrm{Pr}(v)$. To have $\lambda_c' = 1$, the term p_1/N denotes the chance of choosing the 2^m codewords with indices $i_1 = \{0,1,\ldots,p_1 - 1\}$, $i_2 = i_3 = \cdots = i_k = 0$ and the same $l = \{1,2,\ldots,p_1 - 1\}$, where $2^m \leq p_1$. To have $\lambda_c' = 0$, the term $(N - p_1)/N$ denotes the chance of choosing the 2^m codewords with indices $i_1 = \{0,1,\ldots,p_1 - 1\}$ and the same i_2, i_3, ..., i_k, and l. If $v \in [1, w - 1]$, it is found that $\mathrm{Pr}'(v) = (p_1/N)\{(v/p_1)\mathrm{Pr}(v - 1) + [1 - (v + 1)/p_1]\mathrm{Pr}(v)\} + [(N - p_1)/N]\mathrm{Pr}(v)$. The term $(v/p_1)\mathrm{Pr}(v - 1)$ denotes the chance of increasing the number of entries in a wrong decoder from $v - 1$ to v due to $\lambda_c' = 1$. This is because there is only one codeword (out of p_1 codewords) having one hit with the address codeword (of a decoder) in v ways when there are $v - 1$ entries in a wrong decoder. Similarly, the term $[1 - (v + 1)/p_1]\mathrm{Pr}(v)$ considers the chance of increasing the number of entries in a wrong decoder from v to $v + 1$. This is because there is only one codeword (out of p_1 codewords) having one hit with the address codeword in $v + 1$ ways when there are

v entries in a wrong decoder. If $v = w$, $\mathrm{Pr}'(v) = (p_1/N)[(v/p_1)\mathrm{Pr}(v-1)+\mathrm{Pr}(v)]+$ $[(N-p_1)/N]\mathrm{Pr}(v)$. After some manipulations, the final form of $\mathrm{Pr}'(v)$ is derived.

For codewords in groups $l = \{1,2,\ldots,p_1-1\}$, $\mathrm{Pr}'(w,t)$ is defined in the same form as $\mathrm{Pr}(w,t)$ but with the $\mathrm{Pr}(w)$ and $\mathrm{Pr}(v)$ terms being replaced by $\mathrm{Pr}'(w)$ and $\mathrm{Pr}'(v)$, respectively.

Because the probability of correctly choosing the correct decoder is $1/(t+1)$, the symbol error probability P_{symbol} is given by

$$P_{\text{symbol}} = 1 - \frac{p_1-1}{p_1}\sum_{t=0}^{2^m-1}\left(\frac{1}{t+1}\right)\mathrm{Pr}'(w,t) - \frac{1}{p_1}\sum_{t=0}^{2^m-1}\left(\frac{1}{t+1}\right)\mathrm{Pr}(w-1,t)$$

The term $(p_1-1)/p_1$ denotes the chance of choosing the 2^m codewords from groups $l = \{1,2,\ldots,p_1-1\}$ and the term $1/p_1$ denotes the chance of choosing the 2^m codewords from group $l = 0$. The probability $\mathrm{Pr}(w-1,t)$ assumes code weight $w-1$ because of the structure of the codewords in group $l = 0$, in which the first pulse of every codeword always locates at the first time slot. So, these codewords always hit with each other at the first time slot. The contribution of the pulse in the first time slot is "erased" and the "effective" code weight becomes $w-1$.

Finally, the chip-synchronous, hard-limiting bit error probability is given by

$$P_{e,\text{hard,multicode}} = \frac{2^m}{2(2^m-1)}P_{\text{symbol}}$$

∎

Figure 5.16 compares the chip-synchronous, hard-limiting error probabilities of the quadratic-congruence carrier-hopping prime codes of $k = 1$, $L = 9$ wavelengths, length $N = p_1 = 103$, and weight $w = 9$ in OOK and 2^m-ary multicode keying for $m = \{1,2,3,4\}$. In general, the error probabilities get worse when m increases. This is because there are more data bits to be decided incorrectly if a symbol decision error occurs for a larger m. The error probabilities in multicode keying are worse than those in OOK for a given bandwidth expansion LN. This is because the hit probabilities in OOK are reduced by half as data bit 0s are not conveyed. This example shows that there is a trade-off between code performance and the choices of m, in the sense that code performance suffers when bit rate or user code obscurity is enhanced. If bit rate or user code obscurity is more important, one should use multicode keying with $m = \{2,3\}$, which provides a good compromise among error probability, hardware complexity, code obscurity, and bit rate.

The aforementioned multicode-keying approach reduces the number of possible subscribers by a factor of p_1. Applying shifted-code keying (e.g., see Section 5.3), time-shifted quadratic-congruence carrier-hopping prime codes can be used to support $p_1^2 p_2 \cdots p_k$ possible subscribers. The main idea is to assign each user one quadratic-congruence carrier-hopping prime codeword and then to use its 2^m cyclic-time-shifted copies to represent the 2^m symbols. Another advantage of this approach is that the intrasymbol cross-correlation functions become 0. So, the performance analysis of the time-shifted quadratic-congruence carrier-hopping prime codes in

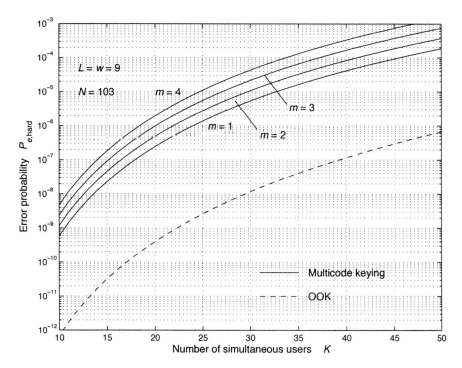

FIGURE 5.16 Chip-synchronous, hard-limiting error probabilities of the quadratic-congruence carrier-hopping prime codes of $L = w = 9$ and $N = 103$ in OOK and multicode keying for $m = \{1,2,3,4\}$.

shifted-code keying is very similar to that in multicode keying, except that the term $\Pr'(v)$ is not needed anymore. The chip-synchronous, hard-limiting error probability of these quadratic-congruence carrier-hopping prime codes with the maximum intersymbol (periodic) cross-correlation functions of 2 in shifted-code keying is then formulated as

$$P_{e,\text{hard,shifted-code}} = \frac{2^m}{2(2^m - 1)} \left[1 - \sum_{t=0}^{2^m - 1} \left(\frac{1}{t+1} \right) \Pr(w,t) \right]$$

where $\Pr(w,t)$ and other probability terms are given in Theorem 5.13.

Figure 5.17 compares the chip-synchronous, hard-limiting error probabilities of the quadratic-congruence carrier-hopping prime codes of $k = 1$, $L = 9$ wavelengths, length $N = 103$, and weight $w = 9$ in 2^m-ary shifted-code keying and multicode keying for $m = \{1,2,3\}$. In general, the error probabilities follow the trends of those in Figure 5.16 as the error probabilities get worse when m increases. However, the error probabilities (solid curves) of shifted-code keying get better than those (dashed curves) of multicode keying for a given m because the time-shifted quadratic-congruence carrier-hopping prime codes have zero intrasymbol cross-correlation

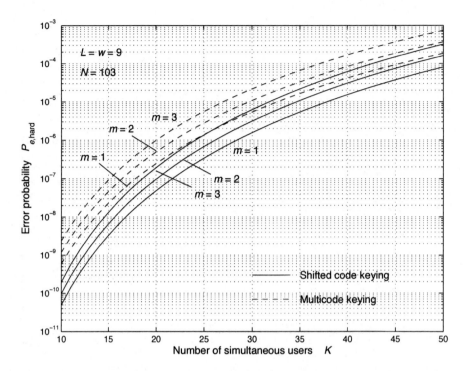

FIGURE 5.17 Chip-synchronous, hard-limiting error probabilities of the quadratic-congruence carrier-hopping prime codes of $L = w = 9$ and $N = 103$ in shifted-code keying and multicode keying for $m = \{1, 2, 3\}$.

functions. In addition, a factor of p_1 more possible subscribers are supported in shifted-code keying.

5.6.3 Spectral Efficiency Study

Similar to Section 5.3, the SE of multicode keying is defined as

$$\text{SE} \propto \frac{Km}{LN}$$

where K is the number of simultaneous users for a given error probability, LN is the bandwidth expansion, and m is the number of bits/symbol in multicode keying or $m = 1$ in OOK. The target is to get the SE as large as possible for better system efficiency or utilization.

Figure 5.18 compares the chip-synchronous, hard-limiting error probabilities of the quadratic-congruence carrier-hopping prime codes in 2^m-ary multicode keying (from Theorem 5.13) and the carrier-hopping prime codes in OOK [from Equation (5.3)] of both $k = 2$, $L = 10$ wavelengths, length $N = p_1 p_2$, and weight $w = 10$ for $p_1 = p_2 = \{17, 23\}$ and $m = \{3, 4\}$. The code parameters are chosen to support

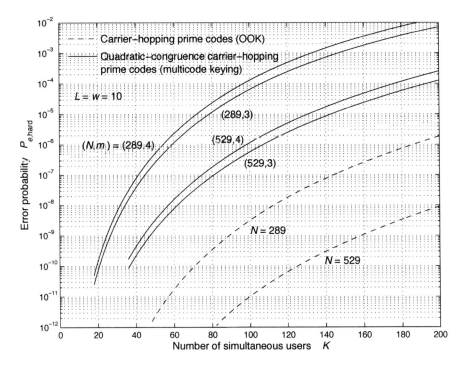

FIGURE 5.18 Chip-synchronous, hard-limiting error probabilities of the quadratic-congruence carrier-hopping prime codes in 2^m-ary multicode keying and the carrier-hopping prime codes in OOK, of both $L = w = 10$ and $N = \{289, 529\}$, for $m = \{3, 4\}$.

the same number of possible subscribers and bandwidth expansion LN for a fair comparison, but the former have the maximum cross-correlation function of 2 and the latter have 1. For example, considering $P_{e,\text{hard}} \approx 10^{-9}$, $m = 4$, and $N = 289$ in the figure, $K = 23$ is supported in multicode keying but OOK supports $K = 88$. Then, $\text{SE}_{\text{multicode}} \propto 23 \times 4/(10 \times 289) = 3.18\%$ and $\text{SE}_{\text{OOK}} \propto 88 \times 1/(10 \times 289) = 3.04\%$. In this example, multicode keying is able to utilize better spectral efficiency, even though OOK supports more simultaneous users.

Table 5.1 summarizes the SEs of both code families for various error probabilities, $P_{e,\text{hard}}$, obtained from Figure 5.18. In general, their SEs get worse when $P_{e,\text{hard}}$ decreases because K also decreases. Also, the SE decreases as N increases for fixed m and $P_{e,\text{hard}}$. This is because K increases more slowly as N gets larger. However, the SE improves with m when N is fixed. From the table, m is found to be a more dominating factor than N in determining the SE. When m gets larger, the effective bit rate increases for a fixed symbol rate, which is related to N. However, the number of decoders increases linearly with 2^m, worsening the hardware complexity and cost. In this example, multicode keying begins to have better SEs than OOK when $m > 3$. By adjusting m, multicode keying allows the trade of system efficiency for hardware complexity; no such trade is allowed in OOK though.

TABLE 5.1

Spectral Efficiencies of the Quadratic-Congruence Carrier-Hopping Prime
Codes in Multicode Keying and the Carrier-Hopping Prime Codes in OOK for
Various Error Probabilities from Figure 5.18

$N = 289$	$m = 4$		$m = 3$		OOK	
	K	SE (%)	K	SE (%)	K	SE (%)
$P_{e,\text{hard}} = 10^{-8}$	32	4.43	34	3.53	114	3.94
$P_{e,\text{hard}} = 10^{-9}$	23	3.18	26	2.70	88	3.04
$P_{e,\text{hard}} = 10^{-10}$	19	2.63	21	2.18	71	2.46

$N = 529$	$m = 4$		$m = 3$		OOK	
	K	SE (%)	K	SE (%)	K	SE (%)
$P_{e,\text{hard}} = 10^{-8}$	56	4.23	62	3.52	200	3.78
$P_{e,\text{hard}} = 10^{-9}$	44	3.33	47	2.67	160	3.02
$P_{e,\text{hard}} = 10^{-10}$	31	2.34	35	1.98	124	2.34

5.7 PRIME-PERMUTED CODES WITH UNIPOLAR CODES

A method of constructing 2-D wavelength-time codes involves combining two families of 1-D optical codes—one for wavelength hopping and another one for time
spreading [13, 16–22, 29]. For ease of representation, the notations $(N, w, \lambda_a, \lambda_c)$ and
$(L \times N, w, \lambda_a, \lambda_c)$ are here used to describe the number of wavelengths L, length
N, weight w, the maximum autocorrelation sidelobe λ_a, and the maximum periodic
cross-correlation function λ_c of the 1-D and 2-D optical codes involved in the constructions, respectively.

In [29], a family of 2-D $(N_{\text{OOC}} \times p^2, w, 0, 1)$ OOC/prime codes was constructed,
where 1-D $(p^2, p, p - 1, 2)$ prime codes (in Section 3.1) over GF(p) of a prime
p were used as the time-spreading codes, and 1-D $(N_{\text{OOC}}, p, 1, 1)$ optical orthogonal codes (OOCs) [30–33] of length $N_{\text{OOC}} = p(p - 1) \Phi_{\text{OOC}} + 1$ and cardinality
Φ_{OOC} were used to determine the wavelengths of the pulses in the time-spreading
codes. The overall cardinality of the OOC/prime codes was given by $\Phi_{\text{OOC}} N_{\text{OOC}} p$.
In [34], a family of 2-D $(p \times p^2, w, 0, 1)$ prime/prime codes with the overall cardinality of $p(p - 1)$ was proposed, where 1-D $(p^2, p, p - 1, 2)$ prime codes were
used for both wavelength hopping and time spreading. In [16], a family of 2-D
$(p \times p(2p - 1), w, 0, 2)$ prime/EQCC codes with the overall cardinality of $p(p - 1)^2$
was proposed, in which 1-D $(p(2p - 1), p, 1, 2)$ extended quadratic-congruence
codes (EQCCs) were used as the time-spreading codes. Following this approach,
a family of 2-D $(p \times p^2, w, 0, 2)$ EQCC/prime codes with the overall cardinality of
$p^2(p - 1)$ was also mentioned in [17]. The problems of these four code families are
that either code cardinality is a linear function of the number of wavelengths or the

number of wavelengths and code length are two dependent parameters. To improve code cardinality, many wavelengths are needed, or their code length and the number of wavelengths must be increased together. The second approach may not be flexible due to hardware limitations. For example, mode-locked lasers with over 100-nm flattened supercontinuum optical spectrum had been reported [27]. In other words, there are more available wavelengths than time slots, especially for 10+ Gbits/s optical coding systems. If the cardinality of wavelength-time codes can be increased by raising the number of wavelengths alone, there is no need to increase the code length or sacrifice the code performance by relaxing the maximum periodic cross-correlation function from 1 to 2 or even higher.

TABLE 5.2

Composition, Property, and Cardinality Comparisons of Prime- and QC-Permuted Codes

Time Spreading	Wavelength Hopping	Property	Overall Cardinality
$(N, w, 1, 1)$ OOC	Prime sequences	$(p \times N, w, 1, 1)$	$p^2 \Phi_{(N,w,1,1)\text{OOC}}$ (optimal)
$(N, w, 2, 1)$ OOC	Prime sequences	$(p \times N, w, 2, 2)$	$p^2 \Phi_{(N,w,2,1)\text{OOC}}$
$(N, w, 1, 2)$ OOC	Prime sequences	$(p \times N, w, 1, 2)$	$p^2 \Phi_{(N,w,1,2)\text{OOC}}$
$(N, w, 2, 2)$ OOC	Prime sequences	$(p \times N, w, 2, 2)$	$p^2 \Phi_{(N,w,2,2)\text{OOC}}$
$(N, w, 1, 1)$ OOC	QC sequences	$(p \times N, w, 1, 2)$	$p^3 \Phi_{(N,w,1,1)\text{OOC}}$
$(N, w, 2, 1)$ OOC	QC sequences	$(p \times N, w, 2, 2)$	$p^3 \Phi_{(N,w,2,1)\text{OOC}}$
$(N, w, 1, 2)$ OOC	QC sequences	$(p \times N, w, 1, 2)$	$p^3 \Phi_{(N,w,1,2)\text{OOC}}$
$(N, w, 2, 2)$ OOC	QC sequences	$(p \times N, w, 2, 2)$	$p^3 \Phi_{(N,w,2,2)\text{OOC}}$ (optimal)

In this section, the constructions of 2-D wavelength-time codes with the use of prime sequences to permutate the wavelengths of the pulses in 1-D unipolar codes are studied. The overall cardinality of these prime-permuted codes is a quadratic function of the number of wavelengths and, at the same time, the number of wavelengths and code length are independent of each other. Table 5.2 summaries the compositions, properties, and cardinalities of these prime-permuted codes. In general, with the use of 1-D $(N, w, \lambda_a, \lambda_c')$ OOCs, such as those in Section 3.7 and [30–33], for time spreading, a family of 2-D $(p \times N, w, \lambda_a, \lambda_c)$ prime-permuted codes can be constructed with an overall cardinality of $p^2 \Phi_{(n,w,\lambda_a,\lambda_c')\text{OOC}}$ [18, 20–22], where p is a prime number. To obtain even larger cardinality, the use of quadratic-congruence (QC) sequences [23, 35] for wavelength permutations are studied in Section 5.9. The compositions, properties, and cardinalities of the resulting QC-permuted codes [22] are also summarized in Table 5.2.

The 2-D $(p \times N, w, \lambda_a, \lambda_c)$ prime-permuted codes in Table 5.2 are constructed by first choosing a family of 1-D $(N, w, \lambda_a, \lambda_c')$ OOCs as the time-spreading codes. Afterward, p wavelengths are assigned to the pulses of each codeword of these OOCs in accordance with the permutation of wavelength indices determined by *shifted* prime sequences, $S_{i,l} = (s_{i,l,0}, s_{i,l,1}, \ldots, s_{i,l,j}, \ldots, s_{i,l,p-1})$, with the jth element defined as [18, 20–22]

$$s_{i,l,j} = ij + l \pmod{p}$$

where i and $l = \{0, 1, \ldots, p-1\}$ for a prime p. There are p^2 shifted prime sequences over GF(p) and they can be separated into p groups (indexed by i). Every prime sequence with $l = 0$ is used as a seed to generate other $p - 1$ shifted prime sequences in its group. These p^2 shifted prime sequences give p^2 permutations in assigning up to p wavelengths to the pulses of each time-spreading $(N, w, \lambda_a, \lambda_c')$ OOC codeword, resulting in an overall cardinality of $p^2 \Phi_{(N,w,\lambda_a,\lambda_c')\text{OOC}}$ in the $(p \times N, w, \lambda_a, \lambda_c)$ prime-permuted codes with code weight $w \le p$.

TABLE 5.3

Shifted Prime Sequences over GF(7)

	Group $i=0$	Group $i=1$	Group $i=2$	Group $i=3$	$\cdots$	Group $i=6$
$l=0$	0000000	0123456	0246135	0362514	$\cdots$	0654321
$l=1$	1111111	1234560	1350246	1403625	$\cdots$	1065432
$l=2$	2222222	2345601	2461350	2514036	$\cdots$	2106543
$l=3$	3333333	3456012	3502461	3625140	$\cdots$	3210654
$l=4$	4444444	4560123	4613502	4036251	$\cdots$	4321065
$l=5$	5555555	5601234	5024613	5140362	$\cdots$	5432106
$l=6$	6666666	6012345	6135024	6251403	$\cdots$	6543210

TABLE 5.4

$(7 \times 13, 4, 2, 2)$ Prime-Permuted Code over GF(7) with 7 Wavelengths and the Time-Spreading $(13, 4, 1, 2)$ OOC Codeword 1011000100000

Group $i=0$	Group $i=1$	Group $i=2$	$\cdots$	Group $i=6$
$\lambda_0 0 \lambda_0 \lambda_0 000 \lambda_0 00000$	$\lambda_0 0 \lambda_1 \lambda_2 000 \lambda_3 00000$	$\lambda_0 0 \lambda_2 \lambda_4 000 \lambda_6 00000$	$\cdots$	$\lambda_0 0 \lambda_6 \lambda_5 000 \lambda_4 00000$
$\lambda_1 0 \lambda_1 \lambda_1 000 \lambda_1 00000$	$\lambda_1 0 \lambda_2 \lambda_3 000 \lambda_4 00000$	$\lambda_1 0 \lambda_3 \lambda_5 000 \lambda_0 00000$	$\cdots$	$\lambda_1 0 \lambda_0 \lambda_6 000 \lambda_5 00000$
$\lambda_2 0 \lambda_2 \lambda_2 000 \lambda_2 00000$	$\lambda_2 0 \lambda_3 \lambda_4 000 \lambda_5 00000$	$\lambda_2 0 \lambda_4 \lambda_6 000 \lambda_1 00000$	$\cdots$	$\lambda_2 0 \lambda_1 \lambda_0 000 \lambda_6 00000$
$\lambda_3 0 \lambda_3 \lambda_3 000 \lambda_3 00000$	$\lambda_3 0 \lambda_4 \lambda_5 000 \lambda_6 00000$	$\lambda_3 0 \lambda_5 \lambda_0 000 \lambda_2 00000$	$\cdots$	$\lambda_3 0 \lambda_2 \lambda_1 000 \lambda_0 00000$
$\lambda_4 0 \lambda_4 \lambda_4 000 \lambda_4 00000$	$\lambda_4 0 \lambda_5 \lambda_6 000 \lambda_0 00000$	$\lambda_4 0 \lambda_6 \lambda_1 000 \lambda_3 00000$	$\cdots$	$\lambda_4 0 \lambda_3 \lambda_2 000 \lambda_1 00000$
$\lambda_5 0 \lambda_5 \lambda_5 000 \lambda_5 00000$	$\lambda_5 0 \lambda_6 \lambda_0 000 \lambda_1 00000$	$\lambda_5 0 \lambda_0 \lambda_2 000 \lambda_4 00000$	$\cdots$	$\lambda_5 0 \lambda_4 \lambda_3 000 \lambda_2 00000$
$\lambda_6 0 \lambda_6 \lambda_6 000 \lambda_6 00000$	$\lambda_6 0 \lambda_0 \lambda_1 000 \lambda_2 00000$	$\lambda_6 0 \lambda_1 \lambda_3 000 \lambda_5 00000$	$\cdots$	$\lambda_6 0 \lambda_5 \lambda_4 000 \lambda_3 00000$

Table 5.3 shows the $p^2 = 49$ shifted prime sequences over GF(7). Table 5.4 shows the $(7 \times 13, 4, 1, 2)$ prime-permuted code generated by using $L = p = 7$ wavelengths

$\{\lambda_0, \lambda_1, \ldots, \lambda_6\}$, and the time-spreading $(13, 4, 1, 2)$ OOC codeword 1101000001000 [32]. The wavelength indices in these 49 prime-permuted codewords are determined by the shifted prime sequences in Table 5.3.

Theorem 5.14

The autocorrelation peaks of these prime-permuted codes over $GF(p)$ of a prime p and weight w are equal to w, where $w \leq p$. The maximum autocorrelation side-lobe of these prime-permuted codes follows that of the time-spreading OOCs in use. By excluding the prime-permuted codewords in group $i = 0$, the autocorrelation sidelobes become 0. The periodic cross-correlation functions of the $(p \times N, w, 1, 1)$ prime-permuted codes are at most 1. The periodic cross-correlation functions of the $(p \times N, w, 1, 2)$ and $(p \times N, w, 2, 2)$ prime-permuted codes are at most 2 [18–22].

Proof As every pulse within a prime-permuted codeword originating from group $i = 0$ of the shifted prime sequences has the same wavelength, the maximum auto-correlation sidelobe is determined by that of the time-spreading OOCs. For groups $i = \{1, 2, \ldots, p-1\}$, all the pulses within a prime-permuted codeword are conveyed with distinct wavelengths, resulting in zero autocorrelation sidelobes. However, the number of prime-permuted codewords is reduced to $p^2 - p$ if those in group $i = 0$ are excluded. The autocorrelation peaks of w are due to the code weight $w \leq p$.

For any two $(p \times N, w, 1, 1)$ prime-permuted codewords coming from two differ-ent time-spreading $(N, w, 1, 1)$ OOC codewords, the periodic cross-correlation func-tion is at most 1 due to the same cross-correlation property of the OOCs. For any two $(p \times N, w, 1, 1)$ prime-permuted codewords coming from the same $(N, w, 1, 1)$ OOC codeword, the periodic cross-correlation function is also at most 1 due to the same cross-correlation property of the shifted prime sequences and the autocorrela-tion sidelobes of at most 1 in the OOCs.

When the time shift τ between any two correlating $(p \times N, w, 2, 2)$ prime-permuted codewords is equal to 0, their periodic cross-correlation function is at most 1 due to the same cross-correlation property of the shifted prime sequences. When $\tau \subset [1, N-1]$, the correlation properties of the time-spreading OOCs are taken into consideration. The periodic cross-correlation function of any two correlating $(p \times N, w, 2, 2)$ prime-permuted codewords is at most 1 if they come from two dif-ferent $(N, w, 2, 1)$ OOC codewords due to the same cross-correlation property of the OOCs. The periodic cross-correlation function of any two correlating $(p \times N, w, 2, 2)$ prime-permuted codewords is at most 2 if they come from the same $(N, w, 2, 1)$ OOC codeword due to the maximum autocorrelation sidelobe of the OOCs. Similarly, the periodic cross-correlation function of any two $(p \times N, w, 2, 2)$ prime-permuted code-words is at most 2 if they come from two different $(N, w, 1, 2)$ OOC codewords or two different $(N, w, 2, 2)$ OOC codewords due to the same cross-correlation property of these OOCs. The periodic cross-correlation function of any two $(p \times N, w, 2, 2)$

prime-permuted codewords is at most 1 if they come from the same $(N, w, 1, 2)$ OOC codeword, but at most 2 if they come from the same $(N, w, 2, 2)$ OOC codeword due to the maximum autocorrelation sidelobe of the OOCs.

The proof on the cross-correlation properties of the $(p \times N, w, 1, 2)$ prime-permuted codes follows the rationale used for the $(p \times N, w, 2, 2)$ prime-permuted codes by replacing the $(N, w, 2, 1)$ OOCs by the $(N, w, 1, 2)$ OOCs.   ∎

Due to the property of GF(p) of a prime p, all p elements of GF(p) occur exactly once in each shifted prime sequence, excluding those in group $i = 0$, and there is at most one location in any shifted prime sequence having an identical element in the same location in other shifted prime sequences (e.g., see Table 5.3). These two conditions are important to maintain the cross-correlation functions of the prime-permuted codes as low as possible. So, the best overall cardinality is achieved when p is a prime number because all p groups, with p shifted prime sequences in each group, can be used for the wavelength permutation (e.g., see Table 5.4). However, this may not be the case when p is not a prime number, whereas those prime sequences with repeated elements will worsen the cross-correlation functions and must be removed. One exception is on the extension field of a prime number, GF(p^n) for an integer $n > 1$, which have the p^n elements in each shifted prime sequence, excluding those in group $i = 0$, nonrepeating and the two aforementioned conditions are still satisfied. The jth element of each shifted prime sequence over GF(p^n) is defined as

$$s_{i,l,j} = ij + l \quad (\bmod \ p^n)$$

For example, the shifted prime sequences over GF(2^3) are shown in Table 5.5, based on the addition and multiplication tables of GF(2^3) in Section 1.1.

TABLE 5.5

Shifted Prime Sequences over GF(2^3)

	Group $i = 0$	Group $i = 1$	Group $i = 2$	Group $i = 3$	$\cdots$	Group $i = 6$
$l = 0$	00000000	01234567	02463175	03657412	$\cdots$	07521643
$l = 1$	11111111	10325476	13572064	12746503	$\cdots$	16430752
$l = 2$	22222222	23016745	20641357	21475630	$\cdots$	25703461
$l = 3$	33333333	32107654	31750246	30564721	$\cdots$	34612570
$l = 4$	44444444	45670123	46027531	47213056	$\cdots$	43165207
$l = 5$	55555555	54761032	57136420	56302147	$\cdots$	52074316
$l = 6$	66666666	67452301	64205713	65031274	$\cdots$	61347025
$l = 7$	77777777	76543210	75314602	74120365	$\cdots$	70256134

For a non-prime p, denote $1 < k_1 < k_2 < \cdots < k_m < p$ as all possible distinct factors of p. There are $p - 1$ groups, excluding group $i = 0$, of p shifted prime sequences with the first k_1 elements in every sequence satisfying the two aforementioned nonrepeating-element conditions. So, by including group $i = 0$, there are in total $\Phi_{group} = p$ valid groups and p shifted prime sequences per group for the wavelength permutation if the first k_1 elements in each shifted prime sequence are used, even though p is non-prime. When $w > k_1$, the overall cardinality is reduced, depending on the actual values of p and w. The number of valid groups, Φ_{group}, of shifted prime sequences with nonrepeating elements for the wavelength permutation can be determined by the following rules:

- $\Phi_{group} = p$ if p is a prime number or a power of a prime number, or if $w \leq k_1$
- $\Phi_{group} = p/k_1$ if $k_1 < w \leq k_2$
- $\Phi_{group} = p/k_2$ if $k_2 < w \leq k_3$

$\vdots$

- $\Phi_{group} = p/k_{m-1}$ if $k_{m-1} < w \leq k_m$
- $\Phi_{group} = p/k_m$ if $w > k_m$

TABLE 5.6
Non-Prime Sequences for $p = 12$

		0	1	2	3	4	5	6	7	8	9	10	11
$i = 0$		0	0	0	0	0	0	0	0	0	0	0	0
$i = 1$		0	1	2	3	4	5	6	7	8	9	10	11
$i = 2$		0	2	4	6	8	10	0	2	4	6	8	10
$i = 3$		0	3	6	9	0	3	6	9	0	3	6	9
$i = 4$		0	4	8	0	4	8	0	4	8	0	4	8
$i = 5$		0	5	10	3	8	1	6	11	4	9	2	7
$i = 6$		0	6	0	6	0	6	0	6	0	6	0	6
$i = 7$		0	7	2	9	4	11	6	1	8	3	10	5
$i = 8$		0	8	4	0	8	4	0	8	4	0	8	4
$i = 9$		0	9	6	3	0	9	6	3	0	9	6	3
$i = 10$		0	10	8	6	4	2	0	10	8	6	4	2
$i = 11$		0	11	10	9	8	7	6	5	4	3	2	1

The top header row is labeled j.

$| \quad w = 2 \quad |$
$| \leftarrow w = 3 \rightarrow |$
$| \leftarrow -w = 4 -- \rightarrow |$
$| \leftarrow ---w = 6 ---\rightarrow \quad |$

For example, Table 5.6 shows the non-prime sequences for $p = 12$, which corresponds to the shifted prime sequences $S_{i,l}$ with $l = 0$ (e.g., compare Table 5.5). Because $p = 12 = 2 \times 2 \times 3$, all possible distinct factors are $k_1 = 2$, $k_2 = 3$, $k_3 = 4$, and $k_4 = 6$. There exist 12 groups of 12 shifted prime sequences per group with nonrepeating elements in each row and column, except the first row and column, of the table when $w \leq 2$, giving $\Phi_{group} = 12$. For $3 \geq w > 2$, the rule states that only $\Phi_{\text{group}} = p/k_1 = 6$ groups (indexed by $i = \{0,1,2,3,4,5\}$) of 12 shifted prime sequences per group can be used. This is because other shifted prime sequences contain repeating elements either in the same row or column (up to the wth column). Similarly, for $4 \geq w > 3$, there are $\Phi_{\text{group}} = p/k_2 = 4$ valid groups (indexed by $i = \{0,1,2,3\}$). For $6 \geq w > 4$, there are $\Phi_{\text{group}} = p/k_3 = 3$ valid groups (indexed by $i = \{0,1,2\}$). Finally, for $w > 6$, there are $\Phi_{\text{group}} = p/k_3 = 2$ valid groups (indexed by $i = \{0,1\}$). From this example, it is sometimes better to trim down the number of wavelengths to the nearest prime number, say $p = 11$, in order to improve the number of valid groups to $\Phi_{\text{group}} = 11$ and to support any code weight w up to 11.

Because each time-spreading OOC codeword can generate $p\Phi_{\text{group}}$ prime-permuted codewords, the overall cardinality of the $(p \times N, w, \lambda_a, \lambda_c)$ prime-permuted codes is given by

$$\Phi(p \times N, w, \lambda_a, \lambda_c) = p\Phi_{\text{group}}\Phi_{(N,w,\lambda_a,\lambda_c')\text{OOC}} \leq p^2 \Phi_{(N,w,\lambda_a,\lambda_c')\text{OOC}}$$

where $\Phi_{(N,w,\lambda_a,\lambda_c')\text{OOC}}$ is the cardinality of the time-spreading $(N, w, \lambda_a, \lambda_c')$ OOCs and $w \leq p$. The maximum overall cardinality is achieved when $\Phi_{\text{group}} = p$, which is possible if p is a prime number or a power of a prime number. In the code cardinality aspect, it is often more beneficial to use the nearest prime number that is less than p, even though the permutation algorithm may work with a non-prime p.

According to Section 3.5 and [18–22, 30–33], the cardinalities of some of the time-spreading OOCs are given by

$$\Phi_{(N,w,1,1)\text{OOC}} = \frac{N-1}{w(w-1)}$$

$$\Phi_{(N,w,2,1)\text{OOC}} = \begin{cases} \frac{2(N-1)}{w^2-1} & \text{for odd } w \\ \frac{2(N-1)}{w^2} & \text{for even } w \end{cases}$$

$$\Phi_{(N,w,1,2)\text{OOC}} = \begin{cases} \frac{N-1}{w} & \text{for odd } w \\ \frac{\frac{N}{w}-1}{w-1} & \text{for even } w \end{cases}$$

$$\Phi_{(N,w,1,2)\text{OOC}} = \frac{2(N-1)}{w(w-1)} \quad \text{coordinate-reversed method}$$

$$\Phi_{(N,w,2,2)\text{OOC}} = w-3 \quad \text{for } N = w^2 - 2w$$

In general, the $(N, w, 1, 1)$ and $(N, w, 2, 2)$ OOCs in [30–33] are optimal because they achieve the cardinality upper bound defined in Section 1.6.

According to Section 1.6, the cardinality upper bound of the 2-D $(p \times N, w, 1, 1)$ prime-permuted codes with the overall cardinality $p^2 \Phi_{(N,w,1,1)\text{OOC}}$ is given by

$$\Phi(p \times N, w, 1, 1) \leq \frac{p(pN-1)}{w(w-1)}$$

$$= p^2 \Phi_{(N,w,1,1)\text{OOC}} + \frac{p(p-1)}{w(w-1)}$$

where $N = w(w-1)\Phi_{(N,w,1,1)\text{OOC}} + 1$. The actual cardinality achieves the upper bound when w approaches p. So, the $(p \times N, w, 1, 1)$ prime-permuted codes are asymptotically optimal in cardinality. However, the $(p \times N, w, \lambda_a, 2)$ prime-permuted codes are not optimal because their actual cardinalities cannot generally approach their corresponding upper bounds even when w approaches p.

5.7.1 Performance Analysis

Because the 2-D $(p \times N, w, 1, 1)$ prime-permuted codes have a maximum periodic cross-correlation function of 1, their chip-synchronous, hard- and soft-limiting error probabilities in OOK are given by

$$P_{e,\text{hard}} = \frac{1}{2} \sum_{h=Z_{\text{th}}}^{w} \frac{w!}{h!(w-h)!} \sum_{i=0}^{h} (-1)^{h-i} \frac{h!}{i!(h-i)!} \left(q_0 + \frac{iq_1}{w} \right)^{K-1} \tag{5.15}$$

and Equation (5.1), respectively, where K is the number of simultaneous users and the decision threshold $Z_{\text{th}} = w$ is usually applied for optimal decision.

Theorem 5.15

For the $(p \times N, w, 1, 1)$ prime-permuted codes over $\mathrm{GF}(p)$ of a prime p with the time-spreading $(N, w, 1, 1)$ OOCs of cardinality $\Phi_{(N,w,1,1)\text{OOC}}$, the hit probabilities, q_j, of having the periodic cross-correlation values of $j = \{0, 1\}$ (in the sampling time) are formulated as [17–22]

$$q_1 = \frac{pw^2(p\Phi_{(N,w,1,1)\text{OOC}} - 1) + (p-1)(w-1)^2}{2pN(p^2\Phi_{(N,w,1,1)\text{OOC}} - 1)}$$

and $q_0 = 1 - q_1$, for $w \le p$.

Proof Let $q_{1,(0)}$ and $q_{1,(i)}$ denote the probabilities of getting one hit in the sampling time of the periodic cross-correlation functions between the prime-permuted codeword (address signature of a receiver) coming from group $i = 0$ and groups $i = \{1, 2, \ldots, p-1\}$, respectively, and an interfering prime-permuted codeword. So,

$$
\begin{aligned}
q_{1,(0)} &= \frac{1}{2} \left[\frac{1}{N} \times \frac{w(p-1)}{p^2\Phi_{(N,w,1,1)\text{OOC}} - 1} + \frac{w(w-1)}{N} \times \frac{1}{w} \times \frac{w(p-1)}{p^2\Phi_{(N,w,1,1)\text{OOC}} - 1} \right. \\
&\quad + \frac{w^2}{N} \times \frac{\Phi_{(N,w,1,1)\text{OOC}} - 1}{p^2\Phi_{(N,w,1,1)\text{OOC}} - 1} \\
&\quad \left. + \frac{w^2}{N} \times \frac{1}{w} \times \frac{(\Phi_{(N,w,1,1)\text{OOC}} - 1)w(p-1)}{p^2\Phi_{(N,w,1,1)\text{OOC}} - 1} \right] \\
&= \frac{w^2(p\Phi_{(N,w,1,1)\text{OOC}} - 1)}{2N(p^2\Phi_{(N,w,1,1)\text{OOC}} - 1)}
\end{aligned}
$$

where the factor $1/2$ comes from the assumption of equiprobable data bit-1 and bit-0 transmissions in OOK. In the denominators, $p^2\Phi_{(N,w,1,1)\text{OOC}} - 1$ denotes the number of possible interfering codewords. The first product term accounts for the hit probability of the address codeword (from group $i = 0$) correlating with an interfering codeword coming from the same $(N, w, 1, 1)$ OOC codeword, without any time shift. The term N represents the number of possible time shifts in a codeword of length N. There are $w(p-1)$ interfering codewords contributing one-hits. Similarly, the second product term accounts for the case with a time shift, with a probability of $w(w-1)/N$. The factor $1/w$ represents the probability of getting one-hits from an interfering codeword of a different group. The third product term accounts for the hit probability of the address and interfering codewords from the same group $i = 0$ but different $(N, w, 1, 1)$ OOC codewords. The factor w^2/N represents the probability of getting one-hits. There are $\Phi_{(N,w,1,1)\text{OOC}} - 1$ interfering codewords (from group $i = 0$) contributing one-hits. Finally, the fourth product term accounts for the hit probability of the address codeword (from group $i = 0$) correlating with an interfering codeword coming from groups $i = \{1, 2, \dots, p-1\}$ and a different $(N, w, 1, 1)$ OOC codeword. There are $(\Phi_{(N,w,1,1)\text{OOC}} - 1)w(p-1)$ interfering codewords (from groups $i = \{1, 2, \dots, p-1\}$) contributing one-hits.

For the address codeword originating from groups $i = \{1, 2, \dots, p-1\}$),

$$
\begin{aligned}
q_{1,(i)} &= \frac{1}{2}\left[\frac{1}{N} \times \frac{w(p-1)}{p^2\Phi_{(N,w,1,1)\text{OOC}} - 1} + \frac{w(w-1)}{N} \times \frac{1}{w} \times \frac{w}{p^2\Phi_{(N,w,1,1)\text{OOC}} - 1} \right. \\
&\quad + \frac{w(w-1)}{N} \times \frac{1}{w^2} \times \frac{w^2(p-2)}{p^2\Phi_{(N,w,1,1)\text{OOC}} - 1} + \frac{w(w-1)}{N} \times \frac{1}{w} \\
&\quad \left. \times \frac{w-1}{p^2\Phi_{(N,w,1,1)\text{OOC}} - 1} + \frac{w^2}{N} \times \frac{1}{w} \times \frac{(\Phi_{(N,w,1,1)\text{OOC}} - 1)wp}{p^2\Phi_{(N,w,1,1)\text{OOC}} - 1} \right] \\
&= \frac{w^2(p\Phi_{(N,w,1,1)\text{OOC}} - 1) + (w-1)^2}{2N(p^2\Phi_{(N,w,1,1)\text{OOC}} - 1)}
\end{aligned}
$$

The derivation follows the rationale used for $q_{1,(0)}$. The first four product terms account for the hit probabilities of the address codeword (from groups $i = \{1, 2, \dots, p-1\}$) correlating with an interfering codeword coming from the same $(N, w, 1, 1)$ OOC codeword, whereas the fifth product term accounts for the case of a different $(N, w, 1, 1)$ OOC codeword. The first product term shows the case of zero time shift between the address and interfering codewords. The second product term shows the case with a time shift, with a probability of $w(w-1)/N$, whereas the interfering codeword is from group $i = 0$. Similarly, the third product term shows the case with a time shift, whereas the interfering codeword is from groups $\{1, 2, \dots, i-1\}$ or groups $\{i+1, i+2, \dots, p-1\}$. The fourth product term is similar to the third term, but the interfering codeword is in the same group $i = \{1, 2, \dots, p-1\}$ as the address codeword.

By combining all groups, the final form of q_1, which is equal to $(1/p)q_{1,(0)} + [(p-1)/p]q_{1,(i)}$, in the theorem is derived after some manipulations. ∎

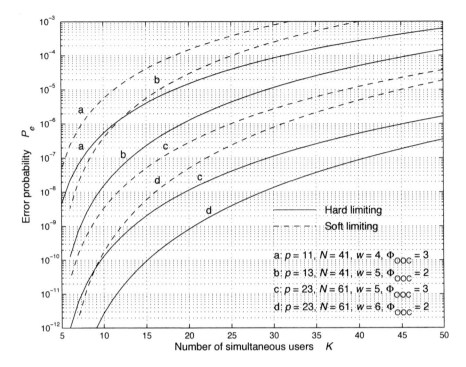

FIGURE 5.19 Chip-synchronous, hard- and soft-limiting error probabilities of the $(p \times N, w, 1, 1)$ prime-permuted codes with the time-spreading $(N, w, 1, 1)$ OOCs for $p = \{11, 13, 23\}$, $N = \{41, 61\}$, and $w = \{4, 5, 6\}$.

Figure 5.19 shows the chip-synchronous, hard- and soft-limiting error probabilities of the $(p \times N, w, 1, 1)$ prime-permuted codes with the time-spreading $(N, w, 1, 1)$ OOCs against the number of simultaneous users K for $p = \{11, 13, 23\}$, $N = \{41, 61\}$, and $w = \{4, 5, 6\}$. In general, the error probabilities improve as p, w, or N increases because of higher autocorrelation peaks or lower hit probabilities. However, the error probabilities get worse as K increases due to stronger mutual interference. As expected, the hard-limiting (solid) curves always perform better than the soft-limiting (dashed) curves because the former reduce the amount of interference.

Because the $(p \times N, w, \lambda_a, 2)$ prime-permuted codes have the maximum periodic cross-correlation function of 2, their chip-synchronous, hard-limiting error probability in OOK follows Equation (5.14).

Theorem 5.16

For the $(p \times N, w, 2, 2)$ prime-permuted codes over GF(p) of a prime p with the time-spreading $(N, w, 2, 1)$ OOCs of cardinality $\Phi_{(N,w,2,1)\text{OOC}}$, the hit probabilities, q_j, of having the periodic cross-correlation values of $j = \{0, 1, 2\}$ (in the sampling time) are formulated as [20]

$$q_2 = \frac{(p-1)(w-1-x)(w-1+x)}{4pN(p^2\Phi_{(N,w,2,1)OOC}-1)}$$

$$q_1 = \frac{pw^2(p\Phi_{(N,w,2,1)OOC}-1)+(p-1)(w-1+x)}{2pN(p^2\Phi_{(N,w,2,1)OOC}-1)}$$

and $q_0 = 1 - q_1 - q_2$, for $w \leq p$, where $x = 0$ for odd w, but $x = 1$ for even w.

Proof Let $q_{j,(0)}$ and $q_{j,(i)}$ denote the probabilities of getting $j = \{0,1,2\}$ hits in the sampling time of the periodic cross-correlation functions between the prime-permuted codeword (address signature of a receiver) coming from group $i = 0$ and groups $i = \{1,2,\ldots,p-1\}$, respectively, and an interfering codeword.

As studied in Sections 1.6 and 3.4, the definition of cyclic adjacent-pulse separations, which was commonly used for constructing 1-D optical codes [1, 30–33, 36–39], can be applied to determine the maximum periodic cross-correlation function. This is because the number of repeated elements in the sets of the cyclic adjacent-pulse separations associated with two correlating codewords determine the number of hits. For instance, if the set of cyclic adjacent-pulse separations of two correlating prime-permuted codewords of odd weight contains $(w-1)/2$ repeated elements in each codeword, their periodic cross-correlation function sees $(w-1)^2/2$ two-hits. Because each element will contribute $w-1$ cyclic adjacent-pulse separations with the other $w-1$ elements, the number of one-hits becomes $w(w-1) - 2(w-1)^2/2 = w-1$ [32].

For the address codeword originating from groups $i = \{1,2,\ldots,p-1\}$ and of odd weight $w \leq p$,

$$q_{2,(i)} = \frac{1}{2} \times \frac{1}{N} \times \frac{(w-1)^2}{2} \times \frac{1}{p^2\Phi_{(N,w,2,1)OOC}-1}$$

where $1/2$ comes from the assumption of equiprobable data bit-1 and bit-0 transmissions in OOK and N is the number of possible time shifts in a codeword of length N. The term $(w-1)^2/2$ represents the total number of two-hits seen by the address codeword of odd weight w. The denominator $p^2\Phi_{(N,w,2,1)OOC} - 1$ represents the number of possible interfering codewords.

The set of cyclic adjacent-pulse separations of a prime-permuted codeword of even weight is derived similar to that of the odd-weight codeword. From [32], the periodic cross-correlation function between two even-weight codewords sees a total of $w(w-2)/2$ two-hits and w one-hits. The derivation of $q_{2,(i)}$ with even weight follows the rationale used for odd weight with $(w-1)^2$ in the numerator being replaced by $w(w-2)$.

Because no two-hit can be generated by interfering codewords from group $i = 0$, the final form of q_2, which is equal to $[(p-1)/p]q_{2,(i)}$, in the theorem is derived after some manipulations.

For the address codeword originating from group $i = 0$,

$$
\begin{aligned}
q_{1,(0)} &= \frac{1}{2} \times \frac{1}{N} \times \left[\frac{w(p-1)}{p^2 \Phi_{(N,w,2,1)\text{OOC}} - 1} + \frac{w(w-1)(p-1)}{p^2 \Phi_{(N,w,2,1)\text{OOC}} - 1} \right. \\
&\quad \left. + \frac{w^2(\Phi_{(N,w,2,1)\text{OOC}} - 1)}{p^2 \Phi_{(N,w,2,1)\text{OOC}} - 1} + \frac{w^2(\Phi_{(N,w,2,1)\text{OOC}} - 1)(p-1)}{\Phi_{(N,w,2,1)\text{OOC}} p^2 - 1} \right] \\
&= \frac{w^2(p\Phi_{(N,w,2,1)\text{OOC}} - 1)}{2N(p^2 \Phi_{(N,w,2,1)\text{OOC}} - 1)}
\end{aligned}
$$

The first product term in the brackets accounts for the hit probability of the address codeword (from group $i = 0$) correlating with an interfering codeword coming from other groups but from the same $(N, w, 2, 1)$ OOC codeword, without any time shift. There are $w(p-1)$ interfering codewords contributing one-hits. Similarly, the second product term accounts for the case with a time shift and there are $w(w-1)(p-1)$ interfering codewords contributing one-hits. The third and fourth product terms account for the hit probabilities of the address codeword (from group $i = 0$) correlating with an interfering codeword coming from group $i = 0$ and groups $i = \{1, 2, \ldots, p-1\}$, respectively, and from a different $(N, w, 2, 1)$ OOC codeword.

For the address codeword originating from groups $i = \{1, 2, \ldots, p-1\}$ and of odd weight $w \le p$,

$$
\begin{aligned}
q_{1,(i)} &= \frac{1}{2} \times \frac{1}{N} \times \left[\frac{w(p-1)}{p^2 \Phi_{(N,w,2,1)\text{OOC}} - 1} + \frac{w(w-1)}{p^2 \Phi_{(N,w,2,1)\text{OOC}} - 1} \right. \\
&\quad \left. + \frac{w(w-1)(p-2) + (w-1)}{p^2 \Phi_{(N,w,2,1)\text{OOC}} - 1} + \frac{w^2(\Phi_{(n,w,2,1)\text{OOC}} - 1)p}{p^2 \Phi_{(N,w,2,1)\text{OOC}} - 1} \right] \\
&= \frac{w^2(p\Phi_{(N,w,2,1)\text{OOC}} - 1) + w - 1}{2N(p^2 \Phi_{(N,w,2,1)\text{OOC}} - 1)}
\end{aligned}
$$

The derivation follows the rationale used for $q_{1,(0)}$. The first three product terms in the brackets account for the hit probabilities of the address codeword (from groups $i = \{1, 2, \ldots, p-1\}$) when it correlates with an interfering codeword coming from the same $(N, w, 2, 1)$ OOC codeword. The first product term shows the case of zero time shift between the address and interfering codewords. The second and third product terms show the cases with a time shift and the interfering codeword coming from group $i = 0$ and groups $i = \{1, 2, \ldots, p-1\}$, respectively. The fourth product term accounts for the hit probability of the address codeword (from groups $i = \{1, 2, \ldots, p-1\}$) when it correlates with an interfering codeword coming from a different $(N, w, 2, 1)$ OOC codeword.

The derivation of $q_{1,(i)}$ of even weight follows the rationale used for odd weight with $w - 1$ in the numerator being replaced by w.

By combining all groups, the final form of q_1, which is equal to $(1/p)q_{1,(0)} + [(p-1)/p]q_{1,(i)}$, in the theorem is derived after some manipulations. ∎

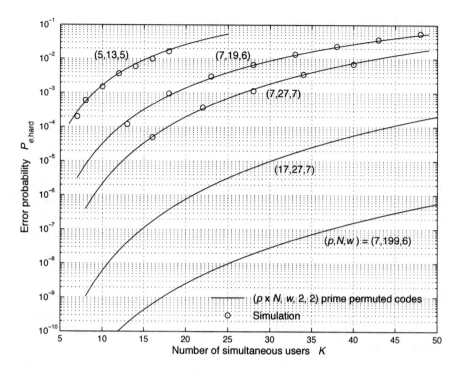

FIGURE 5.20 Chip-synchronous, hard-limiting error probabilities of the $(p \times N, w, 2, 2)$ prime-permuted codes with the time-spreading $(N, w, 2, 1)$ OOCs for $p = \{5, 7, 17\}$, $N = \{13, 19, 27, 199\}$, and $w = \{5, 6, 7\}$.

Figure 5.20 plots the chip-synchronous, hard-limiting error probabilities of the $(p \times N, w, 2, 2)$ prime-permuted codes with the time-spreading $(N, w, 2, 1)$ OOCs against the number of simultaneous users K for $p = \{5, 7, 17\}$, $N = \{13, 19, 27, 199\}$, and $w = \{5, 6, 7\}$. In general, the error probabilities improve as p, N, or w increases because of higher autocorrelation peaks or lower hit probabilities. However, the error probabilities get worse as K increases due to stronger mutual interference. Also plotted in the figure are the computer-simulation results, which closely match the theoretical results. The computer simulation is performed by randomly assigning each simultaneous user one of the prime-permuted codewords in the code set, and OOK modulation is used for transmitting each data bit 1 with a codeword. The total number of data bits involved in the simulation is at least 100 times the reciprocal of the target error probability in order to provide enough iterations.

Theorem 5.17

For the $(p \times N, w, 1, 2)$ prime-permuted codes over GF(p) of a prime p with the time-spreading $(N,w,1,2)$ OOCs of cardinality $\Phi_{(N,w,1,2)\text{OOC}}$, the hit probabilities, q_j, of having the periodic cross-correlation values of $j = \{0,1,2\}$ (in the sampling time) are formulated as [21]

$$q_2 = \frac{w(w-1)(w-2+x)}{4N(p^2\Phi_{(N,w,1,2)\text{OOC}}-1)}$$

$$q_1 = \frac{pw^2(p\Phi_{(N,w,1,2)\text{OOC}}-1)-w(w-1)[p(w-3+x)+1]}{2pN(p^2\Phi_{(N,w,1,2)\text{OOC}}-1)}$$

and $q_0 = 1 - q_1 - q_2$, for $w \leq p$, where $x = 0$ for odd w, but $x = 1$ for even w.

Proof The proof is similar to that of Theorem 5.16. Let $q_{j,(0)}$ and $q_{j,(i)}$ denote the probabilities of getting $j = \{0,1,2\}$ hits in the sampling time of the periodic cross-correlation functions between the prime-permuted codeword (address signature of a receiver) coming from group $i = 0$ and groups $i = \{1,2,\ldots,p-1\}$, respectively, and an interfering prime-permuted codeword.

Assuming that the time-spreading $(N,w,1,2)$ OOCs are constructed by the coordinate-reversed method in Section 3.5.2, in which $(w-1)/2$ sets of the $(N,w,1,1)$ OOCs of odd weight w or $w/2$ sets of the $(N,w,1,1)$ OOCs of even weight w, and their coordinate-reversed images are unionized [32]. The construction does not change the autocorrelation property and the resulting $(N,w,1,2)$ OOCs still have $\lambda_a = 1$. Furthermore, the periodic cross-correlation function of any two $(N,w,1,2)$ OOC codewords is at most 1, but at most 2 if a $(N,w,1,2)$ OOC codeword correlates with its coordinate-reversed image.

For the address codeword originating from groups $i = \{0,1,\ldots,p-1\}$ and of odd weight $w \leq p$,

$$q_{2,(0)} = q_{2,(i)} = \frac{1}{2} \times \frac{1}{N} \times \left[\frac{\frac{w(w-1)}{2}}{p^2\Phi_{(N,w,1,2)\text{OOC}}-1} + \frac{\frac{w-3}{2} \times w(w-1)}{p^2\Phi_{(N,w,1,2)\text{OOC}}-1} \right]$$
$$- \frac{w(w-1)(w-2)}{4N(p^2\Phi_{(N,w,1,2)\text{OOC}}-1)}$$

where $1/2$ comes from the assumption of equiprobable data bit-1 and bit-0 transmissions in OOK and N is the number of possible time shifts in a codeword of length N. The denominator $p^2\Phi_{(N,w,1,2)\text{OOC}} - 1$ represents the number of possible interfering codewords. The first product term in the brackets accounts for the hit probability of the address codeword, with its $(N,w,1,2)$ OOC codeword coming from one of the $(w-1)/2$ sets, correlating with an interfering codeword, with its $(N,w,1,2)$ OOC codeword being the coordinate-reversed image of that of the address codeword. The factor $w(w-1)/2$ represents the total number of two-hits seen by the address codeword of odd weight w. The second product term accounts for the hit probability of the address codeword correlating with an interfering codeword coming from a different $(N,w,1,2)$ OOC codeword, which is from one of the other $(w-1)/2-1 = (w-3)/2$

sets. The factor $w(w-1)$ represents the total number of two-hits seen by the address codeword.

Because there are $[(w-1)/2] \times w(w-1) = w(w-1)^2/2$ two-hits in the second product term when the address codeword is of even weight, the derivations of $q_{2,(0)}$ and $q_{2,(i)}$ with even weight follow the rationale used for odd weight by replacing $(w-2)$ in the numerator by $(w-1)$.

For the address codeword originating from group $i = 0$,

$$
\begin{aligned}
q_{1,(0)} &= \frac{1}{2} \times \frac{1}{N} \times \left[\frac{w^2(p-1)}{p^2 \Phi_{(N,w,1,2)\text{OOC}} - 1} \right. \\
&\quad \left. + \frac{w^2 p(\Phi_{(N,w,1,2)\text{OOC}} - 1)}{p^2 \Phi_{(N,w,1,2)\text{OOC}} - 1} - \frac{2 \times \frac{w(w-1)(w-2)}{2}}{p^2 \Phi_{(N,w,1,2)\text{OOC}} - 1} \right] \\
&= \frac{w^2(p\Phi_{(N,w,1,2)\text{OOC}} - 1) - w(w-1)(w-2)}{2N(p^2 \Phi_{(N,w,1,2)\text{OOC}} - 1)}
\end{aligned}
$$

The first product term in the brackets accounts for the hit probability of the address codeword (from group $i = 0$) correlating with an interfering codeword coming from the same $(N, w, 1, 2)$ OOC codeword. There are $w^2(p-1)$ interfering codewords contributing one-hits. The second product term accounts for the hit probabilities of the address codeword (from group $i = 0$) correlating with an interfering codeword coming from a different $(N, w, 1, 2)$ OOC codeword. There are $w^2 p(\Phi_{(N,w,1,2)\text{OOC}} - 1)$ interfering codewords contributing one-hits. The only difference between the second and last product terms is that the numerator of the latter, $w(w-1)/2 + (w-3)/2 \times w(w-1) = w(w-1)(w-2)/2$, represents the number of interfering codewords contributing two-hits.

For the address codeword originating from groups $i = \{1, 2, \ldots, p-1\}$ and of odd weight $w \le p$,

$$
\begin{aligned}
q_{1,(i)} &= \frac{1}{2} \times \frac{1}{N} \times \left[\frac{w(w-1) + w^2(p-1)}{p^2 \Phi_{(N,w,1,2)\text{OOC}} - 1} \right. \\
&\quad \left. + \frac{w^2 p(\Phi_{(N,w,1,2)\text{OOC}} - 1) - 2 \times \frac{w(w-1)(w-2)}{2}}{p^2 \Phi_{(N,w,1,2)\text{OOC}} - 1} \right] \\
&= \frac{w^2(\Phi_{(N,w,1,2)\text{OOC}} p - 1) + w(w-1)(3-w)}{2N(p^2 \Phi_{(N,w,1,2)\text{OOC}} - 1)}
\end{aligned}
$$

The first product term in the brackets accounts for the hit probability of the address codeword (from groups $i = \{1, 2, \ldots, p-1\}$) correlating with an interfering codeword coming from the same $(N, w, 1, 2)$ OOC codeword. There are $w(w-1)$ interfering codewords coming from the same group $i = \{1, 2, \ldots, p-1\}$ of the address codeword, and $w^2(p-1)$ interfering codewords coming from different groups, contributing one-hits. The second product term accounts for the hit probability of the address codeword (from groups $i = \{1, 2, \ldots, p-1\}$) correlating with an interfering codeword coming from a different $(N, w, 1, 2)$ OOC codeword. There are

$w^2 p(\Phi_{(N,w,1,2)\text{OOC}} - 1) - 2 \times w(w-1)(w-2)/2$ interfering codewords contributing one-hits and $w(w-1)/2 + (w-3)/2 \times w(w-1) = w(w-1)(w-2)/2$ interfering codewords contributing two-hits, out of $w^2 p(\Phi_{(N,w,1,2)\text{OOC}} - 1)$ possible number of hits.

Following the rationale used for odd weight, the one-hit probabilities, $q_{1,(0)}$ and $q_{1,(i)}$, for even weight are derived by replacing $w-2$ in the numerator by $w-1$.

By combining all groups, the final forms of q_1 and q_2, which are equal to $q_j = (1/p)q_{j,(0)} + [(p-1)/p]q_{j,(i)}$ for $j = \{1,2\}$, in the theorem are derived after some manipulations. ∎

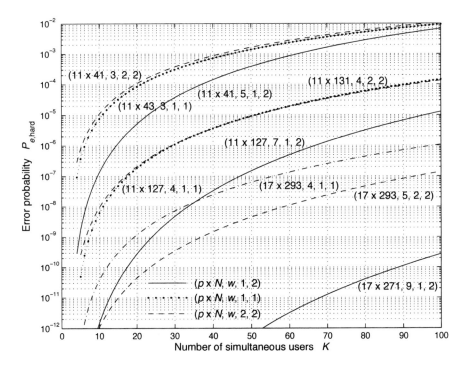

FIGURE 5.21 Chip-synchronous, hard-limiting error probabilities of the $(p \times N, w, 2, 2)$, $(p \times N, w, 1, 2)$, and $(p \times N, w, 1, 1)$ prime-permuted codes for $p = \{5, 11, 13, 17\}$, $N = \{13, 41, 73, 111\}$, and $w = \{3, 4, 5, 7, 9\}$.

Figure 5.21 plots the chip-synchronous, hard-limiting error probabilities of the $(p \times N, w, 1, 2)$, $(p \times N, w, 1, 1)$, and $(p \times N, w, 2, 2)$ prime-permuted codes with the time-spreading $(N, w, 1, 2)$, $(N, w, 1, 1)$, and $(N, w, 2, 1)$ OOCs, respectively, against the number of simultaneous user K for $p = \{5, 11, 13, 17\}$, $N = \{13, 41, 73, 111\}$, and $w = \{3, 4, 5, 7, 9\}$. The code parameters are chosen so that the same number of wavelengths, and similar code cardinality and length are used for a fair comparison. In general, the error probabilities improve as N, w, or p increases because of higher autocorrelation peaks or lower hit probabilities. However, the error probabilities get worse as K increases due to stronger mutual interference. In theory, codes with the maximum cross-correlation function of 2 (or $\lambda_c = 2$) should always perform worse than those with $\lambda_c = 1$ for similar K, L, N, and w values. However, Figure 5.21 shows the opposite in some cases. This is because the $(p \times N, w, 1, 2)$ prime-permuted codes can support heavier code weight than the $(p \times N, w, 1, 2)$ prime-permuted codes for similar code length and cardinality, and this compensates for the worsening in performance due to larger λ_c. As a result, the $(p \times N, w, 1, 2)$ prime-permuted codes generally perform better than their $(p \times N, w, 1, 1)$ counterparts. For example, for the same N, the $(11 \times 41, 5, 1, 2)$ codes have $w = 5$, while the $(11 \times 41, 3, 1, 1)$ prime-permuted codes have $w = 3$ only, corresponding to a code-weight difference of 2. Their performance difference increases with the code-weight difference. Furthermore, even though the number of two-hits occurring in the $(p \times N, w, 1, 2)$ prime-permuted codes is more than that of their $(p \times N, w, 2, 2)$ counterparts, the former have the flexibility of carrying heavier code weight, a property inherited from the $(N, w, 2, 1)$ OOCs, for the same code length and similar code cardinality. This compensates for the larger number of two-hits and results in code better performance than the latter. It is found that the two-hit probability q_2 in the $(11 \times 41, 3, 2, 2)$ prime-permuted codes (see Theorem 5.16) is at least $1/p$ times smaller than the one-hit probability q_1 in the $(11 \times 43, 3, 1, 1)$ prime-permuted codes (see Theorem 5.15). In addition, the cardinality of the former is about two times greater than that of the latter due to their time-spreading OOCs. Combining both effects, the $(11 \times 41, 3, 2, 2)$- and $(11 \times 43, 3, 1, 1)$-curves match closely when the same L and w and similar N are assumed, and so do the $(11 \times 131, 4, 2, 2)$- and $(11 \times 127, 4, 1, 1)$-curves.

5.8   PRIME-PERMUTED CODES WITH BIPOLAR CODES

In this section, 2-D $(L \times N, w, 1, 1)$ prime-permuted codes, which use bipolar codes, such as Walsh codes, maximal-length sequences, and modified maximal-length sequences, for wavelength hopping and bipolar Barker or Gold sequences for time spreading, are studied [13, 17–19, 40]. To improve code performance, these prime-permuted codes also support code-inversion keying (CIK), in which data bit 0s are transmitted with wavelength-conjugate codewords [41], in additional to OOK.

As listed in Table 5.7, three families of 2-D $(L \times N, w, 1, 1)$ prime-permuted codes are obtained from the permutations of multiwavelength (bipolar) codewords algebraically onto the time slots of unipolar 1-D time-spreading $(N, w, 1, 1)$ OOC codewords, bipolar Barker sequences, and bipolar Gold sequences, respectively [13, 17–19]. The permutations are controlled by the shifted prime sequences over $GF(p)$ of a prime p in order to keep the periodic cross-correlation functions of the 2-D prime-permuted codes at most 1. Other benefits are the flexible relationship of code length N and the number of wavelengths L and that the code cardinality is a quadratic function of the number of wavelengths. The choice of the 1-D time-spreading codes (unipolar versus bipolar) affects the modulation format (OOK versus CIK) and the selection of the bipolar codes for wavelength hopping, as explained in the following.

If the 1-D $(N, w, 1, 1)$ OOCs are used for time spreading, the wavelengths used for wavelength hopping are determined by the multiwavelength codewords, which are

TABLE 5.7

Code Composition, Modulation Format, and Cardinality of the $(L \times N, w, 1, 1)$ Prime-Permuted Codes over GF(p) of a Prime p, where Φ Denotes the Cardinality of the Time-Spreading Codes

Time Spreading	Wavelength Hopping	Modulation	Cardinality
$(N, w, 1, 1)$ OOCs	Unipolar version of Walsh codes or maximal-length sequences of length L	OOK	$p^2 \Phi_{OOC}$
Barker sequence (weight w & length N)	Bipolar version of Walsh codes or modified maximal-length sequences of length L	CIK	$p^2 \Phi_{Barker}$
Gold sequences (weight w & length N)	Bipolar version of Walsh codes or modified maximal-length sequences of length L	CIK	$p^2 \Phi_{Gold}$

obtained by carrying every "$+1$" element in the selected bipolar codewords with a wavelength whose index is related to the code element's location, but the "-1" elements are not represented by any wavelength [13, 17]. Table 5.8 shows two examples of the bipolar codes [2, 42, 43] that can be used as the multiwavelength codes. The maximal-length sequence $(+1, +1, +1, -1, -1, +1, -1)$ of length 7 gives the multiwavelength codeword C_0, which contains wavelengths λ_1, λ_2, λ_3, and λ_6, as the "$+1$" elements are found at the 1st, 2nd, 3rd, and 6th locations. By cyclic-shifting this maximal-length sequence 6 times, 7 multiwavelength codewords, listed as C_0 to C_6, are generated. For the Walsh code of length 8, eight wavelengths are used to represent the seven multiwavelength codewords, as listed in Table 5.8.

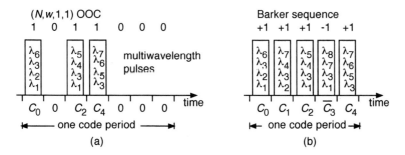

FIGURE 5.22 A 2-D prime-permuted codeword obtained by putting (a) the multiwavelength codewords C_0, C_2, and C_4, from the maximal-length sequences in Table 5.8, onto nonzero time slots of the time-spreading $(7, 3, 1, 1)$ OOC codeword 1011000 and (b) the multiwavelength codewords C_0, C_1, C_2, $\overline{C}_3$, and C_4, from the modified maximal-length sequences in Table 5.10, onto time slots of the time-spreading Barker sequence $(+1, +1, +1, -1, +1)$, where L is the number of wavelengths, which depends on the length of the multiwavelength codewords.

TABLE 5.8

Multiwavelength Codes, Based on the Maximal-Length Sequences of Length 7 and Walsh Code of Length 8

	Maximal-Length Sequences	Wavelengths
C_0	$(+1,+1,+1,-1,-1,+1,-1)$	$\lambda_1 \lambda_2 \lambda_3 \lambda_6$
C_1	$(-1,+1,+1,+1,-1,-1,+1)$	$\lambda_2 \lambda_3 \lambda_4 \lambda_7$
C_2	$(+1,-1,+1,+1,+1,-1,-1)$	$\lambda_1 \lambda_3 \lambda_4 \lambda_5$
C_3	$(-1,+1,-1,+1,+1,+1,-1)$	$\lambda_2 \lambda_4 \lambda_5 \lambda_6$
C_4	$(-1,-1,+1,-1,+1,+1,+1)$	$\lambda_3 \lambda_5 \lambda_6 \lambda_7$
C_5	$(+1,-1,-1,+1,-1,+1,+1)$	$\lambda_1 \lambda_4 \lambda_6 \lambda_7$
C_6	$(+1,+1,-1,-1,+1,-1,+1)$	$\lambda_1 \lambda_2 \lambda_5 \lambda_7$

	Walsh Code	Wavelengths
C_0	$(+1,-1,+1,-1,+1,-1,+1,-1)$	$\lambda_1 \lambda_3 \lambda_5 \lambda_7$
C_1	$(+1,+1,-1,-1,+1,+1,-1,-1)$	$\lambda_1 \lambda_2 \lambda_5 \lambda_6$
C_2	$(+1,-1,-1,+1,+1,-1,-1,+1)$	$\lambda_1 \lambda_4 \lambda_5 \lambda_8$
C_3	$(+1,+1,+1,+1,-1,-1,-1,-1)$	$\lambda_1 \lambda_2 \lambda_3 \lambda_4$
C_4	$(+1,-1,+1,-1,-1,+1,-1,+1)$	$\lambda_1 \lambda_3 \lambda_6 \lambda_8$
C_5	$(+1,+1,-1,-1,-1,-1,+1,+1)$	$\lambda_1 \lambda_2 \lambda_7 \lambda_8$
C_6	$(+1,-1,-1,+1,-1,+1,+1,-1)$	$\lambda_1 \lambda_4 \lambda_6 \lambda_7$

After the time-spreading and multiwavelength codewords have been selected, an algebraic permutation algorithm is used to assign these multiwavelength codewords onto the nonzero time slots of the time-spreading $(N, w, 1, 1)$ OOC codewords. The algebraic permutation is based on the p^2 shifted prime sequences over $GF(p)$ of a prime p (e.g., see Table 5.3). Figure 5.22(a) shows an example of such a 2-D prime-permuted codeword. The code weight w of the time-spreading $(N, w, 1, 1)$ OOCs can be as large as p. The use of these OOCs dictates OOK as the modulation format in these 2-D prime-permuted codes.

Listed in Table 5.9 is the OOK-based $(L \times 7, 3, 1, 1)$ prime-permuted code generated by using the seven multiwavelength codewords $\{C_0, C_1, \ldots, C_6\}$ from the maximal-length sequences of length $L = 7$ or Walsh code of length $L = 8$ in Table 5.8, and the time-spreading $(7, 3, 1, 1)$ OOC codeword 1011000. Due to the construction, L also denotes the number of wavelengths used in these 49 $(L \times 7, 3, 1, 1)$ prime-permuted codewords.

Theorem 5.18

The autocorrelation peaks and sidelobes of the $(L \times N, w, 1, 1)$ prime-permuted codes

TABLE 5.9

OOK-Based ($L \times 7$, 3, 1, 1) Prime-Permuted Code over GF(7), Based on the Multiwavelength Codes in Table 5.8 and Time-Spreading (7, 3, 1, 1) OOC Codeword 1011000

Group $i=0$	Group $i=1$	Group $i=2$	Group $i=3$	$\cdots$	Group $i=6$
$C_0 0 C_0 C_0 000$	$C_0 0 C_1 C_2 000$	$C_0 0 C_2 C_4 000$	$C_0 0 C_3 C_6 000$	$\cdots$	$C_0 0 C_6 C_5 000$
$C_1 0 C_1 C_1 000$	$C_1 0 C_2 C_3 000$	$C_1 0 C_3 C_5 000$	$C_1 0 C_4 C_0 000$	$\cdots$	$C_1 0 C_0 C_6 000$
$C_2 0 C_2 C_2 000$	$C_2 0 C_3 C_4 000$	$C_2 0 C_4 C_6 000$	$C_2 0 C_5 C_1 000$	$\cdots$	$C_2 0 C_1 C_0 000$
$C_3 0 C_3 C_3 000$	$C_3 0 C_4 C_5 000$	$C_3 0 C_5 C_0 000$	$C_3 0 C_6 C_2 000$	$\cdots$	$C_3 0 C_2 C_1 000$
$C_4 0 C_4 C_4 000$	$C_4 0 C_5 C_6 000$	$C_4 0 C_6 C_1 000$	$C_4 0 C_0 C_3 000$	$\cdots$	$C_4 0 C_3 C_2 000$
$C_5 0 C_5 C_5 000$	$C_5 0 C_6 C_0 000$	$C_5 0 C_0 C_2 000$	$C_5 0 C_1 C_4 000$	$\cdots$	$C_5 0 C_4 C_3 000$
$C_6 0 C_6 C_6 000$	$C_6 0 C_0 C_1 000$	$C_6 0 C_1 C_3 000$	$C_6 0 C_2 C_5 000$	$\cdots$	$C_6 0 C_5 C_4 000$

over $GF(p)$ of a prime p with the time-spreading $(N, w, 1, 1)$ OOCs are equal to w and 1, respectively, where $w \leq p$. The periodic cross-correlation functions of the codes are at most 1 [13, 17].

Proof The proof follows that of Theorem 5.14. In essence, the prime-permuted codewords originating from different time-spreading $(N, w, 1, 1)$ OOC codewords follow the OOC's autocorrelation-sidelobe and cross-correlation properties, which are both at most 1. The prime-permuted codewords coming from the same OOC codeword follow the cross-correlation property of the shifted prime sequences, which is also at most 1. Finally, the autocorrelation peaks of w are due to the code weight $w \leq p$. ∎

As studied in Section 5.7, the overall cardinality of these OOK-based prime-permuted codes depends on the number of valid groups, Φ_{group}, of the shifted prime sequences over $GF(p)$, the number of multiwavelength codewords Φ_λ, and the cardinality of the time-spreading $(N, w, 1, 1)$ OOCs $\Phi_{(N,w,1,1)\text{OOC}}$. Due to the property of $GF(p)$ of a prime p, all elements of $GF(p)$ occur exactly once in each shifted prime sequence, excluding those in group $i = 0$, and there is at most one location in any shifted prime sequence having an identical element in the same location in other shifted prime sequences (e.g., see Table 5.3). These two conditions are important to maintain the periodic cross-correlation functions of the prime-permuted codes as low as possible in Theorem 5.18. So, the best overall cardinality is achieved when p is a prime number and Φ_λ is also equal to p, which matches the number of the shifted prime sequences in each group. This is because all p groups, with p shifted prime sequences in each group, can be used for wavelength permutation (e.g., see Table 5.9). By the same argument, extension fields of a prime number, $GF(p^n)$ for an integer $n > 1$, also carry the same nonrepeating-element property [e.g., see $GF(2^3)$ in Table 5.5], resulting in the best overall cardinality. The permutation algorithm also works with a non-prime p but with reduced cardinality. Details and general rules on how a non-prime field can be used to obtain valid groups of shifted prime sequences are given in Section 5.7.

In summary, the overall cardinality of these OOK-based $(L \times N, w, 1, 1)$ prime-permuted codes is given by

$$\Phi_{overall} = \Phi_{\lambda} \, \Phi_{group} \, \Phi_{(N,w,1,1)OOC} \leq p \, \Phi_{group} \, \Phi_{(N,w,1,1)OOC} \leq p^2 \, \Phi_{(N,w,1,1)OOC}$$

where $N = w(w-1) \Phi_{(N,w,1,1)OOC} + 1$, according to Section 5.7 [30–33].

In the code cardinality aspect, it is often more beneficial to use the nearest prime number that is less than p, even though the permutation algorithm may work with a non-prime p, as discussed in Section 5.7.

With the use of bipolar codes for time spreading, this kind of 2-D $(L \times N, w, 1, 1)$ prime-permuted codes now support CIK by means of transmitting a wavelength-conjugate codeword for every data bit 0, resulting in code-performance improvement [18, 19]. In addition, the "+1" elements of the time-spreading bipolar codewords are transmitted with multiwavelength codewords, and the "−1" elements are transmitted with their wavelength-conjugates. To ensure zero interference among the multiwavelength codewords, each bipolar codeword used in wavelength hopping must have equal numbers of "+1" and "−1" elements. Nevertheless, there is no such requirement in the OOK-based prime-permuted codewords because nothing is transmitted for data bit 0s. While the maximal-length sequences do not satisfy this requirement, modified maximal-length sequences and Walsh codes do.

Shown in Table 5.10 are the seven modified maximal-length sequences of length 8, which are generated by padding an extra "−1" to the end of the maximal-length sequence $(+1, +1, +1, -1, -1, +1, -1)$ and its six cyclic-shifted copies [2]. Also shown are the wavelength mappings of the multiwavelength codewords, C_i, in accordance with the locations of the "+1" elements in the sequences, whereas $\overline{C}_i$ denotes the wavelength-conjugate of C_i for $i = \{0, 1, 2, \ldots, 6\}$. The Walsh code of length 8 is also shown in Table 5.10. For both cases, $L = 8$ wavelengths $\{\lambda_1, \lambda_2, \ldots, \lambda_8\}$ are needed.

To select suitable time-spreading bipolar codes, their "even" and "odd" correlation functions, which are distinguished by the four possible patterns of two consecutive data bits, are considered [44]. The even definition represents the case of receiving two consecutive bit 1s or 0s. The odd definition represents the case of receiving a bit 1 followed by a bit 0, or vice versa. A suitable candidate is the family of Barker sequences because they have even and odd autocorrelation sidelobes of at most 1. The Barker sequences of length 3, 5, 7, 11, and 13 are given as $(+1, +1, -1)$, $(+1, +1, +1, -1, +1)$, $(+1, +1, +1, -1, -1, +1, -1)$, $(+1, +1, +1, -1, -1, -1, +1, -1, -1, +1, -1)$, and $(+1, +1, +1, +1, +1, -1, -1, +1, +1, -1, +1, -1, +1)$, respectively [44].

To generate the CIK-based prime-permuted codes, the multiwavelength bipolar codes are permuted onto the time slots of the time-spreading bipolar codes of length N and the permutation patterns are controlled by the p^2 shifted prime sequences over $GF(p)$ of a prime p, where $N \leq p$ [13, 18, 19].

TABLE 5.10
Multiwavelength Codes and Their Wavelength-Conjugates, Based on the Modified Maximal-Length Sequences and Walsh Code of Length 8

Modified Maximal-Length Sequences	Wavelengths	Wavelengths
$(+1,+1,+1,-1,-1,+1,-1,-1)$	$C_0 = \lambda_1\lambda_2\lambda_3\lambda_6$	$\overline{C}_0 = \lambda_4\lambda_5\lambda_7\lambda_8$
$(-1,+1,+1,+1,-1,-1,+1,-1)$	$C_1 = \lambda_2\lambda_3\lambda_4\lambda_7$	$\overline{C}_1 = \lambda_1\lambda_5\lambda_6\lambda_8$
$(+1,-1,+1,+1,+1,-1,-1,-1)$	$C_2 = \lambda_1\lambda_3\lambda_4\lambda_5$	$\overline{C}_2 = \lambda_2\lambda_6\lambda_7\lambda_8$
$(-1,+1,-1,+1,+1,+1,-1,-1)$	$C_3 = \lambda_2\lambda_4\lambda_5\lambda_6$	$\overline{C}_3 = \lambda_1\lambda_3\lambda_7\lambda_8$
$(-1,-1,+1,-1,+1,+1,+1,-1)$	$C_4 = \lambda_3\lambda_5\lambda_6\lambda_7$	$\overline{C}_4 = \lambda_1\lambda_2\lambda_4\lambda_8$
$(+1,-1,-1,+1,-1,+1,+1,-1)$	$C_5 = \lambda_1\lambda_4\lambda_6\lambda_7$	$\overline{C}_5 = \lambda_2\lambda_3\lambda_5\lambda_8$
$(+1,+1,-1,-1,+1,-1,+1,-1)$	$C_6 = \lambda_1\lambda_2\lambda_5\lambda_7$	$\overline{C}_6 = \lambda_3\lambda_4\lambda_6\lambda_8$

Walsh Code	Wavelengths	Wavelengths
$(+1,-1,+1,-1,+1,-1,+1,-1)$	$C_0 = \lambda_1\lambda_3\lambda_5\lambda_7$	$\overline{C}_0 = \lambda_2\lambda_4\lambda_6\lambda_8$
$(+1,+1,-1,-1,+1,+1,-1,-1)$	$C_1 = \lambda_1\lambda_2\lambda_5\lambda_6$	$\overline{C}_1 = \lambda_3\lambda_4\lambda_7\lambda_8$
$(+1,-1,-1,+1,+1,-1,-1,+1)$	$C_2 = \lambda_1\lambda_4\lambda_5\lambda_8$	$\overline{C}_2 = \lambda_2\lambda_3\lambda_6\lambda_7$
$(+1,+1,+1,+1,-1,-1,-1,-1)$	$C_3 = \lambda_1\lambda_2\lambda_3\lambda_4$	$\overline{C}_3 = \lambda_5\lambda_6\lambda_7\lambda_8$
$(+1,-1,+1,-1,-1,+1,-1,+1)$	$C_4 = \lambda_1\lambda_3\lambda_6\lambda_8$	$\overline{C}_4 = \lambda_2\lambda_4\lambda_5\lambda_7$
$(+1,+1,-1,-1,-1,-1,+1,+1)$	$C_5 = \lambda_1\lambda_2\lambda_7\lambda_8$	$\overline{C}_5 = \lambda_3\lambda_4\lambda_5\lambda_6$
$(+1,-1,-1,+1,-1,+1,+1,-1)$	$C_6 = \lambda_1\lambda_4\lambda_6\lambda_7$	$\overline{C}_6 = \lambda_2\lambda_3\lambda_5\lambda_8$

Shown in Table 5.11 is the $(8 \times 5, 5, 1, 1)$ prime-permuted code generated using the shifted prime sequences over GF(7) in Table 5.3; 7 multiwavelength codewords of length 8, such as the modified maximal-length sequences or Walsh code in Table 5.10; and the time-spreading Barker sequence $(+1,+1,+1,-1,+1)$ of length 5. As illustrated in Figure 5.22(b), the "$+1$" and "-1" elements of the Barker sequence are represented by multiwavelength codewords, C_i's and $\overline{C}_i$'s, correspondingly, where the index $i = \{0,1,\ldots,6\}$ is determined by the elements of the shifted prime sequences. For CIK, the code in Table 5.11 is for the transmission of data bit 1s, a wavelength-conjugate form is used to transmit data bit 0s. For example, if codeword $C_0C_1C_2\overline{C}_3C_4$ are transmitted for a bit 1, the wavelength-conjugates, $\overline{C}_0\overline{C}_1\overline{C}_2C_3\overline{C}_4$, are transmitted for a bit 0.

Theorem 5.19

The autocorrelation peaks of the $(L \times N, w, 1, 1)$ prime-permuted codes over GF(p) of a prime p with the time-spreading bipolar codes are equal to w, where $w = N \leq p$. The absolute values of the autocorrelation sidelobes and periodic cross-correlation functions of the codes are both at most 1 only if the time-spreading bipolar codes

TABLE 5.11

CIK-based $(8 \times 5, 5, 1, 1)$ Prime-Permuted Code over GF(7), Based on the Multiwavelength Codes in Table 5.10 and Time-Spreading Barker Sequence $(+1, +1, +1, -1, +1)$

Group $i = 0$	Group $i = 1$	Group $i = 2$	Group $i = 3$	$\cdots$	Group $i = 6$
$C_0C_0C_0\overline{C}_0C_0$	$C_0C_1C_2\overline{C}_3C_4$	$C_0C_2C_4\overline{C}_6C_1$	$C_0C_3C_6\overline{C}_2C_5$	$\cdots$	$C_0C_6C_5\overline{C}_4C_3$
$C_1C_1C_1\overline{C}_1C_1$	$C_1C_2C_3\overline{C}_4C_5$	$C_1C_3C_5\overline{C}_0C_2$	$C_1C_4C_0\overline{C}_3C_6$	$\cdots$	$C_1C_0C_6\overline{C}_5C_4$
$C_2C_2C_2\overline{C}_2C_2$	$C_2C_3C_4\overline{C}_5C_6$	$C_2C_4C_6\overline{C}_1C_3$	$C_2C_5C_1\overline{C}_4C_0$	$\cdots$	$C_2C_1C_0\overline{C}_6C_5$
$C_3C_3C_3\overline{C}_3C_3$	$C_3C_4C_5\overline{C}_6C_0$	$C_3C_5C_0\overline{C}_2C_4$	$C_3C_6C_2\overline{C}_5C_1$	$\cdots$	$C_3C_2C_1\overline{C}_0C_6$
$C_4C_4C_4\overline{C}_4C_4$	$C_4C_5C_6\overline{C}_0C_1$	$C_4C_6C_1\overline{C}_3C_5$	$C_4C_0C_3\overline{C}_6C_2$	$\cdots$	$C_4C_3C_2\overline{C}_1C_0$
$C_5C_5C_5\overline{C}_5C_5$	$C_5C_6C_0\overline{C}_1C_2$	$C_5C_0C_2\overline{C}_4C_6$	$C_5C_1C_4\overline{C}_0C_3$	$\cdots$	$C_5C_4C_3\overline{C}_2C_1$
$C_6C_6C_6\overline{C}_6C_6$	$C_6C_0C_1\overline{C}_2C_3$	$C_6C_1C_3\overline{C}_5C_0$	$C_6C_2C_5\overline{C}_1C_4$	$\cdots$	$C_6C_5C_4\overline{C}_3C_2$

have even and odd autocorrelation sidelobes bounded by 1 [13, 18, 19].

Proof The periodic cross-correlation function of any two 2-D prime-permuted codewords coming from different groups of the shifted prime sequences follows that of the shifted prime sequences, which is at most 1. The periodic cross-correlation function of any two prime-permuted codewords coming from the same group follows the autocorrelation sidelobe of the time-spreading bipolar codes, which is at most 1. The autocorrelation sidelobes of the prime-permuted codewords coming from group $i = 0$ follow that of the time-spreading bipolar codes. Because the multiwavelength codewords in each of the prime-permuted codewords coming from groups $i = \{1, 2, \ldots, p - 1\}$ are all distinct, the autocorrelation sidelobes become 0. Finally, the autocorrelation peaks of w are due to the code weight $w = N \leq p$. ■

According to Theorem 5.19, the requirement of having low periodic cross-correlation functions in the CIK-based prime-permuted codes is to use time-spreading bipolar codes with low even and odd autocorrelation sidelobes. So, Gold sequences, which have good autocorrelation properties can also be used in place of Barker sequences. Gold sequences of length N can produce $N + 2$ codewords with three cross-correlation values: -1, $-f(s)$, and $f(s) - 2$, where $f(s) = 2^{(s+1)/2} + 1$ for an odd integer s but $f(s) = 2^{(s+2)/2} + 1$ for an even s, and $s > 0$ is the maximum degree of the generator polynomial used to generate Gold sequences [44]. For example, the nine Gold sequences of length 7 are $(+1, +1, -1, +1, -1, -1, -1)$, $(+1, +1, -1, -1, -1, +1, -1)$, $(+1, +1, +1, -1, +1, -1, +1)$, $(+1, -1, +1, -1, -1, +1, -1)$, $(-1, -1, +1, +1, +1, -1, -1)$, $(-1, -1, -1, -1, -1, -1, +1)$, $(-1, +1, +1, +1, -1, +1, +1)$, $(+1, -1, -1, +1, +1, +1, +1)$, and $(-1, +1, -1, -1, +1, +1, -1)$.

Listed in Table 5.12 are the $(8 \times 7, 7, 1, 1)$ prime-permuted code generated by

TABLE 5.12

CIK-Based $(8 \times 7, 7, 1, 1)$ Prime-Permuted Code over GF(7), Based on the Multiwavelength Codes in Table 5.10 and Time-Spreading Gold Sequence $(+1, +1, +1, -1, +1, -1, +1)$

Group $i = 0$	Group $i = 1$	Group $i = 2$	$\cdots$	Group $i = 6$
$C_0 C_0 C_0 \overline{C}_0 C_0 \overline{C}_0 C_0$	$C_0 C_1 C_2 \overline{C}_3 C_4 \overline{C}_5 C_6$	$C_0 C_2 C_4 \overline{C}_6 C_1 \overline{C}_3 C_5$	$\cdots$	$C_0 C_6 C_5 \overline{C}_4 C_3 \overline{C}_2 C_1$
$C_1 C_1 C_1 \overline{C}_1 C_1 \overline{C}_1 C_1$	$C_1 C_2 C_3 \overline{C}_4 C_5 \overline{C}_6 C_0$	$C_1 C_3 C_5 \overline{C}_0 C_2 \overline{C}_4 C_6$	$\cdots$	$C_1 C_0 C_6 \overline{C}_5 C_4 \overline{C}_3 C_2$
$C_2 C_2 C_2 \overline{C}_2 C_2 \overline{C}_2 C_2$	$C_2 C_3 C_4 \overline{C}_5 C_6 \overline{C}_0 C_1$	$C_2 C_4 C_6 \overline{C}_1 C_3 \overline{C}_5 C_0$	$\cdots$	$C_2 C_1 C_0 \overline{C}_6 C_5 \overline{C}_4 C_3$
$C_3 C_3 C_3 \overline{C}_3 C_3 \overline{C}_3 C_3$	$C_3 C_4 C_5 \overline{C}_6 C_0 \overline{C}_1 C_2$	$C_3 C_5 C_0 \overline{C}_2 C_4 \overline{C}_6 C_1$	$\cdots$	$C_3 C_2 C_1 \overline{C}_0 C_6 \overline{C}_5 C_4$
$C_4 C_4 C_4 \overline{C}_4 C_4 \overline{C}_4 C_4$	$C_4 C_5 C_6 \overline{C}_0 C_1 \overline{C}_2 C_3$	$C_4 C_6 C_1 \overline{C}_3 C_5 \overline{C}_0 C_2$	$\cdots$	$C_4 C_3 C_2 \overline{C}_1 C_0 \overline{C}_6 C_5$
$C_5 C_5 C_5 \overline{C}_5 C_5 \overline{C}_5 C_5$	$C_5 C_6 C_0 \overline{C}_1 C_2 \overline{C}_3 C_4$	$C_5 C_0 C_2 \overline{C}_4 C_6 \overline{C}_1 C_3$	$\cdots$	$C_5 C_4 C_3 \overline{C}_2 C_1 \overline{C}_0 C_6$
$C_6 C_6 C_6 \overline{C}_6 C_6 \overline{C}_6 C_6$	$C_6 C_0 C_1 \overline{C}_2 C_3 \overline{C}_4 C_5$	$C_6 C_1 C_3 \overline{C}_5 C_0 \overline{C}_2 C_4$	$\cdots$	$C_6 C_5 C_4 \overline{C}_3 C_2 \overline{C}_1 C_0$

using the shifted prime sequences over GF(7) in Table 5.3; 7 multiwavelength codewords of length 8, such as the modified maximal-length sequences or Walsh code in Table 5.10; and time-spreading Gold sequence $(+1,+1,+1,-1,+1,-1,+1)$. For CIK, the code in Table 5.12 is for the transmission of data bit 1s, its wavelength-conjugates is used for transmitting data bit 0s. For example, if codeword $C_0 C_6 C_5 \overline{C}_4 C_3 \overline{C}_2 C_1$ are transmitted for a bit 1, the wavelength-conjugate $\overline{C}_0 \overline{C}_6 \overline{C}_5 C_4 \overline{C}_3 C_2 \overline{C}_1$ is for a bit 0. Because there are 9 Gold sequences of length 7, the same permutation algorithm used in Table 5.12 can also be applied to the other 8 Gold sequences and the overall cardinality of the CIK-based prime-permuted code in this example becomes $9 \times 49 = 441$.

Similar to the OOK-based counterparts, the overall cardinality of these CIK-based prime-permuted codes depends on the number of valid groups, Φ_{group}, of the shifted prime sequences over GF(p), the number of multiwavelength codewords Φ_λ, and the cardinality of the time-spreading bipolar codes Φ_{bipolar}. The best overall cardinality is achieved when p is a prime number or a power of a prime number. In such cases, Φ_λ is equal to p and matches the number of shifted prime sequences in each group. So, all p groups (of p shifted prime sequences in each group) can be used for wavelength permutation (e.g., see Tables 5.11 and 5.12). The permutation algorithm also works with a non-prime p but with reduced cardinality, as explained in the OOK-based prime-permuted codes and Section 5.7.

In summary, the overall cardinality of these CIK-based $(L \times N, w, 1, 1)$ prime-permuted codes is given by [13, 18, 19]

$$\Phi_{\text{overall}} = \Phi_{\text{group}} \Phi_\lambda \Phi_{\text{bipolar}} \leq p^2 \Phi_{\text{bipolar}}$$

where $\Phi_{\text{bipolar}} = N + 2$ for the time-spreading Gold sequences of length N, and $\Phi_{\text{bipolar}} = 1$ for any time-spreading Barker sequence.

5.8.1 Performance Analysis

For the OOK-based 2-D $(L \times N, w, 1, 1)$ prime-permuted codes over GF(p) of a prime p with the time-spreading $(N, w, 1, 1)$ OOCs of cardinality $\Phi_{(N,w,1,1)OOC} = (N-1)/[w(w-1)]$, the chip-synchronous, hard-limiting error probability follows Equation (5.15). The hit probabilities, q_j, of having the periodic cross-correlation values of $j = \{0, 1\}$ (in the sampling time) follow Theorem 5.15 because $(N, w, 1, 1)$ OOCs are also used for time spreading.

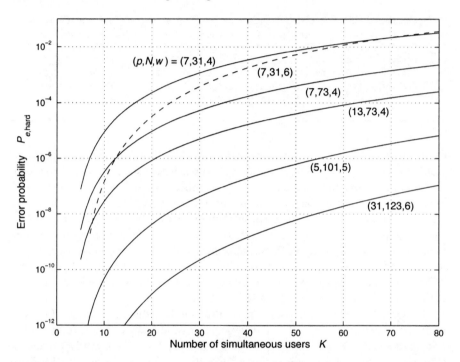

FIGURE 5.23 Chip-synchronous, hard-limiting error probabilities of the OOK-based $(p \times N, w, 1, 1)$ prime-permuted codes with the $(N, w, 1, 1)$ OOCs for various N, w, and p.

Figure 5.23 plots the chip-synchronous, hard-limiting error probabilities of the OOK-based $(L \times N, w, 1, 1)$ prime-permuted codes with the time-spreading $(N, w, 1, 1)$ OOCs against the number of simultaneous users K for length $N = \{31, 73, 101, 123\}$, weight $w = \{4, 5, 6\}$, and number of wavelengths $L = p = \{5, 7, 13, 31\}$. In general, the error probabilities improve as p, w, or N increases because of higher autocorrelation peaks or lower hit probabilities. However, the error probabilities get worse as K increases due to stronger mutual interference. The $(7, 31, 4)$- and $(7, 73, 4)$-curves indicate that error probability is a relatively strong function of N. When K is small, both curves differ by more than two orders of magnitude in error probability. From the $(7, 31, 4)$- and $(7, 31, 6)$-curves, the performance improvement due to the increment of w is only noticeable when K is small. These two curves converge as K increases because interference gets stronger and overshadows the improvement caused by the increment of w. The $(7,73,4)$- and $(13,73,4)$-curves show performance improvement by solely increasing $p = 7$ to $p = 13$. Because p is related to the number of wavelengths and also the number of multiwavelength codewords, the one-hit probability q_1 gets smaller when p gets larger. The $(7,31,6)$-curve has better performance than the $(7,73,4)$-curve, and w becomes a dominating factor when K is small. However, the advantage of using $w = 6$ diminishes and N plays a more important role when the amount of interference increases even slightly.

Theorem 5.20

The chip-synchronous, soft-limiting error probability of the CIK-based 2-D ($L \times N, w, 1, 1$) prime-permuted codes over GF(p) of a prime p with $L = p + 1$ wavelengths and the time-spreading Barker sequence of length $N = w \le p$ is formulated as [13, 18, 19]

$$
P_e = \frac{1}{2} \left[\sum_{i_{-1} > i_{+1} + N} \Pr(i_{+1}, i_{-1}) + \frac{1}{2} \sum_{i_{-1} = i_{+1} + N} \Pr(i_{+1}, i_{-1}) \right]
$$
$$
+ \frac{1}{2} \left[\sum_{i_{+1} > i_{-1} + N} \Pr(i_{+1}, i_{-1}) + \frac{1}{2} \sum_{i_{+1} = i_{-1} + N} \Pr(i_{+1}, i_{-1}) \right]
$$

where the number of simultaneous users $K > i_{+1} + i_{-1}$,

$$
\Pr(i_{+1}, i_{-1}) = \frac{(K-1)!}{i_{+1}! i_{-1}! (K - 1 - i_{+1} - i_{-1})!} q_{+1}^{i_{+1}} q_{-1}^{i_{-1}} (1 - q_{+1} - q_{-1})^{K - 1 - i_{+1} - i_{-1}}
$$

and the hit probabilities of having the periodic cross-correlation values of "+1" and "−1" (in the sampling time) are given by

$$
q_{+1} = q_{-1} = \frac{pN + N - 1}{2p(p+1)}
$$

Proof In the CIK-based prime-permuted codes, there are two sources of mutual interference. One source is from the time-spreading bipolar codes and another source is from the multiwavelength bipolar codes. Let $q_{1,(0)}$ and $q_{1,(i)}$ denote the probabilities of getting one hit in the sampling time of the periodic cross-correlation functions between the prime-permuted codeword (address signature of a receiver) coming from group $i = 0$ and groups $i = \{1, 2, \ldots, p - 1\}$, respectively, and an interfering prime-permuted codeword.

Because the prime-permuted codewords coming from group $i = 0$ consists of distinct multiwavelength codewords, the interference caused by the multiwavelength codewords are always 0. So,

$$q_{1,(0)} = \frac{p^2 - p}{p^2 - 1} \times \frac{N}{p} = \frac{N}{p+1}$$

where the factor $1/2$ is not needed due to CIK. The term $p^2 - p$ represents the number of prime-permuted codewords coming from group $i = 0$, in which they have zero cross-correlation values due to distinct multiwavelength codewords. The denominator $p^2 - 1$ represents the number of possible interfering codewords. The factor N/p accounts for the number of elements, out of a total of p elements, in each shifted prime sequence used to generate the prime-permuted codes due to code weight $w = N \leq p$.

Similarly, for the address codeword originating from groups $i = \{1, 2, \ldots, p - 1\}$,

$$\begin{aligned} q_{1,(i)} &= \frac{p^2 - 2p}{p^2 - 1} \times \frac{N}{p} + \frac{p}{p^2 - 1} \times \frac{N}{p} + \frac{p - 1}{p^2 - 1} \times \frac{N(N - 1)}{p - 1} \times \frac{1}{N} \\ &= \frac{Np - 1}{p^2 - 1} \end{aligned}$$

The first product term accounts for the hit probability when the interfering codeword comes from a different group, excluding group $i = 0$, than that of the address codeword. The second product term accounts for the hit probability when the interfering codeword comes from group $i = 0$. The third product term accounts for the hit probability when the interfering codewoed comes from the same group as that of the address codeword.

By combining these one-hit probabilities with the cross-correlation property of the time-spreading Barker sequence, the periodic cross-correlation function between any two CIK-based prime-permuted codewords can be either "+1" and "−1," and their corresponding hit probabilities are given by

$$q_{+1} = q_{-1} = \frac{1}{2} \left[\frac{1}{p} q_{1,(0)} + \frac{p - 1}{p} q_{1,(i)} \right] = \frac{pN + N - 1}{2p(p + 1)}$$

where the factor $1/2$ comes from the assumption of equiprobable data bit-1 and bit-0 transmissions.

A decision error occurs when a data bit-1 is received but the receiver output is less than or equal to 0, or when a data bit-0 is received but the receiver output is larger than or equal to 0. So, the probability of having a certain cross-correlation value for a given number of interfering codewords i_{+1} contributing "+1"-hits and a given number of interfering codewords i_{-1} contributing "−1"-hits follows a trinomial distribution and is given as $\Pr(i_{+1}, i_{-1})$ in the theorem. Furthermore, the chip-synchronous, soft-limiting error probability is given by $P_e = (1/2)\Pr(\text{error}|\text{data bit } 1) + (1/2)\Pr(\text{error}|\text{data bit } 0)$. The final form of P_e in the theorem is derived after some manipulations, where the factor $1/2$ in the second summations of the two brackets is due to identical probability of deciding a bit-1 and bit-0 in the receiver. ∎

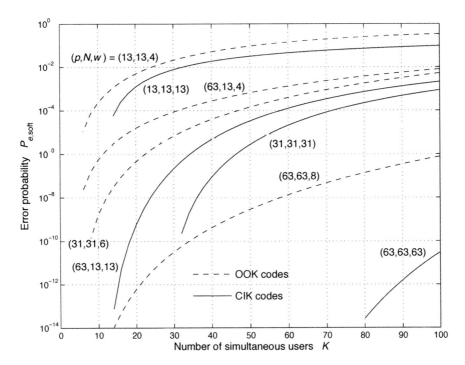

FIGURE 5.24 Chip-synchronous, soft-limiting error probabilities of the CIK-based $(L \times N, w, 1, 1)$ prime-permuted codes with the time-spreading Barker sequence of length $N = w$ and the OOK-based $(L \times N, w, 1, 1)$ prime-permuted codes with the time-spreading $(N, w, 1, 1)$ OOCs for $L = p + 1$ and various N, w, and p.

Figure 5.24 plots the chip-synchronous, soft-limiting error probabilities of the CIK-based $(L \times N, w, 1, 1)$ prime-permuted codes with the time-spreading Barker sequence of length $N = w$ and the OOK-based $(L \times N, w, 1, 1)$ prime-permuted codes with the time-spreading $(N, w, 1, 1)$ OOCs against the number of simultaneous users K for length $N = \{13, 31, 63\}$, weight $w = \{4, 8, 13, 31, 63\}$, and number of wavelengths $L = p + 1$, where $p = \{13, 31, 63\}$. The chip-synchronous, soft-limiting error probability of the OOK-based codes is given in Equation (5.1) with q_1 from Theorem 5.15. To have a fair comparison, the code parameters are chosen such that the bandwidth expansion LN and overall cardinality of both code families are as identical as possible. So, $\Phi_{(N,w,1,1)OOC} = 1$ and length $N = p$ are assumed in the time-spreading $(N, w, 1, 1)$ OOCs, and weight w is chosen to be the largest integer satisfying the cardinality bound, which is given as $w(w-1) \leq (N-1)/\Phi_{(N,w,1,1)OOC}$. In general, the error probabilities improve as N, w, or p increases because of higher autocorrelation peaks or lower hit probabilities. However, the error probabilities get worse as K increases due to stronger mutual interference. The CIK-based codes always outperform the OOK-based codes. This is because the weight of the former is equal to its length, while the weight of the latter is always less than its length. Heavier weight means higher autocorrelation peaks and better discrimination against mutual interference. However, the trade-off is the requirement of transmission on every time slot and data bit.

Because the cross-correlation functions of Gold sequences are not fixed, Gaussian approximation is here used to compute the soft-limiting error probability of the CIK-based $(L \times N, w, 1, 1)$ prime-permuted codes with the time-spreading Gold sequences.

Theorem 5.21

For the CIK-based 2-D $(L \times N, w, 1, 1)$ prime-permuted codes over $GF(p)$ of a prime p with $L = p + 1$ wavelengths and the time-spreading Gold sequences of length $N = w \leq p$ and cardinality $\Phi_{\text{bipolar}} = N + 2$, the Gaussian error probability is given by [44]

$$P_{e,\text{Gaussian}} = Q\left(\sqrt{\text{SIR}}\right) = Q\left(\sqrt{\frac{N^2}{(K-1)\sigma^2}}\right)$$

according to Section 1.8.2, where $Q(x) = (2\pi)^{-1/2} \int_x^\infty \exp(-y^2/2) dy$ is the complementary error function and the signal-to-interference power ratio (SIR) is defined as the ratio of the autocorrelation peak, which is equal to N in this case, squared to the total interference variance $(K-1)\sigma^2$. By the Central Limit Theorem, this approximation is valid for a large number of simultaneous users K.

The chip-asynchronous and chip-synchronous interference variances contributed by each interfering codeword are formulated as [19]

$$\sigma_{\text{asyn}}^2 \approx \frac{2[(N+2)(N+p^3-p)+1-N-p]}{3p^3(N+2)-3p}$$

$$\sigma_{\text{syn}}^2 \approx \frac{(N+2)(N+p^3-p)+1-N-p}{p^3(N+2)-p}$$

Proof According to [44, Equation (10.15)] and [45], the chip-asynchronous interference variance contributed by each interfering codeword can be generally approximated as

$$\sigma_{\text{asyn,general}}^2 \approx \frac{2}{3N} \sum_{\tau=-(N-1)}^{N-1} \left|\Theta_{\mathbf{x},\mathbf{x}'}(\tau)\right|^2$$

in which $\Theta_{\mathbf{x},\mathbf{x}'}(\tau)$ is the discrete periodic cross-correlation function between two distinct CIK-based prime-permuted codewords, $\mathbf{x} = [\mathbf{x}_0\ \mathbf{x}_1\ \dots\ \mathbf{x}_j\ \dots\ \mathbf{x}_{N-1}]$ and $\mathbf{x}' = [\mathbf{x}'_0\ \mathbf{x}'_1\ \dots\ \mathbf{x}'_j\ \dots\ \mathbf{x}'_{N-1}]$, in matrix form, with a τ-shift and given by [46]

$$\Theta_{\mathbf{x},\mathbf{x}'}(\tau) = \begin{cases} \frac{1}{L}\sum_{j=0}^{N-1-\tau}[\mathbf{x}'_j]^T\mathbf{x}_{j+\tau} & \text{for } 0 \leq \tau \leq N-1 \\ \frac{1}{L}\sum_{j=0}^{N-1+\tau}[\mathbf{x}'_{j-\tau}]^T\mathbf{x}_j & \text{for } -(N-1) \leq \tau \leq 0 \\ 0 & \text{otherwise} \end{cases}$$

The column vectors $\mathbf{x}_j$ and $\mathbf{x}_j'$ represent the multiwavelength bipolar codewords located in the jth time slots of $\mathbf{x}$ and $\mathbf{x}'$, respectively. If $\mathbf{x} = \mathbf{x}'$, $\Theta_{\mathbf{x},\mathbf{x}}(\tau)$ becomes the discrete autocorrelation function of $\mathbf{x}$ and the autocorrelation peak is located at $\tau = 0$. The factor $1/L$ is used to normalize the cross-correlation function as each of the column vectors $\mathbf{x}_j$ and $\mathbf{x}_j'$ carries L wavelengths.

Let $\sigma_{\text{asyn},0}^2$ and $\sigma_{\text{asyn},i}^2$ denote the chip-asynchronous interference variances seen by a receiver with the address codeword originating from group $i = 0$ and groups $i = \{1, 2, \ldots, p-1\}$, respectively. So,

$$\sigma_{\text{asyn},0}^2 \approx \frac{2N}{3} \times \frac{\Phi_{\text{bipolar}} - 1}{p^2 \Phi_{\text{bipolar}} - 1} + \frac{2}{3} \times \frac{\Phi_{\text{bipolar}}(p^2 - p)}{p^2 \Phi_{\text{bipolar}} - 1}$$

where the denominator $\Phi_{\text{bipolar}} p^2 - 1$ represents the number of possible interfering codewords and $\Phi_{\text{bipolar}} = N + 2$ for the time-spreading Gold sequences of length $N \leq p$. The first product term accounts for the variance of interference created by the time-spreading Gold sequences when the address and interfering codewords are from group $i = 0$. The term $2N/3$ comes from the calculation of $\sigma_{\text{asyn,general}}^2$, in which the discrete cross-correlation value of Gold sequences is equal to $|\Theta_{\mathbf{x},\mathbf{x}}(\tau)|^2 = N^2$ [44]. The second product term accounts for the variance of interference created by the shifted prime sequences when the address and interfering codewords are from different groups. The term $2/3$ comes from the calculation of $\sigma_{\text{asyn,general}}^2$, in which $|\Theta_{\mathbf{x},\mathbf{x}}(\tau)|^2 = N$ because the cross-correlation functions of the shifted prime sequences from different groups are at most 1. The term $p^2 - p$ is due to p groups of p shifted prime sequences in each group.

Similarly, for the address codeword originating from groups $i = \{1, 2, \ldots, p-1\}$,

$$\sigma_{\text{asyn},i}^2 \approx \frac{2}{3} \times \frac{p-1}{\Phi_{\text{bipolar}} p^2 - 1} + \frac{2}{3} \times \frac{(\Phi_{\text{bipolar}} - 1)p}{p^2 \Phi_{\text{bipolar}} - 1} + \frac{2}{3} \times \frac{\Phi_{\text{bipolar}}(p^2 - p)}{p^2 \Phi_{\text{bipolar}} - 1}$$

The first product term accounts for the variance of interference created by the autocorrelation sidelobes of the time-spreading Gold sequences and the shifted prime sequences when the address and interfering codewords are from the same group $i = \{1, 2, \ldots, p-1\}$ and the same Gold sequence. From [44], the maximum autocorrelation sidelobe of Gold sequences contributes $|\Theta_{\mathbf{x},\mathbf{x}}(\tau)|^2 = N^2$. Also, the use of the p shifted prime sequences in the same group requires the variance being scaled by $1/N$. These give the factor $2/3$ in the first product term. The second product term accounts for the variance of interference created by the cross-correlation functions of Gold sequences and the shifted prime sequences when the address and interfering codewords are from the same group $i = \{1, 2, \ldots, p-1\}$ but different Gold sequences. So, the derivation follows the rationale used for the first product term in $\sigma_{\text{asyn},0}$. Also, the variance is scaled by $1/N$ due to the use of the shifted prime sequences in the same group. Finally, the derivation of the last product term follows the rationale used for the last product term in $\sigma_{\text{asyn},0}$ because both terms account for the case when the address and interfering codewords are from different groups of the shifted prime sequences.

By combining all groups, the chip-asynchronous variance is given by $\sigma_{asyn}^2 = (1/p)\sigma_{asyn,0}^2 + [(p-1)/p]\sigma_{asyn,i}^2$, and the final form in the theorem is derived after some manipulations.

According to Section 1.8.5, for optical codes with the maximum periodic cross-correlation function of 1, the chip-synchronous and chip-asynchronous interference variances can be related by [1]

$$\sigma_{syn}^2 \approx \frac{3}{2}\sigma_{asyn}^2$$

Alternatively, because the chip-synchronous variance can generally be defined as [44]

$$\sigma_{syn,general}^2 \approx \frac{1}{N}\sum_{\tau=-(N-1)}^{N-1} |\Theta_{x,x'}(\tau)|^2$$

the variance is also found to be $3/2$ of the chip-asynchronous variance by following the rationale used for the derivation of σ_{asyn}^2. ∎

Figure 5.25 plots the chip-asynchronous and chip-synchronous, Gaussian-approximated error probabilities of the CIK-based $(L \times N, w, 1, 1)$ prime-permuted codes with the time-spreading Gold sequences of length N against the number of simultaneous users K for $L = p+1$ and $N = w = p = \{7, 31, 63\}$. In general, the error probabilities improve as p increases because of lower hit probabilities and higher autocorrelation peaks. However, the error probabilities get worse as K increases due to stronger mutual interference. The chip-asynchronous case always performs better than the chip-synchronous case because the chip-asynchronous variances are equal to two-thirds of the chip-synchronous variances. The performance difference increases with p. Also plotted in Figure 5.25 are the computer-simulation results, which closely match the theoretical results. The computer simulation is performed by randomly assigning each simultaneous user one of the prime-permuted codes in the code set, and CIK modulation is used for transmitting each data bit 1 and 0 with a codeword and its wavelength-conjugate, respectively. The total number of data bits involved in the simulation is at least 100 times the reciprocal of the target error probability in order to provide enough iterations.

To have a fair comparison, Gaussian approximation is here applied to the CIK-based prime-permuted codes with the time-spreading Barker sequence. Because there is only one Barker sequence of any length and the autocorrelation sidelobes of each Barker sequence is at most 1, the chip-synchronous interference variance of the CIK-based $(L \times N, w, 1, 1)$ prime-permuted codes with Barker sequence of length $N \leq p$ is formulated as

$$\begin{aligned}
\sigma_{syn,Barker}^2 &= \frac{1}{p} \times \frac{p^2-p}{p^2-1} \times \frac{N}{p} + \frac{p-1}{p} \times \left[\frac{p-1}{N(p^2-1)} + \frac{p^2-p}{p^2-1} \times \frac{N}{p}\right] \\
&= \frac{N^2p+p-1}{Np(p+1)}
\end{aligned}$$

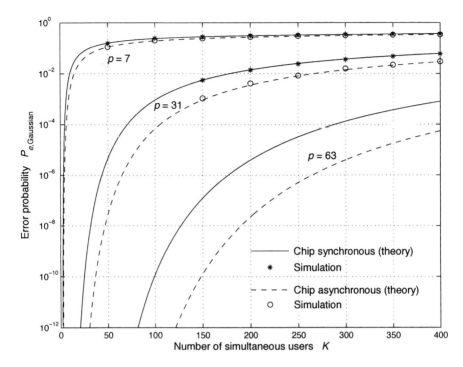

FIGURE 5.25 Chip-synchronous and chip-asynchronous, Gaussian error probabilities of the CIK-based $(L \times N, w, 1, 1)$ prime-permuted codes with the Gold sequences for $L = p + 1$ and $N = w = p = \{7, 31, 63\}$.

by following the proof of Theorem 5.21 with $\Phi_{\text{bipolar}} = 1$. The first product term accounts for the case when the address codeword comes from group $i = 0$ of the shifted prime sequences. Because the codewords in group $i = 0$ are orthogonal, interference is created by the interfering codewords in other groups. The term N/p is the fraction of codewords that have non-zero cross-correlation values in the shifted prime sequences when the address and interfering codewords are from different groups. The second product term accounts for the case when the address codeword comes from groups $i = \{1, 2, \ldots, p - 1\}$. The first term inside the brackets is for the interfering codeword coming from a different group than that of the address codeword. The factor $1/N$ accounts for N possible time-shifts in a codeword of length N. The second term in the brackets is for the interfering codeword coming from the same group as that of the address codeword.

For example, the chip-synchronous variances of the CIK-based $(L \times N, w, 1, 1)$ prime-permuted codes with $L = p + 1$ and the Barker and Gold sequences of length $N = p$ are computed as $\sigma_{\text{syn}}^2 = 0.8903$ and 0.9980 for $p = 7$, $\sigma_{\text{syn}}^2 = 0.9697$ and 0.9997 for $p = 31$, and $\sigma_{\text{syn}}^2 = 0.9846$ and 0.9999 for $p = 63$, respectively. As p increases, the variance of the CIK-based codes with Barker sequences approaches that of the latter and their interference variances get larger. With such small differences in the variances, the performances of both code families are almost identical, while the former support N times more codewords.

5.9 QUADRATIC-CONGRUENCE-PERMUTED CODES

The 2-D $(p \times N, w, \lambda_a, 2)$ QC-permuted codes [22] over $GF(p)$ of a prime p listed in Table 5.2 are constructed by first choosing a family of 1-D $(N, w, \lambda_a, \lambda_c')$ OOCs as the time-spreading codes with the maximum periodic cross-correlation function $\lambda_c' = \{1, 2\}$. Afterward, p wavelengths are assigned to the pulses of these OOCs in accordance with the permutation of wavelength indices determined by shifted QC sequences, $S_{i_2,i_1,l} = (s_{i_2,i_1,l,0}, s_{i_2,i_1,l,1}, \ldots, s_{i_2,i_1,l,j}, \ldots, s_{i_2,i_1,l,p-1})$, with its jth element defined as

$$s_{i_2,i_1,l,j} = i_1 j + i_2 + \frac{lj(j+1)}{2} \quad (\text{mod } p)$$

where i_1, i_2, and $l = \{0, 1, \ldots, p-1\}$ for a prime p. There are p^3 shifted QC sequences over $GF(p)$ and they can be separated into p groups (indexed by l) with p^2 sequences (indexed by i_1 and i_2) per group [23, 35]. Group $l = 0$ contains the p^2 shifted prime sequences over $GF(p)$ (see Section 5.7). A QC-operator, such as $lj(j+1)/2$, is applied to these shifted prime sequences in order to generate the corresponding shifted QC sequences in other groups $l = \{1, 2, \ldots, p-1\}$.

These p^3 shifted QC sequences give p^3 permutations in assigning up to p wavelengths to the pulses of each time-spreading OOC codeword, resulting in an overall cardinality of $p^3 \Phi_{(N,w,\lambda_a,\lambda_c')OOC}$ in the $(p \times N, w, \lambda_a, 2)$ QC-permuted codes with code weight $w \leq p$.

For illustration, Table 5.13 shows the $p^3 = 125$ shifted QC sequences over $GF(5)$, whereas group $l = 0$ contains all 25 shifted prime sequences over $GF(5)$.

Theorem 5.22

The autocorrelation peaks of the $(p \times N, w, \lambda_a, 2)$ QC-permuted codes over $GF(p)$ of a prime p are equal to w, where $w \leq p$. The autocorrelation sidelobes of the codes are at most 1 and 2 if the time-spreading $(N, w, 1, \lambda_c')$ and $(N, w, 2, \lambda_c')$ OOCs are used, respectively, where $\lambda_c' = \{1, 2\}$. By excluding the codewords coming from group $(l = 0, i_1 = 0)$ of the shifted QC sequences, the autocorrelation sidelobes become 0. The periodic cross-correlation functions of the QC-permuted codes are at most 2, but at most 1 only if the correlating codewords come from the time-spreading $(N, w, 1, 2)$ OOCs and the same group $(l = 0, i_1 = 0)$ of the shifted QC sequences [22].

Proof Because pulses in a QC-permuted codeword coming from group $(l = 0, i_1 = 0)$ of the shifted QC sequences are conveyed with the same wavelength, the maximum autocorrelation sidelobe follows that of the time-spreading OOCs. However,

TABLE 5.13
Shifted QC Sequences over GF(5)

Group $l=0$	$i_1=0$	$i_1=1$	$i_1=2$	$i_1=3$	$i_1=4$
$i_2=0$	00000	01234	02413	03142	04321
$i_2=1$	11111	12340	13024	14203	10432
$i_2=2$	22222	23401	24130	20314	21043
$i_2=3$	33333	34012	30214	31420	32104
$i_2=4$	44444	40123	41302	42031	43210
Group $l=1$	$i_1=0$	$i_1=1$	$i_1=2$	$i_1=3$	$i_1=4$
$i_2=0$	01310	02044	03223	04402	00131
$i_2=1$	12421	13100	14334	10013	11242
$i_2=2$	23032	24211	20440	21124	22303
$i_2=3$	34143	30322	31001	32230	33414
$i_2=4$	40204	41433	42112	43341	44020
Group $l=2$	$i_1=0$	$i_1=1$	$i_1=2$	$i_1=3$	$i_1=4$
$i_2=0$	02120	03304	04033	00212	01441
$i_2=1$	13231	14410	10144	11323	12002
$i_2=2$	24342	20021	21200	22434	23113
$i_2=3$	30403	31132	32311	33040	34224
$i_2=4$	41014	42243	43422	44101	40330
Group $l=3$	$i_1=0$	$i_1=1$	$i_1=2$	$i_1=3$	$i_1=4$
$i_2=0$	03430	04114	00343	01022	01441
$i_2=1$	14041	10220	11404	12133	13312
$i_2=2$	20102	21331	22010	23244	24423
$i_2=3$	31213	32442	33121	34300	30034
$i_2=4$	42324	43003	44232	40411	41140
Group $l=4$	$i_1=0$	$i_1=1$	$i_2=2$	$i_2=3$	$i_1=4$
$i_2=0$	04240	00424	01103	02332	03011
$i_2=1$	10301	11030	12214	13443	14122
$i_2=2$	21412	22141	23320	24004	20233
$i_2=3$	32023	33202	34431	30110	31344
$i_2=4$	43134	44313	40042	41221	42400

because pulses in a QC-permuted codeword coming from other groups are conveyed with distinct wavelengths, the autocorrelation sidelobes are equal to 0. The number of shifted QC sequences that can be used for wavelength permutation is reduced to $p^3 - p$ if those in group ($l = 0, i_1 = 0$) are excluded.

The cross-correlation property can be derived by considering two correlating QC-permuted codewords with different compositions of the shifted QC sequences and time-spreading OOCs. If both correlating codewords are from two different time-spreading $(N, w, 2, 2)$ OOC codewords or two different shifted QC sequences (in any same or different groups), the periodic cross-correlation function is at most 2 due to the maximum autocorrelation sidelobe of the OOCs or the maximum cross-correlation function of the shifted QC sequences, whichever is larger.

However, the periodic cross-correlation function is at most 1 only if the two correlating codewords are from two different time-spreading $(N, w, 2, 1)$ OOC codewords or two different shifted QC sequences in the same group ($l = 0, i_1 = 0$). This is because the maximum autocorrelation sidelobe of the OOCs and cross-correlation function of the shifted QC sequences in group ($l = 0, i_1 = 0$) are both at most 1.

The proofs on the autocorrelation and cross-correlation properties of the $(p \times N, w, 1, 2)$ QC-permuted codes follow those of the $(p \times N, w, 2, 2)$ QC-permuted codes by replacing the $(N, w, 2, 1)$ OOCs by the $(N, w, 1, 2)$ OOCs.

Finally, the autocorrelation peaks of w are due to code weight $w \leq p$.   ∎

The number of the shifted QC sequences that can be used in the wavelength permutation is at most p^3. So, the overall cardinality of the $(p \times N, w, \lambda_a, \lambda_c)$ QC-permuted codes of $w \leq p$ is given by

$$\Phi(p \times N, w, \lambda_a, 2) \leq p^3 \Phi_{(N, w, \lambda_a, \lambda_c')OOC}$$

where $\Phi_{(N, w, \lambda_a, \lambda_c')OOC}$ is the cardinality of the time-spreading $(N, w, \lambda_a, \lambda_c')$ OOCs, and some of their cardinalities are listed in Section 5.7. The maximum cardinality of the QC-permuted codes is achieved when p is a prime number by following the reasoning in Sections 5.7 and 5.8.

According to Section 1.6, the cardinality of the 2-D $(p \times N, w, \lambda_a, 2)$ QC-permuted codes is upper-bounded by

$$\begin{aligned}
\Phi(p \times N, w, \lambda_a, 2) &\leq \Phi(p \times N, w, 2, 2) \\
&= \frac{p(pw^2 - 2pw - 1)(pw^2 - 2pw - 2)}{w(w-1)(w-2)}
\end{aligned}$$

where $\Phi_{(N, w, 2, 2)OOC} = w - 3$ and $N = w^2 - 2w$ [33]. The upper bound is $p(pw^2 - 2pw - 1)(pw^2 - 2pw - 2)/[p^3 w(w-1)(w-2)(w-3)]$ times the actual maximum overall cardinality, which is equal to $p^3 \Phi_{(N, w, 2, 2)OOC} = p^3(w - 3)$. This factor is nearly equal to 1 for a large w. Because $\Phi_{(N, w, 2, 2)OOC}$ is optimal [33], the $(p \times N, w, 2, 2)$ QC-permuted codes are asymptomatically optimal in cardinality when w is large.

5.9.1   Performance Analysis

Because the $(p \times N, w, 2, 2)$ QC-permuted codes have the maximum periodic cross-correlation function of 2, their chip-synchronous, hard-limiting error probability in OOK follows Equation (5.14).

Theorem 5.23

For the $(p \times N, w, 2, 2)$ QC-permuted codes over GF(p) of a prime p with the time-spreading $(N, w, 2, 2)$ OOCs, the hit probabilities, q_i, of having the periodic cross-correlation values of $i = \{0, 1, 2\}$ (in the sampling time) are formulated as [22]

$$q_2 = \frac{p^3 w^3 - p^2 (3p+1)w^2 + p^2(2p+1)w - w^2 + 2w - 1}{4p^2 N[p^3 \Phi_{(N,w,2,2)\text{OOC}} - 1]}$$

for odd weight $w \le p$ or

$$q_2 = \frac{p^3 w^3 - p^2 (3p+1)w^2 + p^2(2p+1)w - \frac{2p^3}{w-3} - w^3 + 5w^2 - 7w + 2}{4p^2 N[p^3 \Phi_{(N,w,2,2)\text{OOC}} - 1]}$$

for even weight $w \le p$,

$$\sum_{i=0}^{2} i q_i = \frac{w^2}{2LN} = \frac{w^2}{2pN}$$

and $\sum_{i=0}^{2} q_i = 1$, where $\Phi_{(N,w,2,2)\text{OOC}} = w - 3$ and $N = w^2 - 2w$ [33].

Proof Let $q_{2,(0)}$ and $q_{2,(1)}$ denote the probabilities of getting two hits in the sampling time of the periodic cross-correlation functions between the QC-permuted codeword (address signature of a receiver) coming from group $(l = 0, i_1 = 0)$ and other groups of the shifted QC sequences, respectively, and an interfering QC-permuted codeword.

For the address codeword originating from any group, other than group $(l = 0, i_1 = 0)$,

$$q_{2,(l)} = \frac{1}{2} \times \frac{1}{N} \times \frac{1}{p^3 \Phi_{(N,w,2,2)\text{OOC}} - 1} \times \left\{ \frac{(w-1)^2}{2} \right.$$
$$+ (p-1) \left[\frac{(w-1)^2}{2} + \frac{w(w-1)}{2} \right] + p \left[(\Phi_{(N,w,2,2)\text{OOC}} - 1) \right.$$
$$\left. \times \frac{(w-1)^2}{2} + (\Phi_{(N,w,2,2)\text{OOC}} - 2) \times \frac{(w-1)}{2} + (w-1) \right] \right\}$$

where the factor $1/2$ comes from the assumption of equiprobable data bit-1 and bit-0 transmissions in OOK and N is the number of possible time shifts in a codeword of length N. The denominator $p^3 \Phi_{(N,w,2,2)\text{OOC}} - 1$ represents the number of possible interfering codewords. The first term in the braces accounts for the number of two-hits contributed by an interfering codeword coming from the same group of the shifted QC-sequences and the same $(N, w, 2, 2)$ OOC codeword as the address codeword. The term $(w-1)^2/2$ comes from the number of repeated elements in the sets of the cyclic adjacent-pulse separations associated with two correlating codewords of odd weight w with cyclic shifts, as applied in the proof of Theorem 5.16 [1, 30–33, 36–39]. The terms in the first pair of brackets account for the number of two-hits contributed by an interfering codeword coming from a different group of the shifted QC-sequences than that of the address codeword, but the $(N, w, 2, 2)$ OOC codeword is still the same. The factor $p-1$ represents the number of different groups. Similarly, the term $(w-1)^2/2$ comes from the number of repeated elements in the sets of the cyclic adjacent-pulse separations (with cyclic shifts). The term $w(w-1)/2$ comes from all elements, whether repeated or nonrepeated, without cyclic shifts. The terms in the second pair of brackets account for the number of two-hits contributed by an interfering codeword coming from any group of the shifted QC-sequences but a different OOC codeword than that of the address codeword. The factor p represents the number of possible groups. The term $[\Phi_{(n,w,2,2)\text{OOC}} - 1](w-1)^2/2$ comes from the cyclic shifts of repeated elements in the sets of the cyclic adjacent-pulse separations (with cyclic shifts), and there are $\Phi_{(N,w,2,2)\text{OOC}} - 1$ different OOC codewords. The term $[\Phi_{(N,w,2,2)\text{OOC}} - 2](w-1)/2$ comes from the cyclic shifts of nonrepeated elements with $\Phi_{(N,w,2,2)\text{OOC}} - 2$ different OOC codewords, and each different OOC codeword contributes $w-1$ two-hits due to the cyclic shifts of nonrepeated elements.

The derivation of the two-hit probability $q_{2,(0)}$ of the address codeword originating from group $(l = 0, i_1 = 0)$ is the same as that of the other groups, except that the first term in the braces is now removed. This is because the cross-correlation function of the shifted QC sequences in this group is 0.

By combining all groups, the final form of q_2, which is equal to $(1/p^2)q_{2,(0)} + [(p^2 - 1)/p^2]q_{2,(l)}$, for odd weight w is derived after some manipulations. The derivation of q_2 with even weight w follows the rationale used for odd weight. ∎

Figure 5.26 plots the chip-synchronous, hard-limiting error probability of the ($p \times N, w, 2, 2$) QC-permuted codes over GF(p) with the time-spreading $(N, w, 2, 2)$ OOCs against the number of simultaneous users K for $N = \{15, 48, 63\}$, $w = \{5, 6, 8, 9\}$, and $p = \{5, 7, 11\}$. The $(15, 5, 2, 2)$ OOCs have two codewords, 010011100100000 and 001100001010100. In general, the error probabilities improve as p, N, or w increases because of higher autocorrelation peak or lower hit probabilities. However, the error probabilities get worse as K increases due to stronger mutual interference. Also plotted in Figure 5.26 are the computer-simulation results, which closely match the theoretical results. The computer simulation is performed by randomly assigning each simultaneous user one of the QC-permuted codewords in the code set, and OOK modulation is used for transmitting each data bit 1 with a codeword. The total number of data bits involved in the simulation is at least 100 times the reciprocal of the target error probability in order to provide enough iterations.

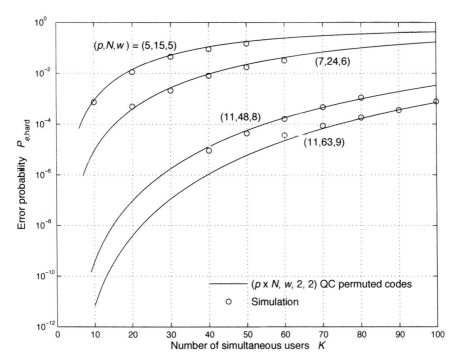

FIGURE 5.26 Chip-synchronous, hard-limiting error probabilities of the $(p \times N, w, 2, 2)$ QC-permuted codes with the time-spreading $(N, w, 2, 2)$ OOCs for various p, N, and w.

Figure 5.27 compares the chip-synchronous, hard-limiting error probabilities of the $(p \times N, w, 2, 2)$ QC-permuted codes with the $(N, w, 2, 2)$ OOCs, the $(p \times N, w, 1, 1)$ prime-permuted codes with the $(N, w, 1, 1)$ OOCs, the $(p \times N, w, 1, 2)$ prime-permuted codes with the $(N, w, 1, 2)$ OOCs, and the $(p \times N, w, 2, 2)$ prime-permuted codes with the $(N, w, 2, 1)$ OOCs, all over GF(p), for $N = \{49, 121, 127\}$, $w = \{4, 5, 6, 7, 8, 12\}$, and $p = \{11, 13\}$. In general, the error probabilities improve as N, w, or p increases, but get worse as K increases. In this example, the $(p \times N, w, 2, 2)$ QC-permuted codes perform the best. This is because the codes can support a larger w when the bandwidth expansion LN is fixed and the same cardinality is used for a fair code comparison. This example shows the benefit to having a larger cross-correlation function. Heavier code weight increases the autocorrelation peaks, compensates for stronger interference due to two-hits, and even provides a net gain in code performance, as shown in this figure.

5.10   2-D OPTICAL ORTHOGONAL CODES

Similar to the 1-D counterparts, 2-D optical orthogonal codes (OOCs), which have periodic cross-correlation functions of at most 1 or 2, have also been constructed by various methods [14, 15, 47–52]. In this section, two families of 2-D OOCs are

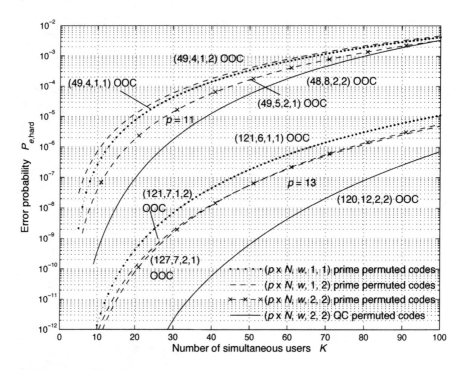

FIGURE 5.27 Chip-synchronous, hard-limiting error probabilities of the $(p \times N, w, 2, 2)$ QC-permuted codes and the $(p \times N, w, 1, 1)$, $(p \times N, w, 1, 2)$, and $(p \times N, w, 2, 2)$ prime-permuted codes for various p, N, and w.

constructed algebraically, for the sake of illustration [4]. One family is based on 1-D OOCs in Section 3.5 [30–33], and the second family is based on Reed–Solomon codes [53–57].

5.10.1   Construction 1: From 1-D (N, w, 1, 1) OOC

This construction begins with a family of 1-D $(N, w, 1, 1)$ OOCs, such as those in Section 3.5 and [30–33], with cardinality t, length $N = w(w-1)t + 1$, which is a prime number, weight w, and the autocorrelation sidelobes and periodic cross-correlation functions of both at most 1. Denote these t OOC codewords as binary $(0, 1)$ sequences with w pulses located at the chip positions

$$\{(x_{i,0}, x_{i,1}, x_{i,2}, \ldots, x_{i,j}, \ldots, x_{i,w-1}) : i = \{0, 1, \ldots, t-1\}\}$$

where $x_{i,j}$ denotes the jth pulse in the ith code.

Binary $(0,1)$ matrices with the ordered pairs, all under modulo-N operations,

$$\{[(x_{i_1,0}+i_3,i_2x_{i_1,0}),(x_{i_1,1}+i_3,i_2x_{i_1,1}),(x_{i_1,2}+i_3,i_2x_{i_1,2}),\dots,$$
$$(x_{i_1,w-1}+i_3,i_2x_{i_1,w-1})]:i_1=\{0,1,\dots,t-1\},$$
$$i_2=\{0,1,\dots,N-1\},i_3=\{0,1,\dots,N-1\}\}$$

and

$$\{[(i_2,x_{i_1,0}),(i_2,x_{i_1,1}),(i_2,x_{i_1,2}),\dots,(i_2,x_{i_1,w-1})]:$$
$$i_1=\{0,1,\dots,t-1\},i_2=\{0,1,\dots,N-1\}\}$$

form a family of 2-D OOCs with cardinality $N(N+1)t$, $L=N$ wavelengths, length $N=w(w-1)t+1$, and weight w [4].

Using $L=N=13$, $w=3$, and $t=2$ as an example, if the two 1-D $(13,3,1,1)$ OOC codewords have their pulses at chip positions $(0,2,8)$ and $(0,3,4)$, the resulting 2-D OOC of $L=13$ wavelengths, length $N=13$ and weight $w=3$ has $N(N+1)t=364$ codewords, denoted by $[(i_2,0),(i_2,2),(i_2,8)]$, $[(i_2,0),(i_2,3),(i_2,4)]$, $[(2+i_3,2i_2),(8+i_3,8i_2)]$, and $[(i_3,0),(3+i_3,3i_2),(4+i_3,4i_2)]$, all under modulo-13 operations, with i_2 and $i_3\in[0,12]$.

Theorem 5.24

The autocorrelation peaks and sidelobes of these 2-D OOCs of weight w are equal to w and 1, respectively. The periodic cross-correlation functions of the codes are at most 1 [4].

Proof Consider the autocorrelation function of a 2-D OOC codeword, say $\mathbf{x}_{i_3,i_2,i_1}$ for $i_1\in[0,t-1]$, $i_2\in[0,N-1]$, and $i_3\in[0,N-1]$. If there exist more than one hit of pulses in any horizontal cyclic shift τ, the ordered pairs are related by

$$(x_{i_1,j}+i_3,i_2x_{i_1,j}+\tau)=(x_{i_1,j'}+i_3,i_2x_{i_1,j'})\quad(\text{mod }N)$$

and must hold simultaneously for some j and $j'\in[0,w-1]$, where $j\neq j'$. Because $x_{i_1,j}\neq x_{i_1,j'}$, no solution can be found. So, the autocorrelation sidelobes are at most 1. The autocorrelation peaks of w are due to the code weight w.

Let $\mathbf{x}_{i_3,i_2,i_1}=[(x_{i_1,0}+i_3,i_2x_{i_1,0}),(x_{i_1,1}+i_3,i_2x_{i_1,1}),\dots,(x_{i_1,w-1}+i_3,i_2x_{i_1,w-1})]$ and $\mathbf{x}_{i_3',i_2',i_1'}=[(x_{i_1',0}+i_3',i_2'x_{i_1',0}),(x_{i_1',1}+i_3',i_2'x_{i_1',1}),\dots,(x_{i_1',w-1}+i_3',i_2'x_{i_1',w-1})]$ be two distinct 2-D OOC codewords with $(i_3,i_2,i_1)\neq(i_3',i_2',i_1')$. If there exists two hits of pulses in any horizontal cyclic shift τ between the two codewords, two of the first components in the ordered pairs, say $x_{i_1,j_1}+i_3=x_{i_1',j_1'}+i_3'$ and $x_{i_1,j_2}+i_3=x_{i_1',j_2'}+i_3'$, must hold simultaneously for a $j_1=\{0,1,\dots,w-1\}$, a $j_1'=\{0,1,\dots,w-1\}$, a $j_2=\{0,1,\dots,w-1\}$, and a $j_2'=\{0,1,\dots,w-1\}$, where $j_1\neq j_1'$ and $j_2\neq j_2'$. The subtraction of these two equations results in $x_{i_1,j_1} - x_{i_1,j_2} = x_{i_1',j_1'} - x_{i_1',j_2'}$, which is valid only when $i_m = i_m'$ for all $m = \{1,2,3\}$. This violates the assumption of distinct $\mathbf{x}_{i_3,i_2,i_1}$ and $\mathbf{x}_{i_3',i_2',i_1'}$. So, the periodic cross-correlation function is at most 1.

For the 2-D OOC codewords with ordered pairs in the form of $(i_2, a_{i_1,j})$, the w pulses in each codeword only carry the same wavelength, where $i_1 \in [0, t-1]$, $i_2 \in [0, N-1]$, and $j \in [0, w-1]$. They are equivalent to 1-D OOCs and then follow the autocorrelation and cross-correlation properties of the latter. ∎

According to Section 1.6, the cardinality upper bound of these 2-D OOCs with cardinality $N(N+1)t$, $L = N$ wavelengths, length $N = w(w-1)t + 1$, weight w, and the maximum autocorrelation sidelobe and periodic cross-correlation function of both 1 is given by

$$\Phi_{\text{upper}} \quad \leq \quad \frac{L(LN-1)}{w(w-1)} = \frac{N(N^2-1)}{w(w-1)} = N(N+1)t$$

The upper bound is equal to the actual cardinality. So, these 2-D OOCs are optimal in cardinality.

5.10.2 Construction 2: From Reed–Solomon Code

Consider a generator polynomial $g(x) = (x - \alpha^1)(x - \alpha^2) \cdots (x - \alpha^{p_1-3})$ with a primitive element α of $GF(p_1)$ of a prime p_1. A Reed–Solomon codeword, $C = (c_0, c_1, \ldots, c_j, \ldots, c_{i,p_1-2})$, of length $N = p_1 - 1$, can be generated, in polynomial form, by evaluating the corresponding coefficients of $c(x) = g(x) = c_0 + c_1 x + \cdots + c_j x^j + \cdots + c_{p_1-2} x^{p_1-2}$, where $c_j \in GF(p_1)$ is the value of the jth code element [53–57].

Given a set of prime numbers $p_k \geq p_{k-1} \geq \cdots \geq p_1$ and the above Reed–Solomon codeword, binary $(0,1)$ matrices, $\mathbf{x}_{i_k,i_{k-1},\ldots,i_1}$, with the ordered pairs [4]

$$
\begin{aligned}
\{&[(c_0 \oplus i_1, ((c_0 \oplus i_1) \odot_{p_2} i_2)(p_1 - 1) + \cdots \\
&+ ((c_0 \oplus i_1) \odot_{p_k} i_k)(p_1 - 1)p_2 \cdots p_{k-1}), \\
&(c_1 \oplus i_1, 1 + ((c_1 \oplus i_1) \odot_{p_2} i_2)(p_1 - 1) + \cdots \\
&+ (c_1 \oplus i_1) \odot_{p_k} i_k)(p_1 - 1)p_2 \cdots p_{k-1}), \\
&(c_{p_1-2} \oplus i_1, (p_1 - 2) + ((c_{p_1-2} \oplus i_1) \odot_{p_2} i_2)(p_1 - 1) + \cdots \\
&+ ((c_{p-2} \oplus i_1) \odot_{p_k} i_k)(p_1 - 1)p_2 \ldots p_{k-1})] : i_1 = \{0, 1, \ldots, p_1 - 1\}, \\
&i_2 = \{0, 1, \ldots, p_2 - 1\}, \ldots, i_k = \{0, 1, \ldots, p_k - 1\}\}
\end{aligned}
$$

form a family of 2-D OOCs with cardinality $p_1 p_2 \cdots p_k$, $L = p_1$ wavelengths, length $N = (p_1 - 1)p_2 \cdots p_k$, and weight $w \leq p_1 - 1$, where "$\oplus$" is a modulo-p_1 addition and "$\odot_{p_j}$" is a modulo-p_j multiplications for $j = \{1,2,\ldots,k\}$.

Using $k = 2$, $p_1 = 5$, $p_2 = 7$, and $\alpha = 2$ as an example, the generator polynomial is given by $g(x) = (x - 2)(x - 2^2) = x^2 + 4x + 3$, under modulo-5 operations, and the Reed–Solomon codeword becomes $C = (c_0, c_1, c_2, c_3) = (0, 1, 4, 3)$. The resulting

2-D OOC of $L = p_1 = 5$ wavelengths, length $N = (p_1 - 1)p_2 = 28$, and weight $w = p_1 - 1 = 4$ has $p_1 p_2 = 35$ codewords, denoted by $\mathbf{x}_{i_2, i_1} = [(i_1, (i_1 \odot_7 i_2)4), (i_1 \oplus 1, 1 + ((i_1 \oplus 1) \odot_7 i_2)4), (i_1 \oplus 4, 2 + ((i_1 \oplus 4) \odot_7 i_2)4), (i_1 \oplus 3, 3 + ((i_1 \oplus 3) \odot_7 i_2)4)]$ for $i_1 \in [0,4]$ and $i_2 \in [0,6]$.

Theorem 5.25

The autocorrelation peaks and sidelobes of these 2-D OOCs of weight w are equal to w and 0, respectively, where $w \leq p_1 - 1$. The periodic cross-correlation functions of the codes are at most 1 [4].

Proof Let $\mathbf{x}_{i_k, i_{k-1}, \ldots, i_1}$ and $\mathbf{x}_{i'_k, i'_{k-1}, \ldots, i'_1}$ be two distinct codewords with $(i_k, i_{k-1}, \ldots, i_1) \neq (i'_k, i'_{k-1}, \ldots, i'_1)$. If there exist two hits of pulses in any relative horizontal cyclic shift τ between the two codewords, then

$$
\begin{aligned}
j_1 &+ ((c_{j_1} \oplus i_1) \odot_{p_2} i_2)(p_1 - 1) + ((c_{j_1} \oplus i_1) \odot_{p_3} i_3)(p_1 - 1)p_2 + \cdots \\
&+ ((c_{j_1} \oplus i_1) \odot_{p_k} i_k)(p_1 - 1)p_2 \cdots p_{k-1} + \tau \\
&= j_1 + ((c_{j_1} \oplus i'_1) \odot_{p_2} i'_2)(p_1 - 1) + ((c_{j_1} \oplus i'_1) \odot_{p_3} i'_3)(p_1 - 1)p_2 + \cdots \\
&+ ((c_{j_1} \oplus i'_1) \odot_{p_k} i'_k)(p_1 - 1)p_2 \cdots p_{k-1}
\end{aligned}
$$

$$
\begin{aligned}
j_2 &+ ((c_{j_2} \oplus i_1) \odot_{p_2} i_2)(p_1 - 1) + ((c_{j_2} \oplus i_1) \odot_{p_3} i_3)(p_1 - 1)p_2 + \cdots \\
&+ ((c_{j_2} \oplus i_1) \odot_{p_k} i_k)(p_1 - 1)p_2 \cdots p_{k-1} + \tau \\
&= j_2 + ((c_{j_2} \oplus i'_1) \odot_{p_2} i'_2)(p_1 - 1) + (c_{j_2} \oplus i'_1) \odot_{p_3} i'_3)(p_1 - 1)p_2 + \cdots \\
&+ ((c_{j_2} \oplus i'_1) \odot_{p_k} i'_k)(p_1 - 1)p_2 \cdots p_{k-1}
\end{aligned}
$$

must hold simultaneously for a $j_1 = \{0, 1, \ldots, p_1 - 1\}$ and a $j_2 = \{0, 1, \ldots, p_1 - 1\}$, where $j_1 \neq j_2$. The subtraction of these two equations results in

$$
\begin{aligned}
&\{[(c_{j_1} \oplus i_1) \odot_{p_2} i_2 - (c_{j_2} \oplus i_1) \odot_{p_2} i_2] - [(c_{j_1} \oplus i'_1) \odot_{p_2} i'_2 \\
&- (c_{j_2} \oplus i'_1) \odot_{p_2} i'_2]\}(p_1 - 1) + \{[(c_{j_1} \oplus i_1) \odot_{p_3} i_3 - (c_{j_2} \oplus i_1) \odot_{p_3} i_3] \\
&- [(c_{j_1} \oplus i'_1) \odot_{p_3} i'_3 - (c_{j_2} \oplus i'_1) \odot_{p_3} i'_3]\}(p_1 - 1)p_2 + \cdots \\
&+ \{[(c_{j_1} \oplus i_1) \odot_{p_k} i_k - (c_{j_2} \oplus i_1) \odot_{p_k} i_k] \\
&- [(c_{j_1} \oplus i'_1) \odot_{p_k} i'_k - (c_{j_2} \oplus i'_1) \odot_{p_k} i'_k]\}(p_1 - 1)p_2 \cdots p_{k-1} = 0
\end{aligned}
$$

which is valid only when $i_m = i'_m$ for all $m = \{1, 2, \ldots, k\}$. This violates the assumption of distinct $\mathbf{x}_{i_k, i_{k-1}, \ldots, i_1}$ and $\mathbf{x}_{i'_k, i'_{k-1}, \ldots, i'_1}$. So, the periodic cross-correlation function is at most 1.

Because all pulses in a codeword are in different wavelengths, the autocorrelation sidelobes are always 0. Finally, the autocorrelation peaks of w are due to the code weight $w \leq p_1 - 1$. ∎

According to Section 1.6, the cardinality upper bound of these 2-D OOCs with cardinality $p_1 p_2 \cdots p_k$, $L = p_1$ wavelengths, length $N = (p_1 - 1)p_2 p_3 \cdots p_k$, weight $w = p_1 - 1$, and the maximum periodic cross-correlation function of 1 is given by

$$
\begin{aligned}
\Phi_{\text{upper}} \quad &\leq \quad \frac{p_1[(p_1 - 1)p_1 p_2 \cdots p_k - 1]}{(p_1 - 1)(p_1 - 2)} \\
&= \quad p_1 p_2 \cdots p_k + \frac{2p_1(p_1 - 1)p_2 \cdots p_k - p_1}{(p_1 - 1)(p_1 - 2)}
\end{aligned}
$$

The upper bound is equal to $1 + [2(p_1 - 1)p_2 \cdots p_k - p_1]/[(p_1 - 1)(p_1 - 2)p_1 p_2 \cdots p_k]$ times the actual cardinality. The factor approaches 1 for a large p_1. So, these 2-D OOCs are asymptotically optimal in cardinality.

5.10.3   Performance Analysis

Because the maximum periodic cross-correlation function of these two families of 2-D OOCs is 1, the chip-synchronous, soft- and hard-limiting error probabilities in OOK follow Equations (5.1) and (5.15), respectively. The one-hit probability is formulated as

$$
q_1 = \frac{w^2}{2LN}
$$

and $q_0 = 1 - q_1$, where the actual forms of w, L, and N are determined by the code parameters of the 2-D OOCs in use.

As the chip-synchronous, soft- and hard-limiting error probabilities are mainly determined by the hit probabilities, the performances of these two families of 2-D OOCs closely follow those of the 2-D prime codes with the periodic cross-correlation functions of at most 1 in this chapter (e.g., see Figures 5.2 and 5.19) if the values of w, L, and N are similar.

5.11   SUMMARY

In this chapter, various families of 2-D asynchronous prime codes, which provide flexible choices of optical codes with different relationships among code length, number of wavelengths, correlation properties, and cardinality, were studied. For the same length, weight, and number of wavelengths, the carrier-hopping prime codes have a larger cardinality than the 1-D prime codes in hybrid WDM-coding and generally perform better, especially when the traffic load is heavy and when there is no central controller to evenly distribute wavelengths to the simultaneous users in the hybrid scheme. The multilevel carrier-hopping prime codes, which have enlarged cardinality and a flexible relationship between code length and cross-correlation functions, were also studied. By partitioning the codes into different subsets, codes with suitable cardinality and performance can be selected. The use of the shifted carrier-hopping prime codes for shifted-code keying were analyzed in terms of error probability and spectral efficiency. The advantages of shifted-code keying are that a lower symbol-rate can support a higher bit rate, no reduction in code cardinality due to the assignment of multiple codes (or symbols) per user is needed, and user code obscurity is enhanced at the expense of code performance and hardware complexity. The extended and expanded carrier-hopping prime codes with hugh cardinality were designed to support high bit-rate optical coding systems, in which the number of time slots is limited and less than the number of available wavelengths. The quadratic-congruence carrier-hopping prime codes improve code cardinality by relaxing the maximum cross-correlation function to 2. The large cardinality supports multicode keying for improving bit rate and user code obscurity at the expense of code performance and hardware complexity. Several families of wavelength-time codes were constructed with the use of shifted prime and quadratic-congruence sequences to permutate the wavelengths of the pulses in various families of time-spreading 1-D unipolar and bipolar codes. Finally, the algebraic constructions of two families of 2-D OOCs were illustrated.

REFERENCES

1. Yang, G.-C., Kwong, W. C. (2002). *Prime Codes with Applications to CDMA Optical and Wireless Networks*. Norwood, MA: Artech House.
2. Prucnal, P. R. (ed.) (2006). *Optical Code Division Multiple Access: Fundamentals and Applications*. Boca Raton, FL: Taylor & Francis Group.
3. Perrier, P. A., Prucnal, P. R. (1988). Wavelength-division integration of services in fiber-optic networks. *Inter. J. Digital Analog Cabled Systems* 1(3):149–157.
4. Yang, G.-C., Kwong, W. C. (1997). Performance comparison of multiwavelength CDMA and WDMA+CDMA for fiber-optic networks. *IEEE Trans. Commun.* 45(11):1426–1434.
5. Yang, G.-C., Kwong, W. C. (2004). A new class of carrier-hopping codes for code-division multiple-access optical and wireless systems. *IEEE Commun. Lett.* 8(1):51–53.
6. Kwong, W. C., Yang, G.-C. (2004). Extended carrier-hopping prime codes for wavelength-time optical code-division multiple access. *IEEE Trans. Commun.* 52(7):1084–1091.
7. Yang, G.-C., Kwong, W. C. (2005). Performance analysis of extended carrier-hopping prime codes for optical CDMA. *IEEE Trans. Commun.* 53(5):876–881.
8. Kwong, W. C., Yang, G.-C. (2005). Multiple-length extended carrier-hopping prime codes for optical CDMA systems supporting multirate, multimedia services. *J. Lightwave Technol* 23(11):3653–3662.
9. Narimanov, E., Kwong, W. C., Yang, G.-C., Prucnal, P. R. (2005) Shifted carrier-hopping prime codes for multicode keying in wavelength-time O-CDMA. *IEEE Trans. Commun.* 53(12):2150–2156.
10. Chang, C.-Y., Yang, G.-C., Kwong, W. C. (2006). Wavelength-time codes with maximum cross-correlation function of two for multicode-keying optical CDMA. *J. Lightwave Technol.* 24(3):1093–1100.
11. Hsieh, C.-H., Yang, G.-C., Chang, C.-Y., Kwong, W. C. (2009). Multilevel prime codes for optical CDMA systems. *J. Optical Commun. Networking* 1(7):600–607.
12. Sun, C.-C., Yang, G.-C., Tu, C.-P., Chang, C.-Y., Kwong, W. C. (2010). Extended multilevel prime codes for optical CDMA. *IEEE Trans. Commun.* 58(5):1344–1350.

13. Kwong, W. C., Yang, G.-C., Liu, Y.-C. (2005). A new family of wavelength-time optical CDMA codes utilizing programmable arrayed waveguide gratings. *IEEE J. Selected Areas Commun.* 23(8):1564–1571.

14. Yang, G.-C., Kwong, W. C. (1996). Two-dimensional spatial signature patterns. *IEEE Trans. Commun.* 44(2):184–191.

15. Yim, R. M. H., Chen, L. R., Bajcsy, J. (2002). Design and performance of 2D codes for wavelength-time optical CDMA. *IEEE Photon. Technol. Lett,* 14(5):714–716.

16. Tančevski, L., Andonovic, I. (1996). Hybrid wavelength hopping/time spreading schemes for use in massive optical LANs with increased security. *J. Lightwave Technol.* 14(12):2636–2647.

17. Kwong, W. C., Yang, G.-C., Baby, V., Brès, C.-S., Prucnal, P. R. (2005). Multiple-wavelength optical orthogonal codes under prime permutations for optical CDMA. *IEEE Trans. Commun.* 53(1):117–123.

18. Kwong, W. C., Yang, G.-C., Chang, C.-Y. (2005). Wavelength-hopping time-spreading optical CDMA with bipolar codes. *J. Lightwave Technol.* 23(1):260–267.

19. Hsieh, C.-P., Chang, C.-Y., Yang, G.-C., Kwong, W. C. (2006). A bipolar-bipolar code for asynchronous wavelength-time optical CDMA. *IEEE Trans. Commun.* 54(7):1190–1194.

20. Tien, J.-H., Yang, G.-C., Chang, C.-Y., Kwong, W. C. (2008). Design and analysis of 2D codes with the maximum cross-correlation value of two for optical CDMA. *J. Lightwave Technol.* 26(22):3632–3639.

21. Wang, T.-C., Yang, G.-C., Chang, C.-Y., Kwong, W. C. (2009). A new family of 2D codes for fiber-optic CDMA system with and without the chip-synchronous assumption. *J. Lightwave Technol.* 27(14):2612–2620.

22. Lin, Y.-C., Yang, G.-C., Chang, C.-Y., Kwong, W. C. (2011). Construction of optimal 2D optical codes using $(n, w, 2, 2)$ optical orthogonal codes. *IEEE Trans. Commun.* 59(1):194–200.

23. Titlebaum, E. L., Sibul, L. H. (1981). Time-frequency hop signals. Part II. Coding based upon quadratic congruences. *IEEE Trans. Aerospace Electron. Systems* 17(4):494–500.

24. Maric, S. V., Titlebaum, E. L. (1990). Frequency hop multiple access codes based upon the theory of cubic congruences. *IEEE Trans. Aerospace Electron. Systems* 26(6):1035–1039.

25. Chen, H.-W., Yang, G.-C., Chang, C.-Y., Lin, T.-C., Kwong, W. C. (2009). Spectral efficiency study of two multirate schemes for optical CDMA with/without symbol synchronization. *J. Lightwave Technol.* 27(14):2771–2778.

26. Deng, K.-L., Runser, R.J., Toliver, P., Glesk, I., Prucnal, P. R. (2000). A highly-scalable, rapidly-reconfigurable, multicasting-capable, 100 Gb/s photonic switched interconnect based upon OTDM technology. *J. Lightwave Technol.* 18(12):1892–1904.

27. Mori, K., Takara, H., Kawanishi, S., Saruwatari, M., Morioka, T. (1997). Flatly broadened supercontinuum spectrum generated in a dispersion decreasing fibre with convex dispersion profile. *Electron. Lett.* 22(21):1806–1808.

28. Chang, C.-Y., Chen, H.-T., Yang, G.-C., Kwong, W. C. (2007). Spectral efficiency study of QC-CHPCs in multirate optical CDMA system. *IEEE J. Selected Areas Commun.* 25(9):118–128.

29. Wan, S. P., Hu, Y. (2001). Two-dimensional optical CDMA differential system with prime/OOC codes. *IEEE Photon. Technol. Lett.* 13(12):1373–1375.

30. Chung, F. R. K., Salehi, J. A., Wei, V. K. (1989). Optical orthogonal codes: Design, analysis, and applications. *IEEE Trans. Info. Theory* 35(3):595–604.

31. Yang, G.-C., Fuja, T. (1995). Optical orthogonal codes with unequal auto- and cross-correlation constraints. *IEEE Trans. Info. Theory* 41(1):96–106.

32. Yang, G.-C. (1995). Some new families of optical orthogonal codes for code division multiple-access fibre-optic network. *IEE Proc. Commun.* 142(6):363–368.

33. Chung, H., Kumar, P. V. (1990). Optical orthogonal codes—New bounds and an optimal construction. *IEEE Trans. Info. Theory* 36(4):866–873.

34. Tančevski, L., Andonovic, I. (1994). Wavelength hopping/time spreading code division multiple access systems. *Electron. Lett.* 30(17):1388–1390.

35. Maric, S. V., Kostic, Z. I., Titlebaum, E. L. (1993). A new family of optical code sequences for use in spread-spectrum fiber-optic local area networks. *IEEE Trans. Commun.* 41(8):1217–1221.

36. Yang, G.-C., Kwong, W. C. (1995). On the construction of 2^n codes for optical code-division multiple-access. *IEEE Trans. Commun.* 43(2–4):495–502.

37. Yang, G.-C., (1996). Variable-weight optical orthogonal codes for CDMA networks with multiple performance requirements. *IEEE Trans. Commun.* 44(1):47–55.

38. Kwong, W. C., Yang, G.-C. (1995). Construction of 2^n prime codes for optical code-division multiple-access. *IEE Proc. Commun.* 142(3):141–150.

39. Kwong, W. C., Yang, G.-C., Zhang, J.-G. (1996). $2^{,n}$ prime codes and coding architecture for optical code-division multiple-access. *IEEE Trans. Commun.* 44(9):1152–1162.

40. Griner, U. N., Arnon, S. (2004). A novel bipolar wavelength-time coding scheme for optical CDMA systems. *IEEE Photon. Technol. Lett.* 16(1):332–334.

41. Proakis, J. G. (1995). *Digital Communications*. (third edition). New York: McGraw-Hill.

42. Dinan, E. H., Jabbari, B. (1998). Spreading codes for direct sequence CDMA and wideband CDMA cellular networks. *IEEE Commun. Mag.* 36(9):48–54.

43. Huang, J.-F., Hsu, D.-Z. (2000). Fiber-grating-based optical CDMA spectral coding with nearly orthogonal m-sequence codes. *IEEE Photon. Technol. Lett.* 12(9):1252–1254.

44. Lam, A. W., Tantaratana, S. (1994). *Theory and Application of Spread Spectrum Systems*. Piscataway, NJ: IEEE Press.

45. Kärkkäinen, K. H. A. (1993). Meaning of maximum and mean-squared crosscorrelation as a performance measure for CDMA code families and their influence on system capacity. *IEICE Trans. Commun.* E76-B(8):848–854.

46. Pursley, M. B. (1977). Performance evaluation for phase-coded spread-spectrum multiple-access communication—Part II: Code sequence analysis. *IEEE Trans. Commun.* 25(8):800–803.

47. Kwong, W. C., Yang, G.-C. (1998). Image transmission in multicore-fiber code-division multiple-access networks. *IEEE Commun. Lett.* 2(10):285–287.

48. Mendez, A. J., Gagliardi, R. M., Feng, H. X. C., Heritage, J. P., Morookian, J.-M. (2000). Strategies for realizing optical CDMA for dense, high speed, long span, optical network applications. *J. Lightwave Technol.* 18(12):1685–1696.

49. Kwong, W. C., Yang, G.-C. (2001). Double-weight signature pattern codes for multicore-fiber code-division multiple-access networks. *IEEE Commun. Lett.* 5(5):203–205.

50. Mendez, A. J., Gagliardi, R. M., Hernandez, V. J., Bennett, C. V., Lennon, W. J. (2004). High-performance optical CDMA system based on 2-D optical orthogonal codes. *J. Lightwave Technol.* 22(11):2409–2419.

51. Yeh, B.-C., Lin, C.-H., Yang, C.-L., Wu, J. (2009). Noncoherent spectral/spatial optical CDMA system using 2-D diluted perfect difference codes. *J. Lightwave Technol.* 27(13):2420–2432.

52. Omrani, R., Garg, G., Kumar, P. V., Elia, P., Bhambhani, P. (2012). Large families of asymptotically optimal two-dimensional optical orthogonal codes. *IEEE Trans. Info. Theory* 58(2):1163–1185.
53. Reed, I. S. (1971). *k*-th order near-orthogonal codes. *IEEE Trans. Info. Theory* 15(1):116–117.
54. Rocha, Jr., V. C. (1984). Maximum distance separable multilevel codes. *IEEE Trans. Info. Theory* 30(3)547–548.
55. Yang, G.-C., Jaw, J.-Y. (1994). Performance analysis and sequence designs of synchronous code-division multiple-access systems with multimedia services. *IEE Proceedings–Commun.* 141(6):371.
56. Lin, S., Costello, Jr., D. J. (2004). *Error Control Coding.* (second edition). Englewood Cliffs, NJ: Prentice Hall.
57. Lin, M.-F., Yang, G.-C., Chang, C.-Y., Liu, Y.-S., Kwong, W. C. (2007). Frequency-hopping CDMA with Reed–Solomon code sequences in wireless communications. *IEEE Trans. Commun.* 55(11):2052–2055.

6 2-D Synchronous Prime Codes

In Chapter 4, 1-D synchronous prime codes were constructed by cyclic-shifting codewords of the 1-D asynchronous prime codes in Chapter 3. Due to code synchronism, the benefits of synchronous prime codes include larger code cardinality and better code performance than their asynchronous counterparts, and supporting more possible subscribers and simultaneous users. This is because in-phase cross-correlation functions are considered, instead of periodic ones. Some codewords of these synchronous prime codes have zero in-phase cross-correlation functions and achieve true orthogonality.

In this chapter, three families of 2-D synchronous carrier-hopping prime codes are first constructed by cyclic-shifting codewords of the carrier-hopping prime codes in Chapter 5 [1, 2]. Afterward, 2-D synchronous multilevel carrier-hopping prime codes are studied [3, 4]. These multilevel codes can be partitioned into a tree structure of levels of subsets of codewords with different cardinalities and in-phase cross-correlation functions for attaining different code performances. Finally, 2-D synchronous prime-permuted codes, which use bipolar Walsh codes as the (synchronous) time-spreading codes, are constructed and analyzed [5–7].

Similar to the 1-D synchronous prime codes in Chapter 4, these 2-D synchronous prime codes also find potential applications, for example, in integrated O-TDMA and synchronous O-CDMA multirate, multimedia networks and in coding-based passive optical networks (PONs). In PONs, the downstream central-station-to-subscribers traffic is synchronous in nature but the upstream subscribers-to-central-station traffic is asynchronous [8, 9]. While 2-D synchronous prime codes can be used for the synchronous downstream traffic, their asynchronous counterparts (in Chapter 5) carry the asynchronous upstream traffic. As both types of codes originate from the same code family, the same encoding and decoding hardware can be used for both traffic directions. Last but not least, the 2-D synchronous prime codes in this chapter can also be used in spectral amplitude coding due to their fixed maximum in-phase cross-correlation function, as discussed in Section 2.4. The codes reduce phase-induced-intensity noise, a major deleterious effect in spectral-amplitude-coding systems, because they are sparse in the number of mark chips (or pulses).

6.1 SYNCHRONOUS ORIGINAL, EXPANDED, AND QUADRATIC-CONGRUENCE CARRIER-HOPPING PRIME CODES

In general, the original, expanded, and quadratic-congruence carrier-hopping prime codes in Chapter 5 can be converted into their corresponding synchronous carrier-hopping prime codes by means of cyclic-shifting the code elements. Let the notation

$(L \times N, w, \lambda_c)$ represent the number of wavelengths L, code length N, code weight w, and the maximum periodic cross-correlation function λ_c of the asynchronous carrier-hopping prime codes. Also, $(L \times N, w, \lambda_c')$ denotes the corresponding code parameters of the synchronous counterparts, except that λ_c' represents the maximum in-phase cross-correlation function.

Based on Sections 5.1, 5.5, and 5.6, given a positive integer k and a set of prime numbers $p_k \geq p_{k-1} \geq \cdots \geq p_1$ and p', the $(w \times p_1 p_2 \cdots p_k, w, 1)$ original carrier-hopping prime codes, $\mathbf{x}_{i_k, i_{k-1}, \ldots, i_1}$, of cardinality $p_1 p_2 \cdots p_k$ and weight $w \leq p_1$, the $(wp' \times p_1 p_2 \cdots p_k, w, 1)$ expanded carrier-hopping prime codes, $\mathbf{x}_{i_k, i_{k-1}, \ldots, i_1, l_2, l_1}$ and $\mathbf{x}_{i_k, i_{k-1}, \ldots, i_1, l_3}$, of cardinality $(w^2 + p')p_1 p_2 \cdots p_k$ and weight $w \leq p'$ (with $p_1 \geq wp'$), and the $(w \times p_1 p_2 \cdots p_k, w, 2)$ quadratic-congruence carrier-hopping prime codes, $\mathbf{x}_{i_k, i_{k-1}, \ldots, i_1, l}$, of cardinality $p_1^2 p_2 \cdots p_k$ and weight $w \leq p_1$ can be generally represented by the ordered pairs

$$\{[(\lambda_0, t_0), (\lambda_1, t_1), (\lambda_2, t_2), \ldots, (\lambda_h, t_h), \ldots, (\lambda_{w-1}, t_{w-1})]:$$
$$i_1 = \{0, 1, \ldots, p_1 - 1\}, i_2 = \{0, 1, \ldots, p_2 - 1\}, \ldots, i_k = \{0, 1, \ldots, p_k - 1\},$$
$$l_1 = \{0, 1, \ldots, w - 1\}, l_2 = \{0, 1, \ldots, w - 1\}, l_3 = \{0, 1, \ldots, p' - 1\},$$
$$l = \{0, 1, \ldots, p_1 - 1\}\}$$

Each (λ_j, t_j) ordered pair represents the transmitting wavelength λ_j and (time) chip location t_j of the jth pulse in each code matrix. The actual equations of λ_j and t_j depend on the specific carrier-hopping prime codes in use and are correspondingly given in Sections 5.1, 5.5, and 5.6.

By applying s cyclic time-shifts to these ordered pairs, binary $(0, 1)$ matrices, $\mathbf{x}_{i_k, i_{k-1}, \ldots, i_1, s}$, $\mathbf{x}_{i_k, i_{k-1}, \ldots, i_1, l_2, l_1, s}$, $\mathbf{x}_{i_k, i_{k-1}, \ldots, i_1, l_3, s}$, and $\mathbf{x}_{i_k, i_{k-1}, \ldots, i_1, l, s}$, with the ordered pairs, in a general form,

$$\{[(\lambda_0, t_0 \oplus s), (\lambda_1, t_1 \oplus s), (\lambda_2, t_2 \oplus s), \ldots, (\lambda_h, t_h \oplus s), \ldots, (\lambda_{w-1}, t_{w-1} \oplus s)]:$$
$$i_1 = \{0, 1, \ldots, p_1 - 1\}, i_2 = \{0, 1, \ldots, p_2 - 1\}, \ldots, i_k = \{0, 1, \ldots, p_k - 1\},$$
$$l_1 = \{0, 1, \ldots, w - 1\}, l_2 = \{0, 1, \ldots, w - 1\}, l_3 = \{0, 1, \ldots, p' - 1\},$$
$$l = \{0, 1, \ldots, p_1 - 1\}, s = \{0, 1, \ldots, p_1 p_2 \cdots p_k - 1\}\}$$

form the synchronous $(w \times p_1 p_2 \cdots p_k, w, 1)$ original, $(wp' \times p_1 p_2 \cdots p_k, w, 1)$ expanded, and $(w \times p_1 p_2 \cdots p_k, w, 2)$ quadratic-congruence carrier-hopping prime codes with cardinalities $(p_1 p_2 \cdots p_k)^2$, $(w^2 + p')(p_1 p_2 \cdots p_k)^2$, and $p_1(p_1 p_2 \cdots p_k)^2$, and weights $w \leq p_1$, $w \leq p'$, and $w \leq p_1$, respectively, where "$\oplus$" denotes a modulo-$p_1 p_2 \cdots p_k$ addition.

In general, the parameters and properties of these synchronous carrier-hopping prime codes remain the same as those of their asynchronous counterparts, except that the maximum in-phase cross-correlation function λ_c' is now considered, in place of the periodic one λ_c, due to code synchronism. As a result, the cardinalities of these synchronous carrier-hopping prime codes are $p_1 p_2 \cdots p_k$ times the cardinalities of the asynchronous ones.

These synchronous original, expanded, and quadratic-congruence carrier-hopping prime codes can be partitioned into $p_1 p_2 \cdots p_k$, $(w^2 + p')p_1 p_2 \cdots p_k$, and $p_1^2 p_2 \cdots p_k$

subsets (indexed by i_1, i_2, ..., i_k, l_1, l_2, l_3, and l), respectively, and each subset has $p_1 p_2 \cdots p_k$ codewords (indexed by s). The first synchronous codeword, such as $\mathbf{x}_{i_k,i_{k-1},\ldots,i_1,0}$, $\mathbf{x}_{i_k,i_{k-1},\ldots,i_1,l_2,l_1,0}$, $\mathbf{x}_{i_k,i_{k-1},\ldots,i_1,l_3,0}$, and $\mathbf{x}_{i_k,i_{k-1},\ldots,i_1,l,0}$, in every subset is from one corresponding asynchronous carrier-hopping prime codeword in Chapter 5, which acts as a seed to generate the other synchronous codewords in the subset.

Using $k = 2$, $p_1 = w = 3$, and $p_2 = 5$ as an example, there are 15 original carrier-hopping prime codewords, denoted by $\mathbf{x}_{i_2,i_1} = [(0,0),(1,i_1 + 3i_2),(2,2\odot_3 i_1 + (2\odot_5 i_2)3)]$ for $i_1 \in [0,2]$ and $i_2 \subset [0,4]$, from Section 5.1. Each of them can generate one subset of $p_1 p_2 = 15$ cyclic-time-shifted copies, which are indexed by $s \in [0,14]$. So, there are in total $(p_1 p_2)^2 = 225$ synchronous original carrier-hopping prime codewords, denoted by $\mathbf{x}_{i_2,i_1,s} = [(0,s),(1,(i_1 + 3i_2)\oplus s),(2,(2\odot_3 i_1 + (2\odot_5 i_2)3)\oplus s]$ for $i_1 \in [0,2]$, $i_2 \in [0,4]$, and $s \in [0,14]$, where "$\oplus$" is a modulo-15 addition. For example, $\mathbf{x}_{2,2,0} = [(0,0),(1,8),(2,13)]$ is one original codeword and $\mathbf{x}_{2,2,2} = [(0,2),(1,10),(2,0)]$ is a copy after two cyclic-time-shifts. The codewords can also be represented as wavelength-time sequences, such as $\mathbf{x}_{2,2,2} = \lambda_2 0\lambda_0 00\ 00000\ \lambda_1 0000$. Some of these synchronous original carrier-hopping prime codewords are listed in Table 6.1 for illustration.

Using $k = 2$, $w = p' = 3$, and $p_1 = p_2 = 11$ as an example, there are 1452 expanded carrier-hopping prime codewords, denoted by $\mathbf{x}_{i_2,i_1,l_2,l_1} = [(l_1,l_1 \odot_{11} i_1 + (l_1 \odot_{11} i_2)11),((l_1 \oplus_3 l_2) + 3,((l_1 \oplus_3 l_2) + 3)\odot_{11} i_1 + (((l_1 \oplus_3 l_2) + 3)\odot_{11} i_2)11),((l_1 \oplus_3 (2\odot_3 l_2)) + 6,((l_1 \oplus_3 (2\odot_3 l_2)) + 6)\odot_{11} i_1 + (((l_1 \oplus_3 (2\odot_3 l_2)) + 6)\odot_{11} i_2)11)]$ and $\mathbf{x}_{i_2,i_1,l_3} = [(3l_3,(3l_3)\odot_{11} i_1 + ((3l_3)\odot_{11} i_2)11),(3l_3 + 1,(3l_3 + 1)\odot_{11} i_1 + ((3l_3 + 1)\odot_{11} i_2)11),(3l_3 + 2,(3l_3 + 2)\odot_{11} i_1 + (3l_3 + 2)\odot_{11} i_2)11)]$ for $i_1 \in [0,10]$, $i_2 \in [0,10]$, $l_1 \in [0,2]$, $l_2 \in [0,2]$, and $l_3 \in [0,2]$, from Section 5.5. Each of them can generate one subset of $(p_1 p_2)^2 = 121$ cyclic-time-shifted copies, which are indexed by $s \in [0,120]$. So, there are in total $(w^2 + p')(p_1 p_2)^2 = 175692$ synchronous expanded carrier-hopping prime codewords, denoted by $\mathbf{x}_{i_2,i_1,l_2,l_1,s} = [(l_1,l_1 \odot_{11} i_1 + (l_1 \odot_{11} i_2)11 \oplus s),((l_1 \oplus_3 l_2) + 3,((l_1 \oplus_3 l_2) + 3)\odot_{11} i_1 + (((l_1 \oplus_3 l_2) + 3)\odot_{11} i_2)11 \oplus s),((l_1 \oplus_3 (2\odot_3 l_2)) + 6,((l_1 \oplus_3 (2\odot_3 l_2)) + 6)\odot_{11} i_1 + (((l_1 \oplus_3 (2\odot_3 l_2)) + 6)\odot_{11} i_2)11)\oplus s]$ and $\mathbf{x}_{i_2,i_1,l_3,s} = [(3l_3,(3l_3)\odot_{11} i_1 + ((3l_3)\odot_{11} i_2)11 \oplus s),(3l_3 + 1,(3l_3 + 1)\odot_{11} i_1 + ((3l_3 + 1)\odot_{11} i_2)11 \oplus s),(3l_3 + 2,(3l_3 + 2)\odot_{11} i_1 + (3l_3 + 2)\odot_{11} i_2)11 \oplus s)]$ for $i_1 \in [0,10]$, $i_2 \in [0,10]$, $l_1 \in [0,2]$, $l_2 \in [0,2]$, $l_3 \in [0,2]$, and $s \in [0,120]$, where "$\oplus$" is a modulo-121 addition. For example, $\mathbf{x}_{5,2,2,1,0} = [(1,57),(3,50),(8,82)]$ and $\mathbf{x}_{5,2,1,0} = [(3,50),(4,107),(5,43)]$ are two original codewords, and $\mathbf{x}_{5,2,2,1,2} = [(1,59),(3,52),(8,84)]$ and $\mathbf{x}_{5,2,1,2} = [(3,52),(4,109),(5,45)]$ are their copies after two cyclic-time-shifts.

Using $k = 2$, $w = 5$, and $p_1 = p_2 = 5$ as an example, there are 125 quadratic-congruence carrier-hopping prime codewords, denoted by $\mathbf{x}_{i_2,i_1,0} = [(0,0),(1,i_1 + 5i_2),(2,2\odot_5 i_1 + (2\odot_5 i_2)5),(3,3\odot_5 i_1 + (3\odot_5 i_2)5),(4,4\odot_5 i_1 + (4\odot_5 i_2)5)]$ and $\mathbf{x}_{i_2,i_1,l} = [(i_1,0),(1\oplus_5 i_1,1\odot_5 l + (1\odot_5 i_2)5),(2\oplus_5 i_1,3\odot_5 l + (2\odot_5 i_2)5),(3\oplus_5 i_1,6\odot_5 l + (3\odot_5 i_2)5),(4\oplus_5 i_1,10\odot_5 l + (4\odot_5 i_2)5)]$ for $i_1 \in [0,4]$, $i_2 \in [0,4]$, and $l \in [1,4]$, from Section 5.6. Each of them can generate one subset of $p_1 p_2 = 25$ cyclic-time-shifted copies, which are indexed by $s \in [0,24]$. So, there are in total $p_1(p_1 p_2)^2 = 3125$ synchronous quadratic-congruence carrier-hopping

TABLE 6.1

Some Synchronous Original Carrier-Hopping Prime Codewords with $k = 2$, p_1 = 3, $p_2 = 5$, and $w = 3$

(i_2, i_1, s)	$\mathbf{x}_{i_2, i_1, s}$	Wavelength-Time Sequences
$(0,1,0)$	$[(0,0),(1,1),(2,2)]$	$\lambda_0 \lambda_1 \lambda_2 000000000000$
$(0,1,1)$	$[(0,1),(1,2),(2,3)]$	$0\lambda_0 \lambda_1 \lambda_2 00000000000$
$(0,1,2)$	$[(0,2),(1,3),(2,4)]$	$00\lambda_0 \lambda_1 \lambda_2 0000000000$
$(0,1,3)$	$[(0,3),(1,4),(2,5)]$	$000\lambda_0 \lambda_1 \lambda_2 000000000$
$(0,1,4)$	$[(0,4),(1,5),(2,6)]$	$0000\lambda_0 \lambda_1 \lambda_2 00000000$
$(0,1,5)$	$[(0,5),(1,6),(2,7)]$	$00000\lambda_0 \lambda_1 \lambda_2 0000000$
$(0,1,6)$	$[(0,6),(1,7),(2,8)]$	$000000\lambda_0 \lambda_1 \lambda_2 000000$
$(0,1,7)$	$[(0,7),(1,8),(2,9)]$	$0000000\lambda_0 \lambda_1 \lambda_2 00000$
$(0,1,8)$	$[(0,8),(1,9),(2,10)]$	$00000000\lambda_0 \lambda_1 \lambda_2 0000$
$(0,1,9)$	$[(0,9),(1,10),(2,11)]$	$000000000\lambda_0 \lambda_1 \lambda_2 000$
$(0,1,10)$	$[(0,10),(1,11),(2,12)]$	$0000000000\lambda_0 \lambda_1 \lambda_2 00$
$(0,1,11)$	$[(0,11),(1,12),(2,13)]$	$00000000000\lambda_0 \lambda_1 \lambda_2 0$
$(0,1,12)$	$[(0,12),(1,13),(2,14)]$	$000000000000\lambda_0 \lambda_1 \lambda_2$
$(0,1,13)$	$[(0,13),(1,14),(2,0)]$	$\lambda_2 000000000000\lambda_0 \lambda_1$
$(0,1,14)$	$[(0,14),(1,0),(2,1)]$	$\lambda_1 \lambda_2 000000000000\lambda_0$
$(1,0,0)$	$[(0,0),(1,3),(2,6)]$	$\lambda_0 00\lambda_1 00\lambda_2 00000000$
$(1,0,1)$	$[(0,1),(1,4),(2,7)]$	$0\lambda_0 00\lambda_1 00\lambda_2 0000000$
$(1,0,2)$	$[(0,2),(1,5),(2,8)]$	$00\lambda_0 00\lambda_1 00\lambda_2 000000$
$(1,0,3)$	$[(0,3),(1,6),(2,9)]$	$000\lambda_0 00\lambda_1 00\lambda_2 00000$
$(1,0,4)$	$[(0,4),(1,7),(2,10)]$	$0000\lambda_0 00\lambda_1 00\lambda_2 0000$
$(1,0,5)$	$[(0,5),(1,8),(2,11)]$	$00000\lambda_0 00\lambda_1 00\lambda_2 000$
$(1,0,6)$	$[(0,6),(1,9),(2,12)]$	$000000\lambda_0 00\lambda_1 00\lambda_2 00$
$(1,0,7)$	$[(0,7),(1,10),(2,13)]$	$0000000\lambda_0 00\lambda_1 00\lambda_2 0$
$(1,0,8)$	$[(0,8),(1,11),(2,14)]$	$00000000\lambda_0 00\lambda_1 00\lambda_2$
$(1,0,9)$	$[(0,9),(1,12),(2,0)]$	$\lambda_2 00000000\lambda_0 00\lambda_1 00$
$(1,0,10)$	$[(0,10),(1,13),(2,1)]$	$0\lambda_2 00000000\lambda_0 00\lambda_1 0$
$(1,0,11)$	$[(0,11),(1,14),(2,2)]$	$00\lambda_2 00000000\lambda_0 00\lambda_1$
$(1,0,12)$	$[(0,12),(1,0),(2,3)]$	$\lambda_1 00\lambda_2 00000000\lambda_0 00$
$(1,0,13)$	$[(0,13),(1,1),(2,4)]$	$0\lambda_1 00\lambda_2 00000000\lambda_0 0$
$(1,0,14)$	$[(0,14),(1,2),(2,5)]$	$00\lambda_1 00\lambda_2 00000000\lambda_0$
$(1,1,0)$	$[(0,0),(1,4),(2,8)]$	$\lambda_0 000\lambda_1 000\lambda_2 000000$
$(1,1,1)$	$[(0,1),(1,5),(2,9)]$	$0\lambda_0 000\lambda_1 000\lambda_2 00000$
$(1,1,2)$	$[(0,2),(1,6),(2,10)]$	$00\lambda_0 000\lambda_1 000\lambda_2 0000$
$(1,1,3)$	$[(0,3),(1,7),(2,11)]$	$000\lambda_0 000\lambda_1 000\lambda_2 000$
$(1,1,4)$	$[(0,4),(1,8),(2,12)]$	$0000\lambda_0 000\lambda_1 000\lambda_2 00$
$(1,1,5)$	$[(0,5),(1,9),(2,13)]$	$00000\lambda_0 000\lambda_1 000\lambda_2 0$
$(1,1,6)$	$[(0,6),(1,10),(2,14)]$	$000000\lambda_0 000\lambda_1 000\lambda_2$
$(1,1,7)$	$[(0,7),(1,11),(2,0)]$	$\lambda_2 000000\lambda_0 000\lambda_1 000$
$(1,1,8)$	$[(0,8),(1,12),(2,1)]$	$0\lambda_2 000000\lambda_0 000\lambda_1 00$
$(1,1,9)$	$[(0,9),(1,13),(2,2)]$	$00\lambda_2 000000\lambda_0 000\lambda_1 0$

prime codewords, denoted by $\mathbf{x}_{i_2,i_1,0,s} = [(0,s),(1,i_1 + 5i_2 \oplus s),(2,2 \odot_5 i_1 + (2 \odot_5 i_2)5 \oplus s),(3,3 \odot_5 i_1 + (3 \odot_5 i_2)5 \oplus s),(4,4 \odot_5 i_1 + (4 \odot_5 i_2)5 \oplus s)]$ and $\mathbf{x}_{i_2,i_1,l,s} = [(i_1,s),(1 \oplus_5 i_1,1 \odot_5 l + (1 \odot_5 i_2)5 \oplus s),(2 \oplus_5 i_1,3 \odot_5 l + (2 \odot_5 i_2)5 \oplus s),(3 \oplus_5 i_1,6 \odot_5 l + (3 \odot_5 i_2)5 \oplus s),(4 \oplus_5 i_1,10 \odot_5 l + (4 \odot_5 i_2)5 \oplus s)]$ for $i_1 \in [0,4]$, $i_2 \in [0,4]$, $l \in [1,4]$, and $s \in [0,24]$, where "$\oplus$" is a modulo-25 addition. For example, $\mathbf{x}_{1,0,1,0} = [(0,0),(1,6),(2,13),(3,16),(4,20)]$ is one original codeword and $\mathbf{x}_{1,0,1,3} = [(0,3),(1,9),(2,16),(3,19),(4,23)]$ is a copy after three cyclic-time-shifts.

Similar to Chapter 4, the peak of the cross-correlation function between any two synchronous carrier-hopping prime codewords can be as high as the autocorrelation peak, but never be found at the expected autocorrelation-peak (or in-phase) location. By synchronizing to the in-phase location, a receiver can distinguish the true autocorrelation peak from adjacent cross-correlation peaks.

Theorem 6.1

The autocorrelation peaks of these synchronous carrier-hopping prime codes of weight w are equal to w. The in-phase cross-correlation functions of the original, expanded, and quadratic-congruence carrier-hopping prime codes are at most 1, 1, and 2, respectively. The in-phase cross-correlation function between any two correlating codewords from the same subset is at most 0.

Proof The in-phase cross-correlation properties of the synchronous carrier-hopping prime codes follow the periodic cross-correlation properties of the corresponding asynchronous codes in Chapter 5. The in-phase cross-correlation values are no greater than their periodic counterparts because the former do not need to consider any time shift between the correlating codewords, due to code synchronism. The zero in-phase cross-correlation value between any two synchronous codewords in the same subset is due to the zero autocorrelation sidelobes in the asynchronous codewords. Finally, the autocorrelation peaks of w are due to the code weight w. ■

6.1.1 Performance Analysis

According to Section 4.2.1, the chip-synchronous, soft-limiting error probability of the synchronous original, expanded, and quadratic-congruence carrier-hopping prime codes with the maximum in-phase cross-correlation function of $\lambda'_c = \{1,2\}$ in OOK follows Equation (4.3).

Theorem 6.2

For the synchronous original, expanded, and quadratic-congruence carrier-hopping prime codes with cardinality $\Phi_{\text{asyn}} p_1 p_2 \cdots p_k$, $L = w$ wavelengths, length $N = p_1 p_2 \cdots p_k$, weight w, and $\lambda_c' = \{1, 2\}$, the hit probabilities, q_i, of having the in-phase cross-correlation values of $i = \{1, 2, \ldots, \lambda_c'\}$ are formulated as

$$q_i = q_i^{\text{asyn}} \times \frac{(\Phi_{\text{asyn}} - 1) p_1 p_2 \cdots p_k}{\Phi_{\text{asyn}} p_1 p_2 \cdots p_k - 1}$$

$$\sum_{i=0}^{\lambda_c'} i q_i = \frac{w^2}{2LN} \times \frac{(\Phi_{\text{asyn}} - 1) p_1 p_2 \cdots p_k}{\Phi_{\text{asyn}} p_1 p_2 \cdots p_k - 1} = \frac{w(\Phi_{\text{asyn}} - 1) p_1 p_2 \cdots p_k}{2 p_1 p_2 \cdots p_k (\Phi_{\text{asyn}} p_1 p_2 \cdots p_k - 1)}$$

and $\sum_{i=0}^{\lambda_c'} q_i = 1$, where q_i^{asyn} and Φ_{asyn} are the hit probabilities and cardinality of the corresponding asynchronous carrier-hopping prime codes in Chapter 5, respectively.

Proof According to the constructions, the cardinalities of the synchronous codes are $p_1 p_2 \cdots p_k$ times those of the asynchronous counterparts, and there exist zero in-phase cross-correlation values if the correlating codewords are from the same subset of $p_1 p_2 \cdots p_k$ orthogonal codewords. So, the numerator $(\Phi_{\text{asyn}} - 1) p_1 p_2 \cdots p_k$ represents the number of interfering synchronous codewords, excluding those orthogonal codewords in the same subset as the address codeword of the receiver in study. The denominator $\Phi_{\text{asyn}} p_1 p_2 \cdots p_k - 1$ represents the number of interfering synchronous codewords.   ∎

Because these synchronous carrier-hopping prime codes have zero in-phase cross-correlation values among the $p_1 p_2 \cdots p_k$ codewords in every subset, orthogonal codewords can be chosen from the same subset when $K \leq p_1 p_2 \cdots p_k$ (for the $\lambda_c' = 1$ codes) or $K \leq \lceil p_1 p_2 \cdots p_k / 2 \rceil$ (for the $\lambda_c' = 2$ codes), resulting in zero mutual interference and error probability, where $\lceil \cdot \rceil$ is the ceiling function. Otherwise, codewords must be chosen from more than one subset, sacrificing code performance. For example, for the $\lambda_c' = 1$ synchronous carrier-hopping prime codes, if there exist $K \in [p_1 p_2 \cdots p_k + 1, 2 p_1 p_2 \cdots p_k]$ simultaneous users, codewords are selected from two subsets in order to limit the amount of mutual interference. In general, if $K \in [(l - 1) p_1 p_2 \cdots p_k + 1, l p_1 p_2 \cdots p_k]$, codewords are selected from l subsets, where $l \in [1, \Phi_{\text{asyn}}]$. This "subset-by-subset" codeword-selection method can optimize the code performance, as shown in Theorem 6.3.

Theorem 6.3

For the synchronous original carrier-hopping prime codes with cardinality $\Phi_{\text{asyn}} p_1 p_2 \cdots p_k$, $L = w$ wavelengths, length $N = p_1 p_2 \cdots p_k$, weight w, and $\lambda_c' = 1$, the chip-synchronous, soft-limiting error probability can be optimized as

$$
\begin{aligned}
P_{e,\text{soft,optimal}}(K) \;=\; & \frac{\left\lfloor \dfrac{K}{p_1 p_2 \cdots p_k} \right\rfloor p_1 p_2 \cdots p_k}{K} \times P_{e,\text{soft}}(K - p_1 p_2 \cdots p_k + 1) \\[2ex]
& + \frac{K - \left\lfloor \dfrac{K}{p_1 p_2 \cdots p_k} \right\rfloor p_1 p_2 \cdots p_k}{K} \\[2ex]
& \times P_{e,\text{soft}}\left(\left\lfloor \dfrac{K}{p_1 p_2 \cdots p_k} \right\rfloor p_1 p_2 \cdots p_k + 1 \right)
\end{aligned}
\tag{6.1}
$$

by applying the subset-by-subset codeword-selection method, where $P_{e,\text{soft}}(\cdot)$ is given in Equation (4.3), and $\lfloor \cdot \rfloor$ is the floor function.

Proof Because the codeword-selection method requires an entire subset of the synchronous original carrier-hopping prime codewords to be assigned to the K simultaneous users before making another subset available, the sources of error probability can be divided into two categories. In the first category, there exist $\lfloor K/p_1 p_2 \cdots p_k \rfloor$ subsets in which all their codewords are selected. As there are $p_1 p_2 \cdots p_k$ codewords per subset, the term $\lfloor \lfloor K/p_1 p_2 \cdots p_k \rfloor p_1 p_2 \cdots p_k \rfloor / K$ represents the probability of picking an interfering codeword from these subsets. The effective number of simultaneous users becomes $K - (p_1 p_2 \cdots p_k - 1)$ by excluding the $p_1 p_2 \cdots p_k - 1$ interfering codewords that are in the same subset as the address codeword of the receiver in study. This is because the codewords in the same subset are all orthogonal. In the second category, there exist $K - \lfloor K/(p_1 p_2 \cdots p_k) \rfloor p_1 p_2 \cdots p_k$ codewords coming from the last subset in which not all its codewords are selected. The effective number of simultaneous users becomes $\lfloor K/(p_1 p_2 \cdots p_k) \rfloor p_1 p_2 \cdots p_k + 1$ by including the address codeword itself and the (non-orthogonal) interfering codewords in different subsets than the address codeword. ∎

Figure 6.1 plots the chip-synchronous, soft-limiting error probabilities of the asynchronous and synchronous original carrier-hopping prime codes for $p_1 = \{37, 101\}$, where $k = 1$, $L = w = 10$, and $N = p_1$. The maximum cross-correlation functions of both code families are 1, but the first function is periodic and the second function is in-phase. From Section 5.1, $q_1^{\text{asyn}} = w^2/(2LN) = w/(2p_1)$, $q_0^{\text{asyn}} = 1 - q_1^{\text{asyn}}$, and $\Phi_{\text{asyn}} = p_1$. In general, the error probabilities improve as p_1 increases because longer code length ($N = p_1$) lowers the hit probabilities. However, the error probabilities get worse as K increases due to stronger mutual interference. In the solid and dashed curves, simultaneous users are assumed to randomly select codewords from the sets of p^2 and p codewords, respectively—the maximum cardinality of both code families. This explains why the dashed curves stop at $K = p_1 = \{37, 101\}$, but the solid curves continue up to $K = p_1^2$. Nevertheless, the performances of the synchronous and asynchronous codes are almost identical because their dominating hit probabilities q_1 and q_1^{asyn} only differ by a factor of $(\Phi_{\text{asyn}} - 1)p_1/(\Phi_{\text{asyn}} p_1 - 1)$, as shown in Theorem 6.2, which is almost equal to 1, especially when p_1 is large.

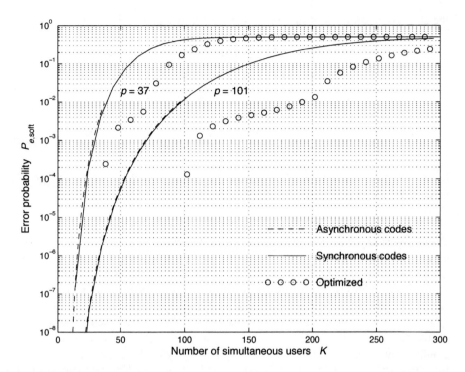

FIGURE 6.1 Chip-synchronous, soft-limiting error probabilities of the asynchronous and synchronous original carrier-hopping prime codes for $k = 1$, $L = w = 10$, and $N = p_1 = \{37, 101\}$.

Figure 6.1 also shows an example of how the performance of the synchronous carrier-hopping prime codes can be optimized as a function of K and the number of orthogonal codewords in each subset. The circles represent the code performance with the selection of orthogonal codewords "subset-by-subset," based on Theorem 6.3. The circles start from $K > p_1$ because synchronous codewords coming from the same subset are orthogonal and then $P_{e,\text{soft}} = 0$ when $K \leq p_1$. Nonzero error probabilities (the circles) appear at $K > p_1$ and gets worse gradually. As synchronous codewords are now selected from more than one subset, code orthogonality is broken slowly as K increases beyond p_1. The synchronous carrier-hopping prime codes always perform better than the asynchronous counterparts, especially when $K \leq p_1$, and support more subscribers at the expense of code synchronism.

6.2 SYNCHRONOUS MULTILEVEL CARRIER-HOPPING PRIME CODES

Similar to those synchronous carrier-hopping prime codes in Section 6.1, there also exists a synchronous version of the multilevel carrier-hopping prime codes in Section 5.2. In this section, synchronous multilevel carrier-hopping prime codes, which have multiple levels of in-phase cross-correlation functions, are constructed. By partitioning the codes into a tree structure of subsets of codewords, the cross-correlation values can be varied to attain different code performances and cardinalities. Subsets of codewords in the lowest level of the tree structure achieve orthogonality.

Based on $GF(p)$ of a prime number p and two positive integers k and n, the synchronous multilevel carrier-hopping prime codes with cardinality $p^{(n+1)k}$, $L = w$ wavelengths, length $N = p^k$, weight $w \leq p$, and the maximum in-phase cross-correlation function $\lambda_c' = n \leq w$ are constructed in the form of binary $(0,1)$ matrices, $\mathbf{x}_{i_{k,n+1},i_{k,n},\ldots,i_{k,1},i_{k-1,n+1},i_{k-1,n},\ldots,i_{1,1}}$, with the ordered pairs [3, 4]

$$\{[(0,x_{i_{k,n+1},i_{k,n},\ldots,i_{k,1},i_{k-1,n+1},i_{k-1,n},\ldots,i_{1,1}},0),(1,x_{i_{k,n+1},i_{k,n},\ldots,i_{k,1},i_{k-1,n+1},i_{k-1,n},\ldots,i_{1,1}},1),$$
$$(2,x_{i_{k,n+1},i_{k,n},\ldots,i_{k,1},i_{k-1,n+1},i_{k-1,n},\ldots,i_{1,1}},2),\ldots,(j,x_{i_{k,n+1},i_{k,n},\ldots,i_{k,1},i_{k-1,n+1},i_{k-1,n},\ldots,i_{1,1}},j),$$
$$\ldots,(w-1,x_{i_{k,n+1},i_{k,n},\ldots,i_{k,1},i_{k-1,n+1},i_{k-1,n},\ldots,i_{1,1}},w-1)]: i_{s,t} = \{0,1,\ldots,p-1\}$$
$$\text{for } s = \{1,2,\ldots,k\} \text{ and } t = \{1,2,\ldots,n+1\}\}$$

The jth code element is given by

$$x_{i_{k,n+1},i_{k,n},\ldots,i_{k,1},i_{k-1,n+1},i_{k-1,n},\ldots,i_{1,1},j}$$
$$= \left\{ \sum_{m=1}^{k} p^{m-1} \left[(j^n i_{m,n+1}) \oplus_p (j^{n-1} i_{m,n}) \oplus_p \cdots \oplus_p (j i_{m,2}) \right] \right\}$$
$$\oplus_{p^k} (i_{k,1}p^{k-1} + i_{k-1,1}p^{k-2} + \cdots + i_{2,1}p + i_{1,1})$$

which determines the chip (time) location of the jth wavelength in a codeword for $j = \{0,1,\ldots,w-1\}$, where "$\oplus_h$" represents a modulo-h addition for $h = \{p,p^k\}$.

In general, the parameters and properties of these synchronous multilevel carrier-hopping prime codes remain the same as those of their asynchronous counterparts in Section 5.2, except that the maximum in-phase cross-correlation function λ_c' is now considered, in place of the periodic one, due to code synchronism. As a result, the cardinality of these synchronous multilevel carrier-hopping prime codes is p^k times the cardinality of the asynchronous ones.

Illustrated in Figure 6.2, the $p^{(n+1)k}$ synchronous multilevel carrier-hopping prime codewords can be partitioned into a tree structure of $n+1$ levels. Starting from the root on the left-hand side, level $n+1$ has one set of $\Phi = p^{(n+1)k}$ codewords of $\lambda_c' = n$. In level n, these $p^{(n+1)k}$ codewords are partitioned into p^k subsets and each subset has $\Phi = p^{nk}$ codewords of $\lambda_c' = n-1$. In level $n-1$, every subset of p^{nk} codewords in level n is further partitioned into p^k subsets, giving a total of p^{2k} subsets and each subset has $\Phi = p^{(n-1)k}$ codewords of $\lambda_c' = n-2$. This partition process continues to level 1, in which there are in total p^{nk} subsets and $\Phi = p^k$ codewords in each subset with $\lambda_c' = 0$. Code orthogonality (or zero mutual interference) is achieved within every subset in level 1, an important characteristic of the synchronous multilevel carrier-hopping prime codes. This partition property allows the selection of codewords of certain cardinality and performance. If code performance is more important than cardinality, codewords from lower levels of the tree structure are selected. If cardinality is more important, codewords from higher levels are used at the expense of code performance.

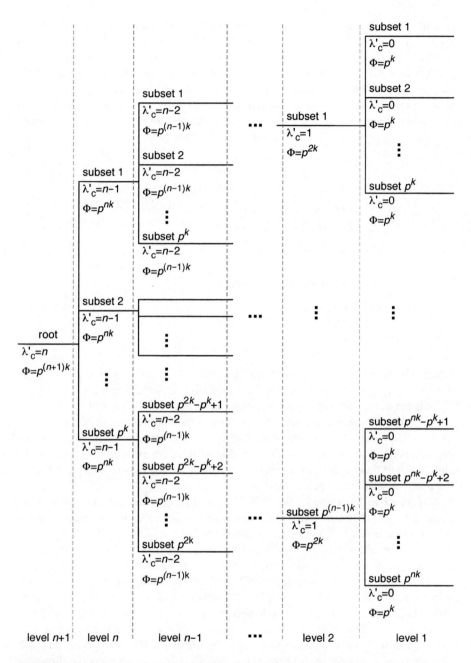

FIGURE 6.2 Tree structure of the synchronous multilevel carrier-hopping prime codes over $GF(p)$ of a prime p and positive integers n and k, where Φ is the code cardinality in each subset.

The synchronous original carrier-hopping prime codes in Section 6.1 belong to one subset in level 2.

Theorem 6.4

The autocorrelation peaks of the synchronous multilevel carrier-hopping prime codes over GF(p) of a prime p and weight w are equal to w, where $w \le p$ [3, 4]. The in-phase cross-correlation functions of the codes are at most n, but at most $l-1$ if the correlating codewords come from the same subset in level $l \in [1, n+1]$.

Proof The in-phase cross-correlation properties of the synchronous multilevel carrier-hopping prime codes follow the periodic cross-correlation properties of the corresponding asynchronous codes in Section 5.2. The in-phase cross-correlation values are no greater than their periodic counterparts because the former do not need to consider any cyclic-shift between the correlating codewords due to code synchronism. The zero in-phase cross-correlation value between any two synchronous multilevel carrier-hopping prime codewords in the same subset of level 1 is due to the zero autocorrelation sidelobes in the corresponding asynchronous codewords in Section 5.2. The autocorrelation peaks of w are due to the code weight $w \le p$. ∎

Using $k=1$, $n=2$, $L=w=4$, and $p=N=5$ as an example, there are 125 synchronous trilevel carrier-hopping prime codewords, denoted by $\mathbf{x}_{i_{1,3}, i_{1,2}, i_{1,1}} = [(0, i_{1,1}), (1, i_{1,3} \oplus_5 i_{1,2} \oplus_5 i_{1,1}), (2, 4i_{1,3} \oplus_5 2i_{1,2} \oplus_5 i_{1,1}), (3, 9i_{1,3} \oplus_5 3i_{1,2} \oplus_5 i_{1,1})]$ for $i_{1,1} \in [0,4]$, $i_{1,2} \in [0,4]$, and $i_{1,3} \in [0,4]$, where "$\oplus_5$" represents a modulo-5 addition. The 25 synchronous trilevel prime codewords with $i_{1,3} = 0$ are listed in Table 6.2. The partitioning of code subsets is done by the use of indices $i_{1,2}$ and $i_{1,3}$. In level 3, all 125 codewords have $\lambda_c' = 2$. In level 2, the 25 codewords with the same $i_{1,3}$ value (e.g., those in Table 6.2) have $\lambda_c' = 1$, but those with different $i_{1,3}$ values have $\lambda_c' = 2$. In level 1, every 5 codewords with the same $i_{1,2}$ and $i_{1,3}$ values have $\lambda_c' = 0$ (e.g., the 5 codewords in every group in Table 6.2).

6.2.1 Performance Analysis

From Section 4.2.1, the chip-synchronous, soft-limiting error probability of the synchronous multilevel carrier-hopping prime codes over GF(p) of a prime p with the maximum in-phase cross-correlation function $\lambda_c' = n$ in OOK follows Equation (4.3).

Theorem 6.5

For the synchronous multilevel carrier-hopping prime codes over GF(p) of a prime

TABLE 6.2

Synchronous Trilevel Carrier-Hopping Prime Codewords over GF(5) with $w = 4$, $i_{1,3} = 0$, and $k = 1$

$(i_{1,2},i_{1,1})$	$\mathbf{x}_{0,i_{1,2},i_{1,1}}$	$(i_{1,2},i_{1,1})$	$\mathbf{x}_{0,i_{1,2},i_{1,1}}$
(0,0)	[(0,0),(1,0),(2,0),(3,0)]	(3,0)	[(0,0),(1,3),(2,1),(3,4)]
(0,1)	[(0,1),(1,1),(2,1),(3,1)]	(3,1)	[(0,1),(1,4),(2,2),(3,0)]
(0,2)	[(0,2),(1,2),(2,2),(3,2)]	(3,2)	[(0,2),(1,0),(2,3),(3,1)]
(0,3)	[(0,3),(1,3),(2,3),(3,3)]	(3,3)	[(0,3),(1,1),(2,4),(3,2)]
(0,4)	[(0,4),(1,4),(2,4),(3,4)]	(3,4)	[(0,4),(1,2),(2,0),(3,3)]
(1,0)	[(0,0),(1,1),(2,2),(3,3)]	(4,0)	[(0,0),(1,4),(2,3),(3,2)]
(1,1)	[(0,1),(1,2),(2,3),(3,4)]	(4,1)	[(0,1),(1,0),(2,4),(3,3)]
(1,2)	[(0,2),(1,3),(2,4),(3,0)]	(4,2)	[(0,2),(1,1),(2,0),(3,4)]
(1,3)	[(0,3),(1,4),(2,0),(3,1)]	(4,3)	[(0,3),(1,2),(2,1),(3,0)]
(1,4)	[(0,4),(1,0),(2,1),(3,2)]	(4,4)	[(0,4),(1,3),(2,2),(3,1)]
(2,0)	[(0,0),(1,2),(2,4),(3,1)]		
(2,1)	[(0,1),(1,3),(2,0),(3,2)]		
(2,2)	[(0,2),(1,4),(2,1),(3,3)]		
(2,3)	[(0,3),(1,0),(2,2),(3,4)]		
(2,4)	[(0,4),(1,1),(2,3),(3,0)]		

p with cardinality $p^{(n+1)k}$, $L = w$ wavelengths, length $N = p^k$, weight $w \le p$, and $\lambda'_c = n$, the hit probabilities, q_i, of having the in-phase cross-correlation values of $i = \{0,1,\ldots,n\}$ are formulated as [3, 4]

$$q_i = \frac{h_{n,i}}{2[p^{(n+1)k} - 1]}$$

$$\sum_{i=0}^{n} i q_i = \frac{w(p^{nk} - 1)}{2[p^{(n+1)k} - 1]}$$

and $\sum_{i=0}^{n} q_i = 1$, where $h_{n,i}$ is the total number of times of getting i hits in the in-phase cross-correlation function, given by

$$h_{n,0} = 2[p^{(n+1)k} - 1] - h_{n,n} - h_{n,n-1} - \cdots - h_{n,1}$$

$$h_{n,1} = w(p^{nk} - 1) - nh_{n,n} - (n-1)h_{n,n-1} - \cdots - 2h_{n,2}$$

$$h_{n,i} = \frac{(h_{n-1,i-1} + h_{n-2,i-1} + \cdots + h_{i-1,i-1})h_{i,i}}{h_{i-1,i-1}}$$

$$h_{n,n} = \frac{w!(p^k - 1)}{n!(w - n)!}$$

Proof The derivations of the synchronous hit probabilities, q_i, are similar to those in Theorem 4.5 (for synchronous 1-D multilevel prime codes in Section 4.2) as code orthogonality in the subsets of level 1 needs to be considered. So,

$$q_i = \frac{1}{2} \times \frac{h_{n,i}}{p^{(n+1)k} - 1}$$

$$\sum_{i=0}^{n} i q_i = \frac{w^2}{2LN} \times \frac{p^{(n+1)k} - p^k}{p^{(n+1)k} - 1} = \frac{w}{2p^k} \times \frac{p^k(p^{nk} - 1)}{p^{(n+1)k} - 1}$$

where the factor $1/2$ comes from the assumption of equiprobable data bit-1 and bit-0 transmissions in OOK, $p^{(n+1)k} - 1$ represents the possible number of interfering codewords, and $p^{(n+1)k} - p^k$ accounts for the number of interfering codewords not coming from the same subset in level 1 of the address codeword of the receiver in study. The hit probability q_i is computed by evaluating $h_{n,i}$ recursively. The equations of $h_{n,0}$ and $h_{n,1}$ come from the rearrangements of $q_i = h_{n,i}/\{2[p^{(n+1)k} - 1]\}$ in $\sum_{i=0}^{n} q_i = 1$ and $\sum_{i=0}^{n} i q_i$, respectively.

Starting from the root of the tree structure, codewords in level $n + 1$ can be partitioned into p^k subsets and only one subset has the same $(i_{k,n+1}, i_{k-1,n+1}, \ldots, i_{1,n+1})$ values as the address codeword. So, there are $p^k - 1$ subsets of interfering codewords contributing at most n hits in the in-phase cross-correlation function, out of a total of w possible hits. This accounts for the equation of $h_{n,n}$. Furthermore, $h_{n-1,i}$ counts the number of times of getting j hits contributed by the interfering codewords in level $n + 1$ with the same $(i_{k,n+1}, i_{k-1,n+1}, \ldots, i_{1,n+1})$ subset as the address codeword. Because the cross-correlation property of the codewords is uniform, the term $(h_{n,i} - h_{n-1,i})/h_{n-1,i-1}$ is always a constant, in which $h_{n,i} - h_{n-1,i}$ counts the number of times getting i hits contributed by the interfering codewords in level $n + 1$ with different $(i_{k,n+1}, i_{k-1,n+1}, \ldots, i_{1,n+1})$ subsets as the address codeword. Continuing down the tree level-by-level, the relationship found in the term $(h_{n,i} - h_{n-1,i})/h_{n-1,i-1}$ holds as a recursive function of n and results in

$$\frac{h_{n,i} - h_{n-1,i}}{h_{n-1,i-1}} = \frac{h_{n-1,i} - h_{n-2,i}}{h_{n-2,j-1}} = \cdots = \frac{h_{i,i} - h_{i-1,i}}{h_{i-1,i-1}}$$

in which $h_{i-1,i} = 0$ is assumed because $h_{i-1,i}$ does not exist, by definition. After some manipulations, the final form of $h_{n,i}$ in the theorem is derived. ∎

To complete the evaluation of the hit probabilities in Theorem 6.5, $h_{n,n}$, $h_{n,n-1}$, ..., and $h_{n,0}$ are found from the following steps:

Step 1: Set $n = 1$.

   a. For $i = 1$, the equation of $h_{n,n}$ gives $h_{1,1} = w(p^k - 1)$.

Step 2: Increase n by one to $n = 2$.

   a. For $i = 2$, the equation of $h_{n,n}$ gives $h_{2,2} = w(w - 1)(p^k - 1)/2$.
   b. For $i = 1$, the equation of $h_{n,1}$ gives $h_{2,1} = w(p^{2k} - 1) - 2h_{2,2} = w(p^k + 2 - w)(p^k - 1)$.

Step 3: Increase $n = j - 1$ by one to $n = j$, for all $j = \{3, 4, 5, \ldots, \lambda'_c\}$.

    a. For $i = j$, the equation of $h_{n,n}$ gives $h_{j,j} = w!(p^k - 1)/[j!(w - j)!]$.

    b. For $i = \{j - 1, j - 2, \ldots, 2\}$, the equation of $h_{n,i}$ gives $h_{j,j-1}$, $h_{j,j-2}$, $\ldots$, and $h_{j,2}$, respectively.

    c. For $i = 1$, the equation of $h_{n,1}$ gives $h_{j,1} = w(p^{jk} - 1) - jh_{j,j} - (j - 1)h_{j,j-1} - \cdots - 2h_{j,2}$.

Step 4: Repeat Step 3 if $n \leq \lambda'_c$; otherwise, go to Step 5.

Step 5: Finally, $h_{n,0} = 2[p^{(n+1)k} - 1] - h_{n,n} - h_{n,n-1} - \cdots - h_{n,1}$ is obtained.

Because these synchronous multilevel carrier-hopping prime codes have zero in-phase cross-correlation values among the p^k codewords in every subset in level 1, orthogonal codewords can be chosen from the same subset when $K \leq p^k$, resulting in zero mutual interference and error probability. Otherwise, codewords must be chosen from more than one subset in level 1, sacrificing code performance. If there exist $K \in [p^k + 1, p^{2k}]$ simultaneous users, codewords are selected from multiple subsets of level 1 but all these subsets of level 1 should come from one subset of level 2 in order to limit λ'_c to 1. Similarly, if $K \in [p^{2k} + 1, p^{3k}]$, codewords from one subset of level 3 are chosen in order to contain λ'_c at 2. In general, if $K \in [p^{lk} + 1, p^{(l+1)k}]$, codewords are selected from one subset of level $l + 1$ in order to limit λ'_c to l, where $l \in [0, n]$.

Figure 6.3 plots the chip-synchronous, soft-limiting error probabilities of the synchronous multilevel carrier-hopping prime codes against the number of simultaneous users K for $L = w = \{10, 15, 20\}$, $N = p = 89$, $k = 1$, and $\lambda'_c = n = \{1, 2\}$. In general, the error probabilities improve as w increases because of higher autocorrelation peaks. However, the error probabilities get worse when n or K increases due to stronger mutual interference. Because the code cardinality is given by $p^{(n+1)k}$, there is a trade-off between code performance and cardinality. The biggest difference in the error probabilities occurs between $n = 1$ and $n = 2$, and the worsening in error probabilities slows down when $n \geq 3$. This is because hit probabilities get worse and cannot depreciate much further as n increases beyond 3. Also note that the error probabilities of the synchronous multilevel carrier-hopping prime codes should be very similar to those of the asynchronous counterparts in Section 5.2 if the code parameters are the same. This is because their hit probabilities are only different by a small factor of $[p^{(n+1)k} - p^k]/[p^{(n+1)k} - 1]$. As p or n increases, the factor is almost equal to 1; the performances of the synchronous and asynchronous multilevel carrier-hopping prime codes become almost identical, similar to the situation in Figure 6.1.

Figure 6.4 shows an example of how the performance of the synchronous multilevel carrier-hopping prime codes can be optimized as a function of K and the number of orthogonal codewords in each subset of level 1. The synchronous trilevel carrier-hopping prime codes with $L = w = \{8, 12\}$, $N = p = \{23, 31\}$, $k = 1$, and $\lambda'_c = n = 2$ are used in this example. In this code set, there are p^3 codewords with

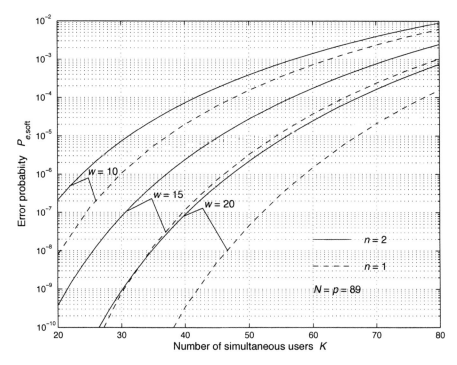

FIGURE 6.3 Chip-synchronous, soft-limiting error probabilities of the synchronous multi-level carrier-hopping prime codes for $L = w = \{10, 15, 20\}$, $N = p = 89$, $k = 1$, and $n = \{1, 2\}$.

$\lambda_c' = 2$ in the root (or level 3). These p^3 codewords can be partitioned into p subsets of codewords in level 2, in which each subset consists of p^2 codewords with $\lambda_c' = 1$. Every subset of p^2 codewords in level 2 can be further partitioned into p subsets with p orthogonal codewords (with $\lambda_c' = 0$) in each subset in level 1. Similar to Figure 6.3, the solid curves show the error probabilities with interfering codewords being randomly selected from all p^3 codewords (of $\lambda_c' = 2$). To optimize the code performance as a function of K, codewords are selected in a subset-by-subset fashion. When $K \leq p$, the codewords are chosen from only one subset of level 1. When $K \in [p+1, p^2]$, the remaining $K - p$ interfering codewords are chosen from another subset in level 1. When $K > p^2$, codewords from more than two subsets of level 1 are selected for the remaining $K - p^2$ codewords. The asterisks and circles represent the optimized performance with the selection of orthogonal codewords "subset-by-subset," based on Theorem 6.3. Nonzero error probabilities (the asterisks and circles) appear at $K > p = \{23, 31\}$ because synchronous codewords coming from the same subset are orthogonal and then $P_{e,\text{soft}} = 0$ when $K \leq p$. Both asterisks and circles get worse gradually as synchronous codewords are now selected from more than one subset and code orthogonality is broken slowly as K increases beyond p. They slowly approach the solid curves as more $\lambda_c' = 1$ codewords are added. Although it is not shown in the figure, the asterisks and circles will overlap with the solid curves when

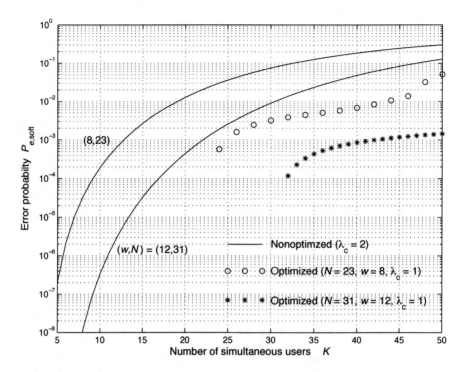

FIGURE 6.4 Chip-synchronous, soft-limiting error probabilities of the synchronous trilevel carrier-hopping prime codes, optimized as a function of K, for $L = w = \{8, 12\}$, $N = p = \{23, 31\}$, $k = 1$, and $n = 2$.

$K > p^2$ because codewords with $\lambda_c' = 2$ are eventually selected. In summary, by partitioning the codewords into multiple levels, the code cardinality and maximum in-phase cross-correlation function are selected to suit different code-performance requirements.

6.3 SYNCHRONOUS PRIME-PERMUTED CODES

In this section, the synchronous prime-permuted codes, which use bipolar codes, such as Walsh codes and modified maximal-length sequences, for wavelength hopping and Walsh codes for time spreading, are constructed [7,10–13]. The main difference from the asynchronous prime-permuted codes in Section 5.8 [5,6] is that Walsh codes are synchronous bipolar codes, which dictate (time) synchronization when they are now used as the time-spreading codes. These synchronous prime-permuted codes improve the code cardinality and performance over those asynchronous ones in Section 5.8, and also support code-inversion keying (CIK) by means of transmitting a wavelength-conjugate codeword for every data bit 0.

The construction of the synchronous prime-permuted codes is similar to that of the asynchronous counterparts in Section 5.8. For the wavelength-hopping part, the wavelengths in every time slot of a codeword are determined by the multiwavelength codewords formed by the bipolar codes in use. To ensure true orthogonality (or zero in-phase cross-correlations) among these multiwavelength codewords, the bipolar codes, such as Walsh codes and modified maximal-length sequences, chosen for wavelength hopping must have the same numbers of "+1" and "−1" elements in each codeword [7]. For example, the multiwavelength codewords and their wavelength conjugates based on the modified maximal-length sequences and Walsh code of length 8 are shown in Table 5.10, in which the wavelength mapping of the multiwavelength codewords, C_i, is determined by the positions of "+1" elements, whereas $\overline{C}_i$ denotes the wavelength conjugate of C_i, for $i = \{0, 1, 2, \ldots, 6\}$. For the time-spreading part, Walsh code of a different length $N \leq p$ is now used. The "+1" elements of each time-spreading Walsh codeword are transmitted with multiwavelength codewords, while the "−1" elements are transmitted with the corresponding wavelength conjugates of the multiwavelength codewords in use. In general, Walsh code of length N can produce N synchronous time-spreading codewords with zero in-phase cross-correlation functions [1,10]. To generate the final synchronous prime-permuted codewords, the multiwavelength codewords are permuted onto the time slots of the time-spreading codewords with the permutation controlled by the shifted prime sequences over $GF(p)$ of a prime p, similar to the procedure discussed in Figure 5.22(b), but the asynchronous Barker sequences are now replaced by synchronous Walsh codes as the time-spreading codewords.

TABLE 6.3

Synchronous Prime-Permuted Codewords over GF(7), Based on the 7 Multiwavelength Codewords of Length 8 in Table 5.8, and the Time-Spreading Walsh Codeword $(+1, -1, +1, -1)$

Group 0	Group 1	Group 2	Group 3	$\cdots$	Group 6
$C_0\overline{C}_0C_0\overline{C}_0$	$C_0\overline{C}_1C_2\overline{C}_3$	$C_0\overline{C}_2C_4\overline{C}_6$	$C_0\overline{C}_3C_6\overline{C}_2$	$\cdots$	$C_0\overline{C}_6C_5\overline{C}_4$
$C_1\overline{C}_1C_1\overline{C}_1$	$C_1\overline{C}_2C_3\overline{C}_4$	$C_1\overline{C}_3C_5\overline{C}_0$	$C_1\overline{C}_4C_0\overline{C}_3$	$\cdots$	$C_1\overline{C}_0C_6\overline{C}_5$
$C_2\overline{C}_2C_2\overline{C}_2$	$C_2\overline{C}_3C_4\overline{C}_5$	$C_2\overline{C}_4C_6\overline{C}_1$	$C_2\overline{C}_5C_1\overline{C}_4$	$\cdots$	$C_2\overline{C}_1C_0\overline{C}_6$
$C_3\overline{C}_3C_3\overline{C}_3$	$C_3\overline{C}_4C_5\overline{C}_6$	$C_3\overline{C}_5C_0\overline{C}_2$	$C_3\overline{C}_6C_2\overline{C}_5$	$\cdots$	$C_3\overline{C}_2C_1\overline{C}_0$
$C_4\overline{C}_4C_4\overline{C}_4$	$C_4\overline{C}_5C_6\overline{C}_0$	$C_4\overline{C}_6C_1\overline{C}_3$	$C_4\overline{C}_0C_3\overline{C}_6$	$\cdots$	$C_4\overline{C}_3C_2\overline{C}_1$
$C_5\overline{C}_5C_5\overline{C}_5$	$C_5\overline{C}_6C_0\overline{C}_1$	$C_5\overline{C}_0C_2\overline{C}_4$	$C_5\overline{C}_1C_4\overline{C}_0$	$\cdots$	$C_5\overline{C}_4C_3\overline{C}_2$
$C_6\overline{C}_6C_6\overline{C}_6$	$C_6\overline{C}_0C_1\overline{C}_2$	$C_6\overline{C}_1C_3\overline{C}_5$	$C_6\overline{C}_2C_5\overline{C}_1$	$\cdots$	$C_6\overline{C}_5C_4\overline{C}_3$

Table 6.3 shows the 49 synchronous prime-permuted codewords generated by using the shifted prime sequences over $GF(7)$ in Table 5.3, 7 multiwavelength codewords of length 8 in Table 5.8, and the time-spreading Walsh code $(+1, -1, +1, -1)$ of length 4. The "+1" and "−1" elements in the time-spreading codeword are represented by the multiwavelength codewords C_i and $\overline{C}_i$, correspondingly, where the index i follows the values of the elements in each shifted prime sequence. Because there are N Walsh codewords of length $N \leq p$ and the same p^2 permutations can be applied, this results in a total of $Np^2 = 196$ synchronous prime-permuted codewords in this example.

For CIK, the synchronous prime-permuted codewords in Table 6.3 are for the transmission of data bit 1s; a conjugate form is used for transmitting data bit 0s. For example, if the codeword $C_2\overline{C}_1C_0\overline{C}_6$ is transmitted for a data bit 1, its wavelength conjugate $\overline{C}_2C_1\overline{C}_0C_6$ will be transmitted for a bit 0.

Theorem 6.6

The autocorrelation peaks of the synchronous prime-permuted codes over $GF(p)$ of a prime p and length N are equal to N, where $N \leq p$. The in-phase cross-correlation functions of the codes are at most 1, but at most 0 if the correlating codewords are from the same group of the shifted prime sequences [7].

Proof Let $\mathbf{x}_{u,g,s}$ and $\mathbf{x}_{u,g,s'}$ be two distinct synchronous prime-permuted codewords originating from the sth and s'th shifted prime sequences in the same gth group, and the same uth time-spreading codeword, where $s \neq s'$, $u \in [1,N]$, $g \in [0, p-1]$, $s \in [0, p-1]$, and $s' \in [0, p-1]$. Their in-phase cross-correlation function is 0 due to the same cross-correlation property of the shifted prime sequences in the same group. The same cross-correlation property is also found in the correlation of $\mathbf{x}_{u,g,s}$ with $\mathbf{x}_{u',g,s}$ or $\mathbf{x}_{u',g,s'}$ due to the same cross-correlation property of the time-spreading Walsh code [12], where $s \neq s'$ and $u \neq u'$.

For any two distinct codewords originating from different groups of the shifted prime sequences (no matter with the same or different time-spreading Walsh codewords), the maximum in-phase cross-correlation function is 1 due to the same cross-correlation property of the shifted prime sequences in different groups.

Finally, the autocorrelation peaks of N are due to the code weight w, which is equal to N in the time-spreading Walsh code. ∎

As studied in Sections 5.7 and 5.8, the overall cardinality of the synchronized prime-permuted codes depends on the number of valid groups, Φ_{group}, of the shifted prime sequences over $GF(p)$, the number of multiwavelength bipolar codewords Φ_λ, and the number of time-spreading Walsh codewords Φ_{Walsh}. Due to the property of $GF(p)$ of a prime p, all elements of $GF(p)$ occur exactly once in each shifted prime sequence, excluding those in group 0, and there is at most one location in any shifted prime sequence having an identical element in the same location in other shifted prime sequences [e.g., see Table 5.3]. These two conditions are important to maintain the in-phase cross-correlation functions of at most 1 in Theorem 6.6. So, the best overall cardinality is achieved when p is a prime number and Φ_λ is also equal to p, which matches with the number of shifted prime sequences in each group. This is because all p groups (with p shifted prime sequences in each group) can be used for wavelength permutation (e.g., see Table 6.3). By the same argument, extension fields of a prime number, $GF(p^n)$ for an integer $n > 1$, also carry the same nonrepeating-element property [e.g., see $GF(2^3)$ in Table 5.5] and result in the best overall cardinality. The permutation algorithm also works with a non-prime p but with reduced cardinality, as explained in Sections 5.7 and 5.8. Details and general rules on how a non-prime field can be used to obtain valid groups of shifted prime sequences are given in Section 5.7.

In summary, the overall cardinality of these synchronous prime-permuted codes is given by [7]

$$\Phi_{\text{overall}} = \Phi_{\text{group}} \Phi_\lambda \Phi_{\text{Walsh}} \leq p^2 N$$

where $N \leq p$. In the viewpoint of cardinality, even though the permutation algorithm works with a non-prime p', it is often more beneficial to use the largest prime number less than or equal to p', as discussed in Section 5.7.

6.3.1 Performance Analysis

Under Gaussian approximation, the error probability of the synchronous prime-permuted codes over $GF(p)$ of a prime p and length $N \leq p$ in CIK is given by [1,7,10,13]

$$P_{e,\text{Gaussian}} = Q\left(\sqrt{\text{SIR}}\right) = Q\left(\sqrt{\frac{N^2}{(K-1)\sigma^2}}\right)$$

according to Section 1.8.1, where $Q(x) = (2\pi)^{-1/2} \int_x^\infty \exp(-y^2/2) dy$ is the complementary error function and the signal-to-interference power ratio (SIR) is defined as the ratio of the autocorrelation peak, which is equal to the code length N in this case, squared to the total interference variance $(K-1)\sigma^2$.

Because the synchronous prime-permuted codes over $GF(p)$ of a prime p have zero in-phase cross-correlation values among the Np codewords in the same group of the shifted prime sequences, orthogonal codewords can be chosen from the same group when $K \leq Np$, resulting in zero mutual interference and error probability. Otherwise, codewords should be chosen from more than one group, sacrificing code performance. If there exist $K \in [Np+1, 2Np]$ simultaneous users, codewords are selected from two groups in order to limit the amount of mutual interference. In general, if $K \in [(l-1)Np+1, lNp]$, codewords are selected from l groups, where $l \in [1,p]$.

For comparison, Gaussian approximation is here applied to the Barker-based asynchronous prime-permuted codes (in Section 5.8), which use an asynchronous Barker sequence of length N for time spreading.

Theorem 6.7

Assuming that codewords are selected "group-by-group" for optimal code performance, the variance of the in-phase cross-correlation functions contributed by each interfering synchronous prime-permuted codeword over GF(p) of a prime p with length $N \leq p$ in CIK is formulated as [7]

$$\sigma^2_{\text{Walsh,syn}} = \frac{(\lceil \frac{K}{Np} \rceil - 1)(K - NP)N^2}{K^2} + \frac{[K - (\lceil \frac{K}{Np} \rceil - 1)Np](\lceil \frac{K}{Np} \rceil - 1)N^2}{K^2}$$

where K is the number of simultaneous users and $\lceil \cdot \rceil$ is the ceiling function.

Also assuming "group-by-group" codeword selection, the variance of the periodic cross-correlation functions contributed by each interfering Barker-based asynchronous prime-permuted codeword over GF(p) of a prime p with length $N \leq p$ in CIK is formulated as [6, 7]

$$\sigma^2_{\text{Barker,asyn}} = \frac{p(\lceil \frac{K}{p} \rceil - 1)(\lceil \frac{K}{p} \rceil N^2 + p - 1)}{Np \lceil \frac{K}{p} \rceil (\lceil \frac{K}{p} \rceil p - 1)}$$

Proof For the Walsh-based synchronous prime-permuted codes in CIK, the interference variance is generally formulated as

$$\sigma^2_{\text{Walsh,syn}} = \frac{(\lceil \frac{K}{Np} \rceil - 1)Np}{K} \times \sigma^2_1 + \frac{K - (\lceil \frac{K}{Np} \rceil - 1)Np}{K} \times \sigma^2_2$$

where

$$\sigma^2_1 = \frac{Np - 1}{K} \times 0 + \frac{K - Np}{K} \times 1 \times \frac{N}{p}$$

$$\sigma^2_2 = \frac{K - (\lceil \frac{K}{Np} \rceil - 1)Np - 1}{K} \times 0 + \frac{(\lceil \frac{K}{Np} \rceil - 1)Np}{K} \times 1 \times \frac{N}{p}$$

The derivation assumes that the synchronous prime-permuted codewords assigned to the K simultaneous users can be divided into two categories, depending on the group relationship between the interfering codewords and the address codeword of the receiver in study. In the first category, the address codeword comes from a shifted prime sequence in which an entire group (of the shifted prime sequences) is used by other interfering codewords. So, the interference generated by each of these interfering codewords has the same variance σ^2_1 with a probability of $[\lceil K/(Np) \rceil - 1]Np/K$. This is because there exist $\lceil K/(Np) \rceil - 1$ such groups with p shifted prime sequences in each group and N time-spreading Walsh codewords, out of K simultaneous users. In the second category, the address codeword comes from a shifted prime sequence in which only a partial group is used by other interfering codewords. So, the interference generated by each of these interfering codewords has the same variance σ^2_2 with a probability of $\{K - [\lceil K/(Np) \rceil - 1]Np\}/K$.

To derive σ^2_1, the term $(Np - 1)/K$ accounts for the probability of selecting an interfering codeword from the same group as the address codeword, and "0" is the interference variance contributed by the zero in-phase cross-correlation value between the codewords. The term $(K - Np)/K$ represents a similar probability, but for those interfering codewords being selected from different groups of the address codeword, "1" is the variance contributed by the non-zero in-phase cross-correlation value between the codewords, and N/p is the fraction of codewords that have such non-zero cross-correlation value. Similarly, for σ_2^2, the term $\{K - [\lceil K/(Np) \rceil - 1]Np - 1\}/K$ accounts for the probability of selecting an interfering codeword from the same group as the address codeword. The term $\{[\lceil K/(Np) \rceil - 1]Np\}/K$ represents a similar ratio, but for those interfering codewords being selected from different groups of the address codeword.

For the Barker-based asynchronous prime-permuted codes (in Section 5.8) in CIK, the interference variance is generally formulated as

$$\sigma_{\text{Barker,asyn}}^2 = \frac{1}{j} \times \frac{jp-p}{jp-1} \times \frac{N}{p} + \frac{j-1}{j} \times \left(\frac{p-1}{jp-1} \times \frac{1}{N} + \frac{jp-p}{jp-1} \times \frac{N}{p} \right)$$

where $j = \lceil K/p \rceil$. These asynchronous codes have the maximum cardinality of p^2 because there is only one Barker sequence of length N. So, j represents the number of groups of codewords in use for a given K and takes on a value from the set of $\{2, 3, \ldots, p\}$. When $K \leq p$, codewords are selected from group 0 (of the shifted prime sequences), according to the group-by-group selection method. Because all codewords from group 0 are orthogonal, the interference variance is equal to 0. For $K > p$, codewords are selected from more than one group and the variance gets worse as more groups are used. So, $\sigma_{\text{Barker,asyn}}^2$ is a function of $j = \lceil K/p \rceil \in [2,p]$, and its first and second product terms account for the interference variances when the address codeword originates from group 0 and group $\{1, 2, \ldots, p-1\}$ with the probabilities of $1/j$ and $(j-1)/j$, respectively. The term $(jp-p)/(jp-1)$ account for the probability that the address and interfering codewords are from different groups. The term N/p is the fraction of the codewords that have non-zero cross-correlation values in the shifted prime sequences when the address and interfering codewords are from different groups. The term $(p-1)/(jp-1)$ accounts for the probability that both codewords are from the same group. The term $1/N$ accounts for the probability of having non-zero cross-correlation values due to the use of the shifted prime sequences in the same group. ∎

Figure 6.5 plots the Gaussian-approximated error probabilities of the CIK Walsh-based synchronous and Barker-based asynchronous prime-permuted codes over $GF(p)$ of a prime p against the number of simultaneous users K for $p = \{11, 17\}$ and $N = \{7, 8, 16\}$. In general, the error probabilities improve as p or N increases because more wavelengths or longer code length is used, resulting in lower hit probabilities or higher autocorrelation peaks. However, the error probabilities get worse when K increases due to stronger mutual interference. In the calculation, simultaneous users are assumed to select codewords "group-by-group" so that the orthogonality of the Walsh-based synchronous codes is applied during codeword selection. So, the codes have $P_{e|G} = 0$ when $K \leq Np$, and the solid curves appear only when $K > Np$. In addition, the error probabilities of the synchronous codes (solid curves) are always better than those of the asynchronous ones (dashed curves). The dashed curves of the

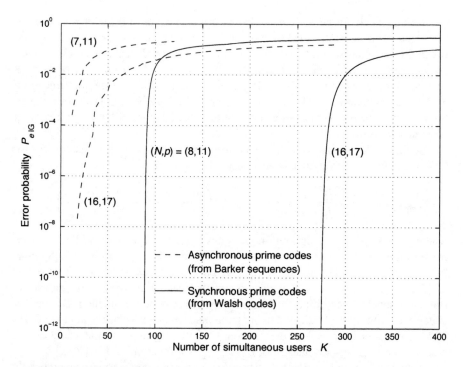

FIGURE 6.5 Gaussian error probabilities of the CIK Walsh-based synchronous and Barker-based asynchronous prime-permuted codes for various p and N.

Barker-based codes stops at $K = p^2$ due to their maximum cardinality. In summary, the Walsh-based synchronous codes support greater numbers of simultaneous users and subscribers at the expense of code synchronism.

6.4 SUMMARY

In this chapter, three families of 2-D synchronous carrier-hopping prime codes were studied. By applying cyclic-time-shifts to codewords of the carrier-hopping prime codes in Chapter 5, the synchronous carrier-hopping prime codes have expanded cardinality and better performance, supporting more number of simultaneous users and subscribers. In addition, code orthogonality is supported due to zero in-phase cross-correlation functions in the synchronous codes. Synchronous multilevel carrier-hopping prime codes allows enlargement of code cardinality by having arbitrary maximum in-phase cross-correlation functions. By properly partitioning the codes into a tree structure of subsets of codewords, the in-phase cross-correlation functions can be varied in order to attain different code performances and cardinalities, and orthogonal codewords are found in the subsets at the lowest level of the tree. Similarly, the Walsh-based synchronous prime-permuted codes have zero in-phase cross-correlation functions, and larger cardinality and better performance than their asynchronous counterparts in Section 5.8.

REFERENCES

1. Yang, G.-C., Kwong, W. C. (2002). *Prime Codes with Applications to CDMA Optical and Wireless Networks*. Norwood, MA: Artech House.
2. Narimanov, E., Kwong, W. C., Yang, G.-C., Prucnal, P. R. (2005). Shifted carrier-hopping prime codes for multicode keying in wavelength-time O-CDMA. *IEEE Trans. Commun.* 53(12):2150–2156.
3. Hsieh, C.-H., Yang, G.-C., Chang, C.-Y., Kwong, W. C. (2009). Multilevel prime codes for optical CDMA systems. *J. Optical Commun. Networking* 1(7):600–607.
4. Sun, C.-C., Yang, G.-C., Tu, C.-P., Chang, C.-Y., Kwong, W. C. (2010). Extended multilevel prime codes for optical CDMA. *IEEE Trans. Commun.* 58(5):1344–1350.
5. Kwong, W. C., Yang, G.-C., Chang, C.-Y. (2005). Wavelength-hopping time-spreading optical CDMA with bipolar codes. *J. Lightwave Technol.* 23(1):260–267.
6. Hsieh, C.-P., Chang, C.-Y., Yang, G.-C., Kwong, W. C. (2006). A bipolar-bipolar code for asynchronous wavelength-time optical CDMA. *IEEE Trans. Commun.* 54(7):1190–1194.
7. Hu, H.-W., Chen, H.-T., Yang, G.-C., Kwong, W. C. (2007). Synchronous Walsh-based bipolar-bipolar code for CDMA passive optical networks. *J. Lightwave Technol.* 25(8):1910–1917.
8. Topliss, S., Beeler, D., Altwegg, L. (1995). Synchronization for passive optical networks. *J. Lightwave Technol.* 13(5):947–953.
9. Feldman, R. D., Wood, T. H., Meester, J. P., Austin, R. F. (1998). Broadband upgrade of an operating narrowband single-filter passive optical network using coarse wavelength division multiplexing and subcarrier multiple access. *J. Lightwave Technol.* 16(1):1–8.
10. Prucnal, P. R. (ed.) (2006). *Optical Code Division Multiple Access: Fundamentals and Applications*. Boca Raton, FL: Taylor & Francis Group.
11. O'Farrell, T., Lochmann, S. (1994). Performance analysis of an optical correlator receiver for SIK DS-CDMA communication. *Electron. Lett.* 30(1):63–65.
12. Xian, Y. Y. (2001). *Theory and Application of Higher-Dimensional Hadamard Matrices*. New York: Kluwer Academic.
13. Lam, A. W., Tantaratana, S. (1994). *Theory and Application of Spread-Spectrum Systems*, Piscataway, NJ: IEEE.

7 Multilength Prime Codes

Most studies on optical coding theory are based on the assumptions that there is only one type of service in a coding-based optical system and the bit rates among services are the same [1–9]. Services, such as data, voice, image, and video, with different bit rates, traffic patterns, and quality-of-service (QoS) requirements are expected to coexist in future systems. The use of single-length, constant-weight optical codes alone will not be able to serve these multirate, variable-QoS, multimedia systems sufficiently or efficiently.

One possible solution is to utilize multiple wavelengths on top of 1-D optical codewords of various lengths in the so-called hybrid WDM-coding scheme [7, 10]. While each wavelength carries 1-D optical codewords of the same length for users of the same bit rate, different wavelengths carry 1-D optical codewords of different lengths for users of different rates. Another method is to collect 1-D or 2-D optical codewords of various lengths together and each user transmits a codeword with length matching the bit rate in use. However, the cross-correlation functions of the codewords can be large and cause strong mutual interference if these codewords are not selected carefully. The third method is to start with long-length codewords and then shorten some of them to suit the bit rate [11]. This approach will require an exhaustive computer search to find out which codewords can be shortened without worsening the cross-correlation functions. In addition, the weights of the shortened codewords may be different from the original ones, unintentionally changing the autocorrelation peaks and complicating the correlation and decision processes. Alternatively, codewords of different lengths can be generated by padding sufficient numbers of 0s to the end of some codewords in order to preserve the correlation properties [7]. However, this approach requires the use of short-length codes, which have small cardinality. In summary, the aforementioned methods fail to satisfy the basic criteria of code construction in this book that the autocorrelation peaks should not be changed unintentionally, the cross-correlation functions should be kept low, and no exhaustive computer search should be used. Furthermore, QoS control is another important issue to consider in multimedia applications. One way to adjust QoS is through code-weight variation, in addition to changing code length [12–14]. It is the general property of (incoherent) optical codes that the weight of a codeword can be changed easily by dropping pulses, while the autocorrelation sidelobes and cross-correlation functions are still preserved.

In this chapter, several families of 2-D multilength prime codes, which support the integration of different types of multirate, multi-QoS services in optical multimedia systems, are studied [7,14–17]. These multilength prime codes are specially designed to have the cross-correlation functions of at most 1 or 2, independent of code length. As a result, code performance improves when code length decreases or code weight increases. Because higher-rate media (e.g., video) are assigned with codewords of length shorter than those of lower-rate media (e.g., voice or data), the former see less mutual interference and then have better QoS, and, in turn, higher priority. This feature supports user prioritization and guarantees the QoS of those media that have high bit rates and require real-time support. This chapter also shows that code weight is a dominating factor and more effective than code length in controlling QoS. Nevertheless, if a user's QoS is boosted by increasing its code weight suddenly, the QoSs of other users suffer. In this aspect, variable-weight coding finds applications in top-priority military transmission and emergency broadcasting, in which real-time handling and high throughput are required but this kind of traffic is usually rare and bursty in nature. Furthermore, a general and exact analytical model under a constant-bit-power assumption is formulated in order to show the effect of power limitation in some laser sources on the performance of multilength codes [18–20]. This accurate model is important in power-sensitive applications, such as in-service monitoring and fiber-fault surveillance in coding-based optical systems and networks, and sensor-identification in coding-based fiber-sensor systems [21–23]. Finally, the constructions of two families of 1-D multilength optical orthogonal codes are illustrated [24, 25].

7.1 MULTILENGTH CARRIER-HOPPING PRIME CODES

As an extension to the single-length counterparts in Section 5.1, the multilength carrier-hopping prime codes are constructed by the introduction of a set of $k-1$ positive integers $t_{k-1} \leq t_{k-2} \leq \cdots \leq t_1$ to control the number of codewords in each length, out of k different lengths. Also, given a set of k prime numbers $p_k \geq p_{k-1} \geq \cdots \geq p_1$ and $p_1 \geq t_1$, binary $(0,1)$ matrices, $\mathbf{x}_{i_1}$, with the ordered pairs [7, 14]

$$\{[(0,0),(1,i_1),(2,2\odot_{p_1} i_1),\ldots,(p_1-1,(p_1-1)\odot_{p_1} i_1)] :$$
$$i_1 = \{t_1,t_1+1,\ldots,p_1-1\}\} \qquad (7.1)$$

matrices, $\mathbf{x}_{i_2,i_1}$, with the ordered pairs

$$\{[(0,0),(1,i_1+i_2p_1),(2,2\odot_{p_1} i_1+(2\odot_{p_2} i_2)p_1),\ldots,$$
$$(p_1-1,(p_1-1)\odot_{p_1} i_1+((p_1-1)\odot_{p_2} i_2)p_1)] :$$
$$i_1 = \{t_2,t_2+1,\ldots,t_1-1\},i_2 = \{0,1,\ldots,p_2-1\}\} \qquad (7.2)$$

$$\vdots$$

and matrices, $\mathbf{x}_{i_k,i_{k-1},\ldots,i_1}$, with the ordered pairs

$$\{[(0,0),(1,i_1+i_2p_1+\cdots+i_kp_1p_2\cdots p_{k-1}),$$
$$(2,2\odot_{p_1} i_1+(2\odot_{p_2} i_2)p_1+\cdots+(2\odot_{p_k} i_l)p_1p_2\cdots p_{k-1}),\ldots,$$
$$(p_1-1,(p_1-1)\odot_{p_1} i_1+((p_1-1)\odot_{p_2} i_2)p_1+\cdots$$
$$+((p_1-1)\odot_{p_l} i_l)p_1p_2\cdots p_{k-1})] : i_1 = \{0,1,\ldots,t_{k-1}-1\},$$
$$i_2 = \{0,1,\ldots,p_2-1\},\ldots,i_k = \{0,1,\ldots,p_k-1\}\} \qquad (7.3)$$

form the multilength carrier-hopping prime codes of $L = p_1$ wavelengths and weight $w = p_1$ with $\phi_1 = p_1 - t_1$ codewords of length $N_1 = p_1$; $\phi_2 = p_2(t_1 - t_2)$ codewords of length $N_2 = p_1p_2$; $\phi_3 = p_2p_3(t_2 - t_3)$ codewords of length $N_3 = p_1p_2p_3$; ...; $\phi_{k-1} = p_2p_3 \cdots p_{k-1}(t_{k-2} - t_{k-1})$ codewords of length $N_{k-1} = p_1p_2 \cdots p_{k-1}$; and $\phi_k = p_2p_3 \cdots p_k t_{k-1}$ codewords of length $N_k = p_1p_2 \cdots p_k$, respectively, where "$\odot_{p_j}$" denotes a modulo-p_j multiplication for $j = \{1, 2, \ldots, k\}$.

There are w ordered pairs for a code matrix (i.e., codeword) of weight w. An ordered pair (λ_v, t_h) records the vertical (v) and horizontal (h) displacements of a pulse (or called a mark chip) from the bottom-leftmost corner of a code matrix. So, λ_v represents the transmitting channel (e.g., fiber or wavelength) and t_h shows the chip (or time-slot) location of a pulse in the code matrix.

To vary the weight of a multilength carrier-hopping prime codeword, say from $w = p_1$ to w', $p_1 - w'$ pulses can be removed randomly from the codeword. Another method is to remove the pulses with the top $p_1 - w'$ wavelengths in order to reduce the number of total wavelengths from p_1 to w'. Because the codewords have at most one pulse per row and column in the code matrices, the autocorrelation-sidelobe and cross-correlation properties are still preserved in this variable-weight operation.

Using $k = 2$, $p_1 = p_2 = 5$, and $t_1 = 2$ as an example, this double-length carrier-hopping prime code has $L = w$ wavelengths, weight $w = p_1 = 5$, and $\phi_1 = p_1 - t_1 = 3$ short codewords of length $N_1 = p_1 = 5$, denoted by $\mathbf{x}_2 = [(0,0), (1,2), (2,4), (3,1), (4,3)]$, $\mathbf{x}_3 = [(0,0), (1,3), (2,1), (3,4), (4,2)]$, and $\mathbf{x}_4 = [(0,0), (1,4), (2,3), (3,2), (4,1)]$; and $\phi_2 = t_1p_2 = 10$ long codewords of length $N_2 = p_1p_2 = 25$, denoted by $\mathbf{x}_{0,0} = [(0,0), (1,0), (2,0), (3,0), (4,0)]$, $\mathbf{x}_{1,0} = [(0,0), (1,5), (2,10), (3,15), (4,20)]$, $\mathbf{x}_{2,0} = [(0,0), (1,10), (2,20), (3,5), (4,15)]$, $\mathbf{x}_{3,0} = [(0,0), (1,15), (2,5), (3,20), (4,10)]$, $\mathbf{x}_{4,0} = [(0,0), (1,20), (2,15), (3,10), (4,5)]$, $\mathbf{x}_{0,1} = [(0,0), (1,1), (2,2), (3,3), (4,4)]$, $\mathbf{x}_{1,1} = [(0,0), (1,6), (2,12), (3,18), (4,24)]$, $\mathbf{x}_{2,1} = [(0,0), (1,12), (2,24), (3,6), (4,18)]$, $\mathbf{x}_{3,1} = [(0,0), (1,18), (2,6), (3,24), (4,12)]$, and $\mathbf{x}_{4,1} = [(0,0), (1,24), (2,18), (3,12), (4,6)]$. To have codewords of $L = 4$ wavelengths and weight $w = 4$, the pulses with the top wavelengths, which have the values of 4 in the first components of the ordered pairs, are dropped. For instance, $\mathbf{x}_4 = [(0,0), (1,4), (2,3), (3,2)]$ and $\mathbf{x}_{2,1} = [(0,0), (1,12), (2,24), (3,6)]$. Some of these codewords are illustrated in Figure 7.1. The codewords can also be represented in terms of wavelength-time sequences, such as $\mathbf{x}_4 = \lambda_0 0\lambda_3\lambda_2\lambda_1$ and $\mathbf{x}_{2,1} = \lambda_0 0000\, 0\lambda_3 000\, 00\lambda_1 00\, 00000\, 0000\lambda_2$.

Using $k = 3$, $p_1 = p_2 = p_3 = 5$, $t_1 = 3$, and $t_2 = 1$ as an example, this triple-length carrier-hopping prime code has $L = w$ wavelengths, weight $w = p_1 = 5$, and $\phi_1 = p_1 - t_1 = 2$ codewords of length $N_1 = 5$, denoted by $\mathbf{x}_{i_1} = [(0,0), (1, i_1), (2, 2 \odot_5 i_1), (3, 3 \odot_5 i_1), (4, 4 \odot_5 i_1)]$ for $i_1 \in [3,4]$; $\phi_2 = p_2(t_1 - t_2) = 10$ codewords of length $N_2 = 25$, denoted by $\mathbf{x}_{i_2, i_1} = [(0,0), (1, i_1 + 5i_2), (2, 2 \odot_5 i_1 + (2 \odot_5 i_2)5), (3, 3 \odot_5 i_1 + (3 \odot_5 i_2)5), (4, 4 \odot_5 i_1 + (4 \odot_5 i_2)5)]$ for $i_1 \in [1,2]$ and $i_2 \in [0,4]$; and $\phi_3 = t_2p_2p_3 = 25$ codewords of length $N_3 = 125$, denoted by $\mathbf{x}_{i_3, i_2, i_1} = [(0,0), (1, i_1 + 5i_2 + 25i_3), (2, 2 \odot_5 i_1 + (2 \odot_5 i_2)5 + (2 \odot_5 i_3)25), (3, 3 \odot_5 i_1 + (3 \odot_5 i_2)5 + (3 \odot_5 i_3)25), (4, 4 \odot_5 i_1 + (4 \odot_5 i_2)5 + (4 \odot_5 i_3)25)]$ for $i_1 = 0$, $i_2 \in [0,4]$, and $i_3 \in [0,4]$. For example, $\mathbf{x}_3 = [(0,0), (1,3), (2,1), (3,4), (4,2)]$, $\mathbf{x}_{2,1} = [(0,0), (1,11), (2,22), (3,8), (4,19)]$,

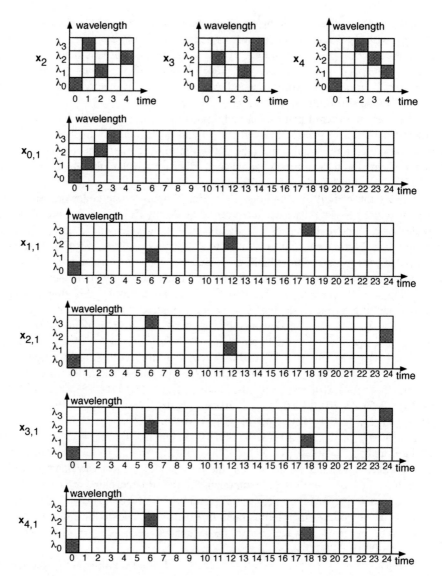

FIGURE 7.1 Some double-length carrier-hopping prime codewords with 4 wavelengths and lengths $\{5, 25\}$, based on $p_1 = p_2 = 5$, and $t_1 = 2$, where dark squares indicate the wavelength-time locations of pulses.

and $x_{3,2,0} = [(0,0),(1,85),(2,45),(3,105),(4,65)]$.

With the multilength carrier-hopping prime codes in use, the amount of mutual interference seen by the address codeword of a receiver consists of the periodic cross-correlation functions among codewords of shorter, same, or longer lengths. The periodic cross-correlation functions of the same-length codes follow those of the single-length carrier-hopping prime codes in Section 5.1 [7, 9, 14–17, 24, 25]. If the address codeword is shorter than the interfering codeword, the periodic cross-correlation function is no larger than those of the same-length (short) codewords because the correlation process only involves a portion of the long interfering codeword. It is more complex to compute the periodic cross-correlation function when the address codeword is longer than the interfering codeword. If the code length is r times longer, a complete periodic cross-correlation function will involve $r + 1$ consecutive OOK transmissions of the short interfering codeword, as illustrated in Figure 7.2 [9, 15, 24, 25]. This kind of concatenated cross-correlation function can be as large as the autocorrelation peak, which is usually equal to the code weight in use, if the codes are not constructed carefully.

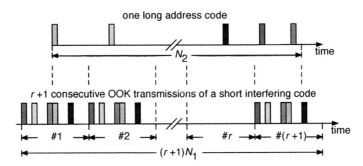

FIGURE 7.2 A complete periodic cross-correlation process of a long address codeword of length $N_2 = rN_1$ and $r + 1$ consecutive OOK transmissions of a short interfering codeword of length N_1.

To preserve zero autocorrelation sidelobes and the periodic cross-correlation functions of at most 1 (independent of code length), the multilength carrier-hopping prime codes are specially designed with the wavelengths in each codeword being used once.

Theorem 7.1

The autocorrelation peaks and sidelobes of the multilength carrier-hopping prime codes of weight w are equal to w and 0, respectively, where $w \leq p_1$. The periodic cross-correlation functions of the codes are at most 1, independent of code length [7, 14].

Proof The multilength carrier-hopping prime codewords, say $x_{i_h,i_{h-1},\ldots,i_1}$, are from the $k = h$ single-length carrier-hopping prime codes in Section 5.1 [7]. So, the autocorrelation and cross-correlation properties of the same-length codewords follow those of the single-length carrier-hopping prime codes in Section 5.1. In addition, the periodic cross-correlation function between a short address codeword (of a receiver) and a long interfering codeword follows that of the same-length (short) carrier-hopping prime codes because the correlation process only involves a portion of the long interfering codeword.

If the length of the long address codeword $x_{i_m,i_{m-1},\ldots,i_1} = [(0,0),(1,i_1 + i_2 p_1 + \cdots + i_m p_1 p_2 \cdots p_{m-1}),(2,2 \odot_{p_1} i_1 + (2 \odot_{p_2} i_2)p_1 + \cdots + (2 \odot_{p_m} i_m)p_1 p_2 \cdots p_{m-1}),\ldots, (w-1,(w-1) \odot_{p_1} i_1 + ((w-1) \odot_{p_2} i_2)p_1 + \cdots + ((w-1) \odot_{p_m} i_m)p_1 p_2 \cdots p_{m-1})]$ is $r = p_{n+1}p_{n+2} \cdots p_m$ times the length of the short interfering codeword $x_{i'_n,i'_{n-1},\ldots,i'_1}$, $r + 1$ consecutive OOK transmissions of the short codeword, denoted by the concatenated ordered pairs $[(0,0),(0,p_1 p_2 \cdots p_n),\ (0,2p_1 p_2 \cdots p_n),\ldots,(0,(p_m - 1)p_{m-1} \cdots p_{m+1}p_1 p_2 \cdots p_n),\ (1,i'_1 + i'_2 p_1 + \cdots + i'_n p_1 p_2 \cdots p_{n-1}),\ (1,p_1 p_2 \cdots p_n + i'_1 + i'_2 p_1 + \cdots + i'_n p_1 p_2 \cdots p_{n-1}),\ \ldots,(1,(p_m - 1)p_{m-1} \cdots p_{n+1}p_1 p_2 \cdots p_n + i'_1 + i'_2 p_1 + \cdots + i'_n p_1 p_2 \cdots p_{n-1}),\ \ldots,\ (w-1,(w-1) \odot_{p_1} i'_1 + ((w-1) \odot_{p_n} i'_2)p_1 + \cdots + ((w-1) \odot_{p_n} i'_n)p_1 p_2 \cdots p_{n-1}),\ (w-1,p_1 p_2 \cdots p_n + (w-1) \odot_{p_1} i'_1 + ((w-1) \odot_{p_2} i'_2)p_1 + \cdots + ((w-1) \odot_{p_n} i'_n)p_1 p_2 \cdots p_{n-1}),\ldots,(w-1,(p_m - 1)p_{m-1} \cdots p_{n+1}p_1 p_2 \cdots p_n + (w-1) \odot_{p_1} i'_1 + ((w-1) \odot_{p_2} i'_2)p_1 + \cdots + ((w-1) \odot_{p_n} i'_n)p_1 p_2 \cdots p_{n-1})]$, are involved to complete one periodic cross-correlation process. If there exist two hits of pulses in any relative horizontal cyclic shift τ between these two codewords, then

$$j \odot_{p_1} i_1 + (j \odot_{p_2} i_2)p_1 + \cdots + (j \odot_{p_m} i_m)p_1 p_2 \cdots p_{m-1} + \tau$$
$$= j \odot_{p_1} i'_1 + (j \odot_{p_2} i'_2)p_1 + \cdots + (j \odot_{p_n} i'_n)p_1 p_2 \cdots p_{n-1} + s p_1 p_2 \cdots p_n$$

$$j' \odot_{p_1} i_1 + (j' \odot_{p_2} i_2)p_1 + \cdots + (j' \odot_{p_m} i_m)p_1 p_2 \cdots p_{m-1} + \tau$$
$$= j' \odot_{p_1} i'_1 + (j' \odot_{p_2} i'_2)p_1 + \cdots + (j' \odot_{p_n} i'_n)p_1 p_2 \cdots p_{n-1} + s' p_1 p_2 \cdots p_n$$

must hold simultaneously for a $j = \{0,1,\ldots,w-1\}$, a $j' = \{0,1,\ldots,w-1\}$, some $s = \{0,1,\ldots,(p_m - 1)p_{m-1} \cdots p_n\}$, and some $s' = \{0,1,\ldots,(p_m - 1)p_{m-1} \cdots p_n\}$, where $j \neq j'$, $i_1 \neq i'_1$, and $m > n$. The subtraction of these two equations results in

$$(j \odot_{p_1} i_1 - j' \odot_{p_1} i_1) + [(j \odot_{p_2} i_2) - (j' \odot_{p_2} i_2)]p_1 + \cdots$$
$$+ [(j \odot_{p_m} i_m) - (j' \odot_{p_m} i_m)]p_1 p_2 \cdots p_{m-1}$$
$$= (j \odot_{p_1} i'_1 - j' \odot_{p_1} i'_1) + [(j \odot_{p_2} i'_2) - (j' \odot_{p_2} i'_2)]p_1 + \cdots$$
$$+ [(j \odot_{p_n} i'_n) - (j' \odot_{p_n} i'_n)]p_1 p_2 \cdots p_{n-1} + (s - s')p_1 p_2 \cdots p_n$$

which is valid only if $i_t = i'_t$ for all $t = \{1,2,\ldots,n\}$. This violates the assumption of distinct $x_{i_m,i_{m-1},\ldots,i_1}$ and $x_{i'_n,i'_{n-1},\ldots,i'_1}$. So, the periodic cross-correlation function is at most 1. ∎

Theorem 7.2

The upper bound of the overall cardinality of the multilength carrier-hopping prime codes of $L = p_1$ wavelengths and weight $w = p_1$ is formulated as [7]

$$\Phi_{\text{upper}} \leq \frac{(p_1 N_k - 1)\,\Phi_{\text{multilength}}}{\phi_k(p_1 - 1) + \sum_{i=1}^{k-1} \phi_i(p_1 \Pi_{j=i+1}^{k} p_j - 1)}$$

where $N_k = p_1 p_2 \cdots p_k$ and the actual overall cardinality is given by

$$\begin{aligned}
\Phi_{\text{multilength}} &= (p_1 - t_1) + p_2(t_1 - t_2) + p_2 p_3(t_2 - t_3) + \cdots \\
&\quad + p_2 p_3 \cdots p_{k-1}(t_{k-2} - t_{k-1}) + p_2 p_3 \cdots p_k t_{k-1}
\end{aligned}$$

The actual overall cardinality approaches the upper bound for a large p_1. So, the multilength carrier-hopping prime codes are asymptotic optimal in cardinality.

Proof According to the definition of cyclic adjacent-pulse separations in Sections 1.6 and 3.4 [1, 2, 4, 7], there must exist $\phi_k w(w-1)$ distinct cyclic adjacent-pulse separations in the $\phi_k = p_2 p_3 \cdots p_k t_{k-1}$ codewords of length $N_k = p_1 p_2 \cdots p_k$ in order to attain the maximum periodic cross-correlation function of 1. This is because there are $w(w-1)$ combinations of nonrepeating cyclic adjacent-pulse separations in each codeword, and all cyclic adjacent-pulse separations in these codewords must be distinct. If one of the $\phi_{k-1} = p_2 p_3 \cdots p_{k-1}(t_{k-2} - t_{k-1})$ codewords of (shorter) length $N_{k-1} = p_1 p_2 \cdots p_{k-1}$ correlates with a codeword of (longer) length N_k, $p_k + 1$ copies of the shorter codeword are involved in order to complete one periodic cross-correlation process. It is equivalent to treat these copies as a concatenated codeword of weight $p_k w$. This concatenated codeword requires $p_k w(p_k w - 1)/\lambda_a$ distinct cyclic adjacent-pulse separations in order to attain the maximum periodic cross-correlation function of 1, where the maximum autocorrelation sidelobe λ_a can be as high as p_k [1, 4, 12]. So, the total number of distinct cyclic adjacent-pulse separations in these ϕ_{k-1} codewords of length N_{k-1} becomes $\phi_{k-1} w(p_k w - 1)$.

In general, $\phi_j w(p_{j+1} p_{j+2} \cdots p_k w - 1)$ distinct cyclic adjacent-pulse separations for the ϕ_j codewords of length N_j for $j = \{1, 2, \ldots, k-1\}$ are required. Because the total number of distinct cyclic adjacent-pulse separations from all cases cannot exceed $L(LN_k - 1)\Phi_{\text{multilength}}$, it is found that

$$\begin{aligned}
\Phi_{\text{upper}} &\leq \frac{L(LN_k - 1)\,\Phi_{\text{multilength}}}{\text{Total cyclic adjacent-pulse separations of all lengths}} \\
&= \frac{w(wN_k - 1)\,\Phi_{\text{multilength}}}{\phi_k w(w-1) + \sum_{i=1}^{k-1} \phi_i w(w \Pi_{j=i+1}^{k} p_j - 1)}
\end{aligned}$$

By applying $L = w = p_1$, the final form of Φ_{upper} is derived after some manipulations.

To show the asymptotic optimal cardinality of the multilength carrier-hopping prime codes, it is found that

$$\frac{\Phi_{\text{multilength}}}{\Phi_{\text{upper}}} \approx \frac{p_1 - t_1}{p_1}\left(1 - \frac{1}{p_1 p_2 \cdots p_k}\right) + \frac{t_1 - t_2}{p_1}\left(1 - \frac{1}{p_1 p_3 p_4 \cdots p_k}\right)$$
$$+ \frac{t_2 - t_3}{p_1}\left(1 - \frac{1}{p_1 p_4 p_5 \cdots p_k}\right) + \cdots + \frac{t_{k-2} - t_{k-1}}{p_1}\left(1 - \frac{1}{p_1 p_k}\right)$$
$$+ \frac{t_{k-1}}{p_1}\left(1 - \frac{1}{p_1}\right)$$

which approaches 1, for a large p_1. ∎

In general, the overall cardinality suffers as k increases because there are more short codewords and then more concatenated cross-correlation functions to consider. So, the overall cardinality can be improved by reducing the number of short codewords.

To fairly compare the cardinalities of the multilength carrier-hopping prime codes and their single-length counterparts in Section 5.1, length N_k and $L = p_1$ wavelengths are used in the latter so that both code families occupy the same maximum bandwidth expansion LN_K. So, the cardinality of these single-length codes is given by $\Phi_{\text{single}} = p_1 p_2 \cdots p_k$. Because $t_{k-1} \leq t_{k-2} \leq \cdots \leq t_1 \leq p_1 \leq p_2 \leq \cdots \leq p_k$, it is found that

$$\frac{\Phi_{\text{multiple}}}{\Phi_{\text{single}}} = \frac{p_1 - t_1}{p_1 p_2 \cdots p_k} + \frac{t_1 - t_2}{p_1 p_3 p_4 \cdots p_k} + \cdots + \frac{t_{k-2} - t_{k-1}}{p_1 p_k} + \frac{t_{k-1}}{p_1} \leq 1$$

This implies that the multilength carrier-hopping prime codes always have smaller cardinality than their single-length counterparts. Equality occurs when $t_1 = t_2 = \cdots = t_{k-1} = p_1$, meaning that the multilength codes become the single-length ones.

7.1.1 Performance Analysis

Because the multilength carrier-hopping prime codes have the periodic cross-correlation functions of at most 1, the hit probabilities and performance of each codeword depend on its length and weight and are also affected by the lengths and weights of the interfering codewords.

Theorem 7.3

When a multilength carrier-hopping prime codeword of weight w_i and length $N_{i'}$ correlates with an interfering codeword of weight w_j and length $N_{j'}$, the one-hit probability is generally formulated as [14]

$$q_{i,i',j,j'} = \frac{w_i w_j}{2LN_{j'}} \tag{7.4}$$

for i and $j \in [1,k]$, and i' and $j' \in [1,k']$, where L is the number of wavelengths, k is the number of different weights, and k' is the number of different lengths in the code set. (This general equation applies to any multilength 2-D optical codes that use all available wavelengths at most once within the heaviest-weight codewords and that have the periodic cross-correlation functions of at most 1.)

To minimize the number of wavelengths L, it is assumed that each heaviest-weight codeword uses all these L wavelength exactly once (or $L = w_{\text{heaviest}}$). The one-hit probability becomes

$$q_{i,i',j,j'} = \frac{w_i w_j}{2 w_{\text{heaviest}} N_{j'}} \tag{7.5}$$

whereas the wavelengths of light-weight codewords are randomly selected from all $L = w_{\text{heaviest}}$ wavelengths with equal probability. This method results in a better one-hit probability than the general case given in Equation (7.4).

Without random wavelength selection, a straightforward method is to always use lower-order wavelengths in light-weight codewords. For example, wavelengths λ_1 to λ_4 are used by codewords of weight 4, while λ_1 to λ_3 are used by codewords of weight 3. The one-hit probability becomes

$$q_{i,i',j,j'} = \frac{\min\{w_i, w_j\}}{2 N_{j'}} \tag{7.6}$$

which is generally worse than that in Equation (7.5).

The chip-synchronous, soft-limiting error probability of the multilength carrier-hopping prime codes of weight w_i and length $N_{i'}$ with the maximum periodic cross-correlation function of 1 in OOK is formulated as [14]

$$P_{e,i,i'} = \frac{1}{2} \sum_{\substack{\sum_{m=1}^{k}\sum_{m'=1}^{k'} l_{m,m'}=w_i}}^{\left(\sum_{m=1}^{k}\sum_{m'=1}^{k'} K_{m,m'}\right)-1} \frac{(K_{i,i'}-1)!}{l_{i,i'}!(K_{i,i'}-1-l_{i,i'})!}(q_{i,i',i,i'})^{l_{i,i'}}$$

$$\times (1-q_{i,i',j,j'})^{K_{i,i'}-1-l_{i,i'}} \prod_{\substack{j=1 \\ (j,j')\neq(i,i')}}^{k} \prod_{j'=1}^{k'} \frac{K_{j,j'}!}{l_{j,j'}!(K_{j,j'}-l_{j,j'})!}$$

$$\times (q_{i,i',j,j'})^{l_{j,j'}}(1-q_{i,i',j,j'})^{K_{j,j'}-l_{j,j'}} \tag{7.7}$$

for the three cases of $q_{i,i',j,j'}$ given in Equations (7.4) through (7.6), where $K_{j,j'}$ is the number of simultaneous users with codewords of weight w_j and length $N_{j'}$, $l_{j,j'}$ is the number of interferers contributing one-hits, and $l_{j,j'} \leq K_{j,j'}$ for $j \in [1,k]$ and $j' \in [1,k']$.

The chip-synchronous, hard-limiting error probability of the multilength carrier-hopping prime codes of weight w_i and length $N_{i'}$ with the maximum periodic cross-correlation function of 1 in OOK is formulated as

$$
\begin{aligned}
P_{e,i,i',\text{hard}} \;=\; & \frac{1}{2}\sum_{m=0}^{w_i}(-1)^m\frac{w_i!}{m!(w_i-m)!}\left(1-\frac{m\,q_{i,i',i,i'}}{w_i}\right)^{K_{i,i'}-1} \\
& \times \prod_{\substack{j=1\\(j,j')\neq(i,i')}}^{k}\prod_{j'=1}^{k'}\left(1-\frac{m\,q_{i,i',j,j'}}{w_i}\right)^{K_{j,j'}}
\end{aligned}
\tag{7.8}
$$

where $q_{i,i',j,j'}$ is given by Equation (7.4) for the general case or by Equation (7.5) for the case of random wavelength selection. For the case of using lower-order wavelengths, the OOK, chip-synchronous, hard-limiting error probability is formulated as

$$
\begin{aligned}
P_{e,i,i',\text{hard}} \;=\; & \frac{1}{2}\sum_{m_1=0}^{w_1}\sum_{m_2=0}^{w_2-w_1}\sum_{m_3=0}^{w_3-w_2}\cdots\sum_{m_i=0}^{w_i-w_{i-1}}(-1)^{\Sigma_{j=1}^{i}m_j}\frac{w_1!}{m_1!(w_1-m_1)!} \\
& \times\frac{(w_2-w_1)!}{m_2!(w_2-w_1-m_2)!}\times\frac{(w_3-w_2)!}{m_3!(w_3-w_2-m_3)!}\times\cdots \\
& \times\frac{(w_i-w_{i-1})!}{m_i!(w_i-w_{i-1}-m_i)!}\times\prod_{j'=1}^{k'}\left(1-\frac{m_1 q_{i,i',1,j'}}{w_1}\right)^{K_{1,j'}} \\
& \times\prod_{j'=1}^{k'}\left[1-\frac{\left(\Sigma_{j=1}^{2}m_j\right)q_{i,i',2,j'}}{w_2}\right]^{K_{2,j'}}\cdots \\
& \times\prod_{j'=1}^{k'}\left[1-\frac{\left(\Sigma_{j=1}^{i-1}m_j\right)q_{i,i',i-1,j'}}{w_{i-1}}\right]^{K_{i-1,j'}} \\
& \times\prod_{j'=1}^{k'}\left[1-\frac{\left(\Sigma_{j=1}^{i}m_j\right)q_{i,i',i,j'}}{w_i}\right]^{\Sigma_{j=i}^{k}K_{j,j'}} \\
& \div\left[1-\frac{\left(\Sigma_{j=1}^{i}m_j\right)q_{i,i',i,i'}}{w_i}\right]
\end{aligned}
\tag{7.9}
$$

where $q_{i,i',j,j'}$ is given by Equation (7.6), $w_1 < w_2 < \cdots < w_k$, and $\Sigma_{j=0}^{i}t_j \leq w_i$.

Proof According to Theorem 7.1, the number of hits in the cross-correlation function between any two multilength carrier-hopping prime codewords is at most 1 and independent of weight and length [7, 14]. When an address codeword (of a receiver) of weight w_i and length $N_{i'}$ correlates with an interfering codeword of weight w_j and length $N_{j'}$, the one-hit probability is generally given by $q_{i,i',j,j'} = w_i[w_j(N_{i'}/N_{j'})]/(2LN_{i'}) = w_i w_j/(2LN_{j'})$ for i and $j \in [1,k]$, and i' and $j' \in [1,k']$. The factor $1/2$ comes from the assumption of equiprobable data bit-1 and bit-0 transmissions in OOK. The factor $w_i w_j(N_{i'}/N_{j'})$ accounts for the number of ways of getting one hit out of $LN_{i'}$ possible wavelength-time combinations. If $N_{i'} > N_{j'}$, $w_j(N_{i'}/N_{j'})$ is the combined weight of the concatenated $N_{i'}/N_{j'}$ copies of the shorter interfering codeword seen by the longer address codeword. If $N_{i'} \leq N_{j'}$, $w_j(N_{i'}/N_{j'})$ is the proportional weight of the longer interfering codeword seen by the shorter address codeword.

In Equation (7.7), $l_{m,m'}$ denotes the number of interfering codewords of weight w_m and length $N_{m'}$ contributing one-hits in the sampling time of the cross-correlation function, out of $K_{m,m'}$ simultaneous users (or codewords), where $m \in \lfloor 1,k \rfloor$ and $m' \in [1,k']$. So, the sum of all $l_{m,m'}$ one-hits must be at least equal to w_i (or $\sum_{m=1}^{k} \sum_{m'=1}^{k'} l_{m,m'} = w_i$) before any decision error occurs. The summation symbol in Equation (7.7) consists of multiple summations such that all possible combinations of the sum of all $l_{m,m'}$ one-hits equal to or greater than w_i are evaluated. The one-hit contributions of these $l_{m,m'}$ interfering codewords are divided into two groups of product terms, depending on whether they have the same w_i and $N_{i'}$ as the address codeword or different w_j and $N_{j'}$ with $(j,j') \neq (i,i')$.

Similarly, in Equation (7.8), the one-hit contributions of the interfering codewords are also divided into two groups of product terms, depending on whether they have the same w_i and $N_{i'}$ as the address codeword or different w_j and $N_{j'}$ with $(j,j') \neq (i,i')$.

In Equation (7.9), the $K_{j,j'}$ simultaneous users with codewords of weight w_j and length $N_{j'}$ have different interference effects than the address codeword of weight w_i and length $N_{i'}$, depending on their weight relationships. If $w_j \geq w_i$, the interfering codewords of w_j can contribute one-hits at up to w_i pulses. This is because only the first w_i lower-order wavelengths are recognized during the correlation process. So, the interference effect of any heavier-weight codeword is simply the same as those codewords of lighter weight w_i. This effect is accounted for by the product term in the power of $\sum_{j=i}^{k} K_{j,j'}$ in Equation (7.9). By the same argument, the interference effect of any interfering codeword of weight less than w_i is restricted to its own weight only, which ranges from w_1 to w_{i-1}. This effect is accounted for by the product terms in the powers of $K_{1,j'}$, $K_{2,j'}$, ..., and $K_{i-1,j'}$ in Equation (7.9). For the first w_1 wavelengths, all interfering codewords will contribute one-hits and then m_1 is found in all these product terms. For the next $w_2 - w_1$ wavelengths, the $K_{1,j'}$ interfering codewords of weight w_1 will not contribute any hit, and then m_2 is not found in the product term associated with $K_{1,j'}$. In general, for the $w_l - w_{l-1}$ wavelengths, the interfering codewords of weights less than w_l will not contribute any hit, and m_l is not found in the product terms associated with $K_{1,j'}$, $K_{2,j'}$, ..., and $K_{l-1,j'}$, where $l \in [2, i-1]$. ∎

Figure 7.3 plots the chip-synchronous, hard-limiting error probabilities, from Equations (7.6) and (7.9) for the lower-order-wavelength case, of the triple-weight, triple-length carrier-hopping prime codes against the numbers of simultaneous users with long-length codewords $K_{3,3}$ and medium-length codewords $K_{3,2}$ of both heavy weight w_3, where $k = 3$, $k' = 3$, $p_1 = 17$, $p_2 = 19$, $p_3 = 23$, $t_1 = 6$, $t_2 = 3$, $w_1 = 9$, $w_2 = 11$, $w_3 = 13$, $N_1 = p_1 = 17$, $N_2 = p_1p_2 = 323$, and $N_3 = p_1p_2p_3 = 7429$.

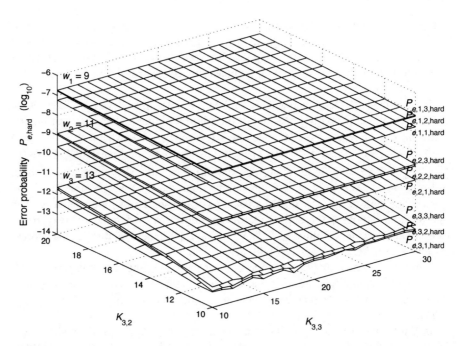

FIGURE 7.3 Chip-synchronous, hard-limiting error probabilities of the triple-weight, triple-length carrier-hopping prime codes (using lower-order wavelengths) versus $K_{3,2}$ and $K_{3,3}$, where $w_1 = 9$, $w_2 = 11$, $w_3 = 13$, $N_1 = 17$, $N_2 = 323$, and $N_3 = 7429$, and $K_{1,1} = K_{1,2} = K_{1,3} = K_{2,1} = K_{2,2} = K_{2,3} = K_{3,1} = 3$.

The numbers of all other simultaneous users are fixed at 3. $K_{i,i'}$ represents the number of simultaneous users with codewords of weight w_i and length $N_{i'}$ for i and $i' \in [1,3]$. The three topmost meshed surfaces correspond to the error probabilities, $P_{e,1,3,\text{hard}}$, $P_{e,1,2,\text{hard}}$, and $P_{e,1,1,\text{hard}}$ (from top to bottom), of codewords with lengths N_3, N_2, and N_1, respectively, and all with light weight $w_1 = 9$. The three middle meshed surfaces correspond to $P_{e,2,3,\text{hard}}$, $P_{e,2,2,\text{hard}}$, and $P_{e,2,1,\text{hard}}$, respectively, with medium weight $w_2 = 12$. The three bottommost meshed surfaces are for heavy weight $w_3 = 13$. In general, the error probabilities improve as code weight increases because of higher autocorrelation peaks. However, the error probabilities get worse as the total number of simultaneous users increases due to stronger mutual interference. In contrast to the single-length carrier-hopping prime codes in Section 5.1, short codewords now generate stronger interference than long codewords, resulting in $P_{e,i,1,\text{hard}} < P_{e,i,2,\text{hard}} < P_{e,i,3,\text{hard}}$, when the same code weight is used. This can be explained by stronger interference created by multiple copies of short codewords toward the cross-correlation functions. Because both medium-length and long codewords see the same number of short codewords, the difference between $P_{e,i,3,\text{hard}}$ and $P_{e,i,2,\text{hard}}$ is small for a given $i \in [1,3]$.

Figure 7.4 plots the chip-synchronous, hard-limiting error probability of the same

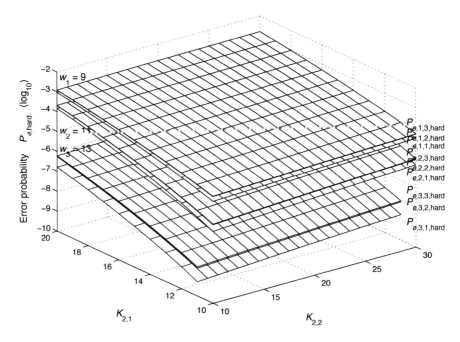

FIGURE 7.4 Chip-synchronous, hard-limiting error probabilities of the triple-weight, triple-length carrier-hopping prime codes (using lower-order wavelengths) versus $K_{2,1}$ and $K_{2,2}$, where $w_1 = 9$, $w_2 = 11$, $w_3 = 13$, $N_1 = 17$, $N_2 = 323$, and $N_3 = 7429$, and $K_{1,1} = K_{1,2} = K_{1,3} = K_{2,1} = K_{2,2} = K_{2,3} = K_{3,1} = 3$.

triple-weight, triple-length carrier-hopping prime codes as in Figure 7.3 against the numbers of simultaneous users with short-length codewords $K_{2,1}$ and medium-length codewords $K_{2,2}$ of both medium weight w_2, where the numbers of all other simultaneous users are fixed at 3. Similar to Figure 7.3, the error probabilities generally improve as the code weight increases or the total number of simultaneous users decreases. From both figures, code weight is shown as a dominating factor and better than code length in controlling code performance and, in turn, QoS.

7.2 MULTILENGTH EXPANDED CARRIER-HOPPING PRIME CODES

The multilength carrier-hopping prime codes require that all available wavelengths be used in the heaviest codewords. However, if a lower code weight is already good enough to achieve a target performance, the restriction implies that there are more wavelengths available than are actually needed. If the number of available wavelengths is more than the weight of the heaviest codewords, each of the multilength carrier-hopping prime codes can be taken as a seed from which groups of multilength expanded carrier-hopping prime codes can be constructed with enlarged cardinality [14, 15].

Let w denote the weight of the heaviest codewords in the multilength carrier-hopping prime codes in Section 7.1, $p' \geq w$ be a prime number, and the number of available wavelengths be $L = wp' \leq p_1$. The w ordered pairs of the multilength expanded carrier-hopping prime codewords, $\mathbf{x}_{i_k,i_{k-1},\dots,i_1,l_2,l_1}$ and $\mathbf{x}_{i_k,i_{k-1},\dots,i_1,l_3}$, are here selected from the ordered pairs in the multilength carrier-hopping prime codewords, $\mathbf{x}_{i_k,i_{k-1},\dots,i_1}$, with the first components in Equations (7.1) through (7.3) matching the values [15]

$$\{l_1, (l_1 \oplus_w l_2) + w, (l_1 \oplus_w (2 \odot_{p'} l_2)) + 2w, \dots, (l_1 \oplus_w ((w-1) \odot_{p'} l_2))$$
$$+ (w-1)w : l_1 = \{0,1,\dots,w-1\}, l_2 = \{0,1,\dots,w-1\}\} \qquad (7.10)$$

and

$$\{l_3 w, l_3 w + 1, \dots, l_3 w + w - 1 : l_3 = \{0,1,\dots,p'-1\}\} \qquad (7.11)$$

respectively, where "$\odot_{p'}$" denotes a modulo-p' multiplication and "$\oplus_w$" denotes a modulo-w addition. This selection process results in the multilength expanded carrier-hopping prime codes of $L = wp' \leq p_1$ wavelengths and weight $w \leq p_1$ with $\gamma_1 = (w^2 + p')(p_1 - t_1)$ codewords of length $N_1 = p_1$; $\gamma_2 = (w^2 + p')p_2(t_1 - t_2)$ codewords of length $N_2 = p_1 p_2$; $\gamma_3 = (w^2 + p')p_2 p_3(t_2 - t_3)$ codewords of length $N_3 = p_1 p_2 p_3$; $\dots$; $\gamma_{k-1} = (w^2 + p')p_2 p_3 \cdots p_{k-1}(t_{k-2} - t_{k-1})$ codewords of length $N_{k-1} = p_1 p_2 \cdots p_{k-1}$; and $\gamma_k = (w^2 + p')t_{k-1}p_2 p_3 \cdots p_k$ codewords of length $N_k = p_1 p_2 \cdots p_k$.

To vary the weight of a multilength expanded carrier-hopping prime codeword, say from w to w', $w - w'$ pulses can be removed randomly from the codeword. Because the codewords have at most one pulse per row and column in the code matrices, the autocorrelation-sidelobe and cross-correlation properties are still preserved in this variable-weight operation.

Using $k = 2$, $w = p' = 3$, $p_1 = 11$, $p_2 = 13$, and $t_1 = 6$ as an example, the double-length carrier-hopping prime codes in Equations (7.1) through (7.3) have $\phi_1 = p_1 - t_1 = 5$ codewords of length $N_1 = p_1 = 11$, denoted by $\mathbf{x}_{i_1} = [(0,0),(1,i_1),(2,2 \odot_{11} i_1),\dots,(10,10 \odot_{11} i_1)]$ for $i_1 \in [6,10]$; and $\phi_2 = t_1 p_2 = 78$ codewords of length $N_2 = p_1 p_2 = 143$, denoted by $\mathbf{x}_{i_2,i_1} = [(0,0),(1,i_1 + 11 i_2),(2,2 \odot_{11} i_1 + (2 \odot_{13} i_2)11),\dots,(10,10 \odot_{11} i_1 + (10 \odot_{13} i_2)11)]$ for $i_1 \in [0,5]$ and $i_2 \in [0,12]$. The corresponding double-length expanded carrier-hopping prime codes have $\gamma_1 = (w^2 + p')(p_1 - t_1) = 60$ codewords of length $N_1 = 11$, denoted by $\mathbf{x}_{i_1,l_2,l_1}$ and $\mathbf{x}_{i_1,l_3}$ for $i_1 \in [6,10]$, $l_1 \in [0,2]$, $l_2 \in [0,2]$, and $l_3 \in [0,2]$; and $\gamma_2 = (w^2 + p')t_1 p_2 = 936$ codewords of length $N_2 = 143$, denoted by $\mathbf{x}_{i_2,i_1,l_2,l_1}$ and $\mathbf{x}_{i_2,i_1,l_3}$ for $i_1 \in [0,5]$, $i_2 \in [0,12]$, $l_1 \in [0,2]$, $l_2 \in [0,2]$, and $l_3 \in [0,2]$. The three ordered pairs of the expanded codewords, $\mathbf{x}_{i_1,l_2,l_1}$, $\mathbf{x}_{i_1,l_3}$, $\mathbf{x}_{i_2,i_1,l_2,l_1}$, and $\mathbf{x}_{i_2,i_1,l_3}$, are chosen from the ordered pairs of the corresponding codewords, $\mathbf{x}_{i_1}$ and $\mathbf{x}_{i_2,i_1}$, with the first components equal to $\{l_1, (l_1 \oplus_3 l_2) + 3, (l_1 \oplus_3 (2 \odot_3 l_2)) + 6\}$ and $\{3l_3, 3l_3 + 1, 3l_3 + 2\}$, respectively. For example, $\mathbf{x}_{i_2,i_1,l_3} = \mathbf{x}_{3,1,2} = [(6,61),(7,95),(8,129)]$ and $\mathbf{x}_{i_2,i_1,l_2,l_1} = \mathbf{x}_{3,6,2,1} = [(1,39),(3,108),(8,125)]$, out of a total of $L = wp' = 9$ wavelengths.

Theorem 7.4

The autocorrelation peaks and sidelobes of the multilength expanded carrier-hopping prime codes of weight w are equal to w and 0, respectively, where $w \leq p_1$. The periodic cross-correlation functions of the codes are at most 1, independent of code length. There are $w(p_1 - t_1)$, $wp_2(t_1 - t_2)$, ..., and $wp_2 p_3 \cdots p_k t_{k-1}$ groups of w codewords in each group and $p_1 - t_1$, $p_2(t_1 - t_2)$, ..., and $p_2 p_3 \cdots p_k t_{k-1}$ groups of p' codewords in each group such that all codewords within a group have zero periodic cross-correlation functions [15].

Proof According to the construction, the w ordered pairs of each multilength expanded carrier-hopping prime codeword are selected from the ordered pairs in its corresponding multilength carrier-hopping prime codeword (in Section 7.1) with their first components matching the values given in Equation (7.10) or (7.11). Based on the proof of Theorem 7.1, the autocorrelation and cross-correlation properties of the multilength expanded carrier-hopping prime codes follow those of the multilength carrier-hopping prime codes.

Furthermore, there exists zero interference among the multilength expanded carrier-hopping prime codewords with the same l_2 but different l_1 values because the pulses in these codewords are all in different wavelengths. There are w groups of w such orthogonal codewords per group, generated from the $p_1 - t_1$, $(t_1 - t_2)p_2$, ..., and $t_{k-1}p_2 p_3 \cdots p_k$ single-length expanded carrier-hopping prime codewords using Equation (7.10). Similarly, the codewords with different l_3 values have zero interference among themselves. There is one group of p' such orthogonal codewords, generated from each one of the $p_1 - t_1$, $(t_1 - t_2)p_2$, ..., and $t_{k-1}p_2 p_3 \cdots p_k$ single-length expanded carrier-hopping prime codewords using Equation (7.11). ∎

According to the construction, the multilength expanded carrier-hopping prime codes have a similar code structure as the multilength carrier-hopping prime codes in Section 7.1. The upper bound of the overall cardinality of the multilength expanded carrier-hopping prime codes of $L = p_1$ wavelengths and weight $w = p_1$ follows Theorem 7.2 by replacing ϕ_i by γ_i such that [15]

$$\Phi_{upper} \leq \frac{(p_1 N_k - 1)\Phi_{multilength}}{\gamma_k(p_1 - 1) + \sum_{i=1}^{k-1} \gamma_i(p_1 \Pi_{j=i+1}^k p_j - 1)}$$

where $N_k = p_1 p_2 \cdots p_k$ and the actual overall cardinality is given by

$$\Phi_{multilength} = (w^2 + p')[(p_1 - t_1) + p_2(t_1 - t_2) + p_2 p_3(t_2 - t_3) + \cdots$$
$$+ p_2 p_3 \cdots p_{k-1}(t_{k-2} - t_{k-1}) + p_2 p_3 \cdots p_k t_{k-1}]$$

Similarly, the asymptotic optimal cardinality of the multilength expanded carrier-hopping prime codes can be shown by evaluating the $\Phi_{multilength}/\Phi_{upper}$ ratio, which is found identical to the one in Theorem 7.2 and approaches 1 for a large p_1.

In general, the overall cardinality suffers as the number of different weights k increases because there are more short codewords and then more concatenated cross-correlation functions to consider. So, the overall cardinality can be improved by reducing the number of short codewords.

To fairly compare the cardinalities of the multilength expanded carrier-hopping prime codes with their single-length counterparts in Section 5.5, length N_k and $L = wp'$ wavelengths are used in the latter so that both code families occupy the same maximum bandwidth expansion LN_k. So, the cardinality of these single-length codewords is given by $\Phi_{\text{single}} = (w^2 + p')p_1p_2 \cdots p_k$. Because $t_{k-1} \leq t_{k-2} \leq \cdots \leq t_1 \leq p_1 \leq p_2 \leq \cdots \leq p_k$, it is found that [15]

$$\frac{\Phi_{\text{multiple}}}{\Phi_{\text{single}}} = \frac{p_1 - t_1}{p_1 p_2 \cdots p_k} + \frac{t_1 - t_2}{p_1 p_3 p_4 \cdots p_k} + \cdots + \frac{t_{k-2} - t_{k-1}}{p_1 p_k} + \frac{t_{k-1}}{p_1} \leq 1$$

This implies that the multilength expanded carrier-hopping prime codes always have smaller cardinality than their single-length counterparts. Equality occurs when $t_1 = t_2 = \cdots = t_{k-1} = p_1$, meaning that the multilength expanded carrier-hopping prime codes become the single-length ones.

7.2.1 Performance Analysis

Because the multilength expanded carrier-hopping prime codes have the periodic cross-correlation functions of at most 1, the chip-synchronous, soft- and hard-limiting error probabilities in OOK follow Equations (7.7) and (7.8), respectively.

Theorem 7.5

When a multilength expanded carrier-hopping prime codeword of weight w_i and length $N_{i'}$ correlates with an interfering codeword of weight w_j and length $N_{j'}$, the one-hit probability is generally formulated as [14, 15]

$$q_{i,i',j,j'} = \frac{w_i w_j}{2LN_{j'}} \left[1 - \frac{(w_{\text{heaviest}}^3 - w_{\text{heaviest}}^2 + p'^2 - p')\phi_{j'}}{(\gamma_{j'} - 1)(w_{\text{heaviest}}^2 + p')} \right]$$

for i and $j \in [1,k]$, and i' and $j' \in [1,k']$, where L is the number of wavelengths, k is the number of different weights, k' is the number of different lengths, w_{heaviest} is the weight of the heaviest codewords, $\phi_{j'}$ is the number of multilength carrier-hopping prime codewords of length $N_{j'}$, and $\gamma_{j'} = (w_{\text{heaviest}}^2 + p')\phi_{j'}$ is the number of multilength expanded carrier-hopping prime codewords of length $N_{j'}$.

To minimize the number of required wavelengths, $L = w_{\text{heaviest}}p'$ is assumed in $q_{i,i',j,j'}$, on the condition that wavelengths of lighter-weight codewords are picked randomly out of all available wavelengths with equal probability.

Proof The derivation of the one-hit probability $q_{i,i',j,j'}$ of the multilength expanded carrier-hopping prime codes is similar to that of Equation (7.4) in Theorem 7.3. So,

$$q_{i,i',j,j'} = \frac{w_i w_j}{2LN_{j'}} \left[\frac{\gamma_{j'} - (w_{\text{heaviest}} - 1)\phi_{j'}}{\gamma_{j'} - 1} \times \frac{w_{\text{heaviest}}^2}{w_{\text{heaviest}}^2 + p'} \right.$$
$$\left. + \frac{\gamma_{j'} - (p'-1)\phi_{j'}}{\gamma_{j'} - 1} \times \frac{p'}{w_{\text{heaviest}}^2 + p'} \right]$$

The terms inside the brackets account for the number of interfering codewords of length $N_{j'}$ contributing one-hits, out of the total number of all interfering codewords of the same length $N_{j'}$. In the first product term, there are $w_{\text{heaviest}}^2/(w_{\text{heaviest}}^2 + p')$ chances of choosing an interfering codeword out of the w_{heaviest}^2 codewords from Equation (7.10). Because there are $w_{\text{heaviest}} - 1$ orthogonal codewords that carry distinct wavelengths, $\gamma_{j'} - (w_{\text{heaviest}} - 1)\phi_{j'}$ represents the number of codewords contributing one-hits, out of $\gamma_{j'} - 1$ codewords. In the second product term, there are $p'/(w_{\text{heaviest}}^2 + p')$ chances of choosing an interfering codeword out of the p' codewords from Equation (7.11). As there are $p' - 1$ orthogonal codewords, $\gamma_{j'} - (p'-1)\phi_{j'}$ represents the number of codewords contributing one-hits, out of $\gamma_{j'} - 1$ codewords. After some manipulations, the final form in the theorem is derived. ∎

Figure 7.5 plots the chip-synchronous, soft-limiting error probabilities of the single-weight, double-length expanded carrier-hopping prime codes against the number of simultaneous users with long-length codewords $K_{1,2}$ for various numbers of simultaneous users with short-length codewords $K_{1,1} = \{0,4,8\}$, where $k = 1, k' = 2$, $p_1 = p_2 = 23, w_{\text{heaviest}} = w_1 = 5, p' = 7, t_1 = 11, N_1 = p_1 = 23$, and $N_2 = p_1 p_2 = 529$. $K_{1,i'}$ represents the number of simultaneous users with codewords of weight w_1 and length $N_{i'}$ for $i' \in [1,2]$. Figure 7.6 is for the same codes but against $K_{1,1}$ for various $K_{1,2} = \{0,100,200\}$. In general, the error probabilities get worse as the total number of simultaneous users $K_{1,2} + K_{1,1}$ increases. The short codewords always perform better than the long codewords because stronger interference is created by multiple copies of the short codewords in the cross-correlation process. However, the improvement is rather small because a short code length $N_1 = 23$ is used, which has poor performance anyway. The dashed curve with $K_{1,1} = 0$ in Figure 7.5 and the solid curve with $K_{1,2} = 0$ in Figure 7.6 show the performances of single-length expanded carrier-hopping prime codes (in Section 5.5) of long length N_2 and short length N_1, respectively. Both figures show that the short codewords dominate the performance and create stronger interference than the long codewords. This contradicts the finding in conventional single-length codes that code performance improves with code length, as seen by comparing the $(K_{1,1} = 0)$-curve in Figure 7.5 and the $(K_{1,2} = 0)$-curve in Figure 7.6.

In general, it is difficult to calculate the code performances as k' increases beyond 2 because there are more different-length interfering patterns and, in turn, more hit probabilities to consider [20]. The calculations can be simplified by evaluating the performance bounds. This is because the best performance (or lower bound) is

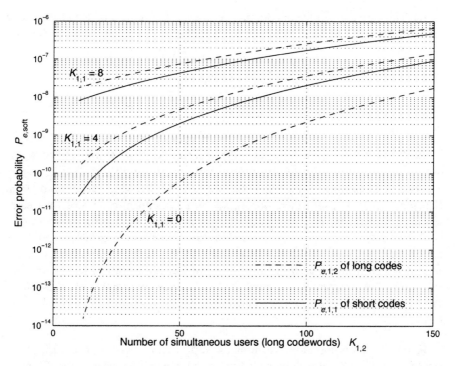

FIGURE 7.5 Chip-synchronous, soft-limiting error probabilities of the single-weight, double-length expanded carrier-hopping prime codes versus $K_{1,2}$ for $w_1 = 5$, $p' = 7$, $t_1 = 11$, $N_1 = 23$, and $N_2 = 529$.

achieved by the shortest codewords, and the worst performance (or upper bound) is achieved by the longest codewords. So, codewords with lengths in between will fall into these two bounds.

Figure 7.7 plots the chip-synchronous, soft-limiting error probabilities of the single-weight, triple-length expanded carrier-hopping prime codes against the numbers of simultaneous users with long-length codewords $K_{1,3}$ and medium-length codewords $K_{1,2}$, where $k = 1$, $k' = 3$, $p_1 = p_2 = p_3 = 13$, $w_{\text{heaviest}} = w_1 = 7$, $p' = 3$, $t_1 = 6$, $t_2 = 3$, $N_1 = p_1 = 13$, $N_2 = p_1 p_2 = 169$, and $N_3 = p_1 p_2 p_3 = 2197$. The number of simultaneous users with short-length codewords is fixed at $K_{1,1} = 5$. In general, the error probabilities get worse as the total number of simultaneous users $K_{1,3} + K_{1,2} + K_{1,1}$ increases. The long codewords always perform the worst and give the performance upper bound because stronger interference is created by multiple copies of the short and medium-length codewords in the cross-correlation process. The short codewords see the least amount of interference from codewords of other lengths and give the performance lower bound. Because both medium-length and long codewords see the same number of short codewords, the performance difference between the medium-length and long codewords is small.

The performances of the multilength expanded carrier-hopping prime codes, es-

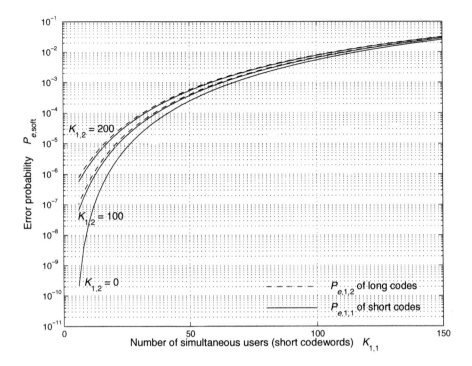

FIGURE 7.6 Chip-synchronous, soft-limiting error probabilities of the single-weight, double-length expanded carrier-hopping prime codes versus $K_{1,1}$ for $w_1 = 5$, $p' = 7$, $t_1 = 11$, $N_1 = 23$, and $N_2 = 529$.

pecially the long codewords, can be enhanced using the orthogonal codewords in the groups listed in Theorem 7.4. As long as codewords with different i_1 values are not using the same wavelengths, there will be no mutual interference. Because there are $w - 1$ codewords not occupying the same wavelengths as a codeword in one group, only $(w - w_1)(p_1 - t_1)p_2p_3 \cdots p_n$ or $(p' - w_1)(p_1 - t_1)p_2p_3 \cdots p_n$ short codewords and $w_1t_1p_2p_3 \cdots p_m$ long codewords that are orthogonal among themselves can be used in the group, where $m > n$ and $w > w_1 > 0$.

7.3 MULTILENGTH QUADRATIC-CONGRUENCE CARRIER-HOPPING PRIME CODES

To expand code cardinality without the need to increase the number of wavelengths, the multilength quadratic-congruence carrier-hopping prime codes are here constructed by adding a quadratic-congruence (QC) operator, such as i^2l or $i(i+1)l/2$ (mod p_1), to the ordered pairs of the multilength carrier-hopping prime codes in Section 7.1, where $l = \{0, 1, \ldots, p_1 - 1\}$ is the group number of the multilength codewords and $i = \{0, 1, \ldots, p_1 - 1\}$ for a prime p_1 [8, 16].

Given a set of $k - 1$ positive integers $t_{k-1} \geq t_{k-2} \geq \cdots \geq t_1$ to control the number

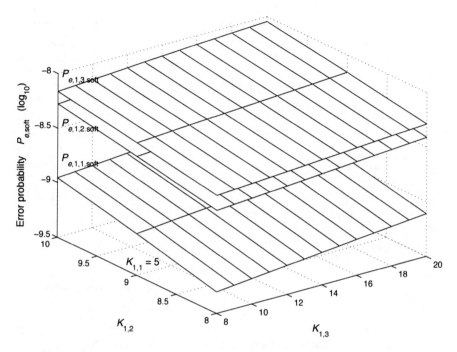

FIGURE 7.7 Chip-synchronous, soft-limiting error probabilities of the single-weight, triple-length expanded carrier-hopping prime codes versus $K_{1,2}$ and $K_{1,3}$ for $w_1 = 7$, $p' = 3$, $t_1 = 6$, $t_2 = 3$, $N_1 = 13$, $N_2 = 169$, $N_3 = 2197$, and $K_{1,1} = 5$.

of codewords in each length, out of k different lengths, a set of k prime numbers $p_k \geq p_{k-1} \geq p_{k-2} \geq \cdots \geq p_1$ to determine the code lengths, and $p_1 \geq t_1$, binary $(0,1)$ matrices, $\mathbf{x}_{i_1,l}$, with the ordered pairs

$$\{[(0,0),(1,(1 \odot_{p_1} l) \oplus_{p_1} (1 \odot_{p_1} i_1)),(2,(3 \odot_{p_1} l) \oplus_{p_1} (2 \odot_{p_1} i_1)),\ldots,$$
$$((p_1-1),(((p_1-1)p_1/2) \odot_{p_1} l) \oplus_{p_1} ((p_1-1) \odot_{p_1} i_1))] :$$
$$i_1 = \{0,1,\ldots,p_1-1\}, l = \{t_1,t_1+1,\ldots,p_1-1\}\}$$

matrices, $\mathbf{x}_{i_2,i_1,l}$, with the ordered pairs

$$\{[(0,0),(1,((1 \odot_{p_1} l) \oplus_{p_1} (1 \odot_{p_1} i_1)) + (1 \odot_{p_2} i_2)p_1),$$
$$(2,((3 \odot_{p_1} l) \oplus_{p_1} (2 \odot_{p_1} i_1)) + (2 \odot_{p_2} i_2)p_1),\ldots,$$
$$((p_1-1),((((p_1-1)p_1/2) \odot_{p_1} l) \oplus_{p_1} ((p_1-1) \odot_{p_1} i_1))$$
$$+((p_1-1) \odot_{p_2} i_2)p_1)] : i_1 = \{0,1,\ldots,p_1-1\},$$
$$i_2 = \{0,1,\ldots,p_2-1\}, l = \{t_2,t_2+1,\ldots,t_1-1\}\}$$

$$\vdots$$

and matrices, $\mathbf{x}_{i_k,i_{k-1},\ldots,i_1,l}$, with the ordered pairs

$$\{[(0,0),(1,((1\odot_{p_1} l)\oplus_{p_1}(1\odot_{p_1} i_1))+(1\odot_{p_2} i_2)p_1+\cdots$$
$$+(1\odot_{p_k} i_k)p_1 p_2\cdots p_{k-1}),(2,((3\odot_{p_1} l)\oplus_{p_1}(2\odot_{p_1} i_1))$$
$$+(2\odot_{p_2} i_2)p_1+\cdots+(2\odot_{p_k} i_k)p_1 p_2\cdots p_{k-1}),\ldots,$$
$$((p_1-1),((((p_1-1)p_1/2)\odot_{p_1} l)\oplus_{p_1}((p_1-1)\odot_{p_1} i_1))$$
$$+((p_1-1)\odot_{p_2} i_2)p_1+\cdots+((p_1-1)\odot_{p_k} i_k)p_1 p_2\quad\cdots p_{k-1})]:$$
$$i_1=\{0,1,\ldots,p_1-1\}, i_2=\{0,1,\ldots,p_2-1\},\ldots,$$
$$i_k=\{0,1,\ldots,p_k-1\}, l=\{0,1,\ldots,t_{k-1}-1\}\}$$

form the multilength quadratic-congruence carrier-hopping prime codes of $L=p_1$ wavelengths and weight $w=p_1$ with $\alpha_1=(p_1-t_1)p_1$ codewords of length $N_1=p_1$; $\alpha_2=p_1 p_2(t_1-t_2)$ codewords of length $N_2=p_1 p_2$; $\alpha_3=p_1 p_2 p_3(t_2-t_3)$ codewords of length $N_3=p_1 p_2 p_3$; $\ldots$; $\alpha_{k-1}=p_1 p_2\cdots p_{k-1}(t_{k-2}-t_{k-1})$ codewords of length $N_{k-1}=p_1 p_2\cdots p_{k-1}$; and $\alpha_k=p_1 p_2\cdots p_k t_{k-1}$ codewords of length $N_k=p_1 p_2\cdots p_k$, respectively, where "$\oplus_{p_1}$" denotes a modulo-p_1 addition and "$\odot_{p_j}$" denotes a modulo-p_j multiplication for $j=\{1,2,\ldots,k\}$.

To vary the weight of a multilength quadratic-congruence carrier-hopping prime codeword, say from $w=p_1$ to w', p_1-w' pulses can be removed randomly from the codeword. Another method is to remove the pulses with the top p_1-w' wavelengths to reduce the total number of wavelengths from p_1 to w'. Because pulse removal in (incoherent) optical codes does not increase the number of hits, the autocorrelation-sidelobe and cross-correlation properties are preserved in this variable-weight operation.

By relaxing the cross-correlation functions to 2, the cardinality of the multilength quadratic-congruence carrier-hopping prime codes is p_1 times that of the multilength carrier-hopping prime codes in Section 7.1. Furthermore, the multilength quadratic-congruence carrier-hopping prime codes can be separated into p_1 groups (indexed by $l=\{0,1,\ldots,p_1-1\}$). Each group has $p_1 p_2\ldots p_j$ codewords of length N_j for every $j=\{1,2,\ldots,k\}$. Codewords coming from the same group l have the periodic cross-correlation functions of at most 1.

Using $k=2$, $L=w=p_1=5$, $p_2=7$, and $t_1=2$ as an example, this double-length quadratic-congruence carrier-hopping prime code has $\alpha_1=p_1(p_1-t_1)=15$ short codewords of length $N_1=p_1=5$, denoted by $\mathbf{x}_{i_1,l}=[(0,0),(1,(1\odot_5 l)\oplus_5 (1\odot_5 i_1)),(2,(3\odot_5 l)\oplus_5(2\odot_5 i_1)),\ldots,(4,(10\odot_5 l)\oplus_5(4\odot_5 i_1))]$ for $i_1\in[0,4]$ and $l\in[2,4]$; and $\alpha_2=p_1 p_2 t_1=70$ long codewords of length $N_2=p_1 p_2=35$, denoted by $\mathbf{x}_{i_2,i_1,l}=[(0,0),(1,((1\odot_5 l)\oplus_5(1\odot_5 i_1))+(1\odot_7 i_2)5),(2,((3\odot_5 l)\oplus_5(2\odot_5 i_1))+(2\odot_7 i_2)5),\ldots,(4,((10\odot_5 l)\oplus_5(4\odot_5 i_1))+(4\odot_7 i_2)5)]$ for $i_1\in[0,4]$, $i_2\in[0,6]$, and $l\in[0,1]$. For example, $\mathbf{x}_{0,2}=[(0,0),(1,2),(2,1),(3,2),(4,0)]$ and $\mathbf{x}_{0,3}=[(0,0),(1,3),(2,4),(3,3),(4,0)]$ have the periodic cross-correlation functions of at most 2 because they are from two different l-groups. However, $\mathbf{x}_{0,2}$ and $\mathbf{x}_{1,2}=[(0,0),(1,3),(2,3),(3,0),(4,4)]$ have the periodic cross-correlation functions of at most 1 due to the same group of $l=2$.

Theorem 7.6

The autocorrelation peaks and sidelobes of the multilength quadratic-congruence carrier-hopping prime codes of weight w are equal to w and 0, respectively, where $w \leq p_1$. The periodic cross-correlation functions of the codes are at most 2, but at most 1 if the correlating codewords come from the same group $l = \{0, 1, \ldots, p_1 - 1\}$, independent of code length [8, 16].

Proof The proof is similar to that of Theorem 7.1. The multilength quadratic-congruence carrier-hopping prime codewords, say $\mathbf{x}_{i_h, i_{h-1}, \ldots, i_1, l}$, are from the $k = h$ single-length quadratic-congruence carrier-hopping prime codes in Section 5.6. So, the autocorrelation and cross-correlation properties of the same-length codewords follow those of the single-length quadratic-congruence carrier-hopping prime codes in Section 5.6. In addition, the periodic cross-correlation function between a short address codeword (of a receiver) and a long interfering codeword follows that of the same-length codewords because the correlation process only involves a portion of the long interfering codeword.

If the length of the long address codeword $\mathbf{x}_{i_m, i_{m-1}, \ldots, i_1, l}$ is $r = p_{n+1} p_{n+2} \cdots p_m$ times the length of the short interfering codeword $\mathbf{x}_{i'_n, i'_{n-1}, \ldots, i'_1, l'}$, then $r + 1$ consecutive OOK transmissions of the short codeword are involved to complete one periodic cross-correlation process, where $i_1 \neq i'_1$ and $m > n$. This periodic cross-correlation function is at most 2, but at most 1 if the codewords are from the same group $l = \{0, 1, \ldots, p_1 - 1\}$ because the correlation and group properties of the quadratic-congruence operator are followed, as shown in Section 5.6. ∎

Optical codes do not usually achieve optimal cardinality when the maximum cross-correlation function is greater than 1, and so are the multilength quadratic-congruence carrier-hopping prime codes.

7.3.1   Performance Analysis

Because the maximum periodic cross-correlation function is 2, the chip-synchronous, hard-limiting error probability of the single-weight, multilength quadratic-congruence carrier-hopping prime codes of weight $w \leq p_1$ and length N_i in OOK is formulated as [16]

$$
\begin{aligned}
P_{e,i,\text{hard}} = {} & \frac{1}{2} \sum_{h=0}^{w} \left\{ (-1)^{w-h} \frac{w!}{h!(w-h)!} \left[q_{0,i,i} + \frac{h q_{1,i,i}}{w} + \frac{h(h-1)q_{2,i,i}}{w(w-1)} \right]^{K_i - 1} \right. \\
& \left. \times \prod_{j=1, \, j \neq i}^{k} \left[q_{0,i,j} + \frac{h q_{1,i,j}}{w} + \frac{h(h-1)q_{2,i,j}}{w(w-1)} \right]^{K_j} \right\}
\end{aligned}
$$

according to Section 1.8.4 and Theorem 7.3, where K_i is the number of simultaneous users with codewords of length N_i for $i \in [1,k]$, and k is the number of different lengths.

Theorem 7.7

The probabilities, $q_{h,i,j}$, of getting $h = \{0,1,2\}$ hits in a quadratic-congruence carrier-hopping prime codeword of length N_i and cardinality α_i correlating with an interfering codeword of length N_j, both of $L = w$ wavelengths and weight $w \leq p_1$, in OOK are generally formulated as [8, 16]

$$q_{2,i,j} = \begin{cases} \frac{w(w-1)(\alpha_i - N_i)}{4N_j^2(\alpha_i - 1)} & \text{for } i = j \\ \frac{w(w-1)}{4N_j^2} & \text{otherwise} \end{cases}$$

$$\sum_{h=0}^{2} h q_{h,i,j} = \frac{w^2}{2LN_j} = \frac{w}{2N_j}$$

and $\sum_{h=0}^{2} q_{h,i,j} = 1$ for i and $j \in [1,k]$, where k is the number of different lengths.

Proof The two-hit probability can generally be derived as

$$q_{2,i,j} = \frac{1}{2} \times \frac{w(w-1)}{2} \times \frac{1}{N_j} \times \frac{1}{N_j} \times \begin{cases} \frac{\alpha_i - N_i}{\alpha_i - 1} & \text{for } i = j \\ 1 & \text{otherwise} \end{cases}$$

where $1/2$ comes from the assumption of equiprobable data bit-1 and bit-0 transmissions in OOK. The term $w(w-1)/2 = \binom{p_1}{2} - (p_1 - w)w - \binom{p_1 - w}{2}$ accounts for the number of times of having two-hits caused by $L = w$ wavelengths after the $p_1 - w$ top wavelengths have been removed. From the definition of cyclic adjacent-pulse separations in Sections 1.6 and 3.4, $\binom{p_1}{2}$ denotes the number of cyclic adjacent-pulse separations generated by the original p_1 pulses in a codeword, $(p_1 - w)w$ denotes the number of such separations among the w pulses after $p_1 - w$ pulses have been removed, and $\binom{p_1 - w}{2}$ denotes the number of such separations among these $p_1 - w$ pulses. The first N_j represents the number of codewords of length N_j in the same l group. The second N_j is the number of time shifts in these codewords. For code orthogonality in each group, two cases are considered, depending on whether the address and interfering codewords are of the same length or different lengths. For $i = j$, there are $\alpha_i - 1$ interfering codewords of the same length N_i as the address codeword and $[(\alpha_i/N_i) - 1]N_i$ interfering codewords come from different groups. So, the probability of choosing such an interfering codeword, out of all codewords of length N_i, becomes $(\alpha_i - N_i)/(\alpha_i - 1)$. For $i \neq j$, there are α_j interfering codewords of length N_j and α_j codewords from different groups because codewords of different lengths always come from different groups. So, the probability of choosing an interfering codeword of length N_j becomes $\alpha_j / \alpha_j = 1$.   ∎

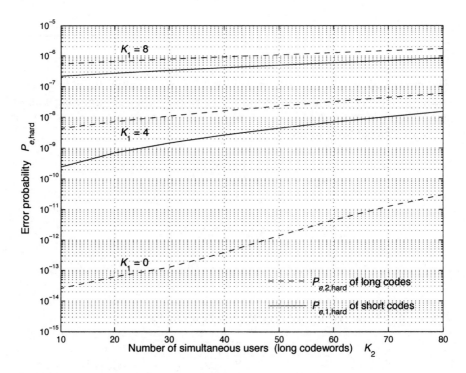

FIGURE 7.8 Chip-synchronous, hard-limiting error probabilities of the double-length quadratic-congruence carrier-hopping prime codes versus K_2 for $t_1 = 11$, $L = w = 7$, $N_1 = 31$, and $N_2 = 1147$.

Figure 7.8 plots the chip-synchronous, hard-limiting error probabilities of the single-weight, double-length quadratic-congruence carrier-hopping prime codes against the number of simultaneous users with long-length codewords K_2 for various numbers of simultaneous users of short-length codewords $K_1 = \{0, 4, 8\}$, where $k = 2$, $p_1 = 31$, $p_2 = 37$, $t_1 = 11$, $L = w = 7$, $N_1 = p_1 = 31$, $N_2 = p_1 p_2 = 1147$. Figure 7.9 is for the same codes but against K_1 for various $K_2 = \{0, 200, 600\}$. In general, the error probabilities get worse as the total number of simultaneous users $K_1 + K_2$ increases. The long codewords perform worse than the short codewords because stronger interference is created by multiple copies of the short codewords in the periodic cross-correlation process. However, the improvement is rather small because a short code-length $N_1 = 37$ is used, which has poor performance anyway. The dashed curve with $K_1 = 0$ in Figure 7.8 and the solid curve with $K_2 = 0$ in Figure 7.9 show the performances of the single-length quadratic-congruence carrier-hopping prime codes (see Section 5.6) with long length N_2 and short length N_1, respectively.

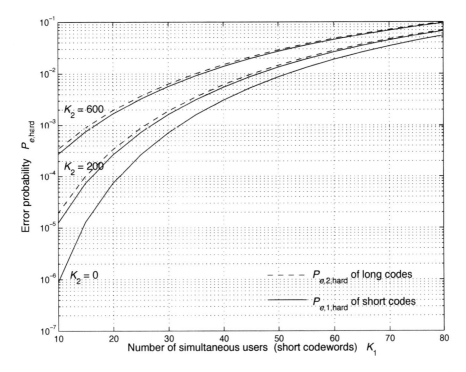

FIGURE 7.9 Chip-synchronous, hard-limiting error probabilities of the double-length quadratic-congruence carrier-hopping prime codes versus K_1 for $t_1 = 11, L = w = 7, N_1 = 31$, and $N_2 = 1147$.

Both figures show that the short codewords dominate the performance and create stronger interference than the long codewords. This contradicts the finding in conventional single-length codes that code performance improves with code length, as seen by comparing the ($K_1 = 0$)-curve in Figure 7.8 and the ($K_2 = 0$)-curve in Figure 7.9.

7.3.2 Multicode Keying

Similar to their single-length counterparts in Section 5.6, the multilength quadratic-congruence carrier-hopping prime codes also support multicode keying due to their enlarged cardinality. In multicode keying, the total amount of interference seen at the receiver of a user consists of the intrasymbol cross-correlation functions generated by the user's other codewords—self-interference by different symbols—and the intersymbol cross-correlation functions generated by the codewords of interferers [8].

To minimize the intrasymbol cross-correlation functions to at most 1, each user is here assigned a set of $2^{m_j} \leq p_1$ codewords of length $N_j = p_1 p_2 \ldots p_j$ from the multilength quadratic-congruence carrier-hopping prime codes with the same indices $(i_2, i_3, \ldots, i_k, l)$ for $j \in [1, k]$. This code-assignment method supports α_j / p_1 sets (or possible users of length N_j) of 2^{m_j} codewords (or symbols per user) in each set for 2^{m_j}-code keying, representing the transmission of m_j bits/symbol.

Definition 7.1

In multicode keying, depending on the code lengths and sets of the multilength quadratic-congruence carrier-hopping prime codes in use, two additional cross-correlation constraints are defined as

- (*Intersymbol cross-correlation*) For two distinct codewords, $\mathbf{x}$ of length N_i and $\mathbf{y}$ of length N_j, from two different code sets, their discrete (periodic) cross-correlation function is no greater than a non-negative integer λ'_c such that

$$\sum_{r=0}^{L-1}\sum_{s=0}^{N_i-1} x_{r,s}y_{r,s\oplus_j\tau} \leq \lambda'_c$$

if $N_i = N_j$, but

$$\sum_{r=0}^{L-1}\sum_{s=0}^{N_i-1} x_{r,s}y_{r,s\oplus_j\tau} \leq \lambda'_c \quad \text{and} \quad \sum_{r=0}^{L-1}\sum_{s=0}^{N_j-1} x_{r,s\oplus_i\tau}y_{r,s} \leq \lambda'_c$$

if $N_i \neq N_j$, where $\tau \in [0, N_i - 1]$, "$\oplus_j$" denotes a modulo-N_j addition, and $x_{r,s} = \{0,1\}$ is an element of $\mathbf{x}$ and $y_{r,s} = \{0,1\}$ is an element of $\mathbf{y}$ at the rth row and sth column.
- (*Intrasymbol cross-correlation*) For two distinct codewords, $\mathbf{x}$ and $\mathbf{x}'$ of the same length N_i, from the same code set, their discrete (in-phase) cross-correlation function is no greater than a non-negative integer $\lambda'_{c,i}$ such that

$$\sum_{r=0}^{L-1}\sum_{s=0}^{N_i-1} x_{r,s}x'_{r,s} \leq \lambda'_{c,i}$$

where $x'_{r,s} = \{0,1\}$ is an element of $\mathbf{x}'$ at the rth row and sth column. (Note: The cross-correlation value at the expected location of the autocorrelation peak of $\mathbf{x}$ is here considered and not a function of any τ-shift.)

■

Theorem 7.8

The chip-synchronous, hard-limiting error probability of the multilength quadratic-congruence carrier-hopping prime codes of $L = w$ wavelengths, weight $w \leq p_1$, and length $N_i = p_1 p_2 \cdots p_i$ in 2^{m_i}-code keying is formulated as [8, 16]

$$P_{e,i,\text{hard,multicode}} = \frac{2^{m_i}}{2(2^{m_i}-1)} \left\{ 1 - \sum_{t=0}^{2^{m_i}-1} \left(\frac{1}{t+1} \right) \frac{(2^{m_i}-1)!}{t!(2^{m_i}-1-t)!} \right.$$

$$\left. \times [\text{Pr}_i(w-1)]^t \left[\sum_{z=0}^{w-2} \text{Pr}_i(z) \right]^{2^{m_i}-1-t} \right\}$$

where $i \in [1,k]$, k is the number of different lengths, and

$$\text{Pr}_i(v) = \frac{w!}{v!(w-v)!} \sum_{s=0}^{v} (-1)^{v-s} \frac{v!}{s!(v-s)!} \left\{ \left[q'_{0,i,i} + \frac{s q'_{1,i,i}}{w} + \frac{s(s-1)q'_{2,i,i}}{w(w-1)} \right]^{K_i-1} \right.$$

$$\left. \times \prod_{j=1,j\neq i}^{k} \left[q'_{0,i,j} + \frac{s q'_{1,i,j}}{w} + \frac{s(s-1)q'_{2,i,j}}{w(w-1)} \right]^{K_j} \right\}$$

The probabilities, $q'_{h,i,j}$, of getting $h = \{0,1,2\}$ hits in a codeword of length N_i and cardinality α_i correlating with an interfering codeword of length N_j, both of $L = w$ wavelengths and weight $w \leq p_1$, in 2^{m_i}-code keying are formulated as

$$q'_{2,i,j} = \begin{cases} \frac{w(w-1)(\alpha_i - N_i)}{2N_i^2(\alpha_i - p_1)} & \text{for } i = j \\ \frac{w(w-1)}{2N_j^2} & \text{otherwise} \end{cases}$$

$$\sum_{h=0}^{2} h q'_{h,i,j} = \frac{w^2}{LN_j} = \frac{w}{N_j}$$

and $\sum_{h=0}^{2} q'_{h,i,j} = 1$.

Proof The derivation of the hit probabilities is similar to that of the OOK case, except that the factor $1/2$ is not needed in multicode keying due to continuous symbol transmission. Similar to Theorem 7.7, the two-hit probability is given by

$$q'_{2,i,j} = \frac{\binom{w}{2}}{N_j} \times \frac{1}{N_j} \times \begin{cases} \frac{\alpha_i - N_i}{\alpha_i - p_1} & \text{for } i = j \\ 1 & \text{otherwise} \end{cases}$$

There are now only $\alpha_j - p_1$ codewords of length N_j that can serve as interfering codewords for the $i = j$ case, instead of $\alpha_j - 1$ in the proof of Theorem 7.7.

A symbol decision error in a decoder occurs when interfering codewords cause the cross-correlation function (in the sampling time) to be greater than or equal to w. A final decision error occurs if more than one decoder has an output intensity of at least w. Given that there are $K_i - 1 + \sum_{j=1,j\neq i}^{k} K_j$ interfering codewords and each generates at most two hits in the sampling time, the hard-limiting probability of having a peak of v appearing at any one of $2^{m_i} - 1$ wrong decoders in the intended receiver is obtained by $\Pr_i(v)$ in the theorem [8]. The probability that t decoders have an output intensity of at least w and $2^{m_i} - 1 - t$ decoders have an output intensity of less than w is given by

$$\Pr_i(w,t) = \binom{2^{m_i} - 1}{t} [\Pr_i(w)]^t \left[\sum_{z=0}^{w-1} \Pr_i(z) \right]^{2^{m_i} - 1 - t}$$

Finally, the chip-synchronous, hard-limiting bit error probability is given by [8, 16]

$$P_{e,i,\text{hard,multicode}} = \frac{2^{m_i}}{2(2^{m_i} - 1)} \left[1 - \sum_{t=0}^{2^{m_i} - 1} \left(\frac{1}{t+1} \right) \Pr_i(w - 1, t) \right]$$

in which the probability of choosing the correct decoder is $1/(t+1)$. Because the first pulse of every codeword always locates at the first chip location, codewords always hit with each other at this location if such a hit occurs. As the intrasymbol cross-correlation function is at most 1, no other hits can be found between any two of the 2^{m_i} codewords of an interferer if the one-hit caused by the first chip locations are excluded. In coding terminology, the contribution of the pulse in the first chip location is erased and the effective weight becomes $w - 1$ inside the $\Pr_i(w - 1, t)$ term, instead of w. ∎

Figure 7.10 plots the chip-synchronous, hard-limiting error probabilities of the single-weight, double-length quadratic-congruence carrier-hopping prime codes in OOK and multicode keying against the number of simultaneous users with short-length codewords K_1 for various m_1 and $m_2 = \{1, 2, 3, 4\}$, where $k = 2$, $p_1 = 31$, $p_2 = 37$, $L = w = 7$, $t_1 = 11$, $N_1 = p_1 = 31$, and $N_2 = p_1 p_2 = 1147$. The number of simultaneous users with long-length codewords is fixed at $K_2 = 15$. Figure 7.11 is for the same codes but against K_2 with a fixed $K_1 = 5$. In general, the error probabilities in both figures follow the trends in those in Figures 7.8 and 7.9. The short codewords always perform better than the long codewords. Additionally in multicode keying, the error probabilities get worse as m_i increases. This is because there are more incorrect data bits if a symbol decision error occurs. The performance in multicode keying is much worse than that in OOK for a given bandwidth expansion LN_1 or LN_2. This is because the hit probabilities in OOK are reduced by half as data bit 0s are not conveyed. This example shows that there is a trade-off between code performance and the choices of m_1 and m_2, in the sense that code performance suffers when bit rate and user code obscurity are enhanced. In summary, if bit rate or user code obscurity is more important, one should use multicode keying with m_1 and $m_2 = \{2, 3\}$, which provide a good compromise among error probability, hardware complexity, code obscurity, and bit rate.

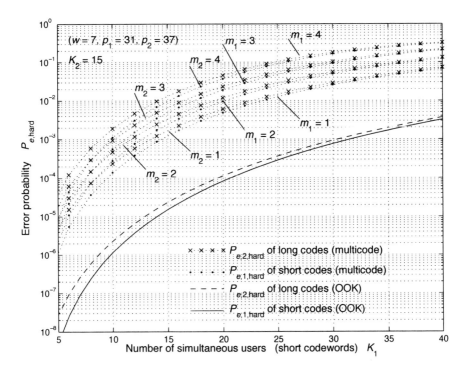

FIGURE 7.10 Chip-synchronous, hard-limiting error probabilities of the double-length quadratic-congruence carrier-hopping prime codes in OOK and multicode keying versus K_1 for $t_1 = 11, L = w = 7, N_1 = 31, N_2 = 1147,$ and $K_2 = 15$.

7.3.3 Spectral Efficiency Study

Modified from Section 5.6, the spectral efficiency of the multilength quadratic-congruence carrier-hopping prime codes in multicode keying is defined as [16]

$$\text{SE} \propto \sum_{i=1}^{k} \frac{K_i m_i}{LN_i}$$

where k is the number of different lengths, K_i is the number of simultaneous users with codewords of length N_i for a given error probability, LN_i is the bandwidth expansion, and m_i is the number of bits/symbol in multicode keying or $m_i = 1$ in OOK. The target is to get the SE as large as possible for better system efficiency or utilization.

Figure 7.12 plots the chip-synchronous, hard-limiting error probabilities of the single-weight, double-length quadratic-congruence carrier-hopping prime codes in multicode keying against the numbers of simultaneous users with long-length codewords K_2 and short-length codewords K_1, where $k = 2, L = w = 12, p_1 = 41,$ $p_2 = 43, t_1 = 20, N_1 = p_1 = 41, N_2 = p_1 p_2 = 1763,$ and $m_1 = m_2 = 5$. In general, the error probabilities of the short and long codewords are found very close

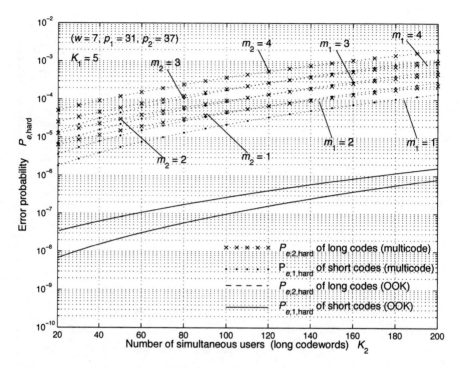

FIGURE 7.11 Chip-synchronous, hard-limiting error probabilities of the double-length quadratic-congruence carrier-hopping prime codes in OOK and multicode keying versus K_2 for $t_1 = 11, L = w = 7, N_1 = 31, N_2 = 1147$, and $K_1 = 5$.

to each other, but the short codewords ($P_{e,1,\text{hard}}$ surface) always perform better than the long codewords ($P_{e,2,\text{hard}}$ surface). The error probabilities get worse as K_1 or K_2 increases. A ($P_{e,2,\text{hard}} = 10^{-9}$)-line is drawn on the $P_{e,2,\text{hard}}$ surface for finding the combinations of K_1 and K_2 that give the error probability of 10^{-9}. This procedure establishes the relationship of SE and code length in Table 7.1. For example, with $K_1 = 5$, $K_2 \approx 48$ is found by locating the intersection point between the ($K_1 = 5$)-plane and the ($P_{e,2,\text{hard}} = 10^{-9}$)-line on the $P_{e,2,\text{hard}}$ surface in Figure 7.12. So, SE $\propto 5 \times 5/(12 \times 41) + 48 \times 5/(12 \times 1763) = 6.21\%$ if $m_1 = m_2 = 5$, $w = 12$, $N_1 = 41$, and $N_2 = 1763$ are assumed.

Table 7.1 compares the SEs of the single-weight, double-length quadratic-congruence carrier-hopping prime codes in multicode keying as a function of K_1, for a fixed $P_{e,2,\text{hard}} \approx 10^{-9}$ in Figure 7.12. The table shows that SE_{total} improves but the total number of simultaneous users $K_1 + K_2$ gets worse as K_1 increases. So, there is a trade-off between the total SE and the total number of simultaneous users, and the combination of K_1 and K_2 affects the total SE. Which combination of K_1 and K_2 should be used depends on which criterion—better spectral efficiency versus more simultaneous users—is more important.

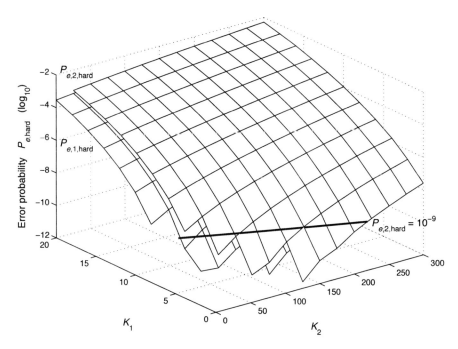

FIGURE 7.12 Chip-synchronous, hard-limiting error probabilities of the double-length quadratic-congruence carrier-hopping prime codes in multicode keying versus K_1 and K_2 for $t_1 = 20$, $L = w = 12$, $N_1 = p_1 = 41$, $N_2 = p_1 p_2 = 1763$, and $m_1 = m_2 = 5$.

7.4   2-D MULTILENGTH PRIME-PERMUTED CODES

Similar to their single-length counterparts in Section 5.7, the 2-D multilength prime-permuted codes use the p^2 shifted prime sequences over GF(p) of a prime p to permutate the wavelengths of pulses in 1-D time-spreading codes algebraically. The time-spreading codes now come from 1-D multilength codes, such as the 1-D multilength optical orthogonal codes (OOCs) in Section 7.6, which have the periodic cross-correlation functions of at most 1, independent of code length [14, 24, 25].

Given a set of k positive integers $t > t_{k-1} > \cdots > t_1$ to control the number of codewords in each length, out of k different lengths, a set of $k - 1$ prime numbers $p_{k-1} \geq p_{k-2} \geq \cdots \geq p_1$ to determine the number of codewords and lengths, and these prime numbers to be relatively prime to $(w - 1)!$, the construction begins with the 1-D multilength OOC codewords, $X_{i_1}, X_{i_2,i_1}, X_{i_3,i_2,i_1}, \ldots$, and $X_{i_k,i_{k-1},\ldots,i_1}$, from Construction 1 of Section 7.6. By mapping the p^2 shifted prime sequences over GF(p) of a prime p with $L = p$ wavelengths onto the pulses of these time-spreading 1-D multilength OOC codewords (in a similar way as in Section 5.7), the resulting 2-D multilength prime-permuted codewords, $\mathbf{x}_{i_1,l_2,l_1}, \mathbf{x}_{i_2,i_1,l_2,l_1}, \mathbf{x}_{i_3,i_2,i_1,l_2,l_1}, \ldots$, and $\mathbf{x}_{i_k,i_{k-1},\ldots,i_1,l_2,l_1}$, of weight $w \leq p$ have $\beta_1 = p^2 t_1$ codewords of length $N_1 = w(w - 1)t + 1$; $\beta_2 = p^2 p_1 (t_2 - t_1)$ codewords of length $N_2 = p_1 N_1$; $\beta_3 = p^2 p_1 p_2 (t_3 - t_2)$ codewords of

TABLE 7.1

Spectral Efficiency Comparison of the Single-Weight, Double-Length Quadratic-Congruence Carrier-Hopping Prime Codes in Multicode-Keying, Based on Figure 7.12 with $P_{e,2,\text{hard}} \approx 10^{-9}$

K_1	SE$_1$ (%)	K_2	SE$_2$ (%)	$K_1 + K_2$	SE$_{\text{total}} =$ SE$_1 +$ SE$_2$ (%)
0	0	219	6.21	219	6.21
1	1.02	184	4.35	185	5.37
2	2.03	149	3.52	151	5.55
3	3.05	115	2.72	118	5.77
4	4.07	81	1.91	85	5.98
5	5.08	48	1.13	53	6.21
6	6.10	16	0.38	22	6.48

length $N_3 = p_1 p_2 N_1$; ...; and $\beta_k = p^2 p_1 p_2 \cdots p_{k-1}(t - t_{k-1})$ codewords of length $N_k = p_1 p_2 \cdots p_{k-1} N_1$, respectively, for $i_1 = \{0,1,\ldots,t-1\}$, $i_2 = \{0,1,\ldots,p_1-1\}$, $i_3 = \{0,1,\ldots,p_2-1\}$, ..., $i_k = \{0,1,\ldots,p_{k-1}-1\}$, where $l_2 = \{0,1,\ldots,p-1\}$ is the l_2th shifted prime sequence in the $l_1 = \{0,1,\ldots,p-1\}$ group [14,25].

To vary the weight of a 2-D multilength prime-permuted codeword, say from w to w', $w - w'$ pulses can be removed randomly from the codeword. Because the codewords have at most one pulse per row and column in the code matrices, the autocorrelation-sidelobe and cross-correlation properties are still preserved in this variable-weight operation.

Using $k = 2$, $L = p = 7$, $w = 3$, $p_1 = 5$, $t_1 = 1$, and $t_2 = 2$ as an example, the time-spreading 1-D double-length OOCs from Construction 1 in Section 7.6 have one short codeword of length $N_1 = w(w-1)t_2 + 1 = 13$, denoted by $X_0 = (0,2,8)$; and 5 long codewords of length $N_2 = p_1 N_1 = 65$, denoted by $X_{0,1} = (0,3,4)$, $X_{1,1} = (0,16,30)$, $X_{2,1} = (0,29,56)$, $X_{3,1} = (0,17,42)$, and $X_{4,1} = (0,43,55)$. With the permutations of $L = 7$ wavelengths controlled by the $p^2 = 49$ shifted prime sequences over GF(7), each 1-D double-length OOC codeword can generate 49 prime-permuted codewords. So, these 2-D double-length prime-permuted codes of weight $w = 3$ have $p^2 t_1 = 49$ codewords of short length $N_1 = 13$, denoted by $\mathbf{x}_{0,l_2,l_1}$, and $p^2 p_1 (t_2 - t_1) = 245$ codewords of long length $N_2 = 65$, denoted by $\mathbf{x}_{i_2,1,l_2,l_1}$, where $l_1 \in [0,6]$ is the group number and $l_2 \in [0,6]$ is the l_2th codewords in each group. Illustrated in Table 7.2 are some of the short 2-D prime-permuted codewords, $\mathbf{x}_{0,l_2,l_1}$, which are represented as wavelength-time sequences, originating from the short OOC codeword $X_0 = 1010000010000$.

TABLE 7.2
Double-Length Prime-Permuted Codes over GF(7) of Short Length $N_1 = 13$, Weight $w = 3$, and $L = 7$ Wavelengths, from the Time-Spreading 1-D Short OOC Codeword 1010000010000

l_2	Group $l_1 = 0$	Group $l_1 = 1$	$\cdots$	Group $l_1 = 6$
0	$\lambda_0 0 \lambda_0 00000 \lambda_0 0000$	$\lambda_0 0 \lambda_1 00000 \lambda_2 0000$	$\cdots$	$\lambda_0 0 \lambda_6 00000 \lambda_5 0000$
1	$\lambda_1 0 \lambda_1 00000 \lambda_1 0000$	$\lambda_1 0 \lambda_2 00000 \lambda_3 0000$	$\cdots$	$\lambda_1 0 \lambda_0 00000 \lambda_6 0000$
2	$\lambda_2 0 \lambda_2 00000 \lambda_2 0000$	$\lambda_2 0 \lambda_3 00000 \lambda_4 0000$	$\cdots$	$\lambda_2 0 \lambda_1 00000 \lambda_0 0000$
3	$\lambda_3 0 \lambda_3 00000 \lambda_3 0000$	$\lambda_3 0 \lambda_4 00000 \lambda_5 0000$	$\cdots$	$\lambda_3 0 \lambda_2 00000 \lambda_1 0000$
4	$\lambda_4 0 \lambda_4 00000 \lambda_4 0000$	$\lambda_4 0 \lambda_5 00000 \lambda_6 0000$	$\cdots$	$\lambda_4 0 \lambda_3 00000 \lambda_2 0000$
5	$\lambda_5 0 \lambda_5 00000 \lambda_5 0000$	$\lambda_5 0 \lambda_6 00000 \lambda_0 0000$	$\cdots$	$\lambda_5 0 \lambda_4 00000 \lambda_3 0000$
6	$\lambda_6 0 \lambda_6 00000 \lambda_6 0000$	$\lambda_6 0 \lambda_0 00000 \lambda_1 0000$	$\cdots$	$\lambda_6 0 \lambda_5 00000 \lambda_4 0000$

Theorem 7.9

The autocorrelation peaks of the 2-D multiple-length prime-permuted codes over GF(p) of a prime p and weight w are equal to w, where $w \leq p$. The autocorrelation sidelobes of the codes are at most 1, but equal to 0 if the codewords in group $l_1 = 0$ are excluded. The periodic cross-correlation functions of the codes are at most 1, independent of code length [14, 25].

Proof As proved in Section 7.6, the time-spreading 1-D multilength OOCs have the periodic cross-correlation functions of at most 1, independent of code length. Also, the maximum cross-correlation function of the shifted prime sequences over GF(p) is 1. Similar to the single-length counterparts in Section 5.7, the 2-D multilength prime-permuted codes have the periodic cross-correlation functions of at most 1 by following the autocorrelation and cross-correlation properties of the time-spreading 1-D multilength OOCs and shifted prime sequences. The autocorrelation sidelobes of any codeword from group $l_1 \in [1, p-1]$ are always 0 because all pulses within each codeword are in different wavelengths. For those codewords in group $l_1 = 0$, the maximum autocorrelation sidelobe is at most 1 due to the same property of the time-spreading 1-D multilength OOCs. Finally, the autocorrelation peaks of w are due to the code weight $w \leq p$. ∎

Similar to other multilength codes in this chapter, the upper bound of the overall cardinality of the 2-D multilength prime-permuted codes over GF(p) of a prime p

with $L = p$ wavelengths and weight $w \le p$ is given by

$$\Phi_{\text{upper}} \le \frac{p(pN_k - 1)\Phi_{\text{multilength}}}{\beta_k w(w-1) + \sum_{i=1}^{k-1} \beta_i w(w\prod_{j=i}^{k-1} p_j - 1)}$$

where $N_k = p_1 p_2 \cdots p_{k-1} N_1$, $N_1 = w(w-1)t + 1$, and the actual overall cardinality is given by

$$\begin{aligned}
\Phi_{\text{multilength}} &= p^2[t_1 + p_1(t_2 - t_1) + p_1 p_2(t_3 - t_2) + \cdots \\
&\quad + p_1 p_2 \cdots p_{k-2}(t_{k-1} - t_{k-2}) + p_1 p_2 \cdots p_{k-1}(t - t_{k-1})]
\end{aligned}$$

To show the asymptotic optimal overall cardinality of the 2-D multilength prime-permuted codes, it is found that

$$\begin{aligned}
\frac{\Phi_{\text{multilength}}}{\Phi_{\text{upper}}} &\approx \frac{t_1}{t}\left[1 + \frac{p_1 p_2 \cdots p_{k-1} - 1}{p_1 p_2 \cdots p_{k-1}(p-1)}\right] + \frac{t_2 - t_1}{t}\left[1 + \frac{p_2 p_3 \cdots p_{k-1} - 1}{p_2 p_3 \cdots p_{k-1}(p-1)}\right] \\
&\quad + \cdots + \frac{t_{k-1} - t_{k-2}}{t}\left[1 + \frac{p_{k-1} - 1}{p_{k-1}(p-1)}\right] + \frac{t - t_{k-1}}{t}
\end{aligned}$$

which approaches 1, for a large $w = p$ and t.

In general, the overall cardinality suffers as k increases because there are more short codewords and then more concatenated cross-correlation functions to consider. So, the overall cardinality can be improved by reducing the number of short codewords.

To fairly compare the cardinalities of the 2-D multilength prime-permuted codes and their single-length counterparts in Section 5.7, length N_k and $L = p$ wavelengths are used in the latter so that both code families occupy the same maximum bandwidth expansion LN_k, giving $\Phi_{\text{single}} = p^2 p_1 p_2 \cdots p_{k-1} t$. As $p_1 \le p_2 \le \cdots \le p_{k-1}$ and $t_1 \le t_2 \le \cdots \le t_{k-1} \le t$, it is found that [14, 25]

$$\frac{\Phi_{\text{multiple}}}{\Phi_{\text{single}}} = \frac{t_1}{p_1 p_2 \cdots p_{k-1} t} + \frac{t_2 - t_1}{p_2 p_3 \cdots p_{k-1} t} + \cdots + \frac{t_{k-1} - t_{k-2}}{p_{k-1} t} + \frac{t - t_{k-1}}{t} \le 1$$

This implies that the multilength codes always have smaller cardinality than their single-length counterparts. Equality occurs when $t_1 = t_2 = \cdots = t_{k-1} = 0$, and the 2-D multilength prime-permuted codes become the single-length ones.

7.4.1 Performance Analysis

Because the maximum periodic cross-correlation function is 1, the chip-synchronous, soft- and hard-limiting error probabilities of the 2-D multilength prime-permuted codes in OOK follow Equations (7.7) and (7.8), respectively.

Theorem 7.10

When a 2-D multilength prime-permuted codeword of weight w_i and length $N_{i'}$ correlates with an interfering codeword of weight w_j, length $N_{j'}$, and cardinality $\beta_{j'}$, both of $L = p$ wavelengths, the one-hit probability is generally formulated as [14,25]

$$q_{i,i',j,j'} = \frac{w_i w_j(\beta_{j'} - 1) - (p-1)\min\{w_i, w_j\}}{2pN_{j'}(\beta_{j'} - 1)}$$

for i and $j \in [1,k]$, and i' and $j' \in [1,k']$, where k is the number of different weights and k' is the number of different lengths.

Proof The one-hit probability of the address codeword (of a receiver) of weight w_i and length $N_{i'}$ originating from group $l_1 = 0$ when it correlates with an interfering codeword of weight w_j and length $N_{j'}$ from any group $l_1 = \{0, 1, \dots, p-1\}$ is derived as

$$
\begin{aligned}
q_{i,i',j,j'}^{(0)} = \frac{1}{2}\Bigg[& \frac{1}{N_{j'}} \times \frac{\min\{w_i, w_j\}(p-1)}{\beta_{j'} - 1} + \frac{w_i w_j - \min\{w_i, w_j\}}{N_{j'}} \\
& \times \frac{w_j(p-1)}{\beta_{j'} - 1} \times \frac{1}{w_j} + \frac{w_i w_j}{N_{j'}} \times \frac{(\beta_{j'}/p^2) - 1}{\beta_{j'} - 1} \\
& + \frac{w_i w_j}{N_{j'}} \times \frac{[(\beta_{j'}/p^2) - 1]w_j(p-1)}{\beta_{j'} - 1} \times \frac{1}{w_j}\Bigg]
\end{aligned}
$$

where the factor $1/2$ comes from the assumption of equiprobable data bit-1 and bit-0 transmissions in OOK. The denominator $\beta_{j'} - 1$ represents the number of interfering codewords of length $N_{j'}$. The first product term in the brackets accounts for the one-hit probability caused by an interfering codeword coming from the same time-spreading OOC codeword as that of the address codeword and aligning with the address codeword with zero time shift with a probability of $1/N_{j'}$. The term $\min\{w_i, w_j\}(p-1)$ counts the number of such interfering codewords. Similarly, the second product term accounts for the same situation but the interfering codeword comes from group $l_1 \neq 0$ with a probability of $1/w_j$ and aligns with the address codeword with a time shift with a probability of $(w_i w_j - \min\{w_i, w_j\})/N_{j'}$. The term $w_j(p-1)$ counts the number of such interfering codewords. The third product term in the brackets accounts for the one-hit probability caused by an interfering codeword coming from the same ($l_1 = 0$)-group but a different OOC codeword than that of the address codeword. The term $w_i w_j/N_{j'}$ denotes the probability of getting one-hits. Because each time-spreading OOC codeword can generate p^2 2-D prime-permuted codewords, the term $(\beta_{j'}/p^2) - 1$ accounts for the possible number of different OOC codewords of length $N_{j'}$. The fourth product term accounts for the one-hit probability caused by an interfering code coming from a ($l_1 \neq 0$)-group and a different OOC codeword than that of the address codeword. The term $w_i w_j/N_{j'}$ represents the probability of getting one-hits. The factor $1/w_j$ represents the probability of getting one-hits caused by an interfering codeword coming from a ($l_1 \neq 0$)-group. The term $[(\beta_{j'}/p^2) - 1]w_j(p-1)$ represents the number of such interfering codewords coming from one of the $p - 1$ ($l_1 \neq 0$)-groups.

Similarly, the one-hit probability of the address codeword originating from group $l_1 = \{1, 2, \ldots, p-1\}$ when it correlates with an interfering codeword from any group is derived as

$$
\begin{aligned}
q_{i,i',j,j'}^{(1)} = \frac{1}{2} \Bigg[& \frac{1}{N_{j'}} \times \frac{\min\{w_i, w_j\}(p-1)}{\beta_{j'} - 1} + \frac{w_i w_j - \min\{w_i, w_j\}}{N_{j'}} \\
& \times \frac{1}{\beta_{j'} - 1} + \frac{w_i w_j - \min\{w_i, w_j\}}{N_{j'}} \times \frac{(p-2)}{\beta_{j'} p^2 - 1} \\
& + \frac{w_i w_j - \min\{w_i, w_j\}}{N_{j'}} \times \frac{1}{\beta_{j'} - 1} + \frac{w_i w_j}{N_{j'}} \times \frac{[(\beta_{j'}/p^2) - 1]p}{\beta_{j'} - 1} \Bigg]
\end{aligned}
$$

The derivation follows the rationale used for $q_{i,i',j,j'}^{(0)}$. The first four product terms in the brackets account for the one-hit probabilities caused by an interfering codeword coming from any group $l = \{0, 1, \ldots, p-1\}$ and from the same time-spreading OOC codeword as that of the address codeword. The first product term accounts for the one-hit probability caused by the interfering codeword aligning with the address codeword with zero time shift with a probability of $1/N_{j'}$. Similarly, the second product term accounts for the one-hit probability caused by an interfering codeword coming from the $(l_1 = 0)$-group and aligning with the address codeword with a time shift with a probability of $(w_i w_j - \min\{w_i, w_j\})/N_{j'}$. The third product term accounts for the one-hit probability caused by an interfering codeword coming from a different $(l_1 \neq 0)$-group than that of the address codeword and aligning with the address codeword with zero time shift. Similarly, the fourth product term accounts for the same situation but both codewords come from the same $(l_1 \neq 0)$-group. Finally, the fifth product term accounts for the one-hit probability caused by an interfering codeword coming from a different OOC codeword than that of the address codeword.

By combining all groups, the final form of $q_{i,i',j,j'}$, which is equal to $q_{i,i',j,j'} = (1/p)q_{i,i',j,j'}^{(0)} + [(p-1)/p]q_{i,i',j,j'}^{(1)}$, in the theorem is derived after some manipulations. ∎

Figure 7.13 plots the chip-synchronous, soft-limiting error probabilities of the single-weight, double-length prime-permuted codes against the number of simultaneous users with long-length codewords $K_{1,2}$ for various numbers of simultaneous users with short-length codewords $K_{1,1} = \{0, 5, 20\}$, where $k = 1$, $k' = 2$, $p_1 = 11$, $t_2 = 3$, $t_1 = 1$, $L = p = w = 5$, $\beta_1 = p^2 t_1$, $\beta_2 = p^2 p_1 (t_2 - t_1)$, $N_1 = w(w+1)t_2 + 1 = 61$, and $N_2 = p_1 N_1 = 671$. $K_{1,i'}$ represents the number of simultaneous users with codewords of length $N_{i'}$ for $i' \in [1, 2]$. Figure 7.14 is for the same codes but against $K_{1,1}$ for various $K_{1,2} = \{0, 20, 200\}$. In general, the error probabilities get worse as the total number of simultaneous uses $K_{1,1} + K_{1,2}$ increases. The short codewords always perform better than the long codewords because stronger interference is created by multiple copies of the short interfering codewords in the cross-correlation process. However, the performance improvement is small because a rather short codeword length $N_1 = 61$ is used, which has poor performance anyway. The dashed curve with $K_{1,1} = 0$ in Figure 7.13 and the solid curve with $K_{1,2} = 0$ in Figure 7.14

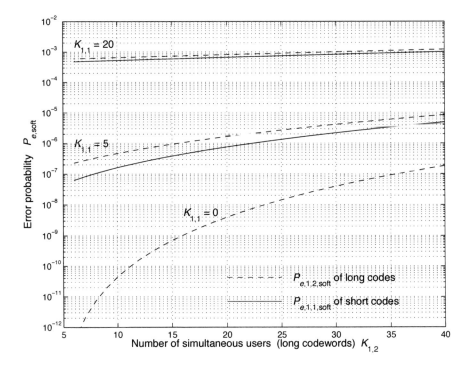

FIGURE 7.13 Chip-synchronous, soft-limiting error probabilities of the single-weight, double-length prime-permuted codes versus $K_{1,2}$ for $t_1 = 1$, $t_2 = 3$, $L = p = w = 5$, $N_1 = 61$, and $N_2 = 671$.

show the performances of single-length prime-permuted codes (in Section 5.7) with long length N_2 and short length N_1, respectively. Both figures confirm that the short codewords dominate the performance as they generate stronger interference than the long codewords. This contradicts the conventional finding in the single-length codes that long codewords perform better than short codewords, as seen by comparing the $(K_{1,2} = 0)$-curve in Figure 7.13 and the $(K_{1,1} = 0)$-curve in Figure 7.14.

In general, it is difficult to calculate the code performances as k' increases beyond 2 because there are more different-length interfering patterns and, in turn, hit probabilities to consider [20]. The calculations can be simplified by evaluating the performance bounds. This is because the best performance (or lower bound) is achieved by the shortest codewords and the worst performance (or upper bound) is achieved by the longest codewords. So, codewords with lengths in between will fall within these two bounds.

7.5   VARIABLE-WEIGHT CODING WITH SAME BIT POWER

In Sections 7.1 through 7.4, the variable-weight, multilength codes are assumed to carry the same optical pulse (or chip) power [7, 9, 12, 14]. So, heavier-weight code-

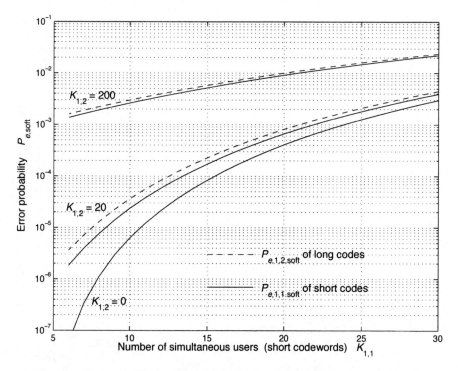

FIGURE 7.14 Chip-synchronous, soft-limiting error probabilities of the single-weight, double-length prime-permuted codes versus $K_{1,1}$ for $t_1 = 1, t_2 = 3, L = p = w = 5, N_1 = 61$, and $N_2 = 671$.

words always have more total power per bit and higher autocorrelation peaks than lower-weight codewords. These translate into better code performance in heavier-weight codewords and, in turn, better QoS. However, there is a realistic problem in some laser sources that the amount of optical pulse power per repetition may be limited. In such situations, the chip power of an optical codeword depends on the code weight in use [18–20, 26, 27]. For example, let w_1 and w_2 be the weights of a family of double-weight codes with the maximum periodic cross-correlation function of 1, where $w_1 > w_2$. If the total bit power P_b of every codeword is limited, then $P_b = w_1 P_{c1} = w_2 P_{c2}$ and this gives $P_{c1} < P_{c2}$, where P_{c1} and P_{c2} are the chip powers of the codewords of weights w_1 and w_2, respectively. Under this same-bit-power assumption, one complete hit is generated when a light-weight (address) codeword is interfered by a heavy-weight codeword. For illustration, if $w_1 = 7$ and $w_2 = 4$, only 4/7 of a complete hit can be obtained in the cross-correlation function because their chip powers are now related by $P_{c1} = P_b/7$ and $P_{c2} = P_b/4$. There must exist at least two heavy-weight interfering codewords at the same time in order to generate one complete hit to the light-weight address codeword. This implies that heavy-weight codewords now carry lessened interference effects and the performance of light-weight codewords can be improved. This contradicts some of the findings in Sections 7.1 through 7.4, in which the same-chip-power assumption is applied. In addition, the QoS functionality in variable-weight coding becomes less predictable because there are more uncertainties on how these codewords perform and interact under the same-bit-power assumption.

To overcome various problems, such as near-far, connector loss, and aging of optical link or components, some power-control mechanisms have been introduced in the physical layer [11, 18–20, 28]. Variable-weight coding with chip-power control allows fine-tuning of QoS in the physical layer at no extra cost and supplements the conventional QoS-control mechanism at higher layers. An exact analytical model will be important because it provides a better understanding of the combined effect of chip-power and code-weight variations on QoS. Such an exact model will also be beneficial to power-sensitive applications, such as in-service monitoring and fiber-fault surveillance in coding-based optical systems and networks, and sensor-identification in coding-based fiber-sensor systems [21–23].

An error-probability upper bound for 1-D optical codes under the same-bit-power assumption was studied by Beyranvand in [27], and an approximation model (or lower bound) for both 1-D and 2-D optical codes was derived by Chen et al. in [18]. An exact model for providing a more accurate relationship of weight-variation and power control in the performance of 1-D and 2-D optical codes is formulated in this section [19]. For the sake of illustration, the following analysis focuses on double-weight, single-length optical codes with the periodic cross-correlation functions of at most 1. The complexity of the analysis grows tremendously when the number of chip powers or code weights increases beyond 2. A general description of the complexity can be found in [20].

Theorem 7.11

For a family of double-weight, single-length optical codes with the maximum periodic cross-correlation function of 1, the same-bit-power, chip-synchronous, hard-limiting error probability of the codewords with heavy weight w_1 in OOK is formulated as [18–20]

$$P_{e,1,\text{hard}} = \frac{1}{2} \sum_{m=0}^{w_1} (-1)^m \frac{w_1!}{i!(w_1-m)!} \left(1 - \frac{mq_{1,1}}{w_1}\right)^{K_1-1} \left(1 - \frac{mq_{1,2}}{w_1}\right)^{K_2} \qquad (7.12)$$

where K_i is the number of simultaneous users with codewords of weight w_i for $i \in [1,2]$, and $w_1 > w_2$. The one-hit probability of the address codeword of weight w_i correlating with an interfering codeword of weight w_j is generally given by

$$q_{i,j} = \frac{w_i w_j}{2LN}$$

for i and $j \in [1,2]$, where L is the number of wavelengths and N is the code length. For the case of 1-D codes, $L = 1$ is set.

The same-bit-power, chip-synchronous, hard-limiting error probability of the codewords with light weight w_2 in OOK is approximated as [18, 19]

$$P_{e,2,\text{hard}} \approx \frac{1}{2} \sum_{t=0}^{w_2} \frac{w_2!}{t!(w_2-t)!} \left\{ \sum_{i=0}^{t} (-1)^i \frac{t!}{i!(t-i)!} \left(1 - \frac{iq_2}{t} \right)^{K_2-1} \right.$$
$$\left. \times \sum_{j=0}^{c(w_2-t)} (-1)^j \frac{[c(w_2-t)]!}{j![c(w_2-t)-j]!} \left[1 - \frac{jq_1}{c(w_2-t)} \right]^{K_1} \right\} \quad (7.13)$$

where $c = \lceil w_1/w_2 \rceil$ and $\lceil \cdot \rceil$ is the ceiling function. The one-hit probabilities are given by

$$q_1 = \frac{w_1(w_2-t)}{2LN} \qquad \text{and} \qquad q_2 = \frac{w_2 t}{2LN}$$

For the case of 1-D codes, $L = 1$ is set.

Proof There is no difference in the amount of interference seen by a heavy-weight address codeword (of a receiver) caused by light- or heavy-weight interfering codewords. This is because light-weight codewords have higher chip power than heavy-weight codewords and then a light-weight interfering codeword will always constitute one complete hit in the cross-correlation function with a heavy-weight address codeword after hard-limiting if any one-hit occurs. So, $P_{e,1,\text{hard}}$ in Equation (7.12) follows Equation (7.8), which is originally derived for the same-chip-power assumption, with $k = 2$ and $k' = 1$ [12, 14].

Furthermore, the chip-synchronous, hard-limiting error probability of a light-weight address codeword due to light-weight interfering codewords is given by [18]

$$P'_{e,\text{hard}} = \sum_{i=0}^{w_2} (-1)^i \frac{w_2!}{i!(w_2-i)!} \left(1 - \frac{iq_{2,2}}{w_2} \right)^{K_2-1}$$

because every hit generated by the light-weight interfering codewords alway gives one complete hit due to the same chip power. However, every hit generated by the heavy-weight interfering codewords only gives w_2/w_1 of one complete hit when they correlate with a light-weight address codeword. There must exist cw_2 heavy-weight interfering codewords in order to obtain one complete hit in each of the w_2 pulses of the light-weight address codeword, where $c = \lceil P_{c2}/P_{c1} \rceil = \lceil w_1/w_2 \rceil$ and $\lceil \cdot \rceil$ is the ceiling function. To account for this, the Markov-chain method [29, 30] in Section 1.8.4 is applied to derive the chip-synchronous, hard-limiting error probability of a light-weight address codeword due to heavy-weight interfering codewords as [18]

$$P''_{e,\text{hard}} \approx \sum_{j=0}^{cw_2} (-1)^j \frac{(cw_2)!}{j!(cw_2-j)!} \left(1 - \frac{jq_{2,1}}{cw_2} \right)^{K_1}$$

By combining $P'_{e,\text{hard}}$ and $P''_{e,\text{hard}}$, the final form of $P_{e,2,\text{hard}}$ in the theorem is derived after some modifications. In $P'_{e,\text{hard}}$, w_2 is replaced by t and $q_{2,2}$ is replaced by q_2 to account for the case that up to t pulses of the light-weight address codeword can be hit by $K_2 - 1$ light-weight interfering codewords in $P_{e,2,\text{hard}}$. Similarly, in $P''_{e,\text{hard}}$, w_2 is replaced by $w_2 - t$ and $q_{2,1}$ is replaced by q_1 to account for the case that up to $w_2 - t$ pulses can be hit by K_1 heavy-weight interfering codewords in $P_{e,2,\text{hard}}$. ∎

Equation (7.13) is an approximated model (or lower bound) due to the approximation used in the $P''_{e,\text{hard}}$ derivation. It is improved as an exact form in Theorem 7.12.

___

Theorem 7.12

The same-bit-power, chip-synchronous, hard-limiting error probability of the double-weight, single-length optical codes with light weight w_2 in OOK in Theorem 7.11 can be more accurately formulated as [19]

$$
P_{e,2,\text{hard}} = \frac{1}{2}\sum_{t=0}^{w_2}\frac{w_2!}{t!(w_2-t)!}\left[\sum_{i=0}^{t}(-1)^i\frac{t!}{i!(t-i)!}\left(1-\frac{iq_2}{t}\right)^{K_2-1}\right.
$$
$$
\left.\times \sum_{l=c(w_2-t)}^{K_1}\frac{K_1!}{l!(K-l)!}q_1^l(1-q_1)^{K_1-l}\frac{S_c(w_2-t,l)}{(w_2-t)^l}\right] \quad (7.14)
$$

where

$$
S_c(w_2,l) = \prod_{k=1}^{c-1}\left[\sum_{i_{c-k}=0}^{w_2-\sum_{j=1}^{k-1}i_{c-j}-1}(-1)^{i_{c-k}}\frac{(w_2-\sum_{j=1}^{k-1}i_{c-j})!}{i_{c-k}!(w_2-\sum_{j=1}^{k}i_{c-j})!}\right.
$$
$$
\times \frac{l-\sum_{j=1}^{k-1}(c-j)i_{c-j}}{[(c-k)i_{c-k}]![l-\sum_{j=1}^{k}(c-j)i_{c-j}]!}\times\left.\frac{[(c-k)i_{c-k}]!}{[(c-k)!]^{i_{c-k}}}\right]
$$
$$
\times S_1\left(w_2-\sum_{j=1}^{c-1}i_{c-j},l-\sum_{j=1}^{c-1}(c-j)i_{c-j}\right)
$$

$$
S_1(w_2,l) = \sum_{i=0}^{w_2-1}(-1)^i\frac{w_2!}{i!(w_2-i)!}(w_2-i)^l
$$

Proof While the probability term $P''_{e,\text{hard}}$ is approximated by means of the Markov-chain method in the proof of Theorem 7.11, it can be exactly derived as

$$
P''_{e,\text{hard}} = \frac{1}{2}\sum_{l=cw_2}^{K_1}\binom{K_1}{l}q_1^l(1-q_1)^{K_1-l}\frac{S_c(w_2,l)}{w_2^l}
$$

where the lower limit of the summation represents the number of heavy-weight interfering codewords needed to generate a decision error, where $c = \lceil w_1/w_2 \rceil$. From [3],

$S_c(w_2,l)/w_2^l$ denotes the hard-limiting error probability caused by l interfering code-words that contribute one-hits, where $S_j(w_2,l)$ accounts for the number of possible interference patterns such that there are at least $j \in [1,c]$ pulses overlapping with each of the w_2 pulses of the light-weight address codeword. Modifying this exact $P''_{e,\text{hard}}$ similar to that in Equation (7.13), the final form of Equation (7.14) results.

The term $S_c(w_2,l)$ is computed by recursively evaluating $S_j(w_2,l)$ for $j \in [1,c]$. When $j = 1$, this corresponds to the same-chip-power assumption and $S_1(w_2,l)$ is given in the theorem [3]. For $j = 2$, the interference patterns are considered, in which each one of the w_2 pulses of the address codeword is getting at least two hits. The number of such patterns can be computed by subtracting the number of interference patterns that have exactly one hit in each of the w_2 pulses from the number of inter-ference patterns that have at least one hit in each of the w_2 pulses. Unionizing these patterns [29, Corollary 6], $S_2(w_2,l)$ is recursively related to $S_1(w_2,l)$ as

$$
\begin{aligned}
S_2(w_2,l) &= S_1(w_2,l) - \binom{w_2}{1}\binom{l}{1}1!S_1(w_2-1,l-1) \\
&\quad + \binom{w_2}{2}\binom{l}{2}2!S_1(w_2-2,l-2) + \cdots \\
&\quad + \binom{w_2}{w_2-1}\binom{l}{w_2-1}(w_2-1)!S_1(1,l-w_2+1) \\
&= \sum_{i_1=0}^{w_2-1}(-1)^{i_1}\binom{w_2}{i_1}\binom{l}{i_1}i_1!S_1(w_2-i_1,l-i_1)
\end{aligned}
$$

Similarly, for $j = 3$, the interference patterns, in which each of the w_2 pulses of the address codeword gets at least three hits, are considered. The number of such patterns are computed by subtracting the number of interference patterns having exactly one two-hits at each of the w_2 pulses from the number of interference patterns having at least one two-hits at each of the w_2 pulses. Unionizing these patterns, $S_3(w_2,l)$ is recursively related to $S_2(w_2,l)$ and, in turn, $S_1(w_2,l)$ as

$$
\begin{aligned}
S_3(w_2,l) &= S_2(w_2,l) - \binom{w}{1}\binom{l}{2}\left(\frac{2!}{2!}\right)S_2(w_2-1,l-2) \\
&\quad + \binom{w_2}{2}\binom{l}{4}\left(\frac{4!}{2!2!}\right)S_2(w_2-2,l-4) + \cdots \\
&\quad + \binom{w_2}{w_2-1}\binom{l}{2(w_2-1)}\frac{(2w_2-2)!}{(2!)^{w_2-1}}S_2(1,l-2(w_2-1)) \\
&= \sum_{i_2=0}^{w_2-1}(-1)^{i_2}\binom{w_2}{i_2}\binom{l}{2i_2}\frac{(2i_2)!}{(2!)^{i_2}}S_2(w_2-i_2,l-2i_2) \\
&= \sum_{i_2=0}^{w_2-1}(-1)^{i_2}\binom{w_2}{i_2}\binom{l}{2i_2}\frac{(2i_2)!}{(2!)^{i_2}}\sum_{i_1=0}^{w_2-i_2-1}(-1)^{i_1} \\
&\quad \times \binom{w_2-i_2}{i_1}\binom{l-2i_2}{i_1}i_1!S_1(w_2-i_2-i_1,l-2i_2-i_1)
\end{aligned}
$$

Continuing the steps, $S_c(w_2, l)$ is generally formulated as [19]

$$
\begin{aligned}
S_c(w_2, l) &= \sum_{i_{c-1}=0}^{w_2-1} (-1)^{i_{c-1}} \binom{w_2}{i_{c-1}} \binom{l}{(c-1)i_{c-1}} \\
&\quad \times \frac{[(c-1)i_{c-1}]!}{[(c-1)!]^{i_{c-1}}} S_{c-1}(w_2 - i_{c-1}, l - (c-1)i_{c-1}) \\
&= \sum_{i_{c-1}=0}^{w_2-1} (-1)^{i_{c-1}} \binom{w_2}{i_{c-1}} \binom{l}{(c-1)i_{c-1}} \frac{[(c-1)i_{c-1}]!}{[(c-1)!]^{i_{c-1}}} \\
&\quad \times \sum_{i_{c-2}=0}^{w_2-i_{c-1}-1} (-1)^{i_{c-2}} \binom{w_2 - i_{c-1}}{i_{c-2}} \binom{l - (c-1)i_{c-1}}{(c-2)i_{c-2}} \frac{[(c-2)i_{c-2}]!}{[(c-2)!]^{i_{c-2}}} \\
&\quad \times S_{c-2}(w_2 i_{c-1} - i_{c-2}, l - (c-1)i_{c-1} - (c-2)i_{c-2})
\end{aligned}
$$

After some manipulations, the final form of $S_c(w_2, l)$ in the theorem is recursively derived. ∎

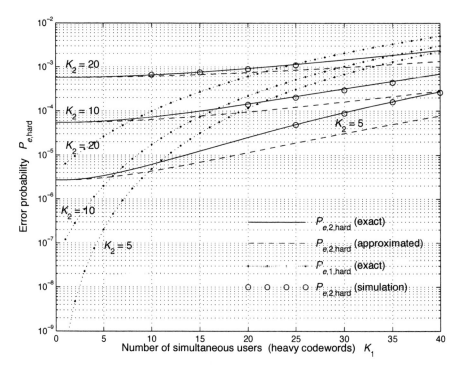

FIGURE 7.15 Same-bit-power, chip-synchronous, hard-limiting error probabilities of the double-weight carrier-hopping prime codes versus K_1 for $L = w_1$, $N = 49$, $w_1 = 5$, $w_2 = 3$, $c = 2$, and $K_2 = \{5, 10, 20\}$.

Figure 7.15 plots the chip-synchronous, hard-limiting error probabilities, $P_{e,1,\text{hard}}$

from Equation (7.12) and $P_{e,2,\text{hard}}$ from Equations (7.13) and (7.14), of the double-weight, single-length carrier-hopping prime codes in Section 7.1 against the number of simultaneous users with heavy-weight codewords K_1 under the same-bit-power assumption for various numbers of simultaneous users with light-weight codewords $K_2 = \{5, 10, 20\}$, where $L = w_1$, $N = 49$, $w_1 = 5$, and $w_2 = 3$. The trends in the error probabilities due to the changes of K_1 and K_2 are here observed with $c = \lceil w_1/w_2 \rceil = 2$. In general, the error probabilities get worse as the total number of simultaneous users $K_1 + K_2$ increases because of stronger mutual interference. While the solid curves show the exact $P_{e,2,\text{hard}}$ from Equation (7.14), the dashed curves show the approximated $P_{e,2,\text{hard}}$ from Equation (7.13). For a given K_2, the dashed (approximated) and solid (exact) curves agree initially when K_1 is small. The dashed curves deviate and get better as K_1 increases. The difference between these two curves reduces as K_2 increases because Equations (7.13) and (7.14) differ only in the $P_{e,\text{hard}}''$ terms, which are determined by K_1 but the probability terms with K_2 remain the same. As K_2 increases, the effect of the $P_{e,\text{hard}}''$ terms is lessened and their $P_{e,2,\text{hard}}$ differences are reduced. In summary, the approximated model provides the performance lower bound of the light-weight codewords and converges to the exact $P_{e,2,\text{hard}}$ (solid) curves when K_2 is large but K_1 is small.

Also in Figure 7.15, the dotted curves represent the exact error probabilities of the heavy-weight codewords, $P_{e,1,\text{hard}}$ from Equation (7.12), for $K_2 = \{5, 10, 20\}$. The dotted curves are shown better than the solid curves (exact $P_{e,2,\text{hard}}$) when K_1 is small, but the opposite is found when K_1 is large. This is because the heavy-weight codewords have more pulses and the probability of all pulses being hit is less than that of the light-weight codewords when K_1 is small. However, each heavy-weight interfering codeword can only contribute w_2/w_1 of one complete hit to the light-weight address codeword. The interference effect of K_1 on the $P_{e,1,\text{hard}}$ curves is c times as strong as the $P_{e,2,\text{hard}}$ curves, especially when K_1 increases, resulting in poorer performance in the former. Also plotted in Figure 7.15, the computer-simulation results (in circles) closely match the solid curves, validating the accuracy of the exact analytical model in Equation (7.14). The computer simulation is performed by randomly assigning each simultaneous user one of the codewords in the code set, and OOK modulation is used for transmitting each data bit 1 with a codeword. The total number of bits involved in the simulation is at least 100 times the reciprocal of the target error probability in order to provide enough iterations.

Figure 7.16 plots the chip-synchronous, hard-limiting error probabilities, $P_{e,\text{hard},1}$ from Equation (7.12) and $P_{e,\text{hard},2}$ from Equations (7.13) and (7.14), of the double-weight carrier-hopping prime codes in Section 7.1 against the number of simultaneous users with light-weight codewords K_2 under the same-bit-power assumption, where $L = w_1$, $N = 121$, $w_1 = \{5, 7\}$, and $w_2 = 3$. The number of simultaneous users with heavy-weight codewords $K_1 = 20$ is here fixed so that the trends in the error probabilities due to the change of K_2 and $c = \lceil w_1/w_2 \rceil = \{2, 3\}$ are observed. In general, the error probabilities improve as c increases because of higher autocorrelation peaks. However, the error probabilities get worse when K_2 increases due to stronger mutual interference. While the solid curves show the exact $P_{e,2,\text{hard}}$

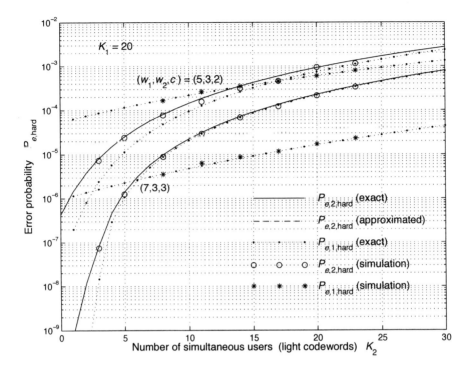

FIGURE 7.16 Same-bit-power, chip-synchronous, hard-limiting error probabilities of the double-weight carrier-hopping prime codes versus K_2 for $L = w_1, N = 121, w_1 = \{5,7\}, w_2 = 3, c = \{2,3\}$, and $K_1 = 20$.

from Equation (7.14), the dashed curves show the approximated $P_{e,2,\text{hard}}$ from Equation (7.13). Also plotted in the figure, the computer-simulation results (in circles) match closely with the solid curves, validating the accuracy of the exact analytical model from Equation (7.14). The solid curves are initially worse than the dashed curves when K_2 is small, but they converge as K_2 increases. The difference between the dashed and solid curves decreases as c increases because each heavy-weight interfering codeword can only contribute w_2/w_1 of one complete hit to the light-weight address codeword. The interference effect of K_1 in the $P''_{e,\text{hard}}$ terms of Equations (7.13) and (7.14) is lessened as c increases, for a given K_2. The approximated (dashed) curves provide the performance lower bound of $P_{e,2,\text{hard}}$ and converge to the exact (solid) curves when K_2 or c is large.

Also in Figure 7.16, the dotted curves represent the exact error probabilities of the heavy-weight codewords, $P_{e,1,\text{hard}}$ from Equation (7.12), for $K_1 = 20$. Their accuracy is also validated by the computer-simulation results (in asterisks). The dotted curves are worse than the solid curve (exact $P_{e,2,\text{hard}}$) when K_2 is small. This is because the light-weight codewords have higher chip power and better immunity against the interference caused by the heavy-weight codewords. However, the worsening of $P_{e,2,\text{hard}}$ is faster than that of $P_{e,1,\text{hard}}$ as K_2 increases. This is because the heavy-weight codewords have more pulses and the probability of all pulses being hit is less than that of the light-weight codewords.

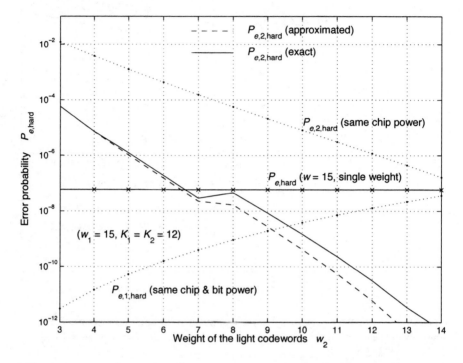

FIGURE 7.17 Same-bit-power, chip-synchronous, hard-limiting error probabilities of the light-weight codewords in the 1-D double-weight OOCs versus w_2 for $N = 307$, $w_1 = 15$, and $K_1 = K_2 = 12$.

Figure 7.17 plots the chip-synchronous, hard-limiting error probabilities, $P_{e,2,\text{hard}}$ from Equations (7.13) and (7.14), of the light-weight codewords in the 1-D double-weight OOCs in Section 7.6 against code weight w_2 under the same-bit-power assumption, where $L = 1$, $N = 307$, $w_1 = 15$, and $K_1 = K_2 = 12$. While the solid curve shows the exact $P_{e,2,\text{hard}}$ from Equation (7.14), the dashed curve is based on the approximated $P_{e,2,\text{hard}}$ from Equation (7.13), which is found as the performance lower bound, as expected. Both curves agree initially, but deviate as w_2 increases. In general, $P_{e,2,\text{hard}}$ improves as w_2 increases because of higher autocorrelation peaks. There exists a twist in each of the $P_{e,2,\text{hard}}$-curves when w_2 changes from 7 to 8 because $c = \lceil w_1/w_2 \rceil$ gets worse from 3 to 2. Shown in the bottom dotted curve is the error probability of the heavy-weight codewords, $P_{e,1,\text{hard}}$ from Equation (7.12), for which the performances are identical for the same-bit-power and same-chip-power assumptions. Shown in the top dotted curve is the error probability of the light-weight codewords, $P_{e,2,\text{hard}}$ from Equation (7.14), with $c = 1$ for the same-chip-power assumption. In general, $P_{e,1,\text{hard}}$ gets worse and $P_{e,2,\text{hard}}$ improves as w_2 increases under both assumptions. Nevertheless, the two dotted curves converge when w_2 approaches $w_1 = 15$ because the double-weight codes become the single-weight codes. The solid-cross line shows the single-weight case with $w = 15$ and $K = 24$ under the same-chip-power assumption, providing a baseline comparison for the two dotted curves. In addition, the solid curve is always better than the top dotted curve, and their $P_{e,2,\text{hard}}$ difference increases when w_2 approaches $w_1 = 15$. In summary, the same-bit-power assumption improves the performance of the light-weight codewords.

7.6 MULTILENGTH 1-D OPTICAL ORTHOGONAL CODES

As discussed in Section 3.5, single-length 1-D optical orthogonal codes (OOCs) can be constructed by several methods, such as projective geometry, disjoint difference sets, and balanced incomplete block designs [1, 2, 4, 6, 12, 24, 25, 31, 32]. In [31], two recursive constructions of the cyclic balanced incomplete block designs in [32] were generalized to form the 1-D OOCs of length rN and weight w with cardinality rt from the 1-D OOCs of length N and weight w with cardinality t, where $N \neq 0 \pmod{w}$, and N and $(w-1)!$ are relatively prime. In this section, two families of 1-D multilength OOCs are recursively constructed by borrowing the method in [31]. The multilength constructions begin with short codewords of length N and then construct long codewords of length rN, both of the same weight w, by dividing the rN time slots into r sections with N time slots in each section [24, 25]. Each one of the w pulses in the short codewords is distinctly mapped onto one of these r sections such that the periodic cross-correlation functions are still at most 1, independent of code length.

7.6.1 Construction 1: Cross-Correlation of One

This construction begins with the 1-D single-length OOCs of weight w, length N_1, and cardinality t, where $N_1 = w(w-1)t + 1$ and $N_1 \neq 0 \pmod{w}$ [1, 2, 4, 6, 12, 24, 25, 31, 32]. Each codeword of these 1-D single-length OOCs can be denoted as $X_{i_1} = (x_{i_1,0}, x_{i_1,1}, \ldots, x_{i_1,j}, \ldots, x_{i_1,w-1})$, where $i_1 = \{0, 1, \ldots, t-1\}$. The code element $x_{i,j} \in [0, N_1 - 1]$ represents the chip (or time-slot) location of a pulse, or so-called mark chip, from the beginning of the codeword.

Given a set of k positive integers $t > t_{k-1} > \ldots > t_1$ to control the number of codewords in each length, out of k different lengths, a set of $k-1$ prime numbers $p_{k-1} \geq p_{k-2} \geq \ldots \geq p_1$ to determine the number of codewords and lengths, and these prime numbers to be relative prime to $(w-1)!$, codewords, X_{i_1}, with pulses at chip locations [24]

$$\{(0, x_{i_1,1} - x_{i_1,0}, x_{i_1,2} - x_{i_1,0}, \ldots, x_{i_1,w-1} - x_{i_1,0}) : i_1 = \{0, 1, \ldots, t_1 - 1\}\}$$

codewords, X_{i_2,i_1}, with pulses at chip locations

$$\{(0, x_{i_1,1} - x_{i_1,0} + i_2 N_1, x_{i_1,2} - x_{i_1,0} + (2 \odot_{p_1} i_2)N_1, \ldots,$$
$$x_{i_1,w-1} - x_{i_1,0} + ((w-1) \odot_{p_1} i_2)N_1):$$
$$i_1 = \{t_1, t_1+1, \ldots, t_2-1\}, i_2 = \{0,1,\ldots,p_1-1\}\}$$

codewords, X_{i_3,i_2,i_1}, with pulses at chip locations

$$\{(0, x_{i_1,1} - x_{i_1,0} + i_2 N_1 + i_3 p_1 N_1, x_{i_1,2} - x_{i_1,0} + (2 \odot_{p_1} i_2)N_1$$
$$+(2 \odot_{p_2} i_3)p_1 N_1, \ldots, x_{i_1,w-1} - x_{i_1,0} + ((w-1) \odot_{p_1} i_2)N_1$$
$$+((w-1) \odot_{p_2} i_3)p_1 N_1): i_1 = \{t_2, t_2+1, \ldots, t_3-1\},$$
$$i_2 = \{0,1,\ldots,p_1-1\}, i_3 = \{0,1,\ldots,p_2-1\}\}$$

$$\vdots$$

codewords, $X_{i_{k-1},i_{k-2},\ldots,i_1}$, with pulses at chip locations

$$\{(0, x_{i_1,1} - x_{i_1,0} + i_2 N_1 + i_3 p_1 N_1 + \cdots + i_{k-1} p_{k-3} p_{k-4} \cdots p_1 N_1,$$
$$x_{i_1,2} - x_{i_1,0} + (2 \odot_{p_1} i_2)N_1 + (2 \odot_{p_2} i_3)p_1 N_1 + \cdots$$
$$+(2 \odot_{p_{k-2}} i_{k-1})p_{k-3} p_{k-4} \cdots p_1 N_1, \ldots, x_{i_1,w-1} - x_{i_1,0}$$
$$+((w-1) \odot_{p_1} i_2)N_1 + ((w-1) \odot_{p_2} i_3)p_1 N_1 + \cdots$$
$$+((w-1) \odot_{p_{k-2}} i_{k-3})p_{k-3} p_{k-4} \cdots p_1 N_1):$$
$$i_1 = \{t_{k-2}, t_{k-2}+1, \ldots, t_{k-1}-1\}, i_2 = \{0,1,\ldots,p_1-1\},$$
$$i_3 = \{0,1,\ldots,p_2-1\}, \ldots, i_{k-1} = \{0,1,\ldots,p_{k-2}-1\}\}$$

and codewords, $X_{i_k,i_{k-1},\ldots,i_1}$, with pulses at chip locations

$$\{(0, x_{i_1,1} - x_{i_1,0} + i_2 N_1 + i_3 p_1 N_1 + \cdots + i_k p_{k-2} p_{k-3} \cdots p_1 N_1,$$
$$x_{i_1,2} - x_{i_1,0} + (2 \odot_{p_1} i_2)N_1 + (2 \odot_{p_2} i_3)p_1 N_1 + \cdots$$
$$+(2 \odot_{p_{k-1}} i_k)p_{k-2} p_{k-3} \cdots p_1 N_1, \ldots, x_{i_1,w-1} - x_{i_1,0}$$
$$+((w-1) \odot_{p_1} i_2)N_1 + ((w-1) \odot_{p_2} i_3)p_1 N_1 + \cdots$$
$$+((w-1) \odot_{p_{k-1}} i_k)p_{k-2} p_{k-3} \cdots p_1 N_1):$$
$$i_1 = \{t_{k-1}, t_{k-1}+1, \ldots, t-1\}, i_2 = \{0,1,\ldots,p_1-1\},$$
$$i_3 = \{0,1,\ldots,p_2-1\}, \ldots, i_k = \{0,1,\ldots,p_{k-1}-1\}\}$$

form the 1-D multilength OOCs of weight $w \leq p_1$ with t_1 codewords of length N_1; $p_1(t_2 - t_1)$ codewords of length $N_2 = p_1 N_1$; $p_1 p_2 (t_3 - t_2)$ codewords of length $N_3 = p_1 p_2 N_1$; $\ldots$; and $p_1 p_2 \cdots p_{k-1}(t - t_{k-1})$ codewords of length $N_k = p_1 p_2 \cdots p_{k-1} N_1$, where "$\odot_{p_j}$" denotes a modulo-$p_j$ multiplication for $j = \{1, 2, \ldots, k-1\}$.

Using $k = 2$, $N_1 = 13$, $w = 3$, $t_2 = 2$, $t_1 = 1$, and $p_1 = 5$ as an example, the 1-D single-length OOC of length $N_1 = 13$ has 2 codewords, denoted by $X_0 = (0, 2, 8)$ and $X_1 = (0, 3, 4)$, which can also be represented as sequences 1010000010000 and

1001100000000, respectively [1]. Based on the construction, the 1-D double-length OOC has one short codeword of length $N_1 = 13$, denoted by $X_0 = (0,2,8)$; and 5 long codewords of length $N_2 = p_1 N_1 = 65$, denoted by $X_{0,1} = (0,3,4)$, $X_{1,1} = (0,16,30)$, $X_{2,1} = (0,29,56)$, $X_{3,1} = (0,17,42)$, and $X_{4,1} = (0,43,55)$.

Theorem 7.13

The autocorrelation peaks and sidelobes of the 1-D multilength OOCs of weight w are equal to w and 1, respectively, where $w \leq p_1$. The periodic cross-correlation functions of the codes are at most 1, independent of code length [25].

Proof According to the definition of cyclic adjacent-pulse separations in Sections 1.6 and 3.4 [1,2,4,7], the 1-D multilength OOC codewords, say $X_{i_h,i_{h-1},...,i_1}$ of length N_h for $h \in [1,k]$, have the cyclic adjacent-pulse separations $x_{i_1,j_1} - x_{i_1,j_2} + ((j_1 - j_2) \odot_{p_1} i_2)N_1 + ((j_1 - j_2) \odot_{p_2} i_3)p_1 N_1 + \cdots + ((j_1 - j_2) \odot_{p_{h-1}} i_h)p_{h-2}p_{h-3}\cdots p_1 N_1 \pmod{N_h}$, for $j_1 \in [0, w-1]$ and $j_2 \in [0, w-1]$, where $j_1 \neq j_2$. Because these separations are in a similar form as those in Construction A in [32], the autocorrelation and cross-correlation properties are inherited. In addition, the periodic cross-correlation function between a short address codeword and a long interfering codeword follows that of the same-length codes because the correlation process only involves a portion of the long interfering codeword.

  If the length of the long address codeword $X_{i_m,i_{m-1},...,i_1}$ is $r = p_n p_{n+1} \cdots p_{m-1}$ times the length of the short interfering codeword $X_{i'_{n-1},i'_{n-2},...,i'_1}$, $r+1$ consecutive OOK transmissions of the short codeword are involved to complete one periodic cross-correlation process, where $i_1 \neq i'_1$ and $m > n$. The cyclic adjacent-pulse separations of these $r+1$ copies are found to be $x_{i'_1,j'_1} - x_{i'_1,j'_2} + s[((j'_1 - j'_2) \odot_{p_1} i'_2)N_1 + ((j'_1 - j'_2) \odot_{p_2} i'_3)p_1 N_1 + \cdots + ((j'_1 - j'_2) \odot_{p_{n-1}} i'_n)p_{n-2}p_{n-3}\cdots p_1 N_1] \pmod{N_m}$ for a $j_1 = \{0,1,\ldots,w-1\}$, a $j_2 = \{0,1,\ldots,w-1\}$, a $j'_1 = \{0,1,\ldots,w-1\}$, and a $j'_2 = \{0,1,\ldots,w-1\}$, and some $s = \{0,1,\ldots,(p_{m-1}-1)p_{m-2}p_{m-3}\cdots p_{n-1}\}$, where $i_1 \neq i'_1$, $j_1 \neq j_2$, $j'_1 \neq j'_2$, and $m > n$. Because these multilength OOC codewords are assumed to have distinct first indices (or $i \neq i'$), this gives $x_{i,j_1} - x_{i,j_2} \neq x_{i',j'_1} - x_{i',j'_2}$ $\pmod{N_1}$. The cyclic adjacent-pulse separations of the long address codeword and the $r+1$ copies of the short interfering codewords are all distinct. By the properties of cyclic adjacent-pulse separations, the periodic cross-correlation functions are at most 1. ∎

7.6.2 Construction 2: Cross-Correlation of Two

This construction begins with the same 1-D single-length OOCs in Construction 1, which have weight w, length $N_1 = w(w-1)t + 1$, and cardinality t, where $N_1 \neq 0$ $\pmod{w}$ [1,2,4,6,12,24,25,31,32]. Given a set of $k-1$ prime numbers $p_{k-1} \geq p_{k-2} \geq \cdots \geq p_1$ to control the number of codewords and lengths, out of k different lengths, with the constraints of $p_1N_1 \neq 0$, $p_1p_2N_1 \neq 0$, ..., and $p_1p_2\cdots p_{k-1}N_1 \neq 0$ (mod w), and these prime numbers to be relatively prime to $(w-1)!$, codewords, X_{i_1}, with pulses at chip locations [24]

$$\{(0, x_{i_1,1} - x_{i_1,0}, x_{i_1,2} - x_{i_1,0}, \ldots, x_{i_1,w-1} - x_{i_1,0}) : i_1 = \{0, 1, \ldots, t-1\}\}$$

codewords, X_{i_2,i_1}, with pulses at chip locations

$$\{(0, x_{i_1,1} - x_{i_1,0} + i_2N_1, x_{i_1,2} - x_{i_1,0} + 2i_2N_1, \ldots, x_{i_1,w-1} - x_{i_1,0} + (w-1)i_2N_1) :$$
$$i_1 = \{0, 1, \ldots, t-1\}, i_2 = \{1, 2, \ldots, p_1 - 1\}\}$$

$$\vdots$$

and codewords, $X_{i_k,i_{k-1},\ldots,i_1}$, with pulses at chip locations

$$\{(0, x_{i_1,1} - x_{i_1,0} + i_2i_3\cdots i_kN_1, x_{i_1,2} - x_{i_1,0} + 2i_2i_3\cdots i_kN_1, \ldots,$$
$$x_{i_1,w-1} - x_{i_1,0} + (w-1)i_2i_3\cdots i_kN_1) : i_1 = \{0, 1, \ldots, t-1\},$$
$$i_2 = \{1, 2, \ldots, p_1 - 1\}, i_3 = \{1, 2, \ldots, p_2 - 1\}, \ldots, i_k = \{1, 2, \ldots, p_{k-1} - 1\}\}$$

form the multilength OOCs of weight $w \leq p_1$ with t codewords of length N_1; $(p_1 - 1)t$ codewords of length $N_2 = p_1N_1$; $(p_1 - 1)(p_2 - 1)t$ codewords of length $N_3 = p_1p_2N_1$; ...; and $(p_1 - 1)(p_2 - 1)\cdots(p_{k-1} - 1)t$ codewords of length $N_k = p_1p_2\cdots p_{k-1}N_1$.

Using $k = 2$, $N_1 = 13$, $w = 3$, $t = 2$, and $p_1 = 5$ as an example, the 1-D single-length OOC of length $N_1 = 13$ has 2 codewords, denoted by $X_0 = (0, 2, 8)$ and $X_1 = (0, 3, 4)$ [1]. Based on the construction, the 1-D double-length OOC has 2 short codewords of length $N_1 = 13$, denoted by $X_{0,0} = (0, 2, 8)$ and $X_{0,1} = (0, 3, 4)$; and 8 long codewords of length $N_2 = p_1N_1 = 65$, denoted by $X_{1,0} = (0, 15, 34)$, $X_{2,0} = (0, 28, 60)$, $X_{3,0} = (0, 21, 41)$, $X_{4,0} = (0, 47, 54)$, $X_{1,1} = (0, 16, 30)$, $X_{2,1} = (0, 29, 56)$, $X_{3,1} = (0, 17, 42)$, and $X_{4,1} = (0, 43, 55)$.

Theorem 7.14

The autocorrelation peaks and sidelobes of the 1-D multilength OOCs of weight w are equal to w and 1, respectively, where $w \leq p_1$. The periodic cross-correlation functions of the codes is at most 1, but at most 2 when a short address codeword correlates with a long interfering codeword [24].

Proof For the case of $k = 2$, the construction of codewords, X_{i_2,i_1}, of length $N_2 = p_1N_1$ follows the 1-D OOC construction of the same length in [32] and so are the autocorrelation and cross-correlation properties. When $i_2 = 0$, each of these codewords contains $(p_1 - 1)N_1$ consecutive tailing zeros. By removing these zeros, short codewords, X_{i_1}, of length N_1 and cardinality t are generated. According to the construction, the chip locations of the pulses of these short codewords are found by shifting the pulses of the 1-D OOCs in [32] by $x_{i,0}$ chips. So, the cyclic adjacent-pulse separations of these codewords are still all distinct, and the autocorrelation and cross-correlation properties are preserved. There are $w(w-1)p_1t$ distinct cyclic adjacent-pulse separations and $w(w-1)p_1t/2$ distinct noncyclic adjacent-pulse separations for its original p_1t long codewords of length is $N_2 = p_1N_1$ in [32]. Because the t short codewords are generated by removing the tailing $(p_1-1)N_1$ zeros from the $i_2 = 0$ long codewords, the periodicity of the codes is broken but the $w(w-1)t/2$ noncyclic adjacent-pulse separations in each of these t codewords are preserved and the aperiodic cross-correlation functions are still at most 1. Because a periodic cross-correlation function is at most twice its aperiodic counterpart, the periodic cross-correlation function between a short address codeword and a long interfering codeword is at most 2.

To generalize the proof for any $k \geq 2$, the same argument with noncyclic adjacent-pulse separations is used. Using $k = 3$ as another example, the construction of codewords, X_{i_3,i_2,i_1}, of length $N_3 = p_1p_2N_1$ follows the 1-D OOC construction of the same length in [24]. The $(p_1-1)t+t$ codewords with the index $i_3 = 0$ have $(p_2-1)p_1N_1$ tailing zeros, which are removed to generate shorter codewords, X_{i_2,i_1}, of length $N_2 = p_1N_1$. Within these $(p_1-1)t+t$ codewords, t of them with the index $i_2 = 0$ have $(p_1-1)N_1$ tailing zeros, which are removed to generate the shortest codewords X_{i_1}, of length N_1. Although the code periodicities are broken in the tailing-zero removal process, the noncyclic adjacent-pulse separations are still preserved. So, the periodic cross-correlation function between a short address codeword and a long interfering codeword is at most 2. This property also holds for the general case of any k by following the same argument.

If the length of the long address codeword $X_{i_m,i_{m-1},...,i_1}$ is $r = p_np_{n+1}\cdots p_{m-1}$ times the length of the short interfering codeword $\mathbf{x}_{i'_n,i'_{n-1},...,i'_1}$, the cyclic adjacent-pulse separations of the long codeword are of the form $x_{i_1,j_1} - x_{i_1,j_2} + (j_1 - j_2)i_2i_3\cdots i_mN_1 \pmod{p_1p_2\cdots p_{m-1}N_1}$ and those of the $r+1$ copies of the short codeword are of the form $x_{i'_1,j'_1} - x_{i'_1,j'_2} + si'_2i'_3\cdots i'_nN_1 \pmod{p_1p_2\cdots p_{m-1}N_1}$ for j_1, j_2, j'_1, and $j'_2 \in [0,w-1]$, and $s \in [0, p_np_{n+1}\cdots p_{m-1}]$, where $j_1 \neq j_2$, $j'_1 \neq j'_2$, $i_1 \neq i'_1$, and $m > n$, based on the construction and the definition of cyclic adjacent-pulse separations in Sections 1.6 and 3.4 [1,2,4,7]. Because these codewords are constructed from 1-D OOCs in [32] and have $i \neq i'$, $x_{i_1,j_1} - x_{i_1,j_2} \neq x_{i'_1,j'_1} - x_{i'_1,j'_2} \pmod{N_1}$ result. This implies that $x_{i_1,j_1} - x_{i_1,j_2} + (j_1 - j_2)i_2i_3\cdots i_mN_1 \neq x_{i'_1,j'_1} - x_{i'_1,j'_2} + si'_2i'_3\cdots i'_nN_1$ $\pmod{p_1p_2\cdots p_{m-1}N_1}$, and all the cyclic adjacent-pulse separations of the long codeword and the $r+1$ copies of the short codeword are distinct for any $i \neq i'$ and $m > n$. So, the periodic cross-correlation function is at most 1. ∎

Similar to other multilength optical codes in this chapter, the upper bound of the overall cardinality of the 1-D multilength OOCs of weight $w \leq p_1$ in both constructions is given by

$$\Phi_{\text{upper}} \leq \frac{(N_k - 1)\,\Phi_{\text{multilength}}}{\phi_k w(w-1) + \sum_{i=1}^{k-1} \phi_i w(w\Pi_{j=i}^{k-1} p_j - 1)}$$

where $N_k = p_1 p_2 \cdots p_{k-1} N_1$ and $N_1 = w(w-1)t + 1$.

The actual overall cardinality of Construction 1 is given by

$$\Phi_{\text{multilength}} = t_1 + p_1(t_2 - t_1) + p_1 p_2(t_3 - t_2) + \cdots + p_1 p_2 \cdots p_{k-1}(t - t_{k-1})$$

To show the asymptotic optimal cardinality of these 1-D multilength OOCs, it is found that

$$\frac{\Phi_{\text{multilength}}}{\Phi_{\text{upper}}} \approx \frac{t_1}{t}\left[1 + \frac{p_1 p_2 \cdots p_{k-1} - 1}{p_1 p_2 \cdots p_{k-1}(w-1)}\right] + \frac{t_2 - t_1}{t}\left[1 + \frac{p_2 \cdots p_{k-1} - 1}{p_2 \cdots p_{k-1}(w-1)}\right]$$
$$+ \cdots + \frac{t_{k-1} - t_{k-2}}{t}\left[1 + \frac{p_{k-1} - 1}{p_{k-1}(w-1)}\right] + \frac{t - t_{k-1}}{t}$$

which approaches 1, for a large w and t.

Similarly, the asymptotic optimal cardinality of the 1-D multilength OOCs in Construction 2 can be shown by applying the actual overall cardinality

$$\Phi_{\text{multilength}} = t + (p_1 - 1)t + (p_1 - 1)(p_2 - 1)t + \cdots + (p_1 - 1)(p_2 - 1)\cdots(p_{k-1} - 1)t$$

into the ratio of $\Phi_{\text{multilength}}/\Phi_{\text{upper}}$, which approaches 1, for a large w and t.

In general, the overall cardinality suffers as k increases because there are more short codewords and then more concatenated cross-correlation functions to consider. So, the overall cardinality can be improved by reducing the number of short codewords.

To fairly compare the cardinalities of the 1-D multilength OOCs in Construction 1 and their single-length counterparts in Section 3.5, length N_k is used in the latter so that both code families occupy the same maximum bandwidth expansion LN_k, giving $\Phi_{\text{single}} = p_1 p_2 \cdots p_{k-1} t$. Because $t_1 \leq t_2 \leq \cdots \leq t$ and $w \leq p_1 \leq p_2 \leq \cdots \leq p_{k-1}$, it is found that

$$\frac{\Phi_{\text{multiple}}}{\Phi_{\text{single}}} \approx \frac{t_1}{p_1 p_2 \cdots p_{k-1} t} + \frac{t_2 - t_1}{p_2 p_3 \cdots p_{k-1} t} + \cdots + \frac{t - t_{k-1}}{t} \leq 1$$

This implies that the 1-D multilength OOCs in Construction 1 always have smaller cardinality than their single-length counterparts. Equality occurs when $t_1 = t_2 = \cdots = t_{k-1} = 0$, and the 1-D multilength OOCs become the single-length ones. The same conclusions also hold in the 1-D multilength OOCs in Construction 2.

7.6.3 Performance Analysis

Because the maximum periodic cross-correlation function of the 1-D multilength OOCs in Construction 1 is 1, the chip-synchronous, soft- and hard-limiting error probabilities in OOK follow Equations (7.7) and (7.8), respectively.

However, the periodic cross-correlation functions of the 1-D multilength OOCs in Construction 2 can be as high as 2 under the condition listed in Theorem 7.14. By modifying [3, Equation (24)], the chip-synchronous, soft-limiting error probabilities of the single-weight, double-length OOCs in Construction 2 with $k = 2$ and length N_1 is formulated as [24]

$$
\begin{aligned}
P_{e,1} &= \frac{1}{2} - \frac{1}{2} \sum_{l_1+l_2=0}^{w-1} \frac{(K_1 - 1)!}{l_1!(K_1 - 1 - l_1)!} q_{1,1,1}^{l_1} (1 - q_{1,1,1})^{K_1 - 1 - l_1} \\
&\quad \times \frac{K_2!}{l_2!(K_2 - l_2)!} q_{1,1,2}^{l_2} (1 - q_{1,1,2})^{K_2 - l_2}
\end{aligned}
$$

and that of length N_2 is formulated as

$$
\begin{aligned}
P_{e,2} &= \frac{1}{2} - \frac{1}{2} \sum_{l_1+l_2=0}^{w-1} \sum_{l_3=0}^{\lfloor (w-1-l_1-l_2)/2 \rfloor} \frac{(K_2 - 1)!}{l_1!(K_2 - 1 - l_1)!} q_{1,2,2}^{l_1} (1 - q_{1,2,2})^{K_2 - 1 - l_1} \\
&\quad \times \frac{K_1!}{l_2! l_3!(K_1 - l_2 - l_3)!} q_{1,2,1}^{l_2} q_{2,2,1}^{l_3} (1 - q_{1,2,1} - q_{2,2,1})^{K_1 - l_1 - l_2}
\end{aligned}
$$

where K_i represent the number of simultaneous users with codewords of lengths N_i for $i = \{1, 2\}$, l_j denotes the number of interfering codewords contributing $j = \{0, 1, 2\}$ hits, and $\lfloor \cdot \rfloor$ is the floor function.

Theorem 7.15

The probabilities, $q_{h,i,j}$, of getting $h = \{0, 1, 2\}$ hits in a 1-D double-length OOCs in Construction 2 of length N_i correlating with an interfering codeword of length N_j, both of weight $w \le p_1$, in OOK are formulated as

$$
\begin{aligned}
q_{1,2,1} &= \sum_{\tau=0}^{N_1-1} \frac{1}{N_1} \left\{ \left(\frac{w^2 \tau}{2N_1 N_2} \right) \left(1 - \frac{w^2}{2N_2} \right)^{p_1-1} \left[1 - \frac{w^2(N_1 - \tau)}{2N_1 N_2} \right] \right. \\
&\quad + (p_1 - 1) \left(1 - \frac{w^2 \tau}{2N_1 N_2} \right) \left(\frac{w^2}{2N_2} \right) \left(1 - \frac{w^2}{2N_2} \right)^{p_1-2} \\
&\quad \times \left[1 - \frac{w^2(N_1 - \tau)}{2N_1 N_2} \right] + \left(1 - \frac{w^2 \tau}{2N_1 N_2} \right) \left(1 - \frac{w^2}{2N_2} \right)^{p_1-1} \\
&\quad \left. \times \left[\frac{w^2(N_1 - \tau)}{2N_1 N_2} \right] \right\} \times \frac{1}{t_2} + \frac{w^2}{2N_1} \times \frac{t_2 - 1}{t_2}
\end{aligned}
$$

$$
q_{2,2,1} = \sum_{\tau=0}^{N_1-1} \frac{1}{N_1} \left\{ (p_1-1) \left(\frac{w^2\tau}{2N_1N_2} \right) \left(\frac{w^2}{2N_2} \right) \left(1 - \frac{w^2}{2N_2} \right)^{p_1-2} \right.
$$

$$
\times \left[1 - \frac{w^2(N_1-\tau)}{2N_1N_2} \right] + \left(\frac{w^2\tau}{2N_1N_2} \right) \left(1 - \frac{w^2}{2N_2} \right)^{p_1-1} \left[\frac{w^2(N_1-\tau)}{2N_1N_2} \right]
$$

$$
+ (p_1-1) \left(1 - \frac{w^2\tau}{2N_1N_2} \right) \left(\frac{w^2}{2N_2} \right) \left(1 - \frac{w^2}{2N_2} \right)^{p_1-2} \left[\frac{w^2(N_1-\tau)}{2N_1N_2} \right]
$$

$$
+ \frac{(p_1-1)(p_1-2)}{2} \left(1 - \frac{w^2\tau}{2N_1N_2} \right) \left(\frac{w^2}{2N_2} \right)^2 \left(1 - \frac{w^2}{2N_2} \right)^{p_1-3}
$$

$$
\left. \times \left[1 - \frac{w^2(N_1-\tau)}{2N_1N_2} \right] \right\} \times \frac{1}{t_2}
$$

$$
q_{1,2,2} = \frac{w^2}{2N_2} \qquad \text{and} \qquad q_{1,1,1} = q_{1,1,2} = \frac{w^2}{2N_1}
$$

for i and $j = \{1,2\}$.

Proof By considering all possible time shifts between a long address codeword (of a receiver) and $p_1 + 1$ copies of a short interfering codeword of length N_1 in their periodic cross-correlation function, the hit probability can be generally written as

$$
q_{h,2,1} = \sum_{\tau=0}^{N_1-1} \Pr(h \text{ hits} | \tau \text{ shifts}) \Pr(\tau \text{ shifts}) = \sum_{\tau=0}^{N_1-1} \frac{1}{N_1} \Pr(h \text{ hits} | \tau \text{ shifts})
$$

where $h = \{1,2\}$. According to Theorem 7.14, the periodic cross-correlation function is at most 1 if both codewords do not have the same first index i_1.

To derive $q_{1,2,1}$, the cross-correlation process between the long address codeword of length $N_2 = p_1N_1$ and $r+1$ copies of the short interfering codeword can be broken into three parts, as illustrated in Figure 7.2, where $r = p_1$ is assumed. In the first part, τ chips of the long codeword overlaps with the end portion of the first copy of the short codeword, where $\tau \in [0, N_1-1]$. In the second part, the middle portion of the long codeword overlaps with $r-1$ copies of the short codeword. In the third part, the rest of the long codeword overlaps with the front $N_1 - \tau$ chips of the last copy of the short codeword. The three product terms inside the summation of $q_{1,2,1}$ account for the three cases of generating the cross-correlation function of 1. The first product term is for getting the one-hit in the first part only. The second product term is for getting the one-hit in the second part only. The third term is for getting the one-hit in the third part only. The factor $1/t_2$ accounts for the probability of choosing long and short codewords with the same i_1 index. For the product term following the summation, the factor $(t_2 - 1)/t_2$ accounts for the probability of choosing codewords with different i_1 indices. The term $w^2/(2N_1)$ comes from $p_1w \times w/(2N_2)$, representing the probability of obtaining one-hits. To explain the terms within the product terms, first note that $w^2 \tau^2/(N_1 N_2)/(2\tau)$ denotes the probability of a pulse in the first copy of the short codeword hitting with a pulse (in the first part) of the long codeword. This is because there are $w\tau/N_1$ chances for the one-hit to take place in the first copy and there are $w\tau/N_2$ chances from the long codeword, and the factor $1/2$ comes from the assumption of equiprobable data bit-1 and bit-0 transmissions in OOK. The probability of getting one-hit is $1/\tau$ because each pulse of the short codewords is assumed to uniformly distribute over their entire lengths and there are w pulses in both codewords. Similarly, $w^2 N_1/(2N_1 N_2)$ denotes the probability of a pulse in the $r-1$ copies of the short codeword hitting with a pulse (in the second part) of the long codeword because of $\tau = N_1$. Finally, $[w^2(N_1 - \tau)^2/(N_1 N_2)]/[2(N_1 - \tau)]$ denotes the probability of a pulse of the last copy of the short codeword hitting with a pulse (in the third part) of the long codeword with a shift of $N_1 - \tau$ chips.

Similarly, the two-hit probability $q_{2,2,1}$ is formulated using the four product terms inside the summation to account for the four cases of getting the periodic cross-correlation value of 2. The first product term accounts for the probability of having one hit in the first part and another hit in the second part. The second term product term accounts for the probability of having one hit in the first part and another hit in the third part. The third term accounts for the probability of having one hit in the second part and another hit in third part. Finally, the fourth term accounts for the probability of having both hits in the second part.

Because $q_{1,2,2}$ denotes the probability of obtaining one hit between two long codewords of length N_2 and weight w with the maximum cross-correlation function of 1, it is found that $q_{1,2,2} = w^2/(2N_2)$.

When a short address codeword of length N_1 correlates with a long interfering codeword of length N_2, only a portion of the long codeword is involved in the cross-correlation process. Because the 1-D multilength OOCs have a cross-correlation function of at most 1, the one-hit probability of a short address codeword is given by $q_{1,1,1} = q_{1,1,2} = w^2/(2N_1)$, independent of code length.   ■

Figure 7.18 plots the chip-synchronous, soft-limiting error probabilities of the 1-D double-length OOCs in Construction 2 against the number of simultaneous users with long-length codewords K_2 for various numbers of simultaneous users with short-length codewords $K_1 = \{0, 3, 5\}$, where $k = 2$, $p_1 = 5$, $t = 10$, $w = 5$, $N_1 = w(w-1)t + 1 = 201$, and $N_2 = p_1 N_1 = 1005$. Figure 7.19 is for the same codes but against K_1 for various $K_2 = \{0, 5, 10, 15\}$. In general, the error probabilities get worse as the total number of simultaneous users $K_1 + K_2$ increases. The short codewords always perform better than the long codewords due to stronger interference created by multiple copies of the short codewords in the cross-correlation function. This contradicts the finding in the conventional single-length codes that code performance improves with code length. The short codewords are affected less by the long codewords, and the former have stronger interference immunity. In other words, the short codewords support higher priority than the long codewords. Furthermore, the dashed curve with $K_1 = 0$ in Figure 7.18 and the dashed curve with $K_2 = 0$ in Figure 7.19 show the performances of single-length OOCs of long length N_2 and short

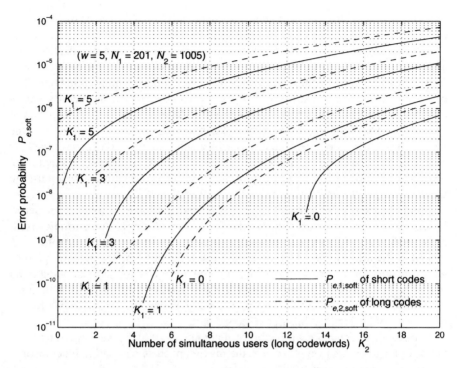

FIGURE 7.18 Chip-synchronous, soft-limiting error probabilities of the double-length OOCs in Construction 2 versus K_2 for $t = 10$, $p_1 = 5$, $w = 5$, $N_1 = 201$, and $N_2 = 1005$.

length N_1, respectively, agreeing with $P_{e,2\text{single}}$ and $P_{e,1\text{single}}$.

In general, it is difficult to calculate the code performances as k' increases beyond 2 because there are more different-length interference patterns and, in turn, hit probabilities to consider. The calculations can be simplified by evaluating the performance bounds. This is because the best performance (or lower bound) is achieved by the shortest codewords, and the worst performance (or upper bound) is achieved by the longest codewords. So, codewords with lengths in between will fall within these two bounds.

7.7 SUMMARY

To support multimedia services with different bit-rates and QoS requirements, several multilength prime codes with low periodic cross-correlation functions were studied. The multilength carrier-hopping prime codes with the maximum periodic cross-correlation function of 1 provided the basis of the codes in this chapter. High-rate media were shown to have better performance than low-rate media because long codewords used by the latter suffer from stronger interference created by multiple copies of short codewords used by the high-rate media. This feature provides user prioritization and guarantees the QoS of those media that carry high bit-rate and

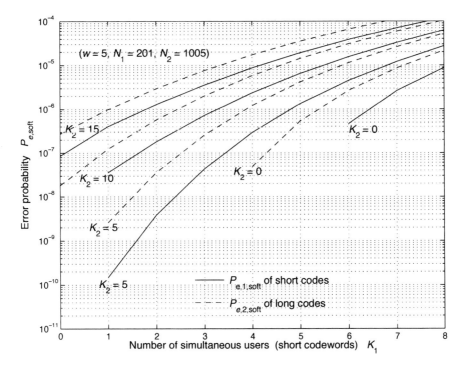

FIGURE 7.19 Chip-synchronous, soft-limiting error probabilities of the double-length OOCs in Construction 2 versus K_1 for $t = 10$, $p_1 = 5$, $w = 5$, $N_1 = 201$, and $N_2 = 1005$.

real-time traffic patterns. To enhance the performance of the low-rate media, subsets of the multilength expanded carrier-hopping prime codes can be used to ensure zero interference among codes. To increase the cardinality, the multilength quadratic-congruence carrier-hopping prime codes with the maximum cross-correlation function of 2 in OOK and multicode keying were studied and their spectral efficiencies were compared. To relax the strict relationship among the number of wavelengths, code length, and cardinality, 2-D multilength prime-permuted codes, which use 1-D multilength OOCs in Section 7.6 for time spreading, were studied.

Code weight was shown as a dominating factor and more effective than code length in controlling code performance and QoS of those users requiring real-time or critical support. One important application of variable-weight coding is emergency broadcasting or top-priority military transmission as these types of traffic require real-time handling and very high throughput, but are rare and bursty in nature. The effect of bit-power-limit, due to laser sources, on 1-D and 2-D double-weight codes were also investigated in this chapter. Because code weight and chip power have different effects on code performance, chip power was shown as another important figure of merit in controlling the performance of codes of different weights. An exact analytical model providing a better understanding of the combined effect of power and code-weight variations to QoS was formulated. The combination of power control and variable weight allows for fine-tuning QoS in the physical layer at no extra cost, in supplemental to the conventional QoS control at higher layers. Such a model will be important for power-sensitive applications, such as in-service monitoring and fiber-fault surveillance in optical networks and sensor identification in fiber-sensor systems with the use of optical codes. Finally, the constructions of two families of 1-D multilength OOCs were illustrated.

REFERENCES

1. Chung, F. R. K., Salehi, J. A., Wei, V. K. (1989). Optical orthogonal codes: Design, analysis, and applications. *IEEE Trans. Info. Theory* 35(3):595–604.
2. Chung, H., Kumar, P. V. (1990). Optical orthogonal codes—New bounds and an optimal construction. *IEEE Trans. Info. Theory* 36(4):866–873.
3. Azizoğlu, M. Y., Salehi, J. A., Li, Y. (1992). Optical CDMA via temporal codes. *IEEE Trans. Commun.* 40(7):1162–1170.
4. Yang, G.-C., Fuja, T. (1995). Optical orthogonal codes with unequal auto- and cross-correlation constraints. *IEEE Trans. Info. Theory* 41(1):96–106.
5. Tančevski, L., Andonovic, I. (1996). Hybrid wavelength hopping/time spreading schemes for use in massive optical LANs with increased security. *J. Lightwave Technol.* 14(12):2636–2647.
6. Fuji-Hara, R., Miao, Y. (2000). Optical orthogonal codes: Their bounds and new optimal constructions. *IEEE Trans. Info. Theory* 46(7):2396–2406.
7. Yang, G.-C., Kwong, W. C. (2002). *Prime Codes with Applications to CDMA Optical and Wireless Networks*. Norwood, MA: Artech House.
8. Chang, C.-Y., Yang, G.-C., Kwong, W. C. (2006). Wavelength-time codes with maximum cross-correlation function of two for multicode-keying optical CDMA. *J. Lightwave Technol.* 24(3):1093–1100.
9. Prucnal, P. R. (ed.) (2006). *Optical Code Division Multiple Access: Fundamentals and Applications*. Boca Raton, FL: Taylor & Francis Group.
10. Perrier, P. A., Prucnal, P. R. (1988). Wavelength-division integration of services in fiber-optic networks. *Int. J. Digital Analog Cabled Systems* 1(3):149–157.
11. Inaty, E., Shalaby, H. M. H., Fortier, P., Rusch, L. A. (2002). Multirate optical fast frequency hopping CDMA systems using power control. *J. Lightwave Technol.* 20(2):166–177.
12. Yang, G.-C. (1996). Variable-weight optical orthogonal codes for CDMA networks with multiple performance requirements. *IEEE Trans. Commun.* 44(1):47–55.
13. Forouzan, A. R., Nasiri-Kenari, M., Rezaee, N. (2005). Frame time-hopping patterns in multirate optical CDMA networks using conventional and multicode schemes. *IEEE Trans. Commun.* 53(5):863–875.
14. Baby, V., Kwong, W. C., Chang, C.-Y., Yang, G.-C., Prucnal, P. R. (2007). Performance analysis of variable-weight, multilength optical codes for wavelength-time O-CDMA multimedia systems. *IEEE Trans. Commun.* 55(7):1325–1333.
15. Kwong, W. C., Yang, G.-C. (2005). Multiple-length extended carrier-hopping prime codes for optical CDMA systems supporting multirate, multimedia services. *J. Lightwave Technol.* 23(11):3653–3662.
16. Chang, C.-Y., Chen, H.-T., Yang, G.-C., Kwong, W. C. (2007). Spectral efficiency study of quadratic-congruence carrier-hopping prime codes in multirate optical CDMA sys-

tem. *IEEE J. Selected Areas Commun.* 25(9):118–128.

17. Chen, H.-W., Yang, G.-C., Chang, C.-Y., Lin, T.-C., Kwong, W. C. (2009). Spectral efficiency study of two multirate schemes for optical CDMA with/without symbol synchronization. *J. Lightwave Technol.* 27(14):2771–2778.

18. Chen, C.-H., Chu, H.-Y., Yang, G.-C., Chang, C.-Y., Kwong, W. C. (2011). Performance analysis of double-weight optical CDMA scheme under the same-bit-power assumption. *IEEE Trans. Commun.* 59(5):1247–1252.

19. Yang, G.-C., Chen, C.-H., Kwong, W. C. (2012). Accurate analysis of double-weight optical CDMA with power control. *IEEE Trans. Commun.* 60(2):322–327.

20. Chen, L.-S., Yang, G.-C., Chang, C.-Y., Kwong, W. C. (2011) Study of power control on double-weight codes with an arbitrary maximum cross-correlation value in variable-QoS optical CDMA. *J. Lightwave Technol.* 29(21):3293–3303.

21. Fathallah, H. A., Rusch, L. A. (2007). Code division multiplexing for in-service out-of-band monitoring. *J. Optical Networking* 6(7):819–829.

22. Rad, M. M., Fathallah, H. A., Rusch, L. A. (2008). Fiber fault monitoring for passive optical networks using hybrid 1-D/2-D coding. *IEEE Photon. Technol. Lett.* 20(24):2054–2056.

23. Rad, M. M., Fathallah, H. A., Rusch, L. A. (2010). Fiber fault PON monitoring using optical coding: Effects of customer geographic distribution. *IEEE Trans. Commun.* 58(4):1172–1181.

24. Kwong, W. C., Yang, G.-C. (2002). Design of multilength optical orthogonal codes for optical CDMA multimedia networks. *IEEE Trans. Commun.* 50(8):1258–1265.

25. Kwong, W. C., Yang, G.-C. (2004). Multiple-length, multiple-wavelength optical orthogonal codes for optical CDMA systems supporting multirate, multimedia services. *IEEE J. Selected Areas Commun.* 22(9):1640–1647.

26. Ghaffari, B. M., Salehi, J. A. (2009). Multiclass, multistage, and multilevel fiber-optic CDMA signaling techniques based on advanced binary optical logic gate elements. *IEEE Trans. Commun.* 57(5):1424–1432.

27. Beyranvand, H., Ghaffari, B. M., Salehi, J. A. (2009). Multirate, differentiated-QoS, and multilevel fiber-optic CDMA system via optical logic gate elements. *J. Lightwave Technol.* 27(19):4348–4359.

28. Yang, C.-C., Huang, J.-F., Hsu, T.-C. (2008). Differentiated service provision in optical CDMA network using power control. *IEEE Photon. Technol. Lett.* 20(20):1664–1666.

29. Leon-Garcia, A. (1994). *Probability and Random Process for Electrical Engineering.* (second edition). Reading, MA: Addison-Wesley.

30. Hsu, C.-C., Yang, G.-C., Kwong, W. C. (2008). Hard-limiting performance analysis of 2-D optical codes under the chip-asynchronous assumption. *IEEE Trans. Commun.* 56(5):762–768.

31. Zhi, C., Pingzhi, F., Fan, J. (1992). Disjoint difference sets, difference triangle sets, and related codes. *IEEE Trans. Info. Theory* 38(2):518–522.

32. Colbourn, M. J., Colbourn, C. J. (1984). Recursive constructions for cyclic block designs. *J. Statistical Planning Inference* 10(1):97–103.

8 3-D Prime Codes

To further enhance code cardinality and coding flexibility, a third coding dimension can be added to 2-D optical codes, resulting in 3-D optical codes [1–6]. In this chapter, 3-D concatenated prime codes and multicarrier prime codes are studied [1, 3, 4], in which the third coding dimension is supported by multiple spatial, fiber-optic, or wavelength-band channels.

8.1   CONCATENATED PRIME CODES

The 2-D carrier-hopping prime codes over $GF(p)$ in Section 5.1 can be treated as wavelength-time matrices of pulses in distinct wavelengths and time slots. This property gives zero autocorrelation sidelobes and periodic cross-correlation functions of at most 1. Nevertheless, the construction cannot be used with any extension field $GF(p^n)$ for $n > 1$. In this section, 3-D concatenated prime codes over $GF(p^2)$ are constructed, in which each codeword is a concatenation of p copies of the time- and wavelength-shifted versions of the carrier-hopping prime codewords in Section 5.1.

Based on the $GF(p)$ of a prime p, each of the concatenated prime codewords, denoted as a wavelength-time matrix $\mathbf{U}_{a,b}$, is constructed with its (i,j)th element (or pulse) determined by the ordered pair [1, 4]

$$
\begin{aligned}
&\{[(\lambda_{aj+ybi,ai+bj \pmod p}, ip+j)] : (a,b) \neq (0,0), a = \{0,1,\ldots,p-1\}, \\
&\quad b = \{0,1,\ldots,p-1\}, i = \{0,1,\ldots,p-1\}, j = \{0,1,\ldots,p-1\}, \\
&\quad y = \{0,1,\ldots,p-1\}\backslash\{A\}\}
\end{aligned}
$$

Each ordered pair $(\lambda_{m,n}, t)$ represents the $\lambda_{m,n}$th wavelength of a pulse at the time-slot location t, where m and $n \in [0, p-1]$, and $t \in [0, p^2-1]$. The set $\{A\}$ contains all integers calculated with $1/r^2 \pmod p$ for $r = \{0,1,\ldots,p-1\}$. The legitimate values of $y = \{0,1,\ldots,p-1\}\backslash\{A\}$ are the remaining field elements in $GF(p)$ after those in the set $\{A\}$ have been excluded. For example, $y = 2$ for $GF(3)$, $y = \{2,3\}$ for $GF(5)$, $y = \{3,5,6\}$ for $GF(7)$, $y = \{2,3,8,10,12,13,14,15,18\}$ for $GF(19)$, and $y = \{2,5,6,8,13,14,15,17,18,19,20,22,23,24,29,31,32,35\}$ for $GF(37)$.

This construction generates $p^2 - 1$ concatenated prime codewords of length p^2 and weight p^2 with the use of p^2 distinct wavelengths, in the form of one wavelength per time slot. These p^2 wavelengths can be partitioned into p groups such that $\lambda_{m,n}$ corresponds to the nth wavelength in group m, where m and $n \in [0, p-1]$. In this way, these 3-D codewords can be transmitted via $m = p$ different (spatial or fiber-optic) channels with the same set of $n = p$ distinct wavelengths being reused in each channel, instead of requiring p^2 distinct wavelengths.

It is the characteristic of the 3-D concatenated prime codes that the code weight w can be varied to be less than p^2 by simply dropping $p^2 - w$ pulses from the codewords, without affecting the cross-correlation properties. Because there is exactly one pulse per row and column in every code matrix, dropping of $p^2 - w$ pulses will automatically reduce the number of wavelengths by the same amount. One pulse-dropping method is to remove the top $p^2 - w$ wavelengths in order to reduce the number of total wavelengths required in conveying the codewords of weight $w \leq p^2$.

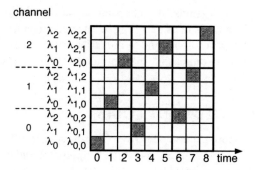

FIGURE 8.1 Concatenated prime codeword $\mathbf{U}_{1,0}$ over GF(3) with $y = 2$.

Using $p = 3$ and $y = 2$ as an example, the eight concatenated prime codewords over GF(3) are given by the ordered pairs: $\{[(\lambda_{aj+2bi,ai+bj \text{ (mod 3)}}, 3i + j)] : (a,b) \neq (0,0), a = \{0,1,2\}, b = \{0,1,2\}, i = \{0,1,2\}, j = \{0,1,2\}\}$. So, $\mathbf{U}_{1,0} = [(\lambda_{0,0}, 0), (\lambda_{1,0}, 1), (\lambda_{2,0}, 2), (\lambda_{0,1}, 3), (\lambda_{1,1}, 4), (\lambda_{2,1}, 5), (\lambda_{0,2}, 6), (\lambda_{1,2}, 7), (\lambda_{2,2}, 8)]$, which can also be represented as a wavelength-time matrix in Figure 8.1. As there is one pulse per row and column in each codeword, these eight concatenated prime codewords can be equivalently written as wavelength-time sequences:

$$
\begin{aligned}
\mathbf{U}_{0,1} &= \lambda_{0,0}\lambda_{0,1}\lambda_{0,2}\lambda_{2,0}\lambda_{2,1}\lambda_{2,2}\lambda_{1,0}\lambda_{1,1}\lambda_{1,2} \\
\mathbf{U}_{0,2} &= \lambda_{0,0}\lambda_{0,2}\lambda_{0,1}\lambda_{1,0}\lambda_{1,2}\lambda_{1,1}\lambda_{2,0}\lambda_{2,2}\lambda_{2,1} \\
\mathbf{U}_{1,0} &= \lambda_{0,0}\lambda_{1,0}\lambda_{2,0}\lambda_{0,1}\lambda_{1,1}\lambda_{2,1}\lambda_{0,2}\lambda_{1,2}\lambda_{2,2} \\
\mathbf{U}_{1,1} &= \lambda_{0,0}\lambda_{1,1}\lambda_{2,2}\lambda_{2,1}\lambda_{0,2}\lambda_{1,0}\lambda_{1,2}\lambda_{2,0}\lambda_{0,1} \\
\mathbf{U}_{1,2} &= \lambda_{0,0}\lambda_{1,2}\lambda_{2,1}\lambda_{1,1}\lambda_{2,0}\lambda_{0,2}\lambda_{2,2}\lambda_{0,1}\lambda_{1,0} \\
\mathbf{U}_{2,0} &= \lambda_{0,0}\lambda_{2,0}\lambda_{1,0}\lambda_{0,2}\lambda_{2,2}\lambda_{1,2}\lambda_{0,1}\lambda_{2,1}\lambda_{1,1} \\
\mathbf{U}_{2,1} &= \lambda_{0,0}\lambda_{2,1}\lambda_{1,2}\lambda_{2,2}\lambda_{1,0}\lambda_{0,1}\lambda_{1,1}\lambda_{0,2}\lambda_{2,0} \\
\mathbf{U}_{2,2} &= \lambda_{0,0}\lambda_{2,2}\lambda_{1,1}\lambda_{1,2}\lambda_{0,1}\lambda_{2,0}\lambda_{2,1}\lambda_{1,0}\lambda_{0,2}
\end{aligned}
$$

in which the $\lambda_{m,n}$ values are ordered in ascending time-slot locations. As in 3-D format, the codewords can be transmitted via $m = p = 3$ different (spatial or fiber-optic) channels with the same set of $n = p = 3$ distinct wavelengths being reused in every channel, instead of $p^2 = 9$ distinct wavelengths, due to the channel partition.

Furthermore, these $p^2 - 1$ concatenated prime codewords, $\mathbf{U}_{a,b}$, can be partitioned into $p + 1$ groups, and there are $p - 1$ codewords in each group. The group partition is determined by

$$
G_g = \begin{cases} (\mathbf{U}_{1\odot g,1}, \mathbf{U}_{2\odot g,2}, \dots, \mathbf{U}_{(p-1)\odot g,p-1}) & \text{for } g = \{0,1,\dots,p-1\} \\ (\mathbf{U}_{1,0}, \mathbf{U}_{2,0}, \dots, \mathbf{U}_{p-1,0}) & \text{for } g = p \end{cases}
$$

where "$\odot$" denotes a modulo-p multiplication. Using the aforementioned 3-D concatenated prime codewords with $p = 3$ and $y = 2$ as an example, the four groups are $G_0 = \{\mathbf{U}_{0,1}, \mathbf{U}_{0,2}\}$, $G_1 = \{\mathbf{U}_{1,1}, \mathbf{U}_{2,2}\}$, $G_2 = \{\mathbf{U}_{2,1}, \mathbf{U}_{1,2}\}$, and $G_3 = \{\mathbf{U}_{1,0}, \mathbf{U}_{2,0}\}$.

Theorem 8.1

The autocorrelation peaks and sidelobes of the 3-D concatenated prime codes over $\mathrm{GF}(p)$ of a prime p are equal to w and 0, respectively, where $w \leq p^2$ [1, 4]. The periodic cross-correlation functions of the codes are at most 2, but at most 1 if the correlating codewords come from the same group $g = \{0, 1, \ldots, p\}$.

Proof Let $\mathbf{U}_{a,b}$ and $\mathbf{U}_{a',b'}$ be two distinct concatenated prime codewords, where $(a,b) \neq (a',b') \neq (0,0)$. Also, let τ_h and τ_v be any relative horizontal and vertical cyclic shifts, respectively, between $\mathbf{U}_{a,b}$ and $\mathbf{U}_{a',b'}$ such that $\tau_h = \tau_1 p + \tau_2$ for τ_1, τ_2, and $\tau_v \in [0, p-1]$. If there exist at most two hits in any relative horizontal and vertical cyclic shifts between $\mathbf{U}_{a,b}$ and $\mathbf{U}_{a',b'}$, one hit comes from the wavelength element in $\mathbf{U}_{a,b}$ with the index $j < p - \tau_2$, and the other hit comes from the index $j \geq p - \tau_2$.

Consider $j < p - \tau_2$. From the construction, if there exist two hits between the wavelength elements of $\mathbf{U}_{a,b}$ and $\mathbf{U}_{a',b'}$ at two time slots, then

$$(aj_1 + ybi_1, ai_1 + bj_1) = (a'j_1' + yb'i_1', a'i_1' + b'j_1' + \tau_v) \pmod{p}$$

$$(aj_2 + ybi_2, ai_2 + bj_2) = (a'j_2' + yb'i_2', a'i_2' + b'j_2' + \tau_v) \pmod{p}$$

must hold simultaneously, where $i_1' = i_1 + \tau_1$, $j_1' = j_1 + \tau_2$, $i_2' = i_2 + \tau_1$, $j_2' = j_2 + \tau_2$, and $i_1' \neq i_2'$. Also, let $a' = a + d \pmod{p}$ and $b' = b + e \pmod{p}$, where d and $e \in [0, p-1]$ and $(d, e) \neq (0, 0)$. Subtracting both equations and after some manipulations, it is found that $l(ye^2 - d^2) = 0$ for $l = i_1 - i_2 = i_1' - i_2'$. Assuming that $e = dr$ $\pmod{p}$, if $l \neq 0$, then

$$y = \begin{cases} 1/r^2 \pmod{p} & \text{for } d \neq 0 \\ 0 & \text{otherwise} \end{cases}$$

which is valid only for $r = \{1, 2, \ldots, (p-1)/2\}$. However, this violates the assumption of $y = \{1, 2, \ldots, p-1\} \setminus \{A\}$. This is because the set $\{A\}$, by definition, contains all integers calculated with $1/r^2 \pmod{p}$ for $r = \{1, 2, \ldots, p-1\}$. So, it is found that

$$\left\{ q : q = \frac{1}{r^2} \pmod{p}, \text{for } r = \left\{ \frac{p+1}{2}, \frac{p+3}{2}, \ldots, p-1 \right\} \right\}$$

$$= \left\{ q : q = \frac{1}{(p-r)^2} \pmod{p}, \text{for } r = \left\{ 1, 2, \ldots, \frac{p-1}{2} \right\} \right\}$$

$$= \left\{ q : q = \frac{1}{r^2} \pmod{p}, \text{for } r = \left\{ 1, 2, \ldots, \frac{p-1}{2} \right\} \right\}$$

This means that $\{A\}$ can be obtained by just checking $r = \{1, 2, \ldots, (p-1)/2\}]$, whereas the remaining $r = \{(p+1)/2, (p+3)/2, \ldots, p-1\}]$ result in an identical set of integers. So, by contradiction, there exists at most one hit between $\mathbf{U}_{a,b}$ and $\mathbf{U}_{a',b'}$, contributed by the element of $\mathbf{U}_{a,b}$ with the index j satisfying the inequality $j + \tau_2 < p$. By a similar argument, there exists at most one hit from the element of $\mathbf{U}_{a,b}$ with the index j satisfying $j + \tau_2 \geq p$. So, the maximum periodic cross-correlation function is 2.

Because the inner product of $\mathbf{U}_{a,b}$ and its cyclic-shifted version is always 0, so are the autocorrelation sidelobes. The autocorrelation peaks of w are due to the code weight $w \leq p^2$.

Assume that there exist two hits in any relative horizontal shift $\tau_h = \tau_1 p + \tau_2$ and vertical shift τ_v between any two codewords $\mathbf{U}_{a,b}$ and $\mathbf{U}_{a',b'}$ in the same group $g = \{0, 1, 2, \ldots, p\}$. From the construction,

$$(a j_3 + y b i_3, a i_3 + b j_3) = (a' j_3' + y b' i_3', a' i_3' + b' j_3' + \tau_v) \quad (\text{mod } p)$$

$$(a j_4 + y b i_4, a i_4 + b j_4) = (a' j_4' + y b' i_4', a' i_4' + b' j_4' \oplus \tau_v) \quad (\text{mod } p)$$

must hold simultaneously, where $i_3' = i_3 + \tau_1$, $j_3' = j_3 + \tau_2$, $i_4' = i_4 + \tau_1 + 1$, $j_4' = j_4 + \tau_2 - p$, $j_3' \neq j_4'$. For any group $g = \{0, 1, \ldots, p-1\}$, it can be found that $a = bg$ $(\text{mod } p)$ and $a' = b'g$ $(\text{mod } p)$, where $b' = b + e$ $(\text{mod } p)$ and $e \in [1, p-1]$. Subtracting both equations and after some manipulations, $el(y - g^2) = 0$ is derived, where $l = j_3 - j_4 = j_3' - j_4'$. Assuming that $g = yr$ $(\text{mod } p)$ and $el \neq 0$, it is concluded that

$$y = \begin{cases} 1/r^2 \quad (\text{mod } p) & \text{for } g \neq 0 \\ 0 & \text{otherwise} \end{cases}$$

This equation is valid only for $r = \{1, 2, \ldots, (p-1)/2\}$, which violates the assumption of $y = \{1, 2, \ldots, p-1\} \backslash \{A\}$. For group p, $b = b' = 0$ and $a' = a + d$ $(\text{mod } p)$ for $d \in [0, p-1]$ and $d \neq 0$. Similarly, subtracting both equations, it is found that $d(j_3 - j_4) = d(i_3 - i_4) = 0$, which violates the assumptions of $d \neq 0$ and $j_3 \neq j_4$. So, the maximum periodic cross-correlation function between any two codewords in the same group $g = \{0, 1, \ldots, p\}$ is 1. ∎

8.1.1 Performance Analysis

Because the periodic cross-correlation functions are at most 2, the chip-synchronous, soft- and hard-limiting error probabilities of the 3-D concatenated prime codes over GF(p) of a prime p with $L = w$ wavelengths, length $N = p^2$, and weight $w \leq p^2$ in OOK follows Equations (3.6) and (3.7) in Section 3.1, respectively.

Theorem 8.2

For the 3-D concatenated prime codes over GF(p) of a prime p with cardinality $p^2 - 1$, $L = w$ wavelengths, length $N = p^2$, and weight $w \leq p^2$, the hit probabilities,

q_i, of having the periodic cross-correlation values of $i = \{0, 1, 2\}$ (in the sampling time) are formulated as

$$q_2 \leq \frac{M(M^2 - 1)}{12p(p^2 - 2)}$$

$$q_1 = \frac{w}{2p^2} - 2q_2$$

$$q_0 = 1 - \frac{w}{2p^2} + q_2$$

where $(M - 1)^2 < w \leq M^2$ for $M = \{2, 3, \ldots, p\}$ and the pulse-dropping method of removing the top $p^2 - w$ wavelengths is assumed.

Proof The derivation of the two-hit probability is similar to that of Theorem 3.2 for the 1-D prime codes (in Section 3.1), which also have the maximum periodic cross-correlation functions of 2. The two-hit probability is generally bounded by

$$q_2 \leq \frac{1}{2} \times \frac{1}{(p^2 - 2)} \times \frac{1}{p^2} \times p \sum_{i=1}^{M-1} i(M - i)$$

$$= \frac{1}{2p(p^2 - 2)} \times \frac{M(M - 1)(M + 1)}{6}$$

where the factor $1/2$ comes from the assumption of equiprobable data bit-1 and bit-0 transmissions in OOK. There are at most $p^2 - 2$ possible interfering codewords and p^2 possible time shifts in a codeword of $N = p^2$. From Theorem 8.1, there are $p + 1$ groups, indexed by $g = \{0, 1, \ldots, p\}$, and the periodic cross-correlation functions are at most 1 for the codewords in the same group. So, the term p represents that there are p groups of codewords, excluding the desired codeword's group, and the summation counts the average number of hits in each of the $g = \{0, 1, \ldots, p\}$ groups. There are $i(M - i)$ hits being overcounted due to this group property. After some manipulations, the final form of q_2 in the theorem is derived.

By applying $q_1 + 2q_2 = w^2/(2LN) = w/(2p^2)$ and $q_0 + q_1 + q_2 = 1$, the final forms of q_1 and q_0 in the theorem are derived after some manipulations. ■

Figure 8.2 plots the chip-synchronous, soft- and hard-limiting error probabilities of the 3-D concatenated prime codes in OOK with $L = w$ wavelengths, weight $w = \{17, 21\}$, and length $N = p^2$ against the number of simultaneous users K for $p = \{7, 11\}$ and $M = 5$. In general, the error probabilities improve as w or p increases because of heavier code weight, longer code length, and more wavelengths, resulting in higher autocorrelation peaks and lower hit probabilities. However, the error probabilities get worse as K increases due to stronger mutual interference. In addition, the hard-limiting error probabilities are always better than the soft-limiting ones due to reduced mutual interference. The difference in error probability enlarges as p increases because of the decrement in the hit probabilities if w is fixed.

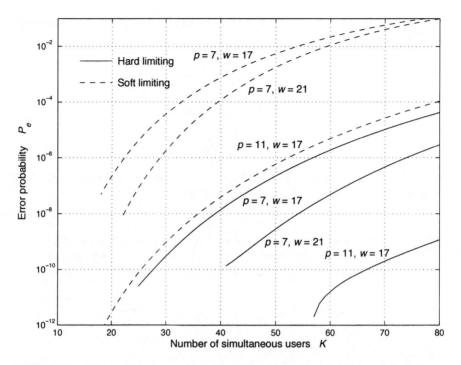

FIGURE 8.2 Chip-synchronous, soft- and hard-limiting error probabilities of the 3-D concatenated prime codes in OOK with $N = p^2$, $L = w = \{17, 21\}$, $M = 5$, and $p = \{7, 11\}$.

8.2 MULTICARRIER PRIME CODES

The 3-D concatenated prime codes in Section 8.1 assume the use of one wavelength per time slot. To relax such restriction, 3-D multicarrier prime codes are here studied. Starting with the $GF(p)$ of a prime p, every multicarrier prime codeword, in the form of a wavelength-time matrix $\mathbf{W}_{a,b} = [\lambda_{aj \oplus ybi, ai \oplus bj}]$, is given by [3, 4]

$$
\begin{bmatrix}
\lambda_{0,0} & \lambda_{a \oplus 0, 0 \oplus b} & \cdots & \lambda_{a(p-1) \oplus 0, 0 \oplus b(p-1)} \\
\lambda_{0 \oplus yb, a \oplus 0} & \lambda_{a \oplus yb, a \oplus b} & \cdots & \lambda_{a(p-1) \oplus yb, a \oplus b(p-1)} \\
\vdots & \vdots & \cdots & \vdots \\
\lambda_{0 \oplus ybi, ai \oplus 0} & \lambda_{a \oplus ybi, ai \oplus b} & \cdots & \lambda_{a(p-1) \oplus ybi, ai \oplus b(p-1)} \\
\vdots & \vdots & \ddots & \vdots \\
\lambda_{0 \oplus yb(p-1), a(p-1) \oplus 0} & \lambda_{a \oplus yb(p-1), a(p-1) \oplus b} & \cdots & \lambda_{a(p-1) \oplus yb(p-1), a(p-1) \oplus b(p-1)}
\end{bmatrix}
$$

The element $\lambda_{aj \oplus ybi, ai \oplus bj}$ represents one wavelength, out of p^2 distinct wavelengths, at the ith (vertical) wavelength group and jth time-slot (horizontal) location in $\mathbf{W}_{a,b}$, where i and $j = \{0, 1, \ldots, p-1\}$, $(a, b) \neq (0, 0)$, $y = \{0, 1, \ldots, p-1\} \backslash \{A\}$, "$\oplus$" denotes a modulo-$p$ addition, and all multiplications are modulo-p. The set $\{A\}$ contains all integers calculated with $1/r^2 \pmod{p}$ for $r = \{1, 2, \ldots, p-1\}$. The legitimate values of $y = \{0, 1, \ldots, p - 1\} \backslash \{A\}$ are the remaining field elements in $\mathrm{GF}(p)$ after those in the set $\{A\}$ have been excluded, and can be found by the same method as in Section 8.1.

While the wavelength groups are indexed by $i = \{0, 1, \ldots, p - 1\}$, the number of wavelength groups, I, can be reduced from p without affecting the periodic cross-correlation functions. Because only p wavelengths (out of p^2 wavelengths) per group are used, $p^2 - 1$ multicarrier prime codewords of length p and weight Ip are constructed with a total of Ip^2 distinct wavelengths, where $I \leq p$. These Ip^2 wavelengths can be partitioned into I groups with p^2 distinct wavelengths per group. Each time slot carries I pulses of I different wavelengths, and one wavelength per group is used. The codewords can then be transmitted via I different (spatial or fiber-optic) channels of p^2 distinct wavelengths, acting as a 3-D code. So, the p^2 distinct wavelengths in every group can be reused in all I (spatial or fiber-optic) channels, instead of requiring Ip^2 distinct wavelengths.

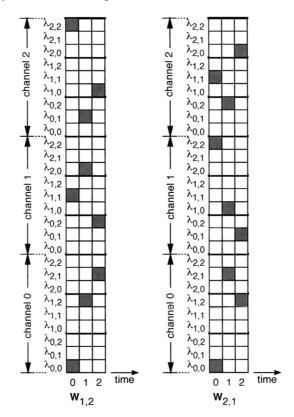

FIGURE 8.3   Two multicarrier prime codewords over GF(3) with $y = 2$.

Using $p = 3$ and $y = 2$ as an example, there are $p^2 - 1 = 8$ multicarrier prime codewords, $\mathbf{W}_{a,b} = [\lambda_{aj \oplus 2bi, ai \oplus bj}]$ for i and $j = \{0, 1, \ldots, p - 1\}$, of length $p = 3$

and weight $Ip = p^2 = 9$ with $Ip^2 = 27$ wavelengths, in the form of 3 groups and 9 wavelengths per group, where a and $b = \{0,1,2\}$, and $(a,b) \neq (0,0)$. The two examples presented in Figure 8.3 are

$$
\mathbf{W}_{1,2} = \begin{bmatrix} \lambda_{0,0} & \lambda_{1,2} & \lambda_{2,1} \\ \lambda_{1,1} & \lambda_{2,0} & \lambda_{0,2} \\ \lambda_{2,2} & \lambda_{0,1} & \lambda_{1,0} \end{bmatrix}
\qquad
\mathbf{W}_{2,1} = \begin{bmatrix} \lambda_{0,0} & \lambda_{2,1} & \lambda_{1,2} \\ \lambda_{2,2} & \lambda_{1,0} & \lambda_{0,1} \\ \lambda_{1,1} & \lambda_{0,2} & \lambda_{2,0} \end{bmatrix}
$$

With $p = 5$ and $y = 2$, there are 24 multicarrier prime codewords, $\mathbf{W}_{a,b}$, of weight 25 and length 5 with 125 wavelengths, in the form of 5 groups and 25 wavelengths per group, where a and $b = \{0,1,2,3,4\}$, and $(a,b) \neq (0,0)$. One example is

$$
\mathbf{W}_{2,1} = \begin{bmatrix} \lambda_{0,0} & \lambda_{2,1} & \lambda_{4,2} & \lambda_{1,3} & \lambda_{3,4} \\ \lambda_{2,2} & \lambda_{4,3} & \lambda_{1,4} & \lambda_{3,0} & \lambda_{0,1} \\ \lambda_{4,4} & \lambda_{1,0} & \lambda_{3,1} & \lambda_{0,2} & \lambda_{2,3} \\ \lambda_{1,1} & \lambda_{3,2} & \lambda_{0,3} & \lambda_{2,4} & \lambda_{4,0} \\ \lambda_{3,3} & \lambda_{0,4} & \lambda_{2,0} & \lambda_{4,1} & \lambda_{1,2} \end{bmatrix}
$$

Theorem 8.3

The autocorrelation peaks and sidelobes of the 3-D multicarrier prime codes over $GF(p)$ of a prime p are equal to w and 0, respectively, where $w = Ip$ and $I \leq p$. The periodic cross-correlation functions of the codes are at most 1 [3,4].

Proof Given any two distinct multicarrier prime codewords, $\mathbf{W}_{a,b}$ and $\mathbf{W}_{a\oplus d,b\oplus e}$, and $(d,e) \neq (0,0)$, the wavelengths of the pulses in the ith groups and jth time slots of $\mathbf{W}_{a,b}$ and $\mathbf{W}_{a\oplus d,b\oplus e}$ are indexed by $(aj \oplus ybi, ai \oplus bj)$ and $((a \oplus d)j \oplus y(b \oplus e)i, (a \oplus d)i \oplus (b \oplus e)j)$, respectively, where d and $e = \{0,1,\ldots,p-1\}$. Assume that there exist two hits in any relative horizontal cyclic shift $\tau_h \in [0, p-1]$ and vertical cyclic shift $\tau_v \in [0, p-1])$ of the two codewords. So,

$$
\begin{aligned}
(i_1, j_1) &= (i_1', j_1' + \tau_h) \\
aj_1 \oplus ybi_1 &= (a \oplus d)(j_1' \oplus \tau_h) \oplus y(b \oplus e)i_1' \\
ai_1 \oplus bj_1 &= (a \oplus d)i_1' \oplus (b \oplus e)(j_1' \oplus \tau_h) \oplus \tau_v
\end{aligned}
$$

and

$$
\begin{aligned}
(i_2, j_2) &= (i_2', j_2' + \tau_h) \\
aj_2 \oplus ybi_2 &= (a \oplus d)(j_2' \oplus \tau_h) \oplus y(b \oplus e)i_2' \\
ai_2 \oplus bj_2 &= (a \oplus d)i_2' \oplus (b \oplus e)(j_2' \oplus \tau_h) \oplus \tau_v
\end{aligned}
$$

must hold simultaneously for $i_1 \neq i_2$ and $i_1' \neq i_2'$. After some manipulations, $i_1(ye^2 - d^2) = d\tau_v \pmod{p}$ and $i_2(ye^2 - d^2) = d\tau_v \pmod{p}$ are derived. The subtraction of these two equations results in $(i_1 - i_2)(ye^2 - d^2) = 0 \pmod{p}$. Rearranging the equation and assuming that $e = dr \pmod{p}$, it is found that

$$y = \begin{cases} 1/r^2 \pmod{p} & \text{for } d \neq 0 \\ 0 & \text{otherwise} \end{cases}$$

From the proof of Theorem 8.1, this equation is valid only for $r = \{1, 2, \ldots, (p-1)/2\}$, which violates the assumption of $y = \{1, 2, \ldots, p-1\} \backslash \{A\}$. So, the maximum periodic cross-correlation function is 1.

Because every pulse in each codeword is conveyed with a distinct wavelength, the autocorrelation sidelobes are equal to 0. The autocorrelation peaks of w are due to the code weight $w = Ip$, where $I \leq p$. ∎

Similar to the wavelength-shifted carrier-hopping prime codes in Section 5.3, the pulses of each of the $p^2 - 1$ 3-D multicarrier prime codewords over GF(p) of a prime p can be cyclic-shifted p times (within their own wavelength groups) to generate p orthogonal wavelength-shifted codewords. This results in a total of $(p^2 - 1)p$ wavelength-shifted multicarrier prime codewords. For example, the pulses in the codeword $\mathbf{W}_{1,2}$, which corresponds to the codeword $\mathbf{W}_{1,2,0}$ without any wavelength-shift, in Figure 8.3 can be cyclic-shifted upward (within their wavelength groups) one time and two times to generate

$$\mathbf{W}_{1,2,1} = \begin{bmatrix} \lambda_{0,1} & \lambda_{1,0} & \lambda_{2,2} \\ \lambda_{1,2} & \lambda_{2,1} & \lambda_{0,0} \\ \lambda_{2,0} & \lambda_{0,2} & \lambda_{1,1} \end{bmatrix} \quad \text{and} \quad \mathbf{W}_{1,2,2} = \begin{bmatrix} \lambda_{0,2} & \lambda_{1,1} & \lambda_{2,0} \\ \lambda_{1,0} & \lambda_{2,2} & \lambda_{0,1} \\ \lambda_{2,1} & \lambda_{0,0} & \lambda_{1,2} \end{bmatrix}$$

respectively.

Because these wavelength-shifted multicarrier prime codewords can be partitioned into $p^2 - 1$ groups and each group has p orthogonal codewords, they can be used for supporting up to $p^2 - 1$ possible subscribers in shifted-code keying with $m = \lfloor \log_2 p \rfloor$ bits per symbol. The maximum intersymbol and intrasymbol cross-correlation functions (see Section 5.3 for their definitions) are equal to 1 and 0, respectively.

8.2.1   Performance Analysis

Because the 3-D multicarrier prime codes over GF(p) of a prime p with $L = Ip^2$ wavelengths, length $N = p$, and weight $w = Ip$ have at most one pulse per row in every code matrix, the (one-hit) probability of the pulses in an interfering codeword overlapping with the pulses in the address codeword (of a receiver) in the sampling time of their periodic cross-correlation function is formulated as [3, 4]

$$q_1 = \frac{w^2}{2LN} = \frac{I}{2p}$$

and $q_0 + q_1 = 1$, where $I \leq p$ and the factor $1/2$ comes from the assumption of equiprobable data bit-1 and bit-0 transmissions in OOK.

Because the maximum periodic cross-correlation function is 1, the chip-synchronous, soft- and hard-limiting error probabilities of the 3-D multicarrier prime codes with $L = Ip^2$ wavelengths, length $N = p$, and weight $w = Ip$ in OOK follows Equations (5.1) and (5.3) in Chapter 5, respectively, where $I \leq p$.

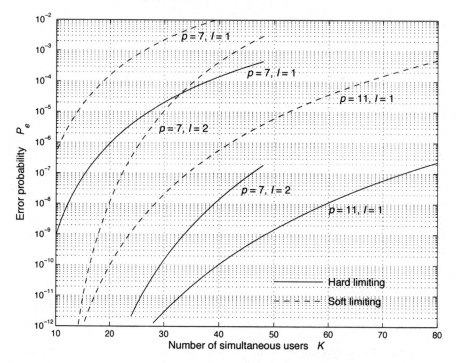

FIGURE 8.4 Chip-synchronous, soft- and hard-limiting error probabilities of the 3-D multicarrier prime codes in OOK with $L = Ip^2$, $w = Ip$, $I = \{1,2\}$, and $N = p = \{7,11\}$.

Figure 8.4 plots the chip-synchronous, soft- and hard-limiting error probabilities of the 3-D multicarrier prime codes in OOK with $L = Ip^2$ wavelengths, weight $w = Ip$, and length $N = p$ against the number of simultaneous users K for $I = \{1,2\}$ and $p = \{7,11\}$. In general, the error probabilities improve as p or I increases because of heavier code weight, longer code length, and more wavelengths, resulting in higher autocorrelation peaks and lower hit probabilities. However, the error probabilities get worse as K increases due to stronger mutual interference. In addition, the hard-limiting error probabilities are always better than the soft-limiting ones due to reduced mutual interference. The difference in error probability enlarges as p increases because of the combining effect of the increment in the autocorrelation peak, which is usually equal to the code weight $w = Ip$, and the decrement in the hit probability $[q_1 = I/(2p)]$.

By partitioning the $p(p^2 - 1)$ wavelength-shifted multicarrier prime codewords over GF(p) of a prime p into $p^2 - 1$ groups (or subscribers) and with each group having p orthogonal codewords (or symbols) for shifted-code keying with $m = \lfloor \log_2 p \rfloor$

bits per symbol, the maximum intersymbol and intrasymbol cross-correlation functions are equal to 1 and 0, respectively. So, the chip-synchronous, hard-limiting error probability of the wavelength-shifted multicarrier prime codes in shifted-code keying follows Theorem 5.6 (in Section 5.3) with $q_1 = w^2/(LN) = I/p$ and $I \leq p$.

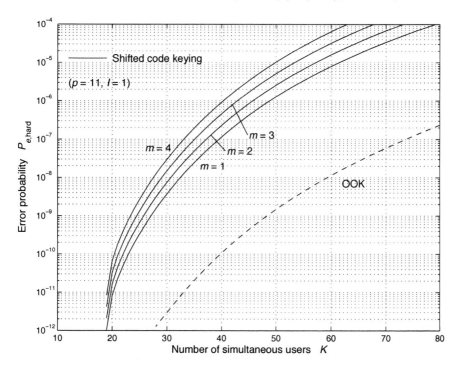

FIGURE 8.5 Chip-synchronous, hard-limiting bit error probabilities of the 3-D concatenated prime codes of $L = Ip^2 = 121$, $w = Ip = 11$, and $N = p = 11$ in OOK and 2^m-ary shifted-code keying for $I = 1$ and $m = \{1,2,3,4\}$.

Figure 8.5 plots the chip-synchronous, hard-limiting bit error probabilities of the 3-D concatenated prime codes in OOK [from Equation (5.3) with $q = I/(2p)$] and the wavelength-shifted 3-D concatenated prime codes in 2^m-ary shifted-code keying [from Equation (5.2) with $q = I/p$], both of $L = Ip^2 = 121$ wavelengths, length $N = p = 11$, and weight $w = Ip = 11$, against the number of simultaneous users K for $I = 1$ and $m = \{1,2,3,4\}$. In general, the error probabilities get worse as K increases because of stronger mutual interference. The worsening in the error probabilities (solid curves) of shifted-code keying is relatively large when compared to those (dashed curves) of OOK because the hit probabilities in the latter are reduced by half as bit 0s are not conveyed. Furthermore, the error probabilities get worse as m increases because more bits will be decided incorrectly if a symbol decision error occurs. The results show that there is a trade-off between code performance and the choice of m. For the benefit of higher bit rate or enhancing user code obscurity, error probability suffers. If bit rate or user code obscurity is not important, one should use

OOK. Otherwise, the choice of $m = 2$ or 3 provides a good compromise among code performance, hardware complexity, and bit rate.

8.3   SUMMARY

In this chapter, the constructions, correlation properties, and performances of the 3-D concatenated prime codes and multicarrier prime codes were studied. While these codes are basically 2-D wavelength-time codes, some wavelengths can be flexibly conveyed by a third coding (e.g., spatial and fiber-optic) channel, due to their special code structure. Using three coding dimensions, coding flexibility is enhanced. Targeted code cardinality and performance are easier to achieve in these 2-D prime codes than in their 1-D or 2-D counterparts, even with short code length.

REFERENCES

1. Hong, C.-F., Yang, G.-C. (1999). Concatenated prime code. *IEEE Commun. Lett.* 3(9):260–262.
2. Kim, S., Yu, K., Park, N. (2000). A new family of space/wavelength/time spread three-dimensional optical code for OCDMA networks. *J. Lightwave Technol.* 18(4):502–511.
3. Hong, C.-F., Yang, G.-C. (2000). Multicarrier FH codes for multicarrier FH-CDMA wireless systems. *IEEE Trans. Commun.* 48(10):1626–1630.
4. Yang, G.-C., Kwong, W. C. (2002). *Prime Codes with Applications to CDMA Optical and Wireless Networks.* Norwood, MA: Artech House.
5. McGeehan, J. E., Nezam, S. M. R. M., Saghari, P., Willner, A. E., Omrani, R., Kumar, P. V. (2005). Experimental demonstration of OCDMA transmission using a three-dimensional (time-wavelength-polarization) codeset. *J. Lightwave Technol.* 23(10):3282–3289.
6. Yeh, B.-C., Lin, C.-H., Wu, J. (2009). Noncoherent spectral/time/spatial optical CDMA system using 3-D perfect difference codes. *J. Lightwave Technol.* 27(6):744–759.

Index